Dynamic Scheduling
With Microsoft® Office Project 2003
The Book by and for Professionals

Eric Uyttewaal, PMP
Executive Director, Microsoft EPM Division
International Institute for Learning, Inc.

Published jointly by J. Ross Publishing and International Institute for Learning

Copyright © 2005 by International Institute for Learning, Inc.

ISBN 1-932159-45-2

Printed and bound in the U.S.A. Printed on acid-free paper.

10   9   8

Library of Congress Cataloging-in-Publication Data

Uyttewaal, Eric.
  Dynamic scheduling with Microsoft Office Project 2003: the book by and for professionals / By Eric Uyttewaal.
      p. cm.
  Includes bibliographical references (p.) and index.
  ISBN 1-932159-45-2 (pbk. : alk. paper)
  1. Microsoft Project. 2. Project management--Computer programs. I. Title.
  HD69.P75P982 2004
  658.4'04'028553--dc22

                    2004023227

Direct all inquiries to J. Ross Publishing, Inc., 6501 Park of Commerce Blvd., Suite 200, Boca Raton, Florida 33487.
Phone: (561) 869-3900
Fax: (561) 892-0700
Web: www.jrosspub.com

International Institute for Learning, Inc. (IIL)

International Institute for Learning (IIL) has earned a reputation as a leader in learning. The content of our curriculum and the experience of our instructors and consultants are unsurpassed. We continue to be at the forefront of innovative learning methods and techniques. We offer a wide variety of delivery mechanisms to ensure that our clients' learning experiences are a perfect fit for their needs and business objectives. These include traditional classroom learning, "virtual" classroom eLearning, and on-demand eLearning. Our curriculum is offered in different languages and can be tailored to meet your specific objectives. We'll work with you closely to provide a learning experience and content that allow you to achieve meaningful and measurable results.

◆ **Traditional Classroom Learning**
   Each year we schedule hundreds of live instructor-led courses and workshops in major cities all around the world. This offers you a convenient way to participate in classes that expose you to a diverse representation of industries and real life experiences. And if you don't see a class scheduled in a city near you, chances are we can schedule that course at a city of your choice. Just call one of our client representatives to discuss a city venue that meets your organization's needs.

◆ **"Virtual" Classroom eLearning**
   Utilizing the latest online learning technologies, IIL brings you a diverse curriculum of live, instructor-led classrooms via the Internet. Interact live with the instructor and fellow classmates, while avoiding the costs and inconvenience of travel. And to maximize the convenience to your schedule, we have scheduled sessions at various times of the day and evening, and even on Saturdays. Never tried virtual eLearning? No problem! Log onto our Website to sign up for one of the many FREE one hour Webinars we've scheduled throughout the year. For more information or to sign up for a Free Webinar, go to www.iil.com.

◆ **On-Demand eLearning and Self-Paced Learning**
   IIL offers a wide variety of courses that give you extraordinary content and the convenience of learning at your own pace. In addition to traditional video, texts and workbooks, we offer content-rich, multimedia training programs. These courses are not only a cost-effective way to bring expertise to your employees, they are also a valuable means for reinforcing your existing training efforts and materials. For a comprehensive listing of IIL's self-paced learning courses, please visit www.iil.com.

◆ **PM Web-Based Methodology**
   IIL has developed a web-based methodology designed to drive continuous project management improvement through the deployment of a common PM process and

methodology. At the heart of IIL's approach for establishing a unified methodology is a robust web-based resource: Unified Project Management® Methodology (UPMM™). It provides online, web access to a repository of information needed to effectively manage projects across the enterprise. It includes intellectual digital assets from leading subject matter experts and over 100 ready-to-use templates. UPMM™ is applicable to many industries, project types and applications, and can be customized and scaled to meet your organization's needs. And, because it is web based, people can access the tool from almost anywhere in the world.

♦ **Computer-Aided Simulation Learning**
A growing number of our courses are utilizing computer-aided simulation. This feature allows participants to learn by making critical decisions in a realistic and safe "virtual" business setting. The consequences of their actions can be seen immediately. It's a thrilling and highly effective method for realizing the potential short- and long-term benefits (or dangers) of specific actions and decisions. Using simulation, the lessons learned are forever ingrained in the participants' minds.

♦ **On-Site Learning and Corporate Solutions**
We work closely with clients to develop learning solutions that are specifically designed to meet precise business objectives and cultural needs. More than 10,000 individuals a year are trained via courses that we deliver at locations specified by our clients. These are scheduled at company locations (on-site) or at specific venues requested by the client. In most cases, such courses are custom-tailored or custom-developed from scratch to squarely address specific client objectives.

For more information about IIL and to request a free copy of our catalog, please visit www.iil.com, or contact Lori Milhaven at 212-515-5121 or Lori.Milhaven@iil.com.

Download Resource Center

Free value-added materials available from the Download Resource Center at:

www.jrosspub.com

At J. Ross Publishing we are committed to providing today's professional with practical, hands-on tools that enhance the learning experience and give readers an opportunity to apply what they have learned. That is why we offer free ancillary materials available for download on this book and all participating Web Added Value™ publications. These online resources may include interactive versions of material that appears in the book or supplemental templates, worksheets, models, plans, case studies, proposals, spreadsheets and assessment tools, among other things. Whenever you see the WAV™ symbol in any of our publications, it means bonus materials accompany the book and are available from the Web Added Value Download Resource Center at www.jrosspub.com.

Downloads available to all readers of *Dynamic Scheduling with Microsoft Office Project 2003* consist of solution files for the Relocation Project exercises, answers to the sample exam questions in Appendix 1, filters to check the quality of your own schedule and about one hundred examples of schedules we certified. There is a solutions manual for professors with the answers to the remaining questions in this book.

Short Table of Contents

Long Table of Contents

Dedication

In Dutch:

Ik draag deze derde editie op aan mijn tweede dochter, Avery. Avery, het is zo'n geweldig plezier je op te zien groeien; als ik in je ogen kijk realiseer ik me dat je sneller wilt opgroeien dan menselijke ontwikkeling toestaat.

Ik draag dit boek ook op aan mijn partner, Shelley. Shelley, je maakt het mogelijk voor me om dit hectische werk te blijven doen. Als ik er niet zeker van kon zijn dat jouw zorg voor onze kinderen alles is wat ze nodig hebben, zou ik niet langer dit beroep kunnen hebben.

In English:

I dedicate this third edition to my second daughter, Avery. Avery, it is such a joy to see you grow up; when I look in your eyes, I realize that you want to grow up faster than human development allows you to.

I dedicate this book also to my partner, Shelley. Shelley, you make it possible for me to continue doing this hectic work. If I could not be absolutely sure that you give our kids everything they need, I could not continue this profession.

What Is New in This Edition

◆ The book has been aligned with the new edition of the PMBOK®, the 2004 edition published in October of 2004 by PMI®. This book is one of the first books published that is aligned with the 2004 PMBOK®.

◆ All text has been reviewed and changed to work with the 2003 release that is now called Microsoft Office Project.

◆ The new features of Project 2003 are discussed throughout and indicated with a 2003 icon to make them easy to find. We maintained the 2002 icons that indicate what was new in the 2002 release, since this 2003 release came so fast.

◆ All screenshots were replaced, as Microsoft has done a complete makeover of the MS Project and Project Web Access interface.

◆ The index has eight times more entries and now also cross-references between the keywords. We put a lot of effort into making the index more consistent and more helpful.

◆ The files that come with the book now contain a macro that helps you find the resource-critical path in a schedule. This macro will make life much easier in resource-constrained schedules.

◆ You can now easily compare your results in the Relocation Project exercises with our solution files. We describe a process to compare two files electronically and have the differences marked.

◆ Project Server has a much more prominent place in this edition, since many organizations are moving towards realizing enterprise project management. People who are using Project 2003 in combination with Project Server will find the things they need to know in this book. People who are using Project 2003 as a standalone application are well served by this book as well.

◆ The checklist of guidelines for valid and dynamic schedules in Chapter 13 has been modified by our team of instructors. Some checks were added, many of them slightly modified. The checklist creates repeatability in project management processes, which can advance the project management maturity of individuals and their organizations. Also:
   ◇ The checklist items refer to the pages in the book where they are discussed in more detail and with procedural steps.
   ◇ The list comes with a corresponding set of filters and macros to perform the checks efficiently. The filters and macros are available for download at

www.jrosspub.com. Please, click the link *WAV Download Resource Center* to enter the download site.

◆ All learning objectives and sample exam questions have been updated again to truly capture the body of knowledge that participants are supposed to master in the Orange Belt course of our IIL certification curriculum.

◆ You will find that the book has a more international character. I invited more technical editors from different countries and their views and local experiences juice up the text in several places.

◆ This edition is written assuming that most readers are now using Windows XP. Some screen captures may differ depending on the operating system being used. The screen shots are made in Windows XP.

Foreword by Harold Kerzner

Over the years, I have been disappointed with books written on the scheduling software. This book, however, uses numerous practical examples from real life projects. You will quickly discover that the author exhibits the necessary experience to give you the insights you need to manage your projects more effectively. In addition, this one book contains all of the necessary information to attain the Orange Belt certificate from the International Institute for Learning, Inc. (IIL). This certificate is quickly gaining worldwide acceptance in the labor market, particularly since Microsoft has started endorsing it in a press release in the fall of 2003.

This book will convince you that project management can be done more efficiently and effectively using scheduling software. Historically, network diagrams were hung in the war rooms of large project teams. These charts provided insight into the downstream impacts of any changes made. Schedulers had to become skilled at identifying the impacts and the associated risks. Project management can be done easier by using Project 2003 and creating a dynamic model of your project. Slippages become immediately visible with a dynamic model. Scenarios can be developed easily with a dynamic model to address the slippages and keep the project on course.

In terms of the Project Management Maturity model I have introduced, this book creates a common language (Level 1) that will help you establishing common processes for the scheduling of projects (Level 2). The summary chapter of the book contains "*guidelines for dynamic schedules*" that reflect the best practices of scheduling with MS Project. If anything, you should consider these for the scheduling of your projects. These guidelines will help you move toward a singular methodology (Level 3). The guidelines are universally applicable to projects of any size and in any industry and are continuously improved (Level 5) with each new edition. Filters are included that help the reader verify the quality of their own schedules. This is where the book has added value over many other books that have been published. It combines the best practices of scheduling with the how-to steps in Project 2003 and tools to check if you did it right.

The scheduling guidelines are an integral part of IIL's MS Project certification curriculum. Organizations are sending their project managers and project office staff to IIL's courses. Some organizations have even made IIL MS Project certificates a requirement for project management positions. The scheduling guidelines have been embraced by a much wider circle of organizations. What seems to be evolving is a body of knowledge on scheduling with Project 2003. This book could very well become the standard.

Harold Kerzner
Cleveland, Ohio

Acknowledgments

I would like to thank all the people I have had the pleasure of meeting during my MS Project courses and consulting. The discussions we had provided valuable input for this book. Many people have opened my eyes to remarkable insights. Where I remembered individuals, I have recognized them in this book. Unfortunately, I have forgotten where many thoughts and insights originated. To all of those who should have been mentioned, I apologize.

Some people were very actively involved in creating this edition of the book and deserve special recognition. First of all I would like to thank the technical editors for their contributions to the accuracy of the text. Because of their help, I have used the word "we" throughout the book when making recommendations. The recommendations are really a culmination of experiences and insights from this team, many of whom are instructors at the International Institute for Learning, Inc. (IIL). Let me thank them individually here:

◆ K. Jeff Turner, The Boeing Company, thank you for your comments that come from deep practical experience and insight. Jeff also created the helpful illustrations on WBS (aircraft), Critical Path and slack calculation.

◆ Brian Kennemer, Microsoft Project MVP, QuantumPM, thank you for your sharp observations on technical accuracy. You made me think again in several places.

◆ Judith W. Firestone, MPM, PMP, Senior Manager, Project Management Office, CSC, thank you for trying out the steps and catching many technical errors. I wished you had more time.

◆ Joël Séguin, Microsoft Project MVP, GO Gestion de projets, as you taught classes for IIL you often sent me tidbits of feedback. I wish I could instill that habit in all instructors. Most of your remarks were incorporated in the book. Thank you.

◆ James Carpenter, Systems Architect, RADASAP, Inc., thank you for your word choice suggestions.

◆ Keith MacMillan, PMP, Senior Instructor, IIL Canada, thank you for your many remarks on where students typically get lost in my verbiage.

◆ Wolfgang Wendl, Senior Instructor, IIL Germany, thank you for your international perspective on project management. It has made the book more international.

◆ Ken Jamison, Engagement Manager, Project Assistants, thank you for going through the text in detail. You often provided very valid remarks. Ken also developed a macro that can find the resource-critical path in a schedule.

◆ Eoin Callan, President & CEO, seaCastle, Inc., thank you for your feedback; I wished you had more time.

◆ Ellen Lehnert, Senior Instructor, IIL, thank you for your recommendations on how to make this information easier to teach and for your bug alerts.

◆ Ken Terry, Senior Instructor, IIL, thank you for your comments.

Technical editors who have been very involved in previous editions are:

◆ Linda Lawlor, Senior Consultant, IIL

◆ John Sullivan, Vice-President, Instructional Design, IIL

◆ Ray Moore, Director, Amethyst Project Management Limited, UK

◆ Frank Walker, TWG Project Management, LLC

◆ Thomas Sauerbrun, Senior Instructor, IIL

In addition to the technical editors, the following people have been involved:

◆ Kelly Sullivan, Editor, IIL, thank you for the English language editing. You improved not only the English, but also the format and the layout.

◆ Paul Mason, thank you for the cartoons that illustrate many of the points made from an angle that always surprises. Whenever I received a batch of new sketches, you gave me some good laughs.

◆ Rina van Adrichem, thank you for creating many of the snapshots, for checking the consistency in words and formats, and for entering all the language edits.

◆ LaVerne Johnson, CEO of IIL, thanks for your confidence that this third edition would be worthwhile again and for your persistence in the negotiations.

◆ Stephen Buda, VP New Business Development and Finance, J. Ross Publishing, Inc., thank you for your belief in the product and for your diligent organizing of everybody involved.

Last but not least, thanks to you, the reader of this book. I hope you will find it time well spent. If you have any comments or suggestions, please send them by e-mail to EricU@iil.com.

Introduction

Microsoft Office Project 2003

Microsoft Project is a tool that helps you plan and control your project. This software can help you create Gantt Charts, network diagrams, resource histograms and budgets. It will provide reports tailored to your needs and allow you to depict the progress of your project. The strengths of the software are:

◆ The ease of use for novice users as well as for power users

◆ The flexibility in scheduling and re-scheduling

◆ The powerful reporting features
   With Project 2003 you can extract almost any information from the project database and present it in concise reports.

◆ The *collaboration* features
   These features help the project manager communicate with team members via the Internet, which is ideal for international project teams. You will need Project Server for this.

Project 2003 is a powerful tool and, like other tools, requires knowledge and skill to use correctly. The software is not a magic bean that will grow a successful project by itself. Experience has taught me that a successful project results from the combination of executive support, competent project management, a committed team and the right tools.

What Is New in Microsoft Office Project 2003?

◆ The first thing that will strike you is the fresh new look of the interface; it has more color and style.

◆ Project 2003 outputs in the web formats of *HTML* and *XML* better than it ever did before. XML in particular will allow you to exchange data with many other line-of-business applications.

◆ Project 2003 has a new **Copy picture to MS Office** feature. This will allow you to create status reports and slideshows for status presentations very quickly.

◆ If that does not help with reporting, you will find a **Print Current view as a Report** wizard on the **Report** Project Guide.

 ◆ The **Help** has been improved dramatically and will even continue to improve as time goes by. The help features search the internet knowledge databases first by default when you are online. Microsoft asks for user feedback on how helpful the help text was. Microsoft rewrites the online help text regularly with that feedback. As you can see, the online help text is subject to continuous improvement.

 ◆ More sources are available directly from the Project 2003 interface: knowledge bases, online research features, online template gallery, online training, directory of solution providers and Microsoft partners, Spotlights (news announcements).

 ◆ If you have a Windows 2003 server, you can set up a shared workspace using the new Windows SharePoint Services (WSS). A shared workspace is like a virtual meeting room. This allows you to collaborate even without Project Server.

 ◆ The *Project Guides* in Project 2003 are easier to work with and also easier to deploy. Deployment now allows relative directory paths instead of absolute paths only. Project Guides are like wizards that guide you through an involved process. The Project Guides are entirely customizable for your organization. You can incorporate your own terminology, methodology and processes in them. Project Guides help new project managers get up and running quickly within your organization. They also foster standardization of processes.

 ◆ There are now two booking types for resources: *proposed* and *committed* booking. This is particularly useful for consulting firms.

 ◆ The Project 2003 interface is much more user-friendly for project managers that connect to Project Server and use filters extensively. The simple lists and tree structure lists that are customized in Project Server now also appear in the custom enterprise fields in MS Project and in Project Web access. In 2003, you don't need a great memory anymore to work with these custom enterprise fields.

 ◆ Last but not least, Project 2003 finally has a feature to compare two versions of the same project. This is a very good feature that will allow students to compare their schedule with the solution schedule provided with the book. Of course, it is also very useful for practicing project managers.

Microsoft Office Project Server 2003

This book is not a complete reference on Project Server. It does describe what you need to know as a project manager when you work with Project 2003 Professional and connect to Project Server.

Project Server is the web-based product that works with MS Project. You could think of Project Server as an add-on of MS Project and that is indeed how it came about. However, when you start to work with Project Server, you will soon realize that turning this statement around is more appropriate; MS Project is an add-on to Project Server. Project Server is the *Enterprise Project Management* (*EPM*) platform for organizations that really want to get serious with project management and gain competitive advantages through project management. When organizations improve their project management practices, they will lower the cost of managing their projects. Organizations, like construction and consulting firms, that have projects as their core business can benefit greatly. There is no doubt in my mind that Project Server will pay itself back quickly for many organizations. Let's have a look at the impressive list of functionality it brings.

Project Server facilitates the communication between the project manager and other project stakeholders:
- The project manager can easily send out time sheets and textual status forms to team members, have them filled in by team members, collect them back and then transfer the data into the project schedule.
- The project manager just needs to save the schedule and an executive can immediately see the latest updates on their portfolio of projects, check on any problems arising and develop what-if scenarios to find solutions.
- Clients, suppliers, banks, government agencies, unions or other stakeholders can also be given access to certain projects through the Internet. You don't need to fumble with emailing *GIF*-images (Graphics Interchange Format) or *PDF*-files (Portable Document Format) any longer.

The project manager needs Microsoft Office Project 2003 Professional to connect to the Project Server database, whereas other stakeholders only need *Internet Explorer* and a license for the web-based application *Microsoft Project Web Access* to access Project Server. Project Server allows the following applications to communicate with each other and acts as *middleware* between them:
- *MS Office Project*
- *MS Office Outlook*
- *MS Office Excel*

- *Internet Explorer*
- *SQL Server database server*
- *SQL Server analysis server*

- *Windows SharePoint Services*
- *Web Server*

What Is New In Microsoft Office Project Server 2003?

Project Server is more than just a postal service. Here is a complete list of benefits you can enjoy by using Project Server, some of which I have marked as new features:

- Better visibility on the status and forecasts of projects for executives
  - ◇ The ultra-flexible reporting tools like the portfolio views, the portfolio analyzer and the portfolio modeler will provide you with much insight into your projects.
  - ◇ The data are stored in a relational database that can be mined efficiently using the OLAP-capabilities of Analysis Server (SQL Server). *OLAP* stands for OnLine Analytical Processing, which allows executives to slice and dice the data, and drill down where they want.

  - ◇ Any grid-like data in Project Web Access views can easily be exported to MS Office Excel or XML with the click of a button. Project managers just need to run a wizard to get an MS Office Word status report or an MS Office PowerPoint presentation on their project ready.
  - ◇ Digital dashboards can now easily be created. A digital dashboard is a one-screen overview of your project portfolio. Dashboards can be created by dragging & dropping your choice of six standard web parts onto the dashboard.

- Providing visibility of the project to other groups of stakeholders:
  - ◇ The administrator can create categories of target groups: team member, project manager, resource manager and executive manager. Each category comes with a set of access rights.
  - ◇ The administrator can give access to certain projects through portfolios of projects.
  - ◇ The administrator can give viewing rights to certain data in the project database through custom views. You can now keep data confidential and away from searching eyes.

- Standardization across the enterprise:
  - ◇ Project Server allows standardization of templates, calendars, fields and views. Project Server allows you to create an enterprise-wide resource pool of thousands of people. With MS Project as a stand-alone tool, you should not go over one hundred resources in the shared resource pool, unless you don't mind waiting five minutes for a schedule to open.

◇ The scalability has improved, because the Project Server database can now be spread over multiple servers.

◆ Modeling of portfolios of projects and integrated program schedules:
Executives can interact with the data to their hearts' content and I would like to meet executives who do that. Most likely they have delegated this to their project office staff. The *project office* is a central support and/or standardization office for project managers within an organization. However, the interface is becoming so intuitive that it is not unthinkable that one day executives will start investigating various scenarios themselves. *Project Web Access* provides a flexible interface that allows you to slice and dice the project data and drill down into the supporting details. Executives and resource managers can thus make analyses to find answers to questions like:

◇ What are our resource needs in the longer term so that we can train existing or hire new employees in a timely manner? In general, resource availability is flexible, as long as the need for the resource is about three months away.

◇ Can we take on another project given the resources we have? If not, when can we take it on? Or, if we were to take it on right now, how much would that make our current projects slip?

◆ Projecting the resource needs of the organization in the long term
Project Server also allows the organization to model their projects and related resource needs in the longer term. This will make your *Human Resources* department very happy.

In 2003, there are now two booking types: *Proposed* versus *Committed*. This allows consulting companies to propose resources without immediately over-allocating them.

◆ Optimization of resource usage in the medium term

◇ Project Server is equipped with skill-based scheduling tools that allow you to optimize the use of your resources. The tools are the *Team Builder*, the *Resource Substitution Wizard* and the *cross-project leveling* features.

◇ The skill-based scheduling has now become much simpler with the arrival of 10 multi-value fields for resources. This makes it easier to capture the multitude of skills that people typically develop over the years.

◆ Foster *collaboration* between project manager and team members

◇ As a project manager, you can collect input from team members through Project Server, like new tasks, new issues, new risks, new documents, changes to the work times and vacation day requests. Project Server creates a two-way street between the project manager and the team members

◇ The document, issue and risk management features now have check in and check out procedures so that the latest version is never lost. When checking in, the editor is prompted to comment on the changes made which provides a complete history for a document. Different versions can be stored.

◆ Integrating *project planning* with *personal planning* for team members:
  ◇ One single *integrated to-do list* of project and non-project tasks in *Project Web Access (PWA)* or in *MS Office Outlook*.
  ◇ Team members can request for vacations and other time off through PWA.
  ◇ Team members can now fill in their *time sheet* in *MS Office Outlook*.

◆ *Delegating tasks*:
  Project Server can accommodate large projects and more than two hierarchical levels in the project team: project manager, team leaders and team members. A team leader can delegate a task to a team member through the delegation feature.
  The delegation feature can also be beneficial for *matrix organizations*.
  Resource managers in matrix organizations don't need MS Project any longer, because with the Web-based Team Builder they can assign their resource to the projects.
  Delegation can now be restricted to only downward in the organizational hierarchy.

◆ Reporting progress electronically in *actual hours* worked, a narrative commentary or both:
  ◇ Time sheets:
    The big benefit of electronic time sheets is one-time data entry. Project Server allows the time sheets to be filled in online or offline by team members and the time sheets in Project Server can include project and non-project tasks. Project managers can automatically transfer the time sheet data into their project schedules.
    Time sheets can now be designed by the project office in this 2003 release. Specific time periods can be designed, and past time periods can be locked so that actuals cannot be changed after the invoices have gone out.
    Non-project time commitments now decrease the availability of resources.
  ◇ Textual status reports:
    The project manager can send out freeform status reports or create template status reports that have the fields he expects to be narrated by the team members.

◆ Baselines can now be locked in by person. Hopefully, we will be able to do this by project in a future release.

◆ Semi-automatic updating of the project schedule:
  ◇ A project manager can create rules that allow updates from trusted sources to be processed automatically.

◇ The project manager can even choose to manage by exception using this feature; if certain thresholds are exceeded, the message is not processed automatically, but called to his attention instead.

◆ Easy administration
This is where Microsoft has made significant strides in this release. The following new features all bring down the amount of effort for the Project Server administrator:

◇ *Active Directory* is a central database of user accounts in the Windows network operating system. The Active Directory can be synchronized with the enterprise resource pool and the synchronization can be scheduled to take place regularly. This will take care of the new hires and the people who left the company. Also, Active Directory security groups of users can be synchronized with Project Server security groups.

◇ Project managers can now check stranded projects in themselves after a power failure or network disconnect.

◇ Administrators can now remove resources entirely.

◇ *OLAP-views* can now be transferred between OLAP-cubes and re-used instead of re-created.

◇ *Portfolio models* are now dynamically refreshed instead of manually.

◆ Enhanced *Application Programming Interface* (*API*) for customizing and integrating into line of business systems. You can now create or retrieve just about any data or object in Project Server.

So, what did we lose?

◆ Project Server does not come any longer with the SharePoint engine built into it. SharePoint has been renamed from *SharePoint Team Services* (*STS*) to *Windows SharePoint Services* (*WSS*). WSS is now packaged as part of the Windows Server 2003 network operating system. You only need WSS on the server computer, so this does not affect you greatly. WSS now provides richly featured document management functionality.

◆ The *workgroup* features have been hidden by default. The workgroup features allow you to send out *time sheets* by email instead of by web. It is clear that Microsoft wants to get rid of it, since this code has not been maintained or upgraded for two releases now.

Is This Book for You?

This book is different from other books written on Project 2003. It not only shows you how to use MS Project, but also adds insights and experiences from real life project management. This book teaches you how to manage projects using Project 2003 instead of teaching you all the features.

The book is intended for the following target groups:

◆ Project managers who use Project 2003 on a day-to-day basis
It is aimed at the novice to intermediate user of MS Project, but I am confident that advanced users will find it worthwhile as well. Advanced users may find better ways to do things, and will find the best practices of scheduling with MS Project. Advanced users may discover better words to explain features to colleagues.

◆ People who schedule and manage a single project
This book is aimed at people who manage a single project at a time with MS Project. We will not delve deep into multi-project management issues. This book is used as the course book in the "Managing a Single Project with Microsoft Office Project 2003" (Orange Belt) course at the International Institute for Learning (IIL). The Blue Belt focuses on managing multiple projects with MS Project and Project Server. The Black Belt course addresses the configuration and customization of *Project Server* from a project office or business analysis point of view.

◆ Students and professors at colleges and universities
For effective delivery of (post-)graduate courses, we added:
  ◇ Cradle-to-grave exercises on an office-relocation project
  ◇ 40 sample exam questions
    In Appendix 1 at the end of the book you will find sample exam questions on Project 2003 that are similar to the questions used in the online exams for the certification curriculum at the International Institute for Learning, Inc.
  ◇ Review questions for self-evaluation of understanding
  ◇ Trouble shooting exercises from real life technical support
  ◇ Case studies from real life consulting
All readers have access to the solutions of the first two items. Professors can request a solution manual from the publisher with the solutions to the remaining items. The publisher will give access to the solution manual if they make this book mandatory reading in their courses.

What You Will Find in This Book

I will present the features to create project schedules efficiently and the features that create effective schedules. These are the features that will benefit you most in practice. At IIL, we constantly ask our course participants what features they use, why they use them and how. We have captured the insights we gained in this book that will give you guidance in how to run your projects in practice.

Many people have asked me for a good process to follow for creating schedules. The structure of the book matches the order of steps we recommend you take. The recommended process is as simple as following the *Short Table of Contents* of this book. The book is aimed at the busy, practicing project manager who needs to get up to speed quickly with MS Project.

This book is entirely based on and aligned with the new 2004 Edition of the PMBOK® published by the PMI. However, I will not explain the concepts of the PMBOK®, but simply refer to them. If you have not read the PMBOK®, I recommend you read it first or, at least, keep it nearby.

I have kept the text as succinct as possible. Less text is more, in my opinion, and the last thing I want is to waste your precious time with too many words. When I read other books, I often find I have to read too many words for the point made. I therefore take pride in writing books that follow the principle of 'less is more', even though the book seems to grow with every edition. I have inserted graphics throughout the text wherever I could save words with an illustration. A picture is worth a thousand words.

This book has an attitude. It is not a complete description of the features of Project 2003. I will recommend certain features and I will argue against using some other features. An important criterion I use for my recommendations is that the schedule you build with Project 2003 should be a good schedule of your project. In our opinion, a good schedule is:

◆ **A model of the project**
   A *model* is a deliberate but smart simplification of the complex reality of the project.
◆ **A valid model of the project**
   A model is *valid* if it reflects the reality of your project and if it forecasts your project well.
◆ **A dynamic model of the project**
   A *dynamic* model updates itself when a change is entered. When one change happens in your project, ideally you would have to update only one field in the model to have a valid representation of your project — again. Changes happen often

during the execution of the project, when you also happen to be very busy. Therefore, a dynamic model is a tremendous help during project execution, because it helps you keep your project schedule alive, hence the title of this book: *Dynamic Scheduling with Microsoft® Office Project 2003*.

Static schedules do not maintain themselves. Some features in MS Project are nice to have, but create schedules that are hungry for maintenance. Therefore, I don't recommend features that continue to need attention from you. I have found the judicious application of features critical in using MS Project. Thousands of students have helped with determining what features in MS Project are most beneficial.

In this book we will cover two main configurations of MS Project currently in use: MS Project used as a standalone tool and Project 2003 Professional used with *Project Server*.

What You Won't Find in This Book

◆ An explanation of all the features in Project 2003. I have made a careful selection of features that will benefit users most when managing a single project. This book is not a complete reference on Project 2003.

◆ An explanation of all there is to know about Project Server. This book will only cover the basics of working with Project Server that project managers need to know.[1]

◆ A discussion on how to manage multiple projects with MS Project.
You will not find much content in this book on:
◇ Managing many small projects
◇ Managing one large, integrated program schedule that consists of subprojects
◇ Managing a portfolio of projects

 Please note that the book is entirely aligned with Project Server. The book is an essential first step on your way towards managing multiple projects. Skipping this book and immediately delving into managing multiple projects is a mistake made often. You need to be able to build a solid model of a single project first. Then you can roll them up into an integrated program schedule or a portfolio and expect to develop scenarios.

---

[1] IIL has separate classes on Project Server; the Blue Belt Professional and Black Belt Professional courses. See www.iil.com and follow the link *Microsoft Project*.

Now that you know that you are reading a book with an attitude, you may be interested in how the attitude came about.

Who Is the Author?

The author is a project management practitioner. Over the past 15 years I have managed many projects using MS Project and I have taught thousands of people in its use. The insights you will find in this book are a combination of the collective wisdom of the clients we met in our consulting and our courses by IIL. When I say 'we' I refer to my team of MS Project and Project Server consultants and instructors at IIL.

In September 1993, I became the first Canadian to be certified in MS Project by Microsoft. At that time, the current version was 3.0. When 4.0 came out, I recertified immediately. My career was progressing well and more eager than ever, I awaited the exam for Project 98 … and waited … and waited. It was never released. I realized that I was probably not the only person who was looking for it. I also observed that many people were wasting a lot of valuable work time in trying to learn MS Project on their own. I realized that organizations needed a meaningful certification curriculum so that they could implement MS Project quickly and thoroughly. Professional development curricula are only thorough if they measure the outcome of the training, and if they provide certificates that are meaningful in the marketplace. I decided to address the need for certification in the marketplace.

In 1998, I developed advanced courses in MS Project. I approached IIL to market them and was hired as Director, MS Project Certification. Since then we have held many certification classes in North America and in Europe. In these workshops, I have had the pleasure of working with some of the finest project managers and project schedulers.

The consulting and training I have done included people from a wide variety of sectors: information technology, telecommunications, banking, automotive, construction, manufacturing, pharmaceutical, international development and government. As a result, you will find a wide variety of examples in this book. It does not cater to one sector in particular. The principles I present in this book are universally applicable across industries.[2]

---

[2] I always appreciate hearing if you think certain recommendations would or would not work for your industry. Please send those observations to me at EricU@iil.com. I promise you a response.

The Project Management Institute (PMI) certified me as a Project Management Professional (PMP) in March of 1994. IIL promoted me to Executive Director, Microsoft EPM Division. I develop the course content, manage the certification curriculum and lead the team of instructors. This team currently consists of thirty instructors in seven different countries.

The Author's Perspective on Scheduling

In my years of consulting and training project managers, I have made some observations:

◆ Some large schedules I have seen did not have a Work Breakdown Structure (WBS). All tasks were on the first (and only) indentation level. Imagine that this book did not have a hierarchy of sections, chapters and paragraphs. A well-known automotive company used schedules like these. (Sorry, no names!) Organizations were not using the basic concept of logical and hierarchical Work Breakdown Structures. Their schedules are difficult to explain to anyone who is not interested in detail activities — like executives.

◆ Many schedules created by "experienced" project managers turned out to have only a few dependencies (links between tasks). Not surprisingly, those schedules had many schedule constraints that anchored the task bars to their dates. Constraints, however, made the schedule very rigid. Every time a change occurred, the entire schedule needed to be reviewed and updated before it depicted the project well again. Isn't this reminiscent of the time when we made schedules on paper to hang on our walls? Such schedules are nice charts of the project, but are definitely not useful dynamic models of the project. These people spend too much time on scheduling. And they are spending this time when they don't have a moment to spare — during project execution. Needless to say, these project managers would inevitably stop updating their schedule after a few weeks into the execution of their project.

◆ Many organizations create schedules that are so complex that it takes weeks to understand them. I am always afraid to ask these project managers how long it took them to create monsters like that. If the *model* of the project is as complex as or even more complex than the reality itself, you do not have a better handle on the reality with the model you created. Modeling is, by its definition, simplifying the reality to get a better handle on it. Too many project managers seem to forget this. If you cannot explain your project schedule to your team, the schedule is simply too complex. If your team understands it, you get much more value from your schedule and scheduling efforts. If other stakeholders can also understand your schedule, even better.

◆ Many organizations invest in making schedules, but abandon them when the project execution starts. The chance that it will be abandoned increases with the complexity of the schedule, with the lack of dependencies or with an abundance of constraints. One aerospace company had never been able to keep any of its schedules alive during project execution. Only after they had one project manager trained in our program (sorry for this plug), this person managed to do that as a primer. Project managers tend to get very busy with fighting fires after the project kicks off. If you don't update your schedule, you don't have accurate forecasts of your project. You need your model to constantly forecast to control your project. A dynamic schedule is easy to maintain and continuously provides forecasts.

◆ Many project managers do not enter resources into MS Project. Even if they do, they often do not check if they over-allocated their resources. The schedule may show finish dates that executives like, which may result in swift approval of the project, but when the workloads are leveled, it becomes painfully clear that the promised dates are not feasible. If you notice that deadlines are often not accomplished in your organization, a lack of modeling resources may very well be the cause of that.

◆ Any organization that shares its resources across projects but does not have a central, shared resource pool will likely suffer from missed deadlines. The cause is the resource impacts across the projects. Many IT departments experience this. IT resources tend to be expensive and they are often shared across all projects. The individual schedules show date forecasts that executives like. When the project execution starts, project managers start stealing each other's resources in order to meet their own deadlines. Doing so wreaks havoc with each other's deadline accomplishment. And if the total workload of the resources has not been modeled across the projects, the dates shown by individual schedules may be too optimistic. With *Project Server* you can set up an enterprise resource pool that can relegate this issue to the past.

◆ Last but not least, in 1994 The Standish Group published a report on the performance of IT projects.[3] They surveyed 365 IT managers representing 8,380 applications from many different industries. Only 1 in 8 projects was delivered successfully. In 1996, the number had improved to 1 in 4, because the shock wave of the first report led to quicker cancellation of dead-end projects. My personal conviction is that the project management concepts are solid and could successfully be applied to IT projects. My personal observation is that many IT project managers, for some weird reason, are not applying the principles of project management or not applying them properly.

---

[3] Chaos, The Standish Group International, 1994, Dennis, MA, page 2-7.

I admit, however, that in certain areas it is necessary to adjust the techniques used. One contribution this book will make in that respect is, for example, that most IT project managers will have to do a Resource Critical Path analysis instead of a Critical Path analysis, since most are in a resource-constrained situation. This relatively new concept is explained in this book.

If you have been bothered by any of these observations, you should read this book cover to cover. This book will provide you with insights and techniques to address them.

These observations on the current state-of-the-art in scheduling led me to believe a certification curriculum was much needed. Such a curriculum can elevate the skills of MS Project users to new heights and improve the accuracy of the forecasts. More projects will be successful. You will experience more reasonable workloads, less burnout and more reliable long-term forecasts of resource needs. The cost of managing projects should decrease and the competitiveness of the organization should increase in the global market place.

Why Do We Need Valid and Dynamic Schedules?

Most project managers create schedules to better forecast their projects. If the schedule is not *valid*, it does not produce reliable forecasts.

There are several reasons why we need schedules to be *dynamic* as well:

♦ Changes happen so frequently in projects that it is hard to keep up with them. If your schedule is not as dynamic as it can be, you will have to review the rest of the schedule whenever you make one change. You will spend too much time keeping it alive. You will likely stop updating it sometime during project execution.

♦ In order to explore *what-if scenarios* in MS Project and in Project Server to solve problems, the schedules need to be dynamic models. If there are many constraints in the schedules, it is hard to assess the impact of proposed solutions. In a typical project, many slippages need to be compensated for.

♦ Schedules of subprojects need to be dynamic *models* when you want to roll them up into a master schedule. Otherwise, you will spend too much time making changes in the master schedule. When dynamic models are rolled up, problems become visible in the master schedule. Problems can easily be resolved by creating *what-if scenarios*.

♦ In order to do schedule *simulation* for quantitative *risk analysis*, you will need dynamic models. *Monte Carlo schedule simulation* is essential to provide more realistic forecasts to executives and clients.

We have made an attempt to quantify the amount of time saved when working with dynamic schedule instead of a rigid schedule. We calculated for a 100 tasks and 3 month project that you will save about 50 hours of effort if you create a dynamic schedule in the first place, see page 217.

We have created a certification curriculum in MS Project and Project server. Organizations can use this curriculum as an instrument to evaluate if their project managers are effective and efficient at managing their projects.

The MS Office Project and Project Server 2003 Curriculum

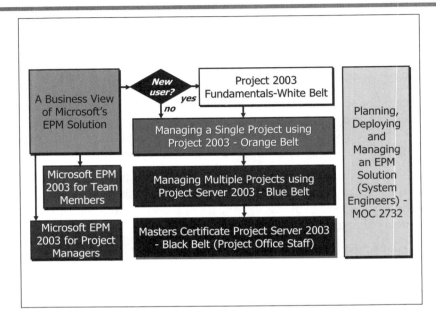

There are three tracks in the curriculum:

◆ The track on the left displays three new workshops on Enterprise Project Management (EPM): an overview course and workshops for team members and project managers. See the next page for more details.

◆ The track in the middle reflects certification curriculum that consists of four levels, each designed with a specific target group in mind:

◇ Microsoft Office Project 2003 Fundamentals (*White Belt*) – for people who are new to MS Project; see page 17.

◇ Managing a Single Project with MS Project (*Orange Belt*) – for project managers who use MS Project regularly; see page 17.

◇ Managing Multiple Projects with MS Project (*Blue Belt Standard*) or with Project Server (*Blue Belt Professional*) – for project managers who manage multiple projects; see page 18.

◇ Masters Certificate in MS Project (*Black Belt Standard*) or Project Server (*Black Belt Professional*) – for project office staff; see page 18.

◆ The track on the right is for Project Server deployment officers; see page 19 for more details.

If you are interested in detailed topical outlines of these workshops, visit www.iil.com and follow the link *Microsoft Project*.

Enterprise Project Management (EPM) Workshops

Many organizations requested more efficient, onsite and custom-made training to support the deployment of Project Server and Project Web Access. The *Enterprise Project Management (EPM)* courses can easily be adapted to the specific needs of your organization depending on your existing business processes and configuration chosen. Typically, these courses will be delivered on your site or in dedicated eLearning sessions. Currently, we offer three EPM-workshops (more are planned for the future):

◆ A Business View of Microsoft's EPM Solution – designed for those who need an introduction to Enterprise Project Management (EPM) with the Microsoft EPM Solution.

◆ Microsoft EPM for Team Members – designed for project team members who need to report progress, issues, risks and documents to their project manager. Team members will learn how they can collaborate online with the project manager.

◆ Microsoft EPM for Project Managers – designed for project managers who use Project 2003 and Project Web Access in an EPM environment. Project managers will learn how they can collaborate online with their team and manage their project efficiently and effectively.

White Belt Workshop

In the 2-day White Belt workshop we get people started on scheduling their projects with MS Project. The White Belt is designed for the person who is new to MS Project and has not had much exposure to it. In this workshop, we have people build a schedule from the ground up and optimize it such that it meets the deadline, and we even have them update the schedule in the simplest way possible. This workshop is meant to raise the confidence level of people when working with MS Project taking them through an entire *project life cycle*. We stay away from the difficult situations and discussions. The White Belt course material is a carefully picked subset of this book.

Orange Belt Workshop

In the 2-day Orange Belt workshop we bring people who make nice charts of their projects to the level of making *dynamic models* that are easy to maintain and to assess impacts with. Dynamic models continue to produce *valid* forecasts until the project is closed. If a person is certified at the Orange Belt level, this means to their employer that the person has demonstrated knowledge to create good schedules of their own projects.

The Orange Belt is tailored to experienced project managers and schedulers. We present all the best practices of scheduling with MS Project and encourage people to check their own schedules to verify if they used those best practices. We enter into intricate discussions on tricky situations that reveal the boundaries of the tool as a modeling tool and present workarounds where available. All in all, the Orange Belt course is a checkup for people who have been using MS Project for years, perhaps even on a day-to-day basis.

The Orange Belt certificate shows that people know how to create good schedules. These schedules are ready for advanced portfolio modeling and optimization. In other words, the Orange Belt course is an essential first step towards *enterprise project management*. The course material of the Orange Belt course is this entire book.

Blue Belt Professional Workshop

The 2-day Blue Belt workshop is designed for people who manage multiple projects simultaneously with Project 2003 Professional in combination with Project Server. These people have successfully managed single projects and ended up managing multiple projects (as a reward?). They can be project managers, program managers, portfolio managers, resource managers and functional managers. Staff members who work in a project office often get involved with the modeling and monitoring of multiple projects as well.

In the Blue Belt Professional, we train project managers who have Project 2003 Professional to work with *Project Web Access* and *Project Server* for managing and controlling their projects.

Black Belt Professional Workshop

The 2-day Black Belt Professional workshop is targeted at people in the project office who focus on decreasing the cost of managing projects in the organization. Project office staff can increase the efficiency of project managers by customizing and standardizing fields, developing views, optimizing resource usage and project portfolios. In other words, the Black Belt Professional is for people who need to know most about the Microsoft EPM tools.

Planning, Deploying and Managing an EPM Solution Workshop

IIL offers a separate track for Project Server deployment officers.[4] It is the track on the right in the overview chart on page 16. This is course 2732 from the *Microsoft Official Curriculum* (MOC) with the impressive title: *Planning, Deploying and Managing an Enterprise Project Management Solution*. Microsoft developed this 5-day course and IIL features it in its assortment. This workshop is meant for system engineers and deployment consultants. It is very technical in nature and aims at preparing people for the installation and configuration of *Project Server* within their organization. Topics range from determining the number of servers and their hardware specifications, deciding which components of Project Server are loaded on which server, installing and configuring the system, testing it, administering and troubleshooting it. You can certify yourself through *Microsoft Learning* with the exam that is associated with this course.[5]

Organizations That Endorse Our Certification Curriculum

◆ Microsoft
In October 2003, Microsoft formally recognized our curriculum for the first time, since we started it in 1998. Microsoft issued a press release in which they announced they would replace the MOUS-certification of MS Project with IIL-certification starting with the 2003 release in October 2003.

◆ *Project Management Institute* (*PMI*)
PMI is offering our Orange Belt workshop in its *Seminars World* offering since 2002.

◆ *Project World*
Project World is offering our Orange Belt workshop at their events since 2002.

◆ *American Council on Education* (*ACE*)
The ACE audited our curriculum in September 2001 and accredited it. Since then people can get (elective) university credits with our IIL-certificates.

[4] Please visit our website www.iil.com for detailed course descriptions and topical outlines.

[5] Please visit www.microsoft.com/learning/

How Many Are Currently Certified?

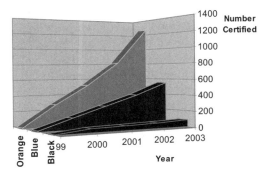

As of December 31, 2003 there were 1271 people certified at the Orange Belt level, 551 at the Blue Belt level and 89 at the Black Belt level. As you can see the curve starts to bend upward; the growth is accelerating. Since October 14, 2003 Microsoft endorses our curriculum and we expect to accelerate even more as a result. We aim at increasing the number of certified people by 50% every year.

The following are some (volunteered and unpaid) quotes from participants:

Orange Belt

Best Project Training I ever attended; very systematical and practical approach for doing Project Management with MS Project. I use the book as an everyday reference. Peter Vogel, Microsoft Services Germany

I want to thank you and all the trainers from IIL for some of the best training I have taken. David W. Weigel, New York State

The knowledge I have gained by taking this course has set me apart from other project managers. I now create dynamic schedules that work! Dino Nosella, Project Manager, SAP Canada, Inc.

The practical and hands-on experience combined with the industry knowledge makes this a very beneficial course for even those who have used MS Project for years. Michele L Bolen, Project Manager, American Red Cross

I found the online Orange Belt course one of the most effective and beneficial software courses I have ever taken. The focus on 'how to use the software to manage a project' was a refreshing contrast to the usual 'how to use the functions of this software'. Tommie G. Cayton, Ph.D., Assistant Director, Project Management, Harcourt

---

Blue Belt

All project plans on this project come through me. It is very - and in most cases, painfully - obvious to me when someone submits a plan who hasn't been through your course. Bill Shepherd, Associate, Booz Allen Hamilton Inc., Oct. 2003

Superb instruction and excellent course content. A must for even experienced MS Project users. Bill Reinhart, Project Manager, SBC/Ameritech, USA

I have managed projects for a number of years, but the course was of such high quality that I now feel the quality and accuracy of my project plans will be enhanced. Dave Kempster, Consultancy & Research Manager, Centrefile Limited, UK

We reviewed a number of training vendors when we determined who to send our folks to and the IIL courses are by far the best quality with regard to content and instruction. David Peeters, PMP, Sr. Project Management Consultant, Alliant Energy

Black Belt

The black belt course was superb! Bryan Menn, Project Manager, University of Texas Health Science Center.

The IIL course teaches real world skills, by instructors with real world experience. Jim Kasper, Project Control Officer, Altaresources

The IIL MS Project Certification series should be required by every project manager who uses the product! Stephanie Iverson, Director Program Management, Marriott Vacation Club International, USA

Although there are millions of copies of MS Project sold, only a few thousand people really know how to use it. If you want to become a real 'master' user of MS Project, this is the class for you. Jacob Myers, Program Manager, Limited Technology Services, USA

This course focuses on teaching Project Managers how to use Microsoft Project to be more productive and proficient. It is extremely valuable. Len Maland, PMP, Senior Program Manager, HP Consulting & Integration Services, May 2002

We are currently experiencing a lot of interest in our certification curriculum not only from the United States, Canada, Mexico and Europe, but also from Brazil and China.

Overall, we are striving towards creating the universally accepted body of knowledge for scheduling projects using MS Project.

What Are the Certification Requirements?

The certification levels have a combination of knowledge and skill tests:

◆ The White Belt candidates must pass the online multiple-choice test. The content of the White Belt test is a subset of this book. Topics are selected from each chapter. White Belt course participants receive a separate course binder.

◆ The Orange Belt candidates must pass the online multiple-choice test. This book contains the entire content of the Orange Belt exam. Sample exam questions can be found on page 705.

◆ The Blue Belt participants must pass the online multiple-choice exam. There is a separate Blue Belt course binder that is handed out to participants in a Blue Belt course.

◆ The Black Belt participants must complete an assignment in which they plan, implement and report on a customization of *Project Server* (Black Belt Professional). This is a test on competency of the individual. There is a separate Black Belt course binder that is handed out to participants in a Black Belt course.

The online multiple-choice tests consist of 30 questions. The questions have to be answered in one hour. The exam is an open-book and open-computer exam so that it reflects the circumstances of the workplace. The test objectives of the online exams are three-fold:

◆ Test your *readiness* to use the basic features
  ◇ Basic features are features most people need when modeling their project, regardless of their industry.
  ◇ Do you know the complete how-to steps of the basic features from memory? If you have to look up all the steps in the interface, you will need more than one hour to answer the exam questions.
◆ Test your *understanding* of the applications
  ◇ Do you understand the behind-the-screens working of MS Project and Project Server?
  ◇ Do you know the basic formulas that MS Project uses to calculate values in the calculated fields?
◆ Test your *practical knowledge* and *skills*
  ◇ Do you know how to model real life situations instead of fictional examples?
  ◇ Can you give sound advice in simple case situations?

With regard to the online exams, our experience shows that the exam discriminates well between people who prepared themselves and those who didn't.

The blend of knowledge tests and skill tests has proven to be very well liked by individuals and has also proven its value for organizations. For example, in the Black Belt assignment, instructors evaluate the candidate's implementation plan for a feature of Project Server. From my personal observations, I can say that IIL-instructors have steered several organizations away from pitfalls in the implementation of Project Server.

Qualification Requirements for Instructors

In order to maintain quality in the delivery of our certification curriculum, we select instructors based on several criteria:

◆ Candidates must have hands-on experience in managing projects.
◆ Candidates must be using MS Project on an almost daily basis.
◆ Candidates must have the *Project Management Professional* (PMP) designation by the *PMI*.
◆ Candidates must have earned credentials in training groups in MS Project.
◆ Candidates must be certified in MS Project in our certification curriculum on one level higher than the level they will be teaching in the curriculum.
◆ Candidates must go through a train-the-trainer process.

If you are interested in becoming an instructor in this curriculum, please send me your resume at EricU@iil.com.

Consulting

In addition to training and certification services, IIL offers consulting. We help people understand how tools like MS Project and Project Server can best be implemented in their organization. Every organization is unique and has its own needs. The output of the consulting can take the shape of:

◆ *Schedule evaluation and certification service*
   We can give you detailed feedback on the quality of the schedules of your project managers based on the checklist in the summary chapter of this book, see page 678. This checklist reflects the best practices of scheduling with MS Project. For about one hundred US dollar per submitted schedule, we will send you one report on the schedule with detailed instructions where your schedule needs improvements, why these improvements are important and how to go about implementing them. If your schedule meets all the requirements in the checklist, IIL will certify your schedule and IIL will send you a certificate for the schedule along with the report.

◆ Implementation of *Project Server*
   Determining hardware needed and establishing the configuration of the servers

considering the projected usage within your organization. Setting up the enterprise codes and resource pool. Designing views and reports needed by executives.

◆ Creation of your project management methodology
A *methodology* can contain processes, templates, best practices, scheduling guidelines, lessons learned or a project management framework specific to your organization. The methodology of your organization can be captured in a custom *Project Guide* such that project managers can consult with the methodology inside MS Project.

◆ Development of *project templates*
Templates can contain custom views, tables, filters and groups. Custom Project guides and macros can be added if the basic functionality in MS Project does not support what is needed in your organization.

◆ *Training* and *certification*
After the tools are developed, people often need training in how to use them. We create new material or adapt our existing course material and train the project managers and schedulers. We can provide custom certification to verify if people acquired the knowledge and skills needed.

◆ *Coaching*, *mentoring* and *help desk*
A final step is often to coach and mentor on the job or provide technical support. People tend to get stuck sometimes when they strike out on their own to model their projects. If so, we are here to help.

Give Us Your Feedback

You are the person who can make the next edition of this book better. Please send me your feedback.

If you have any questions or if you would like to discuss any recommendations we make in this book, don't hesitate to contact me at EricU@iil.com.

Thank you for the time you will spend reading this book. I hope you will find it well worth the effort! If you did, please let me know, since it motivates me to write the next edition. And if you didn't, please let me know why.

Eric Uyttewaal, PMP
Executive Director, Microsoft EPM Division
International Institute for Learning
EricU@iil.com
www.iil.com

About This Book

Learning Objectives

The following are the learning objectives we aim to accomplish with this book. After reading this book you will:

◆ Understand project management terminology aligned with the PMBOK® 2004 edition [6]

◆ Be able to create a valid and dynamic model of your own project:
   ◇ Choosing the options and creating the project calendar
   ◇ Entering tasks, estimates, dependencies, constraints, resources and assignments

◆ Be able to assess if you implemented the best-practices of scheduling established by IIL based on research of over one thousand real life schedules

◆ Know how to optimize the schedule to meet deadlines and budget restrictions while keeping the workloads of the resources within their availability

◆ Be able to create reports and custom views for the project that meet the need of stakeholders

◆ Know how to efficiently update the schedule when the project is running to continuously forecast the project cost and finish date

In general, you should feel very comfortable with Project 2003 and have a good understanding of how the tool functions and behaves. This knowledge will enable you to efficiently and effectively manage your project(s) after you finish reading this book. We will now outline the topics that will address these objectives.

---

[6] See the PMBOK® Guide, 2004 Edition, published by the PMI.

Outline of This Book

First you initiate the project, then you plan it, and while you execute it, you monitor and control it. At the end, you close it out. Sometimes you may have to re-plan the project while it is running. The illustration shows

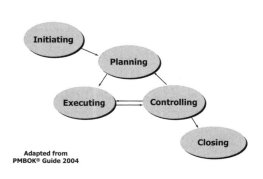

Adapted from
PMBOK® Guide 2004

these five process groups as distinguished by the Project Management Institute (PMI) in the Guide to the Project Management Body of Knowledge (PMBOK®), 2004 Edition. I omitted the word *monitoring* in the process group *monitoring and controlling* for the sake of simplicity. I will often refer to *Planning* as the *planning phase*. *Executing* and *Controlling* take place concurrently, and I will refer to them as the *execution phase*.

We have used the process groups to structure this book. In fact, we are treating the creation of the project plan as a mini-project in itself, and we mapped all the steps to create a schedule with MS Project to these process groups. The result can be seen in the

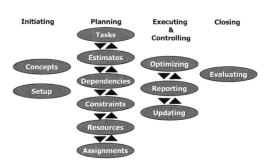

illustration that provides an overview of the contents of this book. Each balloon is a chapter. The overview illustration will be shown at the start of every chapter to indicate where we are. It will pull us back into overview mode before we delve into the details of the next chapter. Each balloon is a step in the process of creating and managing a project using MS Project. We recommend you use these same sequential steps when you model your own project with Project 2003.

We will now elaborate on each step (ellipse).

Initiating

Concepts (Chapter 1)

In this chapter, we will explain some basic concepts of project management. Even though this book is not meant to be a project management theory book, we will provide as much background information as you need to utilize Project 2003 well.

In this chapter, we will also explain the different purposes for using Project 2003. In this book, we will aim at accomplishing the most ambitious one — forecasting a project by building a dynamic model in Project 2003.

Setup (Chapter 2)

In this chapter, we will introduce the Project 2003 interface. We will discuss file management, templates and views. Then we will start creating a new project. This includes naming the project and entering the project start or finish date. We will invite you to think about the default settings that are active in Project 2003, because some important options need to be set at this stage before any tasks are entered. We will create the project calendar at this stage.

Planning

In this section, we will develop and enter all the schedule data into Project 2003. This step involves most of the effort in creating the schedule. There are six types of data that Project 2003 needs to create the schedule. We will discuss each of these in the next six chapters.

Tasks (Chapter 3)

Tasks answer the question: *What needs to be done?* The task list is developed from the deliverables that together with the tasks form the Work Breakdown Structure (WBS). The structure can have several hierarchical levels like in an organizational chart. In MS Project the levels are called outline levels. This chapter will explain how to create and enter the structured list in Project 2003. We will also discuss how to reorganize the task list by moving and copying.

Estimates (Chapter 4)

Estimates answer the question: *How long will the task take?* They can be made in business days (duration) or in person days (work). There are many factors to consider when estimating. We will provide a process in this chapter that will hopefully make estimating easier. We will also discuss the human side of estimating that may bias the estimating. We will discuss some difficulties that occur in practice. We will suggest how to handle these biases and difficulties.

Dependencies (Chapter 5)

Dependencies deal with the question: *In what sequence do the tasks have to be done, and how will the tasks affect each other?* Dependencies are the logical cause-and-effect relationships between tasks that are very important for creating dynamic schedules. Scheduling with project management software does not require the user to enter dates for each task, even though many people do so. By entering dependencies instead, you can build a very powerful, dynamic model of the project. If you change the duration of one task, Project 2003 will reschedule all affected dependent tasks. It will do this on every change you make. The core secrets of dynamic schedules will be revealed in this chapter.

Constraints (Chapter 6)

Constraints are the answer to the question: *What limitations are imposed on the schedule?* Constraints can be dates imposed on the project or promises to meet certain dates. Constraints can also be used for restricting Project 2003's freedom to move task bars around in the timescale, if the practical circumstances require this. In addition to constraints, we will also discuss the feature of deadlines. The Gantt Chart can be finalized after this chapter, and we will also show you how to create a printout of it.

Resources (Chapter 7)

Resources are the answer to: *Who will do the work?* Resources can be human resources, facilities, machines or materials. In this chapter, we will discuss all these types of resources and how to enter them into Project 2003. We will explore the cost side of managing projects in this chapter. We will conclude it with how to print the list of resources.

Assignments (Chapter 8)

This last type of project data answers the question: *Who does what?* Tasks and resources have a many-to-many relationship: multiple resources can be assigned to work on one task, and many tasks can be assigned to one resource.

Human resources do the work and have to be assigned to the appropriate tasks. We will discuss the mechanics of assigning human resources. We will also discuss assigning material resources, which is typically done to complete the cost picture of the project.

Project 2003 does its own thing when you work with assignments. Behind the screens it uses a formula to recalculate data you may have entered when you assign or change assignments. We will explain the when and how and provide you with the insight to help you predict what Project 2003 will do. Of course, from then on you will be in the driver seat and make the tool do what you want it to. The goal of this chapter is to make Project 2003 work for you instead of you working for Project 2003. If you found that MS Project did not do what you wanted, this is the chapter to read.

Executing, Monitoring and Controlling

Optimizing the Schedule (Chapter 9)

After entering all the data, Project 2003 shows a schedule that ends before or after the project deadline. The schedule may be under or over the budget. The first draft of the schedule hardly ever meets time and cost constraints. Changes may have to be made to stay within the deadline, the budget or the availability of resources; this is called optimizing the schedule.

We will present three different approaches for optimizing schedules. You should choose the approach that best fits your own project.
◆ Optimizing for Time
◆ Optimizing for Time and Cost
◆ Optimizing for Time, Cost and Resources
Each approach also includes consideration of *scope* and *quality*.

In *Optimizing for Time* we will explain the Critical Path method briefly and show how to highlight the Critical Path in your schedule. Sometimes the Critical Path is fragmented, and we will show you how to make it complete so that it explains the entire duration of the project. The Critical Path method applies to *logic-constrained schedules*, or schedules that are entirely driven by network logic only. We will then present many different ways in which you can reduce the duration of your project.

In *Optimizing for Time and Cost* we will make the optimization a bit more complex (or more interesting in my professionally deformed opinion) by incorporating the cost dimension of projects. We will explore the methods available to bring down the cost without compromising too much on scope, quality or time.

Optimizing is more complex when you also want to ensure that the required resources are available and not overloaded with work. Over-allocating resources can compromise the scope of the project or the quality of the deliverables and will often lead to missing deadlines. In the section on *Optimizing for Time, Cost and Resources* we will start to include the issue of over-allocations by leveling the workloads. We will also introduce the new concept of a Resource-Critical Path which is needed for this type of optimization. As you will see, the Resource Critical Path will appear like a regular Critical Path but will also take resource constraints into account. The Resource-Critical Path allows you to find the tasks that truly drive the finish date of the project in a *resource-constrained schedule*. Thus, the Resource-Critical Path allows you to shorten your schedule, just as the Critical Path allows you to do this in *logic-constrained schedules*.

After reading this chapter, you will be ready to print and distribute the plan to stakeholders.

Reporting (Chapter 10)

In this chapter, we will not change the data in the schedule; we will only create different appearances of the schedule designed for the respective stakeholder groups. Views and reports can, for example, be used to communicate to resources what to do, what to deliver, and when and with whom to cooperate. Filters can hide certain tasks and display other tasks, and can be used to provide the overview to executives — or the detail of a specific problem to the team members. Tables can be used to communicate certain data by inserting or deleting fields. The task or resource records can be grouped by any commonalities found in the data. Different formats can be applied to lead the eye of the reader to the important parts of the report.

The first reports of the project will be used to get the project approved. After that, project managers typically produce status reports periodically.

Updating (Chapter 11)

As soon as the project is approved, a baseline schedule is set based upon the approved schedule. The baseline schedule serves as the standard of comparison to track progress.

Progress information has to be entered into MS Project, which is known as *updating* the plan. Just like bookkeeping, this should be done on a regular basis. An updated schedule shows the actual performance compared to the baseline.

After updating, you need to establish whether another round of optimizing is needed in case there is slippage. During the *execution phase* of the project, status reports will support the decision making in the project, such as modifying the activities. They will also support the decision making about the project, i.e. approving the next phase.

During the executing and controlling phase of the project, many cycles will be made through the last three project management activities of optimizing, reporting and updating. Delivering a project involves many cycles of making progress (updating), monitoring the progress (reporting) and taking corrective actions (optimizing).

Closing

Evaluating (Chapter 12)

It is important to take some time to look back and see what went well, what went wrong and why. In this chapter, we will discuss what to evaluate in your project and why.

Evaluating your projects is the only way to become a better project manager. It can prevent you from running into the same traps with your next project. Looking back can also improve your skills in setting dependencies and estimating. These are the hardest skills to acquire as a project manager.

Summary (Chapter 13)

In this chapter, you will find a summary of scheduling guidelines to create *valid* and *dynamic* schedules for your project, as discussed throughout the book. These reflect the results of our search for best practices in well over one thousand real life schedules. You can use this chapter as a handy reference to the appropriate pages if you need more explanation on specific topics.

Appendix 1: Certification Curriculum Sample Exam Questions

This appendix contains sample exam questions on Project 2003. These questions are representative of the Orange Belt exam we conduct in the certification curriculum at the International Institute for Learning. The answers to these sample questions are available for download at www.jrosspub.com. Please, click the link *WAV Download Resource Center* to enter the download site.

Appendix 2: Files Available For Download

This appendix describes all files available for download, including about one hundred examples of excellent real life schedules that reflect the best practices of scheduling with MS Project. You will find schedules from a wide variety of industries. The schedules are listed with the names of the people who created them and allowed us to publish them. The schedules are available for download at www.jrosspub.com. Please, click the link *WAV Download Resource Center* to enter the download site.

Exercises

You will find exercises at the end of each chapter. Several projects will be worked out step-by-step or evaluated throughout the exercises to familiarize you with the best practices of scheduling with MS Project.

End of Chapter Exercises

◆ **Review**
These exercises are meant to consolidate the knowledge you gained in each chapter. These questions review the theoretical concepts. Most answers can be found literally in the text of the book itself.

◆ **Hands-on exercise project: The Relocation Project**
You can test yourself and see if you can create a schedule with Project 2003 in the *Relocation Project* exercises. The relocation project is an imaginary office move that you will lead as the project manager. You will be moving about 100 co-workers to a new location that you have yet to find. The solutions to these exercises are available for download at www.jrosspub.com. Please, click the link *WAV Download Resource Center* to enter the download site. These exercises are meant to provide a checkup to see if you also gained the skills with the knowledge.

◆ **Troubleshooting**
These exercises will help you understand some of the pitfalls in MS Project. These exercises help you prepare for providing technical support to other MS Project users. All the troubleshooting exercises are situations I have run into over the years of staring at people's troubled schedules. We have reviewed well over one thousand schedules, since we first started certifying schedules in 1999. The typical troubleshooting situation is one in which the schedule stubbornly refuses to do what the creator expects.

◆ **Case studies**
The case studies are meant to give an idea of what is going on in the practice of

project management in other organizations. They deal with the implementation of MS Project in particular. The case studies are from our consulting experience. In all cases, I have disguised the organizations involved.

End of Book Exercises

In Appendix 1, you can find sample exam questions as used in the certification curriculum at the International Institute for Learning. If you want to check if you answered the multiple-choice questions correctly, compare them to the answers available for download at www.jrosspub.com. Please, click the link *WAV Download Resource Center* to enter the download site.

Professors can acquire a separate solution manual that contains all the answers to the review questions, multiple-choice questions, troubleshooting exercises and discussions on the case studies. This solution manual is only available to professors that use this book in their courses; please contact the publisher, *J. Ross Publishing*. The solution manual will be available for download at www.jrosspub.com. Please, click the link *WAV Download Resource Center* to enter the download site.

Conventions in This Book

Symbols and Typeface

 The light bulb shows a tip or recommendation to the user. It may be a time saver or a way of achieving better project control information.

 An exclamation mark shows a warning to the user of Project 2003. Heeding the warnings may keep you out of trouble and avoid unexpected results, loss of data or quirks in Project 2003.

 The 2003 icon indicates that the feature is new in the *Project 2003* release, in both the *Project 2003 Standard* and the *Project 2003 Professional* edition. For people who are upgrading to Project 2003 from Project 2002 and just want to focus on new features, this is the thing to look for.

 The 2003 Pro icon is for users of Project 2003 Professional who are upgrading from Project 2002 Professional. This icon marks the new features in Project 2003 Professional.

 The 2002 icon indicates that the feature was new in the *Project 2002* release, in both the *Project 2002 Standard* and the *Project 2002 Professional* edition. I kept these icons in this 2003 book for those people who are upgrading from Project 2000 to Project 2003.

The 2002 Pro icon indicates features that were new in the Project 2002 Professional edition that is normally used with *Project Server*.

File Words in bold type can literally be found on your screen in Project 2003 — either as a menu item or as a label or phrase in a dialog box.

Quotes Italicized words are literal references. These can be literal quotes from people, data you literally need to enter into Project 2003 or literal words from the index at the back of the book. The indexed keywords are italicized so that you can find them easily in the text.

<file name> Any text enclosed within the arrow brackets is text that should not be taken literally, because it refers to another thing. For example, <file name> refers to the name of the project file you currently have opened. File names often show up in menu items or in dialog boxes.

Word Choice and Step Formulation

You will notice I use the words MS Project and Project 2003 often. I typically use *MS Project* when the feature was available in previous releases; I use *Project 2003* when it is a feature that is new in Microsoft Office Project 2003. I apologize to Microsoft's marketing department for not using the official name *Microsoft Office Project 2003* all of the time; the book would have been 10 pages longer.

We have not used creativity in formulating the stepwise instructions; in fact, we have followed very rigid guidelines to be as clear and consistent as possible in this respect. It is difficult enough to interpret technical books and consistent formulation might help you. These formulation guidelines are:

◆ For menu items, we always use the verb "*Choose*" as in:
Choose **File, Save As**; the **Save As** dialog appears.
In order to easily follow the procedural steps in this book, you may want to always display the full menus instead of the most frequently used menu items only. You can do this by choosing **Tools, Customize, Toolbars**, clicking tab **Options** and checking ☑ **Always show full menus**. Since we will suggest new menu items to you, it will be easier to follow the steps if you change to full menus.

◆ For the toolbars, we always use the verb "*Click*" as in:
Click **Open** 📂 on the **Standard** toolbar.
In this book, we assume you use the toolbars in their default layout. If you cannot find toolbar buttons that we refer to, you should consider resetting the toolbars to their default appearance by choosing **View, Toolbars, Customize**, click tab **Toolbars**, select a toolbar to reset and then click [Reset...]. While you are in this dialog, you might consider giving the Standard and Formatting toolbar each their own space, instead of having them share one row (which cuts both of them off). You can do this by clicking the tab **Options**, and selecting ☑ **Show Standard and Formatting toolbars on two rows**.

◆ For buttons in dialog boxes, we always use the verb "*Click*" as in:
Click [💾 Save].

◆ For tab pages in dialog boxes, we always use the verb "*Click*" with the name of the tab as in:
Click **Advanced**

◆ For shortcut key combinations on your keyboard, we always use the verb "*Press*":

◇ For a single keystroke: Press [F2].

◇ For two keystrokes: Hold down [Alt] and press [F].

◇ For three keystrokes: Hold down [Alt] + [Shift] and press [→].

◆ For entering text with your keyboard into fields that have a name, we always use "*Key in*" as in:
Key in a file name of your choice in the field **File Name**.

◆ For check boxes that are checked or not and where the user can choose one or more, we always use the verb "*Check*" or "*Clear*" as in:
Check ☑ **Display Help on Startup**
Clear ☐ **Display Help on Startup**

◆ For radio buttons where the user has to choose only one option from two or more, we always use the verb "*Select*" as in:
Select ◉ **Automatic**.

◆ For lists with a label or with a screen tip, we always use the following convention:
Select from the list **Field Name** | ID ▼ | a column to be inserted where *Field Name* is the label next to the field or the screen tip that appears when you rest your mouse pointer on it.

Alternative Options or Alternative Steps

Whenever you have two options that do different things I have separated them with a lowercase "*or*". For example:
*Choose **File, Save** to save current changes into same file, or choose **File, Save As** to save it in a different file.*

If you have two alternative step procedures that accomplish the same goal, I have separated them with an uppercase "*OR*" on a separate line. For example:
press [F3]
OR
*select the item **All Tasks** from the list* | All Tasks ▼ | .

Screenshots and Illustrations

We used many illustrations in this book. Most illustrations only show a small part from a larger schedule. This allowed us to keep the illustrations concise and to the point.

The procedural steps include dialog boxes that are inserted in the steps right at the place where you should encounter them. This is to ensure that you are in the right dialog box before proceeding with the next step. Otherwise, you could easily get lost in intricate steps.

Where screenshots of MS Project views are shown, we have tried to show only the relevant portion of the screen. Where we did print the full screen, you will see the **Standard** and **Formatting** toolbars on two rows. If you want to display them on two rows as well on your computer, choose **View, Toolbars, Customize**, click tab **Options**, and select ☑ **Show Standard and Formatting toolbars on two rows**.

We have annotated the screenshots with blue lines and callouts, so you can easily find the option or field referred to in the text. The annotations can even contain extra tips, so you may still find them worthwhile after reading the text.

Meet the Cartoon Characters…

Throughout this book you will find little stories with cartoons. One of the main characters in these stories is Bob, a very dynamic and successful project manager. This is Bob (any resemblance to actual people is purely coincidental):

As you can see, the man is busy communicating in several different ways at the same time. The smile on his face radiates success. Notice the certificate on the wall.

The second project manager looks rather confused and overwhelmed. His name is Nob (any resemblance to actual people is, again, purely coincidental):

As you can see, Nob has not mastered the latest communication technology, which is epitomized by the way he uses the computer monitor. For him it is just a bulletin board for yellow stickies.

Bob and Nob will share their project adventures with us. You will find several stories and cartoons on their experiences. Each chapter typically starts with one. I hope you will enjoy the cartoons during this serious project management stuff. Every time I received a new batch from the creator, Paul Mason, I had some good laughs.

For the cartoons, I needed a successful project manager, and a loser. Paul and I discussed what their gender should be. There was no way we could come out unscathed by using both a male and a female. Was the successful project manager going to be a man and the loser a woman? Or was the loser going to be a man and the winner a woman? We realized it was a lose-lose situation, and eventually we decided to make both of them men. I apologize to those women who would have liked to see the successful project manager be female. The stories that come with the cartoons apply to both genders.

Throughout the book I will randomly use *he* or *she* in my examples.

Chapter 1 Concepts of Project Management

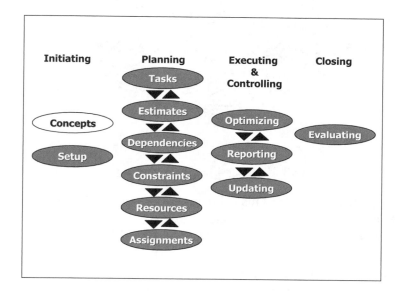

The first *Initiating* phase starts with the *concepts* of project management. The first step is making sure every reader is clear on these concepts. Many concepts in this chapter are taken straight from the Guide to the Project Management Body of Knowledge (PMBOK®), 2004 Edition.

After reading this chapter you will:

◆ be aware of the Guide to the Project Management Body of Knowledge (PMBOK®)
◆ understand how projects relate to integrated program schedules and portfolios
◆ understand a schedule as a model of the real world project
◆ be able to recognize and analyze the driving forces in projects
◆ be able to determine the purpose of a schedule you are about to create
◆ know what project management software can do for you

Why Can't It Just Do What I Want It To?

Nob is in agony when Bob enters his cubicle. "What's wrong?" Bob asks. Nob perks up when Bob shows this interest and quickly assesses Bob as a possible source to help relieve some of his work pressures. Nob explains: "I was busy entering my estimates. I tried entering a work estimate of 20 person days here in the Work field, but when I do that MS Project changes the duration of the five-day task to ten days. I have just been fighting with the tool for hours. Why can't it just do … what I want it to?"

Bob sits down and says: "Let's see what is going on. Did you want to enter 20 days of effort on this task number 134? Let me try it … oh, I see. The duration changed indeed. You did not want the duration to change? Well, let's change the duration back to five days. Wow! That changed the work to ten days. What's going on here? Oh, I remember learning something about a task field called 'Type.' Supposedly, it allows you to control what MS Project recalculates. Let's first set the 'Type' to 'Fixed Duration' and then enter the work estimate again. See … it tells you now that you need four resources to work on the task. Do you have four resources?" Nob thinks and says, "No, I will only have three people for this task." Bob: "Okay, let's change the type to 'Fixed Work' and remove one resource. It now tells you that you will need almost seven business days to finish this task; does that sound right?"

"Yeah, I guess so!" Nob says, somewhat in awe of Bob's mastery of the tool.

Projects

A project is *a temporary endeavor undertaken to create a unique product, service or result.*[7] A project is the vehicle to create change. Project teams create unique deliverables. When the deliverables are ready, the project is over. A project team is a temporary organization within an existing organization or between organizations.

A project has the following characteristics:

◆ A project is *temporary* by definition.
  The end date of the project is forecasted before the project begins. A temporary team creates the deliverables of the project.
◆ The objective is to create a *unique* product, service or result.
  It has a verifiable objective that is a relatively new or unique challenge for the organization in the sense that it has not been done to those specifications before. The project product can be divided into *deliverables* that are components of the project product, handbooks or software applications to support the new service, or a variety of documents or electronic files as the result of research.
◆ *Progressive elaboration*
  The project plan is elaborated progressively, which goes hand in hand with the unique nature of a project and the looming time constraint. The plan is developed in steps and completed in increments.

Some organizations have projects as their core operations, like construction, aerospace and consulting companies. There are full-time project managers in these companies. In other organizations, projects are often used to implement changes (like relocations and reorganizations) or for creating new systems (such as information and financial systems). The line manager of today often has one or more projects in progress. To manage any project endeavors, Project 2003 can be a helpful tool to create a solid project schedule and budget.

Examples of Projects

We will give many examples of projects from different industries.

---

[7] See the PMBOK® Guide, 2004 Edition, published by the PMI.

◆ **Organizational change projects**
  ◇ Implementing a new financial system (*ERP*)
  ◇ Implementing a *Six Sigma quality system*
  ◇ Implementing supply chain management
  ◇ Designing and implementing a project management methodology
  ◇ Creating a *Project Management Office* (*PMO*)
  ◇ Relocating the office
  ◇ Business process re-engineering
  ◇ Designing and implementing a new job classification system

◆ **Regulations implementation projects**
  ◇ Projects to meet new environmental policy standards
  ◇ Realizing equal opportunity regulations in the workplace
  ◇ Airport security projects
  ◇ Sarbanes-Oxley corporate reporting (USA)

◆ **Event projects**
  ◇ Organizing a conference
  ◇ Writing the yearly financial report
  ◇ Creating a press conference
  ◇ A formal presentation to investors

◆ **New product development**
  ◇ Developing a new pharmaceutical drug
  ◇ Developing new computer hardware
  New product development typically involves *Research and Development* (*R&D*).

◆ **Information systems projects**
  ◇ Programming a desktop application
  ◇ Implementing a LAN or WAN
  ◇ Developing the company's e-commerce website

◆ **Construction projects**
  ◇ Designing and constructing buildings
  ◇ Designing and constructing new infrastructures like bridges and roads
  ◇ Construction of a new plant
  ◇ Assembly of a new manufacturing line

◆ **Education projects**
  ◇ Developing and testing new courseware
  ◇ Organizing training workshops across several sites

◆ **Maintenance-type projects**
  Project managers who schedule maintenance projects often deal with many small
  projects or "jobs". Sometimes the maintenance project is huge and can stop an entire

plant, as is the case when a condenser needs to be replaced in a coal-fueled power plant. Such a project can take up to five weeks during which operations are suspended. Every day early or late has huge financial consequences. Therefore, the project needs to be planned carefully.

Managing Multiple Projects

When you start to manage multiple projects, the projects can be similar projects or related subprojects. A program is a group of related subprojects that need to be managed in a coordinated way. There are often dependencies between these projects. The schedule is an *integrated program schedule*, and the appropriate term is *program management*. Projects can be integrated into programs for a variety of reasons:

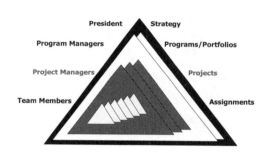

- ◆ A need for overall reporting on all projects
- ◆ A need to model the logical impacts each project has on other projects (*cross-project dependencies*)
- ◆ A need to monitor resource utilization when the projects share the same resources; when resources are shared, projects will impact each other through resource availability

A portfolio of projects consists of projects that support the strategy of the organization. Portfolios often are similar projects that use the same pool of resources. With *portfolio management*, you optimize the mix of projects given the scarce resources of the organization. As you can see, the level of complexity within a portfolio is less; however, the total investment in a portfolio is often much larger than for one integrated program.

This book will deal with managing a single project only and not address issues related to managing multiple projects, be they integrated programs or portfolios.[8] However, unless you know how to create and manage a single project effectively, there is very little hope in managing multiple projects simultaneously.

---

[8] The Blue Belt course is for people who manage multiple projects simultaneously with MS Project. Please visit www.iil.com and follow the link *Microsoft Project*.

Guide to the Project Management Body of Knowledge

The Project Management Institute (PMI) has issued the Guide to the Project

Adapted from
PMBOK® Guide 2004

Management Body of Knowledge, or PMBOK®. The PMBOK® has become a global standard on project management. Most multi-national companies have embraced the PMBOK® as their glossary. Each project has to deal with all nine knowledge areas as specified in the PMBOK® (see the illustration on the left). This book is entirely based on and aligned with the 2004 Edition of the PMBOK® published by the PMI. If you have not read the PMBOK®, I recommend you read it first or, at least, keep it nearby.

The PMBOK® Guide 2004 describes project management as "*the application of knowledge, skills, tools and techniques to project activities to meet the project requirements.*"

The Pulling Forces of a Project

All the areas in which project managers need to have knowledge and skills can also be seen as the areas that require attention from the project manager. The areas even pull the project in opposite directions and can be traded off against each other. The illustration on the left shows this.

MS Project, as a stand-alone tool, isn't a tool to help you in all these areas. For example, Project 2003 does not have many features to manage the quality, risk and procurement side of projects. It does not capture data on risk events, quality standards or contracts.

The five areas that can be managed well with Project 2003 are:

- *Scope*: what to accomplish
- *Time*: the deadline
- *Cost*: the budget
- *Resources*: availability (or capacity) and workloads of the resources, but only up to about 100 resources in a shared resource pool with MS Project as a standalone tool. If you use MS Project in combination with Project Server, you can build much larger shared resource pools of thousands of resources.

Communication is an information flow to and from project stakeholders. While Project 2003 provides many flexible reporting features, *Project Server* dramatically enhances real time communication with project stakeholders. You can also create libraries of documents and link them to tasks or projects. Project Web Access is now a richly featured document management system. It can handle different versions of your MS Project schedule and other types of documents. The latest version of a document is protected by checking out and checking in procedures. When checking the document back in, you are prompted to add comments on the changes you made.

An important activity in *risk management* is to identify adverse events, then rank, monitor and manage them. MS Project standalone can do PERT analysis and, yes, there are add-ons that do *Monte Carlo simulation*. Monte Carlo simulation can help you quantify the time risk of a schedule. We will explain both in chapter 9 Optimizing, see page 419. Project Server 2003 now has risk event management capability, and it already had issue management features.

In project *procurement management* you want to create and track your contracts. There is no feature in Project 2003 that is designed to manage contracts, but what you can do is create links to contract documents (like MS Office Word files) using the hyperlink feature. Project 2003 and *Project Server* are not a procurement management system by themselves.

The area of *quality* can be managed only somewhat with Project 2003. Quality control activities can be scheduled, but the tool does not capture quality standards or requirements for deliverables, for example. The application is not a *quality management* system. Of course, you should always ask yourself if a change to the schedule could also have any quality impacts.

At this point we have to ask ourselves: *Why are we scheduling? Why do we create a model of our project?*

Why Do We Schedule?

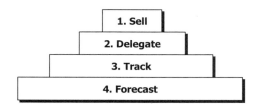

There are four reasons why people prepare schedules of their projects. The reasons can be ranked by level of challenge with the least challenging first:

◆ **Sell**

Project managers may want to sell upper management on an idea in order to start a new project and manage it. Or, a consulting firm may try to sell a new project to a client. The selling is supported by making the timing of milestones visible in a high-level Gantt Chart. Gantt charts built for this purpose often look very slick. Selling requires the least amount of detail in your schedule and does not require the schedule to be dynamic. The expected result would be that you win the contract.

◆ **Delegate**

When you have a detailed Work Breakdown Structure (WBS), you can easily delegate by assigning activities to team members. In this case, the schedule is used as an easy vehicle to communicate commitments to team members. When you have all the assignments, you can easily create to-do lists for each resource to establish responsibilities; who is doing the work? The benefits of a schedule as a delegation instrument are that everybody knows what to do and when to do it. The expected result is a sense of direction in your project.

◆ **Track**

In order to track your project; you enter the current status regularly into your MS Project schedule. The output of tracking is a status report. A status report shows how far the project has progressed. Tracking allows you to report to stakeholders what has been accomplished. Tracking a project has the benefit that you can learn from past mistakes. If you don't track, you will lack the facts to learn from. The main benefit is for future projects.

♦ **Forecast**

You can use MS Project to model your project in such a way that you forecast the project end date and the total cost. You have to create the schedule in such a way that it immediately shows what impact actual events have on the project end date and cost as you enter progress information. Forecasting also requires that you enter the progress in such a way that the forecasts are updated. The main benefit of forecasting is that you benefit from this immediately in your current project. You will have answers for:

◇ When will deliverables be available?
◇ On what dates will individual resources be needed?
◇ When will the project be done?
◇ What will the project cost?

These four levels are listed in order of increasing challenge or difficulty. The farther down the list, the more ambitious you are with MS Project. Forecasting is the most ambitious goal you can have when using scheduling software. If you want to predict the outcome of your project, you have to set up your schedule in a particular way. For example, you have to use dependencies wherever applicable. We will provide you with all the guidelines to help you set up schedules that will give you this predictive power. The summary chapter of this book contains the complete checklist of guidelines. Forecasting is what most project managers aspire to accomplish with MS Project.

Notice that there is no hard hierarchy implied in these purpose levels even though the pyramid of the chart might suggest this. For example, in order to forecast, you don't need to track; the higher levels don't hinge on lower levels.

First, we need to deal with a well-known saying on project planning that does not reflect well on it.

Dwight Was Right, But Is He Still?

"In preparing for battle, I have always found that plans are useless, but planning is indispensable."

President Dwight D. Eisenhower (1890-1969)

In the time in which President Dwight Eisenhower lived (1890-1969), project plans only existed on paper. Paper plans are static in nature and dead as soon as they are written. They are a snapshot of the project and capture the vision of the project when the plan was written. A plan printed on paper is a project-plan-of-the-past. At best, paper plans are "*history-books-written-ahead-of-time*". In his time, Dwight was right.

With the advent of computers, we can now create plans that are alive and dynamic. Let's start thinking of a project plan as an online database that contains the most current status together with prediction algorithms. This project-plan-of-the-future is an up-to-date electronic model of your project. The model allows you to make forecasts at any time during the life of the project.

Such a dynamic model is a powerful tool for project managers. I like to think that, if Dwight were still alive, he would likely admit: "*In preparing for the global marketplace, I have found that planning is indispensable and dynamic models are the critical success factor*".

Scheduling Is Modeling

As a project manager, you should attempt to create a dynamic model of your project situation, not just draw a chart that you hang on your wall and that is just nice to look at. Nice charts are very useful for selling purposes, but not for managing purposes. The differences between a *static chart* and a *dynamic model* of your project are:

◆ **A model is a simplification of the reality.**
Architectural models are small three-dimensional versions of the final building. A model is built at a fraction of the cost of the final build. Similarly, project models should be simple versions of large, complex realities. Simplification is a legitimate and essential activity when modeling.

◆ **A dynamic model has to be kept up-to-date.**
A schedule that is not maintained is static and will be useless soon after it is ready. Dynamic models are never finished; they are living documents and should be kept alive until the project ends. If they are not or cannot be kept alive, they don't deserve the label *dynamic model*.

◆ **A dynamic model needs to be responsive.**
In order for schedules to be easily kept up-to-date, they need to be responsive. A responsive model updates itself as much as it can. Schedules can do this if they are created with as many dependencies as needed and as few fixed dates as possible. Fixed dates are known as *constraints* in MS Project.

◆ **A dynamic model has predictive power.**
Schedules need to show the latest forecasts of the finish date and the final expenses of the project. Only then can a schedule truly be a powerful decision-support system for the project manager. It is nice to have a prediction that holds true in, let's say, 9 out of 10 cases. This requires the model to use empirical, actual data that are translated into forecasts using algorithms. An example of such an algorithm is the 15% rule on *earned value* from Fleming and Koppelman.[9] The 15% rule states that if you are 15% into your project, you should be able to predict the final cost of your project within a margin of plus or minus 10%.

◆ **A dynamic model needs to be accessible online and in real time.**
Project Server is one example of a new class of business intelligence tools arriving in the marketplace that allow you to slice and dice the data any way you want. *Project Server* allows you to drill down into the project database to see supporting detail. Once you have found the root-cause of problems, you can develop scenarios to resolve them. These powerful and dynamic features are accessible through a user-friendly interface that executives can use to keep their finger on the pulse of their portfolio of projects. Executives could do their own analysis and what-if scenario development using data that are as up-to-date as data can get (real time data). But best of all, with its web-based access, no longer are project reports tied to regular reporting periods and static formats. They can be viewed at any time and from any place with intranet or internet access.

In the chapters that follow, we will show you how to create a dynamic model of your projects — a model that meets all the criteria of a dynamic model as just explained.

---

[9] See their book *Earned Value Project Management*, PMI, 2000.

The next thing we will do is explore the field of forces that surrounds our project. This will help us model the important aspects of our project.

How Strong Are the Forces in My Project?

As we described in the previous paragraphs, scheduling treated as a modeling activity is supposed to simplify the reality of the project. One of the first things a project manager needs to do is find out how strong each of the forces is. Recognizing the dominant force and modeling the project accordingly can determine the success of the schedule early in the project life cycle. For example, if a nuclear power station has to be renovated, it is clear that the *scope* and the *quality* cannot be tampered with, because of the immense consequences an error could or would have (see the illustration). Meeting the quality standards of the International Atomic Energy Agency will be a dominant force, even if this leads to higher than anticipated cost and/or a delay in the project.

Remodeling a Nuclear Power Station

For most projects, however, the dominant force is less obvious. Sometimes two forces seem to be equally important. Therefore, a good question to ask before starting is: *Which force is dominant?* Or, if that question is difficult to answer, ask yourself first: *Which force is least important?*

Depending on whether scope, time, cost, quality or resources is the dominant force, different schedules will be the result. If the deadline is very hard, you may want to enter it as a constraint into the model and schedule regular status meetings. If the deadline is soft, you may choose to let it float freely. If the budget is very tight, you want to model all expenses in detail. If the resource availability is very limited, you want to capture all workloads. If quality is the dominant force, you could add more testing tasks. As you can see, being aware of the dominant force in your project is worth the effort.

Project Management Software

In any project, the following seven questions are important:
1. *What needs to be done?*   Deliverables and Tasks
2. *How long will it take?*   Duration Estimates or Work Estimates
3. *In which order?*   Dependencies
4. *When must it happen?*   Constraints
5. *Who is going to do it?*   Resources and Assignments
6. *When will it happen?*   Start and Finish Dates
7. *How much will it cost?*   Rate * Assignment Effort

The user will have to enter the answers to the first five questions, and Project 2003 will automatically answer the last two questions by creating the schedule and the budget.

Notice that when you schedule electronically, you hardly ever enter start or end dates for tasks. You enter durations and dependencies instead. The software then calculates the start and finish dates by itself based upon those durations and dependencies. A schedule with dependencies is flexible and knows how to update the other tasks automatically when preceding tasks are changed. If you have been entering dates, we recommend you reconsider doing this from now on. If you want to change your habit, we recommend you select the **Start** and **Finish** column and press $\boxed{\text{Delete}}$. You can easily re-display the start and finish dates for read-only purposes to the left and right of task bars in the timescale. You can do this by choosing **Format, Bar Styles**, selecting the type of tasks in the list at the top and on the tab **Text** in the field **Left** you select the list item **Start** and in the field **Right** the item **Finish**. If you do this, you will definitely not be tempted any longer to enter dates while you can still view the resulting dates. Entering dates leads to many constraints.

Based upon resource cost rates and assignments you enter, the software calculates the total cost, per deliverable and for the whole project. MS Project calculates a lot of data automatically for you.

Scheduling software is efficient in reporting. The software behaves like a database in that you can pull data from the database to focus on any deliverable, any period or any resource you want. The type of information in a report can be changed as well, like scheduled dates or cost figures. Reports allow you to compare actual against planned progress.

Review Questions

1. What are the two main ways in which projects differ from other things such as programs, operations, task forces, committees, work groups and departments?

2. Are there organizations that never have any projects?

3. Are there organizations that only have projects?

4. What is the difference between project management and program management?

5. Which knowledge areas does the PMBOK® cover?

6. What are the forces that pull your project in different directions and that you constantly need to trade off between as a project manager?

7. What is the strongest pulling force in your current project? And, what is the weakest pulling force?

8. What are the differences between a *static chart* and a *dynamic model* of your project?

9. Why do you intend to create a schedule of your current project? Is it for selling, delegating, tracking or forecasting purposes?

10. What is the difference between tracking a project and forecasting a project?

11. What is the minimum data you need to enter into MS Project to generate a complete and dynamic schedule?

Chapter 2 Setting Up a Project

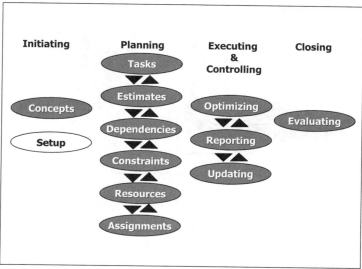

Now that we have reviewed the terminology and some basic concepts, we are ready to explore the application interface of MS Project and set up a new project.

After reading this chapter you will:
- be familiar with the MS Project interface
- understand where MS Project stores the data:
  - ◇ be familiar with the file types MPP/MPT and the Global.MPT file when you work with MS Project as a standalone tool
  - ◇ understand the structure of the relational database of MS Project when you work with Project Server
- be familiar with the MS Project views
- know how to use a project template
- be able to set up a new project and choose the appropriate options
- be able to create the project calendar
- know the best practices for setting up new project schedules

"Have You Been Choked by a Template Lately?"

Nob: "Hey Bob, I opened up this template that our project office put together and I found 300 tasks in there! Do we really have to use them? What the heck were these guys thinking?"

Bob: "Well my friend, the project office didn't put them together for nothing!"

Nob: "But come on ... 300 tasks for a software modification project; that is ridiculous!"

Bob: "Listen man ... the templates are part of this expensive methodology our company purchased. You don't want to be seen throwing that money away!"

Nob: "Spending the money was not MY decision!"

Bob: "Why don't you comb through the templates and use whatever seems applicable and just delete the rest."

Nob: "You can't do that, can you?"

Bob: "Of course you can ... they just made these templates as reminders of everything that MIGHT be necessary in your project. If it is not applicable, it is not applicable! That is how I deal with these templates."

Nob: "I am not sure..."

Bob: "They made more templates than necessary on purpose, because it is always easier to delete than to add!"

Nob: "How did you get so smart???"

Microsoft Office Project 2003 Standard and Professional

MS Project comes in two editions: *Microsoft Office Project 2003 Standard* and *Microsoft Office Project 2003 Professional*. The professional edition can connect to a Project Server database which provides the capability to implement *Enterprise Project Management* (*EPM*). The word '*Enterprise*' refers to the entire organization or a subset of the organization, e.g. the IT-department. EPM is a system to manage projects effectively within that (part of the) organization. EPM typically consists of:

◆ *Portfolio management* to support the strategic direction of the organization.

◆ *Resource management* to use the resources optimally

◆ *Project management* to help project managers manage their projects. The system provides ways for the project manager to collaborate with team members and other stakeholders.

When working with project schedules, there are differences between using Project 2003 with Project Server and using Project 2003 by itself as a standalone tool. We will call it *MS Project standalone* when it is used by itself, which is without Project Server; even Project 2003 Professional can be used as a standalone tool. We prefer the term *standalone*, because it describes the situation better than the term *Standard*.

Working with Files in Project 2003 as a Standalone Tool

File Types

MS Project can store its data in project files and project template files among other file types. Project templates are like regular project files, but with an added protection against accidental changes. The protection is that when you open a template, the template first copies itself and you continue to work with the copy. The original template stays the same. Project templates are standardized schedules and are used in organizations that run similar projects over and over, like construction companies.

Project files (.MPP) and project template files (.MPT) can contain:
◆ *Data*: tasks, estimates, dependencies, constraints, resources, assignments
◆ *Objects*: views, tables, filters, groups, fields, calendars, reports, forms, maps, toolbars (including the menu bar) and modules (Visual Basic)

◆ *Project-specific options*: these relate to the project only and are stored in the individual project. You can easily recognize which options are local in the **Tools, Options** dialog. Where the section heading has the suffix *for <name of current file>*, the option is local and stored with the project.

A special template exists, the default template file, called *Global.MPT*. It contains all the default objects, like views, tables and filters that you use for reporting purposes. Also, the *Menu Bar* and *Toolbars* that reside in the *Global.MPT* are the menu bar and toolbars that you are currently using in the MS Project interface. The menu bar and the toolbars are active in all your projects. The *Global.MPT* could contain a custom menu bar and custom toolbar objects, if desired. The *Global.MPT* is always open when MS Project is running. The *Global.MPT* objects are available for use in new project schedules.

The differences between a *project template* and the *Global.MPT* template are that:
◆ The *Global.MPT* cannot contain schedule data like tasks and dependencies.
◆ Only the menu bar in the *Global.MPT* is active.
◆ Only the toolbars in the *Global.MPT* are accessible through the menu items **View, Toolbars**.

The file extensions have been well thought out by Microsoft:
◆ A project file has an **.MPP** extension, which stands for **M**icrosoft **P**roject **P**roject.
◆ A template file has an **.MPT** extension, which stands for **M**icrosoft **P**roject **T**emplate. Project and template files can contain project data, as well as objects and options. You can view the available objects in the Organizer by choosing **Tools, Organizer**.

Objects can be transferred from one file to another with the *Organizer* on the **Tools** menu.

When you *migrate* from Project 2002 to Project 2003, the first time you run Project 2003, you will be asked if you want to *upgrade* your Project 2002 *Global.MPT* to Project 2003:
◆ Automatically: All the objects in your Project 2002 *Global.MPT* will be transferred. Choose this option if you have custom objects that you would like to keep.
◆ Manually: You can transfer selected objects to your Project 2003 *Global.MPT*.
◆ Not at all: In this case you get the new and default Project 2003 *Global.MPT* installed. Choose this option if you would like to throw out your own custom Project 2002 objects and start with fresh 2003 objects.

The *global options* and the default project-specific options are stored in the *Windows Registry*.

Opening a Project File in Project 2003 Standalone

1. Choose **File, Open**; the **Open** dialog appears:

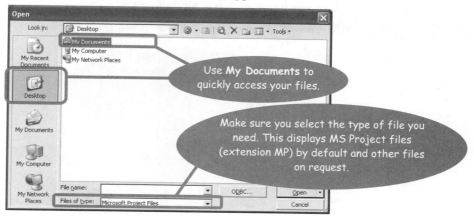

2. If the project is on a drive or directory other than the current one, navigate to it using the **Look in** list at the top of the dialog.

3. Double-click on the name of the file to open.
   OR

   Single-click on the file name and click | Open ▾ |.

Saving Changes in an Existing MPP File

1. Click **Save** 💾 on the **Standard** toolbar OR choose the menu items **File**, **Save**.

2. If your file exists already, the file on your hard disk will be updated with the changes. If the file does not exist, the **Save As** dialog will appear automatically.

Saving a New File with MS Project Standalone

1. If you save a schedule for the first time or if you opened the file read-only and save it, you are prompted for a file name in the **Save As** dialog:

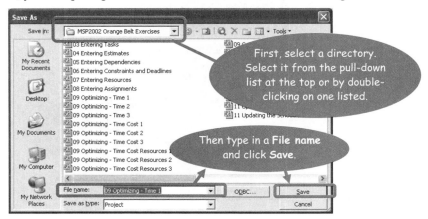

 2. Click [**Save**]. Each project file will be saved with the extension **.MPP** by default.

Saving an MPP File in a New Directory or Under a New Name

1. Choose **File**, **Save As**; the **Save As** dialog appears (see the previous screenshot).

2. Select the drive and directory from the list **Save In** at the top of the dialog.

3. At the bottom of the dialog, type a name in the field:
    File Name: [_____▼].

4. Click [**Save**].

Closing a File

1. Choose **File, Close**. If you have made changes to an open project, MS Project will prompt you to save the changes and the **Microsoft Project** dialog appears.

2. To save your changes, click [Yes] the **Save As** dialog appears if the project hasn't been saved before.
   To discard changes, click [No]
   To interrupt closing the file, click [Cancel]

Sharing All Project-Related Files: Shared Workspace

 Shared workspaces are a new feature that can be used with MS Project standalone. This feature requires *Windows SharePoint Services* (*WSS*) to be installed on a Windows 2003 server that is accessible for your team. You can save the schedule into a workspace that you share with others on this server. Other team members can easily retrieve the schedule by checking it out and contributing to it. The shared workspace allows people to collaborate on schedules and other project-related documents.

 Project Server also allows other people to open your schedule, but Project Server does not provide a collaborative, virtual work space. A shared workspace emulates a physical meeting room in which people work together. A virtual workspace is an easier way for team members to collaborate with you on the creation of the *project charter*, *scope statement*, *project schedule* and *budget*.

 Note that a *shared workspace* in WSS is not the same as the *workspace* feature in MS Project (found under **File, Save Workspace**). The MS Project workspace is simply a set of files that can be opened all in once by opening the workspace file (MPW-file). The WSS shared workspace is like a meeting room table on which a group of people collaborate. The WSS shared workspace first needs to be created by the WSS administrator.

You can use the shared workspace through the Project 2003 interface or through Internet Explorer. Internet Explorer will give you a richer interface and a more intuitive experience. Therefore, we will discuss it first.

Accessing the Shared Workspace with Internet Explorer

1. Start Internet Explorer

2. In the **Address** field enter the URL of the shared workspace (the WSS administrator can provide this). The following screen appears:

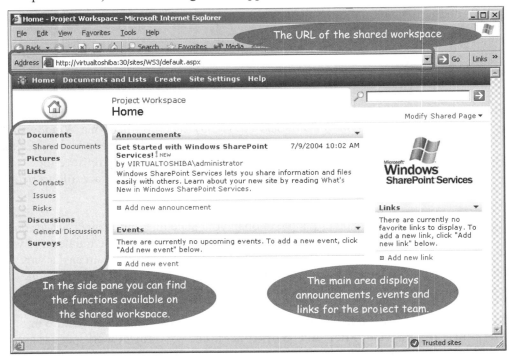

If you applied the **Project Workspace** template when you created the shared workspace site in the previous procedure, you can now do any of the following (If you applied a different template, you will have less or different choices.):

◆ View current announcements or create a new announcement by clicking **Add new announcement** in the main window. This is like a pin board in the kitchenette, near the coffee machine or other watering holes.

◆ View the upcoming events or add a new event by clicking **Add new event** in the main window. This is like calendar of events you would pin up in the gathering places.

◆ Access documents by clicking **Shared Documents** in the side pane on the left. If you want to change one, you will have to check it out and indicate what you changed in the document when checking it back in. This is like the company library or company document management system. Access rights can be different for each individual and can range from read-only, read-write to re-design the shared workspace site.

◆ Access posted pictures by clicking **Pictures** in the side pane on the left. Nice for posting pictures of all members of a remote team. This is a who-is-who gallery often seen in hallways of organizations.

◆ Access **Lists** of **Contacts, Issues** or **Risks** by clicking the item of your choice in the side pane on the left. The list of contacts can be synchronized automatically with the Windows *Active Directory*. Notice that you can create new types of lists that may be beneficial for the team.

◆ Join into a discussion by clicking one of the discussion threads listed under **Discussions** in the side pane on the left. This works similar to discussion groups on the Internet, though they are only accessible for your team members or other stakeholders in your project (that were granted access).

◆ Respond to a posted survey or create a new survey to poll your team by clicking on **Surveys**. This is a very powerful tool to gage opinions on a variety of matters.

◆ Add *Intranet* or *Internet* links with relevant (or fun) material for the project team by clicking **Add new link** in the side pane on the right hand side.

 You can set alerts delivered by email that are automatically triggered and sent to you when documents are changed, new risks are identified or other things happen that you want to monitor.

Accessing the Shared Workspace with Project 2003

The obvious thing you may consider doing is to post your project-related documents, like project charter, scope statement, budget, schedule, drawings, contracts and status reports to the shared workspace such that they can be reviewed. You can even allow certain documents to be modified by other team members. Team members can check these documents out and back in. When checking back in, they will be asked what they changed in the document. We will explain how you can save a schedule to the shared workspace:

1. Start or switch to Project 2003

2. Create the schedule and choose **File, Save**
   OR
   Open an existing schedule to share with the team and choose **File, Save As**

3. Click **My Network Places**, which displays a list that includes the shared workspace website. Double click that website.
   OR
   Enter the URL of the shared workspace (your WSS administrator can help you with that) in the filename dialog and click [Open ▾]

4. The listing in the dialog now lists the folders available on the SharePoint site as in following screenshot:

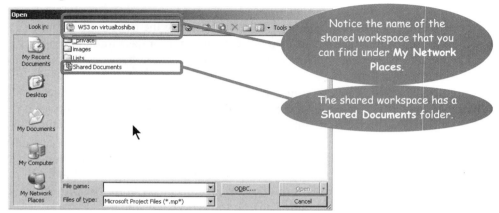

5. Double click the **Shared Documents** folder
    If you save a schedule to a different folder it will not be accessible for other people; they will not see it listed, and you will be the only one working with it.

6. Enter a name for the schedule and click [Save].

Notice that the side pane changes and now displays information about the shared workspace and buttons to manipulate the workspace:

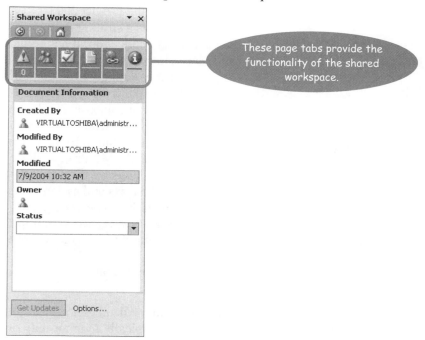

You will also find new menu items on the **File** menu: **Check out** and **Version History**. On the Tools menu you will find the item **Shared Workspace** enabled.

Any *Windows SharePoint Services* (*WSS*) compatible application allows you to perform these same functions as we discussed in Project 2003. All *Microsoft Office 2003* applications are WSS-compatible.

Working with Schedules from the Project Server Database

When we use MS Project in standalone mode, the projects were stored as separate files on your file directory system. When you use *Project Server*, the projects are stored into one *SQL Server* database.

Notice that you should not use the word *file* for a schedule in the context of the Project Server database, since there is only one file in a Project Server EPM system and that is the SQL Server database file that contains all the schedules. It is better to use the word *schedule*.

MS Project as a Relational Database Application

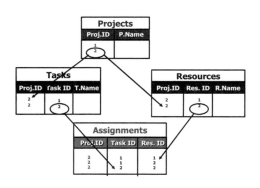

At first glance, the Project 2003 application bears a striking resemblance to a spreadsheet application. It has columns and rows. However, instead of seeing it as a spreadsheet, we suggest you think of Project 2003 itself as an application to access a relational database. A relational database has several different tables that are related to each other through fields they have in common. In MS Project, these are the ID fields.[10] You can see this in the illustration. The tasks and assignments tables have a so-called one-to-many relationship, since one task can be assigned to multiple resources. Similarly for resources, one resource can be assigned to multiple tasks. It is the one-to-many relationships in the data that are hard to manage within a spreadsheet application.

There are three reasons for seeing the application as a relational database application:

1. **There are four types of data.**
   There are four distinct types of data, or *data-entities*, in the database: projects, tasks, resources and assignments. In a spreadsheet table, you typically monitor only one type of data.

2. **The data have one-to-many relationships.**
   The data entities are related and have one-to-many relationships between them.

3. **Each data entity has its own table.**
   Projects can be found in the Projects table. *Tasks* can be found in the task table that can be seen in any of the task views. *Resources* are stored in the resource table and can be seen in the resource views. *Assignments* are in their own table as well, but do not have separate views in MS Project. Assignments can be found in between the tasks in the *Task Usage* view or in between the resources in the *Resource Usage* view.

Project 2003 Professional users store their projects in *SQL Server* as the relational database instead of in MPP-files. In a relational database, you can see each data entity in

---

[10] In fact, the **Unique ID** field contains the unique identifiers, because the **ID** values are just row numbers that constantly change when items are inserted or moved.

its own table. The (simplified) data model for the Project Server database is shown in the illustration. A multi-project database, like Project Server, has an extra table at the top that contains all projects. The *Projects* table is where Project Server stores all the project-level data, like project name, project manager and project start and finish date, among others, for all projects in the database.

Entering an Account to Connect to the Project Server Database

Project Server keeps all projects in a *SQL Server* database. The Project Server administrator manages this database and the security, which determines who can read or write each schedule in the database. This is done through accounts in the Project Server database. The Project Server administrator has to set up an account for you as the project manager in the Project Server database. Then you can configure Project 2003 as a project manager in such a way that it uses this database account to establish a connection between Project 2003 and the Project Server database. Project 2003 will then be able to open schedules from the Project Server database and save changes back into the database.

1. In Project 2003 Professional, choose **Tools, Enterprise Options, Microsoft Office Project Server Accounts**. The **Project Server Accounts** dialog appears.

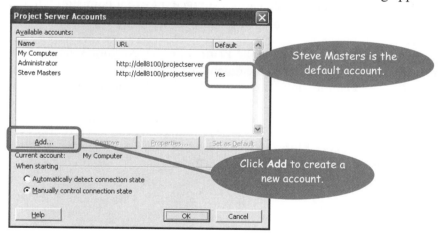

2. Click [Add...]; the **Account Properties** dialog appears:

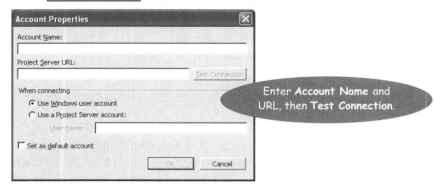

3. Enter the **Account Name**, which is a descriptive name of your own choice.

4. Enter the **Project Server URL** following the syntax:
    http://<server>//ProjectServer
    where *<server>* is the name (like *Toshiba08*) or the IP address (like *63.118.100.55*)
    of the computer on which Project Server is installed.

5. Under **When connecting**, select either
    ⦿ **Use Windows user account** (account you logged into your computer with), or
    ⦿ **Use a Project Server account** and enter the **User name**.

6. Click [OK] and you are back in the **Project Server Accounts** dialog. You
    can select one of your accounts to be the default account and you can even select
    Automatically detect connection state if you don't want to be prompted any longer
    for which account to use. If you will always connect to Project Server and have only
    one Project Server account, you could select this to start the system faster.

7. Click [OK] and choose **File, Exit** to close MS Project. We have now created
    an account to connect to Project server while offline.

Connecting to the Project Server Database

1. Restart Project 2003 Professional and the **Project Server Accounts** dialog appears (if you selected ◉ **Manually control connection state** in previous steps; if you selected ◉ **Automatically detect connection state** it is skipped):

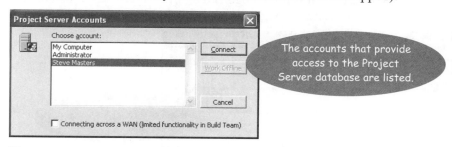

2. You connect MS Project to the Project Server database in which case you need to identify yourself to the secure database by selecting an account which we will discuss from here.

   OR

   If you want to work with your file without a connection to the *Project Server* database, you can select **My Computer** and click [Work Offline].

3. If you select ☑ **Connecting across a WAN** (Wide Area Network), the bandwidth of your connection typically is low. This option limits the number of resources from the enterprise resource pool that you will see at a time.

4. Double-click the account you want to use from the list.
   OR

   Select the account and click [Connect]. The **Project Server Security Login** dialog appears for a moment if you use *Windows authentication*. If it stays you are using a Windows account that is not recognized by the Project Server database or you are using *Project Server authentication* and you have to enter the **Password**.

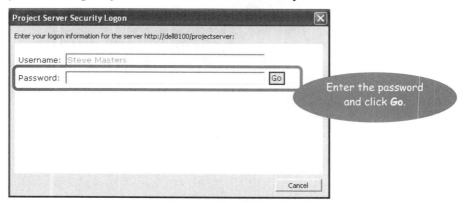

5. Enter the password and click [Go] to open the connection.

 The account you choose will make the MS Project application talk to the Project Server database and allow it to retrieve schedules from it and save your schedule to it.

 When you choose to work offline, you can be productive on a laptop while on a plane or wherever you don't have access to the server computer. In order to have your project schedules accessible offline, you first need to save them offline onto your laptop. Open the file you want to work on offline in Project 2003 and choose **File, Save offline**. While your schedule is offline, it is checked out such that nobody can change it. When you come back from your trip, you choose **File, Save online** to synchronize the Project Server database.

Two Global Containers in the Enterprise Environment

MS Project standalone uses the *Global.MPT* as a container for the default objects. This container is accessible across all your projects. You can copy objects into your Global.MPT that you want to standardize on across your projects.

An important difference between MS Project standalone and Project Server is that in an *enterprise* environment, you have a second global container of default objects, the so-called *Enterprise Global*. This container is accessible to all project managers across the enterprise and serves up the corporate standards to you in terms of templates, calendars, views, tables and filters.

You can see this second container if you choose **Tools, Organizer**; at the bottom left of the dialog in the list **Views available in** you can now see **Global (+non-cached Enterprise)**. The term *+non-cached Enterprise* is Microsoft speak for the second enterprise containers. When connected, you have access to default objects in two containers simultaneously instead of just the local **Global** one. It uses only the local **Global** when you work offline.

The second container, the Enterprise Global, provides extra views that typically have a name that starts with the word *Enterprise*. These views are standard views that your *project office* has created and you cannot change them. If you do make changes, they will be discarded.

As you can see, with this complex situation of your own local Global.MPT and the Enterprise Global, you have the best of both worlds; you can still customize your own work environment by making changes to your local objects (Global.MPT), but the organization can also help you along by providing standard objects (*Enterprise Global*). Project managers do not need to re-invent the wheel and can use best-practice views developed by the project office.

Opening a Project Schedule from the Project Server Database

When you work with MPP files, you need to know how to navigate your file system. With Project Server, there is a different dialog box. When opening a schedule, you have to select the project from a list of projects in the database. When saving a project, you have to give it a title under which you can retrieve it from the database.

1. Choose **File, Open** and the **Open from Microsoft Office Project Server** dialog will appear. It lists all projects you have access to in the Project Server database which are at least the ones you have created yourself. The *Project Server administrator* manages the access rights and could help you if you have trouble finding your schedules.

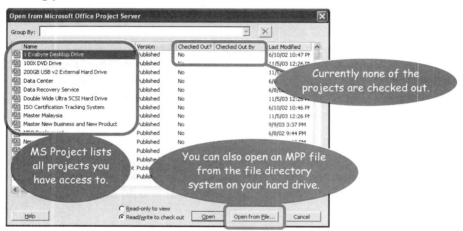

2. Select the project to open with a single click.
    OR
    If you want to open an MPP file, click Open from File… and the same steps apply as when opening a project file in Project 2003 used standalone.

3. Select whether you want to open the project:
    ⦿ **Read-only to view**: You will not be able to save changes. By the way, schedules from a Project Server 2002 database can only be opened read-only in Project 2003 until the database is upgraded to 2003.
    ⦿ **Read/write to check out**: You will be able to save changes if nobody else has the schedule checked out currently; the column **Checked Out?** should display **No**.

4. Click Open .

If you want to open a project read/write, you can double click the project name in the list and it will open right away.

Saving a New Project to the Project Server Database

1. Choose **File, New** to create the schedule.

2. Choose **File, Save As** and the **Save to Project Server** dialog appears:

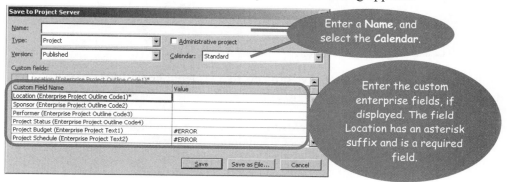

3. In the field **Name**, enter a descriptive name for the project that will be clear to other users of the database with many project schedules in it. If you enter a name that already exists in the database, you will receive the following prompt when attempting to save:

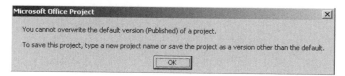

4. Under **Type**, select to save the project as a **Project** or as a **Template**.

5. Under **Version**, select the version identifier for this project. Project Server makes an important distinction between the *Published version* and other versions. The published version is the one that is the latest and active version; only the published version receives time sheet actuals and notes. Other versions are for archiving purposes.

6. Under **Calendar**, select one of the corporate calendars your project should be based on.

7. Under **Custom Field Name**, there can be one or more custom fields that allow, or even require you to describe your project in more detail. The fields that are required

have an asterisk suffixed to their name. In this release, the dialog box is much wider and the asterisk is easier to find. If you forgot to enter a value in a required field and you attempt to save, you will see the following message. The message is vague about which field is required. So, now you have to find the asterisk(s):

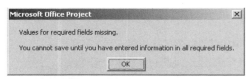

8. Click [Save].

With Project 2003, you cannot save projects to a Project Server 2002 database. The database first needs to be migrated to 2003.

The steps for saving changes and closing schedules are similar for Project Server schedules and MPP-files (MS Project standalone); choose **File, Save** and **File, Close**, respectively.

The Microsoft Office Project 2003 Interface

The Main Screen

MS Project has many different screen areas that pop up when they are needed (and sometimes when they are not). In order for you to follow the procedural steps, you have to know the names of these screen parts. I have labeled them in the next screenshot:

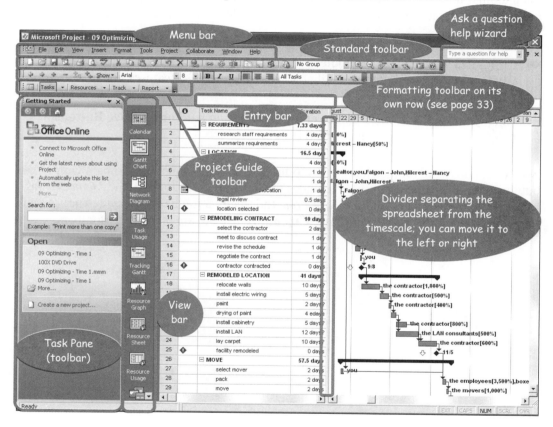

Working with the Menus

To choose a menu item, just click on it with the mouse OR hold down the [Alt] key and press the underscored character of the menu item.

Working with the Toolbar

Toolbars are a great shortcut to commonly used features. To invoke the action of the toolbar buttons, click with the primary mouse button on the tool you need. If you are not sure which tool you need, place the mouse pointer on top of a button without clicking, and a tool tip will remind you what the button does. An example of a tool tip for the tool is: Go To Selected Task.

Each toolbar now has on the right-hand side an extra button (or when there are more tools on the toolbar that are currently not visible). This button allows you to:

◆ Access the hidden tools.

◆ Customize your toolbar very quickly by choosing **Add or Remove Buttons, Customize**. Customizing the toolbar allows you to access features you use often with one click.

◆ Reset your toolbar to its original setting by choosing **Add or Remove Buttons, Customize**, click tab **Toolbars**, and click Reset... .

Notice that the word *toolbar* has started to include more than just the toolbars with buttons over the years; it now also includes the *Project Guide* toolbar, the *Menu Bar* (as a special type of toolbar), and the *Task Pane* (not really a toolbar but a side pane). All of these are listed in the **View, Toolbars, Customize** list and are technically toolbars.

Working with the Task Pane

Project 2003 includes the *Task Pane* feature from Microsoft *Office 2003*. The *Getting Started* task pane is now the same across all Microsoft Office 2003 applications. The Getting Started pane appears when you start the MS Project application.

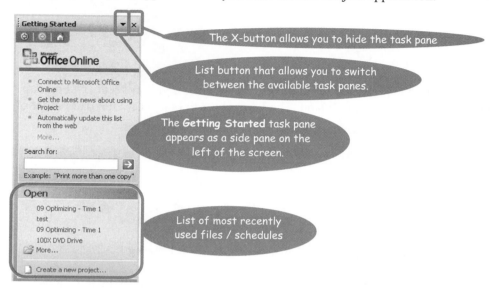

The X-button allows you to hide the task pane

List button that allows you to switch between the available task panes.

The **Getting Started** task pane appears as a side pane on the left of the screen.

List of most recently used files / schedules

Apart from the **Getting Started** task pane, there are several other task panes available:
◆ Search results, see page 98
◆ Help, see page 98
◆ New project, see page 105
◆ Shared workspace, see page 61

Working with the View Bar

The view bar on the left is meant to quickly change views. To display or hide the view bar choose **View, View Bar** or right-click on the view bar and choose **View Bar**. You may see buttons for all views, if your screen is big enough (or your screen resolution is high enough).

Working with Scroll Bars

The scroll bar looks like the illustration to the right and consists of three parts:

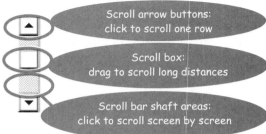

As you are dragging the timescale scroll boxes, you will see a yellow feedback box pop up that will tell you where you will land. The vertical scroll box shows the ID number of the task you are browsing to:

```
ID:    4
Name: LOCATION
```

The horizontal scroll box tells you the date you are traveling to:

```
Aug 1 '01
```

Right-Mouse Clicks and Double-Clicks

For those who are right-handed, the right-mouse button (as opposed to the left-mouse button) under your middle finger can pop up shortcut menus that relate to a particular

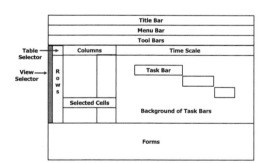

screen area. You can *right-click* on all the places that are labeled in the illustration to the left. It is a stylized version of a Gantt Chart; you can make many more right-clicks in other views. Try them out instead of clicking yourself silly through the menus. Save your mouse muscles!

Alternatively, you can *double-click* in these places; this will take you to the most likely shortcut for that area and display a dialog box right away.

Moving Around in a Project

The following convention is used: [Alt] + [→] means hold down [Alt] and press [→].

Move to	By keyboard	By mouse
Next row	[Enter ↵] or [↓]	Click
Next column	[Tab] or [→]	Click
Display next minor time unit in the timescale, or Display previous	[Alt] + [→] [Alt] + [←]	Click the arrow button [▶] on the scroll bar of the timescale, or click [◀]
Next screen in timescale	[Alt] + [Page Up] or [Alt] + [Page Dn]	Click to the left or right of the scroll box [ ] in the horizontal scroll bar
The start date of the project	[Alt] + [Home]	Left align the scroll box [ ] in the horizontal scroll bar
The end date of the project	[Alt] + [End]	Right align the scroll box [ ] in the horizontal scroll bar
The first task of the project	[Control] + [Home]	Drag the vertical scroll box [ ] to the top
The last task of the project	[Control] + [End]	Drag the vertical scroll box [ ] to the bottom
A specific task and task bar, resource or date	[F5] OR [Control] + [F]	**Edit, Go To** OR **Edit, Find**
The other view in a split window	[F6]	Click in the other view to make it active
Move the timescale to a task bar	[Control] + [Shift] + [F5]	Click **Go To Selected Task** on the **Standard** toolbar

Moving Around in a Dialog Box

The following convention is used: `Alt` + `Tab` means hold down `Alt` and press `Tab`.

Action	By keyboard	By mouse
Move to next field in a dialog box, or	`Tab`	Click in the field
Move to previous field	`Shift` + `Tab`	
Move to any field in a form	`Alt` + press underlined letter of the field name	Click in the field
Increase or decrease value in a field	`↑` `↓`	Use the spin button
While the tab label is selected, move to the next tab in the direction of the arrow	`Alt` + `↑` `Alt` + `↓` `Alt` + `←` `Alt` + `→`	Click on the tab

Selecting Data

The following convention is used in the table: `Alt` + `Tab` means hold down `Alt` and press `Tab`.

Select	By keyboard	By mouse
An entire row or record (task or resource)	`Shift` + space bar	Click on a row heading
An entire column	`Control` + space bar	Click on a column heading

When you select an entire row as explained in the previous table, all the fields of a task (about 240!) are selected, even if they are not visible. It is important to select a task in its entirety before moving or copying it. Remember that MS Project is a relational database, as discussed on page 66.

Project 2003 Views

The *View* of a project is a predefined layout that presents the project from a certain angle. The views allow you to enter or edit data, review or report your project.

View	Shows
Calendar	The tasks shown as bars on a calendar
Enterprise Gantt Chart	This view is essentially the same as the Gantt Chart unless this view was customized within your organization. The word *Enterprise* indicates that it is a view, which is standard across the entire enterprise.
Gantt Chart	The tasks over time, plus spreadsheet columns
Network Diagram	The network of dependencies between tasks (dependencies are shown as arrows)
Task Usage	Tasks with their assigned resources and the effort or cost over time
Tracking Gantt	The original (baseline) schedule versus the most recently revised schedule
Resource Graph	The workloads for resources in a bar chart format
Resource Sheet	The spreadsheet with resource information
Resource Usage	Resources with their assigned tasks with the workloads or cost over time

We will discuss each of these views on the pages that follow.

Calendar View

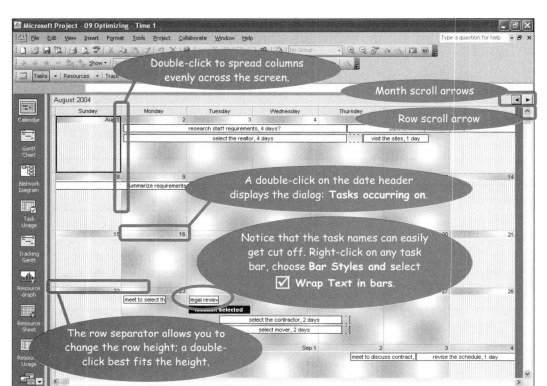

To apply the view, choose **View, Calendar** or click ▦ on the *View bar*.

The calendar view shows the schedule in a format that is similar to conventional calendars that people hang on their walls. Therefore, everybody understands this type of layout. In my experience, not everybody understands Gantt Charts intuitively. That is where this calendar view adds value. We recommend you use it to communicate to-do lists to individual team members (unless you use Project Server). If you apply the filter **Using Resource...** from the list │All Tasks ▾│ on the **Formatting** toolbar, you can display all tasks for one team member. We will explain this in more detail in chapter 10 on reporting, see page 593.

Notice that the *Calendar* view is different from the *Project Calendar*. The Calendar view, like the Gantt Chart, displays task bars, whereas the Project Calendar is used to define the working times and holidays.

To See All Tasks on a Day

The calendar view is not suitable for showing the entire schedule. As you can see in the next screenshot, not all task bars always show within a day. This occurs if too many tasks take place on the same day; each day box has a limited height. If there is too little room vertically, MS Project displays a down arrow ▾ in the date heading, as in:

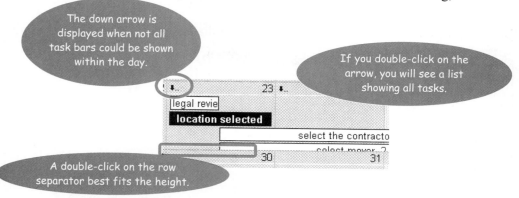

Point to the area where the down arrow is displayed and double-click; a list showing all the tasks on that day appears:

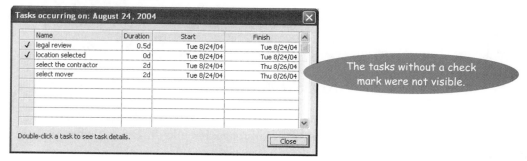

Notice the check mark in front of the tasks that were visible in the calendar view; the ones without a check mark were invisible!

To show all the task bars on any day, position your mouse pointer on any of the horizontal grid lines and double-click when you see the mouse pointer ⬍ .

To Create Tasks

Creating new tasks in this view is not recommended, because the new tasks end up at the end of the task list. You will still have to move them to the right place in the *Work*

Breakdown Structure in the Gantt Chart. If you insist, you can create new tasks by dragging the shape of a new task bar on the dates where you want it. Double-click on it to give it a task name. Notice that the task will have a constraint that is visible on the **Advanced** tab, and you should replace it with appropriate dependencies. Two strikes against this method.

To Edit the Data of a Task

1. Double-click on a task bar; the **Task Information** dialog appears:

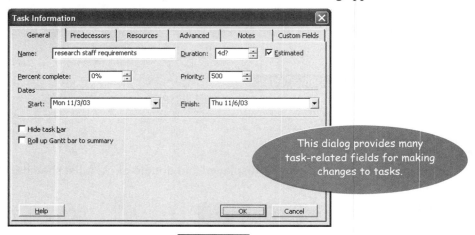

2. Make the changes, and click OK.

To Move Task Bars

You can move task bars horizontally and vertically within a day or between days. You can move a task bar by pointing to the border of a task bar and dragging it when you see the mouse pointer ⊕.

Unless you stay within the same day, you are creating *Start No Earlier Than* constraints on the tasks; just like in the Gantt Chart. *Constraints* are undesirable in schedules, since they make schedules less dynamic. We recommend you show restraint using constraints.

Gantt Chart

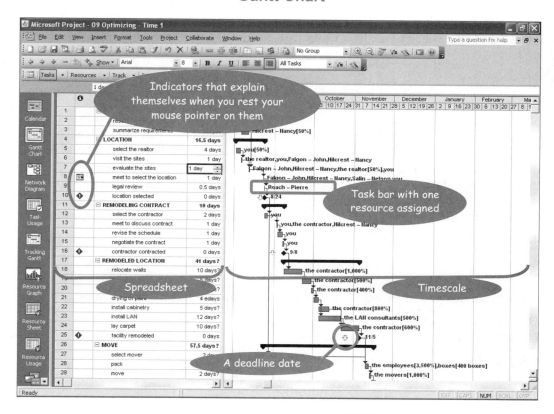

To apply the view, choose **View, Gantt Chart** or click ⊞ in the *View Bar*.

The *Gantt Chart* shows tasks over time. The duration of each task is reflected in the width of its task bar. The Gantt Chart also shows the list of deliverables and tasks, which is commonly referred to as the Work Breakdown Structure (WBS). The WBS typically has a logical hierarchy of summary tasks with detail tasks indented beneath them.

Notice that most items in the schedule explain themselves in a screen tip that pops up when you rest your mouse pointer over them. For example:

◆ The icons in the **Indicators** ❶ column explain problems in the schedule,
◆ When the task name is cut off, you can pop up the complete name
◆ The timescale time units will tell you which year you are in

◆ The task bars inform you of the type of task (summary, detail, milestone, deadline, task name, start, finish and duration),

◆ The dependency arrows inform you which two tasks are linked by the dependency and if there is lag

The Gantt Chart is one of the best views to use when creating or modifying tasks in your project.

To See More Spreadsheet or Timescale

You can change the amount of the spreadsheet you see on the left of the screen and the length of the timescale on the right of your screen. Revealing more of the spreadsheet will be at the expense of the timescale on the right. You can do this by pointing to the divider line between the spreadsheet and the timescale (see page 75). When you see the mouse pointer change to a ◀▶, click and hold down to drag it to the desired position.

If you double-click on the divider, it will jump to the nearest split between two columns. This allows you to clean up the look of the view.

Collapsing and Expanding Levels

Click the minus button ⊟ next to a summary task name to hide its detail tasks
OR press [Alt] + [Shift] + [-] .
Click the plus button ⊞ of a summary task to reveal its detail tasks
OR press [Alt] + [Shift] + [+].

Zooming the Timescale

To zoom the timescale into smaller time units in order to see the details, click **Zoom In** 🔍 on the **Standard** toolbar. When zoomed in, use the **Go to selected task** tool 🖎 to move the timescale to the task bar.
To zoom the timescale out to larger time units in order to get an overview, click **Zoom Out** 🔍 on the **Standard** toolbar.

To fit the entire project duration within the timescale so you always see task bars when you are paging up or down, choose **View, Zoom** and select ◉ **Entire Project**.

Finding the Task Bars

If you don't see any task bars in the Gantt timescale, the timescale is just displaying a time period when no tasks happen to be scheduled. If you put the horizontal scroll box of the timescale at the extreme left on the scroll bar, you will always see the start date of the project. You can also press [Alt] + [Home] on the keyboard.

If you hold the primary mouse button down on the scroll box in the horizontal scroll bar, it will tell you the exact date. It will include the year you currently have on your screen, which is handy in case the timescale does not reveal the year.

 If you quickly want to see the task bar of a task, click on the task and then the tool **Go To Selected Task** on the **Standard** toolbar.

Network Diagram

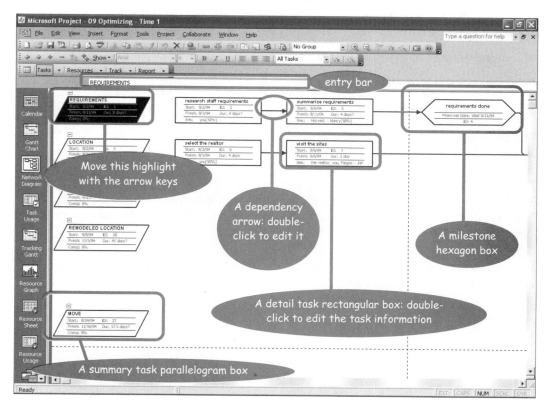

To apply the view, choose **View**, **Network Diagram** or click on the *View Bar*.

The *Network Diagram* shows the network of dependencies between tasks. The dependencies are depicted as arrows. However, when you enter this view for the first time, you often don't see many, in which case you need to **Zoom Out** 🔍 (on **Standard** toolbar) to see more boxes and arrows. When you zoom out far, the text becomes illegible. If you rest the mouse pointer on a task box, a screen tip pops up that allows you to read the task data. An example of such a screen tip is:

print	
Start: Thu 4/6/00	ID: 6
Finish: Fri 4/7/00	Dur: 2 days
Res:	

To zoom back in, use **Zoom In** 🔍 on the **Standard** toolbar.

By default, the Network Diagram displays the different types of tasks in boxes with distinct shapes:

◆ summary tasks in a parallelogram   ▱

◆ detail tasks in a rectangle   ▭

◆ milestones in a hexagon   ⬡

The critical tasks have a red border instead of the (default) blue. More on critical tasks on page 434.

This view is typically used to check the logic in the network. To follow the logic, just use the arrow keys on your keyboard to move the highlight from task to task. If the text is too small, keep your eyes on the *entry bar*, see page 87. The entry bar will show the name of the task.

You can easily add and delete dependencies in this view. We will therefore discuss this view in more detail on page 238.

Task Usage

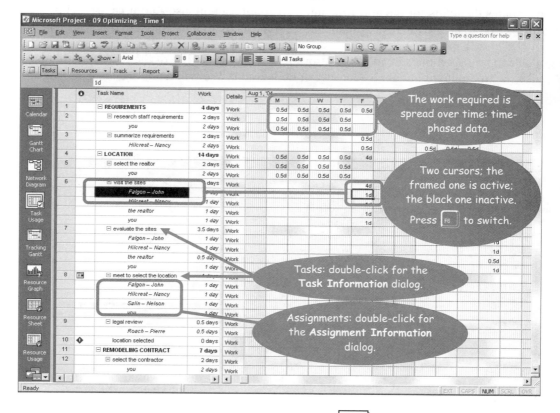

To apply the view, choose **View**, **Task Usage** or click on the *View Bar*.

Notice how the *Task Usage* view shows the assignments in between the tasks. You can differentiate the *assignments* from *tasks* by:
◆ the lack of ID numbers,
◆ the italicized type of the text, and
◆ the lighter yellow background color.

The Task Usage and Resource Usage views are the only views that display the assignments as separate line items.

The timescale on the right shows how MS Project schedules the tasks and assignments. It shows the detailed numbers behind the task bars of the Gantt Chart. This view helps in understanding the Gantt Chart and troubleshooting it, if needed.

If you click **Zoom Out** 🔍 on the **Standard** toolbar, Project 2003 immediately calculates the totals for the new time unit. To zoom back in, use **Zoom In** 🔍. This allows you to create interesting management reports by month, for example.

You can report on the spread of the effort or cost across the life of the project with this view: a time-phased budget by activity or deliverable. We will detail the steps on page 599.

Tracking Gantt

To apply the view, choose **View, Tracking Gantt** or click ⊞ on the *View Bar*.

The *Tracking Gantt* view is used during the execution of the project to track the progress against the original schedule (the *baseline*). Notice that in this view all task bars are split into two halves, a top half that represents the current schedule and a bottom half for the baseline. If you don't have a baseline in your schedule, it only shows the thin top task bars for the current schedule. We will discuss the use of this view extensively in chapter 11 on updating schedules, see page 628.

Resource Graph

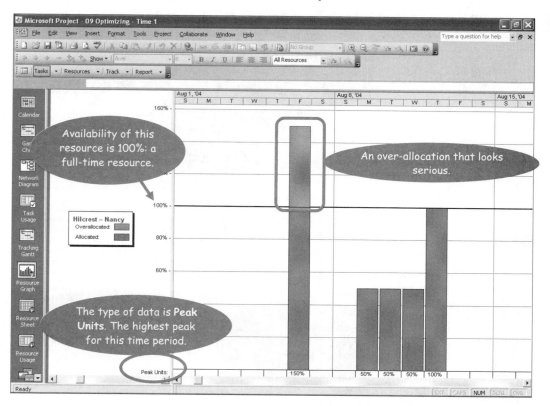

To apply the view, choose **View, Resource Graph** or click ![icon] on the *View Bar*. The *Resource Graph* shows bar charts of the workload over time for all resources, but one resource at a time. This view is also called a *workload histogram*. By pressing [Page Dn] or by using the bottom left horizontal scroll bar you can browse from resource to resource.

If you don't see any bars in the timescale pane, hold down [Alt] and press [Home] to jump to the project start date. If you still don't see any, use **Zoom Out** ![icon] on the **Standard** toolbar until you do.

Notice that the Resource Graph shows the **Peak Units** by default. *Peak Units* means that if you zoom out and go from days to weeks, the highest daily bar will be shown as the peak for the week. This helps you find any over-allocation. However, the more you zoom out, the more pessimistic the depiction of the workload becomes; if you are double-booked during only a one hour meeting task, the entire quarter will depict you to be double-booked. You can change the Peak Units by choosing **Format, Details**. If you select *Work*, you will see the "real" totals of the work hours charted for the time period shown, OR right-click in the chart area and choose **Work** from the pop-up menu.

Resource Sheet

To apply the view, choose **View, Resource Sheet** or click [icon] on the *View Bar*.

The *Resource Sheet* is used to enter the resources needed in a project. Resources can be human resources, facilities, machines and material resources.

Important fields in the Resource Sheet are:

◆ *Name*: Name of the resource.

◆ *Type*: You can indicate if a resource is:
   ◇ a material resource (*Material*) that is consumed on tasks, or
   ◇ a human resource that works on tasks (*Work*).

◆ *Max. Units*: The maximum units represents the maximum availability of the resource to the project expressed as a percentage (default) or in decimals depending on the setting in **Tools, Options,** tab **Schedule**, field **Show assignment units as a**. For example, a full-time individual would be "100%" available (percentage) or be shown as "1" (decimals).

Resource Usage

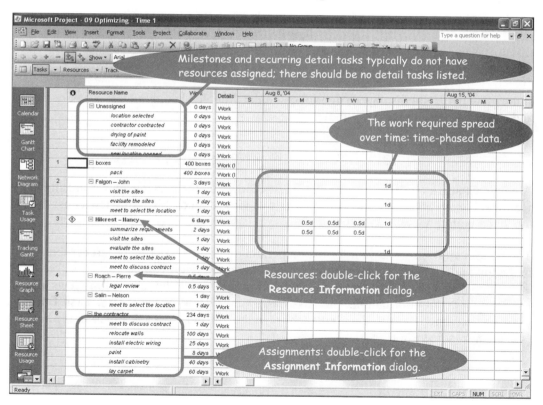

To apply the view, choose **View, Resource Usage** or click ⊞ on the *View Bar*.

The *Resource Usage* view shows the amounts of work or cost over time. As in the Task Usage view, this view shows the assignments as separate line items. You can differentiate the *assignments* from *resources* by:

◆ the lack of ID numbers,
◆ the italicized type of the text, and
◆ the lighter yellow background color.

This view allows you to analyze the workloads and solve any over-allocations. We will discuss the how-to on page 473.

Navigating the Views

To Switch Views

Click the view on the view bar.
OR
Choose **View**; a check mark in front of one of the views means that it is the current view on your screen. Click on the view you want to switch to.
OR
If the view bar is not displayed, right-click on the thin blue bar at the left of your screen and select the view in the pop-up menu.

Single View Versus Combination View

A *single view* is a one-view screen. The views shown on the previous pages are single views. A *combination view* is a screen with two views. A combination view consists of a top and a bottom view.

The bottom view only shows information pertaining to the tasks (or resources) selected in the top view. This interaction between top and bottom view can be very useful for data entry with a sheet view in the top and a form view in the bottom. Form views allow you to enter detail information. The *Task Entry* view (**View, More Views, Task Entry**) is a combination view with the **Gantt Chart** in the top and the **Task Form** in the bottom (see the next screenshot).

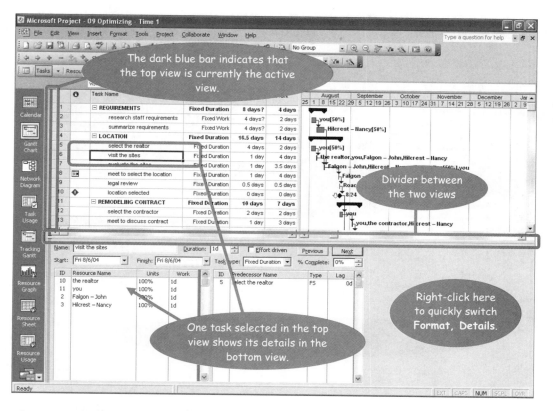

The **Task Entry** view allows you to enter detailed information on tasks. You can enter resource assignments and predecessors. The task you select in the top view, the *Gantt Chart*, is shown in detail in the bottom view, the *Task Form*. The top and bottom views interact; whatever you select in the top is shown in more detail in the bottom. This makes combination views well suited for analysis of schedules:

◆ With a task view in the top and a resource view in the bottom (or vice versa), you can check assignments.

◆ With a resource view in the top and a task view in the bottom you can check over-allocations (**View, More Views, Resource Allocation**), as shown in the next screenshot.

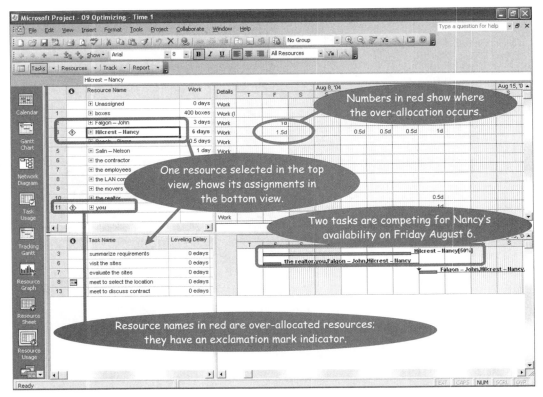

The *Resource Allocation* view has the *Resource Usage* in the top view and the *Leveling Gantt* view in the bottom. This combination view allows you to analyze and resolve over-allocations. The interaction between the top and bottom view is such that the assignments on the task selected in the top view are shown in detail in the bottom.

To Create a Combination View

You can create a custom combination view by splitting the window. Choose **Window, Split**. This menu item then changes into **Remove Split**.
OR
You can point with the tip of the mouse pointer to the sliding window handle at the bottom right of your screen (the tiny little horizontal bar under the scroll down button).

The mouse pointer will become a double-headed arrow ⇕. Drag it up or double-click on it to display the bottom view. You now have two views on the screen, one in the top and one in the bottom. You can change the size of each view by pointing to the divider line between the views; the mouse pointer should change to ⇕. Hold down and drag when you see this mouse pointer. To move the cursor between the views, press [F6] or click in the other view.

 You can drag both the horizontal border and the vertical dividers at the same time. Put your mouse pointer on the intersection between the two divider lines:

Intersection of the divider lines

You should see the mouse pointer. Drag both dividers to the sizes of the views you need.

To Exchange One of the Views in a Combination View

Please note that not all views can be in the bottom of a combination view and not all combinations make sense.

1. Click on the view you want to exchange. This will make the view active. You should see the blue thin vertical bar on the far left of the screen jump to the view you clicked on.

2. Choose **View** and select the view you want to apply.
   OR
   Click on the view in the view bar on the left side of your screen.

To Switch Back to a Single View

Drag the view divider line to the top (or to the bottom depending on which view to keep) using the mouse pointer ⇕.
OR
Double-click on the view divider when you see the mouse pointer ⇕ to keep the top.
OR
Choose **Window, Remove Split** to keep the top.
OR
Hold down [Shift], choose **View** and select another view.

Using Help

Help Task Pane

2003 Choose **Help**, **Microsoft Project Help** and the **Project Help** side pane appears:

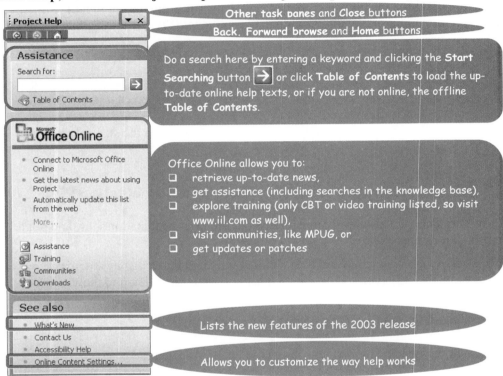

Other task panes and Close buttons

Back. Forward browse and Home buttons

Do a search here by entering a keyword and clicking the **Start Searching** button → or click **Table of Contents** to load the up-to-date online help texts, or if you are not online, the offline **Table of Contents**.

Office Online allows you to:
- ❑ retrieve up-to-date news,
- ❑ get assistance (including searches in the knowledge base),
- ❑ explore training (only CBT or video training listed, so visit www.iil.com as well),
- ❑ visit communities, like MPUG, or
- ❑ get updates or patches

Lists the new features of the 2003 release

Allows you to customize the way help works

To Search for Help Information Online and Offline

1. Choose **Help, Microsoft Project Help** and the **Project Help** side pane appears.

2. In the side pane under **Search for** enter the *keywords* you want to search on; more words will give more accurate results (and the shortest list to dig through). Microsoft recommends entering between 2 and 7 keywords. The search engine will search the online help database first, since it will be most up-to-date, most comprehensive and best formulated. In the online help, people who use the help texts are constantly asked: *Was this information helpful? Yes/No*, and the help texts are subjected to continuous improvement with these quality surveys. In this way, **Help** may become

helpful eventually! If an Internet connection is not available, the local help files are consulted. The *Search Results* pane appears that will tell you if the online help database was accessed:

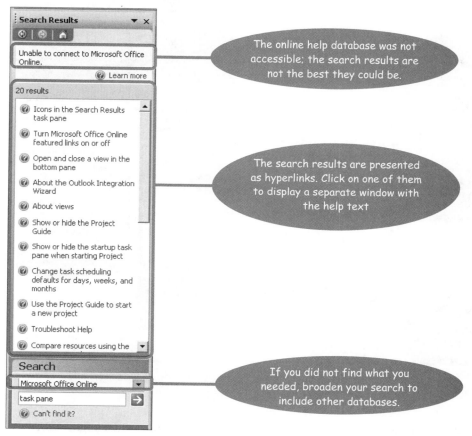

 3. Click one of the help topics listed; you can easily recognize them by their icon ⊚. Each of the help topics is a hyperlink. When clicked, the link will display a separate pane on the right hand side of the screen with the help text. If you did not find what you needed, you can consult other places and databases, since there the pane now displays a list button Microsoft Office Online ▼ with other sources.

4. To close off the help panes, click the **Close** button ✕.

One example of the new (and continuously improved) *Office Online* help in the *Internet Explorer* interface is:

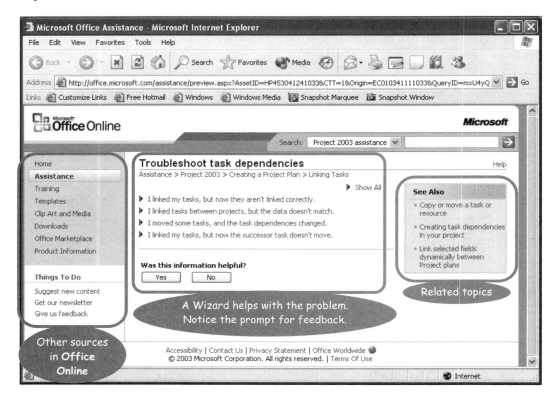

Help on Fields

You just need to rest your mouse pointer on a column heading and a small screen tip pops up, like:

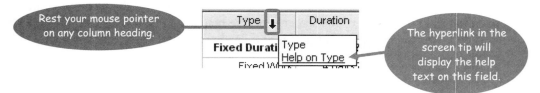

The underlined keywords (hyperlink) in the screen tip will give you access to help text that explains the field.

Help with Scheduling: Planning Wizard

The *Planning Wizard* can help you find your way around MS Project. The Wizard gives you choices of things to do if there could be ambiguity. It presents choices to solve the problem.

We recommend keeping it on and when you start to get annoyed with a certain type of message, select ☑ **Don't tell me about this again** at the bottom left of the dialog:

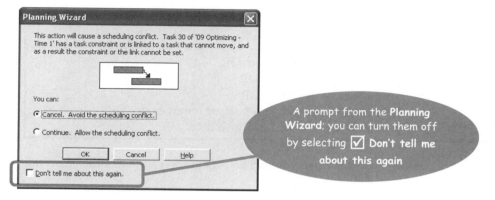

A prompt from the **Planning Wizard**; you can turn them off by selecting ☑ **Don't tell me about this again**

There are three categories of messages and every time you "tell MS Project off", it will turn that message in the category off until they are all gone and the category will be turned off as well at that time in **Tools, Options, General**.

Or you can turn the Wizard off right now by choosing **Tools, Options, General** and clearing ☐ **Advice from Planning Wizard.**

Help When Making Changes: Smart Tags

Whenever you see a small graphical tag appear to the left of where you made changes to the schedule, you are given additional choices. These pop-ups are called *smart tags*. Smart tags ask for clarification when you can end up with unintended side effects. Depending on the situation, different smart tag graphics appear. Below you will find a table of them:

Graphic	Appears when
☒	You press ⌊Delete⌋ on a task name
◈	You change the duration, OR You change the work, OR You change the units, OR You add a resource to a task, or remove one, OR You change the start or finish date

An example of the choices you get when you increase a duration and click the smart tag button is:

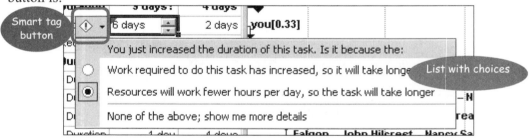

Technical Specifications of Your System and Technical Support

1. Choose **Help, About Microsoft Office Project**. If you are not sure if you have *Project 2003 Standard* or *Project 2003 Professional*, you can verify that in this dialog.

2. Your options here are:

   ◇ Click | System Info... | to get the *technical specifications* of your computer system

   ◇ Click | Tech Support... | to get contact information on *how to reach real technical support* people on the telephone.

◊ Click Disabled Items... to get a list of *disabled items* in MS Project that were disabled, because they stopped MS Project from functioning properly. You can re-enable them if you think the cause has been resolved.

Setting Up a New Project Schedule

The process for preparing a new project schedule is:
1. Creating a new project schedule from the ground up
   OR
   from a project template see page 109.
2. Describing the project in the dialog boxes, see page 106:
   ◊ **Project, Project Information**
   ◊ **File, Properties**
3. Setting the options, see page 111. Options to consider are:
   ◊ Date order
   ◊ **Tools, Options**
   ◊ **Tools, Level Resources...**
4. Setting the *project calendar* in the dialog **Tools, Change Working Time**, see page 116:
   ◊ Working hours
   ◊ Business days
   ◊ Holidays

The *Project Guide* is a toolbar and its buttons display side panes. The side panes act as wizard interfaces that hold your hand and step you through a process. They ask for information in a series of prompts in the right order. You can display the project guide toolbar by right-clicking on any toolbar and choosing **Project Guide**. The toolbar appears and looks like this:

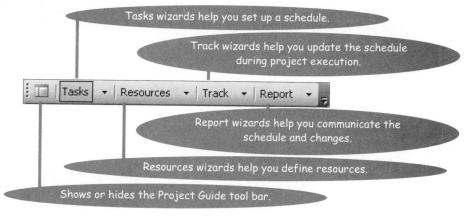

Upon clicking Tasks , the side pane changes to:

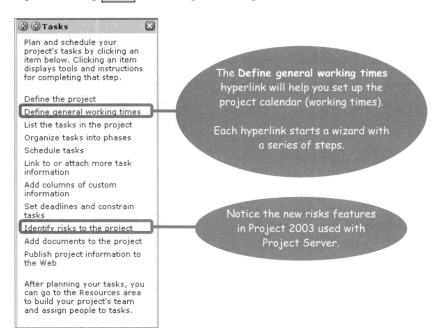

This side pane now provides hyperlinks to perform certain functions, like **Define the project** and **Define general working times**. Clicking a hyperlink will start the series of prompts of the wizard.

 In Project 2003, you don't need to display the side pane first, you can use one of the list buttons ▾ on the Project Guide toolbar to start a particular wizard immediately.

The Project Guide wizards do not cover all the steps that we suggest as a process for setting up a new project and we will therefore discuss these steps in more detail here.

Creating a New Project Schedule

Click **New** 📄 on the **Standard** toolbar. This creates a blank project right away and displays the **Tasks** Project Guide.
OR
Choose **File, New**: a new project appears as well as the *New Project task pane* on the left side of the screen. This MS Office Project task pane is similar to the **New Document** task pane in *MS Office Word* and the **New Workbook** task pane in *MS Office Excel*. As you can see it is a standard across the MS Office 2003. The **New Project** pane looks like:

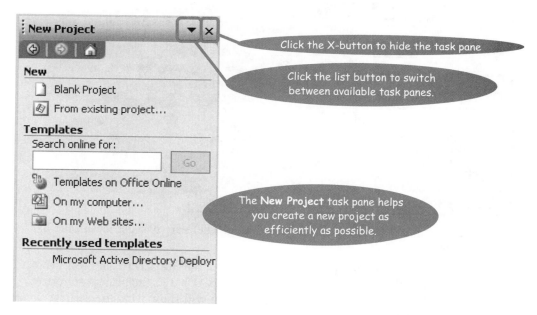

By clicking on one of the blue hyperlinks in the **New Project** task pane, you can create:

◆ a **Blank Project** or
◆ a new project:

  ◇ **From existing project**, or
  ◇ from **Templates**

  - Templates on Office Online; at the time this book was written 15 project templates were posted, some of which created by *Microsoft Partners* or *Solution Providers*. This is a website to visit once in a while, because the list will grow.

- **On my computer** lists the templates on your hard drive and the *Enterprise Templates* if you use *Project 2003 Professional* connected to *Project Server*.

- **On my Web sites** displays the **New from Templates on my Website** dialog in which you can enter the URL of your website like:
http://<name of your web server>/<web site name>.

◇ from one of the **Recently used templates**.
This hyperlink is only displayed when you have accessed templates before.

Describing the Project

1. Choose **Project, Project Information** and the **Project Information** dialog appears:

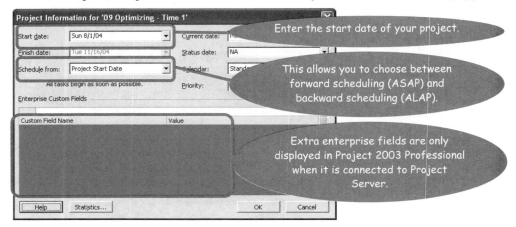

2. Enter the basic project information in this dialog. There are two choices in the list **Schedule from**:

◇ **Project Start Date** (*forward scheduling*): Enter the **Start Date** and MS Project will schedule all tasks *As Soon As Possible* (ASAP) after the project start date. After you have entered all the data, MS Project will show what the earliest finish date will be for the project.

◇ **Project Finish Date** (*backward scheduling*): Enter the **Finish Date** and MS Project will schedule all tasks *As Late As Possible* (ALAP) working backward from the project finish date. After you have entered all the data, MS Project will show what the target start date of the project should be.

The choice you make depends on what you know most certainly about your project: the start date or the finish date. Neither approach will prevent the common occurrence that the initial schedule is too long. You usually have to squeeze the project into a time box that is available for the project. This makes the choice between entering the start or the finish date less important, and most people leave it to the default scheduling from the project start date forward. Click [OK].

3. Choose **File, Properties** and the **<name of your project> Properties** dialog appears:

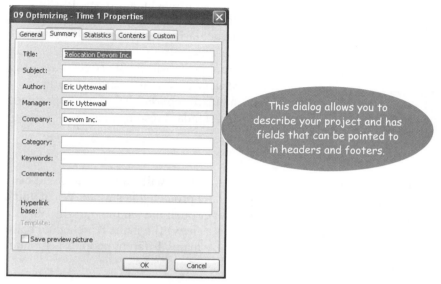

This dialog allows you to describe your project and has fields that can be pointed to in headers and footers.

4. Click the tab **Summary** and enter in this dialog:
   ◇ the name of the project in the field **Title**,
   ◇ your name as the **Author** and/or **Manager** and
   ◇ the project objective or a description of the final project product in the **Comments** field. Try to come up with a single sentence that captures the essence of your project.

5. Click [OK].

 The entries in the **File, Properties** dialog can be used in the headers and footers of each report you create by referring to them. They save time; particularly when an entry changes and all your ten reports will be updated automatically.

Creating a New Schedule from a Project Template

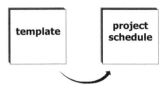

Open template copies the template

Project templates are useful as a jumpstart on your project plan. If you run similar projects over and over again, templates are particularly useful. Templates can be created centrally by your *project office* to promote consistent *Work Breakdown Structures*, common project options, standard reports, shared project calendars and standard resource names.[11]

 Templates are protected from accidental changes, so they will stay the same and can be used over and over again. The way the templates are protected is simple. When you open a project template, Project 2003 copies it; you never open the template itself. When saving the template, you will always be asked for a (new) file name or schedule name. This way the templates are safe and can be used by many different people. Template files have the extension **.MPT**.

---

[11] If you use Project Server, you would standardize on the resource names through the *Enterprise Resource Pool*.

Using a Project Template

1. Choose **File, New**: a new project appears as well as the *New Project task pane* on the left side of the screen.

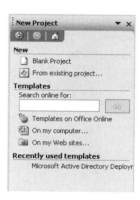

2. In the section **Templates**, click **On my computer** and you will see the following dialog in MS Project used standalone:

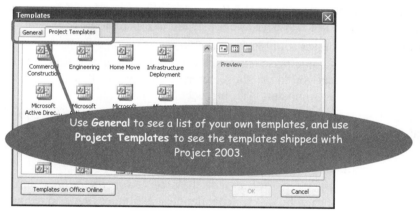

Use **General** to see a list of your own templates, and use **Project Templates** to see the templates shipped with Project 2003.

OR

In Project 2003 Professional with *Project Server*, you will see an extra tab **Enterprise Templates** as in the next dialog:

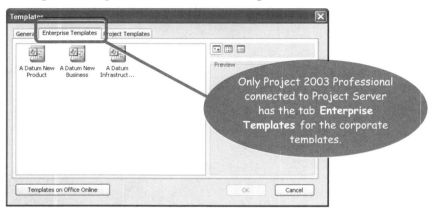

3. These tabs contain:

    ◇ Tab **General** lists the *user templates* you created yourself for your own purposes. General templates are stored in the directory as set in **Tools, Options, Save, User templates**. If you were to fill in a subdirectory under *Workgroup Templates*, you would see it appear as another tab in this dialog.

    ◇ Tab **Enterprise Templates** (only in Project 2003 Professional with *Project Server*) lists the enterprise templates used in your organization. Your organization may expect you to use these enterprise templates that were custom-made for you to jumpstart your projects.

    ◇ Tab **Project Templates** lists 25 templates that are shipped with Project 2003. It has ready-to-go templates for several industries.

4. Double-click on a template OR select one template and click ⬛ OK ⬛; the template copies itself and opens. It appears with the *project-specific options* and *project calendar* set. There may be tasks, dependencies, estimates, generic resources and assignments, as well as custom views and reports.

Setting the Options

The way Project 2003 operates is controlled by the settings in **Tools**, **Options**. The steps to change the options are:

1. Choose **Tools, Options...**; the **Options** dialog appears:

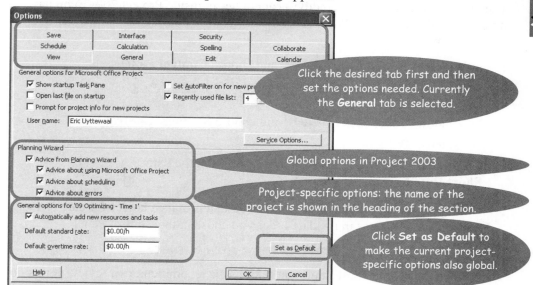

2. Select the category of options by clicking one of the tabs.

3. Set the options.

4. Click [OK] to accept the changes and close the dialog.

There are two types of options:

◆ *Global options* that take effect in all projects: These options are stored in the *Windows Registry*.

◆ *Project-specific options* that affect the active project only: You can recognize these, because they start with a section divider showing the name of the project schedule. These options are stored in the project file (.MPP) or in the schedule (*Project Server* database).

 By clicking [Set as Default] you can make project-specific options the default for new projects. This button saves the project-specific options as they are currently set into the *Windows Registry* as well. When you create a blank new project, the Windows Registry is consulted. For existing project schedules, the project-specific options will not be overridden by clicking this button, because they were already saved with the project.

Setting the Date Order

The date order (ddmmyy or mmddyy) cannot be set inside Project 2003. You have to set it in the Windows *Control Panel*. This means that it will affect the date order in all of your Windows applications.

1. In Windows XP, click **start** and choose **Control Panel**, click ● Regional and Language Options and click [Customize...]
    OR
    In Windows 2000, click **Start** and choose **Settings, Control Panel,** click ●Regional Options

2. Click the tab **Date** and select the date order from the list:
    Short Date Format M/d/yy ▾.

3. Click [OK]; all lists in Project 2003 that provide choices for date formats will now only show items in the date order you chose in the Control Panel.

Options for a New Project

This table indicates the most important options we recommend you review at this point.

Tab	Set to
View	**Date Format:** Mon 1/31/00 ▾
	To avoid confusion about dates in international projects, a date format should be chosen with the month spelled out, i.e., 31 Jan '00. Americans will interpret a date like 7-8-2000 as July 8, 2000. Europeans, South Americans and people from Québec, however, will interpret it as August 7th and think they have an extra month.
General	**User Name** [ ] Enter your name; if you are connected to Project Server, it will be filled in already.
	☑ **Advice from Planning Wizard**
	Meant for novice users. Clear if the Wizard doesn't help you … or annoys you.

Calendar	**Hours per Day** `8.00` ⊟
	MS Project uses this number to convert days that are entered in the **Duration** and **Work** fields into hours. This number should represent the hours worked by a *Full-Time Equivalent* (*FTE*) employee.
	Hours per Week `40.00` ⊟
	MS Project uses this number to convert weeks into hours. If this number does not reflect your situation, the schedule will not be accurate. It should correspond to the **Hours per Day** setting.
	Days per Month `20` ⊟
	MS Project uses this number to convert months into days. This number should reflect your situation.
	`Set as Default` Sets the calendar options entered as the default settings for any new schedules you create. Your other existing schedules are not affected, because this option is stored in the project schedule, as you can see in the label of the section divider **Calendar Options for <schedule name of the project>**.
Schedule	☑ **Show Scheduling Messages** will give helpful messages when it notices a problem in the schedule.
Calculation	◉ **Automatic** will ensure that you see the effect of the last changes immediately. With the current speed of computers, the need for manual calculation is evaporating.

The **Calendar** option **Hours per Day** has to be decided upon first and cannot be changed without re-entering all durations. You have to specify how many work hours a workday has. It uses this setting to convert between time units; the *time unit conversion factors*. For example, if the **Hours per Day** is set to 8 hours and you enter a duration of 5 days, MS Project knows this equals 8 * 5 = 40 hours. If you then change the **Hours per Day** setting to 7h/d, MS Project changes the duration to 5.71 days (= 5 * 8 / 7). You must consider this option before entering any tasks. If you start with the wrong number, MS Project will interpret the durations you enter incorrectly which may result in a schedule that is too optimistic or pessimistic.

There is one way to keep the current durations without having to re-enter all durations again when you change the **Hours per Day** setting. Before changing the **Hours per Day**, copy all durations to one of the extra fields (**Text1** for example), change the **Hours**

per Day and then copy the durations from the **Text1** field back into the **Duration** field. Make sure you have the task field **Type** set to **Fixed Units** for all tasks (see page 185).[12]

When options are global, it means that they apply to all your projects, existing and new. You can see if an option is global in the **Options** dialog box by reading the labels in the section heading. If the name of the project is mentioned, the option is project-specific and not global.

Typically, at the start of each chapter, we will discuss the options relevant for that chapter.

Leveling Option: Automatic or Manual

Workload *leveling* is changing the schedule in such a way that the workloads of the

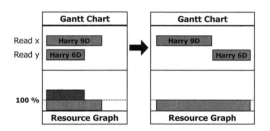

resources are within their availability at any given time. In the illustration, you can see that on the left Harry has to work full-time on two tasks that are scheduled in parallel. It causes a workload that exceeds his availability of 100%, which is called an *over-allocation*. The over-allocation was solved on the right by delaying the task *Read y* until after *Read x*. Delaying tasks is something MS Project can help you with; it is called *automatic leveling*. There are other ways to level the workloads; we will discuss them in Chapter 9 on optimizing, see page 419. These other ways can result in a shorter schedule, but require more effort from you.

---

[12] My colleague Linda Lawlor came up with this trick.

1. Choose **Tools, Level Resources…**; the **Resource Leveling** dialog appears:

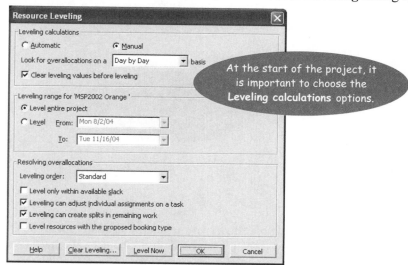

At the start of the project, it is important to choose the **Leveling calculations** options.

2. At the top in **Leveling calculations**, select ⊙ **Manual**. This will allow us to trigger an automatic leveling of the workloads when we are ready for it.

We recommend you use manual leveling at this time. If you select automatic leveling, MS Project will constantly make changes to your schedule as it tries to keep the workloads leveled. When we come to chapter 9 on optimizing schedules (see page 486), we will generate some scenarios using the leveling features in MS Project and discuss the dialog box in more detail. We will also explain methods to level the workloads yourself (see page 473).

Setting the Project Calendar

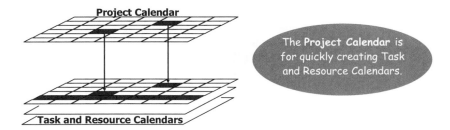

The **Project Calendar** is for quickly creating Task and Resource Calendars.

The **Tools, Change Working Time** dialog allows you to set the *project calendar*. On the project calendar, you can model the *workweek*. The default project calendar is called *Standard*. On the project calendar you indicate:

◆ *Business days*
  Which days are working days in a regular workweek?

◆ Standard *working hours*
  What are the typical working hours for full-time project team members?

◆ National and corporate *holidays*
  What days are nonworking days throughout the year?

In addition to the project calendar there are:

◆ *Task calendars*
  These can be used to schedule individual tasks. For example, outdoor construction tasks can only take place when the weather permits, and a task calendar could be created for all tasks affected by winter weather. An office move can only take place during the weekend. We will discuss task calendars on page 290.

◆ *Resource calendars*
  These are calendars for each individual person. A resource calendar typically contains individual working days and vacations, sometimes the working hours are individualized as well. We will explain resource calendars on page 330.

The business days, working hours and national holidays of the project calendar will be transferred to all resource calendars. The changes you make on the project calendar apply to every task and every resource in the project (unless you have overwritten those settings in the task or resource calendars). At this point, we will only edit the project calendar; later we will create task calendars and resource calendars. All tasks will be scheduled using the project calendar unless:

◆ they have their own task calendar, or
◆ they have resources assigned (with resource calendars).

The task and resource calendars override the project calendar

In summary, the project calendar has two functions:

◆ It is a time-saving device to change all task and resource calendars.
◆ It is used to schedule tasks without a task calendar or resources assigned.

One Project Guide has a wizard that prompts for the working times, hours per day, business days and holidays. You can access it by right-clicking on any toolbar and choosing **Project Guide**; a toolbar appears. Click the **Tasks** tool, the side pane changes and one of the hyperlinks shown is **Define general working times**.

Hours per Day Option versus Working Time

The following is very confusing to many people. If you change the number of hours per day in **Tools, Options, Calendar**, Project 2003 does not update the working times in the project calendar by itself. Project 2003 uses the hours per day option for conversion purposes only. When you enter a duration of *1w*, it will convert it to hours. If the setting in **Tools, Options** is 40h/w, then it knows that 1w = 40h. It converts all the estimates you enter, since it stores the numbers in minutes.

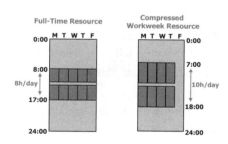

In the project calendar, you can indicate the regular working hours for a full-time resource. Project 2003 uses these settings to schedule the 40 hours of effort within the working hours. Forty hours of effort for a full-time resource will take 5 business days (Monday–Friday). Forty hours of effort for a compressed *workweek* resource who works 10 hours a day, will only need 4 business days (see the illustration). The conclusion is that the **Tools, Options Calendar, Hours per Day** setting needs to be aligned manually with the working hours in the project calendar.

Entering the Business Days

1. Choose **Tools, Change Working Time...**; the **Change Working Time** dialog appears where you can determine the working days of the *workweek*:

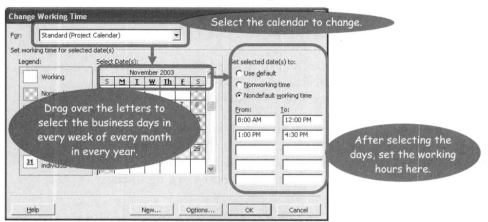

2. Select at the top of the dialog under:

   For: | Standard (Project Calendar) |

   the **Standard (Project Calendar)**, as this is the calendar that acts as the project calendar.

3. If the options on the right-hand side in this dialog are grayed out, it likely is because you are connected to *Project Server* and are using one of the *Enterprise calendars*. Your project office is responsible for maintaining the enterprise calendars, not you. That is one less task for you!

4. If you have a Monday to Friday workweek, select the workdays of the week by dragging over the letters that stand for the days of the week. Click and hold down on the **M** for Monday and stop at the **F** for Friday: | M | T | W | Th | F |.

   Select one of two options:
   ⦿ **Use default**; this sets all weekdays to working days with default working hours of **8:00 AM-12:00 PM** and **1:00 PM-5:00 PM**, or
   ⦿ **Nondefault working time** if you need to change these working hours, you may as well do this at the same time and enter the new working times in the **From** and **To** fields. Make sure you also click | Options... | to adjust the *time unit conversion factors*.

5. Click on the | S | for Saturday, then hold down | Control | and click on the | S | for Sunday and select ⦿ **Nonworking time**.

When you select the days by their letter at the top, you have selected "eternity"! The changes you make apply to those days in every week in every month of every year! However, MS Project's eternity only lasts until 2049 which is well past our retirement age ... hopefully.

Entering the Working Hours

1. Choose **Tools, Change Working Time…**; the **Change Working Time** dialog appears where you can model the working hours of the *workweek*.

2. Select from the list: **For:** Standard (Project Calendar) ▼; **Standard (Project Calendar)**; this is the calendar that acts as the project calendar.

3. If the options on the right-hand side in this dialog are grayed out, it likely is because you are connected to *Project Server* and are using one of the *Enterprise calendars*. Your project office is responsible for maintaining the enterprise calendars.

4. If you did not set the hours per day in **Tools, Options**, do this first by clicking Options… to adjust the *time unit conversion factors*. Upon clicking OK you will be returned to this dialog.

5. Select the workdays Monday through Friday by dragging with the mouse from the **M** to the **F** on M T W Th F .

6. MS Project has a default calendar with 8 hours per day and working hours from 8:00 AM-12:00 PM and 1:00 PM-5:00 PM. For any diversion from these factory set defaults, select ◉ **Nondefault working time**.

7. Type the normal work times into the boxes:
   From: **To**:

   The dates in the calendar now have a gray hatch pattern in the background and are **Edited working hours**.

8. Click OK
   OR

   select another *calendar* from the list and answer Yes to the prompt to save the changes.

Entering the Holidays

1. Choose **Tools, Change Working Time...**; the **Change Working Time** dialog appears.

2. Select at the top of the dialog under **For:** Standard (Project Calendar) the **Standard (Project Calendar)**, as this is the calendar that acts as the project calendar.

3. If the options on the right-hand side in this dialog are grayed out, it likely is because you are connected to *Project Server* and are using one of the *Enterprise calendars*. Your project office is responsible for maintaining the enterprise calendars.

4. Take out your calendar to find the national or company holidays. Go to the first month in which there are holidays by clicking on the scroll arrows ⋀ or ⋁ in Windows XP, or ▲ or ▼ in Windows 2000
   OR
   by pressing [Page Up] or [Page Dn]
   OR
   To go faster, drag the scroll box ▤ (Windows XP) or ▢ (Windows 2000).

5. Select the holidays by dragging over them or by holding down [Control] and clicking and dragging over them. Simply dragging down includes the weekend days as well, if you need to select just the weekdays you have to use the [Control] key.

6. Select ⊙ **Nonworking time**; the days are now gray, like the weekend days (nonworking). Repeat steps 3 and 4 for the rest of the holidays.

The holidays set in the project calendar are carried over to the individual resource calendars and also to the task calendar, if you create it by making a copy of the Standard (Project Calendar).

Even if the project calendar is changed after resource calendars are created, the changes will show up automatically in the resource calendars. This is not the case for task calendars.

The national holidays and the company holidays should be marked in the project calendar. Days should be marked as nonworking days if they apply to (almost) everybody involved in the project. These typically are either national holidays or company holidays. On the *resource calendar*s, the project calendar can still be overridden, and certain holidays can be set back to be working days for certain resources. Therefore, the project calendar should merely be considered and used as a time saver for creating and changing resource calendars.

The calendar information is saved in the project schedule. If you want to distribute a project calendar among colleagues, you have to transfer it to them via the Organizer (see page 208).
OR
If you have *Project Server* you would adjust the *Standard (Project Calendar)* object in the *Enterprise Global*.

Checks on Setting Up a Project

Here are some checks to verify if you used the best practices when setting up a new project:

◆ Does the **File, Properties**, tab **Summary, Comments** field contain a succinct description of the objective or final product of the project?
The description is visible as a **Note** on the project summary task. You need to have some background information on the project to properly evaluate the schedule. It doesn't hurt to have a one-liner on your project ready for when you need to explain to a board member what your project is about in an elevator between the third and the fifth floor.

◆ Do the working hours on the **Tools, Change Working Time, Standard (Project Calendar)** correspond to the **Tools, Options, Calendar, Hours per day**?
For example, working times of 8:00 AM-12:00 PM and 1:00 PM-5:00 PM are consistent with 8 hours per day and 40 hours per week. If the settings are inconsistent, your forecasts are either too optimistic or too pessimistic. Also, you might see decimals in the task durations.
The quickest way to check consistency is by choosing **Tools, Change Working Time**. The button | Options... | will take you directly to the **Tools, Options, Calendar** dialog. If the hours-per-day setting is wrong, please see the text after the table on page 112 for a trick to make these two settings correspond. If the working hours are wrong, you can correct them with the steps on page 119.

Exercises

Review

1. Does MS Office Project function more like MS Office Excel or MS Office Access? Why?

2. What is the function of the *Global.MPT* file?

3. Does Project Server have a global container for objects?

4. In which situations would you recommend the use of project templates?

5. What view would you use for:

	Recommended view
Entering tasks?	
Entering resources?	
Entering assignments?	
Checking the network logic?	
Viewing workloads?	
To-do lists?	

6. Why would you use a split view (combination view) in Project 2003?

7. What steps do you recommend as a process when creating a new project schedule?

8. How do the settings **Tools, Options, Calendar, Hours per day** and the working hours in **Tools, Change Working Time, Standard (Project Calendar)** relate to each other?

9. How can you change the default calendar, i.e., how can you edit the *Standard Project Calendar* in the *Global.MPT*?

Relocation Project — Scope Statement

You are put in charge of relocating your office. You have to find a new location and organize the move. The following is the *scope statement* created for the project. Your CEO has already signed the scope statement.

Scope Statement for the Relocation Project of DEVOM, Inc.
Project accounting code: MOVE001

The Business Need
DEVOM, Inc. is growing and needs larger facilities to accommodate the expanding workforce.

The Project Objectives
- To be moved and operational in the new location by November 1, 2006
- To stay within the available budget of $100,000 for labor cost
- To have an 80% satisfaction rate from the personnel for the new work environment

The Project Deliverables and Requirements
- A project plan (including WBS, Network Diagram, Gantt Chart, budget, resource list and assignments)
- A new rented or leased location that has a maximum capacity of 150 work spaces
  - The location should be accessible to disabled people
  - The location should have parking facilities for at least 150 cars
  - The location should have modern work cubicles and an open workspace
- Contracts with the landlord, the general contractor and the moving company
- The physical move of people and equipment

The Project Constraints
- The work on the project is to be started no earlier than August 1, 2006
- The personnel have to be asked for input as to the location and facilities needed
- The disruption to the normal operations of DEVOM should be minimized and may not exceed a loss of 200 person days caused by the project
- Clients will have to be able to contact DEVOM at any time by phone, fax and e-mail
- The purchase of new materials and equipment shall be budgeted and approved separately
- The new location will be within the boundaries of the city and its suburbs
- The need for expansion is so urgent that the project has priority over normal operations
- Any changes to the project objectives will require the approval of the CEO

The Project Assumptions
◆ The market will continue to grow at the same rate
◆ The current furniture can be reused
◆ The current workstations can be reused
◆ The current LAN and servers will be replaced

Date: ……......................

Your signature   signature N.R. Salin:

                                                            NRSalin

....
Project Manager, Relocation Project   CEO, DEVOM, Inc.

You decide to make a project plan and to put the schedule in Project 2003 to keep track of them.

1. Fill in the date and sign the scope statement to take charge of this project.

2. Create a new MS Project file.

3. Set the start date for the project to *August 1, 2006* in the **Project Information** dialog.

4. Display the file **Properties** dialog.

5. The title of the project is *Relocation Devom Inc.*

6. You are the responsible project manager; enter your own name under **Manager**.

7. Enter *Devom Inc.* under **Company**.

8. Formulate one sentence that captures the essence of the relocation project and enter it in the field **Comments**.

9. Close the dialog and save the file as *Relocation.MPP*.

Relocation Project — Tools, Options

Continue to work in the file *Relocation.MPP* and enter only the following options:

Page tab	Set to
Schedule	☑ *Show scheduling messages*
	Show assignment units as a: Decimal[13]
	Duration is entered in: Days
	Work is entered in: Days
	Default task type: Fixed Duration
	☐ *New tasks are effort driven*
	☑ *Tasks will always honor their constraint dates*
View	*Date Format: Jan 28 '02* [14]
General	*User name: <your name>* [15]
	☑ *Automatically add new resources and tasks*
Calculation	*Calculation mode:* ◉ *Automatic*
Calendar	*Hours per day: 7.5* [16]
	Hours per week: 37.5 [17]
	Days per month: 20

---

[13] In this project we will use mostly individual and group resources and will therefore use decimals rather than percentages.

[14] If you don't see *mmddyy* here, you could go to the Control Panel to change the date order.

[15] Enter your own name here instead of <your name>. This will allow you to refer to this field in the headers and footers of all reports you create.

[16] Enter this by typing instead of using the spin buttons.

[17] Same.

Relocation Project — The Project Calendar

Continue to work with your file *Relocation.MPP* and enter the following data:

1. Set the working hours on the **Standard (Project Calendar)** to:
   8:00 to *12:00* and
   13:00 to *16:30*

2. Enter the following national holidays for the months August, September and October in the **Standard (Project Calendar)**. Since this project takes place in the US, enter the following national holidays of the United States:
   ◇ *Labor Day, September 4th, 2006*
   ◇ *Columbus Day, October 9th, 2006*
   ◇ *Veterans Day, November 11th, but observed on November 10th in 2006*

3. Compare your file with the solution file *03 Entering Tasks.MPP* available for download at www.jrosspub.com. Please, click the link *WAV Download Resource Center* to enter the download site.

Troubleshooting

Open the file *Wrong Hours per Day.MPP* available for download at www.jrosspub.com. Please, click the link *WAV Download Resource Center* to enter the download site. Correct the **Hours per day** setting in the **Tools, Options, Calendar** to 7 hours per day without affecting the durations.

Chapter 3 Entering Tasks

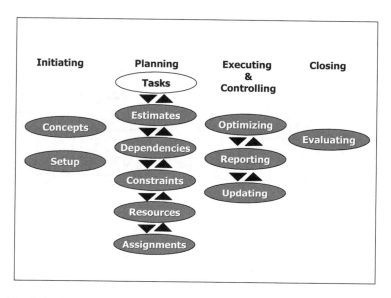

We have finished the *Initiating* phase and will now begin the *Planning phase* by entering *Tasks* (see the white balloon in the illustration). In fact, we will start with entering the deliverables. We recommend you enter the data in the order shown in this overview: first tasks, then estimates, dependencies, constraints, resources and finally, assignments.

After reading this chapter you will:

◆ understand what a Work Breakdown Structure (WBS) is and its importance as the foundation of the project schedule
◆ be able to create and change an indented WBS in MS Project
◆ be able to create summary tasks, detail tasks, milestones, split task bars, recurring tasks and overhead tasks
◆ be able to establish the right level of detail in the WBS
◆ know how to edit, copy and move tasks
◆ be able to check the WBS of the project schedule using scheduling best practices

Deliverables That Make a Difference

Bob has Monica in his office; she is one of his team members. They are discussing the WBS that Monica forwarded to Bob. After chit-chatting, Bob opens the serious part of the meeting with "Overall your plan looks really good, but I would like to have a look at the way you formulated your deliverables. Can we do that?" Monica nods and unfolds her schedule in front of Bob. Bob runs his finger along the WBS, stops at one item and asks, "Here is the planning phase, and I don't see a deliverable in it. Isn't the deliverable here your *project plan*?" Monica nods again. "Can we replace the word 'planning' then with the words 'project plan'?" Monica shrugs her shoulders indifferently but asks, "Why do you find that important?" Bob answers: "It's important to me, because now I know that I will get a project plan from you, since you identified it as a deliverable in your WBS." "Oh, I see!" Monica says.

Bob runs his finger further down and stops at the element *subcontracting:* "What is your deliverable here?" he asks. "Well, the signed contracts, I suppose....," Monica replies. "Yes, I would think so. Can we replace the word *subcontracting* with the words *signed contracts*?" Bob suggests. "Sure, if you think that is important," Monica says.

Bob makes other changes like '*moving to new location*' to '*new and operational location*', '*marketing*' to '*30% increase in revenue*', '*renovation*' to '*renovated facility*', '*material procurement*' to '*procured materials*', '*developed prototype*' to '*prototype development*', and '*closing*' to '*customer approval*'.

Monica concludes: "You are pretty anal about this, aren't you?" "Yes, my dear," Bob says, "and I have found that anal retentiveness makes a world of difference in this case!"

Work Breakdown Structure

The list of tasks in MS Project typically contains a logical grouping. If you group the activities by deliverable, you can keep a better overview of the entire project. A deliverable-oriented grouping also enables you to get good reports from MS Project, like the effort or cost by deliverable. This grouping is known as the *Work Breakdown Structure (WBS)*. The WBS is a breakdown of the project product into deliverables that, together, define the *scope* of the project.[18] Once you know the deliverables, you can then identify the activities to create those deliverables.

The WBS is the most important document in a project plan, since all other project management documents need the WBS as input. Also, the WBS is a *"contract"* between:

◆ The project manager and the customer in *external projects* like consulting projects.
◆ The project manager and executives (*project sponsor*) in an *internal project* like system development projects.

---

[18] See the PMBOK® Guide, 2004 Edition, published by the PMI.

The next illustration shows a WBS for an aircraft manufacturer:[19]

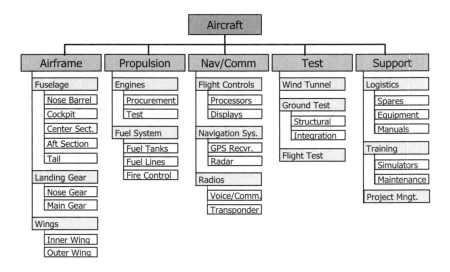

The *WBS* specifies explicitly what should be done. Implicitly, it also specifies what should NOT be done, since it wouldn't be shown. If the client requests output during project execution, the WBS should contain the output to be delivered. If it is not in the WBS, it is *out of scope* and you can then make a case to the client that the requested deliverable was not agreed upon. Therefore, if it is not explicitly in (the WBS), it is implicitly out (of scope). Or, in other words, if it is not in the WBS, it is not in the project. This is the *generally accepted project management practice*. In Project 2003 you can capture the scope of the project in the **Task Name** column by creating an indented list of deliverables and tasks.

In past projects, you may have been forced by your client to deliver something that was never promised; this is commonly known as *scope creep*. From those projects, you have probably learned to specify explicitly in the project plan which elements are out of scope. Otherwise, you will continue to be burned by scope creep. If you expect any

---

[19] Jeff Turner contributed this WBS chart.

possible misunderstanding about the scope of the project, it is a good idea to also document the deliverables that you consider to be out of scope.

Out of scope elements can be captured using the **Task Notes** on the **Standard** toolbar or in the **File, Properties, Summary** tab, **Comments** field. We recommend paying careful attention to clarifying what is in scope and what is out of scope to manage the expectations of your client carefully and early in the life of the project. Working out a detailed WBS with your client ensures a veritable meeting of the minds. Time spent on your WBS is generally time well spent.

Deliverables are tangible components of the project product that are handed over to the client during or at the end of the project. The deliverables are often broken down further into their components and eventually into tasks (activities). It is important to note that the PMBOK® Guide 2004 defines deliverables as: *Any unique and verifiable product, result, or capability to perform a service that must be produced to complete a process, phase or project.*[20] In other words, a deliverable is not a deliverable if it is not *verifiable*. This means that by incorporating deliverables in the WBS and formulating them properly, you create verifiability in the project. You basically clarify what you are going to produce. When you ask your client to sign off on the WBS, you have established how *contract* completion will be verified. This will decrease misunderstandings early in the project that become fatal near the end. Misunderstandings typically result in nasty disputes near the end of the project and often in litigation when you are a contractor.

In the previous illustration, the *WBS* is shown as a chart, the *WBS chart*. MS Project does not have such a view, but *WBS Chart Pro*[21] is an add-on tool you can buy that will allow you to lay out the WBS in such a graphic format. The graphic format is easy to read and understand for most people, because it resembles an organizational chart.

Breaking Down into Phases or Deliverables?

According to its definition, a WBS is supposed to be deliverable-oriented. You may not be used to thinking in terms of *deliverables*, and sometimes it is difficult to identify the deliverables in a project. However, if you put some effort into finding the deliverables, you will be surprised at how easy it is to find them. Consider for example an office relocation project and ask yourself: *what are the deliverables in this project?* If you cannot identify deliverables, you can always divide a project into *phases*. Phases are

---

[20] See the PMBOK® Guide, 2004 Edition, published by the PMI.

[21] WBS Chart Pro is available from Critical Tools, Inc. Please refer to www.CriticalTools.com.

distinct periods in the life of a project, a much vaguer concept than deliverables. Vagueness does not help us control projects. Phases are merely time-oriented groupings of tasks that do not necessarily provide verifiability. Many people tend to use phases, because it is easier or, because they prefer a chronological breakdown of the project. Establishing chronology is in essence sequencing and scheduling, which is a different project management activity than breaking down the work. Most IT life-cycle methodologies are phase-oriented and lack an emphasis on deliverables.

A WBS should be a *logical breakdown*, not a *chronological breakdown*. After the WBS is done, the sequencing and scheduling can start.

Another reason to stay away from chronological breakdowns is, because there are many iterative processes in practice. Iterative processes repeat themselves with steps of progressive elaboration. For example, a requirements document is created during the requirements phase, refined in the analysis phase, and finalized in the development phase. This example makes it clear that a chronological approach in a WBS will tie your brain in a knot. In a deliverable-oriented breakdown you simply add a few more activities (with dependencies to their driving tasks).

In small projects, we recommend creating a deliverable-oriented WBS rather than a phase-oriented WBS. Particularly in IT project schedules, we find too often only phases and no deliverables. As per the PMI definition, a WBS with only phases and activities without deliverables is not a WBS. A deliverable-oriented WBS is often clearer to all, establishes verifiability and has activities that are focused on producing components of the project product. Deliverables are often tangible and are easier to assign to teams than phases. An office relocation project could be broken down into phases or into deliverables, as shown in the illustration. In most projects, you can do either, and we then recommend using the deliverable-oriented breakdown rather than the phase-oriented breakdown.

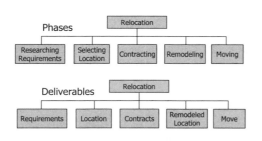

Deliverables provide more direction to the team; they focus the team members better. Imagine you were made responsible for either "researching requirements" or for delivering the "list of requirements" in the office relocation project. The latter is a concrete deliverable; it is verifiable and therefore creates a firmer commitment. Imagine you are subcontracting out work; wouldn't you prefer to commit a subcontractor to delivering something rather than doing something without a specific end result? Deliverables specify the end result better than phases. If you commit a subcontractor to a phase, you may end up with nothing, because you did not ask for a deliverable. If that is true for a subcontractor, wouldn't that be true for employee team members as well?

Another reason to use a deliverable-oriented WBS is that deliverables make it easier to formulate milestones. Deliverables typically have an associated event, for example, when the deliverable is *completed, handed over, sent, published, received, signed off* or *approved*. One of these events is most important for the deliverable in your project and you simply capture it by inserting a milestone. Examples of milestone names are *requirements summarized, report ready, preliminary design accepted* and *document delivered*. As you can see, they all refer to a deliverable. You typically create one milestone for each deliverable.

Phases and Deliverables in Large Projects

In large projects, you often see that the first breakdown level is phases, which are broken down into deliverables on the next level. The *WBS* then contains both phases and deliverables, with the deliverables on the lower level. This is a deliverable-oriented breakdown as well, because there are deliverables in the WBS. You don't need to do away with the phases specified in your project life cycle or methodology. You just have to add the deliverables to them as the next breakdown level to arrive at a "real" WBS, as shown in the next illustration:

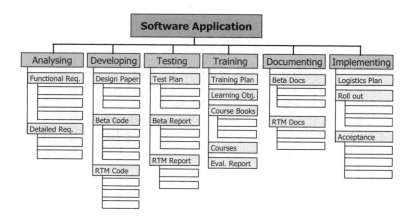

Breaking Down the Work

In the top-down approach, you enter the deliverables first and then you determine all the tasks needed to accomplish the deliverables. In the bottom-up approach, you brainstorm about all the tasks and then you group them under their deliverables. Each deliverable becomes a summary task.

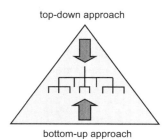

top-down approach

bottom-up approach

The two opposite approaches can lead to the same result. A person who is a novice at the type of project often prefers the bottom-up method. An experienced project manager usually takes the top-down approach. It requires experience to start from the top-down. Either approach can be successful; there is no one best way.

While breaking down the work, it is important to keep in mind that the *WBS* should be a *logical hierarchy*.

A WBS as a Logical Hierarchy

If a WBS is a true logical hierarchy, this means that: [22]
◆ There should be more than one level in the WBS.
   A hierarchy is only a hierarchy if it has multiple levels.
◆ The most important items are on the highest level.
   Each hierarchy has a grading order. The grading order for a WBS is the importance of the items. The importance of an item determines on which level it is inserted into the WBS. Generally speaking, the importance decreases from the project product to phases, to deliverables and finally, tasks.
◆ Within each branch, there should be at least two items on each level.
   If there is only one item in a branch, it should be removed since it is unnecessary detail. You may have to reword the item you keep.
◆ There should be no duplication or logical overlap between items.
   If there are duplications or overlaps between phases, deliverables or activities, the WBS does not have a logical breakdown. Of course, there can be an overlap in the

---

[22] These checks have been adapted from the Practice Standard for Work Breakdown Structures, published by PMI, 2001.

schedule, which is a *chronological* overlap. You should remove only the logical overlaps from the WBS.

◆ Each group of sub elements should completely capture its summary task (top-down check).

We recommend this top-down check, particularly if you used the bottom-up approach to create the WBS. You can easily forget a deliverable or detail task needed to create the deliverable. Use your project team effectively to catch those; many eyes always see more than just one pair.

◆ Each element should relate to its summary tasks on all higher levels (bottom-up check).

We recommend this bottom-up check, particularly if you used the top-down approach to create the WBS. Sometimes engineers and programmers like to hobby during their work time and create wonderful little things that weren't solicited.

An *organizational chart* is a better known example of a logical hierarchy than a WBS. For an organizational chart, a logical hierarchy means that an organization should have multiple levels with the most important person at the top. Nobody should be left out of an organizational chart. You won't find one person in two different positions and you won't find subordinates who don't report to anybody.[23]

However, a WBS should not follow the lines of an organization. Do not break down the project work by *functional group*.[24] Eventually, the deliverables will be assigned to functional groups in the *Responsibility Assignment Matrix*. Again, this is a different project management activity than breaking down the work in the WBS.

---

[23] Yes, I could think of some exceptions as well, but let's not get into that. The existence of 'exceptions' just confirms that there is a 'rule'.

[24] This important point was made by Frank Walker, TWG Project Management, LLC.

From WBS Chart to WBS List

The *WBS chart* has to be converted to an indented list of tasks. The next illustration shows how the chart is converted to an indented list. The chart is rotated 90 degrees and the lower levels then become indentation levels. The add-on tool, *WBS Chart Pro,* mentioned before, does this automatically for you.

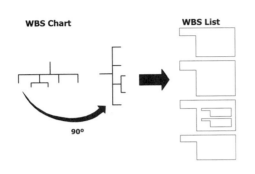

The Gantt Chart view or the Network Diagram view can be used for entering the tasks. You may find the Gantt Chart view the most comfortable window for creating the WBS, because you can create and see the levels of the breakdown structure. The hierarchical levels are shown through indentation of the tasks in the list. The farther indented to the right, the lower the level of the task, and the less important the item is. To switch to the Gantt Chart choose **View, Gantt Chart**.

In an organizational chart, the more important a person is, the higher their level. This is similar in a WBS; the more important a deliverable is, the higher its level should be in the WBS.

Choosing the Options

To set the options that relate to the WBS and tasks, choose **Tools, Options** and consider the following options:

Tab	Option
Schedule	**Default task type** Most people enter the duration immediately[25], and Project 2003 should not change it, unless required. If you normally enter duration estimates, we recommend setting it to **Fixed Duration**. On a task-by-task basis you can still decide what type serves you best and switch the task to it.
	☐ **New Tasks are effort driven** This option changes the number of resources assigned (*assignment units*); we recommend you turn it off. This option works similar as **Fixed Work** tasks, and we recommend you use that task type instead.
	Set as Default Sets the options as the default setting for any new schedules you create. The existing schedules are not affected, because these options are stored in the project schedules, as you can see in the section divider label **Scheduling Options for <schedule name of the project>**.

---

[25] The PMBOK® Guide, 2004 Edition, published by the PMI has *Activity Duration Estimating* as one of the core planning processes after all.

Categories of Tasks

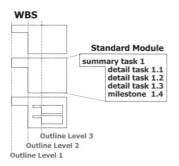

WBS

Standard Module

summary task 1
    detail task 1.1
    detail task 1.2
    detail task 1.3
    milestone 1.4

Outline Level 3
Outline Level 2
Outline Level 1

If you analyze an indented list of tasks, you will find that a standard building block or module recurs. The module consists of a summary task (the deliverable or phase) with subtasks (the detail tasks and a milestone). The summary task summarizes the cost, work and duration of all its sub-tasks. That is where the name *Summary task* originates.[26] These standard modules can even be nested inside one another, thus creating the next indentation level, as the illustration also shows. The indentation level is captured in the field *Outline Level*. The first level is outline level 1, the next indentation outline level 2, etceteras.

Build your plan in a modular way and use the following standard module of tasks. Your WBS will consist of several of these standard modules:

Standard Module	Example
Summary task 1	REPORT
Detail task 1.1	Gather data
Detail task 1.2	Categorize data
Detail task 1.3	Write report
Milestone 1.4	Report ready

 Please note that most project managers indent the milestones on the same level as the detail tasks. The milestone relates to the deliverable, and should be subordinated just like other detail tasks.

---

[26] The label "*summary task*" is not a very fortunate choice of words, because a summary task is seldom a task (activity), but more likely a deliverable or phase. A better term would perhaps have been "*summary item*". The label "*detail task*" is similarly flawed; detail tasks can be milestones that are events instead of tasks. The term "*detail item*" would be more appropriate to refer to the lowest level in the WBS. Perhaps the column title *task name* of the field *Name* should be renamed to *WBS*, and the current field *WBS* should be renamed to *WBS-code*.

We will now discuss the categories of tasks in more detail:

- ◆ *Summary task*

  To make a plan better understood by stakeholders, it is recommended that you group detail tasks and give each group a label that summarizes it. Summary tasks are often deliverables that give the list a logical and hierarchical structure.

  MS Project will sum the costs and work from the detail tasks up to their summary tasks. MS Project summarizes the duration of the detail tasks as well, but not through addition. If tasks are scheduled in parallel, the summary task duration is not the sum of the durations of its detail tasks, but the time span those detail tasks take. For example, suppose a deliverable has two tasks scheduled in parallel. One task has a duration of 5 days, the other 8 days in parallel. The summary task of the deliverable would indicate a duration of 8 days. MS Project calculates the summary duration and fills it in for each summary task. It is a *calculated field* that you cannot change. MS Project "summarizes" the duration of the detail tasks; this is why it is called "*summary task*" instead of "*subtotal task*".

- ◆ *Detail tasks*

  A detail task is any item that is <u>not</u> a summary task, in other words, any task that doesn't have lower level subtasks indented beneath it. *Detail Tasks* or *Activities* are the chunks of work that you would typically assign to resources. Detail tasks are by definition on the lowest level of the *WBS*.

- ◆ *Milestones*

  A milestone is any important date in your schedule. Milestones are often evaluation points or critical points that executives and clients monitor. A milestone can be a date on which a deliverable has to be ready. A milestone has a zero duration; it is a point in time, an event and not an activity.[27] As a general rule of thumb, we recommend you enter at least one *milestone* for each deliverable. You insert one milestone among the detail tasks of each deliverable summary task. Also, most people will indent the milestone on the same level as the other detail tasks of the deliverable.

Even though as practitioners we make the distinction between *summary tasks*, *detail tasks* and *milestones*, MS Project simply expects that we enter all of these in the field called *Task Name* (known in the database as the field *Task*). This misleads some people

---

[27] You can mark tasks with non-zero durations as "*milestones*" also. This creates hard-to-explain gaps between task bars in the timescale. We recommend you use *lag* on dependencies instead, see page 223.

to think that you should only enter tasks in this field, and not phases, deliverables or milestones.

Styles of Task Bars

Each category of task has a distinctive shape and color in the timescale of the Gantt views. The illustration on the left shows the different task *bar styles*. You can change the shape and color of the task bars through the menu items **Format, Bar Styles**. The appearance of the bars in the current view is shown in this dialog. MS Project has other types of tasks: split task bars and recurring tasks. In a split task bar, the task has extra stop and resume dates. Recurring task bars have many splits that are not connected with dots; see the illustration for how it looks. Some more remarks:

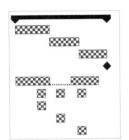

◆ *Summary task bar*
A summary task bar indicates its start and end point with small triangles. Notice that the summary task bar summarizes all its detail tasks and milestones. It starts when its first detail task starts and it ends when its last detail task or milestone ends.

◆ *Detail task bar*
A detail task bar is shown as a simple rectangular bar. A detail task is the lowest level of task in the WBS. The length of a detail task bar represents its estimated duration.

◆ *Milestone diamond*
Milestones appear as black diamonds and figure prominently in the Gantt Chart. Milestones have a zero duration.

◆ *Split task bars*
A split task bar has multiple parts connected by dots. The work on a split task bar is scheduled to be interrupted and resumed at a later date.[28] For example, when

---

[28] The tool **Split Task** [icon] on the **Standard** toolbar should be called *split task bar*, because the tool really splits the *task bars* rather than *tasks*. If it were to split tasks, you would end up with multiple tasks.

electricians wire a building, they have to come back to install the switch plates after the inspection. Another example is when a resource has to interrupt work on a task to attend a one-day meeting. Splits are often not planned, but occur when you update your schedule during execution. In fact, we would like to discourage you from splitting task bars during the *planning phase*, since splits typically need to be rescheduled constantly (because the meeting doesn't move, but the rest of the tasks do). As a result, planned splits often require too much maintenance of your schedule. For more on split task bars, see page 153.

◆ *Recurring task bars*
Recurring task bars have multiple parts that occur at a regular interval. Recurring tasks are useful to model things you do regularly, such as *team status meetings*, *schedule updates*, *change request reviews* and *status reports*. Recurring tasks are in fact summary tasks with detail tasks indented beneath. See page 154 for more explanation. Recurring tasks are often used to capture overhead tasks, which we discuss more on page 156.

Formulation of the WBS Elements

Attention needs to be paid to the wording you choose for each *WBS element*:

◆ *Summary task*
Summary tasks can be deliverables or phases. We recommend you use *nouns* for *deliverables*, for example *location* or *design*. A noun is any word in the English language that you can put "*the*" in front of. You could also add an adjective and call it *new location* or *final design*. Adjectives can improve the measurability of deliverables, which is desirable.
If you use *phases*, use the *imperfect tense* (*-ing*). This tense best indicates that something is ongoing, which is typical of phases. Examples are *Researching* or *Remodeling*.

◆ *Detail tasks*
We recommend you use verbs for detail tasks. The preferred tense for the verb is the *present tense* (or *imperative tense*). The present tense indicates action, and that is exactly what you want, because you will delegate the task to your team members. Examples are *contact the publisher*, *evaluate the alternatives* or *purchase equipment*. As you can see, detail tasks can be interpreted as an order, a command, or an instruction (imperative tense or present tense). Hopefully, a resource assigned to the task will interpret it as a request, which is what you want as the project manager. The only word missing in the request is the word 'please'… One of the blessings of the English language is that the imperative and present tense are

identical. In other languages, project managers face a more difficult choice between imperative and present tense.

◆ *Milestones*
Typically, the milestone is formulated using the syntax:
< deliverable> <perfect tense verb>
where *< deliverable>* is a noun that describes the deliverable, and the *<perfect tense verb>* describes what happened to the deliverable at that point in time. The tense for the verb used in milestones is the *perfect tense* (that so happens to be similar to the *past tense* in English). Typical verbs for milestones are *delivered, accepted, completed, done, sent, shipped* and *finished*. Alternatively, you could use the word *ready* to indicate completion, as in *report ready*. Or you could use the word *sign-off* as in *requirements sign-off*. Examples of milestones are *module completed, server installed, printer delivered* or *report accepted*.

◆ *Recurring tasks*
We recommend using plural *nouns* for recurring tasks, for example *team status meetings, meetings with client, meetings with sponsor, meetings with executives, schedule updates, change request reviews* and *status reports*. The plural indicates there is more than one. Recurring tasks will become summary tasks. You could also use *present tense* verbs to capture recurring tasks, since they are activities, in essence. Examples are: *review change requests* or *meet with team*. However, if there is a concrete deliverable resulting from the activity, we recommend you use a noun; for example, use *status reports* rather than *write status reports*.

A few more general guidelines:

◆ Avoid the overuse of acronyms.
If you do use an acronym, please spell it out the first time you use it, so the reader knows what the letters stand for as they are repeated throughout the schedule. Otherwise, the schedule can be too cryptic to read and understand.

◆ Used mixed (upper and lower) case in the task descriptions.
In this way, acronyms will stand out as acronyms, and there's no confusion as to whether *prepare bad report* is an instruction to prepare a report of poor quality or a report for *Ballistic Aerodynamic Deflection*.

When you apply these guidelines, it is important that you apply them consistently throughout the entire WBS. For example, if you choose nouns for recurring tasks, try to use nouns for all recurring tasks.

You may think to yourself, *Why should I follow these guidelines? I will call the items whatever I want!* To those who take this attitude, I would just like to say that if you do follow these simple guidelines, you will ensure that your WBS will be clear to your team members and any other stakeholders. Team members may not have been schooled in our profession of project management and therefore need this simplicity. Furthermore, your WBS will be the part of the project plan that you share first and most frequently with stakeholders. Make sure it is as clear as it can get.

If you find yourself explaining it all the time, it is not (yet) a good communication piece. Ideally, a WBS should be self-explanatory. If needed, provide a legend of abbreviations with it. If a WBS is not self-explanatory, you could consider adding a *WBS dictionary*. A WBS dictionary provides a narrative explanation of each deliverable in the WBS, sometimes even certain tasks. In the WBS dictionary, the requirements or acceptance criteria for the deliverables can be spelled out. In large projects, a WBS dictionary is a common practice.

Sharper Formulation of Deliverables

The deliverables are supposed to create *measurability* and *verifiability* in the project plan. This is where project management becomes an art, because capturing deliverables in a few words so that they reflect their acceptance criteria is truly an art. We found that most schedules can be greatly improved in this respect. The challenge project managers face is aligning the expectations of all project stakeholders. A properly formulated WBS that is signed off by all stakeholders is the best guarantee that alignment has been achieved. It can only be achieved when the deliverables are formulated as specifically as possible.

The following are examples of deliverables that we came across in real life schedules (in the left column) and our suggestions for a tighter formulation (in the right column). In our view, the right-hand column exhibits deliverables that are easier to verify on completion:

Ambiguously formulated deliverable	Better verifiable, measurable deliverable
Closing	*customer approval of the project product*
Subcontracting	*signed contract*
moving to new location	*operational, new location*
higher revenue	*30% increase in revenue marketing*
Renovation	*renovated facility*
Planning	*project plan*
material procurement	*procured construction materials*
prototype development	*developed prototype*
Training	*300 trained application users*
Staff	*50 newly hired staff members*
Implementation	*New workstations operational for entire team*

The Right Level of Detail

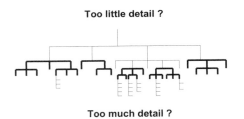

Too little detail ?

Too much detail ?

One of the biggest challenges in breaking down the work is finding the appropriate level of detail. The WBS should have neither too little detail nor too much! In the illustration, the right level is the bold lines on the middle levels. Notice that they are not necessarily on one particular level in the WBS. If one deliverable is bigger, this deliverable ends up with extra levels, as you can see in the middle of the illustration. Finding the right level of detail for each deliverable is an art for the project manager.

Adding levels generally improves the accuracy of the estimates; however a larger WBS also requires more work from the project manager to update the schedule during project execution. At 7:00 o'clock in the evening, you will probably go home instead of update your schedule if this will take another hour. Validating that you have found the right level of detail in your WBS and project schedule will help you keep your schedule alive during project execution when you are very busy.

Here are some guidelines for determining if you have found the right level of detail.[29]

Too Little Detail?

If you think you have a schedule that does not have enough detail levels, ask yourself the following questions while you go through your *WBS*:

◆ Is it clear how the *deliverable* will be created and what the activities involved are? If you have to answer *no* to this question, you will need more detail tasks.

◆ Do these activities correspond to meeting the *acceptance criteria* for the deliverable? If you have to answer *no*, you may need more detail tasks.

◆ Can I *estimate* the duration, effort and cost of the detail tasks? If you find estimating too hard without breaking them down into smaller tasks, you should break them down.

◆ Can I find the *dependencies* between the tasks? Each detail task will end up being a node in a network of dependencies. Dependencies are links between tasks that capture how they affect each other. Dependencies are an abstract concept; however finding the dependencies is easy once you have found the right level of detail. In order to set the dependencies you need, you may have to add more detail tasks or milestones.

◆ Can I *assign* the detail task to somebody? Eventually, we will assign each detail task to a resource, and if you can't assign it to an individual, you may have too little detail in the WBS. If you cannot assign the deliverables in large projects to organizational departments, you may need to add the components of those deliverables, or perhaps even the detail tasks.

We will discuss estimating, dependencies and assignments in later chapters.

Too Much Detail?

If you think you may have a WBS that is too detailed, ask yourself the following questions while you go through the list of tasks:

◆ Is this line item necessary in the WBS? If it is not, get rid of it while you can. If you don't eliminate it now, you will be dragging it behind you until the end of the project.

---

[29] For more guidelines, see the *Practice Standard for Work Breakdown Structures*, PMI, 2001.

◆ Is this line item merely a reminder to myself?
A WBS is not meant to be memory support. A WBS is supposed to capture tasks with significant effort involved. Reminders can be entered in the **Notes** field using the **Task Notes** tool on the **Standard** toolbar.

◆ Is this line item a to-do list item or a real task that will take significant effort?
If the items do not take much time or effort, you have not created a WBS, but a to-do list. To-do list items are what you list on a sheet of paper at the start of the day to organize your work for that day. To-do items can be entered in the **Notes** field using **Task Notes** on the **Standard** toolbar.

◆ Is this line item an acceptance criterion? These items can be entered in the **Notes** field using **Task Notes** on the **Standard** toolbar. *Acceptance criteria* are typically captured in a checklist format and belong in the notes. The task name could then read *complete checklist.*

◆ Will I continue to update all these detail tasks when I am busy during project execution?
If you think you may not be able to update all the tasks during the *execution phase*, this is the time to remove them from the WBS or roll them up into a higher level task.

◆ Do I have at least two detail tasks for each summary task?
If you have only one detail task within a summary, you can leave it out, since you are only restating what the summary task does. Each breakdown level should have at least two detail tasks. On average, each summary task has 5 to 7 detail tasks.

We recommend keeping your schedule lean and mean! Only by doing so, will you be able to keep it alive as a forecasting model during the hectic *execution phase* of the project.

Not Longer Than a Reporting Period

If you report the status of your project every week, your reporting period is one week. Detail task durations should not be longer than one reporting period.[30] If a detail task is longer than a reporting period, you may notice an out-of-control task only two reporting periods later. At that time it may already be so bad that it carries over another reporting period. This simple rule allows you to ask your team members at status time the very

---

[30] Contribution from Frank Walker, TWG Project Management, LLC.

pointed question: *Is this task done now, or are we still working on it?* As a project manager, you know that if a task is still in progress in two consecutive status meetings, there may be a bigger problem that requires your immediate attention.

An exception to this rule is the *overhead tasks* that can stretch over the entire project duration (see page 156 for more information).

The 1%-10% Rule

There is another guideline that we came up with. I call it the *1%-10% rule.* The duration of any detail task should be between a minimum and a maximum duration. The minimum duration is 1% of the project duration (rounded). The maximum is 10% of the project duration (rounded).

For example, if you have a project that you think will take 3 months; you can calculate the range for the right level of detail. Three months is about 60 business days. The minimum duration is 1% of 60 or 0.6 day; let's use half a day. Detail tasks should not last less than half a day. If they are smaller, you should lump them together into larger tasks. The maximum is 10% of 60 or 6 days; let's round it to one week. Detail tasks have to be one week or less in duration.

You can find the project duration easily by:
choosing **Project, Project Information** and clicking $\boxed{\text{Statistics...}}$.
OR
clicking the **Project Statistics** tool $\sim\!\!\!\!\wedge$ on the **Tracking** toolbar.
OR
viewing the **Duration** field of the project summary task, you can display the project summary task by choosing **Tools, Options, View,** ☑ **Show project summary task.** This task will appear at the top of the list as a task with ID number 0.

If you find tasks that are longer than 10% of the project, you can:

◆ Check if the resources are working part-time on it. If you can change their involvement into full-time, the duration will decrease. See page 385 for the how-to.

◆ Split the task into multiple subtasks. See page 470 for detailed steps.

The beauty of this rule is that it can be applied to projects of any size, unlike other guidelines for the size of *work packages*. Other authors often suggest a maximum guideline of 40 or 80 hours for each work package. This absolute guideline is not universally applicable, because a fast-track, one-week project would not be helped by this guideline. We believe the 1%-10% rule has a more universal applicability.

There are some types of tasks to which the 1%-10% rule should not be applied:
◆ *Summary tasks*
◆ *Overhead tasks (level of effort tasks)*
◆ *Recurring detail tasks*
◆ *Milestones*

Notice that the 1%-10% rule should only be applied to the durations and not to the work values (effort). If there are many part-time assignments or many multiple assignments per task, the boundaries for work estimates should be narrower or wider than for the duration. In general, the minimum and maximum values for work are harder to indicate, which is why we stayed away from that.

Why Is the Right Level of Detail Important?

The rationale behind finding the right level of detail is to create enough checkpoints for monitoring and controlling the progress of the project. *Systems theory* tells us that we need feedback loops to control a process. In project management, we need several feedback loops to control a project, and ten is the number we recommend as a minimum. This may seem like a lot, but it really isn't. We have to look at this from the perspective of the client or the executives. In the ten-period project shown in the illustration, the first status report normally becomes available halfway through the second status period. If the report shows a problem, the client would suggest that an action must be taken. You will take the action in the rest of the second period, and you will likely see the results of this corrective action appear in the third period. The report on the third period becomes available in the fourth period. So problems in the first period will be corrected visibly for the client or executives only in the fourth period. There is always a delay in determining the problem, taking action and seeing the result of the action. If you have ten *checkpoints,* clients really only have six or so *manage-points.* You need, therefore, a safe number of reporting periods. Ten periods seems to work in most projects as a minimum. Building in at least ten formal feedback loops seems like a good norm when communicating with clients and executives.

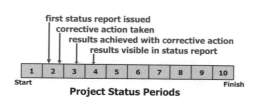

first status report issued
corrective action taken
results achieved with corrective action
results visible in status report

| 1 | 2 | 3 | 4 | 5 | 6 | 7 | 8 | 9 | 10 |

Start   Finish
Project Status Periods

Clients and executives tend to get too nervous when you don't give them visibility on your project and enough chances to make a difference in your project. As a result, they will start micro-managing you as the project manager.

Of course, successful project managers make sure they have at least 1000 manage-points with their own team. They know what the status of their project is at any time if they are in touch with their team. You can ask them the status 24 hours a day, 7 days a week. (Don't do this though!) Successful project managers continuously check up with their team and do much communication on the work floor. This increases the number of feedback loops dramatically and thus the chance for successful completion of the project. Successful project managers don't use their own status reports to find out what is happening in their project. And if they did, they wouldn't be successful.

Entering Tasks

We will discuss how to enter:
- Summary tasks (see below)
- Detail tasks (see below)
- Milestones (see next page)
- Split task bars (see page 153)
- Recurring tasks (see page 154)
- Overhead tasks (see page 156)

Entering Summary Tasks

For summary tasks you only need to enter the name, since most other fields are calculated. These tasks summarize their subtasks in terms of duration, work and cost.

1. Choose **View, Gantt Chart**.

2. Click on the cell in the **Task Name** column where you want to enter the name of the summary task. A summary task typically is a deliverable or a phase on the level above the deliverables.

3. Type the name of the summary task. It is preferably formulated with a *noun*. You can insert an adjective in front of it to reveal acceptance criteria for the deliverable. If the one adjective is not enough, use **Task Notes** 📝 on the **Standard** toolbar to add more explicit acceptance criteria.

4. Press ⌨ to go to the next task.

 The name is normally the only thing you need to enter for summary tasks. A summary task will only start summarizing when tasks are indented beneath it on the next row. At that time it will also get its characteristic task bar ▼━━━▼ .

Entering Detail Tasks

For detail tasks you typically enter the task name and the duration estimate. We will discuss estimating in more detail in the next chapter.

1. To insert a new row for a detail task, click on any cell in the row before where you want to insert a new task (row).

2. Choose **Insert, New Task**, or press ⌨.

3. Enter the **Task Name**; make sure you use a *present tense* verb for it.

4. Press ⎡Tab⎤ to go to its **Duration** field and enter an estimate and press ⎡Tab⎤.

5. If necessary, indent it under its summary task by clicking **Indent** ⇨ on the **Format** toolbar OR **Outdent** ⇦ to outdent the task.

 We recommend you list the tasks in their chronological order as much as you can. Don't force this ranking though, because you will always have difficulties with tasks that are meant to be done in parallel, for example *train staff in software* and *install software*. In those cases, we recommend you let the *logical* structure of the breakdown prevail over the chronology of the tasks. Most projects have tasks that run in parallel. The more tasks you can do in parallel, the faster you will finish the project!

 Don't enter **Start** or **Finish** dates for detail tasks; this will automatically add schedule constraints to those tasks, which will make the schedule rigid. Let the task bars move freely, based upon their dependencies. This will be elaborated in chapter 5 on dependencies (see page 215) and chapter 6 on deadlines and constraints (see page 271).

Entering Milestones

For milestones, you typically first enter the name of the milestone, then you enter a zero in the duration field and finally you enter a deadline date or perhaps a constraint date. You typically would insert one milestone for each deliverable. The milestone should capture an important event for this deliverable, like being *sent, approved* or *delivered*.

1. In the **Gantt Chart**, click any cell of the task prior to which you want to insert a milestone and press ⎡Ins⎤.

2. Enter the name of the milestone in the **Task Name** field; use the perfect tense that typically has an –ed ending in English, as in *delivered*.

3. Enter a **Duration** of 0 (zero). This will toggle the field **Milestone** from No to Yes behind the screen which marks the task as a milestone.

4. If necessary, adjust the indentation level to the same level as the detail tasks above it by using the **Indent** ⇨ and **Outdent** ⇦ tools on the **Formatting** toolbar.

5. Click **Task Information** ⎡☰☰⎤ on the **Standard** toolbar or hold down ⎡Shift⎤ and press ⎡F2⎤; the **Task Information** dialog appears.

6. Click the tab **Advanced**; the dialog should now look like:

7. If you have a deadline, enter this target date in the field **Deadline** and press ⌊Enter ⏎⌋. The deadline shows up in the Gantt Chart timescale as a green ⇩. When the milestone is pushed past its deadline date, a red ◆ will appear in the **Indicators** column.
    OR
    Set a constraint under **Constraint Type** by selecting a type of constraint from the list. Enter a date under **Constraint Date**. A constraint will prevent the network of dependencies from changing the date of the milestone. However, constraints can cause scheduling conflicts. We recommend you observe restraint in adding constraints, since they tend to be maintenance-hungry.

In chapter 6 we will have an in-depth discussion on constraints and deadlines, see page 271.

There is also a **Mark task as milestone** feature in the **Task Information** dialog box. Click **Task Information** 📄 on the **Standard** toolbar, and click the tab **Advanced**. This feature will change a regular detail task bar into a diamond. It will shrink a task bar from 10 days into a 0-day diamond in the timescale while keeping the 10-day duration in the spreadsheet. When dependencies stem from the task, it looks like there is a gap between the task and its linked task. We don't recommend you use this. The **Mark task as milestone** feature stores a *Yes* or *No* in the *Milestone* field. Instead of using ☑ **Mark task as milestone**, we recommend you use the field *Marked* or one of the extra *Flag* fields to handpick tasks that are important for reporting purposes.

Entering Split Task Bars

You can split any existing task bar into two or more parts or you can add a second task bar to an existing one. You can simply do the latter by drawing a second bar in the timescale to the right or to the left (but not before the project start date) of the existing task bar. Just click, hold down and drag to where you want the second part of the task bar.

To split an existing task bar into two parts:

1. Click **Split Task** ⬚ on the **Standard** toolbar; a yellow pop-up window appears and the mouse pointer now looks like: ⊩ .

2. Point to a task bar and click and drag the split part to where you want the split to start. The new start and finish dates of this part appear in the yellow pop-up window when you release the mouse:

Task: ▨▨▨▨▨▨▨▨▨	
Start:	Wed 4/5/00
Finish:	Sat 4/8/00

3. Drop it where you want it by releasing the mouse button; the task bar is now split into two parts. Notice that the two parts are connected by dots: ▰▰▰▰....▰▰▰

To remove a split, just drag the right-most part of the bar to the left and reconnect it to its original bar part. If you have split it multiple times and you want to re-connect the parts, just keep doing this.

Should we use *split task bars*?

◆ You often create a split around another task in your schedule, often a *meeting* or *training* that takes place on a fixed date. You cannot set dependencies on the start or the finish of the dotted split to move it when the split task moves. Because of this, split task bars tend to be very maintenance-hungry in a schedule. We therefore recommend using them sparingly during the *planning phase*.

◆ During project execution, you will see enough split bars appear when you start updating your schedule with actual progress. This will happen when resources are reassigned temporarily, for example. Progress comes about in a haphazard way.

◆ Instead of splitting task bars when you are planning your project, we recommend you split the task into multiple tasks (line items). For example, electricians cable a building, but after the inspection, they have to come back to install the switch plates. You could do this with one task through splitting its task bar, but the schedule would be more dynamic if you split the task into two tasks: *pull cables* and *install switch plates* and set dependencies on these tasks. You can set a dependency from the activity *inspect electric wiring* to *install switch plates* task, and you have a fully dynamic model. (What was the title of this book again?)

Entering Recurring Tasks

Recurring tasks are tasks that take place repeatedly and regularly, for example every other week (biweekly) or monthly. Typical examples of recurring tasks are *status meetings* or *progress meetings*.

1. Choose **Insert, Recurring Task**; the **Recurring Task Information** dialog appears:

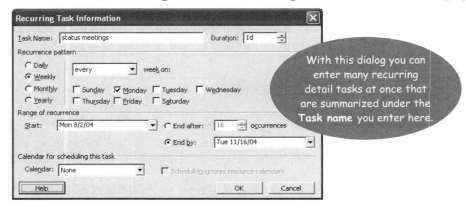

2. Type the name in the **Task Name** field.

3. Type the duration in the **Duration** field or use its to change the duration with pre-set increments.

4. Under **Recurrence Pattern** select the interval at which the task recurs and the dialog changes and presents appropriate choices for the selected interval.

5. Under **Range of recurrence** choose the period or the number of occurrences. Make sure that the *status meetings* or *meetings* with the client, sponsor or executive span the entire duration of the project and keep spanning it. We have found that this is often not the case in the schedules we evaluated for certification.

6. Click OK .

Some remarks about *recurring tasks*:

◆ Notice that recurring tasks are, in fact, a special kind of summary task, but have a different task bar than regular summary tasks. A recurring summary task bar only displays all the task bars of its detail tasks.

◆ Notice that the duration of the *recurring summary task* has no meaning; it encompasses the entire period of its detail tasks.

◆ MS Project sets constraints on each *recurring detail task* that will keep them on their dates in the timescale. Even though we recommend against using constraints in schedules, there is nothing wrong with constraints on recurring detail tasks. They are a legitimate exception to the rule. Recurring detail tasks are typically not hooked up into the network of dependencies, and only scheduling constraints will keep them on the proper dates.

◆ If one occurrence accidentally falls on a national holiday (as entered in the project calendar), MS Project will ask you what to do with it: drop it or move it to the next business day.

◆ The number of recurrences for meetings may need to be adjusted several times (every time the project duration changes significantly). We will therefore discuss an alternative way to capture overhead activities on page 156 that makes your schedule more dynamic.

◆ The recurring detail tasks will not be included in the leveling process, because MS Project sets the field **Level Assignments** to *No* as a default. If you assign resources to the *recurring detail tasks* and level the workloads fully, you will still see slight *over-allocations* on the dates of the recurring detail tasks. To resolve this, use **Edit, Fill, Down** to enter *yes* in the field **Level Assignments** for all recurring detail tasks and level the workloads again. If you do this however, you may see that the recurring detail tasks (like meetings) are rescheduled when you let MS Project level the workloads. You can prevent this by filling down a very high priority number (1000) as well on the recurring detail tasks in the field *Priority* and setting the **Leveling order** to **Priority, Standard.** We will discuss leveling in more detail on page 473: Workload Leveling.

Three questions are important with regard to *recurring tasks*:

◆ When do you need recurring tasks?
Normally, recurring tasks are used for regular meetings, like status meetings. You could also use them for overhead tasks, but we will elaborate on those on page 154.

◆ Will you set *dependencies* on them?
Dependencies are only necessary when deliverables are due for a meeting and you want to capture that in the model. You can make the deliverables predecessors of the detail meeting task. In practice, we have found that project managers normally do not set dependencies on recurring tasks, which is fine.

◆ Will you *assign* resources to them and level the workload?
Assigning resources is okay, but MS Project will not level recurring tasks by default!

Entering Overhead Tasks

Overhead tasks are tasks that are ongoing during the entire project, for example *project management, technical support* and *quality control.* You can enter overhead tasks by inserting tasks that extend over the duration of the project:

◆ *long-duration tasks* (long task bar), or
◆ *recurring tasks*

This table provides pros and cons for each approach:

Long task bar	Recurring tasks
Easier to schedule with; you only need to remember one assignment percentage to prevent over-allocations with other tasks.	Will cause over-allocations and will not allow automatic leveling unless **Level Assignment** is changed to **Yes** (is **No** by default) and **Priority** set to 1000 and the **Priority, Standard** leveling order is used.
Easy to maintain; when you extend them, you don't need to assign resources again.	When you extend them, you may have to assign resources to the new ones.
Every time the project duration changes significantly, its duration needs to be adjusted.	Every time the project duration changes significantly, recurring detail tasks need to be added or removed.

As you will probably conclude from the table yourself, we recommend entering overhead tasks as long-duration tasks rather than recurring tasks. Overhead tasks modeled as long task bars require less maintenance effort. We can even improve the model further.

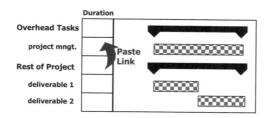

There is a way to prevent having to update the duration of the long task bar every time the project duration changes. At the top of the list, insert the summary *overhead tasks* on the first outline level. Indent below it all the overhead detail tasks, like *project management*. Below the overhead task and also on the first outline level, insert a new and extra summary task that will summarize the rest of the project. It should summarize all deliverables and tasks but exclude the overhead tasks. (By the way, you cannot use the *project summary task* for this, since it will not allow the project to shrink.) Copy the duration from the new summary task, then paste link it into the duration field of the *project management* task by choosing **Edit, Paste Special**, ⊙ **Paste link**. The linked duration updates itself automatically from now on when the project duration extends or shrinks, and you don't need to constantly adjust it. Now you have captured the overhead effort of your project in a way that is almost free of maintenance.

Creating an Outline

Outline Structure

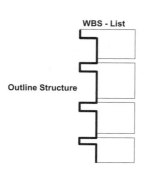

The logical hierarchy of the WBS is entered into MS Project as a list of tasks. The hierarchy of the chart is preserved through indentation in the list of tasks (see the illustration). The more to the left, and less indented, the more important the item is. The tasks on a lower level are indented to the right. The tasks on the lowest level are called *detail tasks*. Detail tasks do not have subtasks. Elements that do have lower level tasks are called *summary tasks*. Tasks can be promoted to a higher level by outdenting them or demoted by indenting them. Thus, an outline structure is created.

Purposes of the *outline structure*:

◆ Outlining makes the plan easier to read and understand. How can you eat a whole loaf of bread? Slice by slice! Similarly, you will digest a large WBS deliverable by deliverable.

◆ Outlining generates extra aggregate information on the summary tasks. MS Project automatically calculates the duration, cost and work fields on the summary tasks. You can immediately see what a deliverable costs. For example, if you are a programmer and you have *software features* as your deliverable, executives can now see how many person hours are spent on a feature and how much it costs. They will use this information when decisions have to be made on which feature will make it in this release of the *software*. With a *deliverable-oriented breakdown structure*, executives can easily make these *trade-off decisions* when you need them to.

◆ Summary tasks can be collapsed and expanded on an as-needed basis, providing just enough detail to perform your analysis or to focus your reports. If you collapse the summary tasks, it provides an *overview* rather than details. Most CEOs like an overview of the phases or deliverables and would prefer to leave the detail tasks for you as the project manager.

Indenting a Series of Detail Tasks

Select the detail tasks by dragging anywhere over them in the spreadsheet.
Click **Indent** on the **Formatting** toolbar.
OR
Hold down Alt + Shift and press →.

After indenting, the summary task shows a duration that summarizes all its detail tasks.

Indenting a task cannot be done by inserting spaces in front of the task name. MS Project will not recognize this as a lower level subtask, even though it may look right. MS Project does not allow you to use the Tab key to create indentation, unlike in *MS Office Word* and *PowerPoint*.

Outdenting Tasks

1. Select the tasks by dragging in the spreadsheet.

2. Click **Outdent** on the **Formatting** toolbar.
   OR
   Hold down Alt + Shift and press ←.

Indenting and Outdenting by Dragging

1. Select the tasks by dragging over them in the spreadsheet.

2. In the **Task Name** column, point to the first characters of the task name; the mouse pointer changes to a two-headed arrow: ↔. Before proceeding, make sure you see this arrow (and not the mouse pointer ✛).

3. Hold down and drag the task to the right for indenting or to the left for outdenting. A vertical gray line gives you feedback on which outline level it will end up on when you release the mouse.

4. Release the mouse button when the gray line appears at the right level of indentation.

To Hide and Re-display Detail Tasks

Click the minus button ⊟ in front of the summary task name to hide its detail tasks.
OR

Select the summary task and hold down [Alt] + [Shift] and press [-].

The detail tasks can be displayed again by clicking the [+].
OR

Select the summary task and hold down [Alt] + [Shift] and press [+].

To Hide All Detail Tasks

Click Show ▾ on the **Formatting** toolbar and select **Outline level 1**.
OR

1. Click on the heading of any column; the entire column should be highlighted now.

2. Click **Hide Subtasks** ▭ on the **Formatting** toolbar. You should now only see the first outline level.

To Reveal the Next Level

Click on the title of any column and click **Show Subtasks** ✛ on the **Formatting** toolbar.
OR

Click Show ▾ on the **Formatting** toolbar, and select the next level down.

To Reveal a Certain Level

1. Click Show ▾ on the **Formatting** toolbar.

2. Select the level you want to see.

 If you are not sure how MS Project counts the levels, please insert the column **Outline Level**, and study the numbers that MS Project displays. The left most level is level 1.

To Reveal All Levels

 Click Show ▾ on the **Formatting** toolbar; a list is displayed with the available outline levels. Click the top item ⁺₊ **All Subtasks**.

What You Do with a Parent, You Do with the Entire Family

 When you manipulate summary tasks, you have to realize that what you do to a summary task affects all its detail tasks as well. If you delete a summary task, you are deleting its detail tasks as well. The same applies to cutting and copying (see page 164). If you indent a summary task, you indent its detail tasks as well.

Changing the WBS

Editing a Task Name

You can replace a task name by typing over it. If you need to make small editorial changes (correct a typo), you are better off editing the task name.

1. Press [F2]. The cursor blinks as a line in the cell, as in the following screenshot (which unfortunately doesn't show the blinking): `write report`.
   OR
   Click once in the field and, after one second, click another time and a blinking insertion point will appear in the cell: `write report`.
   OR
   Click in the entry bar at the top of the screen; the cursor blinks as a vertical line: `✗✓ write report`.

2. Move the cursor by clicking with the mouse or by using the arrow keys on the keyboard. Or use the [Home] to jump to the start of the cell and [End] to jump back to the end. Or hold down [Control] and press [←] to jump one word to the left, or [→] to jump to the right.

3. Make the changes.

4. Press [Enter ↵] to accept the changes and finish the editing. The red-cross and green-checkmark buttons in the entry bar should now disappear.

 If MS Project seems stuck and does not allow you to click on menu items, chances are that you are still in the middle of an editing process. Check if you see blinking insertion points or the red-cross and green-checkmark buttons ✗✓ in the entry bar. Press [Enter ↵] or click on another cell to finish the editing. Now you can proceed to the menu items again.

Inserting Multiple Tasks

We already discussed how to insert one task; you press [Ins]. Here we will discuss how to insert multiple tasks at once:

1. Point to the row heading before which you wish to insert multiple tasks, click and drag down to highlight as many rows as you need inserted.

2. Press [Ins] and the number of rows you had selected are inserted as blank rows.

 If you insert tasks between linked tasks, MS Project may set dependencies automatically if the **Autolink** option is turned on. Choose **Tools, Options**, tab **Schedule** to verify if the option **Autolink inserted or moved tasks** has a checkmark or not. Always check the dependencies after adding, copying or moving tasks (or turn **Autolink** off, if you don't want MS Project to think and link for you).

Deleting Tasks

1. Select the tasks by dragging over their row headings (where you see their ID numbers).

2. Choose the menu items **Edit, Delete Task** OR press [Del].

 Notice that the [Del] key deletes cells instead of entire rows just like in *MS Office Excel* (unless you selected row headings first).

Copying or Moving Tasks

For copying or moving tasks, it is important to select the entire task (including its fields that are hidden from view). You have to select it by clicking on its row heading (the first column with the ID numbers and the gray color), if you want to copy or move the whole task. It will highlight all the visible data of the task and select all 240-some fields of a task, including the ones that are not displayed.

The gray color of the first column tells you that the column is *locked*, which means:
◆ that it will not scroll off the screen,
◆ that its data cannot be edited, and
◆ that you can select the entire task by clicking on it.

Some people use this locked first column to display the *WBS-codes* (field **WBS)** instead of the erratic *ID* field. Other people lock the *Task Name* column to prevent task names from scrolling off of their screen.

If the first column is not gray, you will have to lock the column first (you cannot do this in an *enterprise view*, since this is the responsibility of the *Project Server* administrator).

Locking the First Column of a Table

1. In the Gantt Chart, choose **View, Table: <name of the table>, More Tables**.

2. Click [Edit...].

3. Check ☑ **Lock first column**.

4. Click [OK] and then [Apply].

5. If you now click on a locked row heading, the whole row should be selected.

Copying Tasks

1. Select the tasks by dragging over the locked row headings by using the ➡ mouse pointer.

2. Release the mouse button when you have selected all tasks to copy; they are now highlighted.

3. Point to one of the selected row headings and the mouse pointer changes to 🔀.
   Hold down the [Control] key, and hold down the primary mouse button and the mouse

pointer changes to where the small plus sign indicates that you are copying. Drag the copied tasks to their new place.

OR

Choose the menu items **Edit**, **Copy Task** or click on the **Standard** toolbar; the task is now stored in the clipboard. Select the task before which you wish to insert. Choose **Edit**, **Paste** or click **Paste** on the **Standard** toolbar.

 To keep the dependencies as they are when copying tasks, choose **Tools, Options**, tab **Schedule** and clear ☐ **Autolink inserted or moved tasks**. Perhaps you should make a habit of checking the dependencies after adding, copying or moving tasks, unless you turn Autolink off for all new projects by clicking Set as Default .

Moving Tasks

1. Select the tasks by dragging over locked row headings using the → mouse pointer.

2. Release the mouse button; the tasks should now be highlighted.

3. Point to one of the selected row headings; you should now see the mouse pointer .

4. Click and hold the primary mouse button; you should now see the mouse pointer

5. Drag the tasks to their new place; a horizontal gray line will indicate where the tasks will end up when you release the mouse.
   OR
   Click on the menu items **Edit**, **Cut Task** or click **Cut Task** on the **Standard** toolbar. The tasks are now temporarily stored in the clipboard. Select the task before you wish to insert the cut ones and choose **Edit**, **Paste** or click **Paste** on the **Standard** toolbar. Notice that MS Project creates new rows and insert the ones cut out.

 To keep the dependencies as they are when moving tasks, choose **Tools, Options**, tab **Schedule** and clear ☐ **Autolink inserted or moved tasks**. Perhaps you should make a habit of checking the dependencies after adding, copying or moving tasks, unless you turn it off for all new projects by clicking Set as Default .

To Copy or Move a Summary Family

Select the summary task by clicking on its row heading. Hold the `Control` key down to copy. Hold down the primary mouse button and MS Project will immediately highlight all its detail tasks and move or copy them as well. Drag the summary task and its subtasks to where you want it.

If you use the clipboard instead, the detail tasks will also be copied or moved.

Checks on the WBS for Your Project

Here is a summary of the best practices for the WBS of your project:

◆ Are there deliverables in the WBS? Is the WBS a *deliverable-oriented* breakdown structure?
   Deliverables should be captured using nouns (perhaps with adjectives, but without verbs). Verbs change a deliverable into an activity. If there are no nouns in the task list, there are no deliverables and the list is not a *WBS*.
   Alternatives for a deliverable-oriented breakdown are a phase-oriented breakdown or an organizational breakdown. From a project control perspective, these are less effective. See page 131 for a detailed discussion.

◆ Is the list of deliverables *complete*, but lean?
   ◇ Are all expected deliverables explicitly included in the WBS? This should also include significant reporting items, like monthly status reports, test plans and test reports.
   ◇ Are the project management deliverables and activities included in the WBS? See page 156 for different ways of doing that.
   ◇ Are *out-of-scope* deliverables that may be expected by the client explicitly excluded from the WBS? We recommend you capture exclusions in the **File, Properties,** tab **General, Comments** field.
   ◇ Are there no unnecessary deliverables in the WBS that were not agreed upon with the *client* or *project sponsor*?

◆ Does the WBS have a *logical hierarchy*?
   If you don't have a logical hierarchy, you may report the wrong cost and duration by phase or by deliverable. You can check if the WBS is a logical hierarchy by expanding the outline level by level using the `Show ▼` tool on the **Formatting** toolbar.

◇ Is the WBS an indented list with multiple hierarchical levels instead of a long list without structure?

◇ Are the most important items on the highest levels in the WBS?
- Are the phases, if present, on a higher level than the deliverables?
- Are the tasks, if present, on a lower level than the deliverables?

◇ Does each summary task have at least two subtasks?

◇ Is there any duplication or logical overlap between deliverables?

◇ Does each group of subtasks capture all the work of their summary task (top-down check)?

◇ Does each item logically relate to its summary tasks on all higher levels (bottom-up check)?

◇ Is the feature **Tools, Options, View, Project Summary Task** used instead of a physical project summary task? MS Project's project summary task has ID number 0 (zero) in the first column.

◆ Are there enough *milestones*?
There are enough milestones when there is roughly one milestone for each deliverable. Milestones allow you to create a high-level, one-page report. Milestone events typically capture when the deliverable is completed, approved, sent, signed-off, published or shipped, for example. You can check this by applying the standard filter **Milestones** and checking if most deliverables have a milestone.

◆ Are the WBS elements properly formulated?
If you use the following guidelines you will ensure that everybody can understand the WBS:

◇ Phases are formulated using the *imperfect tense* (-ing).

◇ Deliverables are formulated using a *noun* (perhaps with an adjective, but without a verb).

◇ Detail tasks are formulated using a *present tense* verb.

◇ Milestones are formulated using the noun of the deliverable and a verb in *perfect tense* (or *past tense* in English). Instead of a verb, the words *ready*, *complete* or *sign-off* can be used. You can apply the filter **03 IIL Milestones** to display only the milestones without the summary tasks.[31]

---

[31] This filter can be found in the file *IIL Project 2003 tools to check Orange Belt schedules.MPP* available for download at www.jrosspub.com. Please, click the link WAV Download Resource Center to enter the download site.

◇ Are the names of the deliverables, tasks and milestones used consistently in the WBS?

◆ Does the WBS have the *right level of detail*?
Too little detail does not provide enough control on your project. There may be too few detail levels in the WBS:

◇ If you cannot estimate the duration or work on the detail tasks.

◇ If you have difficulties finding the dependencies between the detail tasks.

◇ If you often *assign* more than one resource per task.

◇ If there are detail tasks that are longer than a reporting period.

◇ If there are detail tasks with durations longer than 10% of the project duration (1%-10% rule). You can check this by applying the filter **02 IIL Level of Detail > 10% of Proj Dur....**[32] You will be prompted to enter what 10% of the project duration is. You can find the project duration by looking at the **Duration** field of the project summary task. The filter will display all detail tasks that are longer than 10% of the project duration. We recommend you split all these tasks into smaller ones.
An exception to the 10% maximum is if you created long tasks to capture overhead effort, like *project management* or *technical support*.

Too much detail will give you too much work updating your schedule during project execution. There may be too many detail levels in the WBS:

◇ If you think there are too many levels or if you think the task list is too long.

◇ If you added reminders, to-do items or acceptance criteria into the task list. Transfer these to the **Notes** field.

◇ If you can't guarantee you will be able to update all detail tasks in the schedule during project execution.

◇ If there are tasks with durations shorter than 1% of the project duration (1%-10% rule). You can check this by applying the filter **01 IIL Level of Detail < 1% of Proj Dur...**[33] You will be prompted to enter

---

[32] This filter can be found in the file *IIL Project 2003 tools to check Orange Belt schedules.MPP* available for download at www.jrosspub.com. Please, click the link *WAV Download Resource Center* to enter the download site.

[33] This filter can be found in the file *IIL Project 2003 tools to check Orange Belt schedules.MPP* available for download at www.jrosspub.com. Please, click the link *WAV Download Resource Center* to enter the download site.

what 1% of the project duration is. You can find the project duration by looking at the **Duration** field of the project summary task. The filter will display all detail tasks that are shorter than 1% of the project duration. *Recurring detail tasks* will not be displayed, since they typically are short and are allowed to be shorter than 1%. You can keep a few of these, but if you keep many, you will have to spend too much effort on updating your schedule during project execution. You then risk that you will let your schedule become obsolete at some point.

◆ Is the WBS clear to all project stakeholders?
All stakeholders, like your customers, suppliers, upper management, team members and support staff, need to fully understand the WBS. If you don't understand it as a project manager, nobody will. If an outside reviewer doesn't understand it, chances are some other stakeholders won't either.

◆ Project management overhead tasks, if present, should extend over the entire duration of the project. It does not make sense to stop managing the project halfway.

   ◇ Do the overhead tasks (like *project management*) extend over the entire duration of the project?

   ◇ Do the *status meetings*, as recurring tasks, continue over the entire duration of the project?

◆ Are there as few as possible task bar splits in the schedule at the end of the *planning phase* of the project?
Task bar splits often require a fair bit of maintenance and should be applied with restraint, see page 153. During the *execution phase*, you will see enough splits appear when updating your schedule with actuals.

Exercises

Review

1. What is the definition of a WBS as per the PMBOK® Guide 2004 by the PMI?

2. What are the differences between a to-do list and a WBS?

3. You ask a person to manage a project. The objective of the project is to write a document. An author, an editor and a graphic artist are on the team. After awhile, the person presents four different first-level breakdowns to you and asks you to choose one. Which one will you choose and why?
   ◆ First draft, final draft, final document
   ◆ Writing, editing, formatting, printing

- ◆ Draft text, edited text, final text, charts
- ◆ Table of contents, body of text, summary

4. Which of the following are proper formulations for deliverables? If you find the wording can be sharpened to improve verifiability, please enter your formulation:

	Your formulation of the deliverable
planning	
research phase	
approved project plan	
pilot	
prototype	
module 36	
deliver code to Harry	

5. Which of the following are proper formulations for detail tasks? If you find the wording can be improved, please enter your formulation:

	Your formulation of the detail task
program module XT607	
print	
design of house	
writing proposal	

6. Which of the following are proper formulations for milestones? If you find the wording can be improved, please enter your formulation:

	Your formulation of the milestone
report ready	
project close	
design approved	
contract sign-off	

7. How do you know you have found the appropriate level of detail in your WBS? Why is finding the right level of detail important?

Relocation Project — Entering the WBS

1. Continue to work with your file *Relocation.MPP* or open the file *03 Entering Tasks.MPP* available for download at www.jrosspub.com. Please, click the link *WAV Download Resource Center* to enter the download site.

2. Check in **Tools, Options,** tab **Schedule**:

   ◇ If the **Default task type** is set to **Fixed Duration**.

   ◇ If the option ☐ **New tasks are effort-driven** is cleared.

3. Enter the WBS into Project 2003 as shown in the next table.[34]

4. Indent the detail tasks under their summary tasks. The summary tasks are the tasks with names in capital letters.

5. Compare your file with the solution file *04 Entering Estimates.MPP* available for download at www.jrosspub.com. Please, click the link *WAV Download Resource Center* to enter the download site. See page 675 of this book for an automated way of comparing and reporting differences between two versions of one schedule.

Below you will find the WBS for the Relocation Project.

ID	Task Name
1.	REQUIREMENTS
2.	research staff requirements
3.	summarize requirements
4.	LOCATION
5.	select the realtor
6.	visit the sites
7.	evaluate the sites
8.	meet to select the location
9.	legal review
10.	location selected

---

[34] Notice that capital letters are used here to indicate which tasks will eventually become summary tasks. MS Project displays the summary tasks in bold type to make them stand out by default. This will happen upon indenting tasks.

ID	Task Name
11.	REMODELING CONTRACT
12.	select the contractor
13.	meet to discuss contract
14.	revise the schedule
15.	negotiate the contract
16.	contractor contracted
17.	REMODELED LOCATION
18.	relocate walls
19.	install electric wiring
20.	paint
21.	drying of paint[35]
22.	install cabinetry
23.	install LAN
24.	lay carpet
25.	facility remodeled
26.	MOVE
27.	select mover
28.	pack
29.	move
30.	unpack
31.	new location opened

[35] You might wonder if *drying of paint* should be entered as a task, because it happens by itself. I merely use it here to illustrate the use of an elapsed duration. Alternatively, you could enter it as lag on the dependency between *paint* and its successor.

Case Study: "My First Time ..."

Norm was proud but tense when he drove home from work. He was assigned to be the project manager on a project for the first time. He felt the assignment was recognition of his outstanding technical expertise. In the evening, he would start breaking down the work. This project, though, was different than other projects he had worked on. He had an idea of what deliverables and activities would be needed, but was worried whether he knew or would find them all. He decided he wanted to stay ahead of his team and create a WBS so his team would be impressed. That night he worked very hard and lost some sleep over his WBS. The next day, he presented it and introduced it as "Here is what we are going to do..." His team was quick to point out that he forgot to incorporate the logistics, documentation and training components in his WBS.

Questions:

1. What do you think about Norm's decision to create a WBS by himself?

2. What led him to do it by himself?

3. Would you have done it by yourself if you were in his shoes? Why?

Troubleshooting

1. Open the file *My Outline.MPP* available for download at www.jrosspub.com. Please, click the link *WAV Download Resource Center* to enter the download site. Explain why the outline does not function as an outline with summary tasks that can be collapsed and expanded.

Chapter 4 Entering Estimates

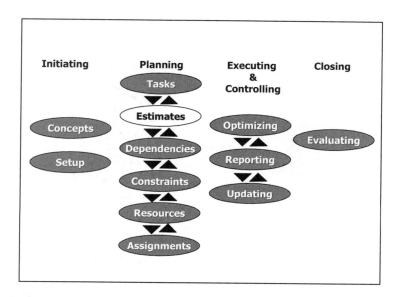

We have the Work Breakdown Structure including the activities (*Tasks*) entered into our project schedule. The next step as highlighted in the illustration above is to enter the estimates.

After reading this chapter you will:

- ◆ know a process for generating estimates
- ◆ know what duration and work/effort estimates are
- ◆ be able to enter duration and work estimates into MS Project
- ◆ understand how MS Project uses the formula $D * U = W$ when assignments are made or changed
- ◆ be aware of the human tendencies in estimating
- ◆ be aware of techniques to handle these human tendencies
- ◆ be aware of practical difficulties in estimating
- ◆ know techniques to address those practical difficulties
- ◆ understand and be able to apply the rolling wave approach
- ◆ understand the difference between pure and gross work time estimates
- ◆ be able to check the estimates of the project schedule using scheduling best practices
- ◆ know how to enter, move and copy data efficiently

Deadly Dates

Nob is bouncing his views on estimating off Bob: "You know the thing I have noticed is that my team members always pad their estimates. Just last week, Brian told me he was really busy and would perhaps not meet his deadline. Since then I have caught him going for a nice long lunch and I heard him chat up a storm at the water fountain. I can't even think of all the times that I saw him goof off in or around his work cubicle. I made it very clear to him that he is holding up my project. He is on my critical path!"

Bob: "What kind of estimate did you ask for?"

Nob: "Well, the normal thing, you know ... I asked for a date he'd be ready!"

Bob: "A date ... !?"

Nob: "Yeah, a date; what's wrong with that?"

Bob: "Well, if you ask for dates, you can be certain that people will pad them."

Nob: "I don't understand that; what do you mean?"

Bob: "Well, it is like a negotiation, you know. If you ask for this date, they will ask for a later date. And when you agree, you basically have a verbal contract that implies that if they meet that date, you will not be able to criticize them in a performance review. People apply the CYA principle."

Nob: "Yeah, you don't need to explain that one to me..."

Bob: "I always ask for a work estimate. I ask them '*How many person days of effort do you need on this task?*' It's an easier question for team members, because they don't need to think of how many hours they are tied up with other tasks or what their work hours will be over the next little while. MS Project will solve all of those problems much quicker and will tell me the date on which they will deliver."

What Are Estimates?

Estimates are predictions of how much time a task will take. The predictions can be made in terms of the duration of a task or in terms of the effort required to perform a task. The difference between duration and effort can easily be demonstrated with an example. If you have 3 carpenters working for 2 business days (duration), the effort is 3 * 2 = 6 person days of effort.

A duration estimate would be expressed in *business days* (working days), which will be the weekdays in most cases. A business day has 8 hours in MS Project by default. A duration estimate can be entered into the field *Duration*; the default time unit is **Days**. To enter a duration of five days (1 week), you could type:

◆   *5 days*
◆   *5d*
◆   *5*
◆   *1w*

Notice that MS Project displays it as *days* and not as *business days*. However, it will help you understand MS Project, if you think of the duration as the number of business days.

An effort estimate would be expressed in *person days* or *person hours*. A person hour is one person working one full hour. The effort estimate is entered into the task-related field *Work* in Project 2003. The default time unit of the **Work** field is **Hours**. To enter effort of 16 hours on a task, you could type:

◆   *16 hours*
◆   *16h*
◆   *16*
◆   *2d* and notice that MS Project will convert this into the default time unit of hours.

Realize that MS Project displays it as *hours* and not as *person hours*. It will help you understand MS Project, if you think of the work as the number of person hours (person days) needed for a task.

Choosing the Options

Before entering the estimates, it is important to be aware of how Project 2003 will function. Choose **Tools, Options** to display the dialog with which you can change MS Project's behavior. We recommend you set or accept the following options.

Tab	Option
Schedule	**Duration is entered in:** Project 2003 will use this as the default time unit for the field **Duration**. With the default duration time unit set to *days*, you can type in *5* instead of *5d* to get 5 days. You don't need to type a *d* in the duration fields. Choose the unit that fits the majority of your inputs. The **Duration** field will display whatever time unit you entered. If you would like to convert all entries to one time unit, choose **Tools, Macro, Macros...**, select the macro **Format_Duration** and click ⟨ Run ⟩ .
	Work is entered in: Same as previous, but for the **Work** field. Realize that the Work field, unlike the Duration field, will convert entries to the default time unit.
	Default task type: Most people enter the duration immediately, and MS Project should not change it, unless required. If you normally enter duration estimates rather than work (effort) estimates, we recommend setting it to **Fixed Duration**.[36]
	☐ **New Tasks are effort driven** When turned on, this option can change *assignment units* (the number of resource assigned); we recommend you turn it off. This option works similarly to the task type **Fixed Work**. We recommend you use the task **Type** instead of **Effort Driven**.
	☑ **Show that tasks have estimated durations** will add a question mark to the durations that you did not enter yourself.

---

[36] The PMBOK® Guide, 2004 Edition, published by the PMI, has *Activity Duration Estimating* as one of the core planning processes.

Tab	Option
	☑ **New tasks have estimated durations** will add a question mark to the durations of new tasks you may create.
	`Set as Default` Sets the options as the default setting for any new schedules you create. The existing schedules are not affected, because these options are stored in the project schedules, as you can see in the section divider label **Scheduling Options for <schedule name of the project>**.
Edit	**Allow cell drag and drop** This allows you to move or copy the selected cells by dragging the selected area by its border. This option is global, as you can see from the label of the section divider **Edit Options for Microsoft Project**.
	View options for Time Units for **Minutes, Hours, Days, Weeks, Months** and **Years** This allows you to change the way time units are shown in your project. The shorter you make the time unit, the more space you save. I set them habitually to the shortest label. Click `Set as Default` if you want these labels to be used in new project from now on.

Difficult Situations

"How do I estimate?" is the question we are asked most often in our project management courses. Estimating is one of the most difficult skills in project management. Estimating is particularly difficult in the following situations:

◆ When the task is entirely new for the organization or when the task is not done very often by the organization, like *moving* or *implementing new hardware* and *software*. For this type of task you may need to contract some outside expertise and have these consultants help you plan the project.

◆ When tasks have uncertain outcomes, like *R&D*-type tasks. How can you map out the remainder of the project if it entirely depends on the results of research you are currently conducting? As a result, *scientists* often hesitate to apply regular project management principles. However, these principles can also be applied to R&D-projects in my view. Apart from applying the common principles, you need to apply special project management techniques for R&D projects like *stage-gate project management* (see page 228), *rolling wave* (see page 198) and *risk management* in these projects.[37]

◆   When a team member is assigned who has little or no experience with estimating the tasks in his area of responsibility. Next we will discuss in more detail how to deal with inexperienced team members.

Estimating is difficult in projects, because, by definition, projects are about creating new things or doing things in a new way. Also, everybody will always have one first time for things that become regular activities. The first time you ask someone that is new to the task how long that task will take, he may be very reluctant to provide an answer. It is, however, more important that people start giving you their estimates than it is for those estimates to be very reliable. Estimating is a skill, and the only way to acquire a skill is by doing. That is how we learned to drive a car. After the team member starts making estimates, he should check how good they were. As a project manager with experience in estimating, you can help in this process of continuous improvement of estimating. You should be a mentor for novice estimators. In chapter 11, we will explain how you can retain your original estimates in the baseline (see page 611).

In MS Project you can capture that you are not sure of the estimate in the duration field. You can have the program treat an estimate like a *"guesstimate"*. You indicate that by adding a "?" to the entry. For example, enter "*3d?*" in the duration field if you are not entirely sure of the 3-day estimate. In its default settings, MS Project will add question marks to those durations that are filled in by the application. These can be default durations of "*1 day?*" or durations calculated by MS Project. It can calculate a duration from the total effort required and the number of people assigned. Unfortunately, MS Project calls durations with a question mark '*estimated durations*'. They really are *default durations* (*1 day?*) or *calculated durations*. You can make them disappear in **Tools, Options** tab **Schedule** as shown in the previous table.

Let's explore the human side of the estimating activity.

---

[37] Risk management is not fully covered in this book, please refer to risk literature or courses (see www.iil.com)

The Human Tendencies in Estimating

We will discuss four common tendencies that people expose in projects when estimating. You will hear things like:

- *"I Can't Predict the Future!"* from team members
- *"I Am Always Off!"* from team members
- *"Can't You Do It?"* from executives and sales representatives
- *"What is the date you'll be done?"* from project managers

"I Can't Predict the Future!"

Often team members have difficulty coming up with estimates. This is particularly true for team members who have never estimated the durations of their tasks or who are new to the type of task to which they are assigned. The latter is very common, because a fundamental characteristic of a project is that the final product is new and unique or produced in a new way. There is always improvisation and on-the-job learning in projects.

What would happen if you were impatient and filled in an estimate yourself when a team member states he cannot come up with one? If the team member is late with the task during project execution, he will simply say: *"I never told you it would be done in only five days; you came up with that yourself!"* You have to get the estimate from the team member; he has to *"own"* it, and then own up to it.

If a team member has difficulty producing estimates, one technique that often works is to ask for two or three estimates instead of one. Here is an interesting paradox; if people cannot give you one estimate, ask for more than one! It works. You may think that is weird, but it is easier to provide a *range estimate* than a *single point estimate*, generally speaking. The second estimate should be a pessimistic estimate: *What if many things went wrong; how long would it take then?* The person will soon consider disasters like *"What if all resources go on strike?"* or *"What if I get run over by a bus?"* or *"What if the whole world crashes down?"*. You can tell the team member that if those things happen, neither of you will be around, the project will not be needed any longer and you don't need the estimate anymore! It is fine to think of those circumstances, but don't consider them in coming up with a pessimistic estimate. Have a good laugh about those extreme situations and move on with estimating.

You probably noticed that I suggest you ask the question: *What if MANY things went wrong; how long would it take then?* "Many things go wrong" is not the same as "everything goes wrong". Therefore, I tend to call it a "pessimistic" estimate rather than a *"worst-case"* estimate. Asking for the worst case will get people thinking of natural disasters and that sort of thing. The estimating becomes humorous and the process may lose credibility. Alternative questions to solicit for pessimistic estimates would be: *"What is a safe estimate?"* or *"In how many days do you feel very confident you can accomplish this?"*

You could even ask for a third estimate, an optimistic estimate: *"What if many things go smoothly; how long would it take you then?"* or *"What would be an aggressive estimate?"*

Asking for more than one estimate gives you a better idea of what to expect. It also helps you determine how much padding or buffer you need to apply to the duration estimate. Best of all, range estimates are much easier for people to make, particularly when you deal with people who want to get it right (engineers maybe?). With a three-point estimate you can even do a *PERT analysis*. Or you can apply *Monte Carlo simulation* to the schedule. We will discuss both starting on page 427.

In summary, when a team member feels insecure about an estimate:

◆ You ask for more than one estimate for the task: a pessimistic one and perhaps even an optimistic estimate.

◆ You could pad the realistic estimate by using the pessimistic estimate instead, so that you have a reasonable probability to realize the padded estimate.

◆ When the target date is not exactly met, you forgive the estimator. You use the padding you applied as the project manager to swiftly forgive the poor person. If you are not forgiving, the person may stop providing estimates altogether. If you cannot get estimates from one of your resources, you are less likely to be successful as a project manager than if you get estimates that are less reliable. When you know the estimate is less reliable, you can pad it to create a feasible schedule.

◆ At the end of the project, you sit down with the team members that were insecure about their estimates and take a look at their original, aggregated estimate and compare it to the factual actual. You help them improve their estimates for the next time around. See the next section on how to do this. Evaluation provides a learning opportunity to become a skilled estimator. Making errors is human, but not learning from them is stupid.

"I Am Always Off!"

People are optimistic or pessimistic by nature. Their personalities greatly affect their estimating. When you have a new team, it will be difficult to determine the *personality factors* of the people that provide you with estimates. Asking for more than one estimate (optimistic, realistic and pessimistic) gives you a better understanding of the time risk of a task.

 In my personal observation, people are quite consistent in their tendency to err toward pessimism or toward optimism. Once you have found out the tendencies of your team members, you should be able to correct their estimates with a *personality factor* as a project manager. You can determine someone's tendency by studying their track record of estimates and actuals realized in their previous projects. You can get a very quick impression if you look at a schedule of a finished project in the resource-related *Actual Work* field and compare it to the *Baseline Work* field. If you divide the **Actual Work** by the resource's **Baseline Work**, you have calculated the person's personality factor. For example, if you find that Rich had 420 hours of actual work and 300 hours in his baseline, you know that from now on you should suggest a factor of 420 / 300 = 1.4 to him to make his work estimates more realistic. The next time you receive an estimate you ask with a smile: *Does that take your 1.4 personality factor into account?* The beauty of this calculation is that the *law of averages* takes effect, since the actual work and baseline work numbers are aggregated from all commitments the resource had in the project. If the number of estimates of a person is more than twenty in the project, the personality factors are fairly accurate.

If you get a date forecast from a young team member who you know is very optimistic, you can ask certain questions to make him realize that the estimate may be optimistic. Ask questions like:

◆ Is this estimate in terms of 100% fully focused work time or does it include the normal workday interruptions?
◆ Does it include continuing to answer your e-mail and voice mail?
◆ Do you have other ongoing responsibilities that will take time as well, like providing technical support, help-desk duties, troubleshooting, attending meetings or training?
◆ Do you have any personal commitments or other work commitments that will take time out of your workday?

Together you may come to the conclusion that time needs to be added before entering the forecast into MS Project.

If the person tends to be pessimistic, you can ask questions that may lead to subtracting time. In any case, you should leave the final decision with the estimator; otherwise you take the ownership and responsibility away from the team member. The team member will not learn from discrepancies, because *"It is not MY estimate!"* Also, the next time, the person may refuse to provide estimates to you, since *"You are going to change them anyway!"* If you think the final estimate is still optimistic and you need an extra time buffer, you can always insert this elsewhere in your schedule.

"Can't You Do It?"

I have seen organizations get stuck in scheduling a project when they use estimates produced by people <u>other</u> than the people who do the work. Examples of people who tend to produce unsolicited "estimates" are:

◆ **Executives and upper management**: *"Can't you do it in two weeks?"*
Project managers all know the stress that occurs when executives impose their "estimates" on a project. Some executives will try to make you feel guilty in order to get you to commit to a crazy deadline. When executives make their guesstimates and impose them as committed dates, your unfortunate fate as a project manager is that they will also do your performance appraisal and you're put in a double-bind position. You are damned if you do commit to their estimate and damned if you don't. However, estimates from executives should really be treated as targets, not as estimates. Enter these as deadlines in Project 2003 (see the discussion of deadlines on page 274) and then create a detailed schedule. If you sincerely feel it cannot be done in the timeframe you were challenged to, you should report this back to the executives.

◆ **Sales representatives**: *"The client gets what she wants."*
Project managers all know the disastrous effects that occur when salespeople present their own "estimates" to the client without consulting you as the project manager. You cannot win in such a situation. These "estimates" are not estimates; they are commitments to please the client and win a sale, often at the project manager's expense. All too often salespeople tell clients what they want to hear just to get the sale (and cash their commission).

Estimates from executives or salespeople often suffer from wishful thinking. As a project manager, you have to come to rely on the estimates of the resources on your team. If you feel the team estimate is high, you can always explore with the team members whether there are other, better, smarter or novel ways of working. In an open discussion, it is often possible to decrease estimates with new ideas. A brainstorm session can do miracles.

Now that we have discussed some of the human tendencies in estimating, let us explore how MS Project handles the estimates you enter.

"What Is the Date You'll Be Done?"

Some project managers habitually ask for dates from their team members and then enter these into their schedule. There are two things wrong with this habit (that seems persistent in some):

◆ You should not enter dates into a schedule, as we discussed on page 53. If you do, you are still living in the age of paper instead of the electronic age.

◆ If you ask for *dates*, you ask for the *most difficult estimate* you could ask for. You are expecting that people can quickly recall their entire to-do list, the dates of their other tasks, dates promised to other project managers, their hours they will be working, co-worker availability, co-worker efficiency, personal commitments, personal vacations, and national holidays. Clearly people cannot process this much information within one second. Project managers need to ask simpler questions if they want to get good estimates. Asking for a duration or effort estimate (work) is much easier for team members.

The Difference Between Duration and Work

The *duration* of a task is the number of time units of working time the task will take. Duration is expressed in *business hours* or in *business days*, even though MS Project will just call it *hours* or *days*.

The *work* is the number of *person hours* or *person days* planned or spent on a task, even though MS Project will just call it *hours* or *days*. Work is synonymous with *effort* in MS Project.

For example, one person who works for 2 *business days* (duration) delivers 2 *person days* of effort (work). Two painters who work for 3 business days (duration) to paint your house spend 2 * 3 = 6 person days of effort (work).

The business days are entered in the *Duration* field and the effort is entered in the *Work* field.

The Formula Behind the Screens

Project 2003 uses the formula: *Duration * Units = Work*.
◆ *Duration* is how many *business days* you have to finish the job.
◆ *Units* are how many *resource units* will do the work.
◆ *Work* is how many *person days* it will take.

The formula is meant to make your life easier, because you only have to provide two out of the three variables in the formula and MS Project will calculate the third one for you. However, if you are not aware of this formula, you cannot predict MS Project, and your life will be more difficult instead.

Given the formula, we recommend you work like this:

◆ You estimate and enter the first value.
The first variable in the formula is a given in most project situations. It is the estimate you first come up with. In most situations, you know the *duration* or *work* first.

◆ You decide on the second value.
The second variable is the one to decide on: for example, when you know you have a job of 6 person days, and you decide to *assign* 2 full-time people (2 * 100%). MS Project can now do the math for you and will calculate a duration of 3 business days.

◆ You let Project 2003 calculate the third value.
The third variable is calculated by MS Project to balance the equation and is automatically entered by the application. MS Project tries to spare you calculating the third value manually with a pocket calculator and entering it.

If you override the third value that is calculated by MS Project and enter a different value, MS Project will recalculate the first or the second value you entered to keep the equation in balance. The field it will recalculate depends on the currently set *Type* of task: *fixed duration*, *fixed units* or *fixed work*.

An Example of an Estimation

Let us assume you want to repaint one room in your house. You wonder on what date you could be done repainting the room; you need to know the number of *calendar days* this project will take.

Estimating the number of calendar days, however, is very difficult and you have to step back and try to estimate the number of workdays (*business days*) the job will take. Once you know the number of business days and on which day of the week you will start, you can convert the business days into calendar days.

Estimating in business days, however, may be difficult as well, because you may not know how many resources will be available. You take another step back and decide to focus on an effort estimate in *person days*. To estimate the effort (work), you realize you must look at parameters like the difference between the old and new color, the number of coats needed, area to be painted, and what you will do with the wallpaper. After you have decided all of those factors, you figure it will take, let's say, 10 person days (see the next illustration).

You still cannot say how many business days this requires, because you have no firm commitments from family members or friends to help you. You ask around, and you find that your significant other is willing to help and that you are going to share the workload. This means that both of you will take 5 person days of effort; 10 person days of effort can be delivered by 2 people in 5 business days.

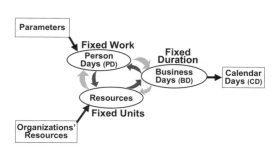

If you start on Monday and you decide not to work on the weekend, you can have your house painted by Friday (5 business days and 5 calendar days). However, if you start on Tuesday, you will be done on Monday of the next week (5 business days but 7 calendar days). You now know what you wanted to know: the project end date.

The last conversion from business days to calendar days is elegantly taken care of by MS Project. Once you have filled in the project calendar, you can count on the eager and rapid cooperation of Project 2003. The challenge in estimating with MS Project lies in solving the puzzle of *person days*, *resource units* and *business days*. We will present a process for solving this puzzle.

A Process for Estimating

Estimating: Types of Tasks

Eventually, MS Project needs to know the start date and the finish date of a task in order to fit it into the time line. To get to those dates, it needs to find out the number of calendar days a job will take, as shown in the illustration. You will find it too difficult to estimate the number of *calendar days*. You will immediately get bogged down with questions like: *When will we start this task? If we start it on a Monday, it will take 2 calendar days, but if we start on a Friday, it will take 4 calendar days!* You don't want to deal with those issues at this point. You should instead try to estimate the number of *business days* and have MS Project do the conversion from business days to calendar days. The software does an excellent job here once you have filled in the project calendar. We filled it in when we set up the new project (see page 116).

In some situations, it is possible to estimate the number of business days (or business hours) directly, for example for tasks like *meeting, training* and *presentation.* For a meeting you set the duration to, let's say, 2 business hours. Activities like these do not shorten in duration when you add more resources to them; these are *Fixed Duration* tasks. On the contrary, meetings tend to take longer with more people attending.

For many other tasks, it is impossible to estimate the number of business days immediately. Those are the tasks for which it is important to know how much effort it will take and how many resources are available to do the work. You have to step back in the process and estimate the amount of effort first in *person days*. MS Project calls effort *Work.*

In order to estimate the work (effort), you may find that you have to look at the *parameters* of the job. For a programming job you can look at how many input screens the application will have. For a construction project you can look at how many cubic feet of concrete you will need to pour. For each job there are relevant parameters to consider. You may have to ask the client to provide some of these.

Looking at the parameters of the job is important. Each industry has its own *metrics* to refine the estimates of a job; this is also known as *parametric estimating*:

◆ The construction industry has its *quantity surveyors*; they can tell exactly how much a brick wall will cost given the square footage and choice of brick. They can derive the footage from the architectural drawings.

◆ The software industry works with *function points*. Once software estimators know the number of function points of an application to be built, they can calculate their estimates. Dividing the function point total by 150 approximates the number of analysts, programmers and technicians they will need. Raising the function point total to the power of 0.4 gives a rough estimate of the time in months that the team will need.[38]

---

[38] These metrics were taken from *"Sizing Up Software"* by Capers Jones, *Scientific American,* December 1998.

Once you have determined the amount of work, you have to decide how many resources will be assigned to the job. After that, you can usually determine how many business days the task will take (duration).

In our example, you estimate the amount of work first, then you decide on the number of resources and the number of business days is calculated as a result. This task is a *Fixed Work* task, because you estimate the work first. Note that for these tasks, the Gantt Chart only starts to make sense after the durations have been calculated, since the task bars in the Gantt Chart depict durations. The durations will be calculated when you *assign* resources to the task by entering the *resource units* of the formula D * U = W.

What you estimate first is entirely up to you, but will typically depend on the situation. If you first estimate the duration, you have a *Fixed Duration* task. This is quite common. In any situation you will have to estimate the first variable, decide on the second and let MS Project calculate the third. The result is that you will know the date the task will be done and the cost of it.

On the next pages we will discuss Fixed Work tasks and Fixed Duration tasks. The Fixed Units tasks are less common when planning a project, and we will postpone discussion of those to page 385. You need Fixed Units mostly when you make changes to assignments as we will see on those pages.

 If you don't intend to enter resources and assignments, you will have to estimate the durations for all tasks, since MS Project needs durations to create the Gantt Chart! If you will assign resources eventually, you can enter work estimates for now. We will discuss assigning resources in chapter 8, see page 367.

Preparing the Gantt Spreadsheet

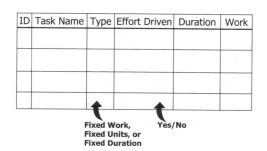

Let us prepare the Gantt spreadsheet so we have the right fields to enter our estimates. The illustration on the left shows which fields we will insert. We recommend you insert them in the order shown in the spreadsheet of the Gantt Chart. You typically have to insert the fields **Type, Effort Driven** and **Work** into the spreadsheet.

We need the following fields in the Gantt spreadsheet:

◆ **ID**

◆ **Task Name**: Note that the database name of this field is simply *Name*. You can see this if you double-click on the column heading.

◆ **Type**: By setting the right task type, you tell MS Project to leave the estimate you entered alone. For example, if you estimate that a task will take 10 person days, you enter 10 days in the *Work* field and you set the task type to *Fixed Work*. The tool may (re)calculate the duration or the *resource units* needed, but never the *Work* when the task type is *Fixed Work*.

◆ **Duration**: To enter the duration for *Fixed Duration* tasks.

◆ **Work**: To enter the effort for *Fixed Work* tasks.

If you have the default **Entry** table displayed, you need to insert the fields **Type, Effort Driven** and **Work**:

1. Choose **View, Gantt Chart**.

2. Click anywhere in the column **Duration** and choose **Insert, Column**.
   OR
   Right-click on the **Duration** column heading and choose **Insert Column...**; the **Column Definition** dialog appears:

3. Select from the list **Field name** ID ▼ the item **Type** and click
   OK . If you type the first characters of the field name, you will get to it quickly; the list is very long. Note that you need to type the characters fairly quickly.

4. Repeat steps 2 and 3 to insert the columns **Effort Driven** and **Work**.

5. Make sure you have the right default task type selected in **Tools, Options, Schedule, Default Task Type** and **Effort Driven** turned off, if possible. These options determine the task type for new tasks you create. Click OK . You are now ready to enter duration and work estimates.

If you started with the wrong default task type, you can change all tasks at once by clicking on a column heading to select all tasks and clicking **Task Information** 🔲 on the **Standard** toolbar. Click the **Advanced** tab, select the type you want from the list **Task type**, and clear ☐ **Effort Driven** (Make sure it is white, not gray. Click another time if it is gray; the checkbox has three states when multiple tasks are selected: on, off and gray for some on, others off). Click [OK].

Fixed Duration Tasks

A *fixed duration task* is a task that has a duration that does not fluctuate with the number of resources assigned to it, or the working hours of those resources. Examples of tasks like these are *status meeting, training, back up computer system* or *drying of paint.* Tasks tend to have a fixed duration when you assign many resources to them (meeting, training) or none (back up computer system, drying of paint). Notice the tendency to use the imperfect tense (-ing) in these task names.

For *Fixed Duration* tasks, enter the duration first. A task such as *meeting* is a prime example of a fixed duration task, because you decide the duration up front (it is more a matter of deciding than of estimating). Then you can decide who you will invite to the meeting and *assign* the number of units (gray arrows in illustration). Once you have assigned the number of *resource units*, MS Project will calculate the total amount of work.

Sometimes you know the maximum number of person hours you are willing to spend in the meeting and you enter it as work (black arrows in the illustration). In this case MS Project will calculate the number of resources needed.

1. Enter the name of the task in the field **Task Name**.

2. Press [Tab]; the cursor moves to the field **Type**. (If you press [Enter ↵], the cursor will move down to the next task.)

3. Select from the task type list [Fixed Units ▼] **Fixed Duration** and press [Tab] to move to the **Effort Driven** field.

4. Change **Effort Driven** to **No** (if you didn't switch the default to *No* in **Tools, Options, Schedule**) and press [Tab] to move to the **Duration** field.

5. Enter in the **Duration** field `1 day?` the number of business days you estimate the task will take. This will override the default duration of **1 day?** that MS Project had entered. You only need to enter the number and MS Project will append *days*.[39] If you want to display a different time unit, for example hours, you have to type the time unit abbreviation as well and you would enter "2h". Valid abbreviations for the time units are: "m" for minutes, "h" for hours, "d" for days, "w" for weeks and "mo" for months. Notice the "m" for minutes versus the "mo" for months.

6. Press `Enter ↵` and then `Home` to position the cursor for the next task.

Fixed Work Tasks

A *fixed work task* is a task that has an amount of effort that is only dependent upon the *parameters* of the job; i.e. what the technical specifications are of the finished work. The amount of effort is not dependent upon the number of resources that will be assigned to the task or the working times (calendars).

Once you determine the amount of work, you will often find that your next step will be to establish how many resources will do the job (black arrows in the illustration). When you know the work and the number of *resource units*, MS Project will derive the number of business days (duration).

In this chapter, we will only discuss the steps for entering work estimates; in chapter 8 we will explain how to assign resources to tasks, see page 367.

Once you know the amount of work (10 person days), you sometimes know in how many business days it needs to be done (gray arrows in the illustration). Let's say you have only 4 business days for the task (duration). From this, MS Project can derive for you the number of resources you need (2.5).

1. Enter the name of the task in the field **Task Name**.

---

[39] *Days* is the default time unit for the *Duration* field as set in **Tools, Options, Schedule.** The default 'abbreviation' for *days* is set in **Tools, Options, Edit.**

2. Press ⌊Tab⌋; the cursor moves to the field **Type**. (If you press ⌊Enter ⤶⌋, the cursor will move down to the next task instead.) Notice that MS Project already entered a *default duration* of **1 day?** in the **Duration** field.

3. Select from the list ⌈Fixed Units ▾⌉ the task type **Fixed Work**. Press ⌊Tab⌋ repeatedly to reach the **Work** field. The field **Effort Driven** is set to **Yes** and cannot be changed for **Fixed Work** tasks.[40]

4. Enter in the **Work** field ⌈0 hrs ▴▾⌉ the number of person hours you estimate the task will take. Review the parameters of the job, if needed. You only need to enter the number and MS Project will append "**hrs**".[41] If you want a different time unit, for example weeks, you have to type the "w" as well and you would enter "3w" for example. Valid abbreviations for the time units are: "m" for minutes, "h" for hours, "d" for days, "w" for weeks and "mo" for months. Notice the "m" for minutes versus the "mo" for months.

5. Press ⌊Enter ⤶⌋ and then ⌊Home⌋ to position the cursor for the next task.

Estimating: Difficulties and Techniques

We already noted that estimating is difficult on page 177. The following factors make estimating difficult and we will discuss what options you have to make it easier:

◆   **In which time unit to estimate**
    You have the choice to estimate the number of *calendar days* (*elapsed time*), *business days* or *person days* (person hours). Sometimes you know the time frame in which the activity has to be ready (calendar days: deadline date), and sometimes you know first how much effort it will take (person days: work). Each situation is different.

◆   **What to include**
    What do your resources include in their estimates? Do they imagine being able to work full-time without interruptions on the task? Do they include personal time, like

---

[40] In my view, this is an indication that these two features work similarly, which makes one of them redundant.

[41] *Hrs* is the default time unit for the *Work* field as set in **Tools, Options, Schedule** and the default abbreviation for hours as set in **Tools, Options, Edit**.

visits to the washroom and calls to their significant other? Do they include time spent in meetings to discuss or present deliverables?

◆ **Unknown events**
In any project, there are always many unknown events. For example, in a project to move a company, the location is often unknown when the move is planned. When estimating, the following questions will erupt:
◇ Will we be able to find a suitable location? How much effort will this cost?
◇ How long will it take to renovate the new location to meet our needs?

◆ **Unknown resources**
During the *planning phase* it is often unclear whether enough resources will be available, who will be available and if they will be available at the time they are needed. Consulting companies often start the search for resources immediately after the ink dried on a new contract.

◆ **Unknown experience and skill level**
Even if you do know which resources you will have on your project, you may not know their experience and skill level. As the project manager, you are often given resources you have not worked with before. For estimating, this creates an extra challenge, because the project manager should look not only at the job, but also at who will do the job. How much skill does the job require? What is the skill level the resource has? Is the estimating resource an optimist or a pessimist by nature?

◆ **Unknown learning curve**
Learning curve theory states that the time needed for repeated deliverables will decrease with each repetition. Therefore, repetitions will affect estimates.

We will discuss each of these difficulties in more detail.

In Which Time Unit to Estimate

You have to choose if you are going to express your estimate in person days, business days or calendar days (elapsed durations):

◆ *Person days*
You can express an estimate in person months, person weeks, person days or person hours. One person day is one person working one full day. The number of person days is the amount of *work* or *effort* needed on the task. For example, if you have to write 20 pages of text and you know it takes you about 2 person hours per page, the total effort is 20 * 2 = 40 person hours. The effort needs to be entered into the field **Work** in MS Project. Person day estimates are (fairly) independent of the number of resources who are going to do the work. Once the job is defined, it just requires a

certain amount of effort to finish it. Person day estimates are needed to calculate the cost of the project. Each person hour applied needs to be multiplied by the appropriate rate to arrive at the cost.

◆ *Business days*
A business day is one working day. The number of hours of a full working day is defined in **Tools, Options, Calendar, Hours per Day**. In the project calendar you can find which days are working days and which are non-working days. The number of full working days a task will take is called the **Duration** of the task, and that is the name of the field where you enter it.

You need to know the number of business days in order to calculate the calendar days needed and the start and finish dates. MS Project also needs the duration in order to create the Gantt Chart. The length of the task bars in the Gantt Chart is driven by the duration of the task (in combination with the project calendar).

◆ *Calendar days*
One calendar day is 24 hours and is simply how everybody thinks of one day, whether educated in project management or not. For example, if paint dries in 2 days, the number of calendar days is 2. The number of calendar days needed is not dependent on the working times, since paint dries during the night and weekend as well. You need to know the number of calendar days if you are asked to commit to a date on which you deliver the project product. Calendar days are also known in MS Project as *elapsed durations*. Unfortunately, MS Project does not have a field that corresponds to the elapsed duration expressed in calendar days.

A working day has 8 hours for most of us, whereas an elapsed day has 24 hours. Saturday and Sundays are not seen as working days in the western world, but they are also elapsed days. An elapsed day is how most people will understand "one day".

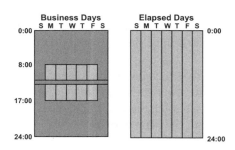

Elapsed durations are used for tasks that go through the night and through the weekend and do not follow working hours, as shown in the illustration.

Examples are backing up a computer system or the drying of paint. At food companies, new products are shelved for months in order to find out if the food preservation procedures are adequate. These months are elapsed months, because they continue over Christmas and through the summer holidays. Defense systems developers will keep a new monitor for a tank in a shake and bake oven for a few days to test its ruggedness. The 2 days are elapsed days. Elapsed activities continue *24 * 7* (24 hours and 7 days a week). If you want to enter an elapsed duration in the *Duration* field, you have to specify the time unit as follows:

Time unit	Enter normally as	Enter in elapsed time as
minutes	*m*	*em*
hours	*h*	*eh*
days	*d*	*ed*
weeks	*w*	*ew*
months	*mo*	*emo*

Instead of typing in "5d" to get 5 days, you have to enter "5ed" to get 5 elapsed days.

What to Include: Pure Work Time or Gross Work Time?

The term *Pure Work Time*[42] expresses an important concept very well. Pure work time is working 100% of your time with 100% focus on the task. Pure work time is 100% productive time without interruptions, also known as *crunch time*!

Pure   Gross

Gross Work Time, on the other hand, includes much time spent on things other than the tasks in the task list of a project. If you look at where you spend your time during a regular workday, you will find that a lot of time is lost on things other than project tasks. It should be clear if the estimate you received from your team members are expressed in pure work time or in gross work time. If the work will be billed to the client, it has to be very clear what should be included in the estimate and what not.

People spent their time at work on the following things:

◆ Time spent on project tasks which is pure work time (for project planning purposes)

◆ Time spent on nonproject, but work-related tasks, for example:
  ◇ Operational tasks
  ◇ Answering e-mails that do not pertain to the project
  ◇ Answering phone calls that do not pertain to the project
  ◇ Company meetings (for example, on employee benefits)
  ◇ Professional development training (not project-related)
  ◇ Providing emotional or technical support for colleagues
  ◇ Introducing and training new staff
  ◇ Changing into the company uniform
  ◇ Troubleshooting and answering support calls (helpdesk)
  ◇ Debugging released versions of software applications (hot fixes, service packs)

---

[42] I learned this term first from my former colleague Brian Petersen.

◆ Time spent that is nonproject and non work-related time, or in other words, time spent on yourself (*personal time*), for example:

◇ Private telephone calls
◇ Chats with colleagues and other passers-by
◇ Daydreaming
◇ Coffee breaks
◇ Visits to the restroom, water fountain, coffee pot and fridge
◇ TGIF,[43] farewell and anniversary lunches for colleagues
◇ Sick leave
◇ Vacation days (this is a special case that can be captured separately in MS Project on the *resource calendar*, see page 332)

All the listed items are included in gross work time. At IIL, we have asked many course participants and it is fairly common that only 70% of the gross work time is spent productively (pure work time), but this percentage can vary significantly from industry to industry. As you can see, there is a difference of 30% between gross and pure. Assuming that you are typically forgiven for a 10% overrun, if you ignore the difference between gross and pure work time, your projects will always be late. Therefore, it is important that you incorporate it in your schedule of the project.

Important questions to ask you are:

◆ Do you, as the project manager, ask your team members explicitly to estimate in pure work time or in gross work time?
If you ask a team member for an estimate, you should ask explicitly for an estimate in *pure work time* or *gross work time*. You can ask a question like: "*Could you tell me how many person hours this would take you in terms of gross work time?*" If you suspect that the team member is not clear on what gross work time means, you should explain it briefly and give examples from the previous list to indicate the difference between pure and gross.

◆ If you don't ask explicitly for pure or gross work time estimates, you have to ask:
Are my resources providing me with estimates in pure work time or in gross work time? If your resources are providing you with pure work time estimates, whereas you always thought they were gross work time estimates, your resources will never meet their deadlines! On the other hand, if you receive gross estimates that you schedule using pure work times on the project calendar, your project schedule will be unnecessarily long.

---

[43] TGIF stands for *Thank Goodness It's Friday*.

It is important that:

- All team members estimate consistently in either pure work time or gross work time; you cannot use a mix of the two. If one estimates in pure work time and another in gross work time, this inevitably leads to misunderstandings that can make the difference between meeting a deadline and missing it.
- Every estimator has the same understanding of what a "*gross working time estimate*" or "*pure working time estimate*" means. Some organizations decide to include the nonproject, work-related time in "pure" working time estimates, though most exclude it. This has to be clarified with any person who estimates or interprets estimates, which is just about every stakeholder in a project.
- Time sheets are filled in consistently as well with pure actual hours worked or gross actual hours worked depending on if you collected pure or gross working time estimates. Otherwise, you cannot compare!

- You consider whether you want the costs in your project to be calculated based upon pure work estimates or gross work estimates. The cost of pure work estimates will turn out to be lower than you may want to report, since personal time is typically included in cost estimates to clients or executives. You will need a multiplication factor to correct this.

The last considerations are why most project managers use gross estimates and gross working times in practice. Of over 1,000 schedules we evaluated for certification at IIL, an estimated 80% used gross working time estimates and gross working times on the project calendar. Particularly if you use the schedule also for developing cost estimates, it is important to use the gross working time system. However, if your team members have a large portion of nonproject work (like operations, maintenance and technical support), gross estimates may be too rough from a cost perspective. In that case, you may want to exclude these from the gross estimates and include the rest.

Only when the collected data are consistent with the project calendar can you produce accurate schedules and *valid* forecasts from these estimates. Project 2003 is set up by default to receive gross work time estimates based on 8 hours for a full workday, because the default working times are 8:00 AM-12:00 PM and 1:00 PM-5:00 PM. If everybody estimates in gross work time based on 8 hours per day, you don't have to change the default settings in MS Project; in any other case, you do have to make changes.

If you want to work with pure work time estimates, you have to do one of the following:

- You can adjust the working times for everybody in the *project calendar* by choosing **Tools, Change Working Time**. You can simply shorten the working times. For example, if you found that the resources are for 75% productive, you could change the working times to reflect 75% * 8 hour * 60 minutes = 6 hours. This could be entered on the project calendar as: 9AM - 12PM and 1PM - 4PM. See page 119 for the detailed steps.

♦ Instead you could decrease everybody's availability from 100% to less than 100%. If you have found that people are productive 70% of their work time, you have to enter this as their availability in the **Max. Units** field in the Resource Sheet. More on this on page 337 under Part-Time Availability.

A separate issue is whether the estimates should include *waiting time*. Waiting time is, for example, the time you have to wait to receive a permit or approval. Many people include these waiting times in their duration estimates. We recommend entering them as lags on dependencies instead. For a definition of lag and how to enter it, see page 223.

Unknown Events: The Rolling Wave Approach

When you have yet to find the new location in an office relocation project, it is hard to estimate how long it will take to remodel it. Perhaps only minor remodeling will be necessary if you find a location in good shape, or maybe you will spend a long time getting an old building up to par.

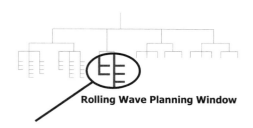

Rolling Wave Planning Window

Some project managers would keep the estimate on the safe side for this part of the project by assuming they have to remodel the new location drastically. They enter just one line item for the remodeling in the *Work Breakdown Structure* (*WBS*) and the uncertain but safe estimate. Once they have an idea which remodeling activities the new location needs, they will start listing the detail activities and create the appropriate level of detail in the WBS. Notice in the illustration that the first 6 deliverables were already detailed to the task level, the next 2 deliverables just came within the *rolling wave planning window* and are currently broken down into tasks, whereas the last 10 deliverables are high level and far in the future still.

This is called the *Rolling Wave* approach; you don't detail the plan until you know well enough what to expect. The project manager will use a planning window when applying the rolling wave technique. A *planning window* is a look-ahead window of a certain number of months. In a project of one year, you could use a planning window of three months, for example. As time goes by, the planning window moves ahead and as soon as a deliverable falls within it, you would break it down to the level of tasks. In this one-year project, you would typically monitor this every month, and add detail to the WBS at the start of every month.

The rolling wave technique is useful to handle the unknown events that are far into the future. This avoids having to redo large portions of the WBS that were uncertain. Often, the planning window is either a three or six month look-ahead window.

 You can even apply the *1%-10% rule* when working with rolling wave planning to find the right level of detail for both the detail schedule and the high-level schedule. You take 1% and 10% of the planning window period to find the right level of detail for the detailed schedule. And you take 1% and 10% of the total project duration to find the right level of detail for the high-level schedule of deliverables.

Unknown Resources

If you don't know which actual resources you will get, you have to make assumptions just for planning purposes. If you don't make assumptions, you cannot finalize your detailed schedule. One common assumption project managers make is that the resources will be available when their project needs them. Of course, it is a good idea to discuss your resource needs with the resource manager, HR or executives as a reality check on this assumption. Make the assumption loud and clear explicitly in the project plan, so no one's lack of memory will come back to haunt you.

"C++ Programmer"   "Winston"
(C++ Programmer)

If you don't know the names of the individuals you will have on your team, you enter them as *generic resources* in terms of roles, functions or positions. The illustration shows that you don't know for sure that you will have *Winston* on your team, and you therefore enter *C++ Programmer* instead. This simple technique will allow you to do your estimates, enter resources and enter the assignments as well. You can now produce a detailed schedule. Once you know the names of the individuals, there are simple techniques to update your schedule to reflect this. We will discuss these techniques on page 401.

 In *Project Server*, you can define *generic resources* in the enterprise resource pool and accumulate the workloads on these generic resources. Generic resources are resources that have the field **Generic** set to **Yes**. This allows you to finalize the loading the resources in a detail schedule.

You may have to formulate certain assumptions about the experience and skill levels of the generic resources.

Unknown Experience and Skill Level

Even if you do know the name of the actual resource that will do the job, you still may not know how much *experience* the person has and at which *skill level* he or she should be classified. This will throw your estimate off and thus, your schedule.

Junior   **Senior**

If this is a major concern, use several resource categories such as *Junior Visual Basic Programmer* and *Senior Visual Basic Programmer*. Assign the junior resource to the easy tasks and the senior resource to the tasks that require experience or skill. Once again, you need to substitute the generic junior and senior resource with the names of the actual individuals. We will discuss these techniques on page 401.

Unknown Learning Curve

Projects create products that are unique. Some say that, because of the lack of repetition, the effect of the learning curve is limited in projects. The number of repetitions in projects is considerably lower than in manufacturing operations. Still, I think, learning plays an important role:

◆ Because the project is new, participants have to be willing to learn. R&D projects and product development projects are prime examples in which learning plays a key role.

◆ There is some repetition in all projects, for example status reports, quality control and time sheets.

◆ In some projects, there is a lot of repetition. In implementation projects the same system is installed in many different locations. The learning curve theory is therefore applicable particularly to implementation projects and their duration estimates.

The amount of learning and the lack of repetition in projects combined imply that resources hired on projects have to be very fast learners. The ability to learn quickly is perhaps even the most important characteristic of good project resources.

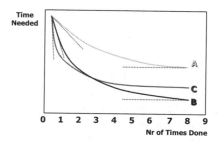

Fast learners (B and C in the illustration on the left) have a *learning curve* that has a steep slope down. The second time they repeat something, the time needed goes down fast. Fast learners can also end up with a faster time per deliverable after many repetitions than slow learners (compare the horizontal dotted lines for A and B). However, it is not a given that the fastest time possible per deliverable is eventually lower for fast learners. To see this, compare the horizontal lines for

B and C. Because of the lack of repetition in projects, the initial learning rate seems to be more important than the eventual fastest time per unit for most projects. We therefore recommend you hire people with a C learning curve for your projects.

In one type of project, implementation projects, there can be many repetitions of installing the same hardware and/or software in many locations. Learning curves are important in this type of project. Also, in this type of project, you probably want the resources that have learning curve B instead of C, because B-resources will eventually be fastest where they go, whereas C-learners are probably bored after the third time.

The learning curve poses difficulties, in terms of estimating. The estimator should not only look at the job, but also at who will do the job in order to produce the right estimate. How much repetition does the job have? Is the resource a slow or a fast learner? How can I maximize the learning by mixing fast and slow learners on an implementation team? These factors complicate estimating and, again, you may have to make some assumptions as to the rate of learning of the resources. Also, don't forget to make these assumptions explicit in your project plan. Otherwise you may end up with a slow learner (and be blamed for late delivery). In addition, if you don't document how you arrived at your estimates, you will not be able to learn from the discrepancies between original plan and actual execution.

Living Document Approach

As we just saw, there are many unknowns in projects: unknown events, unknown resources, unknown experience and skill levels and unknown learning curves. A common way to deal with all unknowns is to make assumptions and treat the project plan as a living document.

When dealing with the unknowns, you can always estimate by making *assumptions*. An assumption is something you treat to be true just for estimating purposes. We recommend you document the assumptions on which you based your estimates. If any of the assumptions that you based your estimate on change, you have a more supportable position for revising your estimate.

The *living document approach* basically says that your detailed project plan is not finished and final until the project is closed. You keep reviewing your assumptions, revising and refining the plan during the entire project life. The project plan "lives" in a sense. You will continue to refine the task list, the estimates and assignments during project execution. *Rolling Wave* is one example of how the living document approach can be implemented.

 Note that the high-level project plan does not change in a living document approach; the *scope* and *quality* requirements, the major *deadlines* and the *budget* may not change at all. The *baseline* may not change. Changes in the high-level project plan only happen through a formal approval process that typically involves your executives and clients. In the living document approach, changes happen at the lower levels of detail. It is important to find the appropriate level of detail whenever you add detail.

Checks on the Estimates

◆ Are the *estimates* reasonable given the work that needs to be performed?
You will need some technical expertise to verify if the estimates are reasonable. If you don't have this technical expertise, you could review the schedules of previous but similar projects. You can ask your team members who have the technical knowledge to peer review each others' estimates or you can ask a *subject matter expert* (*SME*) to review the estimates.

◆ Are the estimates that you collected consistent with the working hours entered in the **Standard (Project Calendar)**?
If they are not consistent the schedule will be too long or too short.

◇ Gross working time estimates should be entered in a schedule with gross working hours (typically 8:00 AM-5:00 PM).

◇ Pure working time is 100% productive time. Pure working time estimates should be entered in a schedule with pure working hours. Note that 100% productive working hours corresponds to a shorter working day, for example, 8:00 AM-3:00 PM. For most organizations, the percentage of totally productive working time lies between 60% and 80% of the working hours.[44]

---

[44] This range is based on answers from thousands of project managers in our classes.

Let's say your normal workday has 8 hours. If you estimate that the productive hours are 70% of the hours worked, the working hours should be 70% * 8h = 5.6 hours, let's say 5.5 hours (68.75%). Working hours that correspond to this are, for example, 9:00 AM-12:00 PM and 1:00 PM-3:30 PM. We prefer that you set working hours like these on the project calendar. You can set other working times, as long as the total number of hours adds up to 5.5. To review the steps to set working hours, see page 116.

Copying and Moving Data

Entering estimates can be a tedious job. We will discuss some quick ways to enter data into MS Project.

Editing Fields of Multiple Tasks at Once

1. Select the tasks by clicking on the first task, holding down Control and clicking on the next ones until they are all selected.

2. Click **Task Information** 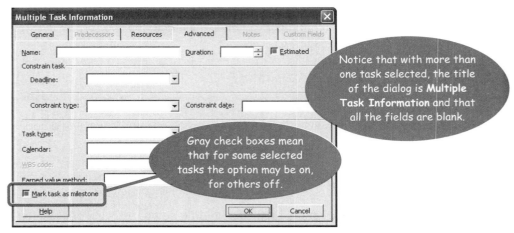 on the **Standard** toolbar,
   OR

   hold down [Shift] and press [F2]; the **Multiple Task Information** dialog appears:

3. Make the changes needed on each tab.

4. Click [OK].

The **Multiple Task Information** dialog can be used as a time saver for many purposes, for example:

◆ Setting the duration of all the milestones to 0 (zero) on the tab **General** and clearing ☐ **Estimated** to make the question mark disappear.

◆ Changing the task type on the **Advanced** tab in the field **Task type**. For example, you can change the type of task from **Fixed Duration** to **Fixed Work** for a series of tasks. This shows up in the field *Type* in the spreadsheet.

◆ You can assign or add a resource to many tasks at once on the tab **Resources**.

◆ Assigning high *priority* numbers to groups of tasks, so they will not likely be delayed when leveling. Choose the tab **General**, and enter a number between 0 and 1000 in the field **Priority** where a higher number reflects a higher priority.

Copying with Fill Down

1. Enter the value that you want to copy down in the top cell.

2. Click and hold down on the top cell and drag down over all adjacent cells you want to fill.
   OR

    Hold down [Shift] and press [↓] to select all cells you wish to fill.
   OR

   Hold down [Control] and click on all nonadjacent cells to fill with the value.

3. Choose **Edit, Fill, Down**.
   OR

   Hold down [Control] and press [D].

Examples in which you can use the fill down feature:

◆ Changing the constraint types for many tasks. To get rid of constraints, fill *As Soon As Possible* in the field *Constraint Type*.

◆ Setting the *Level Assignments* field for all the detail recurring tasks to *Yes* to include them in the workload leveling.

◆ In the resource sheet you can fill down the department (field *Group*) for the resources.

Fill Up or Fill Down Using the Fill Handle

1. Enter the value you wish to fill in the top or the bottom cell of the area to fill into.

2. Make sure you have the cell selected and at the bottom right of the cell you will see a fill handle [1 day?] Fill handle

3. Point to the fill handle; watch the mouse pointer : [1 day?] crosshair mouse pointer

4. When you see a crosshair mouse pointer, click and hold down and drag over the cells to be filled.

 You can even enter a pattern of values in some cells, select the cells that define the pattern and drag the fill handle; MS Project will copy and repeat this same pattern as many times as you drag up or down. MS Project works like *MS Office Excel* in this regard.

Copying, Moving or Clearing Cells

When copying or moving cells, you have to make sure that the receiving cells can accommodate the type of data you paste in. MS Project will warn you if the cells cannot receive it and will refuse the data if it does not make sense. For example, you cannot copy dates into the duration field.

Copying Cells

1. Select the cells and point to the border of the selected area. Make sure the mouse pointer changes from a plus sign ⊕ to a ↖ .

2. Hold down [Control] and drag the cells to their place.

You cannot use copy and paste to copy one cell and paste it into many other cells, like you can in *MS Office Excel*. It will only paste the value into the first cell of all copy-to cells you selected in MS Project.

Moving Cells

1. Select the cells and point to the border of the selected area. Make sure the mouse pointer changes from a plus sign ⊕ to ↖ .

2. Click, hold down and drag the cells to their new place.

If you personally classify as "mouse-challenged" or as a "careless clicker", you should consider turning this *cell drag and drop* option off. You can do so by choosing **Tools, Options,** tab **Edit** and clearing ☐ **Allow Cell Drag and Drop**.

Clearing Cells

The [Delete] key clears the content from the cells. When you press [Delete] in the task name column, a smart tag ✗ will appear to ask if you wanted to delete the entire task. Since you knew what you were doing, you can conveniently ignore it.

OR

Select the cells (not the row heading — the locked first column) and choose **Edit**, **Clear, All**. This menu can also be used to selectively clear only the formatting, only the content, only the notes or only the hyperlinks of a task.

Clearing Rows

You can delete entire rows with the ⌊Delete⌋ key by selecting one or more entire rows by selecting the rows first and then pressing ⌊Delete⌋. You can select multiple adjacent tasks by dragging over their row headings. You can select non-adjacent tasks by ⌊Control⌋ plus clicking on tasks.

Copying or Moving the Data in a Column

1. Select the whole column by clicking on its column heading.

2. Click **Copy Cell** 🗐 on the **Standard** toolbar or choose **Edit, Copy**.

3. Select the column in which you want to paste the data.

4. Click **Paste** 🗐 on the **Standard** toolbar to paste the contents.

Make sure the copy-to column can receive data of that type: dates can be copied into date columns, text into text and numbers into number columns. The *Duration* column looks like a number column, but it is a text column, since there are letters in it for the time unit, like *5 days*. You will receive an error message from MS Project if it cannot paste the data.

Copying Between Projects

Copying Tasks or Resources Between Projects

1. Open the project to copy from.

2. Select the tasks or resources by dragging over their ID numbers (the first column with the gray color) to select entire tasks or resources.
    OR

    You can select non-adjacent tasks or resources by holding down ⌊Control⌋ and clicking on the ID-number of tasks or resources.

3. Choose the menu items **Edit, Copy** or click 🗐 on the **Standard** toolbar. The data are now temporarily stored in the clipboard.

4. Open the project to be copied to.

5. Select the row before which to insert the data and choose the menu items **Edit, Paste** or click **Paste** 📋 on the **Standard** toolbar.

Copying Cells Between Projects

 The steps are the same as the previous steps, except that you select cells instead of entire rows. If you do this, you have to be careful to paste the data into a blank area of the sheet; otherwise existing line items may be overridden. Choose **Edit, Undo Entry** or click **Undo Entry** 🔄 on the **Standard** toolbar when an accident occurs.

Copying Objects Between Projects

Objects are views, reports, calendars and other things that change the appearance of the data or affect the scheduling, see also page 57. You copy objects between projects using the *Organizer*.

1. Choose **Tools, Organizer**; the **Organizer** dialog appears:

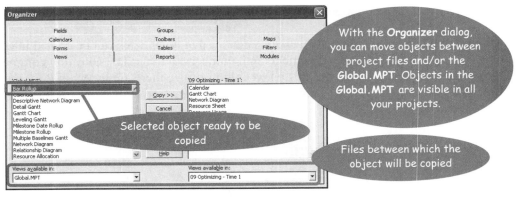

2. Click on the tab of the type of objects to transfer.

3. Select from the lists at the bottom of the dialog the schedule from which to copy the object and in the other list the schedule to copy to.

4. Select the object and click [Copy >>] to copy from left to right or [<< Copy] to copy from right to left.

5. Click [Close] or [Cancel] when done.

The organizer allows you to copy objects to other project schedules or to the *Global.MPT* the global template. Any objects you put into this *global template* are visible in all your projects, unless they have the same name as other objects that are part of the project schedule.

With the organizer you can, for example:

♦ Make your project calendar (tab **Calendars**, object **Standard**) available to other project managers. If you have filled it in for several years into the future, others will be thankful to you.

♦ Create a standard report and make it available to colleagues.

♦ Share views, tables and filters with other people that would like to present similar reports as you do.

Exercises

Review Questions

1. Why is estimating the duration of project activities difficult?

2. Would you estimate the cost of activities and enter these estimates into the task-related field **Cost** in MS Project? If yes, why? If not, how would you get the cost numbers?

3. You are the project manager. When you are working with your team members on estimating the tasks, somebody makes one of the following statements to you. What would you say?

Somebody's statement	Your response
Your team member says: "I can't give you an estimate, because I can't predict the future! I don't possess higher powers."	
Your team member says: "Listen, we went over this already. I am not going to give you any more estimates, because my estimates are always off! My estimates don't help you anyway!"	
Your executive says: "You are one of our most experienced and best project managers. Can't you do this project in three weeks?"	

4. In your own words, what is the difference between *Duration* and *Work*?

5. What formula is working behind the screens of MS Project that relates *Duration* to *Work*?

6. Rank the following time units in terms of difficulty to estimate in for most detail tasks in a typical project and then for your own projects:

Time unit	Difficulty for most projects	Difficulty for your own projects
Business days		
Calendar days		
Person days		

7. What is the difference between a pure work time estimate and a gross work time estimate?

8. Somebody gives you an estimate of 100 person hours of effort for a task and says that the estimate assumes uninterrupted and fully focused work time. You just created a new project schedule that has all options set to the default settings in MS Project.
    a. What other fields or dialog boxes would you have to change in order to get a valid finish date forecast for this task from MS Project?
    b. In which field would you enter this estimate in MS Project?

9. What are two easy ways to change the task type to *Fixed Work* for a series of tasks that you selected in the task list by holding down the [Control] key and clicking?

10. One of your fellow project managers has created a project calendar that has all the national holidays and the company holidays filled in for the next five years. You would like to use that same project calendar for your projects. Explain in detailed steps how you would go about that in MS Project.

Relocation Project — Entering Estimates

Continue to work with your file *Relocation.MPP* or open the file *04 Entering Estimates.MPP* available for download at www.jrosspub.com. Please, click the link *WAV Download Resource Center* to enter the download site.

1. Insert the fields *Type*, *Duration* and *Work* in the Gantt spreadsheet in the order they appear in the column headings of the next table.

2. Check in **Tools, Options,** tab **Schedule** if the time unit for **Work is entered in** is set to **Days**.

3. Enter the data from the table below into the Relocation project file. The tasks with a zero duration will become milestones. Where no data is provided you don't enter anything; MS Project will fill in the default duration of *1 day?* and the default work of *0 days*. Leave these as they are; you cannot blank them out.

ID	Task Name	Type	Duration	Work
1.	REQUIREMENTS	Fixed Duration[45]		
2.	research staff requirements	Fixed Work		2 d
3.	summarize requirements	Fixed Work		2 d
4.	LOCATION	Fixed Duration		
5.	select the realtor	Fixed Duration	4 d	
6.	visit the sites	Fixed Duration	1 d	
7.	evaluate the sites	Fixed Duration	1 d	
8.	meet to select the location	Fixed Duration	1 d	
9.	legal review	Fixed Duration	0.5 d	
10.	location selected	Fixed Duration	0 d	
11.	REMODELING CONTRACT	Fixed Duration		
12.	select the contractor	Fixed Duration	2 d	
13.	meet to discuss contract	Fixed Duration	1 d	
14.	revise the schedule	Fixed Duration	1 d	

---

[45] Notice that you cannot change the **Type** of a summary task; it is set by MS Project to **Fixed Duration**. No **Durations** or **Work** numbers are provided for summary tasks, because these are calculated by MS Project.

ID	Task Name	Type	Duration	Work
15.	negotiate the contract	Fixed Duration	1 d	
16.	contractor contracted	Fixed Duration	0 d	
17.	REMODELED LOCATION	Fixed Duration		
18.	relocate walls	Fixed Work		100 d
19.	install electric wiring	Fixed Work		25 d
20.	paint	Fixed Work		8 d
21.	drying of paint	Fixed Duration	4ed[46]	
22.	install cabinetry	Fixed Work		40 d
23.	install LAN	Fixed Work		60 d
24.	lay carpet	Fixed Work		60 d
25.	facility remodeled	Fixed Duration	0 d	
26.	MOVE	Fixed Duration		
27.	select mover	Fixed Duration	2 d	
28.	Pack	Fixed Duration	2 d	
29.	Move	Fixed Work		20 d
30.	Unpack	Fixed Duration	2 d	
31.	new location opened	Fixed Duration	0 d	

Compare your file with the solution file *05 Entering Dependencies.MPP* available for download at www.jrosspub.com. Please, click the link *WAV Download Resource Center* to enter the download site. See page 675 of this book for an automated way of comparing and reporting differences between two versions of one schedule.

---

[46] Notice the "*e*" in "*4ed*"; this is an elapsed duration that continues through the night and weekend.

Case Study — Escalated Estimates

Mildevices, Inc. is a manufacturer of military products. The company makes navigation and intelligence products. LCD screens and consoles are some of its major products. Mildevices has engineering and manufacturing staff. There is a project control office with 25 project management staff members, and this office reports directly to the Vice President of Operations. The project control staff supports the engineers in delivering the projects.

Upper management typically initiates a new project. One executive becomes the project sponsor and finds an engineer that she will appoint as the project manager. The project manager puts the budget together with his team, and the budget is submitted for approval by the executives.

Executives typically cut the budget proposed by the engineers, because they are concerned with the bottom line of the company. The engineers find that the cuts are applied arbitrarily and often feel they end up with impossibly tight budgets. As a consequence, they start to increase their estimates in order to end up with reasonable budgets. In subsequent projects, the executives react to this in turn by cutting the proposed budgets even more. The new cuts are done in a way that makes even less sense to the engineers. As a result, the project managers now jack up their estimates even further and hide their padding in the estimates wherever they can. At this stage, the openness and the mutual trust are gone between the executives and project managers.

One of the schedulers in the project office, Debbie, says this about these developments: "The numbers the engineers receive back from senior management are so ridiculously low that they just laugh at them." Inevitably, she says, budget overruns take place.

QUESTIONS:

1. In your opinion, is the estimating done in a professional manner at Mildevices?

2. What type of problem is this? Is it predominantly an organizational problem, a cultural problem or a financial problem?

3. If a project manager asked you for advice, what would you recommend to break this escalating spiral?

4. If an executive asked you for advice, what would you recommend to break this escalating spiral?

Chapter 5 Entering Dependencies

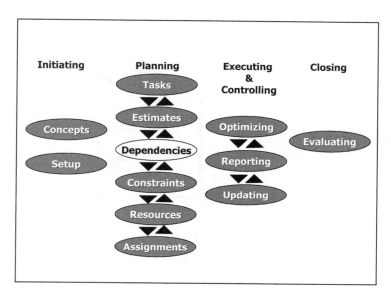

We have the tasks and the estimates entered into our project schedule and are ready to enter the dependencies, as the white highlight shows above. *Dependencies* are relationships between tasks.

After reading this chapter you will:
- know what dependencies are and think of them in terms of cause and effect
- realize how important dependencies are for dynamic schedules
- be able to enter dependencies into an MS Project schedule
- be able to choose the right type of dependencies
- be able to determine if you need a lag or lead on a dependency, expressed in absolute or relative terms
- be able to set multiple predecessors or successors on a task
- know the best practices for the network logic in project schedules
- be able to check if the network logic of a schedule follows the best practices
- be able to format the Network Diagram view in an attractive way

The Beauty of Logic

Bob is working away at his desk when Nob enters his office: "What'ya up to, Bob?" he says.

Bob: "I am creating the schedule for this new project that I got last week. I am trying to figure out the dependencies between the tasks. It always takes me quite a bit of time to find all of them."

Nob: "Yes, as far as I am concerned it takes too much time. I don't bother with linking everything to everything anymore. It is too much work!"

Bob: "At this time in the planning of the project, I am tempted to say that you are right. It is a lot of work and I don't get much benefit from it right now."

Nob: "So why are you always killing yourself on all those dependencies?"

Bob: "I do it, because I have the time to find them during the planning phase!"

Nob: That's not a good reason … if you are looking for some work, just ask; I can keep you very busy!"

Bob: "I was just joking … I spend the time on dependencies, because during the entire project execution phase, I benefit from them … and that is when I don't have time for anything anymore! These dependencies keep my schedule valid and up-to-date. Whenever I enter a change or whenever I update the schedule with actual progress, they adjust the remaining schedule. I set them once when I have the time, and I benefit from them when I don't have time. They allow me to be proactive.…"

Dependencies

The Principle of Dynamic Schedules

A *dynamic schedule* is not just a fashionable term. A schedule is only dynamic if the schedule can easily be kept up-to-date when you are busy during project execution. Think of a schedule as a dynamic model that you continue to work with until the project is over. Ideally, when <u>one</u> thing changes in your real life project, you would have to change only <u>one</u> field in your MS Project model to have *valid* forecasts again. This is the *principle* of *dynamic schedules*. You will only come close to this ideal if your schedule meets the following *requirements*:

◆ You find and enter all the *relationships* between the tasks that may impact your forecasts. These relationships are called "*dependencies*" and are discussed in this chapter.

◆ You minimize the number of *hard dates* in your schedule. Hard dates or *fixed dates* are called *schedule constraints* in MS Project. We will discuss constraints in the next chapter.

Finding the dependencies between the tasks and entering them into your schedule takes a considerable effort. A legitimate question therefore is: *Why is it important to realize this principle of dynamic scheduling as much as you can in your schedules?*

Many changes occur in every project. Every time a change happens, you need to change your schedule to reflect the new reality. If you have a static model, you need to review all future tasks every time and make many changes to their dates. If you have a dynamic model, you don't need to make many changes; ideally only one. If you did an excellent job on dependencies, you probably don't even need to review the future tasks and rely almost blindly on the dependencies to adjust their dates appropriately. Network logic tends to stay the same during the entire project. In other words, *do the logic once well, and your life will be swell.*

Expected Gains from Dynamic Schedules

Let's see if we can approximately quantify how much time you gain with applying the principle of dynamic scheduling and how much time you have to invest to make the model dynamic. Imagine a schedule with 100 tasks. It will take approximately 8 hours of effort to discuss, identify and set all the dependencies and make the model dynamic.

How many changes occur? This is the hard question. We do know for sure that each task needs to be updated at least once, and about 30% of them twice. This already results in 130 changes to the schedule, if you enter them all individually.

Other changes that typically happen in projects are:
◆ Clients change their mind on requirements
◆ Deliverables are dropped, others are added
◆ Activities that were overlooked are inserted
◆ Activities that cannot be done are dropped
◆ Resources get sick or are reassigned
◆ Resources are interrupted with higher priorities

Let's be conservative and say that these things cause 50 more changes, to a total of 180 changes for a 100 task schedule. Entering 180 changes in a dynamic model would take you about 8 hours, since you only need to revise one (or two) fields for each change.

Entering 180 changes in a static model will require you to review the rest of the schedule every time. Therefore, you have to review and adjust on average 50 tasks in a static schedule with every change. If adjusting 50 tasks takes you about 2 hours for each change, the total time spent to keep the schedule alive will be 180 * 2 = 360 hours. Working with a static schedule becomes a fulltime job and does not allow project managers to help their team members any longer.

What you will see in practice therefore is that people who work with static schedules get smart and enter 5 changes at a time and only then review the rest of their schedule. In other words, they update their schedule only 180 / 5 = 36 times instead of 180 times. Notice that the schedule is not all the time up-to-date any longer. Even in this case they will spend at least 36 * 2 = 72 hours on their schedule. The difference in effort spent on a static schedule versus a dynamic schedule is at least: 72 - 16 = 56 hours for a 100 task schedule, which is the gain you can expect from applying the *principle* of *dynamic scheduling*.[47] This is time you will be spending with your family or friends instead of with MS Project.

The expected gains from applying the principle of dynamic scheduling are:

◆ 56 hours of project management time on a 100-task project
You can adjust the averages and calculation for the typical project in your

---

[47] The assumptions and averages shown here are the result of discussions within the team of project managers and instructors at IIL. If you believe the assumptions, averages or calculations are wrong, we would like to hear from you. Please email EricU@iil.com.

organization and multiply the saved hours by the number of projects your organization has, and you will get an idea about the potential for immediate savings.

◆ The number of 56 hours saved for a 100-task schedule does not include how much easier it is to develop scenarios with a dynamic model as opposed to a static model. Every time the project slips, you will have to develop scenarios to find solutions for this; the dynamic model will be much more helpful than a static model.

◆ Another advantage of working with dependencies instead of with dates is that you set dependencies during the *planning phase* of the project when you have time and that you reap the benefits of them during the *execution phase* when you don't have time.

◆ Lastly, a dynamic model can be up-to-date all the time. If you use Project Server as a communication platform, executives can see *real time status* in the projects.

Organizations may need to invest in training and certification to ensure that their project managers apply the principle of dynamic scheduling properly and that people indeed adjust their behavior and habits. In general, certificates motivate individuals to learn seriously and adjust their habits, when needed. That is why we offer an MS Project certification curriculum at IIL.

Hopefully, we have convinced you at this point that finding the dependencies is the way to go.

What Are Dependencies?

A *dependency* is a relationship between the (start or) finish of one task and the start (or finish) of another task. The dependency reflects the cause and effect *relationship*

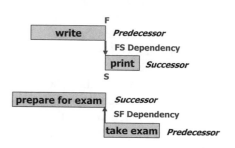

between the two tasks. The result of the first dependency shown in the illustration is that the finish of the independent task *write* (predecessor) drives the start of the dependent task *print* (successor). In other words, when the finish date of *write* changes, the start date of *print* will move with it.

Many people think of dependencies as the *chronological* sequencing of tasks. In the example discussed, the cause and effect relationship indeed happens to match the chronology. If you belong to that category as well, you may get stuck on the concept of dependencies. I once met a project manager with 15 years of experience who was still struggling with the difference between a predecessor and a successor. He thought the predecessor is always the task that is scheduled earlier in time; he held a chronological concept of dependencies. He became confused when he saw that successors are sometimes scheduled earlier than predecessors, like in the second example in the illustration: *prepare for exam* and *take exam*. As a result, he never truly understood the difference between a predecessor and a successor. It is <u>not</u> a matter of chronology!

The words *predecessor* and *successor* are in fact misleading, because they imply chronology. This project manager took the terms too literally.

So, dependencies are not about chronology, but about cause and effect. Think of the predecessor as the independent driving task (driver) and of the successor as the dependent driven task (follower). In order to find the predecessor, the right question to ask is *"Which task drives the other task?"* When you try to identify dependencies with your team members, we suggest you use the terms *driver* and *follower*, instead of *predecessor* and *successor*. You then enter the dependencies into the **Predecessors** and **Successors** fields in MS Project.

The whole network of dependencies is also called the *network logic*. The word "*logic*" provides a much better reference to the cause-and-effect character of dependencies.

Why Should I Use Dependencies?

Most people thought in terms of dates when they scheduled on paper. You may now be used to entering start and finish dates into MS Project. However, it is not necessary to

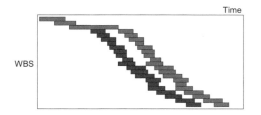

indicate start and end dates when you work with Project 2003. We even strongly recommend <u>not</u> entering start and finish dates, because they create schedule constraints (hard dates). Instead, MS Project only needs to know what the cause and effect is between the tasks. Entering the logic between the tasks is also called *entering dependencies*. In the illustration, you can see that the duration of the third task was extended, and that all the dependent tasks were immediately rescheduled as a result.

The main benefit of making all the dependencies between the tasks explicit is that when the duration or start date of one task changes, Project 2003 can recalculate the entire schedule for you.

If you don't use dependencies, you have to review and redo the future portion of the schedule by hand. This may seem acceptable during the *planning phase* when you still have the time, but it becomes impossible during the execution of the project. During execution, too many things change and they change continuously. I have seen too often that early in the *execution phase* of the project, the Gantt Chart was dumped in a drawer and never looked at again. Too many people abandon their schedule, and this typically happens sometime during project execution. I have even come across companies that have never been able to keep any of their schedules alive during project execution. And it is during project execution that you reap the greatest benefits from your schedule: the continuous forecasts of project end date and final cost. The schedule has to be a dynamic model of your project to gain those benefits, and it is only a dynamic model if it has all the dependencies set. A schedule without dependencies is just a nice chart, a one-time screenshot of your project, and no more than that. These schedules are typically used as wallpaper in work cubicles. Schedules that are not updated during project execution are, in fact, also wallpaper.

Choosing the Options

Tab	Option
Schedule	☑ **Autolink inserted or moved tasks** With Autolink on, MS Project itself will set or break dependencies inside a chain of Finish-to-Start dependencies. It assumes that you want sequential dependencies for the tasks you inserted or moved inside a chain.
	Set as Default Sets the option as the default setting for any new schedules you create. The existing schedules are not affected, because this option is stored in the project schedules, as you can see from the label of the section: **Scheduling Options for <schedule name of the project>**.

To access these options, choose **Tools, Options** and click the tab **Schedule**.

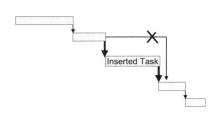

Autolink works inside a chain of sequentially dependent tasks. If you insert a task inside the chain as shown in the illustration, MS Project will immediately incorporate it in the chain of dependencies. It breaks one dependency (the one crossed out) and sets two new ones (the thick black arrows).

If you move a task, it closes the chain by cutting two dependencies and creating one new one, and it incorporates the task in the chain of dependencies (cutting one dependency and creating two new ones) at the destination.

This feature is very helpful during the *planning phase* of the project. However, during the execution of the project, it may be better to turn it off. MS Project makes its own decisions on which dependencies to set or break. To the uninformed scheduler, they may seem arbitrary.

Types of Dependencies

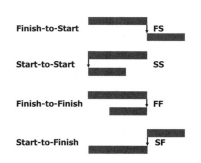

You will be using mostly FS-dependencies that run from the finish (F) of the driver to the start (S) of the follower. The driver task (predecessor) can be linked from its start or from its finish. The follower task can be linked to its start or to its finish. This gives a total of four different possibilities and four types of dependencies. The dependencies are characterized by the following abbreviations: FS, SS, FF and SF as shown in the illustration.

Examples for each type of dependency:

◆ *Finish-to-Start (FS):*
  ◇ The foundation has to be poured before erecting the walls. Similarly, the walls need to be up before the roofing can begin.
  ◇ A report has to be written before it can be printed. If the finish date of the writing slips, the start date of the printing should slip with it. However, the printing of a book cannot easily be rescheduled which is a tough realization for

me while typing these words and trying to meet tight deadlines. In a case like that, we may need constraint dates as well, which we will discuss in the next chapter.

◆ *Start-to-Start* (*SS*):

◇ When you pour concrete, you want it to be leveled right away before it cures. There is an SS link between the tasks *pour concrete* and *level concrete.*

◇ Two days after the carpenters start to break out old drywalls and put up new ones, the electricians can start (SS plus 2 days).

◆ *Finish-to-Finish* (*FF*):

◇ If you train people in how to use a new software application, you would like to have the software installed just as they return to their workstations. There is an FF link between *train users* and *install application.*

◇ After the writing is finished, the editing will be ready in 2 days. (FF plus 2 days).

◇ You conduct a series of workshops and only need 1 day after the end of the last workshop to complete the evaluation report for all courses (FF plus 1 day).

◆ *Start-to-Finish* (*SF*):

◇ The fixed start date of the exam will force the preparation to end, whether you are ready or not.

Absolute Lead or Lag Time

When you want the follower (successor) to wait some time before it starts, you can add a *lag* to a dependency. The lag is expressed in *business days* just like the duration. Lag time acts as if the dependency has a duration, and it always keeps the two task bars apart by the amount of lag time. For example, if you apply for a building permit, you often

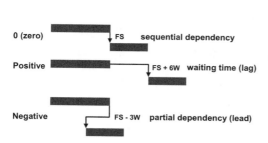

have to wait 6 weeks before you can start construction. This would be an FS dependency with a lag of 6 weeks between the tasks *apply for permit* and *dig the foundation,* as shown in the second example in the illustration.

The beauty of dependencies is that the lag can be negative. A negative lag is called a *lead*, since the start of the successor will be earlier than the finish of the predecessor. In such a *partial dependency*, the follower (successor) is dependent upon the partial completion of its predecessor. As a result, the task bars overlap each other in time. For example, if you write a report, you could finish the entire report before you send it to the editor. You could also send the first half of the report and then write and edit concurrently. This would be an FS dependency between *write report* and *edit report* with a lead of, say, 3 weeks. MS Project only has one field called *Lag*, and you will enter leads as negative lags, so in this case you would enter *FS-3W*.

Note that in the previous illustration lag and lead are shown only on the FS dependency; they can be applied to all other types of dependencies as well.

You can even enter the lag as an elapsed time and MS Project will schedule the follower accordingly. *Elapsed time* is *24 * 7* time and ignores the non-working hours of evenings and weekends. You can enter an *elapsed lag* by entering, for example, "*2ed*" instead of "*2d*" in the **Lag** field. If the driver finishes at the end of Friday, a lag of *2ed* will cause the FS follower to start on Monday (weekend days count as elapsed days), whereas *2d* will make it start on Wednesday (Monday and Tuesday count as business days). For more details on elapsed durations, see page 192.

Relative Lead or Lag Time

You can also express the amount of *lead* or *lag* as a percentage of the duration of the driver task (predecessor), as you can see in the illustration. The follower task bar (successor) takes a relative position to the driver task bar (predecessor). With this feature it is possible to have a successor start halfway through the duration of the predecessor and to keep it at the halfway mark. It will stay at the halfway point even if the duration of the driver task is changed later on!

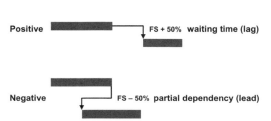

For example, we have two tasks *write report* and *edit report*. After the first half of the report is written, we want to send it to the editor. We need an FS-50% dependency between *write report* and *edit report* in this case (the second example in the illustration).

In the food sector, the shelf life of new food products has to be tested, but these tests are long. Follower tasks, like the marketing of the food product, are often started at 50% of the duration of these shelf-life tests when it starts to look like the shelf life will be good. If the test turns unfavorable later, marketing is stopped before big expenses are made.

In construction projects, the electrical engineering design often starts when the civil engineering design is 60% complete: SS+60% or FS-40%. The lag is relative to the duration of its driver task.

Multiple Predecessors and Successors

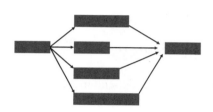

Each task can have more than one predecessor and successor as the illustration shows. This will allow you to schedule several activities concurrently. Tasks that do not have a logical relationship should, in general, be scheduled in parallel. This creates a network of dependencies where some parallel tasks or chains of tasks will take longer than other shorter ones. An example of activities that can take place in parallel is installing systems at several different sites.

Choosing the Right Type of Dependency

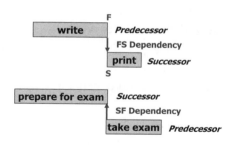

Sometimes when you are creating your project model, you may not be certain about the type of dependency to use. Of the two types used in the illustration, the best one depends on the situation that is modeled. If the situation allows you to postpone the exam when you are not ready preparing for it, the FS dependency is the best. An example is the PMP exam[48] or our IIL online exams[49] which

---

[48] PMP® stands for Project Management Professional, an accreditation by the Project Management Institute (PMI). See www.pmi.org for more information.

[49] Our White, Orange and Blue Belt courses have a one hour online exam associated with 30 multiple-choice questions. If you request extensions timely, your request is normally honored.

can be postponed if you are not ready to take them. If you cannot postpone taking the exam, as is the case for a university exam, the Start-to-Finish is the best one. The moment an exam starts, the preparation will have to stop, as I often experienced when I was in university. I tended to count backwards in preparing for an exam: *What is the latest date I have to start preparing for the exam so that everything will be fresh in my memory?* Of course, there were always unforeseens that haunted me.

You could argue that, when you schedule backward, the SF dependency should be the dependency you use most often. After all, in *backward scheduling*, the finish date drives every task in the project. However, Project 2003 does not change the default dependency to SF when you switch to backward scheduling. In *forward scheduling*, you will use the FS dependency most often, which is the default in MS Project.

Steps for Choosing the Right Type of Dependency

The following seven questions will assist you in choosing the right dependency:

1. *Which task drives the other?* or *What do you need to do this task?*
   To determine which task is the predecessor, ask yourself: "*Which task drives the other?*". People often ask themselves: "*What should be scheduled first or earliest?*" This question asks for the chronology of tasks. Remember, dependencies are not about chronology, but about cause and effect. Another good question to ask is "*What do you need to do this task?*", since people easily come up with things they need completed before they can start.

2. *Does the start or the finish of the predecessor drive the other task?*
   This question helps to find the type of dependency you need, an F or an S dependency.

3. *Does the predecessor drive the start or the finish of the successor?*
   Once you know the answer to this question, you know the type of dependency you need: FS, SS, FF or SF.

4. *Should there be a gap or an overlap between the two tasks?*
   If your answer is *no*, you are ready with this dependency. If the answer is *yes*, you need to continue with the next questions.

5. *Do you need a positive lag or a negative lag (lead)?*
   A positive lag delays the successor in time (farther to the right in the timescale) and creates a gap in an FS-dependency. A negative lag (lead) schedules the successor earlier in time (farther to the left in the timescale) and creates an overlap in an FS-dependency. If negative, you will need to type a "–" (minus) and a number in the **Lag** field.

6. *Is the lag an absolute number of days (weeks), or is the lag relative to the duration of the predecessor?*

  ◇ If absolute, you have an additional question: *Should it be in business days or in elapsed days?*
  If absolute, you enter the number of business days (or weeks) while including the time unit, for example "*5d*" (business days) or "*5ed*" (*elapsed days*).

  ◇ If relative, you enter a percentage in the **Lag** field, like "*50%*" or "*-30%*" (including the percentage sign).

7. *How much should the lag or lead be?*
  At this point you should know the complete dependency definition, for example "*FS+50%*", "*SS+3d*", or "*FF+2ed*".

Often dependencies follow the flow of data, information or deliverables (documents) that are passed on between team members. For example, the detailed design document is passed on from the software architect to the software programmer. So an alternative question you could ask to find the dependencies is: *What does this person need in order to do this activity?[50]* Or better yet, ask the person to identify what she needs from other people to do the task, and you will slowly but surely identify all dependencies from the end of the network to the beginning of it.

Categories of Dependencies

Different situations need different categories of dependencies:
- *Decision point dependencies*
- *Hard and soft dependencies*
- *External dependencies*
- *Resource dependencies*

We will discuss each of these in more detail.

---

[50] See page 50 in the article "*Information Driven Project Management*" in *PM Network*, September 2001, PMI.

Decision Point Dependencies

Decision points are important nodes in the network of dependencies. Decision points are also called "*gates*". If your schedule has decision points, you are using *gate project management* also known as *stage-gate project management*.

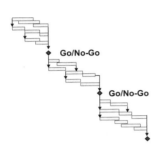

Gates are to dependencies what central stations are to railroads; many tracks are coming together and springing from them, as you can see in the illustration. All the deliverables (reports) that are needed for making the right decision are drivers (predecessors) for the decision point. All activities that rely upon the decision being made are followers of the decision point (dependent successors). What you will see in a schedule with decision points is that several sub networks of dependencies are linked together at the decision points.

Hard and Soft Dependencies

Some tasks have to be done in an absolute sequence, while others have a preferred

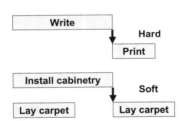

sequence. Hard or mandatory dependencies are dependencies that have an absolute sequence. Common sense dictates creating these hard dependencies. For example, two activities *write* the report and *print* it, require a hard dependency. It does not make sense to schedule the printing in any other way than driven by the finish date of the writing. (If you do find another way to do this, let me know; you will make authors really happy)

Soft or discretionary dependencies are a matter of preference from a practical or personal point of view. For example, the two tasks *installing cabinetry* and *laying the carpet* are not necessarily dependent on each other. The project manager may prefer to set a dependency to make sure that the cabinetmakers do not spill glue that damages the new carpet. However, if you are in a time crunch, you could do both tasks in parallel. You could ask the cabinetmakers to cover the new carpet with plastic and still gain time in your project.

Project 2003 does not have a special feature for creating soft dependencies. If you remember where you created the soft dependencies, it will be easier to optimize the schedule later on. You can document the soft, discretionary dependencies in the **Notes** field; click **Task Notes** 🖾 on the **Standard** toolbar.

External Dependencies

External dependencies are needed when there are impacts from outside your control. You have an *external dependency* when you:

◆ Need to receive goods or materials from a supplier
◆ Require input from another department or project

In general, when you are dependent on an event that is outside of your control, you are dealing with an external dependency.

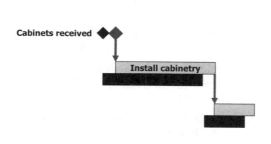

In the illustrated example on the left, you could leave the milestone out when you schedule the external dependency. If you do this and the cabinets arrive late, it would just show as a slipped start date on the task *install cabinetry*. Who will get blamed for the slip in the schedule? The installers would receive the blame. In the case of external dependencies, we recommend you insert an extra milestone for the event in your schedule with a Start No Earlier Than schedule constraint. The constraint will keep the milestone diamond on the date you have agreed to. We will discuss constraints in the next chapter. Then create dependencies from the milestone into your activities.

The advantage is that if the shipment of cabinets arrives late, it is immediately clear that this was beyond your control. If the milestone were omitted, it would look like the installers started working late on their task in an updated schedule, which would reflect badly on your performance as a project manager. It is a simple technique that keeps the fingers pointed at the right people in the case of a slippage or, worse, a contract dispute.

Resource Dependencies

Resource dependencies force tasks to be sequenced, because you will have work overloads if you don't sequence them. A resource dependency occurs when two tasks compete for the same resource. If you cannot find another solution for the overload, one task has to be delayed in order to keep the workload reasonable for the resource. Of course, you could force the sequence by setting an extra *logical dependency* as shown in the illustration, but the two tasks are really independent and could be done in any order. Harry could either read report X or Y first. We don't think you should model resource dependencies by setting extra logical dependencies. What happens if you reassign one of Harry's tasks to Sam? Will you remember to take the logical dependency out again? We added some question marks to the illustration for this reason. You should at least write yourself a reminder in the **Note** field if you hard-code resource dependencies by creating extra logical dependencies.

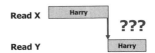

If one of the two tasks is reassigned, the dependency should be removed as well, because it was only created to keep Harry's workload reasonable. It was not created, because of any other logical reason. If you forget to cut the dependency, you end up with a schedule that is suboptimal. Removing soft dependencies is often forgotten. Also, MS Project has special features to keep the workloads leveled and we would invite you to use those features instead. We will discuss them on page 473. In the same chapter, we will also explain how to optimize a schedule with many resource dependencies, see page 512.

Entering Logic

Project 2003 offers a variety of ways to enter dependencies into the schedule. Dependencies can be entered either in the Gantt Chart or in the Network Diagram. In both views, the tools and forms work very similarly. We will discuss:

- Using the *Planning Wizard*
- Using the *Link tool*
- Using the mouse
- Using the *Task Information* dialog
- Using the *Task Form*

We will now discuss these different ways in more detail starting with the Gantt Chart view.

Entering Dependencies in the Gantt Chart

Using the Planning Wizard

Before we list the steps, let us make sure the Planning Wizard is still on. Check **Tools, Options**, tab **General**, ☑ **Advice from the Planning Wizard**. Check the sub checkboxes as well.

2002 The Planning Wizard will remind you to implement the principle of *dynamic scheduling*, since it will prompt you if you want to link tasks when:

- You enter a start date into the field **Start** that immediately follows the finish date of a nearby task above or below, or
- You drag a task bar after the task bar of a nearby task above or below. This can be a very quick method and we will explain it in more detail.

The steps for dragging task bars are:

Point to the middle of the task bar; make sure you see a four-headed arrow: ✥.

1. Click and hold down to drag the bar *horizontally* to where you want it scheduled. Make sure you see a horizontal two-headed arrow:  .

2. Look at the yellow pop-up window to see what the new dates will be:

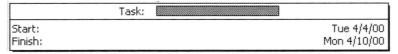

3. Release the mouse when the task bar is scheduled on the date you want, but this should be near the end of another nearby task bar that is above or below it. The following dialog will appear:

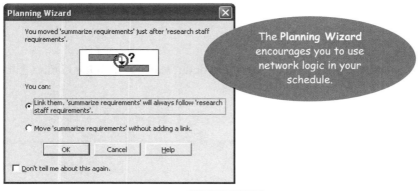

The **Planning Wizard** encourages you to use network logic in your schedule.

4. Select ⦿ **Link them** and click [OK].

Using the Link Tool

With the link tool you can create a waterfall of multiple dependencies with one click after selecting the tasks.

To Set a Dependency

1. Select adjacent tasks by dragging over their task names. You can select more than just two tasks.
   OR

   If the tasks are not adjacent, select the driver (predecessor) first, hold down [Control] and click on the follower (successor). You can click on the task name in the spreadsheet or on its task bar in the timescale. You can click on as many tasks as you want to link. The only thing to remember is that you select the tasks in the order in which you want the tasks to be linked (from driver to follower), even if the driver is lower in the list. Let go of the [Control] key when you have them all selected.

2. Click **Link Tasks** 🔗 on the **Standard** toolbar OR hold down ⌊Control⌋ and press ⌊F2⌋; the tasks are now Finish-to-Start dependent.

This method allows you to set *Finish-to-Start* dependencies only.

To Delete a Chain of Dependencies Between Tasks

1. If the tasks are adjacent, select all predecessors and successors by dragging over their task names.
    OR

    If the tasks are not adjacent, select the predecessor first and then hold down ⌊Control⌋ and click the successor. You can click on the task name or on the task bar, and you can click on more than two tasks that you want unlinked.

2. Click **Unlink Tasks** 🔗 on the **Standard** toolbar or hold down ⌊Control⌋ + ⌊Shift⌋ and press ⌊F2⌋.

To Delete All Dependencies on one Task

Select the task and click **Unlink Tasks** 🔗 on the **Standard** toolbar.

You can easily delete all dependencies in the entire schedule if you select all tasks first by clicking on any column heading and then click **Unlink Tasks** 🔗 on the **Standard** toolbar. Be careful with this, because it can wreck many hours of work in a large schedule faster than you can blink your eye.

Using the Mouse

This method is useful if you have many dependencies pointing up instead of down and also when you want to create parallel paths.

To Draw Dependencies

1. If necessary, click *Zoom In* 🔍 on the **Standard** toolbar to make the task bars wider/longer. This method is easier if the task bars are wide enough.

2. Point to the center of the predecessor task bar; make sure you see a four-headed arrow mouse pointer like ✥ . (Near the front of the task bar you will see another mouse pointer: ％▸ and near the back: ▸ .)

3. Click and hold down and drag vertically toward the successor task bar making sure the mouse pointer now looks like . Notice the yellow feedback pop-up window that tells you between which two tasks you are about to set a Finish-to-Start dependency:

Finish-to-Start Link	
From Finish Of:	Task 5
To Start Of:	Task 6

 If you drag horizontally, you are rescheduling the task bar and you are setting a schedule constraint that will make your schedule static instead of dynamic!

4. Release the mouse button inside the task bar of the successor. A dependency is set and shows up as an arrow. The task bar of the successor moves out to just after the finish date of the predecessor's task bar. A *Finish-to-Start* dependency is set:

 If you drag into the edge of the screen, the screen starts scrolling very fast in the Gantt Chart. It launches like a missile. Microsoft needs to slow it down a bit.

This method of setting dependencies allows you to set FS dependencies only, but you can change to another type of dependency with the next steps.

To Edit or Delete the Dependency

1. Point with the tip of the arrow mouse pointer precisely to the dependency arrow you want to change, as in the next screenshot:

2. Dependency arrows can overlap each other, so wait one second until the yellow feedback window pops up to confirm which dependency you are on.

Task Link: Finish-to-Start (FS)	Lag: 0d
From: (ID 5) write	
To: (ID 6) print	

3. If you have the proper dependency arrow selected, double-click and the **Task Dependency** dialog appears:

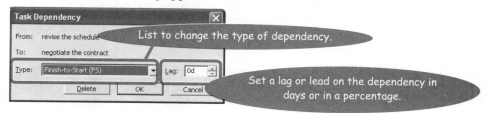

4. Select the type of dependency using the list **Type** Finish-to-Start (FS)
AND
Enter a positive *lag* or a negative lag (*lead*) time, if needed. You can also enter a percentage in the **Lag** field. The percentage will be taken from the duration of the predecessor task and treated as lag time.
OR
Click Delete to get rid of the dependency.

Using the Task Information Dialog

You may need this method if the predecessor and successor are a screen or more apart.

1. Select the successor task.

2. Click **Task Information** on the **Standard** toolbar or hold down Shift and press F2 ; the **Task Information** dialog appears.

3. Click the **Predecessors** tab; the dialog should now look like:

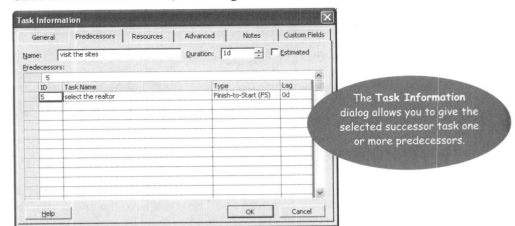

The **Task Information** dialog allows you to give the selected successor task one or more predecessors.

4. Click in the **Task Name** field in an empty row and select the predecessor task from the list. [▼].
    OR
    Enter the ID number of the predecessor in the **ID** field.

5. Select the type of dependency in the **Type** field.

6. Enter a (negative or positive) lag in the **Lag** field. You can also enter a percentage in the **Lag** field. The percentage will be taken from the duration of the predecessor task and then treated as the lag time.

7. Click [OK] and the dependencies are entered into the schedule.

This method is interesting if you want to give one task multiple predecessors. Unfortunately, the dialog does not have a successors tab to set successors on it at the same time. The next method allows you to set multiple predecessors and successors on a task at the same time.

Using the Task Form

1. In the Gantt Chart display the **Task Form** by choosing **Window, Split**; the **Task Form** appears in the bottom of the screen.

2. Click on the **Task Form** and choose **Format, Details, Predecessors & Successors** to view all dependencies of the selected task. Your screen should now look like:

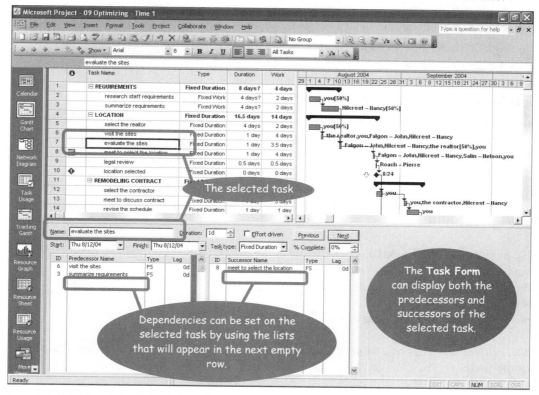

3. Click in the field **Predecessor Name** or **Successor Name** in an empty row and use the list [▼] to create the dependency.
   OR
   Type the ID number of the predecessor or successor task in the **ID** field.

4. Set the type of dependency in the **Type** field and add a positive *lag* or negative lag (*lead*) in the **Lag** field, if necessary. You can also enter a percentage in the **Lag** field. The percentage will be taken from the duration of the predecessor and treated as lag time.

5. Click [OK   ]; the data are entered into the project database only after this button is clicked.

The **Task Form** allows you to set many dependencies on a task at the same time. You can also set predecessors and successors on it all at once. The Task Form allows you to see exactly how dependencies run as well. The arrows in the Gantt timescale can run on top of one another and the Task Form can show you exactly how they run.

To delete a dependency on the Task Form, select the task name, and when it is highlighted press the [Delete] key on your keyboard. Then click [OK] to enter this into the database.

Entering Dependencies in the Network Diagram

The Network Diagram

To apply the view, choose **View, Network Diagram**. The Network Diagram can display an overview of all the dependencies you have set; the dependencies are depicted as arrows.

By default, the **Network Diagram** displays the different types of tasks in differently shaped nodes:
- Summary tasks in a parallelogram
- Detail tasks in a rectangle
- Milestones in a hexagon

The critical tasks have a red border instead of the (default) blue. The color and the shape of the nodes can be changed by choosing **Format, Box Styles** (see page 257).

To navigate through the Network Diagram, the **Network Diagram** toolbar is handy.

Displaying the Network Diagram Toolbar

1. Right-click on any toolbar and the pop-up menu appears with all available toolbars.
   OR
   Choose **View, Toolbars**.

2. Choose **Network Diagram** and the following toolbar is displayed:

This toolbar makes many useful features directly accessible. Tools we recommend are:

◆ 🔧 **Show Link Labels / Hide Link Labels** to display or hide little labels on the dependencies that reveal the type of the *dependency* and the *lag*, if any.

◆ 🖼 **Hide Fields** to display just the ID number for each task in a very small node.

Gaining an Overview of the Network

The problem is that even large screens cannot display large networks in their entirety. In the past networks like these would be printed on plotters and hung like wallpaper in rooms. However, the point of this book is that we don't want to live in the paper age any longer, and we have to find a way to see the entire network while keeping the task details legible:

◆ If you have the window split, remove the split window. Choose **Window, Remove Split** or point to the divider between the top and bottom view and double-click when you see the mouse pointer ⬍.

◆ You can also get more task nodes by using **Zoom Out** 🔍 on the **Standard** toolbar. However, the text becomes illegible when zoomed out too far. To zoom back in, click **Zoom In** 🔍 on the **Standard** toolbar. If you point the mouse pointer to a task node, a pop-up window appears that allows you to read the task data. The screen tip that pops up looks like this:

print	
Start: Thu 4/6/00	ID: 6
Finish: Fri 4/7/00	Dur: 2 days
Res:	

◆ Hide all the fields except the ID number in all nodes of the network:
    Click **Hide Fields** 🖼 on the **Network Diagram** toolbar.
    OR
    Choose **Format, Layout...**, and check ☑ **Hide all fields except ID**.
    OR
    Right-click and choose **Hide Fields** from the pop-up menu.
    You can now see many more nodes on your screen to get an overview of the entire network. The ID number may seem like too little information, but if you hover your mouse pointer over a node, a pop-up window will display the rest of the fields and values so that you can orient yourself in the big network.
    To read and analyze one part of the network, you can zoom back into the detail by selecting the node to view in detail and clicking **Hide Fields** again. MS Project always keeps the selected task on the screen when toggling between hiding and

redisplaying the fields. Toggling back and forth is perhaps the easiest way to analyze the network and this button allows you to do this.

◆   Get rid of all the fields in a task node except the task name. Removing the other fields makes the node a lot smaller. See the steps on page 254. If your network has up to about 50 tasks, this would be a good way to gain the overview. Also, when you use the **Hide Fields** feature, you will see many more nodes.

Using the Mouse to Set Dependencies

Once you have gained the overview and start to identify places where you are missing important links, you can create them right here in the Network Diagram.

1.   Point to the center of the predecessor node and make sure the mouse pointer is a plus sign: ✛.

2.   Click and hold down the primary mouse button, and drag towards the node of the successor; the mouse pointer should change into a ⊕. Even if the node is not visible, you can drag against the side of the screen, which will then start scrolling automatically. Unlike in the Gantt Chart, the screen does not scroll too fast in the Network Diagram.

3.   Release the mouse button in the center of the successor node; an arrow appears and the dependency is now set.

This method allows you to set FS dependencies only, but you can easily change the type by double-clicking on a dependency arrow, see page 241.

If you release the mouse button outside of the successor node, a new task is created! For those who like to build the task list and the network at the same time, this is a great feature. If this happens inadvertently, press [Del] right away, while the new task is still selected, to get rid of it.

Using the Link Tool to Set Dependencies

When you use the **Link** tool, you have to select the tasks in the order in which you want to link them. In other words, you select the predecessor first, then its successor, then the successor of the successor, etc.

1.   Hold down [Control] and click on all tasks to link.
     OR
     You can select multiple tasks quickly by dragging a box around them. As soon as

you hold down the mouse, the mouse pointer will change to a **+** . When you drag, you are drawing a box with a gray border. Any tasks that you enclose in the box will be selected upon releasing the mouse button. You can even select another set of tasks by holding down `Control` before you drag again.

2. Click **Link Tasks** 🔗 on the **Standard** toolbar to link the tasks.

 As in the Gantt Chart, you can also set dependencies in the Network Diagram using the **Task Information** dialog or the **Task Form**. The steps are the same as for the Gantt Chart (please refer to pages 235 and 236, respectively).

To Edit or Delete a Dependency in the Network Diagram

1. Point with the tip of the mouse pointer to the dependency arrow you want to delete. This should look like this:

2. Double-click and the **Task Dependency** dialog appears:

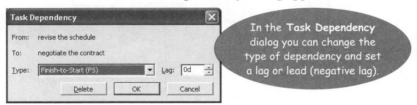

3. Change the **Type** of the dependency using the list `Finish-to-Start (FS)` ▼
AND
set a **Lag** time, if needed. The *Lag* can be negative which creates an overlap (*lead*) or positive which creates a gap. You can also enter a percentage in the **Lag** field. The percentage will be taken from the duration of the predecessor task and then treated as the lag time. The percentage can be negative or positive.

 4. Note that you can also get rid of the dependency, by clicking `Delete` . When you delete a dependency arrow, all dependent tasks are rescheduled to their As Soon As Possible date under forward scheduling. They may zip all the way to the project start date and disappear from your screen. We recommend you create the new dependency first and then delete the old dependency to prevent nodes from disappearing from your screen.

Following Down the Paths in the Network

The Network Diagram has an invisible grid, like a spreadsheet. When you press the arrow keys to move the cursor, they will only take you to the visible "cells" in the grid, the task nodes. If you leave the layout challenge to MS project, it uses this invisible grid:

1. If you have automatic repositioning on, the nodes are rearranged with every change you make. It will be very difficult to check the logic in the network when the nodes keep jumping all over the place. We recommend turning it off by choosing **Format, Layout...**; the **Layout** dialog appears:

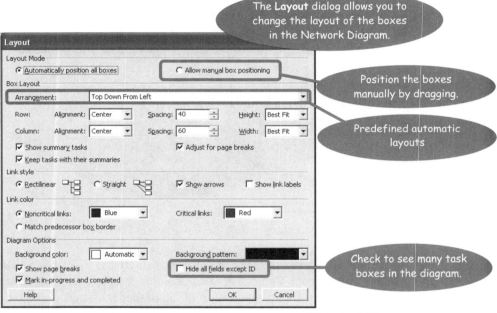

2. Select ⦿ **Allow manual box positioning** and click ⟨ OK ⟩.

3. To see if the logic of the dependencies makes sense, use the arrow keys to follow a chain of dependencies. Click on the first task node in a chain and press → to follow the chain forward. When there is a split, you press → once more to move into one path, and then you can switch between the chains by pressing ↓ or ↑
   OR
   press ← to go backward and press ↓ or ↑ to switch chains.

4. Use the methods discussed before to delete, add or modify dependencies, if necessary.

To find all the successors of a particular task quickly, hold down [Shift] and click a task node and all its successors will be highlighted. If you then choose **Window, Split**, and display the Gantt Chart in the bottom view, you will see the entire chain, which makes checking the logic even easier.

Logic on Summary Tasks

What are the advantages and disadvantages of setting dependencies on summary tasks?

Advantages of summary dependencies

◆ Setting dependencies on summary tasks seems easier and quicker.
◆ Summary logic is high-level logic that executives sometimes like to see.
◆ In certain situations, you can make do with one summary dependency instead of setting several dependencies on detail tasks. When detail tasks all start at the same time independently of each other, one dependency on their summary task makes sense. In the next screenshot, tasks 19 to 21 are all driven by the dependency on their summary task, 18.

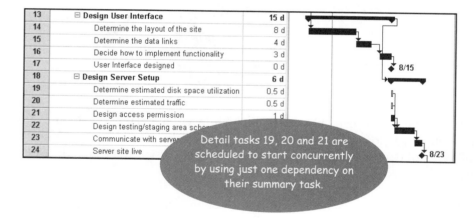

Detail tasks 19, 20 and 21 are scheduled to start concurrently by using just one dependency on their summary task.

Disadvantages of summary dependencies

◆ It is too difficult to check if the network of dependencies is complete. The check is simple if you only have dependencies between detail tasks; you just have to find the detail tasks and milestones without an entry in the predecessor or successor field. If you have logic both on summary tasks and detail tasks in parallel, you cannot perform this simple check any longer. Checking the logic then becomes a very painstaking and laborious process. Yes, I have been there, done that and will not likely do it ever again!

◆ The *Critical Path* is more difficult to find when the dependencies run over detail tasks and summary tasks in parallel. When you follow the Critical Path, a critical detail task may not have any successor. It looks like the Critical Path stops, and you may not realize that the Critical Path continues through a dependency on the summary task. (For a discussion on the Critical Path see page 427.) In the next screenshot, task 17 appears to be the end of the Critical Path, but really continues via the summary dependency to task 21:

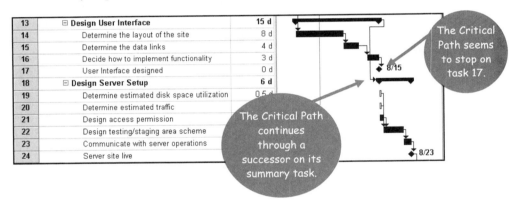

◆ On summary tasks, you can only set rough, high-level logic. High-level logic often does not allow you to create the tightest schedule possible.

◆ Not all types of dependencies can be used on summary tasks; you cannot link FF or SF to summary tasks.

 Even though there seem to be some advantages to setting dependencies on summary tasks, they don't measure up against the disadvantages. Time gained with setting fewer dependencies is lost threefold when checking the logic and analyzing the Critical Path. We therefore recommend that you keep the logic on detail tasks and milestones only.

Checks on Dependencies

We discussed the techniques to enter dependencies. All the dependencies together are called the *network* or the *logic*, sometimes the *network logic*. Now you need to check the network to determine if it will indeed give you the benefit that you created it for in the first place. This benefit was that if you change one field in the schedule, the rest of the schedule is updated automatically, so that you immediately have a *valid* schedule of your project again. We called this the *principle of dynamic schedules*.

The schedule will update itself only if the answers to the following questions are all *yes*:

◆ Is the network of dependencies complete?
  We will discuss this in more detail on page 246.
◆ Is the network logic simple enough?
  We will discuss this in more detail on page 251.
◆ Are there no circular dependencies?
  There should be none, because a schedule with circular dependencies will not be dynamic, but entirely static. MS Project cannot recalculate the schedule any longer as soon as a circular dependency is created. How could it schedule two tasks where A drives B, but B also drives A? The application will warn you if you try to create circularity in the logic within a single schedule. When you set dependencies across schedules, circular dependencies can still easily occur. They will manifest themselves in the master schedule that contains the subschedules. We are venturing out into multiple project management, which is discussed in detail in the Blue Belt course.[51]
◆ Does the logic of the network make sense?
  The schedule is now entirely driven by dependencies. After all the previous checks are done, you should perform one more high level check to see if the resulting schedule actually makes sense. You can check this best by showing only the first outline levels of the Work Breakdown Structure and checking if the timing of the deliverables (or phases) makes sense on this high level. You can use the Show ▾ button on the **Formatting** toolbar to display **Outline level 2** or **Outline level 3** depending on the size of your project. Even though you may not be an expert in the field of this project, you can always pick up on common sense things like *design* scheduled before *construction*, *write* before *print*, etc. Realize that if you followed our recommendations and minimized the number of constraints and set all dependencies, the start and finish dates of the tasks are entirely driven by the

---

[51] Visit www.iil.com and follow the link *Microsoft Project* for more information.

network of dependencies. If the resulting schedule does not make sense, you probably overlooked an essential dependency.

In the next screenshot it looks like the *move* starts too early, perhaps because of a *missing dependency* in a schedule where all tasks are scheduled *As Soon As Possible* (*ASAP*). However, if you expanded the *move* summary task it would become clear that the actual move takes place in the week of November 7 and all the essential logic seems to be there:

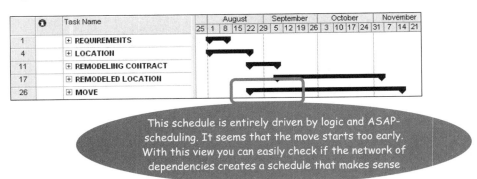

This schedule is entirely driven by logic and ASAP-scheduling. It seems that the move starts too early. With this view you can easily check if the network of dependencies creates a schedule that makes sense

We will now elaborate further on the first two questions to check the network logic.

Is the Network of Dependencies Complete?

The network is complete if the task bars of all detail tasks and milestones are tied up at both ends. The network can have multiple starting points, but only one ending point. Only with one ending point in the network can the Critical Path calculation be correct in a single project. The Critical Path is the most widely used technique to manage the time dimension of a project. We will explain it in more detail in Chapter 9 on optimizing.

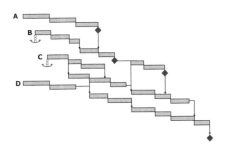

A typical network will look like the illustration. Unlike other authors, we do not require the network to start with just one starting point. We find that this makes the network unnecessarily complex and that it does not provide additional benefits. When you have multiple starting points, the thing to check is if these detail tasks (A, B, C and D in the illustration) have a missing predecessor. If they don't have a logical predecessor, you need to determine if they can indeed start on the project start date or if they need a Start No Earlier Than constraint (under forward scheduling). You can see that A and D start at the project start date, but B and C have a constraint (anchor), since they start later. B and C do not have a driver (predecessor) and may need one. In the over 1,000 schedules we evaluated in our certification curriculum, we found in about 50% that there were starting points in the network that should have had a predecessor. So, you always have to check on the starting points carefully.

Why a Complete Network Is Important

There are two reasons why you should complete the network logic in your schedule:

◆ If you forget to set dependencies, the schedule will not update itself properly when you make a change to it. The schedule is not a dynamic schedule. Having a dynamic schedule is very important during the *execution phase* of the project. When you enter actual progress, you want the rest of the schedule to update itself automatically so that you immediately have a *valid* model of the project again. You need the schedule to update itself every time you enter the status of the project. Project managers who do not carefully check the logic of their schedule during the planning phase typically abandon their schedule sometime during project execution. They have to spend too much time keeping the schedule valid. They have to check their entire schedule every time they enter actual progress. They soon find that they don't have enough time to do this at every status cycle. See page 217 for how much time you might save with complete logic in your schedule.

◆ With an incomplete network you will most likely not have a meaningful *Critical Path*. Or worse, MS Project might lead you to think that tasks are critical that really aren't critical at all and get you to monitor the wrong tasks closely. Project managers also need to see their critical tasks, because they harbor possibilities for shortening the project and bringing it in on time. For more on the *Critical Path Method,* see page 428. In over 1,000 schedules we evaluated in our certification curriculum, we found that in about 50% of them, the project manager had not identified the real critical path.

Checks to Perform on the Completeness of the Network

To check if the network is complete, ask yourself the following questions:

◆ Is the logic set only on detail tasks and milestones?
If dependencies run over summary tasks and detail tasks in parallel, it is too hard to check if the network is complete. It is also too hard to trace the Critical Path and understand it. Only with a complete network will the schedule be a fully dynamic model of the project. Therefore, we recommend that you keep the logic on the detail

tasks and milestones only. You can check if there are dependencies on summary tasks by applying the filter **04 IIL Summary Tasks with Dependencies**.[52] We discussed this point in more detail on page 243.

◆ Are all the starts of the detail tasks linked to at least one other task or milestone? Exceptions are:
  ◇ All tasks that can start when the project starts or that are driven by external forces or deliveries rather than by hand-offs within the project.
  ◇ External delivery milestones with a **Start No Earlier Than** constraint date. (see page 229)
  ◇ Recurring tasks (see page 154)
  ◇ Overhead tasks (see page 156)

You can verify if all starts are linked by applying the filter **05 IIL Detail Tasks without Predecessors**.[53] Note that if the project manager used SS or FF dependencies, the filter is not conclusive. There will be another check on those.
OR
Display the **AutoFilter** buttons by clicking ▼= on the **Format** toolbar. In the **Predecessors** column heading, click the button ▼ and choose the blank item in the list. Now all tasks without an entry in the predecessor field will be displayed, including summary tasks (this is where the IIL filter is better). Notice that the column heading title appears in blue to remind you that an *AutoFilter* is in effect.

◆ Are all the ends of the detail tasks linked to at least one other task or milestone? Exceptions are:
  ◇ The project end milestone
  ◇ Recurring tasks, see page 154.
  ◇ Overhead tasks, see page 156.

A *loose end*, *hanger* or *dangling task* is a detail task that does not have its finish tied to any other task. In any project there should only be one loose end, the project finish milestone (ignoring the summary, recurring and overhead tasks).

---

[52] This filter can be found in the file *IIL Project 2003 tools to check Orange Belt schedules.MPP* available for download at www.jrosspub.com. Please, click the link *WAV Download Resource Center* to enter the download site.

[53] This filter can be found in the file *IIL Project 2003 tools to check Orange Belt schedules.MPP* available for download at www.jrosspub.com. Please, click the link *WAV Download Resource Center* to enter the download site.

You can verify if all ends are linked up by applying the filter
06 IIL Detail Tasks without Successors.[54] Note that if the project manager used
SS or FF dependencies, the filter is not conclusive. There will be another check on
those.
OR

Display the **AutoFilter** buttons by clicking on the **Format** toolbar. In the
Successors column heading, click the button and choose the blank item in the
list. Now all tasks without an entry in the successor field will be displayed, including
summary tasks (this is where the IIL filter is better). Notice that the column label
appears in blue to remind you that an AutoFilter is in effect.

◆ Do you have SS and FF dependencies properly linked up?
Project managers often forget to give every task a successor when they use SS or
FF dependencies:

People often forget to set a dependency on the
finish of the predecessor in an SS dependency
(see the question marks in the illustration at
the left). The finish must also be linked;
otherwise the predecessor in an
SS dependency could still continue even
though the project is already finished, since
you have not linked it to anything. If you just
checked that each detail task has a successor,
you will not find these loose ends. In the
illustration *pour concrete* has an SS successor,
but its finish is not tied to any other task.

---

[54] This filter can be found in the file *IIL Project 2003 tools to check Orange Belt schedules.MPP*
available for download at www.jrosspub.com. Please, click the link *WAV Download Resource
Center* to enter the download site.

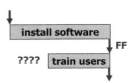

People also often forget to set a dependency on the start of the successor in an FF dependency (see the question marks in the illustration at the left). The task *train users* has an FF predecessor, but its start is not linked to any other task which means that you don't need to find a trainer or create course material for the task *train users*, which is just hard to believe. You are probably missing a link. Alternatively, the start date can be held in place by a schedule constraint.

Again, if you just checked that each detail task has a successor, you will not find these loose ends. If you used SS or FF dependencies in your schedule, you should filter and display all those tasks with SS and FF dependencies and check on loose ends manually. You can do this check by applying the filter **07 IIL Detail Tasks with SS or FF**.[55] Since the filter will display both the predecessor and successor involved in the SS or FF dependency, you can check if they are hooked up properly to other tasks by revealing the **Predecessors** and **Successors** fields. What you should look for is:

◇ Does a task with SS in the **Successor** field also have an FS or FF successor that ties up its end?

◇ Does a task with FF in the **Predecessor** field also have an SS or FS predecessor that ties up its start?

If the answer to either question is *no*, you have found a missing link.

◆ Are there tasks with an unreasonably large amount of *Total Slack*?
You can check this by doing a descending sort on **Total Slack** by choosing **Project**, **Sort, Sort by...** and selecting **Total Slack** from the **Sort by** list. Check if the tasks with most slack were expected to have a lot of slack. If not, you have found missing logic.[56] Even after you have given all detail tasks a successor, you should still apply this check, because even if each task has a successor, it does not guarantee that you haven't forgotten important links. Checking the **Total Slack** will actually lead you

---

[55] This filter can be found in the file *IIL Project 2003 tools to check Orange Belt schedules.MPP* available for download at www.jrosspub.com. Please, click the link *WAV Download Resource Center* to enter the download site.

[56] This check was contributed by Frank Walker, TWG Project Management, LLC.

to where you forgot to set important dependencies in your model of the project. This check is very effective in catching missing logic in schedules. Remember that if you miss just one essential dependency, your critical path is wrong, your forecasts are not *valid* and your model is not *dynamic*.

◆ When a change is entered into the schedule, does it update the rest of the schedule automatically and appropriately through dependencies?
Is the entire schedule still *valid*? Where the schedule is not valid, an essential dependency might be missing. If you have to check the entire schedule after each change, you don't have a dynamic model. Remember, the logic should be helpful especially during project execution when you update your schedule regularly.

Exceptions to the Rule of a Complete Network

Certain tasks do not need links:
◆ *Summary tasks,* see page 243 for why.
◆ *Recurring detail tasks,* like status meetings
◆ *Overhead tasks*, like *project management* or *quality control*. These are also known as *hammock tasks*, because their start and end dates are really driven by or "hung up on" other tasks.

All other detail tasks and milestones need to have at least one successor. If you cannot find logical links to other detail tasks in your schedule, you should create a link to the project end milestone. If you don't have a project end milestone, you should create one even if this only serves the purpose of hooking up all your loose ends. Certain tasks can only be linked to the project end milestone. Examples are:
◆ Tasks to inform other departments or organizations (FYI tasks)[57]
◆ Tasks that create entirely independent parts of a system, which can easily and quickly be assembled without much effort. If it will take effort, you should definitely consider creating a detail task for assembling the final product.

Is the Network Logic Simple Enough?

A network that is too complex to understand and maintain is not helpful in managing the project. Redundant dependencies clutter the view unnecessarily. They make the network overly complicated. If the network is complicated, team members will not try to understand or use it. Thus, the value of the network of dependencies decreases.

---

[57] FYI = For Your Information

Many project managers fall prey to the following fallacy: *All tasks are related to each other, and I have to set dependencies everywhere I notice relationships*. Yes, indeed all tasks are related to each other (that is how you arrive at a complete network of dependencies eventually). Most tasks, however, are only related <u>indirectly</u> to each other, i.e. via other tasks. You only have to link the tasks that have a *direct relationship*.

The following questions will help you determine if the network is simple enough:

◆ Are there dependencies that leapfrog each other? Dependencies that skip over the back of multiple dependencies within a chain are redundant. These are the indirect relationships. Remove them.

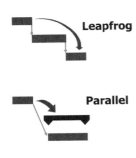

◆ Are there dependencies that run in parallel on detail tasks and their summary tasks? If that is the case, keep the detail task dependency and remove the parallel dependency on the summary task. See page 243 for why logic should be kept to the detail level.

◆ Can you, as the project manager, explain the network to your project team? If you cannot explain it, the network is too complex. If you can explain the network, you can immediately show a team member who else will be affected if their task slips. This is a very powerful method to motivate team members to deliver on time and to facilitate coordination within your team.
A clear network also allows you to do a quick impact analysis of suggestions made by executives. Imagine that your project sponsor of a software development project comes to you during the *execution phase* and asks: *What if we wait for the new release of this operating system?* or *What if we use this new line of more powerful computers?* With a simple network, you will be able to indicate the impacts very clearly by following the dependency arrows from the components that will be affected by such a change in direction. You may be able to stem some unwanted turbulence, or immediately negotiate for more time or money.

Limitations of Dependencies

There are some technical limitations when creating dependencies:

◆ **You can set only one link between two tasks**

It is impossible to set more than one link between two tasks. You will receive the following error message:

◆ Therefore you cannot hook up both the start and the finish of two tasks using an SS as well as an FF dependency. For example, you may have set an SS dependency between *relocate the drywall* and *wire the electricity*. If relocating the walls takes longer than planned, your model may show that the electricians finish earlier than the carpenters, which is unreasonable. If you could set an FF dependency between the same tasks, the problem would be solved. What you can do, though, is insert an extra milestone and run two FF dependencies to and from that milestone. This is a workaround for this limitation.

◆ **You cannot set links on all parts of a split task bar**

You cannot set dependencies on all parts of a split task bar; you can only link to the start of the first part and from the finish of the last part. Therefore you cannot create very dynamic models with split task bars. This is the reason why we don't recommend the use of split task bars when you are planning the project; you will see enough splits appear when you update during project execution.

◆ **You cannot link to the finish of a summary task**

You cannot set an FF or SF dependency to a summary task as the successor, because the finish date of a summary task is always calculated. However, you can link <u>from</u> the finish of the summary task. Remember that we don't recommend logic on summary tasks, see page 243, so this limitation should not bother you at all.

◆ **Percentage lags only apply to the duration of the predecessor task**

You cannot set a *lag* that takes a percentage of the duration of the successor task; the percentages are always taken from the duration of the predecessor. So you cannot create a dependency that drives, for example, the halfway point of a successor.

Printing the Network Diagram

Printing the Network Diagram can be helpful in communicating the flow of the logic to team members and other stakeholders. Prior to printing, you can change the appearance of the view to suit your needs.

 The Project Guide toolbar has a new link on the **Report** side pane, called **Print current view as a report**. Since this wizard is easy on your intuition, I will not elaborate on it further, other than by saying: try it out! Next we will discuss some things that this wizard does not address.

The Layout of the Nodes

You can customize which fields are shown, the border of the nodes and the font.

Displaying Just the Task Name in Each Node

Change the layout of the fields on the task nodes in such a way that only task names will show. This will allow you to see many more nodes within one screen.

1. Choose the menu items **Format, Box Styles** and the **Box Styles** dialog appears:

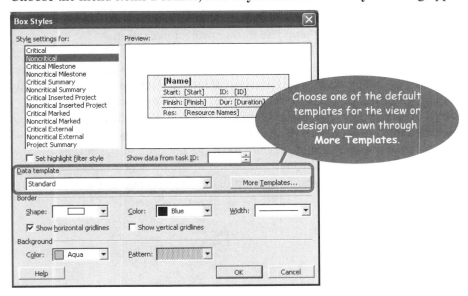

2. Click [More Templates...], and the **Data Templates** dialog opens:

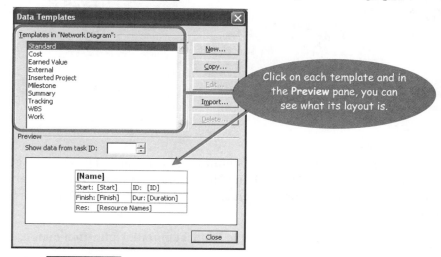

Click on each template and in the **Preview** pane, you can see what its layout is.

3. Click [New...], and the **Data Template Definition** dialog opens:

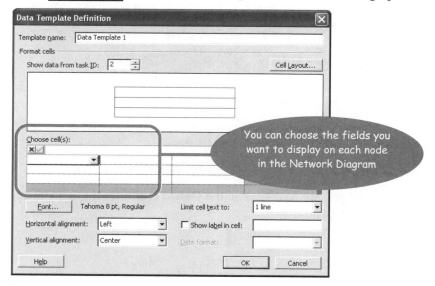

You can choose the fields you want to display on each node in the Network Diagram

4. Enter a name for this template in the field **Template Name**, for example *Task Names Only*.

5. Click | Cell Layout... |, and the **Cell Layout** dialog opens:

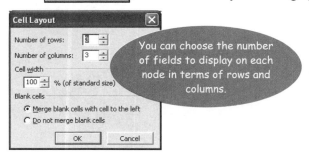

6. Set the **Number of rows** and **Number of columns**. If you want a layout with task names only, select **Number of Rows: 1** and **Number of Columns: 1.** If you have long task names, set the **Cell width** percentage to greater than 100%. All nodes will have the same width.

7. Click | OK |. You are now back in the **Data Template Definition** dialog.

8. In the table-like area below **Choose cell(s)**, click on a cell in the grid; a list button appears:

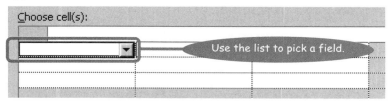

9. Select from this list the field to display. If you want task names only, select the field **Name**. You have now created a new layout template.

10. If you have long task names, set **Limit cell text to** more than one line.

11. Click | OK |, and you are now back in the **Data Templates** dialog; you can see the newly created template listed:

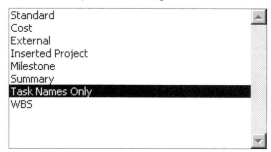

12. Click **Close**, and you are now back in the **Box Styles** dialog.

13. Now we have to apply this template to the different types of tasks; notice that within one Network Diagram view you can apply several templates to different types of task making it look exactly like you imagined. Select under **Style Settings For** all the different types of tasks by dragging over them or selecting them more specifically by holding down Control and clicking.

14. Under **Data Template** display the list and select the data template you just created.

15. Click **OK**, and the **Network Diagram** view now shows nodes with only the task names, which fits many more nodes within one screen.

Instead of applying a data template to all the tasks, you can use different data templates for different types of tasks. To select specific task types hold down Control and click in the **Format, Box Styles** dialog. If you select only the noncritical items, the list would look like:

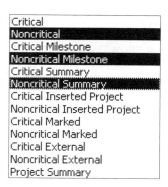

This allows you to create fancy Network Diagrams with dates on the milestones, but durations on the detail tasks, costs on the summary deliverables, etc, all within one view.

Changing the Border of the Nodes

You can use different border formats for different types of tasks.

1. Choose **Format, Box Styles**, and the **Box Styles** dialog appears.

2. In the list **Style Settings for** select the type of task for which to change the border.

3. In the bottom section, **Border**, you can choose the **Shape, Color** and **Width**. The **Preview** area in the top right shows what it will look like when done. You can also choose a fill **Background Color** and even a **Pattern**.

4. If you have more than one data field inside the nodes, you can choose to:
   ☑ **Show horizontal gridlines** and/or
   ☑ **Show vertical gridlines**.

5. Click ⬚ OK ⬚ .

Changing the Font

1. Choose the menu items **Format, Box Styles**, and the **Box Styles** dialog appears.

2. Click ⬚ More Templates... ⬚ , and the **Data Template** dialog opens.

3. In the list **Templates in <schedule name>** select the data template for which to change the font.

4. Click ⬚ Edit... ⬚ , and the **Data Template Definition** dialog opens.

5. Click ⬚ Font... ⬚ , and select the font type and size you need.

6. Click ⬚ OK ⬚ , and you are now back in the **Data Template Definition** dialog.

7. Click ⬚ OK ⬚ , and you are now back in the **Data Template** dialog.

8. Click ⬚ Close ⬚ , and you are now back in the **Box Styles** dialog.

9. Click ⬚ OK ⬚ , and you should now see the new font applied.

The Layout of the Diagram

Showing the Type of Dependency on Each Arrow

It is often helpful to see the type of dependency displayed for each task relationship, like in the following screenshots:

◆ Without *lag*: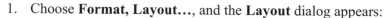

◆ With lag:

With that information, it is much easier to verify the network logic and check if it makes sense.

Click **Show Link Labels** 🔲 on the **Network Diagram** toolbar.
OR

1. Choose **Format, Layout…**, and the **Layout** dialog appears:

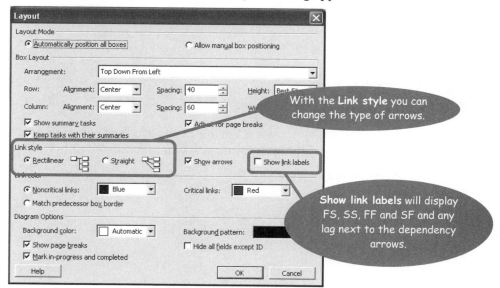

2. Under **Link style** check ☑ **Show link labels**.

3. Click [OK], and you will now see **FS** attached to each Finish-to-Start arrow, as well as **SS**, **FF** and **SF** to their respective arrows. You will also see any **Lag** (*lead*) displayed.

Changing the Type of Arrow

Click **Straight Links** ⌐ on the **Network Diagram** toolbar.
OR

1. Choose **Format, Layout...**, and the **Layout** dialog appears.

2. In the **Link style** section, select the type of arrow: ⦿ **Rectilinear** or ⦿ **Straight**.

3. Click [OK].

Displaying Progress Marks

You can indicate the status of a task with diagonal lines in the nodes:

◆ not started:

◆ in progress:

◆ completed:

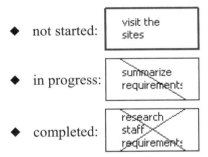

You can toggle these on and off by choosing **Format, Layout...** and selecting or clearing at the bottom the option ☑ **Mark in-progress and completed** or by clicking 🖫 on the **Network Diagram** toolbar.

Hiding the Summary Tasks

Summary tasks look like parallelograms in the **Network Diagram** view:

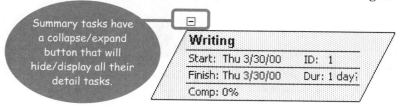

If you set all the logic between detail tasks, which is what we recommend, you can remove the summary tasks from the screen to remove clutter. Click **Hide Summary Tasks** on the **Network Diagram** toolbar to hide the summary task nodes.

Collapsing and Expanding Summary Tasks

The summary tasks can be collapsed to hide all the detail tasks that belong to the summary. Click ⊟ at the top left of the summary node or click the node and hold down [Alt] + [Shift] and press [-].

They can be expanded again by clicking ⊞ or holding down [Alt] + [Shift] and pressing [+].

Notice that if you collapse a summary task, you hide the detail tasks and also their dependencies. The network may now appear to have loose ends that may not really be loose ends. All real loose ends need to be tied up. Before checking the logic in the Network Diagram, we recommend you expand all summary tasks, by clicking Show ▾ on the **Formatting** toolbar and selecting **All Subtasks** from the list.

Improving the Layout of the Nodes

MS Project attempts to arrange the nodes as well as it can. By default, the nodes are laid out from the top left to the bottom right, but MS Project has several layout arrangements to choose from. You can improve the layout by choosing a different arrangement, or you can move nodes manually.

1. Choose **Format, Layout...**, and the **Layout** dialog appears:

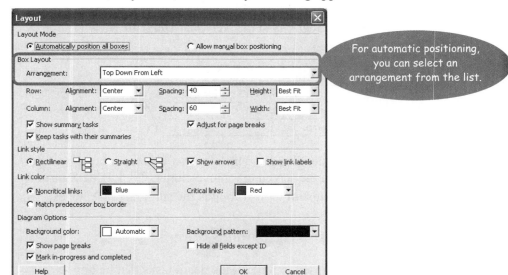

2. Make sure that under **Layout Mode, ⊙ Automatically position all boxes** is selected; otherwise you have to choose **Format, Layout Now** every time to see the effect of a different arrangement.

3. Under **Arrangement** use the list:

   Top Down From Left

   to change the layout of the nodes.

4. Click   OK   , and the layout of the nodes changes according to your choice. If the layout is not satisfactory, try other layout arrangements.

 There are also time-phased arrangements available by day, week or month; these are also known as *Time-Scaled Network Diagrams*. Unfortunately, MS Project does not show a timescale. The time-scaled view is useful when optimizing the network.

Improving the Layout of a Selection of Nodes

If you are manually arranging the nodes, you may still want to position groups of nodes in the selected arrangement.

1. Choose **Format, Layout...** and select **⊙ Allow manual box positioning**. Select an **Arrangement** from the list and click   OK   .

2. Select the nodes by dragging a lasso around them.
   OR

   Hold down [Control] and click on them.

3. Click **Layout Selection Now** 🖧 on the **Network Diagram** toolbar. MS Project rearranges the nodes as best it can and according to the arrangement that is currently selected in the **Format, Layout...** dialog.

Laying Out Single Nodes Manually

1. Choose **Format, Layout...**, and the **Layout** dialog appears:

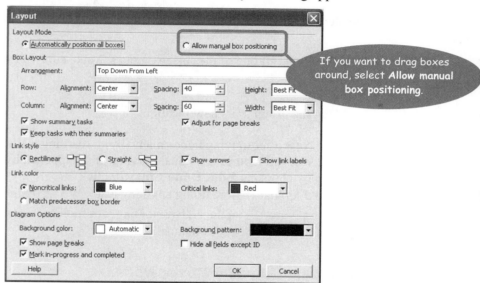

2. Select ⦿ **Allow manual box positioning**.

3. Click [OK].

4. Point to the border of the node you want to move, and make sure that the mouse pointer changes to ⁺↕⟨

5. Click and hold down and drag the node to its new location.

Laying Out Groups of Nodes Manually

1. First you have to select all nodes to move as a group. Click on the first node and hold down [Control]; then click on the other nodes. The nodes are highlighted to show they have been selected.
    OR
    Click and hold down to drag a lasso around all the task nodes to select.
    OR
    Hold down [Shift] and click on the border of a summary task to select it and all its detail tasks.
    OR
    Hold down [Shift] and click on the border of a detail task to select its entire chain of successors.

2. Click and hold down on the border of one of the selected nodes. Make sure you see the mouse pointer ⁺↑⁺↖.

3. Click and hold down to drag the group to its new location.

 Do not choose **Format, Layout Now** after moving nodes manually; it rearranges the entire **Network Diagram** and undoes all laborious manual moving. If it happened by accident, you can undo the mess by choosing **Edit, Undo Entry** or click **Undo Entry** ↺ on the **Standard** toolbar (before doing anything else). We recommend you use the tool **Layout Selection Now** ⊞ on the **Network Diagram** toolbar instead of **Format, Layout Now** after you have moved nodes manually.

Aligning the Manually Moved Nodes

You can select a number of nodes and then align all nodes with the task that is the first one in the chain or the earliest one in time.

1. First you have to select all nodes to move as a group by dragging a lasso around all the nodes to be selected.
    OR
    Click on the first node, hold down [Control] and click on the other nodes; the nodes are highlighted to show they have been selected.

2. Click **Align** Align ▾ on the **Network Diagram** toolbar and choose the way to align the selected tasks. The task nodes should now be aligned.

Exercises

Review

1. Why should a project manager set all the dependencies in her schedule?

2. What are the criteria for a good and solid network of dependencies that creates an entirely dynamic schedule?

3. If you are dependent upon supplies to arrive for one deliverable in your project, what would you recommend in terms of scheduling this situation?

4. What are the different ways to set dependencies? There are 9 different ways discussed in this book. Please provide at least 4 ways.

5. Are the following valid entries in the lag field? Yes or no? Why?
   A. 5d
   B. –3d
   C. +30%
   D. +5ed

6. Should you allow logic on summary tasks? If yes, why? If no, why not?

7. How would you schedule *ordering materials* and *receiving materials* with an order time of 3 weeks? Would you use a Finish-to-Start dependency with a 3-week lag? Or would you split the task bar for 3 weeks? Explain your answer.

8. For each of the following situations determine:
   ◇ Which task is the predecessor and successor: A or B?
   ◇ What type of dependency do you need: FS, SS, FF or SF?
   ◇ Would you advise to add a lead or a lag to the dependency? If so, as a relative lag or absolute lag? And how much?

	Predecessor (A or B)	Type of Dependency	Add Lag? Relative/absolute? How much?
You *gather requirements* (A) and then you *analyze requirements* (B).			

	Predecessor (A or B)	Type of Dependency	Add Lag? Relative/absolute? How much?
After you *apply for a permit* (A), you have to wait 3 weeks for *permit received* (B).			
Halfway through *perform system analysis* (A) we typically start *programming code* (B).			
You have to *pour foundation* (A) and let the concrete dry before you *lay bricks* (B) to erect the walls.			
One day after the finish of *conduct courses* (A), *write evaluation report* (B) has to be completed.			
Prepare for the PMP exam (A) and *take the PMP exam* (B).			

9. You have a task, *test unit,* with a 10-day duration, and you hesitate between using a FS-5d or a SS+5d dependency with this task as the predecessor. The FS-5d dependency will give the successor a different start date than the SS+5d when:
    a. The start date of *test unit* changes
    b. The finish date of *test unit* changes (while its start date stays the same)
    c. The duration of *test unit* changes
    d. The finish date or the duration of *test unit* change

10. You have two tasks, *survey clients* and *summarize survey results,* and you hesitate between using a FS-30% or a SS+70% dependency between the two tasks. The FS-30% dependency will cause a different start date of the successor than the SS+70% dependency when:
    a. The start date of *survey clients* changes
    b. The finish date of *survey clients* changes (while its start date stays the same)
    c. The duration of *survey clients* changes
    d. None of the above gives a difference in impact between FS-30% and SS+70%

Relocation Project — Dependencies

Continue to work with your file *Relocation.MPP* or open the file
05 Entering Dependencies.MPP available for download at www.jrosspub.com. Please,
click the link *WAV Download Resource Center* to enter the download site.

Enter the following dependencies using the **Link** tool on the **Standard** toolbar:

1. The tasks *research staff requirements* and *summarize requirements* are sequentially
    dependent.

2. The tasks of the deliverable *LOCATION* are all sequentially dependent upon each
    other.

3. The tasks of the deliverable *REMODELING CONTRACT* are all sequentially
    dependent upon each other. The dependency between *select contractor* and *meet to
    discuss contract* has a lag of 5 days; it will take a time frame of 5 days to get the
    participants together to meet.

4. The tasks *relocate walls* through *install cabinetry* of the deliverable *REMODELED
    LOCATION* are sequentially dependent upon each other.

5. The tasks of the deliverable *MOVE* are all sequentially dependent upon each other.

Enter the following dependencies by holding down ⌊Control⌋ and clicking to select the tasks
and using the **Link** tool:

6. In the deliverable *REMODELED LOCATION* the tasks *install cabinetry* and *install
    LAN* can take place concurrently after the paint dries. *Drying of paint* is the
    predecessor for both tasks.

7. After the tasks *install cabinetry* and *install LAN* are finished, the carpet can be put in
    place. *Lay carpet* is the successor for both tasks.

8. After the carpet is laid (*lay carpet*), the milestone *facility remodeled* is
    accomplished.

You forgot to set the dependencies between the deliverables (phases). Stay in the
Gantt Chart or switch to the **Network Diagram** to enter these dependencies:

9. The task *evaluate the sites* can start after *summarize requirements* is finished.

10. The task *select the contractor* can start after the milestone *location selected* is
    accomplished.

11. The task *select mover* can start after *location selected*.

12. The task *relocate walls* can start after the milestone *contractor contracted*.

13. The task *pack* can start after the milestone *facility remodeled*.

Compare your file with the solution file *06 Entering Constraints and Deadlines.MPP* available for download at www.jrosspub.com. Please, click the link *WAV Download Resource Center* to enter the download site. See page 675 of this book for an automated way of comparing and reporting differences between two versions of one schedule.

Case Study: CoalPower

CoalPower power station has approached you to do a 2-day introductory workshop in MS Project. CoalPower is a first-time client and it seems this 2-day contract will be its only need for training and consulting for awhile, even though the organization is large and has multiple plants. The key players at CoalPower are:

◆ Andy is the plant manager. You find out that he and you share a similar cultural heritage, and you find an easy basis for conversation with him. Andy sits in on the first part of the workshop you are conducting on-site. He is only interested in the big picture of what MS Project can do for the organization. Andy is concerned about the frequent delays in the engineering projects, as you found out when you talked one-on-one during a lunch break.

◆ Norm manages the engineers, who manage repair, maintenance and construction projects in the power station. They also design the modifications that are needed. You have had difficulties in negotiating with Norm. He told you, only after you had closed your consulting contract, that you will have to travel an extra 250 miles to get to the site of the plant.

◆ Dave and Harry manage the major maintenance projects like the replacement of the $2M turbine condensers. Replacing these condensers will stop the operations in the entire plant. They have been planning their projects mostly off the top of their heads. Norm is getting increasingly anxious about this and has told them, "If you get sick, nobody knows what to do or how to do it. I need to see a detailed plan of your projects!"

◆ Art is the technical drawing expert. He designs most of the small modifications and creates the technical drawings. Art is overworked and has, at any given time, 50 projects on his plate. Norm often criticizes him for not delivering the drawings when Norm wants them.

Questions

Dave and Harry are struggling with the whole concept of scheduling and what benefits it will provide to them:

1. Do you expect them to be motivated to use the tool? Why?

2. How will they benefit from scheduling their projects with MS Project?

3. What do you think of Norm's approach of forcing them to schedule their projects?

4. How important are dependencies in their schedule?

Art approaches you during one of the breaks to talk one-on-one:

5. What is his main concern in scheduling his projects?

6. How should he model his many projects in MS Project? Address in particular whether he should use dependencies in his schedule:

   a. Between the tasks within one project

   b. Between his projects

7. How will Art benefit from modeling his projects in MS Project?

Chapter 6 Entering Deadlines, Constraints and Task Calendars

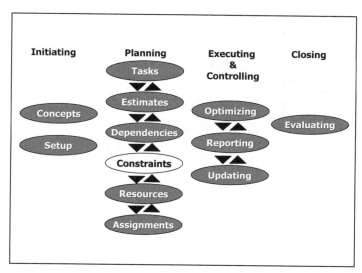

The Gantt Chart is starting to take shape, and there may be certain constraint dates that we may have to add to the model to make it stay within the boundaries of our reality. Also, we may want to capture deadline date. Constraints, deadlines and task calendars are the topics of this chapter; they are all features that capture specific dates.

After reading this chapter you will:

♦   know the difference between constraints and deadlines
♦   know the different types of schedule constraints
♦   know in which situations to use constraints and deadlines
♦   be able to choose the right type of constraint
♦   be able to enter schedule constraints and deadlines into the project model
♦   know the advantages and disadvantages of using constraints
♦   know the advantages and disadvantages of using deadlines
♦   be able to recognize when task calendars are better than constraints
♦   be able to create a task calendar and restrict the scheduling of a task with it
♦   be able to check if we used scheduling best practices with regards to deadlines, constraints and task calendars
♦   know how to format and print the Gantt Chart view

Dancing with a Rock!

Bob: "Hey Nob, did you hear about this feature of deadlines in MS Project? It is a beautiful feature! I can put all the dates that I committed to into my schedule and my schedule still floats back and forth freely. And when a deadline date is not met, a red flag appears."

Nob responds: "Why would you want your schedule to float freely; do you like it to change all the time? I don't like that!"

Bob: "Why don't you like that? The dependencies will make sure that your forecast dates are always valid!"

Nob: "When I have assigned a task to Mary to start on March 12 that task better start on March 12 or all hell will break loose and all kinds of things will start slipping!"

Bob: "Are you able to schedule so rigidly? Does it work like that for you?"

Nob: "Well … there is no project that runs exactly according to schedule, but if we don't try to run it like that, it never happens …"

Bob: "Well, I am probably trying as hard as you are to run projects according to their schedule, but I do expect the schedule to change constantly … except for the tasks coming up in the next two weeks! I always receive change requests from the client and I can easily incorporate those. How do you handle change requests?"

Nob: "I reject, resist or retard them … as much as I can!"

Bob: "As soon as I receive a change request, I enter it into my dynamic project schedule and I can see immediately what the impacts are on the project end date and on the budget. When I show it to the executives, I can often get an immediate decision from them on the change request. That works very well for me! This is partly thanks to using deadlines instead of constraints! Deadlines are life-giving, and constraints are life-sucking, as far as I am concerned! Working with a schedule that has many constraints is like trying to dance with a rock … it does not move!"

What Are Deadlines and Schedule Constraints?

A constraint is a date that restricts MS Project in scheduling a task. A deadline is a date you commit to that does <u>not</u> restrict the scheduling of a task.

It is possible to force tasks to be scheduled on certain dates, which is necessary for certain tasks like *attend meeting, attend conference* and *monitor seminar*. Fixing dates is a matter of putting a schedule *constraint* on the task. You could consider a Must Start On constraint for the aforementioned tasks. A *Must Start On* is a hard constraint, and MS Project cannot reschedule tasks with hard constraints. Constraints affect the network of dependencies. The more constraints you create, the less freely your network will flow back and forth when you enter changes. Therefore, the more constraints you have in your schedule, the more effort you will spend keeping the schedule *valid*.

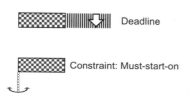

Deadline

Constraint: Must-start-on

Deadlines, on the other hand, do not restrict the timing of task bars. Deadline dates stay visible in the timescale as down-facing green arrows ⇩. When you miss a deadline date MS Project displays a visual indicator ◆ in the ❶ **Indicators** column.

We recommend, therefore, that you enter dates that you committed to as deadline dates rather than as constraint dates. When you want to track a soft target date for a specific task, you can set a deadline date for that task. Since deadlines don't restrict the scheduling, they don't require continuous and immediate maintenance either, like scheduling conflicts caused by constraints do.

We will discuss deadlines first and then constraints (starting on page 277).

Deadlines

Entering Deadlines

1. Choose **View, Gantt Chart**.

2. Double-click on the task.
   OR
   Click on the task for which you want to set a deadline. Click **Task Information** 🔲 on the **Standard** toolbar or hold down ⎵Shift⎵ and press ⎵F2⎵; the **Task Information** dialog appears.

3. Click the **Advanced** tab; the dialog should now look like:

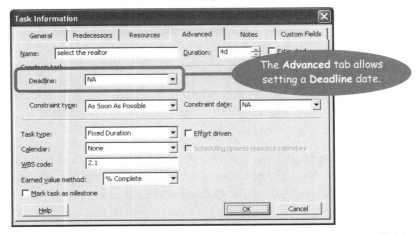

4. Under **Constrain task**, type the deadline date in the **Deadline** field or use the pull-down calendar to click on a date.

5. Click ▭ OK ▭ and you will now see an arrow ⇩ in the timescale that represents the deadline date you entered. If you rest your mouse pointer on it, you will see its screen tip.

 If you have to be done before November 1, you have to enter October 31 as the deadline date. The deadline time will by default be at the end of the day on the date you enter. If you enter November 1 as the deadline date, the task will be done by 5:00 PM on November 1. You could add the time to the deadline date instead.

 You can move deadline dates by simply dragging the ⇩ in the timescale to a new date. You can start dragging as soon as you see the four-arrow mouse pointer ✥ .

The symbol for a deadline ⇩ does not stand out in the timescale; particularly when there are many dependency arrows. We suggest you change it to a solid symbol and more striking color in the **Format, Bar Styles...** dialog, tab **Bars**.

To remove a deadline, simply delete the date from the **Deadline** field on the **Advanced** tab of the **Task Information** dialog.

Managing Deadlines

You will not get automatic warning messages from Project 2003 if deadlines are not met. What you do get is an exclamation icon ◆ in the **Indicators** column. MS Project raises a red flag when a deadline is missed.

Also, if you use the list of filters All Tasks ▾ on the **Formatting** toolbar and apply the filter **Tasks with Deadlines**, you can quickly display tasks with deadlines and see which deadlines are slipping. Press F3 to get rid of the filtering.

Choosing the Options

To access the options, choose **Tools, Options** from the menu.

Tab	Option
Schedule	☑ **Tasks will always honor their constraint dates** This option makes tasks obey their schedule constraints. We recommend you keep this option on to make sure your schedule observes the few real and hard constraint dates that you may have in it.
	Set as Default Sets the option as the default setting for any new schedules you create. The existing schedules are not affected, because this option is stored in the project schedules, as you can see from the label of the section divider: **Scheduling Options for <schedule name of the project>**.

Scheduling Regimes

Before discussing the types of constraints, we need to discuss the basic scheduling regime you choose. The two choices are:

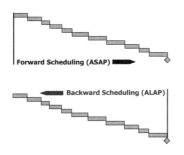

◆ *Forward Scheduling* from the project start date. You do forward scheduling if you entered the project start date and want the model to tell you what the expected finish date is for the project. Under forward scheduling, tasks are scheduled *as soon as possible* (*ASAP*) by default.

◆ *Backward Scheduling* from the project finish date. You schedule backward if you entered the project finish date and want to find out when to start the project to meet this date. Under backward scheduling tasks are scheduled *As Late As Possible* (*ALAP*) by default.

You can see whether you are scheduling forward or backward by checking the **Project, Project Information** dialog in the list **Schedule from**. It shows there that you **Schedule from** either the **Project Start Date** (*forward scheduling*) or from the *Project Finish Date* (*backward scheduling*).

If you change from forward to backward scheduling after you have entered tasks, the constraint for these tasks will stay ASAP; new tasks will be ALAP. Combining ASAP tasks with ALAP tasks in one schedule sometimes creates unexpected results; which of the two tendencies is stronger?

Schedule Conflict

A schedule conflict is when MS Project cannot find an acceptable and feasible schedule for you based on the input you provided to it. For example, your schedule is currently 12 weeks long, but you have set a Finish No Later Than constraint for the project in week 11. Typically a schedule conflict occurs when a constraint date is not met. MS Project will immediately tell you when there is a schedule conflict with the following message:

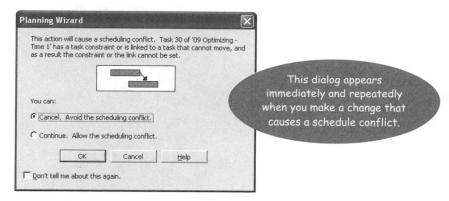

This dialog appears immediately and repeatedly when you make a change that causes a schedule conflict.

OR

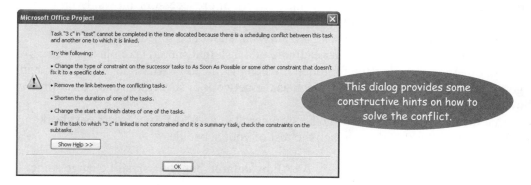

This dialog provides some constructive hints on how to solve the conflict.

You are forced to deal with the issue, because one of the two dialog boxes will keep popping up (unless you check ☑ **Don't tell me about this again**).

If you don't understand why your schedule has a conflict, please click Show Help >> or use the checklist with schedule troubleshooting questions in the Summary chapter on page 676.

Types of Constraints

The eight types of constraints can be characterized as tendencies, one-sided constraints or rigid constraints:

Tendencies
- *As Soon As Possible* (*ASAP*; the default under forward scheduling)
- *As Late As Possible* (*ALAP*; the default under backward scheduling)

One-sided constraints [58]
- *Start No Earlier Than (SNET)*
- *Finish No Earlier Than (FNET)*
- *Start No Later Than (SNLT)*
- *Finish No Later Than (FNLT)*

Rigid constraints
- *Must Start On (MSO)*
- *Must Finish On (MFO)*

Tendencies

MS Project has forward scheduling as its default regime. Under *forward scheduling* MS Project uses **As Soon As Possible** (ASAP) for the tasks; MS Project will pull task bars in the timescale as far to the left as the network of predecessors allows. Even when the regime is ASAP, you can still schedule certain tasks **As Late As Possible** (ALAP). For example, in a move project, *packing equipment* should be scheduled ALAP just before the move. *Training* is another example of a task that should take place as late as possible; otherwise people have forgotten it when they need it. ALAP task bars will tend to go to the right in the timescale as much as the network of successors and constraints allows.

Note that the one ALAP task tends to be stronger than its ASAP successors, so check that the one ALAP task did not hijack the rest of your schedule.

Under backward scheduling, tasks are ALAP by default, but you can still change some tasks to ASAP scheduling.

---

[58] Why they formulated these constraint names in the negative (no earlier than, no later than) instead of in the positive (later than, earlier than) is beyond me. It just makes it more difficult to understand.

Even though ALAP and ASAP do not have a *Constraint Date*, they have a tremendous impact on the schedule and are in that sense "constraining".

One-Sided Constraints

This group of one-sided constraints limits the movement of task bars to only one direction, either to the left (no earlier) or to the right (no later):
◆ Start No Earlier Than (SNET) and Finish No Earlier Than (FNET) constrain free movement of the task bars towards the left in the timescale; the start date (SNET) or finish date (FNET) cannot go to the left of the No Earlier Than date.
◆ Start No Later Than (SNLT) and Finish No Later Than (FNLT) constrain free movement of the task bars towards the right in the timescale; the start date (SNLT) or finish date (FNLT) cannot go to the right of the No Later Than date.

Rigid Constraints

The last group of rigid constraints, Must Start On (MSO) and Must Finish On (MFO), fix the task bar entirely to the date indicated and deny any free movement. Constraints like these severely affect the schedule.

Note that the task bar can still grow or shrink in size when you revise the estimate. This will make the other, unconstrained end of the task bar move.

No Earlier Than Constraints

An example of a *Start No Earlier Than* (*SNET*) constraint is when raw materials will not be delivered until a certain date. You can start the activity for which you need the raw materials no earlier than the delivery date.

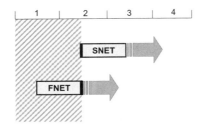

An example of a *Finish No Earlier Than* (*FNET*) is when you need a final approval for the deliverable. You know the approval can take place during the next board meeting planned on the first day of every month. You enter an FNET constraint on the first of the next month. The *No Earlier Than* constraints are restricted from moving earlier in time (to the left in the timescale). They can be pushed to the right by the network without a limit. Under *As Soon As Possible* (*ASAP*) scheduling they will not be able to cause a schedule conflict; in other words, they are *soft constraints* under *forward scheduling*.

Under *backward scheduling*, the project finish date is hard. As you enter dependencies you will see that the *As Late As Possible* (*ALAP*) task bars will be pushed out earlier in time (moving to the left in the timescale). They can be pushed to the left as far as the *No Earlier Than* date allows. If pushed any further, Project 2003 will alert you to a *schedule conflict*. *No Earlier Than* constraints are therefore said to be *hard constraints* under backward scheduling.

A tiny little red dot in the icon 🔳 in the **Indicators ❶** column will tell you if a constraint is hard. If the dot is blue, it is a soft constraint.

No Later Than Constraints

An example of a *Start No Later Than* (*SNLT*) constraint might be the backing up of a computer system that can be scheduled at a later time, but would have to start no later than, let's say, midnight in order to be finished on time. An example of a *Finish No Later Than* (*FNLT*) constraint is when you commit to deliver a report no later than March 13, and this date is a do-or-die date.

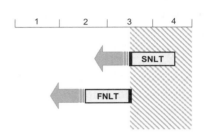

The *No Later Than* constraints are restricted from moving beyond the date specified (moving to the right in a timescale view). They can be allowed earlier by the network all the way up to the start date of the project. Under *As Late As Possible* (*ALAP*) scheduling these constraints will not be able to cause a schedule conflict. In other words, they are soft under backward scheduling.

 Under forward scheduling, the project start date is hard. As you enter dependencies, you will see that the *As Soon As Possible* (*ASAP*) task bars will be pushed out to the right in the timescale (to later in time). They can be pushed out as far as the No Later Than constraint date allows. If pushed any further, Project 2003 will warn you that there is a *schedule conflict*. Therefore, No Later Than constraints are said to be *hard constraints* under forward scheduling.

 A tiny little red dot in the icon 🔲 in the **Indicators ❶** column will tell you if a constraint is hard. If the dot is blue, it is a soft constraint.

Must Constraints

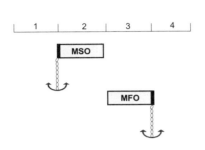

An example of a *Must Start On* (MSO) constraint is holding an important meeting that must start on January 9 at 9:00 AM.

An example of a *Must Finish On* (MFO) constraint is when you have a contractual date by which you must move out of an office space or pay a steep penalty.

Where you use an MSO constraint, the start will always be on the date indicated. With an MFO constraint, the finish will always be on the date specified. MSO and MFO constraints can easily cause *schedule conflicts*. These constraints are always *hard constraints* under both forward <u>and</u> backward scheduling. They should be used only when you absolutely need them to keep the schedule *valid*. Let's explore some situations.

In Which Situations Do You Need Constraints?

Deadlines do not need a lot of maintenance while the project is running, but constraints do. Every time you have a major change in your schedule, you may either have to update all the constraint dates downstream, or you will have to solve all the schedule conflicts. If you don't solve scheduling conflicts right away, MS Project will keep nagging you with messages until you do. Constraints require immediate attention when you may not have time. If a task doesn't have any constraints, its dependencies push it into place in the timescale.

We recommend, therefore, that you enter only the constraints that are absolutely necessary. However, you can enter many deadlines in your schedule without many disadvantages.

Constraints should <u>not</u> be used to model temporary availability of resources. A better place to indicate temporary availability is through availability profiles. We will discuss them on page 335. Constraints should not be used either to create a limited scheduling window for certain tasks, for example to force an *office move* task to the weekend. A better way to do that is through a *Task Calendar*, which we will discuss on page 290.

Task calendars create a more *dynamic model* than constraints, because you can mark every weekend as a target for the move task, whereas with constraints you would be restricted to one particular weekend. If one weekend cannot be met the Task Calendar will force it to the next weekend and will update all dependent forecasts.

Constraints can be set for:

◆ *External dependencies*
On page 229, we recommended that an external dependency be entered as an extra milestone and that the milestone can be held in place by a Start No Earlier Than (SNET) constraint.

◆ *Weather restrictions*
For example, if you have to get road construction done before the rainy or winter season starts, a constraint can help. Constraints can also help for outdoor construction activities that can only start after the winter is over.
MS Project has another feature that is called Task Calendars to schedule these situations; see page 290.

◆ *Group activities*
Meetings, presentations, training or, in general, tasks that involve a group of people may require constraints. In order to get a group together, you have to set a date; otherwise the event will not happen. When the date is agreed upon, a constraint should be set on that date so MS Project does not move it off of its date. Often, you will use Must Start On or Must Finish On constraints here.

◆ Certain milestones (see the following section).

Types of Milestones

Milestones are used in a schedule to indicate events like decisions, approvals, target dates and ceremonies. The type of constraint needed will depend on the "*hardness*" of the milestone. The hardness of a milestone is the resistance you will experience in practice when you try to move its date. For *soft dates*, you can use the *deadline* feature instead of constraints. For *hard dates*, use the feature of *schedule constraints*. The harder the date, the harder the constraint should be. The hardest constraints are *Must Start On* (*MSO*) and *Must Finish On* (*MFO*).

The different types of milestones used in schedules are (listed from soft to hard):

◆ *Decision points*
These are important events on which decisions about the remainder of the project are made. The decision can be:

◊ Go/No-go: A no-go decision will end the project. A go decision will authorize spending for the next phase.

◊ Go-left/Go-right: The how-to or direction is determined for the rest of the project. You will often find this type of milestone in R&D projects where the research findings determine the direction (the deliverables) for the rest of the project.

If there is a target date or a deadline for the decision point, we recommend using the deadline feature that was discussed on page 274. The decision will typically not be taken until the required information is available. That is why these dates are often *soft* dates.

◆ *Target dates*
These are soft deadlines that are inserted to break up a long series of tasks. They focus the efforts on finishing a component of a deliverable. The project manager decides with the team where to insert these target dates. Teams need several target dates on components of their deliverable in order to meet the deadline of the overall deliverable. Target dates are interim evaluation points. It is like driving from Ontario to Florida and checking to see if you are still on schedule at the end of every day. Target dates function as reminders and should keep everyone focused and on track. For target dates, we recommend the use of the deadline feature and no constraints.

◆ *Do-or-die dates*
These are *hard* deadlines and are often contractual dates by which you are committed to hand over a deliverable. There may even be a penalty clause in the contract if the date is not met. These dates should be clear in the schedule at all times. We recommend you enter these into the schedule as deadlines as much as possible in order to keep the schedule dynamic. However, if one is a very hard contractual date (with a huge penalty associated), you could consider a Finish No Later Than (FNLT) constraint. This allows it to float up to the constraint date and never pass it without immediately notifying you with a pop-up dialog box.

◆ *Deliveries*
We recommend you enter the delivery dates of raw materials, supplies or client deliverables as separate milestones in the *Work Breakdown Structure*. We discussed these external dependencies on page 229. The delivery date you agreed upon with the vendor, supplier or client should be entered as an event milestone with a Start No Earlier Than (SNET) constraint.

◆ *Ceremonies*
Ceremonies are short official events to which many people are invited. If the duration of the ceremony is negligible, it can be entered as a milestone with a zero duration. An example might be the official ribbon cutting to open a new plant. The date of a ceremony is often hard, because ceremonies are public events. The

schedule needs a Must Start On (MSO) constraint for these events. If the ceremony has a duration, it is no longer a milestone, but a task and will still need a constraint.

◆ *Project end date*
This is the delivery date for the project product. Meeting the project end date is always a challenge in project management. All the chains of dependencies come together in the project end milestone. A Must Finish On (MFO) or a Finish No Later Than (FNLT) constraint is often set on the project end date. You will immediately receive a scheduling conflict message when this date is in jeopardy. In many projects, a deadline date could do the trick as well. You will then only see the red exclamation icon ◆ appear in the ❶ **Indicators** column if the deadline is missed.

The **Deadlines** feature reminds you of the date agreed upon without constraining the schedule. It is a feature we strongly recommend using over schedule constraints. The more constraints you have, the more time you will spend on maintaining your schedule. And you will have to do this during project execution, when you don't have much time. The fewer constraints you have, the more dynamic your schedule will be.

Constraints

Entering Constraints

If you have to be done before November 1, you have to enter October 31 as the constraint date. The constraint time will be at the end of the day on the date you enter. If you enter November 1 as the date, the task will be done by 5:00 PM on November 1.

You can set constraint dates in a variety of ways:
◆ Dragging task bars:
This method will allow you to set only *Start No Earlier Than* (*SNET*) constraints under forward scheduling or only *Finish No Later Than* (*FNLT*) constraints under backward scheduling.
◆ Entering dates:
Under forward scheduling you can enter a start date that will set an SNET constraint, or you can enter a finish date that will set a *Finish No Earlier Than* (FNET) constraint. Under backward scheduling, entering a start date will create a *Start No Later Than* (*SNLT*) constraint; a finish date creates an *FNLT* constraint. This is probably too much to remember.
◆ Using the task fields *Constraint Type* and *Constraint Date*:
This is where you can select the type of constraint from a list and the date from a pull-down calendar.
◆ Using the **Advanced** tab on the **Task Information** dialog.

As is often the case in MS Project, you can enter constraints in several different ways. The first two ways are easy and quick, but do require you to know and predict which constraints MS Project will set. Therefore, we recommend using the last two ways, but we will discuss all four in more detail.

Setting Constraints by Dragging Task Bars Horizontally

These steps assume that you drag the bar to the right; later in time.

1. Point to the middle of the task bar; make sure you see a four-headed arrow: ⊕.

2. Click and hold down to drag the bar *horizontally* to where you want it scheduled. Make sure you see a horizontal two-headed arrow at this point: ▰▰◄▻▭ .

3. Look at the yellow pop-up window to see what the new dates will be:

4. Release the mouse when the task bar is scheduled on the date you want. The Planning Wizard may prompt you:
   ◇ if you want to keep the link and set a constraint when you moved it away from its predecessor, or
   ◇ if you want to set a link instead of a constraint when you moved it just behind another bar.

   Answer the prompt of the Planning Wizard and click ⎿ OK ⏌.

5. It has a **Start No Earlier Than** constraint on it to keep it in its new place. (Under backward scheduling it will be a **Finish No Later Than** constraint.)

If you drag *vertically*, you will see the mouse pointer ⊛ , and you are creating dependencies instead of constraints!

Setting Constraints by Entering Dates

In the field **Start** you can pick a date from the drop-down calendar. By default, this creates a *Start No Earlier Than* (*SNET*) constraint on the task under *forward scheduling*, and it creates a *Start No Later Than* (*SNLT*) constraint under *backward scheduling*. In the field **Finish**, you can pick a date from the drop-down calendar. By default, this creates a *Finish No Earlier Than* (*FNET*) constraint on the task under *forward* *scheduling*, but it creates a *Finish No Later Than* (*FNLT*) constraint under *backward scheduling*.

Many people use the **Start** and **Finish** fields to schedule all their tasks. Most do not intend to create constraints, but are unaware that MS Project does. Their schedules become rigid and require a lot of work to maintain. If dependencies are used instead, schedules require a lot less maintenance. We don't recommend using the **Start** and **Finish** fields at all for data entry. In addition, using them will require you to memorize what type of constraint will be set both under forward and under backward scheduling. We would even go as far as recommending that you eliminate those fields from the entry table. You can do this by clicking on their column heading and pressing [Delete].

Setting Constraints Using the Task Fields

We recommend you use either this method or the next method to set constraints.

1. Insert the field *Constraint Type* by clicking in the column before which you wish to insert and choosing **Insert, Column**. The **Column Definition** dialog appears:

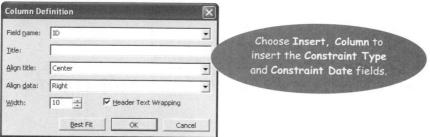

2. Select from the list **Field name:** the item **Constraint Type**. You can quickly get to this field name in the long list by typing the first characters of the name of the field.

3. Click OK .

4. Repeat these steps to insert the field **Constraint Date** as well.

5. You can now enter any type of constraint in the Gantt spreadsheet by selecting the type from the list in the field **Constraint type** 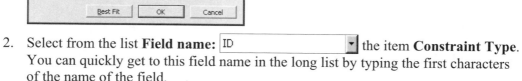 and picking the date from the drop-down calendar in **Constraint date** [NA].

Setting Constraints Using the Task Information Dialog

1. Select the task.

2. Click **Task Information** 📄 on the **Standard** toolbar
    OR

    hold down ⌨️Shift and press ⌨️F2.

3. The **Task Information** dialog appears. Click the **Advanced** tab; the dialog should now look like:

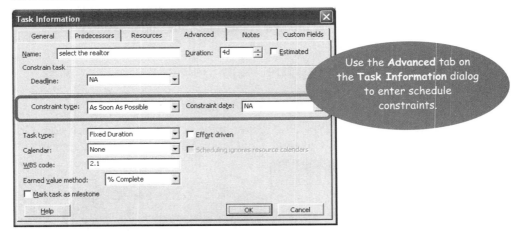

4. Select the type from the **Constraint type** pull-down list and select a date from the **Constraint date** drop-down calendar.

5. Click [OK].

To Check All the Scheduling Constraints

1. In the Gantt Chart choose the menu items **View, Table: <name of currently applied table>**, **More Tables**; the **More Tables** dialog appears:

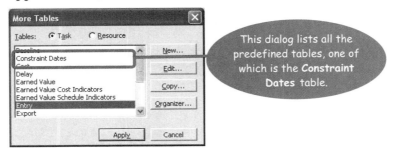

2. Select the **Constraint Dates** table in the list.

3. Click Apply. You can now see the fields **Constraint Type** and **Constraint Dates** to check all constraints on the tasks.

4. You can apply a filter that displays all the tasks that have a constraint date. Use the All Tasks list on the **Formatting** toolbar to apply the filter called **Tasks with Fixed Dates**.

5. When done, press F3 to remove the filtering.

To Remove Constraints

You can remove constraints one by one, but if you want to delete them fast, you can use the fill-down feature. This is useful if you inadvertently entered dates in the **Start** and **Finish** fields without wanting the constraints that came with them.

1. To remove all constraints, click on a column heading in the Gantt chart
   OR

   To remove constraints on certain tasks, select them all by holding down Control and clicking on all of them.

2. Click on the **Standard** toolbar to display the **Multiple Task Information** dialog.

3. Click tab **Advanced** and in the list **Constraint Type,** select the right constraint type: **As Soon As Possible** under forward scheduling or **As Late As Possible** under backward scheduling.

4. Click OK.

Make sure you don't remove real *constraint dates* that are necessary to keep your project schedule *valid*.

Limitations of Constraints

◆ You can only set *FNLT* and *SNET* constraints on summary tasks.
   MS Project does not allow other types of constraints on summary tasks, because summary tasks would not be summarizing their detail tasks any longer. Personally, I try to use constraints sparsely and I have not missed the other types for summary tasks.

◆ You can set a *maximum of one constraint* per task.
Sometimes it would be nice to set two constraints on a task when the task has to be done in a *window of opportunity*. For example, you can only do a test when a specialized lab is available. You cannot model this expensive test with constraints, because you can only set one constraint on a task.
You can use the feature of *Task Calendar* that allows you to create a calendar for the task that reflects all the windows of opportunity. You can apply it to the task using the field *Task Calendar.* We will discuss task calendars next. Task calendars essentially allow you to set multiple constraints per task.

Using Task Calendars

MS Project allows you to schedule tasks using *Task Calendars*. Examples:

◆ In a construction project, you could create a winter weather task calendar to schedule all outdoor construction activities affected by winter weather, as shown in the illustration to the right.

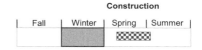

◆ In R&D projects, you can schedule testing with a task calendar when you are only given certain windows of opportunity to use the lab. You may need this if you use expensive testing labs. You assign the task calendar to the test activity.
◆ You can make sure that an office move takes place during a weekend instead of weekdays with a task calendar.
◆ You can make sure that demolition activities take place in evening hours or during the weekend.

Task calendars are good for tasks with or without resources assigned. If resources are assigned, the resource calendars and the task calendar may fight with each other, and if there are conflicts between the calendars, the following message will appear:

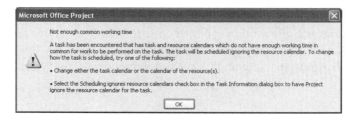

Also, the **Indicators** ❶ column will display the icon when there is an unresolved conflict between calendars. You cannot leave these conflicts unresolved.

The order of precedence between the calendars is:
1. *Task calendar*
2. *Resource calendar*
3. *Project calendar*

In other words, task calendars override resource calendars, which override the project calendar. There is a task field *Ignore resource calendar,* but it does not seem to do more than make the calendar conflict icon disappear.

Creating a task calendar for each individual task, as some people do, is not recommended; it would guarantee hardship when troubleshooting and changing the schedule. They have created a static model; they still live in the age of paper schedules.

Creating a New Task Calendar

When you work with MS Project Professional edition, all calendars are typically created beforehand by project office staff. As a project manager, you can only create new task calendars if you have the right to open and change **Enterprise Global** by choosing **Tools, Enterprise Options, Open Enterprise Global**. If this menu item is grayed out for you, you will have to lobby the project office staff.

Once you have it open, the steps will be the same as for MS Project Standard edition, which are:

1. Choose **Tools, Change Working Time**; the **Change Working Time** dialog appears:

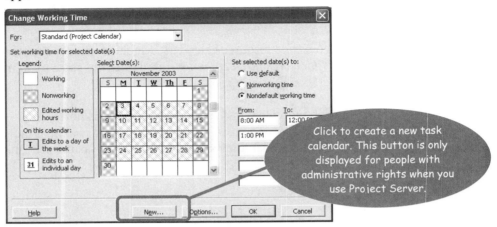

2. Select a base calendar that is closest to what you need for the new task calendar in the list: **For** ┃Standard (Project Calendar)┃▾┃.

3. Click ┃ N**e**w... ┃ at the bottom of the dialog; the **Create New Base Calendar** dialog appears:

4. Enter a descriptive name for the task calendar that reflects its settings and select either:
   ⦿ **Create new base calendar,** or
   ⦿ **Make a copy of** the calendar you selected under step 2 (that's the why of the step).

5. Click ┃ OK ┃; you have now created a new task calendar.

6. Enter the working days, working times or holidays on the new task calendar and click ┃ OK ┃ when done.

Using a Task Calendar

Double-click on a task; the **Task Information** dialog appears. Click the **Advanced** tab, and select the task calendar under **Calendar**. You can also check the option
☑ **Scheduling ignores resource calendars** here if that is your decision in case of conflicts.

OR

1. Right-click on the column heading before which to insert the column *Task Calendar* and choose **Insert Column** from the pop-up menu
    OR
    Click anywhere on the column before which you wish to insert the column *Task Calendar* and choose from the menu **Insert, Column**.

2. The **Column Definition** dialog appears in which you can select the item **Task Calendar** from the list **Field Name**:

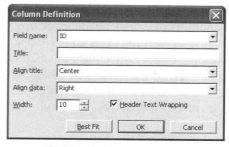

3. Click [OK] to close the dialog.

4. Click in the **Task Calendar** field [None ▼] of a task and select a task calendar from the list provided.

5. The task will now display a task calendar icon 🗓 in the **Indicators ❶** column.

Checks on Deadlines, Constraints and Task Calendars

Next you will find some checks to verify if you have applied best practices in the use of deadlines and constraints in your dynamic model of the project:

◆ Is the project deadline date captured in the schedule?
  It can be set using the **Deadline** feature date or using the **Constraint** feature in MS Project. The deadline or constraint date needs to be set on the project finish

milestone. Whether you use a deadline or a constraint depends on how hard the project target finish date is.

◆ Are there as few as possible *Task Calendars* in the schedule?
Task Calendars have a very specific purpose as we discussed on page 290 and should only be used in those situations.

◆ Does the schedule have as few as possible schedule constraints?
Constraints make the schedule rigid and jeopardize a dynamic schedule. However, constraints are legitimate on:

◇ *Recurring detail tasks*, like *status meetings 1, status meetings 2, etc.*

◇ External dependencies, such as *delivery of supplies* or *arrival of materials.*

◇ Activities that have to take place on a certain agreed-upon date, like *deliver presentation* and *conduct training.* In general, these are activities in which a group of people is involved.

◇ Do-or-die-by dates, like the *December 31, 1999* deadline for Y2K projects as we all perceived it before that date.

◇ Activities affected by (winter) weather conditions, i.e., in Canada asphalting streets *starts no earlier than April 1st*, because of the cold. You can also use the feature of **Task Calendars** for these situations in MS Project (see page 290). Task Calendars would be a better way in the case of the multi-year planning of infrastructural works; unlike constraints, task calendars will push a job automatically out to the next year, if it does not fit within this year any more.

You can display all tasks that have constraints by applying the filter **10 IIL Constraints other than ASAP**.[59] The filter will not display recurring detail tasks, because recurring detail tasks should have constraints.

Formatting the Gantt Chart View

In this section we will prepare the Gantt Chart view for printing. There are three wizards available that can get you where you want quickly:

◆ **Print Current view as a Report** wizard on the **Report** Project Guide
First display the Project Guide toolbar, if needed, by right-clicking on any toolbar

---

[59] This filter can be found in the file *IIL Project 2003 tools to check Orange Belt schedules.MPP* available for download at www.jrosspub.com. Please, click the link *WAV Download Resource Center* to enter the download site.

and choosing **Project Guide** from the pop-up menu. Click Report ▾.
The Wizard does not provide you all the options you may need to get a good report:

◇ It only offers to set a date range for the timescale, whereas the **Format, Timescale** dialog offers more versatility.

◇ This wizard does not allow you to choose exactly which columns you want and in which order; it only provides the **File, Page Setup, View** options.

◇ It only allows you to display a certain outline level; it does not prompt you to apply filters.

◆ **Copy Picture to Office Wizard** on the **Analysis** toolbar
This wizard has potential, but still does not take the trial and error hassle out of the reporting on your project. Often the picture is so small that you cannot read it. This is because the wizard does not provide a facility to adjust the timescale (time units, skip factor for time units, zoom factor/size). I would recommend you first make it look good on the screen and then you use this wizard to quickly export what you see on the screen to *MS Office Word*, *MS Office PowerPoint* or *Visio*.

◆ **Gantt Chart Wizard** on the **Formatting** toolbar.
With the **Gantt Chart Wizard** on the **Formatting** toolbar you can choose format options for the *Gantt Chart* by answering prompts. This wizard allows you to enjoy some of the gems hidden in the illustrious **Format, Bar Styles** dialog. Some of the things you can accomplish with this wizard are:

◇ Display the Critical Path by coloring the critical task bars red. For more information on the Critical Path, see page 438. This can also be done through the menu items **Format, Bar Styles**, tab **Bars**.

◇ Display text of your choice to the left of, to the right of or inside the task bars for summary tasks, detail tasks and milestones. This can also be done through the menu items **Format, Bar Styles**, tab **Text**.

◇ Change the shape and color of the task bars for summary tasks, detail tasks and milestones. This can also be done through the menu items **Format, Bar Styles**, tab **Bars**.

To Adjust the Text Styles

Text styles can be applied to certain task types. The dialog is similar to the
Format, Font dialog except that the font dialog is used for formatting only those tasks
that are selected, whereas the **Text Styles** dialog allows you to format based on the type
of task.

1. Choose **Format, Text Styles…**; the **Text Styles** dialog appears:

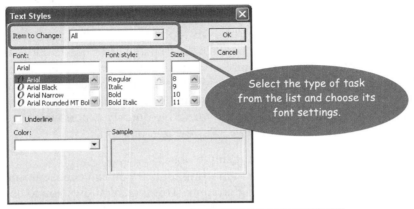

2. From the list **Item to Change:** `All` ▼ at the top, select the type
   of task to change. Then select the format using **Font, Font style, Size** and **Color**.

3. Click [OK].

 If you select the item **All**, all the text will be affected, even the text styles you set
previously.

 The Gantt Chart Wizard allowed you to color the critical task bars red. With the
Text Styles dialog you can color the text of the task names of the critical tasks red as
well to make them appear uniform and stand out whether you look in the spreadsheet or
in the timescale.

To Wrap Task Names Around

You can double the row height of only the tasks with long names (skip the first step if
you want to do this) or you can double the height of all rows. The task names will wrap
around automatically.

1. Select the tasks to adjust the row height by holding down and clicking the row headers of the tasks to adjust.
    OR
    Select the entire spreadsheet by clicking on the table selector at the intersection of the row and column headings in the top left corner of the spreadsheet: ☐.

2. Point to one of the selected row dividers in the row headings (normally the ID column); make sure you see the double-headed arrow mouse pointer ✚.

3. Drag the divider down to at least double the row height. MS Project will automatically wrap the text onto the second line, but only wrap the words in the text fields, like **Task Name, Notes** and the extra fields (**Text1, Text2**, etc.).

 You will double the number of pages in your printout if you double the row height for all rows.

 You can now wrap the text in the column headings as well. Double-click on the column heading and check ☑ **Header Text Wrapping**. If the column width is too narrow for the title, it will start wrapping automatically.

To Adjust the Column Width

Double-click on the heading of the column to adjust; the **Column Definition** dialog shows up. Click 　Best Fit　; the column width automatically takes the appropriate width for all tasks in the project, even the ones not currently visible on the screen.
OR
Point to the divider in the column heading, and make sure you see a double-headed mouse pointer as shown in the next screenshot; then double click:

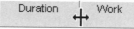

The width of the column is now wide enough to accommodate the widest text in the field for the entire project (up to a maximum of about 150 characters).

 The text in the column headings will wrap automatically if the option ☑ **Header Text Wrapping** is checked in the **Column Definition** dialog. Double-click on the column heading to display this dialog.

To Position the Pane Divider on a Column Split

You can put the divider between the spreadsheet and the Gantt Chart exactly on the border of a column.

1. Point with the mouse pointer anywhere on the vertical divider that separates the spreadsheet from the timescale; you should now see the mouse pointer ◄▐►.

2. Drag it close to the column split where you want it.

3. While you continue to see the mouse pointer ◄▐►, double-click and the divider now jumps to the column split that is closest to it.

To View the Whole Project Timescale

1. Choose **View, Zoom**; the **Zoom** dialog appears:

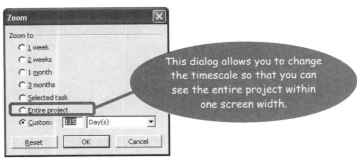

2. Select ⦿ **Entire Project**.

3. Click   OK   .

To Format the Timescale

Click **Zoom Out** 🔍 on the **Standard** toolbar to zoom out until you can see all the task bars. If you zoom out too far, you can use **Zoom In** 🔍 on the **Standard** toolbar to zoom back in on the details.

If you want to customize the timescale to your exact preference:

1. Double-click on the timescale itself 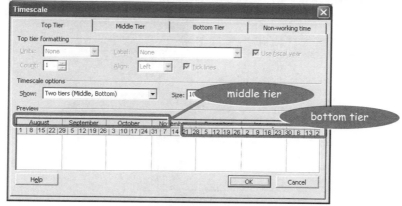.

   OR
   Choose the menu items **Format, Timescale**; the **Timescale** dialog appears:

 2. If you want to display the third tier, you need to select **Three tiers** in the **Show** list. Choose the settings for the **Top Tier** (top of the timescale), the **Middle Tier** (middle) and the **Bottom Tier** (bottom) by clicking on the appropriate tabs. The **Count** is like an increment. If it is set to "2" in a day-by-day timescale, it will go from the 1st to the 3rd and so forth. As a result, only every other day will be displayed.

3. Click OK.

 Having three tiers in the timescale now allows you to show the fiscal year and calendar year timescales next to each other so that there can be no misunderstanding about the exact dates. You can set the start month of the fiscal year in **Tools, Options, Calendar** under **Fiscal year starts in**.

To Format the Task Bars

1. Double-click anywhere in the background of the timescale area.
   OR
   Choose **Format, Bar Styles**, and the **Bar Styles** dialog appears:

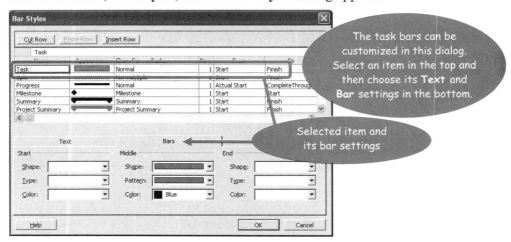

2. In the list in the top half (see next screenshot), select the type of task for which you want to change the appearance:

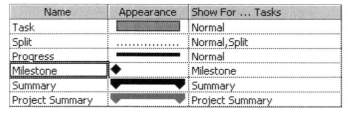

Name	Appearance	Show For ... Tasks
Task		Normal
Split	....	Normal,Split
Progress		Normal
Milestone	◆	Milestone
Summary		Summary
Project Summary		Project Summary

3. Choose your settings for the selected task type at the bottom of the dialog on the **Text** and **Bars** tabs.

4. Click [OK].

Some remarks about this powerful, but not so intuitive dialog box:

◆ MS Project first creates in the Gantt Chart the task bar listed at the top, and then draws the second task bar on top of the first one. If they overlap, only the second bar can be seen fully. Therefore, the order in which the items are listed is important. Lower ones can cover higher ones in the list.

◆ Under **Show For ... Tasks**:

◇ The word *Normal* is used for a rest category, the default type of task. It means a task that is not a summary task, not a milestone, not a flagged and not any of the other task types shown in the pull-down list.

◇ You can use the listed items. You can also type in the word **Not** in front of each item to create an exception for that type of task. "**Not Summary**" means format the task bars as specified for any task type except for summary tasks.

◇ You can specify multiple criteria separated by a comma. The comma functions as a *logical and*, in other words when it says **Normal, Split**, it means that it will apply this bar style only to normal tasks that have a split. Any other tasks are not affected.

◆ The lists you can display in the fields **From** and **To** have all the regular task fields in them, but also some additional ones specifically for the timescale, like the **CompleteThrough** date and **Negative Slack**. Neither one is a regular task field you can display in the spreadsheet. The **CompleteThrough** is used in the Tracking Gantt to display progress bars. For an application of the **Negative Slack** item, see page 434.

◆ On the **Text** tab in the bottom half of the dialog, you can add text to the left or right of or even inside the task bars. You will find the following default settings in the Gantt Chart:

◇ **Resource Names** are put to the right of the detail task bars.

◇ The **Start** dates are shown to the right of the milestone diamonds.

 If you follow our advice and remove the **Start** and **Finish** columns from the spreadsheet, you could consider adding them as text next to the bars in the timescale, where you can see them, but not change them (and accidentally set constraints that you don't need).

To Show Milestone Diamonds on Summary Task Bars

1. Select the milestones by holding down [Control] and clicking on each milestone in the **Task Name** column.

2. Click **Task Information** 📇 on the **Standard** toolbar, and the **Task Information** dialog appears. Click the tab **General**; the dialog now looks like:

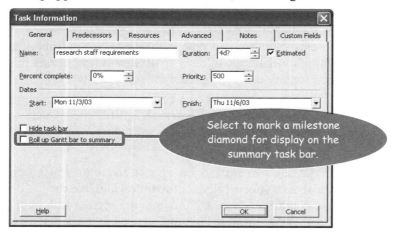

3. Check ☑ **Roll up Gantt bar to summary**.

4. Click OK .

5. Select the summary task, click **Task Information** 📇 again and make sure that the option ☑ **Show rolled up Gantt bars** is selected:

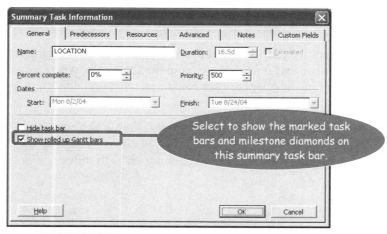

6. Click OK .

To Adjust the Page Setup

Notice that the page setup settings are view specific. For each view listed in the **View** menu, you can set different settings that are stored in the view object itself.

Setting the Page Orientation

1. Choose **File, Page Setup**, and the **Page Setup** dialog appears. Click the tab **Page**:

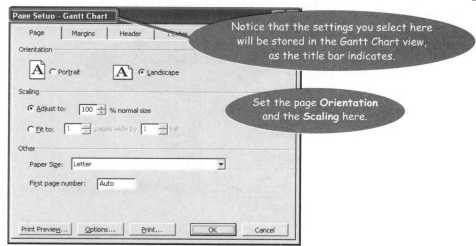

2. Select ◉ **Portrait** or ◉ **Landscape** as the *page orientation*.

3. Click [OK].

Setting the Margins

1. Choose **File, Page Setup**, and the **Page Setup** dialog appears. Click the tab **Margins:**

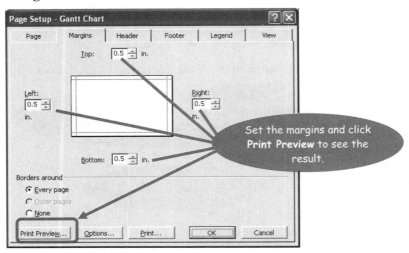

2. Set the margins you need. Click Print Preview... to check if the settings are right.

3. In print preview, click Close to return.

Creating a Header, Footer or Legend

1. Choose **File, Page Setup**, and the **Page Setup** dialog appears. Click the tab **Header, Footer** or **Legend**:

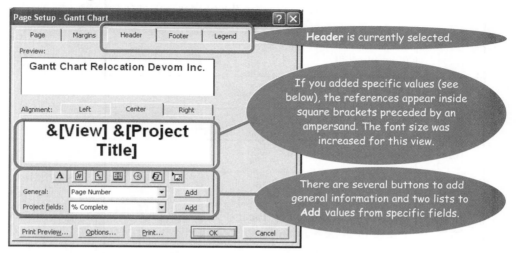

Header is currently selected.

If you added specific values (see below), the references appear inside square brackets preceded by an ampersand. The font size was increased for this view.

There are several buttons to add general information and two lists to **Add** values from specific fields.

2. Under **Alignment** click the tab **Left**, **Center** or **Right** and position the cursor inside the text box where you want to add a reference to project data. You can even press [Enter ↵] to create extra lines.

3. Select a reference from the **General** list at the bottom and click [Add]. The reference is inserted at your cursor position. Add as many text references as needed; most refer to data entered in the **File, Properties** and the **Project, Project Information** dialogs and all start with an ampersand (&). You can also type literal text, like: *Page &[Page] of &[Pages]*, which will print as *Page 1 of 9*.

4. Using the list **Project fields** at the bottom, you can insert project-level information, like the **Baseline Finish** and forecast **Finish** date, or the **Baseline Cost** and forecast **Cost,** or calculated values, like the **% Complete** and **Remaining Duration** for the project.

5. Click one of the buttons to add information quickly:

Button	For
A	font, size and style In order to format the text in the header, select the text first and then click **A**.
	page number
	total number of pages
	date: the system date
	time: the system time
	the schedule name
	Takes you into a dialog for inserting a graphic image into the header, footer or legend; often used to insert the *project logo*

6. Click OK or Print Preview...

Exercises

Review Questions

1. What is the difference between constraint and deadline dates in the way MS Project treats these dates?

2. What is the main output from a project model that is scheduled forward? What about one that is scheduled backward?

3. Which of the following constraints can cause a scheduling conflict? In the next table, add a check mark in the cells where scheduling conflicts could occur:

	In a forward scheduled project	In a backward scheduled project
ASAP		
ALAP		
FNET		
FNLT		
MFO		
MSO		
SNET		
SNLT		

4. Would you set a constraint in the following situations? If so, which type of constraint? In the next table, indicate the type if you would recommend using a constraint.

Situation	Type of constraint
You have a *board meeting* coming up on January 16 in which a go/no-go decision will be taken on the next stage of your project. The board expects certain reports to be ready.	
A vendor needs to deliver custom-made computers to you that you need for testing activities in your project (*computers delivered*).	
You have planned a *"project burial"* ceremony to close off your project. You have invited senior executives and other dignitaries for this special day.	
A testing lab is only available to your project from March 1 to March 15.	

5. Why would you want to minimize the number of constraint dates in your project model?

6. As a car manufacturer, you would like to use an outdoor test lab that consists of a 10 km highway stretch on which different weather conditions can be simulated. The lab is fully booked, but there is a window of opportunity for your project from November 10-17 in 2006 or after April 1st in 2007. How would you model this in MS Project?

7. Is there a way in which you can easily display the entire project duration in the timescale on your screen? If so, what are the steps in MS Project to accomplish this?

Relocation Project — Constraints and Deadlines

1. Continue to work with your file *Relocation.MPP* or open the file *06 Entering Constraints and Deadlines.MPP* available for download at www.jrosspub.com. Please, click the link *WAV Download Resource Center* to enter the download site.

2. Set deadlines on the following milestones:

ID	Milestone	Deadline Date
10	location selected	August 20, 2006
16	contractor contracted	August 30, 2006
25	facility remodeled	October 25, 2006
31	new location opened	November 1, 2006

3. Enter the following constraints:

ID	Task	Constraint
8	meet to select the location	Start No Earlier Than August 23, 2006
28	pack	As Late As Possible

4. The CEO, *Mr. Salin,* is out of the country until *August 23*, 2006. The task *pack* should be scheduled *As Late As Possible*; otherwise the equipment may be packed days before the actual move takes place over the weekend. You want the employees to be packed as late as possible on the Friday before the weekend.

5. Compare your file with the solution file *07 Entering Resources.MPP* available for download at www.jrosspub.com. Please, click the link *WAV Download Resource Center* to enter the download site. See page 675 of this book for an automated way of comparing and reporting differences between two versions of one schedule.

6. Save your file for the next exercise.

Relocation Project — Printing the Gantt Chart

With the tasks, estimates, dependencies and constraints completed, we now have entered all the data needed to print a Gantt Chart.

1. Continue to work with the file from the previous exercise.

2. Format the timescale of the Gantt Chart in the following way:

	Middle Tier	**Bottom Tier**
Units	Months	Days
Label	Jan '00	1, 2,...
Count	1	7
Align	Center	Center
Size	100 %	100 %

3. Format the header, footer and legend of the Gantt Chart in the following way:

Page Tab	Section	Set to	Font
Header	Center	&[View] &[Project Title]	Arial, Bold, 20
Footer	Left	&[Manager] &[Company]	Arial, Regular, 8
	Right	&[Date]	Arial, Regular, 8
Legend	Legend on	◉ None	

4. Compare your file with (a printout of) the solution file *07 Entering Resources.MPP* available for download at www.jrosspub.com. Please, click the link *WAV Download Resource Center* to enter the download site.

Chapter 7 Entering Resources

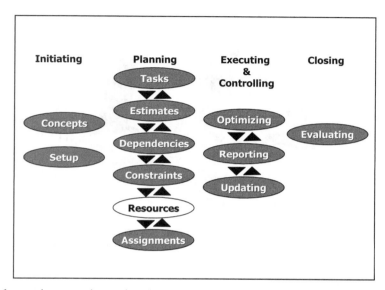

With the tasks, estimates, dependencies, constraints (and deadlines) entered, we now have a Gantt Chart that is a dynamic model of the project. You could stop here if resources, their workloads and their costs are of little concern to you. If they are important in your schedule, you may have to add them to the model and *assign* them to tasks. The result is called a *resource-loaded schedule.*

After reading this chapter you will:
◆ know what resources are and when to add a resource to the project model
◆ know the different types of resources: human, facilities, machines and materials
◆ be aware of important resource-related fields
◆ be able to efficiently enter the resources into the schedule using the enterprise resource pool, download resources from your address book, or manual data entry
◆ know to use generic resources if you don't know who will be on your team
◆ know how to enter the different types of resource availability
◆ be able to create resource calendars
◆ know the cost management features of MS Project
◆ be able to check the list of resources against scheduling best practices
◆ know how to create a resource report

Selling the Project Manager

Joe is the sales representative for the company Bob works for. Joe deals with the clients, and when a contract is closed, he typically introduces Bob to the client as the project manager. Bob looks after the creation and delivery of the project product.

Joe enters Bob's office in a whirlwind of enthusiasm. "Hey, Bob, I got the contract!"

Bob: "Well congrats, Joe, you brought another one in. Thanks for keeping me employed."

Joe: "Yeah, I had to make some concessions though; they wanted the final prototype two weeks earlier. I thought that, with your experience, you could handle that!"

Bob: "Two weeks ... that is three weeks from now! Didn't you realize that my team has at least one more week to go on our current project?"

Joe: "Oh Bob, you have pulled it off before. I am counting on you! And I am offering to help out on the weekends myself!"

Bob: "Well, no thank you. I won't commit to your deadline. I have worked enough weekends to last me a lifetime! And, by the way, what would you help us with?"

Joe: "How am I going to get the prototype done? Why don't you want to do it?"

Bob: "Well, perhaps I am not willing to work weekends, because ... there is no sales commission coming to me when you make ridiculous promises to clients to close the deal. You made the promise without consulting me; now it is your problem, not mine."

What Is a Resource?

Resources are *people*, *facilities*, *machines* or *materials* necessary to create the project product.

Each activity typically needs one or more resource. If you find an activity doesn't need resources, we recommend you model it as a *lag* on a dependency instead of as a task in your schedule. For example, the task *drying of paint* does not need resources and would be better modeled as a lag (see page 223 for the how-to steps). In this way, each task bar actually represents discrete effort.

Apart from resources, there are also *responsible* people. A *resource* and *responsible person* differ in that:
◆   The responsible person does not necessarily spend time and effort on project activities like resources do.
◆   Resources also include facility, machine and material resources.
◆   Resources are normally assigned to activities on the lowest level in the *Work Breakdown Structure*, whereas responsibilities are normally assigned on a higher level.

Responsibilities

Responsibilities for deliverables are typically captured in a *Responsibility Assignment Matrix*[60] also called *RAM* or *Responsibility Chart*. MS Project does not have special features to create a chart like that, but responsibilities can be captured in other ways.

Each deliverable needs a responsible person. Deliverables are captured as summary tasks, and if you *assign* a person to summary tasks, the assignment will create effort (work) for the responsible person during the entire duration of the summary task, which you probably don't want.

---

[60] See the glossary of the PMBOK® Guide, 2004 Edition, Project Management Institute.

If you want to indicate responsibilities in your schedule without adding effort, you can accomplish this in one of three ways:

◆ You can assign the responsible people to the milestone of the deliverable. Since milestones have a duration of zero and therefore no effort, there is no problem assigning responsibilities to milestones. You will find more on how to create assignments in the next chapter.

◆ You can assign the resource to the summary task if you set the **Units** to 0% (zero percent) to prevent this assignment from adding to the work value. By default, the resource name does not show up in the timescale for summary tasks, but you can change this in the **Format, Bar Styles** dialog: select **Summary**, click tab **Text** and in the field **Right** select **Resource Names** from the list. This will make the name of the resource appear for example as *Andrea [0%]* next to the task bar in the timescale. The extra *[0%]* for the zero units does not look all that great, but you cannot get rid of it.

◆ MS Project has enough extra text fields to capture responsibilities. Use the extra **Text1** field, for example, and rename it *Responsible Person* by choosing **Tools, Customize, Fields**. If you click [Value List...], you can even create a pick list for this field. You can also display names of the responsible people to the left of the task bars in the timescale using the **Format, Bar Styles** dialog. This method has the fewest complications and may therefore be the best method. We recommend displaying the names to the left of the task bars, since the names of resources are displayed to the right by default. In this way, it is clear who is responsible and who is a resource.

MS Project accommodates defining resources in the **Resource Sheet** and assigning resources in the **Gantt Chart** view. We will discuss assigning in the next chapter, and we will discuss defining the resources here.

When to Add a Resource

A resource should only be entered as a resource in the model of the project if you expect that the resource may significantly affect the quality, duration or cost of the project. If the resource will not have an impact on quality, duration or cost, you can keep your model leaner by leaving the resource out. If you add resources and *assign* them to the tasks, you have created a *resource-loaded schedule*.

A resource that is *easy to replace* will not likely affect the schedule. In fact, in construction, contractors rarely allow their schedule to be driven by a lack of resources. Generally, it is easy to find bricklayers, carpenters and electricians. Resources that are scarce could increase the duration of the project. Resources will increase the duration of your project:

◆ If they are not available when you need them. For example, you need a sign-off and the busy executives are out of the country, which may affect the duration of your project. Materials that have to come from afar can also affect the schedule. Generally speaking, the more borders that need to be crossed, the more time risk there is.

◆ If human resources are assigned to many tasks and become over-allocated, their workloads need to be leveled. *Experts* are an example of resources that are often over-allocated. Leveling often leads to longer projects.

 If you over-allocate resources, they may affect the duration of the project. Sometimes over-allocations can be solved within the project duration, and sometimes they will extend the project duration. If you find that limited resource availability affects the scheduling of tasks, you have a *resource-constrained schedule* also known as a *resource-limited schedule*.[61]

To manage the cost of the project, you have to define all the *people*, *facilities*, *machines* and *materials* that have a significant cost associated with them in the resource sheet. For example, if you need outside legal advice, you will pay high hourly rates that you need to capture for your project budget; a corporate lawyer in New York will set you back $450 per hour (and that was when this book was written). You do not have to enter small expenses into your MS Project model. MS Project is not meant to be accounting software. There are several reasons for this:

◆ MS Project is a modeling tool with which you deliberately simplify the reality. Accountants cannot afford themselves to simplify; they need to reflect the reality as precisely as they (humanly) can. Project managers, on the other hand, should focus on the big picture from a 10,000-foot distance.

◆ Project managers use averaging when they model their project. Project managers may average levels of effort, for example. Averaging makes accountants cringe. Accountants want facts like bills and nothing else.

◆ Project managers can afford to ignore dollars and cents. They can leave details out, but accountants cannot. Project managers would estimate small expenses in one big category and manage them as a category. Project managers have to stay away from the details to keep their sanity, or they risk letting their schedule get out-of-date.

---

[61] See the glossary of the PMBOK® Guide, 2004 Edition, Project Management Institute.

◆ Accountants are obsessed with the past, whereas project managers are obsessed with the future. In a sense, accountants are the historians of the company whereas the project managers are the "futurologists" of the company. The future has no facts, only the past has facts.

◆ Project managers need only be concerned with expenses that have to be paid from the project budget. Accountants have to be concerned about any expenses within the company. Resources you won't pay for from your project budget can be left out of the schedule. If you use a boardroom that is paid for by the corporation, you would not add it as a resource to the resource sheet from a cost perspective. On the other hand, if you will be paying the rent for a training room from your project budget, you should add the training room as a resource to the resource sheet in MS Project.

In general, accountants do not necessarily make good project managers, as you can see. However, project managers do need some people with an accounting orientation on their team as project control officers. Project managers need to collect actual values to monitor the project and also to learn from the project once it is completed.

Choosing the Options

Choose **Tools, Options** and click on the tab where you want to change settings.

Tab	Option
General	☑ **Automatically add new resources and tasks** This allows entering a new resource wherever and whenever you need a new resource, without having to answer a prompt asking if you really want to create the new resource. In Project Professional with Project Server, you probably don't have the proper access rights to create new resources in the enterprise resource pool as a project manager, and we recommend the option be turned off to prevent accidentally creating many local resources in your project.
	Default standard rate By entering a rate you can reduce the amount of typing you have to do. If the standard rate is set to $50/hr, you don't need to enter a rate for any resource that is $50/hr.
	Default overtime rate By entering a rate you can reduce the amount of typing you have to do.

Tab	Option
	Set as Default This sets the options as the default setting for any new schedules you create. The existing schedules are not affected, because the options are stored in the project schedule (as indicated in the section divider label **General Options for <current schedule name>**).
Schedule	**Show assignment units as a: Percentage** or **Decimals** Units of resources can be expressed as a percentage or in decimals in the **Max. Units** field (availability) and in the assignment **Units** field (workload). This option is a global option and applies to all your projects, existing or new. For example, you have a resource that is available half-time to your project. This option gives you the choice of entering this as *50%* (percentage) or as *0.5* (decimal) in the **Max. Units** field. For part-time resources, **Percentages** seem to make the most sense. Let's consider a situation in which you have 3 carpenters available to your project. You could enter them as a group and enter *300%* (percentage) or as *3* (decimal). For consolidated resources the **Decimals** seem easier to understand. As you can see it would be better for us if this option wasn't global option, but project-specific. You can switch this option at any time; it is entirely your preference.

Types of Resources

MS Project knows only two types of resources: **Work** resources and **Material** resources. These are the two choices given in the resource field **Type**. In practice, you will come across four types of resources: *human, facility, machine* and *material*.

Important questions for each type are:
- Should the resource add to the total amount of effort in the project?
- Should the resource be included in workload leveling?
- Does the resource have a time-related or a unit-related cost?
- Should **Work** or **Material** be chosen in the resource-related field **Type?**

We will discuss these questions for each type of resource:

- *Human resources* are people whose efforts should add up in the *Work* field. The total amount of work per week should be reasonable, which means it is within, or close to their weekly availability. If there are over-allocations, their workloads should be leveled. Human effort costs money, and human resources should be given a standard rate and an overtime rate and cost-per-use rate, if applicable. They have a time-related cost and the rate needs to be appended with "/h" (per hour), "/w" (per week), "/mo" (per month) or "/y" (per year). Human resources need to be entered as **Work** resources.

◆ *Facilities* should not add to the total amount of effort of the project (**Work**). We, therefore, have to make them **Material** resources. The cost of facilities is typically time-related, like monthly rent, for example. Facilities therefore need a standard rate per time unit, and perhaps a cost-per-use rate. Only **Work** resources can have a time-related rate unfortunately. If you want to calculate time-related cost, you could use a workaround, which we will discuss on page 349.

If you enter facilities as material resources, MS Project cannot prevent double reservations by leveling their "workload"; you would not want two different meetings held in one room at the same time. You have to keep an eye on the reservation of the facility yourself. You could choose to enter the facility as a **Work** resource to level its "workload", but this will start adding its "effort" to the amount of **Work** in the project as well, which is not desirable.

◆ *Machines* are similar to facilities in terms of points just made. Machines should not add to the effort of the project and should be entered as **Material** resources. Machines typically have a time-related cost and thus need a standard rate per time unit, but only **Work** resources can have a time-related rate. We have a workaround, which we will discuss on page 349.

If you enter a machine as a material resource, MS Project cannot monitor whether the machine is in use already. You will have to keep an eye on that yourself, just like with facilities.

◆ *Material* resources are *consumable* resources. They should not add to the amount of effort (**Work**) of the project. Materials do not have a capacity like humans or facilities do and do not need to be leveled. Materials do cost money and typically have a unit-related cost only. Materials should be entered as a **Material** resource. The cost per unit should be entered in the **Std. Rate** field without a time unit.

As you can see, Project 2003 only has two types of resources that can be found in the field *Type*: *Work* and *Material* resources. However, there are four fundamentally different types of resources in practice. *Human resources* are typically work resources with effort, leveling and time-related cost. *Material resources* typically do not have effort or leveling and have a per-unit cost. So far, so good. *Facility resources* should not add to the effort, but their capacity should be leveled and they often have time-related cost. We have found a way to enter time-related cost for material resources which we will discuss in detail on page 349; therefore we recommend that they be entered as **Material** resources. The same is true for *machine resources*.

What If You Don't Know Who You Will Get?

In the *planning phase*, you often don't know exactly who is going to do the task. However, if you know you are going to need a programmer, you can enter this resource, for the time being, under the generic name *programmer* in the resource sheet. If you need more precision in your model, you can create *junior* and *senior* generic resources, such as *junior programmer* and *senior programmer*.

 In Project Professional with *Project Server*, the *enterprise resource pool* will be set up by your *project office*. The project office will have added the generic resources that you may need. If you cannot find the resource you need, you would ask your project office to add the generic resource. You need the proper access right to edit the enterprise resource pool. If you are blessed with the rights to maintain the enterprise resource pool, you can open it by choosing **Tools, Enterprise Options, Open Enterprise Resource Pool**. From there the steps are similar to entering resources into MS Project standalone as explained next.

 Not knowing the exact names of the individuals should not stop you from creating a *resource-loaded* schedule. Once you know who you will get on your team, you can reassign the tasks from the *generic resources* to the real individuals. There are several easy ways to accomplish this and we will discuss these ways on page 401.

Change the View to Enter Resources

1. Choose **View, Resource Sheet**.
2. Check if the table **Entry** is active. Choose **View, Table: <name of currently displayed table>, Entry**.

Resource Fields

You will find the following fields in the Resource Sheet. If the field is *required* (as opposed to *optional*), an entry is expected. If a field is *enumerated*, a list with pre-defined options will be presented once you cursor into the field.

Indicator
This field will display indicators for a variety of situations. If a resource is over-allocated, this column will show an ⟐ icon.

Resource Name — required field

Note that the name of the field in the database is *Name*. This is where you enter the name of the resource. We recommend using a standard naming convention to prevent duplicating resources inadvertently. The convention should allow you to sort the resource names. We recommend the convention *last name - first name* when the list gets long. Notice the use of a hyphen (-) instead of the comma (,) because the comma is used to separate multiple entries in a field (also called the *list separator*, which is set in the *Control Panel*). If you use the comma in the resource name field, MS Project will reject this, because it thinks you are trying to enter multiple resources in one row.

What you type in this field will show up in the lists used for assigning resources, like the **Assign Resources** dialog. Only the names entered in this field will show in lists like that. It is therefore imperative that you:

◆ Make the resource names easy to recognize.

◆ Make each resource name unique in this field. If you have more than one *John Smith*, you can look at other fields in the Resource Sheet like **Group** to find out who is who. In the Gantt Chart you cannot distinguish between one *John Smith* and the other, therefore you have to make them unique in the **Resource Name** field.

◆ Sort the resource list alphabetically. You can do this by choosing **Project, Sort, Sort by** and in the **Sort** dialog selecting **Name** in the **Sort by** list and checking ☑ **Permanently renumber resources**. The **Assign Resources** dialog sorts its resources automatically in MS Project.

Type — required, enumerated field

The type of resource can be **Work** (default) or **Material**. Work resources are people. Material resources are facilities, equipment or materials. Examples of material resources are *desktop computers*, *electric cable*, *meeting room* or *concrete*.

Material Label — optional field

The label you type in (for a material resource only!) will show up in several other views and reports. For example, the label *desktop computers* will show on the y-axis in the Resource Graph view to indicate the number of units needed over time. In the timescale of the Gantt Chart, it will show up to the right of the task bars. The label is particularly important for bulk resources to indicate the unit of measurement. For example:

◆ Concrete is measured in *cubic feet (USA), cubic meters (Europe)* or *80-pound bags of mix*

◆ Cable in *yards* (USA) or *meters* (Europe)

When *500* units of the bulk resource *concrete* are assigned, the material label will show up in the Gantt timescale as *500 cubic feet*. The material label defines what one unit is for the bulk resource.

Initials — optional field
In previous versions of MS Project this field was very useful, because you could assign resources to tasks by typing their initials, but nowadays you can point and click when assigning. Initials may still be of use for reporting purposes.

Group — optional field

This field can be used for a variety of purposes, for example to capture the name of the department to which the resource belongs. If you enter department names as the group, you can filter all the tasks for a department. Better still; with the group feature, you can group resources together in their respective departments and see department totals for work and cost. Note that the **Group** field and the group feature (**Project, Group by**) are two different things.

Max. Units (*Maximum Units*) — required field for **Work** resources
This is the maximum availability of the resource to the project. A resource that is available full-time to the project needs 100% in the **Max. Units** field and 50% for a resource available half-time. For a *consolidated resource* the **Max. Units** is the total number of team members on the team. You don't need to enter availability for material resources.

Std. Rate (*Standard Rate*) — optional field
Enter the standard rate for regular work in this field. For example, if you enter *10.50/h*, it means the person earns $10.50 per hour. You don't need a time unit for material resources; the rate will be calculated per unit of material you assign to the task; we will discuss assigning in the next chapter.

You can use the following time units:

If you type	You will see	Which means
m	min	minutes
h	hr	hours
d	day	days
w	wk	weeks
mo	mon	months
y	yr	years

Ovt. Rate (Overtime Rate) — optional field
Enter the rate for overtime work in this field. Do this only:
◆ if you will pay for overtime instead of compensating with extra time off, and
◆ if you will pay a higher rate than the standard rate.
MS Project expects you to indicate separately how many overtime hours are worked on each assignment; those hours will be charged against the overtime rate. Material resources cannot have an overtime rate.

Cost/Use (Cost-per-Use or *Per-Use-Cost)* — optional field
Enter in this field the rate that has to be paid every time the resource is used, which means on each task it is assigned. It can be an *up-front fee*. For example, if you need a *bulldozer* transported to your site, this may cost $200 up front before it does any work. The cost per use will be incurred on every task the resource is used (assigned). The cost is calculated as the Cost/Use rate times the number of units assigned.

Accrue At — optional, enumerated field
Select **Start**, **End**, or **Prorated** to indicate when the costs are incurred. Tab to the **Accrue at** field and a pull-down button ▾ appears. Select one of the following options from the list:

Accrue at	Incurs the Cost	Example
Start	As soon as the task starts.	*actors*
Prorated	The cost is incurred as the task progresses; the cost goes up with the **% Complete**.	*employees*
End	As soon as the task finishes.	*consultants*

The accrual options only pertain to the standard rate and overtime rate; the cost per use is always accrued at the start of the task.

Base Calendar — optional, enumerated field
Select a calendar from the list. The *base calendar* specifies the general working hours and working days for the resource. You can create new base calendars. You can override the base calendar and set individual working hours in the resource calendar. Base calendars are useful in international projects; you can base the resources working in the UK on the *UK base calendar* and the resources in the USA on the *USA base calendar*. These base calendars would have to be created first, which is typically done by your project office. Material resources cannot have a base calendar.

Code — optional field

Type an alphanumeric code, such as an accounting code. This is used to charge the expenses for the resource to a particular cost account. It can be useful for the finance department, but often the tasks or assignments, and not the resources, will be coded to charge to the cost accounts.

Generic — optional, enumerated field

The yes/no field *generic* which can be inserted in the resource sheet allows you to mark a resource as a generic resource. This is usually done by the *Project Server* administrator. Generic resources are roles, positions or function labels (like *carpenter* or *system analyst*); they are not names of individuals (like *Mary Cameron* or *Ben Yong*). Project managers will use generic resources in their initial planning and will replace them with the names of the individuals as soon as they find out whom they will get on their team. Generic resources are very useful for longer term planning. Your human resources department will be delighted if you present them with long-term resource needs instead of what you need next week.

Inactive — optional, enumerated field

The yes/no field *inactive* indicates if the resource is still active in the enterprise resource pool or is inactive and kept for historical purposes only.

Entering Resources

You can enter the resources into the resource sheet in three ways:

♦ Use the shared *enterprise resource pool*. The resources in this pool can be shared by all projects saved in the enterprise database of Project Server. The resources in the enterprise resource pool can be imported from the *company directory* (*Active Directory*)

♦ Download the resources from your *address book*.

♦ Key in the (rest of the) resources manually.

The **Resources** Project Guide will provide all these options to enter resources. Display the Project Guide toolbar by right-clicking on any toolbar and choosing **Project Guide**. Click Resources ▾ , then click the hyperlink **Specify people and equipment for the project**, and you will be presented with the three ways to enter resources. You may think that if you use Project Server, you only need to know how to use the enterprise resource pool, but you overlook that projects often need extra resources that are unique to the project and that are not in the enterprise resource pool; these are called *local resources*. You have to enter them yourself. But let's start with the easy way.

Using the Enterprise Resource Pool

The enterprise resource pool can only be used if *Project Server* has been set up. One of the steps in configuring Project Server is setting up the *enterprise resource pool.* If you also want to do skill-based scheduling, this will take a lot of thinking and planning, since it is no longer a matter of entering names of the resources. Your Project Server administrator needs to do the following:

1. Enter a proper *Resource Breakdown Structure (RBS)*. An RBS is similar to the organizational chart of the organization. It can be a part of the entire organization if you only intend to model the projects of the IT department in the Project Server database, for example. The RBS needs to be developed and entered in the field *Enterprise Resource Outline Code 30* that has permanently been renamed to *RBS* by Microsoft.

2. Give all resources an RBS code (*RBS-code*) using the field RBS (*Enterprise Resource Outline Code 30*).

3. Identify the generic resources you need for longer term resource planning and for use in project templates.

If your organization wants to do *skill-based scheduling*, you also need to do the following:

4. Identify strategic *resource skills* and perhaps even *skill sets*. Each skill needs to be coded. If you want to work with skill sets, you need to do this for each type of skill. You may find for example in a multinational company that it is important to capture the *language skills* as well as the *technical skills* for each person. Also, each resource may speak multiple languages and can have multiple technical skills, like *C++ programming* skills and *Visual Basic programming* skills. In such a case you can use one of ten available *multi-value* skill fields (*Enterprise Resource Outline Code 20-29*).

5. Enter all skills for the actual and generic resources in the *enterprise fields* you customized for skill-based scheduling.

The skill-based scheduling features in Project Server can be very beneficial by saving a lot of time for a variety of people:

◆ *Team Building* and *Resource Substitution*
When project managers first open a project template, they typically will find that only generic resources are assigned to the tasks. The *Resource Substitution Wizard* allows them to quickly find available resources with the right skill set to replace the generic resources. The result is a fully *resource-loaded schedule* with warm bodies instead of zombies (*generic resources*).

◆ *Resource Modeling*
Resource managers can list and analyze the long-term need for the different types of resources. They can analyze resource utilization.

◆ *Resource Management*

Resource managers can now staff projects with resources through *Project Web Access* (runs inside Internet Explorer) with the new web-based *Team Builder* tool and don't need to know Project Professional any longer. They can find resources that are still available even if they work for other resource managers. When *project managers* are faced with a resource leaving the project, they need to quickly find an available resource with the right skill set. They can group the resources by department, location or skills.

◆ *Portfolio Modeling*
Executives can develop scenarios to analyze the impact on meeting deadlines, for example, if they are considering taking on an extra resource or an extra project. To develop these scenarios, you can allow resources to be reassigned in certain projects, whereas assignments in other projects are not affected. You can work with project priority numbers. If you want Project Server to calculate these scenarios automatically, you have to enter the skills available in the resource pool and the skills required for the assignments.

As you can see, the skill-based scheduling features of *Project Server* rely heavily on properly coded skills and skill sets in the enterprise resource pool. If you want skill-based scheduling, you have to spend a considerable amount of thinking and planning before you can take advantage of these features.

Even without skill-based scheduling, project managers can easily connect to the enterprise resource pool and retrieve the resources they need. They will at least use generic resources to indicate to the resource managers what they need. They should establish a connection between *Project 2003 Professional* and *Project Server* which we explained on page 67. Then they create a project and save it to the Project Server database, and the features of **Tools, Build Team from Enterprise...** (*Team Builder*) and **Tools, Substitute resources...** (*Resource Substitution Wizard*) will be available and use the enterprise resource pool.

Download the Resources from the Active Directory

The *Active Directory* refers to the list of user accounts in the Windows Server network operating system. A new feature in Project Server 2003 is that you can now download the resources into the enterprise resource pool from the Active Directory. You can even set up an automatic regular synchronization between the resource pool and the Active Directory in such a way that when employees leave or new ones arrive, the enterprise resource pool is automatically updated by the Active Directory. In this way, you only need to maintain one database, the Active Directory. This is a topic we discuss in grand detail in the Planning, Deploying and Managing an Enterprise Project Management Solution.[62]

Downloading the Resources from Your Address Book

If you are using *MS Office Outlook* for your contact information and address list, you may be able to download the resource names easily from that list. This means you don't have to retype all of them. MS Office Outlook even has powerful import features in the menu items **File, Import and Export**, and if you keep your addresses in another contact management application or database, you should be able to import them. From MS Office Outlook you can import them to MS Project using the following steps:

1. Choose **View, Resource Sheet**.

2. Display the toolbar by right-clicking on any toolbar and clicking on **Resource Management.** The Resource Management toolbar is displayed:

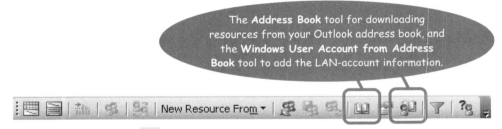

The **Address Book** tool for downloading resources from your Outlook address book, and the **Windows User Account from Address Book** tool to add the LAN-account information.

3. Click **Address Book** 📖 on the **Resource Management** toolbar.

---

[62] See our website www.iil.com.

4. Click [OK]; the **Select Resources** dialog appears:

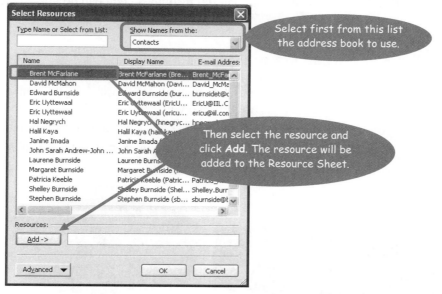

Select first from this list the address book to use.

Then select the resource and click **Add**. The resource will be added to the Resource Sheet.

5. Select the address list from **Show Names from the:** [Contacts ▼], and the names of the resources are now shown in the big list.

6. Type in the first character(s) of the name of the person to add in the field **Type name or select from list**; the list scrolls immediately to the person. Press the arrow keys [↓] or [↑] to highlight the right resource. Press [Enter ↵] or click [Add ->].
OR
Double-click on the resource name; the resource is now added to the list of people at the bottom that will be transferred into the resource sheet in MS Project.

7. Repeat the previous step for all resources you would like to add.

8. Click [OK]; the resources are now added to the end of the resource list. You can always go back into the address list to pick up more resource names. You may want to sort the list alphabetically again to make it easy to find one.

9. If you want to add the **Windows User Account** information, select the resource and click **Windows User Account from Address Book** on the **Resource Management** toolbar to pick up Windows user account information for the resource. If the **Windows User Account** is in the *Enterprise Resource Pool* it will allow enterprise resources to log into *Project Server* without entering their user name and password again.

You will still have to add any project-specific human resources that were not in your address list, as well as facility, machine and material resources. You can do this with the next steps.

Keying in the Resources Manually

An easy way to enter data in certain cells is to drag over all cells in which you want to enter resource information. Multiple cells are selected with one cell still white, which is the input cell. Enter the data in this input cell and use the [Tab] key to make the cursor move to the next cell until you have entered them all. You can even select a nonadjacent series of cells by holding down the [Control] key while dragging.

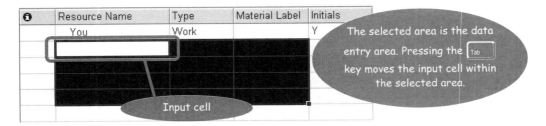

The selected area is the data entry area. Pressing the [Tab] key moves the input cell within the selected area.

Input cell

Here are more precise instructions for the different fields:

1. We recommend you customize the table first so that it has the right columns and in the right order in which to enter data:

   ◇ Delete all columns you will not need by clicking on their column headings and pressing [Del] on your keyboard.

   ◇ Insert new fields by right-clicking on the column heading before which you want to insert a new column; a pop-up menu appears. Choose **Insert Column**; the **Column Definition** dialog appears:

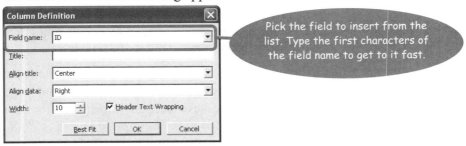

Pick the field to insert from the list. Type the first characters of the field name to get to it fast.

◇ Select the field from the **Field Name** list `ID` ▼ and click `OK` . Repeat these steps for all the fields you need.

◇ You can drag a column around by its heading if you want to move it. First click the column heading and when you see the mouse pointer , drag the column to its desired place.

2. Enter the name of the resource in the field **Resource Name** and press:

`Enter ↵` to go down (to the next row), or

`Tab` to go to the right (to the next column).

3. If the resource is a material resource (facilities, machines or materials), change the field **Type** from **Work** to **Material** and enter the unit of measure for the material resource in the field **Material Label**, for example *cubic yard* for resource *concrete*. If you change the type of the resource, you will lose any rates you may have typed in for the resource. This is because **Work** resources require a time-related rate, like *$50/h*, whereas **Material** resources need a per-unit cost, like *$150 per door*.

4. For **Work** resources only, enter the availability on the resource calendar or in the field **Max. Units**. MS Project assumes that material resources are available in unlimited quantities (i.e. that we live in a rich country).

5. Enter the cost rates in the fields **Std. Rate, Ovt. Rate** and **Cost/Use** and determine when the cost will be accrued by choosing **Start**, **Prorated** or **End** in **Accrue at**.

6. Enter the **Base Calendar** field and a list button will appear. Select the appropriate base calendar for the resource from this list. Normally this would be *Standard* unless more *base calendars* were created which is useful in international projects. You can create other base calendars by choosing **Tools, Change Working Time…** and clicking the button `New…` . This *New* button is not available when you use Project Server, because base calendars are supposed to be prepared centrally by the project office. You may have to ask them to create another base calendar, which we will explain in more detail.

Base Calendars and Resource Calendars

A *resource calendar* is a calendar that is specific for an individual. You can enter individual working times and vacations in a resource calendar. There is a resource calendar available for each resource, but you do not need to modify one unless you expect it to have a significant impact on the schedule. All resource calendars will have

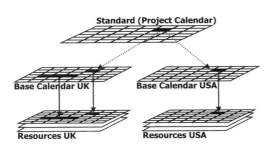

the settings that you entered in the project calendar (see page 116). Apart from the project calendar, there can be one or more *base calendars* on which resource calendars can be based. For example, you will need base calendars if your team members are in different countries. You would create a base calendar for each country and then base each resource on his country calendar (see the illustration). If resources belong to different companies, you may also need multiple base calendars.

Creating a Base Calendar

The *Standard (Project Calendar)* is the default base calendar for all resources. You can create new *base calendars* (and new *task calendars*) in the following way:

1. Choose **Tools, Change Working Time...** ; the **Change Working Time** dialog appears:

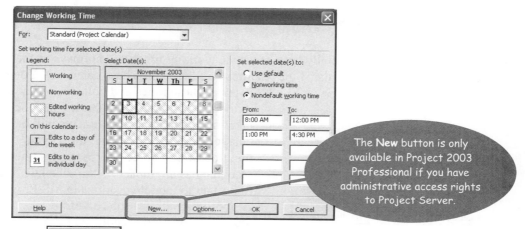

2. Click **New...** . This button may not available in *Project 2003 Professional*, since base calendars are often created centrally by your project office. The **Create New Base Calendar** dialog appears:

3. In the dialog you can choose to copy the *Standard (Project calendar)* as a starting point for the new base calendar. This is a one time affair; the *Standard* calendar will not continue to be synchronized with the base calendar (see dotted arrows in illustration), unlike the base calendars; they will continue to update all the resource calendars (see solid arrows in illustration). Enter a name and select either ⦿ **Create new base calendar** or ⦿ **Make copy of Standard** and click **OK** .

4. You are now back in the **Change Working Time** dialog, but with the newly created base calendar shown in the list **For:** at the top of the dialog. Enter the working times for the base calendar and the holidays. Click **OK** .

5. You are now back in the **Resource Sheet** view; if not, please switch to this view. In the resource-related field **Base calendar** you can select the new base calendar from the list and assign it to certain resources. The resources are now based on the

calendar and MS Project will schedule their work accordingly. If you marked the Christmas days off as holidays, no work will be scheduled on those days.

Editing a Resource Calendar

The resource calendar will initially have the same working times and holidays as the project calendar (or base calendar if the resource was based on a base calendar). You can override these times and holidays on each individual resource calendar. If someone takes a vacation, the assignments will be delayed until the resource returns. The duration of the project increases, and the resource has an impact on the schedule. It is important to model vacations in MS Project. A poorly timed vacation can easily jeopardize precious deadlines. Entering resource vacations is not a lot of work, so there is no good reason not to.

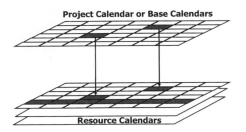

To edit a resource calendar you can:

Double click on a resource and in the **Resource Information** dialog, click on tab **Working Time**. This will allow you to do one resource at a time.
OR
If you want to edit several resource calendars in a row:

1. Choose **Tools, Change Working Time…**; the **Change Working Time** dialog appears:

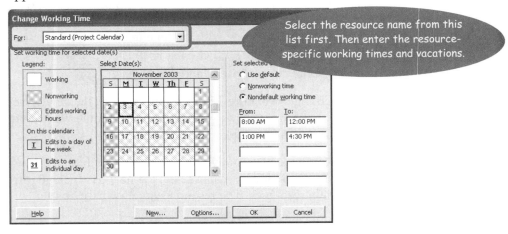

2. Select the resource for which to set the calendar in the list

   For: | Standard (Project Calendar) ▾ |

   If you don't find any resource names in this list, you have not entered the resources yet into your schedule.

3. Change the working times by selecting the day(s) | M | T | W | Th | F |, selecting
   ⦿ **Nondefault working time** and typing the working time in the boxes:

   From: **To:**

   | | |
   | | |

4. To enter a vacation for the individual, highlight the days (you can select multiple days by holding down [Control] while clicking and/or dragging). Then select
   ⦿ **Nonworking time**.

5. Select the next resource from the list **For** at the top to enter another resource calendar or click [OK] when you are done with all resources.

You can even change days that were marked as holidays or weekend days on the **Standard (Project Calendar)** back to working days for a resource. If you want to change a day back to what it is in the project calendar, you have to select the day first and then select ⦿ **Use Default**.

The task-related field **Ignore Resource Calendar** is by default set to *No* for all tasks. This field determines if MS Project will use the *resource calendar* when scheduling assignments. The field is useful when the task also has a *task calendar*. The task calendar overrides the resource calendar. With the new field you can let MS Project know that you have resolved the conflict between the resource calendar and the task calendar. If you leave it set to *No*, the calendar conflict icon 📇 will stay visible in the **Indicators ❶** column. If you change it to *Yes*, it will go away. The schedule should be the same.

The working hours in resource calendars can become very intricate and require a lot of data entry, such as resources working day or night shifts in alternating weeks. You have to ask yourself if you would prefer to manage these shift resources as a consolidated resource instead of as individual resources. If you choose the latter option, your schedule might become very maintenance-hungry. Fortunately, shift work is less prevalent in projects than in the ongoing operations of manufacturing companies. We don't recommend you model the exact working hours of individual resources. There seems to be little gain in that in terms of accuracy of the forecasts and a lot of effort to keep them up to date.

The *Fixed Duration* tasks will look at the resource calendars, but may extend the task duration and task bar when one of the assigned resources is not available. This surprises many people. MS Project does prompt you before extending a fixed duration.

The Max. Units of a Resource

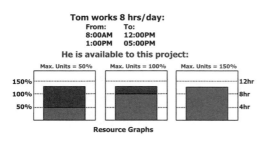

Tom works 8 hrs/day:
From: To:
8:00AM 12:00PM
1:00PM 05:00PM
He is available to this project:

Resource Graphs

The maximum units (**Max. Units**)of resources determine what percentage of one's work hours is available to the project. In the illustration you can see that Tom works 8 hours per day and if the **Max. Units** is 50% there would be a steep over-allocation (dark gray). If the **Max. Units** is set to 100%, there is a small over-allocation. If it is 150% there is remaining availability. You can see that the percentage entered in the **Max. Units** field determines what will constitute an over-allocation for the resource.

Note that the **Max. Units** percentage is relative to the working hours entered on the resource calendar. The working hours can change from week to week. In other words, if you enter 50% as the maximum units, the person would be available 4 hours per day during full-time working hours. If the working hours are only half during certain days, the availability would be only 2 hours per day during those weeks.

Resource Availability

The availability of resources varies from one resource to another and from week to week. The different types of availability are:

◆ *Temporary*, see page 335
   For example, somebody can be "loaned" to a project for only one month.

◆ *Varying availability,* see page 336
   This is a resource that is, for example, available full-time one month, but only half-time the next month.

◆ *Part-time*, see page 337
   This is a person who works fewer hours a day or fewer days a week than a

full-time-equivalent resource as defined in the **Tools, Options, Calendar, Hours per Day** setting.

◆ *Full-time*, see page 338
By default MS Project considers a full-time person to be someone who works 40 hours and 5 days a week. Microsoft has designated this the *default workweek*, and any diversions from this are called *exceptions*.

◆ *Compressed workweeks* (see page 338):
◇ *4-40 workweek* or *every Friday off*
A person works only 4 days per week, but 10 hours per day.
◇ *9-80 workweek* or *alternating Fridays off*
This type of workweek means that a person works for 9 days a total of 80 hours and then takes 1 day off, normally a Friday.

◆ *Overtime*, see page 340
If the deadline is in jeopardy, resources can be asked to start working overtime to compensate for the lack of progress. This is typically not entered during the *planning phase*, but during the *execution phase*.

◆ *Consolidated resources*, see page 343
Consolidated resources are multiple resources that are entered into the schedule as one group instead of as individuals. For example, you can enter 5 Visual Basic programmers as 5 separate individuals, but you can also enter them as one team of 5 (consolidated resource).

On the next pages, we will discuss how each of these resource availabilities can be entered into Project 2003. In many cases, you will have to edit the resource calendar. As a project manager in the *Project Server* environment you may not have the proper access rights to add or change resource availability in the enterprise resource pool, but you still need to know how to do this for the resources that are private to your project, called *local resources*.

Temporary Availability

An example of temporary availability is when a specialized test lab is only available in the month of May for a project team. If a resource is available only during a certain period, you can enter this *temporary availability* in the **Resource Information** dialog box:

1. Double-click a resource in the Resource Sheet view
   OR
   Select the resource, click **Resource Information** 📇 on the **Standard** toolbar

2. Click the tab **Working Time**; the dialog should now look like:

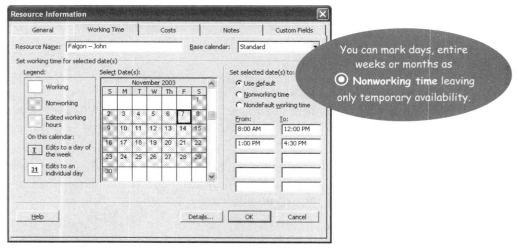

3. Now mark all days in every month that the resource is not available as
   ⊙ **Nonworking time**.

Notice that, unfortunately MS Project does not allow you to mark all weekdays
| M | T | W | Th | F | as ⊙ **Nonworking time**, because it forces you to have at least
one working day. This would have been nice to have, since you would just need to turn
the days on which the resource is available to ⊙ **Use default** settings from the *Standard
(Project Calendar)* or to ⊙ **Nondefault working time**.

Varying Availability

In MS Project you can easily model *varying availability*. You can set up an entire profile
of availability, such as 80% in April, 50% in May, 100% in June, etc. To enter the
availability profile:

1. Double-click a resource in the Resource Sheet
   OR
   Select the resource, click **Resource Information** 📇 on the **Standard** toolbar

2. Click the tab **General**; the dialog should now look like:

3. In the fields **Available from** and **Available to** enter the dates when the resource is available and to what maximum in the field **Units**.

 In an availability profile, you only need to enter the **Available to** dates and MS Project will enter the corresponding **Available from** dates automatically; it takes the next day.

 The **Max. Units** field in the Resource Sheet can only display one percentage of all percentages entered in the availability profile. The one number displayed in the **Max. Units** field will be the availability percentage as per the current date in the **Project, Project Information** dialog. As time goes by, the field **Max. Units** will display all the different values from the availability profile.

Part-Time Availability

Part-time resources can be:

◆ People who work, for example, 4 hours each workday.
The working-time hours in the resource calendar can be set to only 4 hours per day. For example, the working hours could be set to 1:00 PM-5:00 PM for an afternoon job. We recommend this method.
OR
They can be entered in the resource sheet with the **Max. Units** set to 4h/8h * 100% = 50%. A problem with this method can be that all assignments will

be at 50% involvement, and the person assigned to a meeting of 2 hours will only spend 2h * 50% = 1 hour in that meeting, which may be unintended.

◆ People who work 4 out of 5 weekdays; enter this into the schedule by changing a weekday to a nonworking day in their resource calendar. Double click on the resource and click tab **Working time**. Click on **M, T, W, T** or **F** and select ⊙ **Nonworking time**.

◆ Someone who is working on multiple projects and only available part-time to your project. The remaining availability is automatically calculated and displayed within your project if you use the *Project Server* enterprise resource pool that you access with Project 2003 Professional. If you look at the remaining availability you can prevent over-allocations.

A resource can also be assigned to work part-time on a task, which we will discuss in the next chapter on page 372.

Full-Time Availability

People who work *full-time* need to have their **Max. Units** set to 100% or 1.

 Their working hours as set in the resource calendar should correspond with the number of **Hours per Day** and **Hours per Week** settings in the **Tools, Options, Calendar**. For example, if the hours per day in **Tools, Options** is set to 7.5 hours/day, the calendar should show, for example, 8:00 AM-12:00 PM and 1:00 PM-4:30 PM (double-click on the resource and click on the tab **Working Time** to check this). If these two settings are out of sync, you will typically see decimals appear in durations, like 1.07 day.

Compressed Workweeks

4-40 Workweek or Every Friday Off

One example of a *compressed workweek* is when a person works 10 hours per day, but only 4 days per week; this is known as a *4-40 workweek*. This is often the case for people who travel a long distance to work; they may travel on Sunday evening and return late on Thursday evening for a three-day weekend.

If there is more than one resource that will work a 4-40 workweek, we recommend you create a base calendar first, see page 330 or page 339. You can then base all 4-40 resources on this base calendar.

If it is just one resource you can do this with the next steps:

1. In the **Resource Sheet** view, double-click on a resource and the **Resource Information** dialog appears.

2. Click the tab **Working Time**; the dialog should now look like:

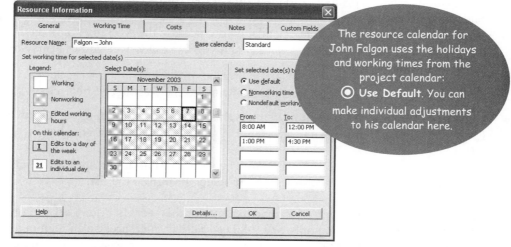

3. Select the working days **M** through **T** for this resource by dragging over them: M T W Th F.

4. Select ⦿ **Nondefault working time**.

5. Enter the longer working hours that correspond to a 10 hour workday in the **From** and **To** fields. For example, the workday could be from 7AM-12PM and 12:30PM-17:30PM.

6. Select the Friday by clicking on the **F** and select the option ⦿ **Nonworking time**.

7. When done, click | OK |; the 4-40 base calendar is now created.

9-80 Workweek or Alternating Fridays Off

Another example of a compressed workweek is if a person works a total of 80 hours over 9 consecutive business days and then takes 1 day off, often a Friday.

If multiple resources work this type of week, we recommend you create a *base calendar* first, and then you can base those resources on the 9-80 calendar:

1. Choose **Tools, Change Working Time**; the **Change Working Time** dialog appears.

2. Click [New...] to create a new base calendar. This button may not available if you are using Project 2003 Professional with *Project Server*; only the person with administrative access privileges to the **Enterprise Global** can create new base calendars. In that case, you have to request that the 9-80 calendar be created for you. If you can create your own base calendars: you increase the working hours on the remaining days to almost 9 hours per day and you can mark every other Friday off as ⦿ **Nonworking time**.

3. To use the 9-80 workweek for a resource, switch to the **Resource Sheet** view.

4. Click in the field **Base Calendar**, which is the second-last column in the resource **Entry** table; a list button ▾ appears. Click ▾ and select **9-80** from the list.
   OR
   Double-click on a resource and the **Resource Information** dialog appears. Click the tab **Working Time**, and in **Base Calendar** select **9-80** from the list.

Notice that there should be two 9-80 calendars: one for this week's Friday off and one for next week's. However, using only one 9-80 calendar is often precise enough in terms of the big picture; you will only loose a bit of accuracy in the forecasts. At least it makes sure that you have incorporated the impact of regular Fridays off work, regardless on which dates these Fridays fall exactly. Sometimes you will loose a day, sometimes you gain a day and the law of averages is going to work for you. Again, project managers should focus on the big picture. If you are in a short project, we recommend you consider adding the second, complementary 9-80 calendar.

Note that for a 10-day task with a 9-80 resource assigned, MS Project will only use 9 business days in the timescale for *Fixed Units* and *Fixed Work* tasks. For *Fixed Duration* tasks, it will use 10 business days in the timescale. Again, MS Project treats Fixed Duration tasks slightly differently.

Overtime Availability

Overtime work is work done outside the regular work hours as indicated in the *resource calendar* (or *project calendar*).

In the initial *planning phase* of the project, you would normally not plan overtime, unless the project is extremely time-constrained right off the bat. Normally the overtime feature is only used during the *execution phase*, when we may try to compensate for slippages.

Overtime can be entered in several different ways depending on whether you pay and what rate you pay for overtime:

◆ If the resource is not paid for overtime, but instead is compensated with extra time off, there are several ways in which you can model this:

◇ You can enter the overtime by increasing the **Max. Units** in the resource sheet to greater than 100%. This is the quick and easy way to enter overtime, and the resource will be working overtime during the entire project.
OR

◇ To be somewhat more precise you can create an *availability profile* in the **Resource Information** dialog , tab **General**; in **Resource Availability** you could specify overtime just for the period in which the resource works more than 100%.
OR

◇ Increase the working time in the resource calendar. For example, somebody works 10 hours overtime in one week, and in the second week the overtime is compensated with time off.
OR

◇ Enter the overtime by changing holidays or weekend days in the resource calendar to working days. Later on, weekdays are set to nonworking days to compensate in time.

◆ If the resource is paid for overtime hours at the regular rate, you only need to check if you kept the over-allocations reasonable. All regular and overtime hours worked are charged at the same standard rate.

◆ If the resource is paid for overtime hours at a higher rate, you have to enter all the hours worked in overtime separately. You enter them on the *Task Form* in the Gantt Chart or in the *Resource Usage* view. We will explain this in more detail next.

Entering Overtime Hours at the Overtime Rate

1. Choose **View, Resource Sheet** and enter the overtime rate in the field **Ovt. Rate**.

2. Choose **View, Gantt Chart**.

3. Choose **Window, Split** to display the **Task Form**.

4. Click on the **Task Form** to make it active.

5. Choose **Format, Details, Resource Work** to display the field **Ovt. Work**. The view should now look like:

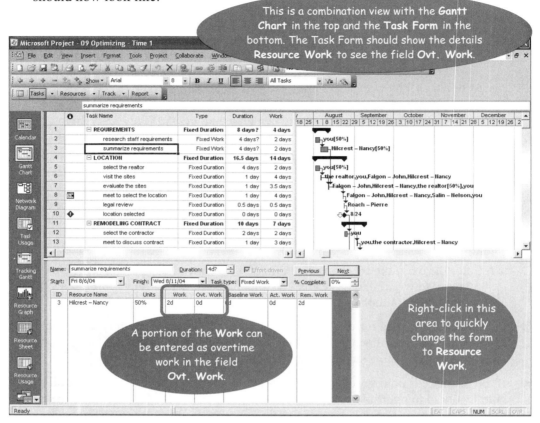

6. Select the task first in the top view, the Gantt Chart, then indicate in the bottom view Task Form in the field **Ovt. Work** how many of the hours shown in the field **Work** will (or should) be worked in overtime.

7. Upon making changes in the Task Form, the [Previous] button transformed to [OK] and when you click it, the data will be entered into the schedule.

OR

Choose **Resource Usage** and then choose **Format, Detail Styles** and select in the list **Available fields** the item **Overtime Work** and click [OK]. In the timescale, you can now enter the overtime hours on the days you think you will have your team members work overtime.

The number of overtime hours has to be reasonable relative to the total number of hours **Work**. If an assignment is 10 hours, you could ask for 2 hours in overtime at most on a weekday and finish the task in 1 business day. If the assignment is 20 hours, you cannot expect a resource to work 8 hours and then 12 hours in overtime to finish within the same day. MS Project would schedule this as one 20-hour workday, which is asking a little too much … for most of us. If the assignment happens to fall on a Friday, you could ask the resource to work in the weekend.

Consolidated Resources

A consolidated resource is a group of pooled individuals, not separate individuals. The group of people is entered as one consolidated resource, one line item. The maximum units are set to the number of *full-time equivalent* individuals who are part of the consolidated resource. Full-time equivalency is defined in the **Tools, Options**, tab **Calendar**, **Hours per Day** setting. For example, if you have 2 full-timers and 2 half-timers on a team, the maximum units for that consolidated resource should be set to 2 * 1 + 2 * 0.5 = 3 or 300%.

Consolidating resources is a beautiful way to keep the devilish details out of your schedule. You basically make an agreement with the team of 3 resources that you will not give them more work than up to 3 full-time equivalent resources. They will have to determine among themselves who will do which task, and because they know each other's expertise best, teams can be very good at that. As a project manager, you will spend a lot less time maintaining detailed resource data and keeping the individual workloads leveled.

Consolidating resources only makes sense if the resources can substitute for each other. If you have experienced and novice resources, you can create two consolidated resources: *junior* and *senior*. For example, if you find that the experience level among your programmers varies widely, create a group of junior and a group of senior programmers. If that does not provide enough precision, you have to revert to modeling resources individually. MS Project is a modeling tool in which you should only capture the most significant parameters of the reality of your project that affect the forecasts.

Cost Management

Cost Situations

Economists distinguish between variable cost and fixed cost:

◆ Variable cost can vary with the amount of time needed, units consumed or number of times used. *Labor cost* is a time-related human resource cost. *Facilities* can also have time-related costs, like rent or lease expenses. *Machines* can have:
  ◇ time-related cost such as rent,
  ◇ unit-related cost such as for paper used in a newspaper printing machine, or
  ◇ use-related cost such as the setup cost of the printing machine. This can be entered in the *Cost/Use* field if the cost is incurred on every use of the resource. Another example is the up-front cost to transport a bulldozer to the construction site.
◆ Fixed costs typically are associated with tasks.
  Examples are expenses for licenses, patents and any fixed-price contracts given to subcontractors.

The following table provides an overview and examples of the different types of costs as well as the way these costs are typically entered in MS Project:

Cost Type	Example	Type	Rate Field	Accrue at
Time related	3 days of work @ 300/d	Work	Std. Rate	Prorated
	2 months rent @ 400/mo	Material [63]	Std. Rate	Prorated
Unit related	3 doors @ 150/door	Material	Std. Rate	Start
Use related	$200 Up front for bulldozer	Material	Cost/Use	Start (by default)
Varying rate	Work @ $300/d, after January 1st $350/d	Work	Cost Rate Table	Prorated
Fixed cost	Fixed-price contract painting the house: $8,500	—	Gantt Chart: Fixed Cost	Gantt Chart: Fixed Cost Accrual [64]

The first thing we have to determine for the expense is what *Type* of resource we should make it: *Work* or *Material.* Then the rate needs to be entered in the appropriate rate field; MS Project has many resource-related rate fields: *Std. Rate*, *Ovt. Rate*, *Cost/Use* and *Cost rate tables*.

In the field *Accrue At*, you determine when the cost will take place:

◆ If you select **Start**, the cost will be scheduled on the start date of the assignment. Actual costs will be incurred on the **Actual Start** date.

◆ If you select **Prorated** the cost is spread across the task duration proportional to the number of hours that are scheduled to be worked on each day. This will only be in effect during the *planning phase*; during the *execution phase*, the *actual costs* are accrued on the dates on which the *actual hours* were worked times the standard rate of the resource.

---

[63] If you make the facility a **Material** resource, you have to enter the *consumption rate* in the assignment **Units** field (see page 349) in order to get a time-related cost. The consumption rate is the number of "*units*" used per time unit.

[64] The task-related field *Fixed Cost Accrual* has the same options as the resource-related field **Accrue At: Start, Prorated or End.**

◆ If you select **End** the cost is accrued on the finish date of the task. Actual costs will be incurred on the **Actual Finish** date.

Material costs are often accrued at the start, whereas facility and machine costs are often accrued as prorated. For human resource costs, employees are typically prorated, whereas cost for consultants is often incurred at the end.

The **Cost/Use** is always incurred at the start of the task which cannot be changed.

MS Project also has task-related cost fields: *Fixed Cost* and *Fixed Cost Accrual*. These are useful for entering firm fixed-price contracts and license costs. Fixed-price contracts often relate directly to a deliverable and license costs are often inputs to detail tasks. It makes sense to enter them in the task-related field **Fixed Cost**.

In practice, you will find more variations:

◆ A resource can have more than one type of cost associated with it. For example, a maintenance man can have a per-use fee of $50 for travel in addition to an hourly rate of $100. In this case, you would enter the per-use fee in the **Cost/Use** field and the hourly rate in the **Std. Rate** (standard rate) field.

◆ The cost rates themselves can change over time; this is known as *varying cost rates* or *rate profile*. In MS Project you can capture a rate profile in the feature *Cost Rate Table*. You can access the cost rate tables for a resource by double-clicking on the resource and clicking the tab **Costs**. Depending on when the effort is scheduled, MS Project will automatically take the appropriate rate to calculate the cost. See page 351 for more.

◆ You can have multiple cost rate tables per resource. MS Project provides up to five tables for each resource, so you can create five rate profiles per resource, see page 351. If you have a *jack-of-all-trades* resource that does systems analysis, programming and occasionally some testing as well, you could specify three different rate profiles (A, B and C) for each of these different activities. This is important if the effort is billed to clients with rates that are different for each type of work. When you *assign* the resource, you have to indicate per assignment which rate profile you would like to use. We will discuss this on page 400.

◆ Materials may have a *consumption rate*. The consumption rate of materials is how many units of the material are used per time unit. For example, you pour concrete that costs $1 per cubic foot and you know that you typically pour 2000 cubic feet a day with the crew you have. This consumption rate can be entered in the assignment-related **Units** field when you assign the resource to the task. In the **Assign Resources** dialog you would enter *2000/day* in the field **Units**. If the duration of the task is 3 days, the cost will be:

3 days * 2000/day * $1/cubic foot = $6000.

The duration of the task will determine the total cost for the task, and if the duration expands, more units of material will be consumed, which will increase the cost of the task. Essentially you have modeled a *time-related cost* for material resources. See page 349 for more details.

◆ You may need to attribute a portion of a large *capital cost* expenditure to a project. For example, you may need to buy expensive test equipment that will be used in future projects as well. You only want part of this capital expense charged to your project, the part that your project should carry as an expense. If you know the amount you can enter it into the task field **Fixed Cost**. MS Project does not have features to calculate of the amount to charge to one project (project-related *depreciation cost)*. You will have to revert to *MS Office Excel* to calculate the contribution per project; see after this list for more detail and tips.

◆ You may encounter discounts when purchasing large volumes of supplies or raw materials; you would need to enter a lookup table with all rate segments. This is something MS Project cannot easily handle. Again, you need to revert to *MS Office Excel.*

◆ You may need to charge taxes or subtract refundable taxes to the cost amounts. Again, MS Project does not have features for this and *MS Office Excel* or your accounting system might help.

See page 352 and following for more ideas on how to handle these last three challenging situations.

Entering Human Resource Costs

In a *Project Server* environment you may not have the proper access privileges as a project manager to add or change resource rates in the enterprise resource pool. However, you will still need to know how to do this for the resources that are private to your project, called *local resources.*

For example, if you temporarily hire a programmer at $300/day, you can enter this in the resource sheet with the following steps:

1. Choose **View, Resource Sheet**.

2. Enter the name of the resource in the field **Resource Name**.

3. Leave the **Type** of the resource set to the default setting of **Work**.

4. Enter the rate in the field **Std. Rate**; for the programmer you would enter *$300/d*.

5. Enter the other cost rates **Ovt. Rate** and **Cost/Use**, if applicable.

6. Select an **Accrue At** option; choose **Start**, **Prorated** or **End**. The accrual determines when the cost will be incurred in the schedule and is important for cash-flow reports.

7. Assign the human resources to the tasks, which we will discuss in the next chapter.

The time-related cost for facilities, like rental and lease, should be entered as material costs.

Entering Material Costs

The cost of material should be incorporated into the project model only:
◆ if it will be paid from your project budget, and
◆ if it is significant enough to keep track of.
If you expect many small expenses, please don't track each expense separately. You don't want to work with MS project as if it is your accounting system, because it is not meant to be an accounting system. We recommend you create a petty cash or expense category and manage it as a separate budget line item. You can enter it as a **Fixed Cost** on the *project summary task* or on a separate detail task, like *manage petty cash*, forcing MS Project to include it in the total project budget.

If a material expense meets those two criteria, you can enter it in this way:

1. Choose **View, Resource Sheet**.

2. Enter the name of the resource in the field **Resource Name**.

3. Click in the field **Type** for the resource and a list button appears |Work   ▼|; select **Material** from this list.

4. Enter a **Material Label**, which will show up in the Resource Graph and other views to remind users that this resource is a material resource. Enter the label in plural, for example *bricks* instead of *brick*, because you typically *assign* more than one unit. You can even enter *thousand bricks* if you will enter the cost of 1000 bricks in the **Std. Rate** field instead of the cost of one brick. For *bulk resources*, you have to enter the *unit of measurement*; for example, for concrete this would be *cubic yards* or *cubic meters*, and for cables it would be *feet* or *meters*.

5. In the **Std. Rate** field, enter the cost per unit for this resource. For the bricks we could enter *$2.00,* for example. You can fill in a **Cost/Use** as well; for the bricks this could be the cost of transportation to the site, let's say *$400.00*. The overtime rate field is neither available nor needed for material resources. Notice that you cannot

enter the time unit (*/h* or */d*) for material resources; use *consumption rates* to model time-related cost for material resources, see page 349.

6. Select the **Accrue At** method to determine on which date the cost will be scheduled in a time-phased view. You can choose **Start**, **Prorated** or **End**. Materials are often accrued at the start. Prorated is spread evenly with the number of hours that resources work on each day of the task duration. The **Cost/Use** is always incurred at the start of the task and cannot be changed.

The next screenshot of the **Resource Usage** view shows how the accrual for material costs works. The 1000 bricks cost $2 each and are accrued at the start of the task: 1,000 * 2 = $2,000. The mortar costs $5 per cubic foot and is accrued evenly with the hours worked on the task. The trowels at $20 each are accrued at the end of the task:

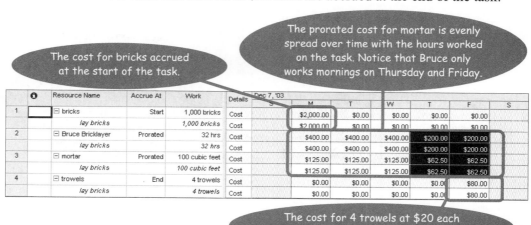

We still need to learn how to assign the number of material resources to the tasks. We will discuss assigning in the next chapter on page 386.

Entering Facility and Machine Costs

This is the most difficult resource situation to enter into MS Project. The use of facilities and machines should not add to the **Work** (effort) of the project. This leads to the conclusion that they have to be entered as **Material** resources. But you cannot enter a time-related rate, like *$400/day*, in the *Standard Rate* field for material resources which is quite common for facilities and machine rental. You can only enter unit- or use-related cost. If you pay a fixed amount for every use of a training room, you can enter that cost in the *Cost/Use* field.

The best way to model time-related cost for facility and machine resources is to enter the resource as a *Material* resource and use the *consumption rate* feature as a work-around to model its time-related cost for the task. The consumption rate is entered into the assignment-related *Units* field, which is found in the *Assign Resources* dialog or the *Task Form*. For example, you organize training and the training room costs your project $600/day. You enter the resource *training room* as a **Material** resource in the Resource Sheet and you enter *600* as the **Std. Rate**. Then you create the *training* task and you assign the training room as the resource, and you enter the consumption rate of *1/d* as the **Units** for the assignment, which means that you will use one room per day (as the consumption rate).

This will appear in the Gantt Chart as follows:

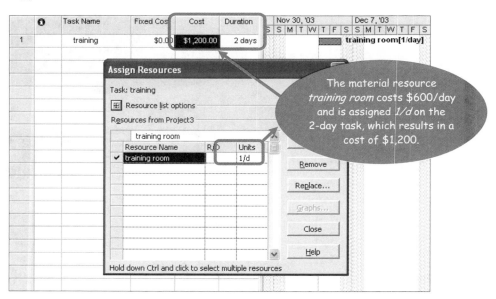

As you can see, we have used the consumption rate feature in MS Project to work around the lack of a specific resource type for facilities. This same workaround can be used to model time-related cost for machines when you rent equipment, for example.

Facility and machine costs are often accrued as prorated or at the end of a task.

Entering Varying Cost Rates

1. Varying cost rates can be entered in the cost rate table in the **Resource Information** dialog.

2. Select a resource and click ; the **Resource Information** dialog appears. Click the tab **Costs** and the dialog will look like:

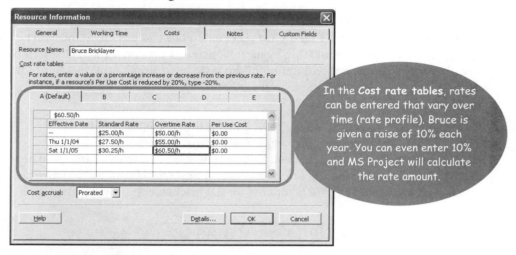

In the **Cost rate tables**, rates can be entered that vary over time (rate profile). Bruce is given a raise of 10% each year. You can even enter 10% and MS Project will calculate the rate amount.

3. Enter the **Effective Date.** Enter the rates that will apply after that date.
   OR
   Enter the percentage with which you want the previous rate to change and MS Project will calculate the new rate for you.

4. Repeat the previous step as many times as the rate will change over time.

5. Click [OK]. MS Project will calculate using the appropriate rate, which depends on when the task is scheduled over time.

In MS Project, you can create rate profiles for all the different types of costs: **Standard Rate**, **Overtime Rate** and **Per Use Cost (Cost/Use)**. This *rate escalation* feature is of particular benefit in multi-year government defense contracts in which new military equipment is envisioned and developed.

Entering Fixed Cost in the Gantt Chart

The fixed cost has to be entered as a task-related cost in the Gantt Chart in the column **Fixed Cost.**

1. Switch to the Gantt Chart view and insert the column **Fixed Cost** or apply the table **Cost**.

2. Enter the fixed cost value in the field **Fixed Cost**. Also indicate when the fixed cost will be accrued in the field **Fixed Cost Accrual.** Your choices are at the **Start** of the task, **Prorated** or at the **End** (finish date). Notice that *Prorated* fixed cost will be spread evenly over the entire duration of the task, regardless of the spread of the effort. All resource-related costs, on the other hand, are spread similarly as the effort is spread.

3. MS Project will then calculate the *total cost* for the task in the field **Cost** as:
   Cost = Fixed Cost + (material costs) + (labor costs).
   The next screenshot shows the **Task Usage** view to illustrate this formula. The total cost of $3,800 for the task *lay bricks* consists of *$600 fixed cost, $2,000* material cost for the bricks and *$1,200* labor cost for the bricklayers:

	Task Name	Fixed Cost	Cost	Duration	Work
1	⊟ lay bricks	$600.00	$3,800.00	5 days	40 hrs
	bricks		$2,000.00		1,000
	brick layers		$1,200.00		40 hrs

The **Cost** for the task is the total of **Fixed Cost**, material cost and labor cost.

Notice that if you enter any cost directly into the **Cost** field for a task, the cost is immediately interpreted as **Fixed Cost** by MS Project and transferred into that field.

Linking a Calculated Cost from MS Office Excel

When you are dealing with *capital costs*, *volume discounts* or *taxes*, we recommend you calculate the cost to attribute to your project in *MS Office Excel*. Then you copy the resulting cost value and paste it into the task-related *Fixed Cost* field or the resource-related *Std.Rate* field of your MS Project schedule. You can even create a dynamic link that will update the schedule automatically when the calculation changes. The steps to do this for the **Fixed Cost** field are:

1. Create the calculation of the cost value in an Excel spreadsheet and save the Excel file (saving is essential if you paste link the number in step 3 instead of a regular paste without a dynamic link). Select the cell with the cost to be charged to the project in the Excel worksheet. Click **Copy** on the **Standard** toolbar in Excel.

2. Switch to MS Project and apply the Gantt Chart view in which you display the field **Fixed Cost**. If needed, create the task and select the cell into which you want to paste the cost.

3. Click **Paste** .
OR
If you expect the number to change several times, you may want to establish a dynamic link between your Excel spreadsheet and MS Project schedule. You can do this by choosing **Edit, Paste Special**, selecting ⦿ **Paste Link** and selecting **Text Data** in the list and clicking OK . The number is now dynamically linked to the spreadsheet. Upon opening the schedule, MS Project will always ask you if you want to update the linked data if the option in **Tools, Options**, tab **Edit**, ☑ **Ask to update automatic links** is checked. If cleared, the update will be automatic upon opening the schedule without a prompt.

 Cells with a dynamic link have a little triangle in the bottom right of the cell. To get rid of a dynamic link, simply select the cell and press ⎡Delete⎤ and a prompt will confirm that you want to remove the link.

Checks on the Resources

The following checks need to be performed to verify whether the resources have been modeled well:

◆ Are all resources identified in the Resource Sheet?
This is the case if all resources that could have a potential impact on the project are entered into the Resource Sheet. There can be impacts on *scope*, *quality*, *duration* or *cost* of the project. Resources and assignments should be entered for projects:

◇ Where it can be expected that limited resource availability or huge workloads will affect the end date of the project.

◇ If you have a cost *budget* for the project and you are responsible for staying within that budget.

◇ If you have a budget expressed in *person months* and you have to stay within this *effort budget*. This is quite common in government IT projects.

◇ If you foresee a *quality* or *scope* impact on the project depending on which resources you will get.

◆ Are all resources named completely and consistently using a naming convention like *<first name> <last name>* or *<last name>-<first name>*?

◆ Are there no overlaps between the resources or duplication of resources?
If there are overlaps or duplications, MS Project will still aggregate the workloads of the resources, but these total numbers will be useless when you check on over-allocations. If Bill Tan is listed twice as a resource (as Bill Tan and William Tan), you would have to sum all time-phased workloads in order to determine if he is over-allocated. The workloads in the Resource Graph and in the Resource Usage can appear to be smaller than they really are when duplicate or overlapping resources exist.

◆ Is the availability of the resources appropriately modeled?
This can be assessed by asking yourself the following questions:

◇ Does the availability of individuals not exceed 120% as captured in the resource field **Max. Units** or the availability profile in the **Resource Information** dialog, tab **General**?
At the International Institute for Learning we set an arbitrary limit and choose the maximum to be 120%. We think it is unreasonable to ask resources for more than 120% availability for periods longer than one week. When you ask resources to work overtime for extended periods of time, their productivity goes down dramatically.[65] So, apart from the fact that it is unreasonable to ask resources for much overtime over extended periods, it does not make sense either. In your organization, the actual threshold may be different from 120%.

◇ If the **Max. Units** are less than 100%, is there a valid reason for this?
Valid reasons are that the project manager works with pure work time estimates (see page 195), that the resources have other ongoing work (or other concurrent projects), or that the resource may be a part-time resource.

◇ Are the vacations of individual resources captured in their resource calendar?
Vacations need to be entered, particularly when there are important deadlines close to the vacations. To check if they are entered, choose **View, Reports, Assignments...**, **Who does what**, click **Edit...**, click tab **Details**, check ☑ **Calendar**, and click **OK**. In print preview, you will now see individual vacations listed under **Exceptions** as well as the exceptions from the *project calendar*. Look careful to verify if the individuals' vacations are listed. You can copy this changed report back into your *Global.MPT* using **Tools, Organizer** to have it ready for future schedule analysis.

---

[65] The OSHA (Occupational Safety & Health Administration) of the U.S. Department of Labor, see www.osha.gov

◆ Are the costs of the resources appropriately modeled?
   The following guidelines will help determine this:

   ◇ Are human resources entered as **Work** resources in the resource field **Type**? Are facilities, machines and materials entered as **Material** resources (see our discussion on page 349)?

   ◇ Do **Material** resources have an appropriate **Material Label** to indicate their unit of measure? For *bulk resources* or *consumable resources* the *material label* should reflect the unit of measure, for example, the material label for cabling could be *yards* or *meters*.

   ◇ Are the rates entered in the appropriate fields?
      - Time-related costs for **Work** resources in the **Std. Rate** field
      - Unit-related cost for **Material** resources in the **Std. Rate** field
      - Time-related cost for facilities and machines as **Material** resources using two fields: the **Std. Rate** field, where you enter the per-unit cost, and the assignment-related *Units* field, where you indicate the number of units used per time unit, for example 2 rooms each day should be entered as *2/day* (for *consumption rate* see page 349)
      - Use-related costs in the **Cost/Use** field
      - Overtime costs in the **Ovt. Rate** field, but only if the overtime is paid and paid at a higher rate than the standard rate. See page 341 for more detail.
      - Rates that vary over time in the **Cost Rate Tables**, see page 351
      - Multiple rates per resource in the five **Cost Rate Tables** and the appropriate cost rate table (A, B, C, D or E) selected for each assignment
      - Task- or deliverable-related fixed costs in the **Fixed Cost** field in the Gantt Chart. See page 352 for more.

   ◇ Is the cost scheduled appropriately?
      This is important for managing the cash-flow of the project: *Can bills be paid when they are supposed to be paid?*
      - Does the resource-related **Accrue At** field reflect when the cost occurs: at the **Start** or at the **End**, or **Prorated** with the time-phased amount of work?
      - Does the task-related **Fixed Cost Accrual** field reflect when the fixed cost will be incurred?

Printing the Resource Sheet

Project 2003 has a new wizard that helps you print reports from a view. The wizard can be accessed from the **Report** Project Guide. Once you have displayed the **Report** side pane, you click the **Print current view as report** hyperlink to start the wizard. Unfortunately, the wizard mostly helps you with the **File, Page Setup** and **File, Print**

choices and little with the choices in the **Format** menu. Next we will discuss additional features not covered by the wizard.

Customizing the Table

1. Choose **View, Table: Entry, More Tables...**; the **More Tables** dialog box appears:

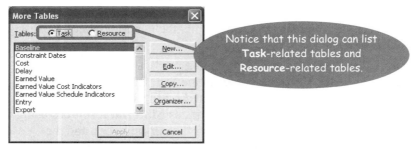

2. Select ⊙ **Resource** to display the list of resource-related tables. Select a table that is close to what you need and click [Copy...]; the **Table Definition** dialog appears:

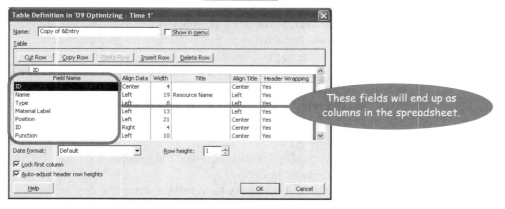

3. Change the **Name** for the new table to a more descriptive name.

4. To add this table to the menu, check ☑ **Show in Menu**.

5. To delete a field from the table, select it and click [Delete Row] or press [Delete].

6. To add a field to the table, click on the row before which to insert it and click [Insert Row] or press [Ins]. Then click in the cell in the column **Field Name** and a list button appears: [▼]. Select the field from the list.

7. Click [OK] and [Apply].

Extra columns you may have used (**Text1, Text2, ... Number1, ... Flag1, ...**) can be permanently renamed by choosing **Tools, Customize, Fields**. This feature allows you to create new fields for resources like *Position* or *Telephone Number*. You can permanently rename these fields in the project database by clicking [Rename...]. This is a better way than simply changing the **Title** in the **Table Definition** dialog which will only be visible in that particular table.

Sorting Resources Alphabetically

Choose **Project, Sort** and pick one of the predefined sorting orders, such as **By Cost, By Name** or **By ID**.
OR
To sort on other fields:

1. Choose **Project, Sort, Sort by...**. The **Sort** dialog appears:

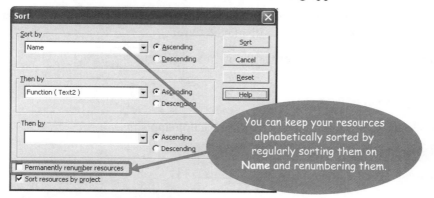

2. Then choose the first sort key in the **Sort by** list and the sorting order ⊙ **Ascending** or ⊙ **Descending**. If necessary, set a second key under **Then by** to break ties that may occur in the sorted list.

3. You can check the ☑ **Permanently renumber resources** option to keep the resources sorted in the chosen order. This will ensure that the resources in all lists where resource names are shown are listed alphabetically.

4. Click [Sort] to effect the sorting.

Formatting the Text

1. Click on the menu items **Format**, **Text Styles**; the **Text Styles** dialog appears:

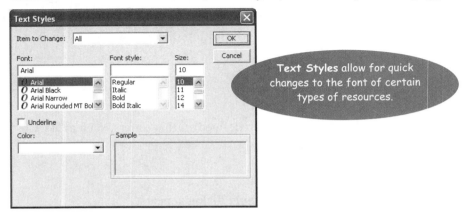

2. Select from the list **Item to Change** the **Over-allocated resources** and notice that by default these critical resources are displayed in red.

3. Choose a font, style, size and color for the item and click   OK .

Formatting the Gridlines

1. Choose **Format, Gridlines…**. The **Gridlines** dialog appears:

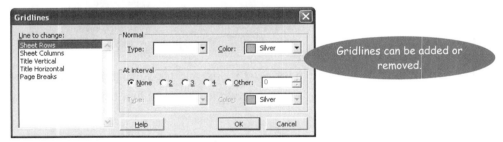

2. Select an item in the list **Line to change** first, then select the **Type** of line for this item, its **Color** and **At Interval**.

3. Click   OK .

Choosing the Page Setup

1. Choose **File, Page Setup...**; the **Page Setup – Resource Sheet** dialog appears. Any changes you make in this dialog are stored in the current view, in our case the Resource Sheet view, as the title of the dialog already suggests.

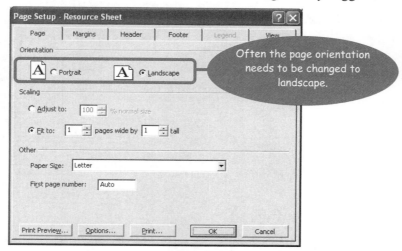

Often the page orientation needs to be changed to landscape.

2. On the tab **Page** you can change:
   ◊ the page orientation from **Portrait** to **Landscape**, and
   ◊ the **Scaling** option to fit the report on a certain number of pages.
3. Click tab **Margins** if you want to adjust the width of the page margin.
4. To insert **Headers, Footers** or a **Legend**, review the instructions on page 305.
5. Select other **View** options you need.
6. Click Print Preview... or Print... to see the results on screen or on paper.

Previewing the Resource Spreadsheet

Choose **File**, **Print Preview** or click **Print Preview** on the **Standard** toolbar; the **Print Preview** screen appears:

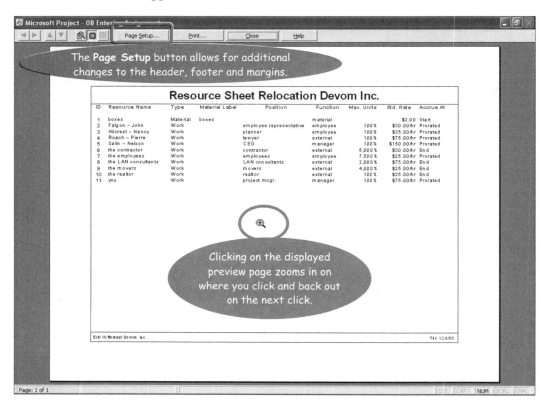

Exercises

Review A

Is it possible to model the following cost situations in MS Project? If so, how? If not, what would be a possible workaround?

1. Up-front fee of $500 for a bulldozer at a rate of $1,000/d for onsite work

2. A consultant who charges $400/d until January 1, then $450/d

3. Car rental with free mileage for the first 100 miles, then a fee of $0.45/mile

4. Penalty of $1,000/d for delivering late

5. Harry, who works as a business analyst at $500/d and as a systems analyst for $400/d

6. Volume discount for materials (for example, if you buy one door, it costs $150; if you buy 10 doors or more, they cost $90 each)

7. Pay an invoice within 30 days or pay a late charge of 10% of the invoice amount extra

8. Overtime hours accumulated throughout the year and paid at the end of the year

9. Courier costs for packages

10. Low and high season hotel room rates (for example, in New York the hotel rates double in December)

Review B

Is it possible to model the following availability situations in MS Project? If so, how?

1. Movers who only work during the weekends

2. A freelancer who typically works on the weekend and delivers the work on Monday

3. Somebody who works a compressed workweek of 10 hours per day and 4 days per week

4. An expert resource that will be available to your project for 10% in March, 20% in April and 50% in May; after that, she is unavailable

5. A part-time resource that only works mornings on Tuesdays and Thursdays

Review C

Which of the following resources should have its workload leveled in MS Project? (Enter Yes or No in the appropriate cell.) Please explain your answer.

Resource	Level Workloads?
1. expert	
2. computer	
3. mortar	
4. boardroom	

Relocation Project — Entering Resources

Continue to work with your file *Relocation.MPP* or open the file
07 Entering Resources.MPP available for download at www.jrosspub.com. Please, click
the link *WAV Download Resource Center* to enter the download site.

In the next table, you will find the resources that will be needed in the relocation project.
Notice that there are generic resources in the list, like *movers*. You found their rates by
telephoning around. There is no **Cost/Use** for these resources.

Resource Name	Type	Material Label	Position	Function	Max. Units	Std. Rate	Accrue at
you[66]	Work		project manager	manager	1	$75/h	Pro-rated
Nelson Salin	Work		CEO	manager	1	$150/h	Pro-rated
John Falgon	Work		employee representative	employee	1	$30/h	Pro-rated
Nancy Hilcrest	Work		planner	employee	1	$35/h	Pro-rated
Pierre Roach	Work		lawyer	external	1	$75/h	Pro-rated
the employees	Work		employees	employee	75	$25/h	Pro-rated
the contractor	Work		contractor	external	50	$30/h	End
the realtor	Work		realtor	external	1	$35/h	End
the movers	Work		movers	external	40	$25/h	End
the LAN consultants	Work		LAN consultants	external	20	$75/h	End
boxes	Material	boxes		material		$2	Start

1. Customize the table for the resource sheet view as shown in the previous table. The
   fields *Position* and *Function* are not standard fields in MS Project. You can use the

---

[66] Fill in your own name instead of "*you*".

fields **Text1** and **Text2** and permanently rename them *Position* and *Function* respectively using the feature **Tools, Customize, Fields**.

2. Enter the resources in the previous table. Use the **Fill Down** feature for the columns *Function* and *Accrue at*.

3. Sort the list of resources on resource *Name* as the first sorting key. Select the option to permanently renumber the resources.

4. You decided that you yourself are going to work regular working hours. You are pressured to jump-start the project by working longer hours, but you decided to resist that pressure. The rest of the team will keep regular working hours as well.

5. *Nancy Hilcrest* will go on a 1-week holiday in the third full week of August 2006.

6. You realize that due to the project requirement that the disruption to normal company operations should be minimal, the move will have to take place over the weekend. For the *Movers*, set all the weekdays to nonworking days and the weekend days to working days, so the move will take place on a weekend. The *Movers* will work 8 hours per day.

7. Compare your file with the solution file *08 Entering Assignments.MPP* available for download at www.jrosspub.com. Please, click the link *WAV Download Resource Center* to enter the download site. See page 675 of this book for an automated way of comparing and reporting differences between two versions of one schedule. Make sure you select to compare the resource information as well by selecting the **Resource Table** named **Entry**.

8. Save your file for the next exercise.

Relocation Project — Printing the Resource Sheet

1. Continue to work with the file from the previous exercise.

2. Apply the following **Format, Text Styles**:

Item to Change	Font	Font Style	Size
All	Arial	Regular	10
Row & Column Titles	Arial	Bold	10

3. Enter the following **File, Page Setup** settings:

Tab	Section	Set to	Font
Page	Orientation	Landscape	
	Scaling	Fit to: 1 pages wide by 1 tall	
Margins	Top, Bottom, Left, Right	1 Inch or 2.5 cm	
	Borders Around	Every page	
Header	Center	&[View] &[Project Title]	Arial Bold 20
Footer	Left	&[Manager] &[Company]	
	Right	&[Date]	Arial Regular 8

4. Apply the following **Format, Gridlines**:

Line to Change	Normal – Type
Sheet Rows	blank (at top of list)
Sheet Columns	blank (at top of list
Title Vertical	blank (at top of list)
Title Horizontal	blank (at top of list)

5. Compare your file with a printout of the solution file *08 Entering Assignments.MPP* available for download at www.jrosspub.com. Please, click the link *WAV Download Resource Center* to enter the download site.

Troubleshooting

1. Open the file *Last Name First Name.MPP* available for download at www.jrosspub.com. Please, click the link *WAV Download Resource Center* to enter the download site. Enter your first name in the resource sheet, and then enter your last name. Questions:
   ◇ Why does the first name show up in two fields?
   ◇ Why does the second entry override the first one?

2. Create a new project file and try entering the resource *Smith, Harry*. Why does Project 2003 not allow you to do that?

Chapter 8 Entering Assignments

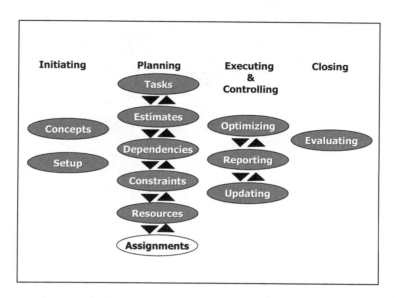

The assignments are the last type of data to enter into our project model (see the white highlight in the illustration above). After completing this chapter, we will have a complete model of our project.

After reading this chapter you will:

◆ know what an assignment is as well as what part-time and full-time assignments are
◆ know the difference between Fixed Duration, Fixed Units and Fixed Work tasks
◆ be able to enter each type of task into MS Project
◆ know how to assign resources using the Assign Resources dialog or the Task Form
◆ be able to enter part-time, full-time, overtime and multiple assignments
◆ know how to make changes to assignments and predict the resulting calculations by MS Project
◆ be able to check if the assignments reflect the best practices of scheduling
◆ know how to create a report of the assignments

Mr. Ambiguity and Friends

Nob is making the rounds in his office. He greets Mary, the system analyst on his project, and gestures for her to sit down with him. "Have you started the system analysis on the web-enabling feature?" he asks.

Mary responds: "No, I haven't actually … perhaps Richard has. Ask him."

Nob walks off to find Richard. He soon finds him: "Hey, Rich, did you start the systems analysis for my project?" Richard replies: "I was actually waiting for Lisa to call a short meeting so we can split up the responsibilities; did you ask her?"

Nob wobbles off to find Lisa. When he finds her, she tells him that she thought Mary was the lead and that she should take the initiative.

Nob: "Mary didn't say she is the lead. I can't believe the miscommunication that is happening to me … again!"

He complains about it to Bob, who asks to see his project plan. Bob only needs one glance and says: "I see what's wrong! You have all three people assigned against this big task 32: *perform system analysis.*"

Nob says: "Yes, all three are responsible for making it happen. They will have to work together on it." "But nobody is taking the initiative, are they?" Bob reacts. Nob: "I just told Lisa to get them organized." Bob fires back immediately: "So you have solved this one, but look at your schedule; you have assigned two or more people to most of your tasks. You will be running around coordinating these people all the time!" Nob: "Well, on the other hand, I kept my task list nice and short, didn't I? Only 100 tasks for this huge project, that is not bad!" Bob wonders out loud: "Yes, but does your schedule work as a delegation instrument? I always assign only one person to a detail activity, except for meetings of course. I may end up with more activities than you do, but I never have to deal with Mr. Ambiguity and his friends!"

What Is an Assignment?

An *assignment* is a combination of one task and one resource. An assignment reflects who works on the task. In the next screen shot you can see the assignments; *Nancy* is assigned to *summarize requirements* and *visit the sites* among others. Assigning resources to tasks is also called *resource loading*, and the result is a *resource-loaded schedule*.

Assignments can be viewed in either the **Task Usage** view, where they show up as resource names indented below the task name, or in the **Resource Usage** view, where they show up as task names indented below the resource name. You can easily recognize the assignment records, because they have no ID number, their text is in italics and their timescale cells have a lighter yellow background; see the next screenshot:

Resource Usage view:
resource record Nancy Hilcrest

3	◇	⊟ **Hilcrest – Nancy**	6 days	Work			0.5d	0.5d	0.5d	1d	
		summarize requirements	*2 days*	Work			0.5d	0.5d	0.5d		
		visit the sites	*1 day*	Work							
		evaluate the sites	*1 day*	Work						1d	
		meet to select the location	*1 day*	Work							
		meet to discuss contract	*1 day*	Work							

Nancy's assignment records: no ID, italic text and light yellow.

Double-click on an assignment and the **Assignment Information** dialog will appear with only assignment-related fields.

Assignment-Specific Fields

Each of the three data entities, *tasks*, *resources* and *assignments*, has its own specific fields. Some fields may be called the same, but contain different information depending on if they belong to the task, resource or assignment. I will discuss three examples in more detail:

◆ *Start* and *Finish* dates (task, resource and assignment-related)
◆ *Max. Units* (resource-related) and *Units* (assignment-related)
◆ *Work* (task, resource and assignment-related)

Start and Finish

Tasks, resources and assignments all have **Start** and **Finish** dates. The start date of a task is not necessarily the same as the start date of its assignments. The start date of an assignment is when one of the resources starts working on the task. If Mary only works the last 2 days of the 5-day task, the start date of her assignment is different from the start date of the task. The start date of a resource is when her earliest assignment starts in the project.

Max. Units and Units

The second example is the resource field **Max. Units** and the assignment field **Units**. The **Max. Units** field of a resource reflects the maximum availability of the resource to the project. For example, the **Max. Units** would be 100% for a person who is entirely

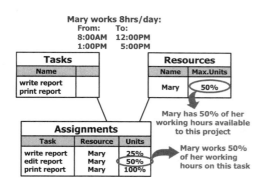

available to the project and 50% for a resource who is available half of her working hours. In the illustration, *Mary* has **Max. Units** of 50%; she has only *50%* of her working hours available to this project. We discussed resource availability on page 334. The assignment-related field **Units** is the percentage of her working hours as set in the resource calendar that the resource is working on the task. In the illustration, Mary works a regular workweek, and a 50% assignment means for her

50% * 8 hours = 4 hours of effort per day on the task *edit report* (and not 50% * 50% = 25%). Four hours per day equals her maximum availability. If Burke works a compressed workweek of 4 days a week and 10 hours per day, a 50% assignment means 5 hours of effort per day on the task. The percentage is always taken from the working hours on the calendar.

The assignment-related field **Units** reflects:
◆ whether a person works full-time or part-time on the task, or
◆ how many individuals of a *consolidated resource* are needed on the task (see page 343 for a definition of a consolidated resource).
In other words, **Max. Units** represents availability, whereas assignment *Units* represents usage.

If you want a resource to work all of her available working hours on the task, simply enter 100% in the field **Units** on the Task Form. If you enter less than 100%, you are asking the resource to work part of her available time on the task; you have created a *part-time* assignment. In the previous illustration, *Mary* will work *50%* of her working hours on the task *edit report*. The assignment units can be changed quickly in the **Assign Resources** 🔲 dialog on the **Standard** toolbar.

Work, Work and Work

The third and last example of how a field is different for tasks, resources and assignments, is the field **Work**. The field **Work** for tasks in the Gantt spreadsheet is not the same as the field **Work** in the Resource Sheet, nor is it the same as the assignment-related field **Work** on the Task Form. They are all called by the same name: **Work**. In the Gantt Chart, **Work** is the total effort of all resources working on the task. In the Resource Sheet, **Work** is the total effort for the resource in the entire project. (For material resources, it is the total number of units used in the project.)

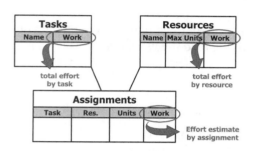

On the Task Form, you can see the assignment-related **Work** field, which displays the effort of one resource on one particular task. This is a very low level estimate and not an aggregate.

Full-Time or Part-Time Assignment

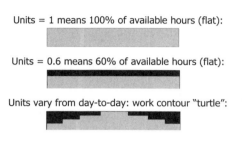

Units = 1 means 100% of available hours (flat):

Units = 0.6 means 60% of available hours (flat):

Units vary from day-to-day: work contour "turtle":

You can see three different *assignments* in the illustration. In the 100% and the 60% assignment, the work of the resource will be spread evenly across the duration of the task; the work (effort) is spread in a flat *pattern*. You can spread the work over the task duration in different, predefined patterns and MS Project calls these *work contours*. There are eight predefined work contours, but you can also spread the work over the task duration yourself by entering the spread in the time-phased **Work** fields.

Some remarks about work contours:

◆ You can apply one of the predefined work contours using the **Assignment Information** dialog. If you double-click on an assignment in either the **Task Usage** or the **Resource Usage** view, the **Assignment Information** dialog will be displayed. You can then select a predefined contour from the list **Work contour**. MS Project will maintain the pattern of the contour when the duration or the work is changed during the planning phase.

◆ You can even fill in on a day-by-day basis how many hours you need from the resource over the duration of the task. You can enter the needed hours directly into the **Work** field in the timescale of the **Task Usage** view. This level of detail is seldom needed in the planning of projects.

If you do decide to enter numbers in the timescale yourself, you will spend a lot of time maintaining your schedule, since MS Project has no clue about your rationale behind the spread. Particularly if you enter the required hours on a day-by-day basis, you will have a lot of data to maintain. We do not recommend it, because the chance is real that you will abandon your schedule during project execution when you are simply too busy to maintain that amount of data.

Choosing the Options

The assignment-related options are shown in the following table. Before creating *assignments*, review them in **Tools, Options**:

Tab	Option
Schedule	**Show assignment units as a:** `Percentage` ▼ **Percentage** is the best choice when you have part-time resources; if there are mostly consolidated resources, **Decimal** is better, since *5 carpenters* is easier to understand than *500% carpenters*. This option is a global option; if you change it to **decimal** in one project, all your projects will use decimal numbers.
	Duration is entered in: `Days` ▼ Choose the default time unit to avoid having to enter the "*d*" of "*5d*" in the field **Duration** if set to **Days**.
	Work is entered in: `Hours` ▼ Choose the default time unit to avoid having to enter the "*h*" of "*5h*" in the field **Work** if set to **Hours**.
	Default task type: `Fixed Units` ▼ Choose the type of task for any new tasks you create. This option is meant to be a time-saver. See the next section titled *Types of Detail Tasks* for more explanation.
	☐ **New Tasks are effort driven** This option can lead to MS Project changing assignment units for you. For now, we recommend you turn it off. See the next section for more explanation.
	`Set as Default` Sets the options except the first one as the default settings for any new projects you create. Existing projects are not affected, because these options are stored in the project schedule. You can read this from the label of the section divider: **Scheduling Options for <schedule name of the project>**.

Types of Detail Tasks

There are three types of detail tasks: *Fixed Duration*, *Fixed Units* and *Fixed Work*. Each task has three variables:

◆ *Duration* is the length of a task expressed in *business days* or *business hours*.

◆ *Units* reflect the number of resource units assigned, which is:

◇ The percentage of the available working hours of a resource. For a resource working half his available hours, it would be 50%, for a resource working all her available hours 100%, and for two resources working all their available hours 200%.

◇ The number of people assigned from a *consolidated resource* (pooled resource). You can change the percentages to **Decimal** numbers via **Tools, Options,** tab **Schedule** in the field **Show assignments as a**. The **Units** field would then display 0.5, 1 and 2 respectively for the previous example.

◆ *Work* is the amount of effort expressed in person hours or person days. A *person day* is one person working full-time for one day.

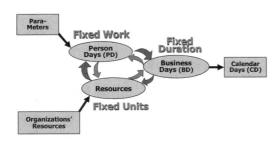

On page 185, we discussed the process of estimating, which is shown in the illustration. We recommended using Fixed Duration or Fixed Work tasks when first entering estimates. It is important to be aware of the task type when you assign resources, because each type of task makes MS Project calculate differently. For example, MS Project will never recalculate the duration on a fixed duration task (unless it prompts you which may happen when one resource is on vacation), and if you add a second resource, it will double the work on the task following the formula *Duration * Units = Work*. We will therefore insert the column **Type**, so we can see at any point what type of task we have.

You may also want to insert the field *Effort Driven*, because you want to keep this field set to *No* (except for Fixed Work tasks, which are effort driven by definition). The Effort Driven attribute works similar to the Fixed Work task type as is already indicated from the fact that Fixed Work tasks are always effort driven.

We recommend keeping **Effort Driven** off to keep things simple; it keeps the number of possibilities we need to know down to three instead of six. Insert the field **Work** as well, and the layout of columns we recommend is as follows when working with assignments:

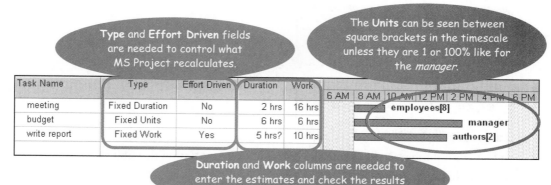

We can now see all three variables of the formula *Duration * Units = Work* with the *Units* visible in the timescale to the right of the task bars following the resource name between square brackets (unless the units are 1 or 100%). If there are multiple resources assigned to a task, you have to add their units to arrive at the total number used in the formula.

You could also insert the column **Resource Names**. This field displays the number of resources as well, but the column is often too narrow when there is more than one person assigned. Let's explore how we can create the recommended layout.

Improving the Entry Table for Assigning Resources

1. Choose **View, Gantt Chart**.

2. Choose **View, Table <current table name>, Entry**; the **Entry** table is applied and it has by default the columns: **𝟢** , **Task Name, Duration, Start, Finish, Predecessors** and **Resource Names** respectively.

3. We will insert the column **Type** before the column **Duration**. Right-click on the column **Duration** and choose **Insert Column...** from the pop-up menu; the **Column Definition** dialog appears:

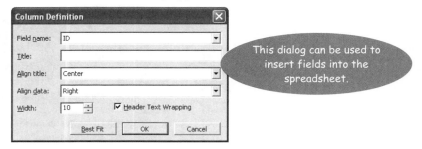

4. Select from the list **Field Name** the column **Type** by typing the first two characters of the field name and click [OK].

5. Repeat steps 3 and 4 for the fields **Effort Driven** and **Work**; we recommend you insert them in the order indicated in the next screenshot:

Task Name	Type	Effort Driven	Duration	Work							
					6 AM	8 AM	10 AM	12 PM	2 PM	4 PM	6 PM
meeting	Fixed Duration	No	2 hrs	16 hrs	employees[8]						
budget	Fixed Units	No	6 hrs	6 hrs							manager
write report	Fixed Work	Yes	5 hrs?	10 hrs						authors[2]	

We are now ready to assign.

Assigning and the Types of Tasks

MS Project uses the following *formula* for these variables: *Duration * Units = Work*

	Duration	* Units	= Work
Fixed Duration meeting	2 h	8	.....
Fixed Units budget	.....	1	6 h
Fixed Work write report	.....	2	10 h

It is not a coincidence that each type of task relates to one of the variables in the formula. As their names indicate, each of the three types fixes one of the three variables in the formula. If you set a task to be Fixed Duration, MS Project will never change this duration. That is a comforting thought, particularly if you have been haunted in the past by numbers being changed by MS Project that ... you did not want changed.

When you enter the second value, MS Project will calculate the third one for you with the formula. For example, if you have a task *meeting* with a fixed duration of 2 business hours, and you invite 8 people to the meeting, MS Project will calculate 2 * 8 = 16 person hours of work. Another example: a task *write report* with 10 person hours fixed work could be worked on by two people and MS Project will calculate a duration of 5 business hours. When entering the data the first time, most of your tasks will be either *Fixed Duration* or *Fixed Work*. The *Fixed Units* task type is useful when you start making changes to the task and you want to keep the number of resources that are working on it the same. For example, if you want to change the amount of work on the *Fixed Duration* task *meeting* to 12 person hours to save some cost, MS Project would change the number of units from 8 to 6 people and thus uninviting 2 people from the meeting. Or it would reduce the units for all assigned individuals from 100% to 75% (some people say 75% mental presence is an accurate model of a meeting …). Since the duration is fixed, changing the units was the only thing MS Project could do. This is probably not what you wanted; you probably want to meet with the same people and have the duration recalculated. In order to accomplish that, we have to change the task type first to *Fixed Units* to tell MS Project that it should not change the *resource units* on the task.

Of course, you could ask yourself at this point: *Why is MS Project recalculating all these values constantly? It makes my life miserable!* The answer is that if it did not calculate them, you would definitely need your calculator when you enter data making many calculations yourself. MS Project tries to help you, and it uses the broad assumption that every resource is equally effective and efficient, which is not true of course. However, in 90% of the cases, this assumption is accurate enough for modeling purposes. Remember that we are deliberately simplifying the reality when we model projects (see page 50). We try to approach reality as closely as possible, but with as little effort as possible. We are not trying to recreate reality in all its complexity in our computer when we schedule. Many project managers seem to forget this once they get going with MS Project.

The following table suggests the best use for each task **Type**:

Type of task	Use in situations like:
Fixed Duration	◆ When the duration is the first thing you estimate. ◆ If the duration does not decrease when human resources are added, such as when backing up a computer system. ◆ Tasks that always have a group of resources assigned, such as *meetings* or *training*. ◆ When the deadline is so tight that it is the primary driver for the duration of the task. You have to make it work within the available time frame. ◆ When the workload is not your problem, e.g., for external resources, such as subcontractors and consultants.
Fixed Units (default)	◆ When the number of resources you have for the task is the first thing you know. ◆ When you cannot get more resources to do the work, for example, you only have two internal resources. ◆ When you want to change the duration or the work on a task while keeping the number of people working on the task the same (assignment units). We will discuss this on page 400. ◆ When you want to keep the resource working on a task at a certain percentage of his available hours.
Fixed Work	◆ When the effort required is the first thing you estimate. ◆ When the effort required is the easiest thing to estimate. This is often the case. For example, you estimate that painting a home takes 12 person days of effort. A software project manager may estimate that coding a module in an application will take 20 person hours. Estimating effort is often easier and more accurate than estimating duration. After all, you don't need to take resource availability and holidays into account.

The formula $D * U = W$ does not apply to:
◆ Tasks that have *assignments* with a *work contour* (that spreads the effort in a certain pattern over the duration of the task).
◆ Tasks with multiple assignments where one assignment is longer than the others or starts later (*multiple, uneven assignments*). In this situation you would find that the formula still applies on the level of each individual assignment.

Three Rules to Make MS Project an Easy Tool for You

We would like to suggest three rules to memorize and follow when you enter or change assignments. If you do so, MS Project will become your obedient servant instead of *an obnoxious piece of software with a bad attitude*. If you don't look at the task *Type* when working with MS Project, it will inevitably recalculate values that you did not want changed. You can even end up in an endless loop with MS Project, if you keep changing the value back that MS Project just recalculated and then change the other value again...

If you want to work pleasantly with MS Project, simply follow these rules:

1. Enter the duration estimate or work estimate and fix that number by setting the task **Type** accordingly. Fixing it prevents MS Project from changing it.
   - ◇ If you enter a **Duration** estimate, set the task **Type** to **Fixed Duration**.
   - ◇ If you enter a **Work** estimate, set the task **Type** to **Fixed Work**.

2. Provide the second value in the formula *Duration * Units = Work* and let MS Project calculate the third value; always provide only two of the three values. If you created a fixed duration task, *assign* the resources you need, and let MS Project calculate the work. If you created a fixed work task, assign the resources and let MS Project calculate the duration. If you entered the duration and the work, MS Project only needs to know who will do the task and it will calculate the number of resources needed (units).

3. Before making a change to any of the three values in the formula, reconsider the task type by asking yourself: *What type of task do I need for this particular change?* More on this next.

Changing an Assignment

Before you change any of the three values in the formula $D * U = W$, you should always first think about the task type you need for that change. With every change, MS Project will recalculate one other value, and it may not recalculate the one you want, if you don't think about it first.

Changes that will trigger a recalculation in the formula $D * U = W$ are, among others:
- ◆ Changing the **Duration** (D) of a task by editing the value or by stretching the task bar with the mouse
- ◆ Adding a resource to a task as well as removing a resource from a task, changes the **Units** (U). Also, changing the 100% allocation into a different percentage is changing the units value.

◆ Changing the **Work** (W) of a task or of one of its assignments

The **Type** of the task and the **Effort Driven** attribute determine how MS Project will react. We suggest these steps when changing an *assignment*:

1. Choose and set the task **Type** first.
   You can determine the appropriate task type by asking yourself: *I will change this value in the formula; which one of the other two values do I want to keep the same?* The answer to this question will tell you which task type you need. For example, if you want to keep the assigned units the same while you change the work, you should set the *Type* to *Fixed Units*. If you want to keep the total amount of work on the task the same while you change the duration, you need *Fixed Work*.

2. Ensure **Effort Driven** is set to *No* except for **Fixed Work** tasks. Fixed Work tasks are effort driven by definition; **Fixed Duration** and **Fixed Units** should not be effort driven.

3. Then edit the value that you wanted to change on the assignment.
   MS Project will recalculate the third value. For example, if you change the **Work** on a **Fixed Units** task, MS Project will recalculate the **Duration**. Note that you never change the value that you fixed with the task type. For example, you never change the duration when the task type is Fixed Duration. If you do this, you are not controlling what MS Project recalculates; it could adjust the **Units** or the **Work**. You have to change the task type first to keep one of the other two variables the same before making the change.

The task **Type** is not something you set once and never look at again. You continue to monitor it in order to control what MS Project calculates. If you reconsider the type of task first before every change, you will always control what MS Project will do and you will even be able to predict it.

Here is an example of how this works. Assume you have a **Fixed Units** task *write* of *4 days* in duration with one resource assigned. This will appear in MS Project as:

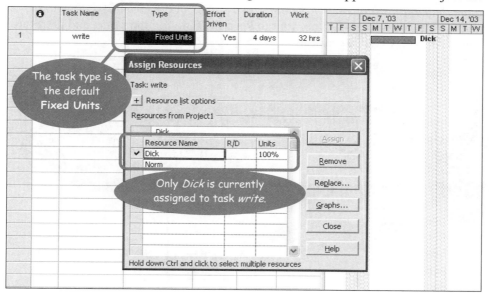

You want to add a second resource and, let's say you want MS Project to keep the **Duration** the same when you add the resource. We should ask ourselves the question: *I will change the Units; which one of the other two values in the formula do I want to keep the same?* The answer is that you want to keep the duration the same, and therefore, you need the task type **Fixed Duration**:

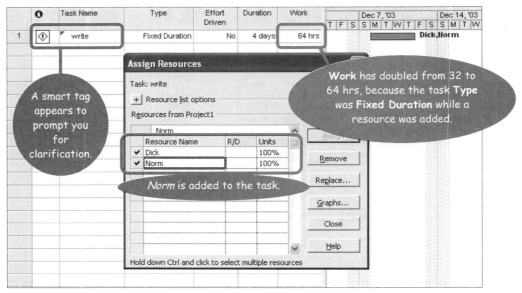

So first you change the task **Type** to *Fixed Duration* and you set **Effort Driven** to *No*, then you add the second resource, which doubles the **Work** (from *32 hrs* to *64 hrs*). If you add a resource to a **Fixed Duration** task, the work goes up. Alternatively, if you add a resource to a **Fixed Work** task, the duration will go down.

You will find that you often want to keep the assigned units the same on a task while changing the duration or the work. In this case, you will need the **Fixed Units** task type. This task type is most common when making changes. For example, if you change the work on a **Fixed Units** task, MS Project will recalculate the duration. If the Duration = 10 days, Units = 1 (fixed), Work = 10 days and you change the work to 5 days, MS Project will decrease the duration from 10 to 5 days; one person can deliver 5 person days of effort (work) within 5 business days (duration). We will also use this task type when we update our schedule (see chapter 11 on page 611).

When there are multiple, uneven *assignments*, one (or more) of the assignments can drive the duration of the task. Before you can make a change, you should find out which assignment drives the duration of the task. Consider changing assignment fields instead of task fields.

Notice that when you apply the task type **Fixed Work** the attribute *Effort Driven* is automatically turned on by MS Project. When you change to a different task type again, the **Effort Driven** attribute stays on and sticks. If you leave it set to *Yes,* it may create unexpected recalculations. You can display the task-related field **Effort Driven** and toggle it to *No.* Effort-driven tasks act very similar to Fixed Work tasks, and it seems to be a redundant field.

To replace a resource with another one, MS Project provides a shortcut that does not trigger recalculations. Use the **Assign Resources** dialog 🔄, select the assigned resource and click ⟨ Replace... ⟩. Select the new one and click ⟨ OK ⟩. This is a better way to go than removing the resource and reassigning somebody else, because this will trigger two recalculations. If the resource calendars are different and you replace a full-time resource with a half-time resource on a **Fixed Work** task for example, the duration will double.

Changing a Fixed Duration Task

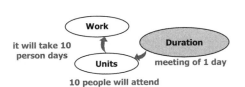

When the duration is fixed, changes in assignments or total work will not affect it. Examples of *fixed duration tasks* are *training* and *meeting*. The duration of a training session or meeting is typically set and will not vary (much) with the number of participants, which makes it a perfect candidate for fixed duration. In the illustration, we see a meeting with a 1 day fixed duration. If the number of attending resources is changed to 10, the total work will be calculated as 10 person days.

1. In the Gantt spreadsheet, enter the task name and set the task *Type* to **Fixed Duration.**

2. Change the work estimate in the field **Work**, or change the number of resources assigned. We will discuss this on page 388.

3. MS Project will have recalculated the third variable in the formula $D * U = W$ (where D = Duration, U = Assignment Units and W = Work).

MS Project sometimes schedules fixed duration tasks with a split task bar when more than one person is assigned. It creates a split when one of the resources is not available while the others are working. This looks strange for a task such as a *meeting*, because the split task bar suggests that there will be two meetings. You can solve this by removing the resource from the task or rescheduling the meeting to when all resources are available.

Changing a Fixed Work Task

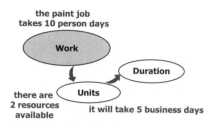

the paint job
takes 10 person days

there are
2 resources
available

it will take 5 business days

Fixed work tasks are very common. A task is a fixed work task if the first thing you estimate is the amount of effort (work). Once you fix the work, MS Project will calculate either the duration or the necessary number of resources. In the illustration, we see the paint job is estimated to take 10 person days of work. When the number of resource assigned is changed to 2 people, MS Project will determine that it will take 5 business days of duration.

1. In the Gantt spreadsheet, enter the task name and set the task **Type** to **Fixed Work.** Enter the total work on the task in the field **Work.**

2. Assign the resources in the number of units required; we will discuss how to do this on the next pages, or enter the duration available for this task.

3. MS Project will have recalculated the third variable in the formula $D * U = W$ (where D = Duration, U = Units and W = Work).

Changing a Fixed Units Task

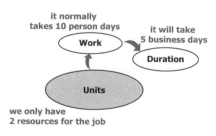

it normally
takes 10 person days

it will take
5 business days

we only have
2 resources for the job

For fixed units tasks, you know the number of resources available for the task. You want the duration or work to be calculated by MS Project. The illustration on the left shows an example in which there are 2 resources available for the job (*Units*). You want to change the estimate to 10 person days of *Work*. MS Project will recalculate the *Duration* to 5 business days. Again, you fix one, change the second and MS Project will recalculate the third.

The **Fixed Units** task type is mostly used when making changes to the task or its assignments. The Fixed Units task type allows you to keep the number of assigned units the same when you change the work or the duration.

1. In the Gantt spreadsheet, set the task **Type** to **Fixed Units.**

2. Change the duration or the work of the task.

3. MS Project will have recalculated the third variable in the formula $D * U = W$ (where D = Duration, U = Units and W = Work).

Overview of Assigning

The following are the many different ways you can *assign* resources to tasks. The methods are listed from simple (and quick) to sophisticated (and cumbersome). The more sophisticated the method, the more detail it allows you to enter about the *assignment*:

◆ **Task Sheet** view
 ◇ Assigning multiple resources is not easy.
 ◇ Adjusting the **Units** of resources is not easy.

◆ **Assign Resources** dialog box
 ◇ You can assign or replace resources.
 ◇ You can specify units or work by assignment.

◆ **Task Information** dialog box
 ◇ You can assign units or work.
 ◇ You can enter multiple assignments simultaneously.
 ◇ You have to display the dialog for every task.

◆ **Task Form** view
 ◇ You can assign units and work.
 ◇ You can enter multiple assignments simultaneously.
 ◇ The form stays on the screen.

◆ **Task Usage** or **Resource Usage** view
 You can assign work "day-by-day" and create workloads on each task that vary over time. You can assign a series of work values on each day in the timescale in the **Task Usage** or **Resource Usage** view.

In the first four ways of assigning, MS Project creates a flat workload. Generally, a flat workload is a good enough approximation of the true workload. If it isn't, you should consider breaking up the tasks into smaller tasks or using the work contour feature. Predefined *work contours* allow you to spread the work across the task duration in a certain pattern. See pages 372 for more on work contours. We don't recommend the last way of assigning resources, because it requires entering too much data, and all data need to be maintained for the life of the project. During project execution, you will have little time to maintain the schedule.

We recommend and will discuss two methods in more detail: **Assign Resources** dialog and the **Task Form** view. The Assign Resources dialog allows you to drag resources onto tasks and is a quick method. The Task Form allows you to enter the units and the work for one or more resources at a time and is a flexible method. Together these two methods will give you the speed and the flexibility you may need.

 MS Project has a **Resources** project guide that helps you with assigning resources to tasks. Display the project guide toolbar by right-clicking on any toolbar and choosing **Project Guide**. Click Resources and then the hyperlink **Assign people and equipment to tasks**. It will make use of the Assign Resources dialog and the Task Form where needed; but you will still need to know how to work with those. We will explain them next.

Assign Using the Assign Resources Dialog

 The **Assign Resources** dialog was already nicely improved in the 2002 release in that:
- It lists all the resources that are assigned to the task at the top of the list. Every time you click on a task, you can now immediately see which resources are assigned instead of scrolling up and down the list.
- It sorts the rest of the list alphabetically, regardless what the sort order is in the resource sheet.
- It provides filtering options to determine who is available.

Assigning Resources by Dragging

1. Click 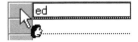; the **Assign Resources** floating dialog appears:

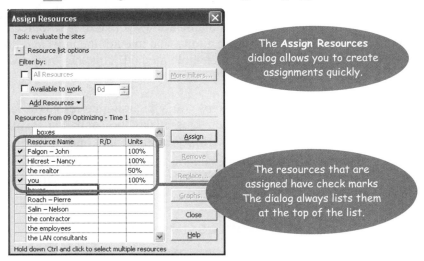

2. Click on the resource to assign.

3. Point to the resource selector [ ] in front of the resource name; the mouse pointer now has a person's (decapitated!) head attached:

4. Hold down the primary mouse button, drag and drop the resource onto the task you want to assign it to. The resource is now assigned; it has a check mark in front of its name. It appears in the field **Resource Names** and to the right of the task bar in the timescale.

When you drag resources onto tasks, MS Project assigns:
◆ The maximum availability (*Max. Units*) of individual resources
◆ Only one unit of *consolidated resources*
You may need to edit the number of units, which will trigger a recalculation by MS Project, so check the task **Type** first.

To Enter the Units on an Assignment

1. Select the task and check what task type it has; it should not be **Fixed Units**, because then you are not controlling what MS Project recalculates.

2. Click ; the **Assign Resources** dialog appears.

3. In the field **Units**, enter the percentage of the resource's available working hours (or the number of resources you need from a *consolidated resource*). You can quickly check the working hours of a resource by double-clicking on its name in the list. Units should be entered as a percentage (recommended for single resources) or as decimals (recommended for consolidated resources). You can work with either percentages or decimals by choosing this in **Tools, Options,** tab **Schedule,** field **Show assignments units as**.

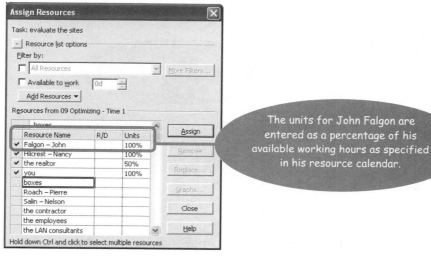

The units for John Falgon are entered as a percentage of his available working hours as specified in his resource calendar.

4. In the field *R/D* you can indicate whether the assignment is a **Request** or a **Demand,** i.e., if the resource is requested to work on the task or must work on the task to complete it successfully. Entering this is only important if your executives use the *Project Server* features of *Resource Substitution Wizard* to increase resource usage or the *Portfolio Modeler* to develop what-if scenarios. You don't need to click Assign again after setting this attribute.

5. Click Assign ; MS Project recalculated the work if it is a **Fixed Duration** task, or the duration if it is a **Fixed Work** task.

Even though the field **Units** asks for units to be entered, you can even enter work in this field and MS Project will calculate the units required. If you want to do so, you have to make sure you include the time unit, as in *5d*, to make it clear to MS Project that it should interpret your entry as person days of work instead of as units.

Assigning Multiple Resources to Multiple Tasks

1. Click 🖳 ; the **Assign Resources** floating dialog appears.

2. Select the tasks to assign by dragging over them.
    OR
    Select them by holding down [Control] and clicking, if you want to randomly select tasks.

3. Select the resource you want to assign or select multiple resources to assign by holding down [Control] and clicking on their names in the **Assign Resources** dialog:

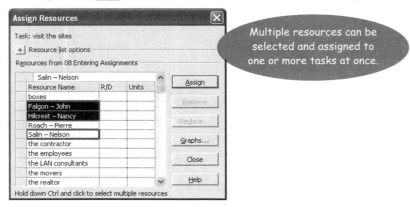

4. Click [Assign]; a check mark appears in front of the name in the resource selector: [✓].

Checking Availability Before Assigning

Since the 2002 release, you can check if the resource is available while you are making the assignments. If you have Project Server you can even check availability across all enterprise projects. We recommend you use this feature to prevent over-allocations from occurring in the first place, rather than sorting them out later. Resolving over-allocations is a nasty job that necessitates awkward meetings.

1. Select the task you are about to assign resources to. This is an important step, because MS Project checks the availability of resources between the start and finish date of the task that is currently selected.

2. Insert the column **Work** by right-clicking on a column heading and choosing **Insert column**. Select **Work** from the list **Field name** and click [OK]. In this field, you can see the total effort required on the task.

3. Click 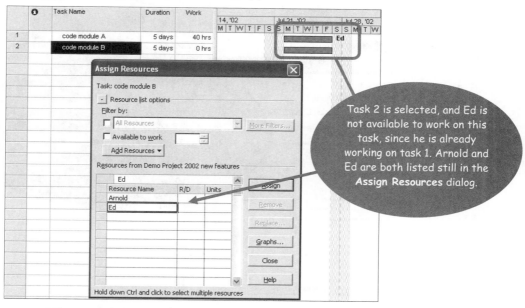; the **Assign Resources** dialog appears.

4. Check ☑ **Available to work** and enter the amount of effort that you need from the resource in the field to the right of it. MS Project will immediately list only the resources with enough availability (between the start and finish date of the selected task). This feature prevents you from having to switch to the Resource Usage view and back before you can make one assignment.
OR

Select the resource(s) in the list and click ⎣ Graphs... ⎦; a chart will appear with the **Work** charted. In the list **Select Graph**, you can change **Work** to **Remaining Availability** to check availability. The graph allows you to verify even within the duration of the task if the resource has enough availability. We recommend you use this for long tasks.

5. The screenshot would look like:

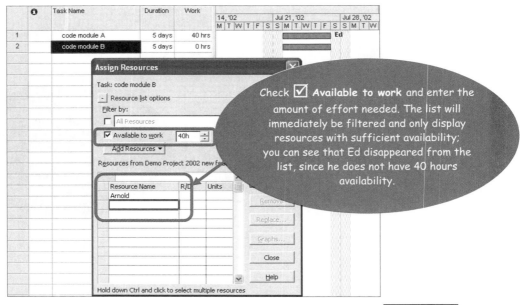

6. Select a resource from the resources that are available and click Assign .

7. Make sure you clear ☐ **Available to work** again so that you see the entire list of resources for the next task.

To Delete an Assignment in the Assign Resources Dialog

1. Display the **Assign Resources** dialog by clicking .

2. Look at the check marks [✓] in front of the resource names that indicate which resources are assigned to the task(s) selected in the spreadsheet:

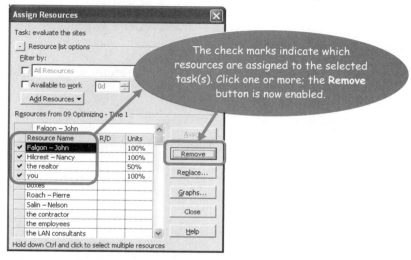

3. Select the resource to be removed.

4. Click [Remove].

Replacing a Resource on Its Assignments

1. Select the task(s) on which to replace a resource.

2. Display the **Assign Resources** dialog by clicking .

3. Select one of the assigned resources to replace.

4. Click [Replace...]; the **Replace Resource** dialog appears.

5. Select a resource and click [OK]; the resource will now be replaced without a recalculation.

If a task is in progress, only the remaining duration of the assignment will be reassigned to the new resource; all *actual hours* worked stay with the original resource. Assignments that are 100% complete will trigger an appropriate prompt:

If you get this prompt, you may need to cancel and first more carefully select the tasks in the future.

Assign Using the Task Form

Fields in the Task Form

◆ *Name*
A descriptive title for the task.

◆ *Duration*
How long the task will take in business days. Type a number followed by an abbreviation for the time unit. For example, *4d* means *4 business days,* which will be shown as *4 days* by MS Project. By default, duration is working time only, but it can also be entered as *elapsed time,* which includes holidays, weekends, vacations and nights (if you enter *4ed* it means *4 elapsed days of 24 hours*).

◆ *Effort Driven*
Effort driven will keep the total amount of work constant while adding or removing resources. This option only kicks in after entering the assignments the first time. It will redistribute the work among the assigned resources when adding or removing resources (keeping the relative workloads the same). Fixed work tasks are always effort driven.

◆ *Start*
MS Project automatically calculates the start date based on task dependencies. If you enter a date instead, MS Project sets a Start No Earlier Than constraint date for the task (under *forward scheduling),* which forces the program to schedule the task on or after that date. We don't recommend entering dates, because the constraints make the model less dynamic.

◆ *Finish*
MS Project calculates the finish date based on the start date plus the total duration. If

you type a date, MS Project sets a Finish No Earlier Than constraint for the task under *forward scheduling*. We don't recommend entering dates.

◆ *Task Type*
Detail tasks come in three kinds: *Fixed Duration* tasks, *Fixed Units* tasks, and *Fixed Work* tasks. Note that MS Project stores this attribute in the task-related field **Type**.

◆ *% Complete*
This percentage shows how much of the task duration is completed. We will discuss this in chapter 11 on updating schedules (see page 611).

To Assign with the Task Form

1. In the Gantt Chart, choose **Window, Split** to display the Task Form,
OR
Double-click on the sliding window handle at the bottom right of the screen:

2. On the Task Form, we need to see at least the fields **Resource Name**, **Units** and **Work**. To display these, click on the Task Form to make it active, then choose **Format, Details, Resource Work**.
OR
Right-click anywhere on the Task Form and choose **Resource Work** from the pop-up menu. The Task Form should now look like:

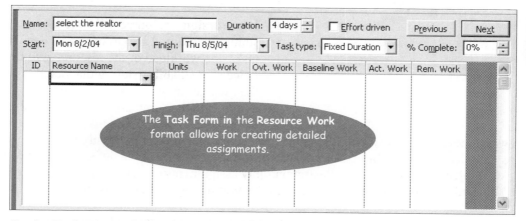

The **Task Form** in the **Resource Work** format allows for creating detailed assignments.

3. On the Task Form, click in the field **Resource Name**, and a list button will appear:

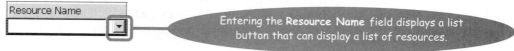

Entering the **Resource Name** field displays a list button that can display a list of resources.

4. Click the list button and select a resource from the list that appears. Enter the **Units** (the percentage of the available working hours) and/or the **Work** (person hours of effort needed). You can assign more than one resource at a time, which is easy to do with this form.

5. Click [OK] once all resources are assigned. All new assignments are entered into the project model simultaneously upon clicking it, which triggers only one recalculation by MS Project. This makes this method better for assigning multiple resources with specific **Units** or **Work** values; you are not triggering a recalculation with every assignment you add or remove, unlike in the **Assign Resources** dialog.

To Delete an Assignment in the Task Form

Display the **Task Form**, select an assigned resource, press [Delete] and click [OK].

Assigning to Summary Tasks

MS Project happily allows you to *assign* resources to summary tasks, but we would like to discourage assigning to summary tasks. The reason is that sooner or later you will end up with over-allocations that cannot be resolved other than by removing the resource from the summary task again. Let me explain this.

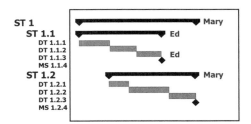

If you assign a resource full-time to a summary task and also to one of its detail tasks, the workload of the resource will be twice its availability during that detail task. In the illustration, you can see that Ed is assigned to the summary task *ST 1.1* and its detail task *DT 1.1.3*. You may think that you would never create a situation like this, but realize that you cannot easily see *assignments* on summary tasks, because they don't show up in the default timescale in MS Project as they do in the illustration; only assignments on detail tasks are displayed. You could change this in the **Format, Bar Styles** dialog, tab **Text**, by the way.

An assignment on both the summary task and its own detail task causes an over-allocation that cannot be solved by MS Project. After all, if MS Project moves the detail task to a later date, the summary task will automatically extend as well and continue the over-allocation. You cannot resolve the over-allocation yourself either, other than by removing the resource from the summary task (or from its detail task). So why bother assigning to summary tasks in the first place, if you normally assign resources to detail tasks?

There is another reason why this might happen to you. A similar over-allocation can happen between the different levels of summary tasks. In the previous illustration you can see that Mary is assigned only to summary tasks *ST 1* and *ST 1.2*. Because *ST 1.2* is subordinate to *ST 1*, the over-allocation cannot be solved again unless you remove the resource from one of the summary tasks. This situation could easily occur if you have several indentation levels. You could say: *Well, I will only assign resources to tasks that are on one certain outline level.* You insert the field **Outline level** and you use that to prevent this type of over-allocation. But why did you add more levels of detail tasks, if you are not going to use them to delegate or model workloads? It looks like you could have saved yourself some time by not creating all those detail tasks in the first place! Updating schedules with summary task assignments is also more cumbersome than when all assignments are on the lowest level. Again, we are back to our principle of modeling; leave things out that do not have added value.

You may be tempted to assign to a summary task if all its detail tasks are scheduled in sequence without gaps in between and all are done by the same resource(s). In this situation, you could be quicker by only assigning to the summary task. However, you will not save many mouse clicks, since you can select all detail tasks and assign the resource(s) to all of them with one click. Therefore, we don't even recommend it for that reason and in that rare situation, because of the substantial risk of stubborn over-allocations.

In short, in our view, there are no situations in which you are better off assigning to summary tasks rather than to detail tasks. We recommend keeping the assignments on the lowest level, the detail level only.

You can, however, assign resources to the *recurring summary tasks* with the **Assign Resources** tool, because MS Project will automatically transfer these to the detail tasks and the assignment on the recurring summary task is no longer there.

Assigning to Recurring Tasks

3 Status Meeting ☒ ☒ ☒ Mark, Brad
  3.1 Status meeting 1 ☒ Mark, Brad
  3.2 Status meeting 2 ☒ Mark, Brad
  3.3 Status meeting 3 ☒ Mark, Brad

If you *assign* a resource to the *recurring summary task* with the **Assign Resources** tool 🔲 , the *assignments* are immediately transferred to the detail tasks. This is done automatically, compliments of MS Project. In the illustration on the left, the resources *Mark* and *Brad* are assigned to the recurring summary task *3 Status Meeting* and are automatically transferred by MS Project to the *recurring detail tasks*. That is where we want the assignments anyway.

You can assign to recurring tasks in situations such as:

◆ Long meetings: They tend to be lengthy and therefore require considerable effort (work) from the resources.

◆ Short meetings: You require attendance at short meetings, and you want to show them as assignments in the to-do lists of team members.

You should only assign to recurring tasks, such as status meetings, if the efforts for these meetings are not included in the work estimates that your team members provided to you.

Assigning to recurring detail tasks can easily result in over-allocations that MS Project's leveling features will not resolve. The reason is that MS Project by default excludes recurring tasks from the leveling process by setting the field **Level Assignments** to **No** for the recurring detail tasks. You could switch it manually to **Yes**, but then your recurring tasks may be rescheduled, which is probably not what you want.

We recommend you keep the meetings short, assign resources and ignore the over-allocations.

Entering Multiple, Uneven Assignments

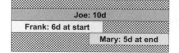

If there are multiple *assignments* on a task, often one of the assignments drives the duration of the task. The assignment that takes the longest or starts the latest will drive the duration of the task. The illustration on the left shows that three engineers, *Joe*, *Frank* and *Mary*, are assigned to develop a prototype. *Joe* will work 10 days, *Frank* only the first 6 days and *Mary* only the last 5 days, so the duration will be 10 days. *Joe* and *Mary* determine or "drive" the duration of the job. There are several disadvantages of this practice:

◆ Leveling workloads manually is very difficult with multiple uneven assignments. It is simpler if there is mostly only one resource assigned per task.

◆ It is unclear who is supposed to take the lead on the task, see the cartoon *Mr. Ambiguity and friends* at the start of this chapter.

To create *multiple, uneven assignments* on a task you need to:

1. Display the Task Form in the Gantt Chart by choosing **Window, Split**.

2. Change the details in the Task Form to show assignment start dates by clicking on the Task Form and choosing **Format, Details, Resource Schedule**
   OR
   right-clicking almost anywhere on the Task Form and choosing **Resource Schedule**.

3. To enter multiple uneven assignments, set the task **Type** to **Fixed Units** in the Task Form. Click OK .

4. Click in the field **Resource Name** and select a resource to assign from the list that appears [   ]. Repeat this for all resources to assign and enter different amounts of **Work** for each assigned resource. Enter a specific **Start** date OR enter a **Delay** for each assignment.

5. Click [OK]; you can see the result of the uneven assignments by choosing **View, Task Usage**. The result of the previous example would look like:

Task Name	Details	Dec 31, 00							Jan 7, 01					
		S	M	T	W	T	F	S	S	M	T	W	T	F
⊟ write	Work		16h	16h	16h	16h	16h			24h	16h	16h	16h	16h
Joe	Work		8h	8h	8h	8h	8h			8h	8h	8h	8h	8h
Frank	Work		8h	8h	8h	8h	8h			8h				
Mary	Work		0h	0h	0h	0h	0h			8h	8h	8h	8h	8h

Mary's assignment is scheduled on the last 5 days of the task duration.

Typically, the resource with the least work finishes early, unless you change the start date of their assignment. In our example, *Mary* drives the task finish date as much as *Joe*.

Generally, we recommend to split one task with multiple, uneven assignments into multiple tasks with a single assignment, if you can. There are two reasons:

◆ The formula $D * U = W$ does not apply to a task with multiple, uneven assignments, but it does apply to the individual assignments.

◆ The project schedule will stay simpler if you split the task into more tasks, creating one task for each resource. Where people need to get together and work as a group, you can create a short meeting task. In the example shown in the screenshot, the meeting would take place on Monday, January 8. We recommend this, because of the misery that Nob experienced by assigning multiple resources to tasks in the story at the start of this chapter. Also, leveling the workloads by hand is simpler when there is only one resource assigned per task.

Changing Assignment Attributes

1. Switch to a usage view, either the **Task Usage** or **Resource Usage**.

2. Double-click on an assignment. *Assignments* have no number, italic text and a light yellow background in the timescale. The **Assignment Information** dialog appears:

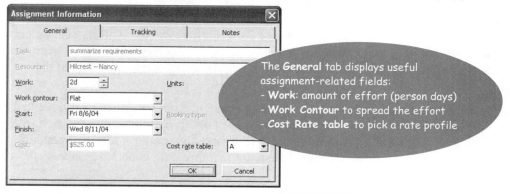

3. Make the changes to the assignment and click ___OK___ .

You can change many assignment-specific attributes. Assignments have about 50 purely assignment-related fields. Some useful examples are:

♦ *Start* and *Finish*: These fields allow you to have one or more resources start later or finish earlier on a task than the rest.

♦ *Delay*: Instead of entering start or finish dates, you could enter a number of days delay for the assignment.

♦ *Work contour*: This allows you to spread the effort on a task in a pattern you choose.

♦ *Cost rate table*: This allows you to select a specific rate profile for each assignment. This is useful for jacks-of-all-trades in small consulting firms that are billed differently for each job.

♦ *Note*: You can document actual findings and lessons learned by assignment. This allows you to create a project archive as you go along.

Replacing Generic Resources with Individuals

We have mentioned before that if you don't know who you will get on your team, you should simply assign generic resources, see page 319. I like to call generic resources "clones". There are several ways in which you can replace generic resources with real individuals of flesh-and-blood:

♦ In the Resource Sheet, type over the generic resource name with the name of the individual.

♦ In MS Project with Project Server, you can use the *Team Builder* to replace generic resources. Choose **Tools, Build Team from Enterprise** and select the generic

Team Resource in the list on the right and the substitute resource in the list **Enterprise Resource** on the left; then click . You cannot replace resources on assignments with actuals; the Team Builder will notify you.

Of course, these two methods will replace the generic resource on all its assignments, so you only want to use them when you have a one-to-one correspondence between the generic resource and the individual. Otherwise, you are going to need one of the following methods:

◆ In the Resource Usage view, drag the assignment from the generic resource to a real person. This method allows you to create just one generic resource for each role, function or position you need on your team and do long-term resource planning where you accumulate workload far into the future onto generic resources.

◆ You can use the [Replace...] button in the **Assign Resources** dialog. First, you select the tasks with the generic resource to replace, then select the generic resource and click [Replace...] and select the substitute resource from the list presented.

◆ In MS Project with *Project Server*, you can use the *Resource Substitution Wizard* to replace all generic resources quickly with real people. This method assumes that you have coded the skills of all resources (including the generic resources) in such a way that the wizard can determine which person has the right qualifications for the job. The Resource Substitution Wizard looks at availability as the second most important factor. So the result can be that a person gets over-allocated by the wizard, and you would still have to apply workload leveling after running the wizard.

Using the Resource Substitution Wizard

This wizard has two functions:
◆ Replace the generic resources in a project template with actual resources.
The generic resources should have codes that reflect their *skills*. If that is the case, the Substitution Wizard can figure out what individual has a matching set of skills if all the resources in the resource pool also have their skills coded.
◆ Optimize the resource allocation across a portfolio of projects.
It can also reallocate resources across any number of projects, optimizing the utilization of your resources. We will not discuss this function here; it is content for the Black Belt Professional course.[67] However, it is good to be aware of this

---

[67] See www.iil.com and follow the link *Microsoft Project*.

alternative use, because the options in the dialog boxes of the wizard might otherwise be confusing.

1. Choose **Tools, Substitute Resources**; the **Resource Substitution Wizard** appears with its **Welcome** screen.

2. Click [Next >] and the **Step 1** dialog appears:

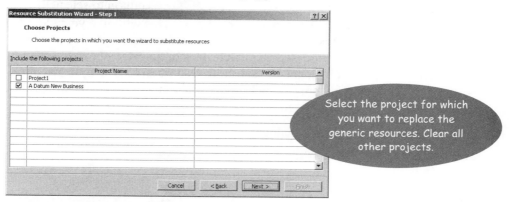

3. Check the project for which you want the wizard to substitute generic resources with real ones, and clear any other projects listed. Selecting other projects is necessary when you want to reallocate resources across projects.

4. Click [Next >]; the **Step 2** dialog appears:

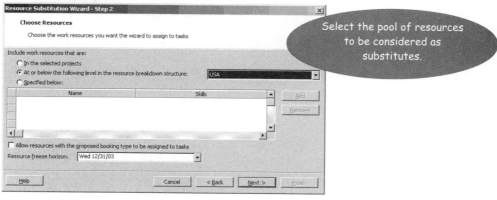

5. Choose the resources that you want the wizard to consider as substitutes. You can choose one of the options:

   ⦿ **In the selected projects**: This option is meant for reallocating resources across multiple projects. Do not use it for replacing generic resources with real ones.

⊙ **At or below the following level in the Resource Breakdown structure**:
Here you can select either a geographical region if you want the resources to live
close to where the project is, or a certain level in the organizational break down
structure. The list displays an organization-specific hierarchy configured during
the setup of Project Server, also known as the *Resource Breakdown Structure.*

⊙ **Specified below**: You have to click the [Add] button to select all
individual resources to consider for substitution. This will give you a lot of
control over the end result, but may not give the tightest schedule possible if you
narrow down the resource pool too much. This option also allows you to
influence the wizard by manually selecting resources, for example, resources
that have enough remaining availability for their tasks in the new project so that
you are not overloading them.

6. Click [Next >]; the **Step 3** dialog appears:

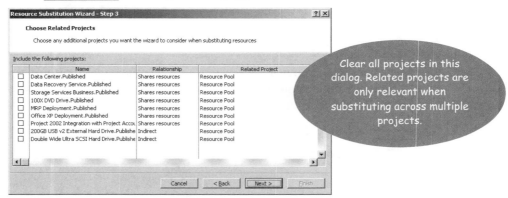

7. Choose the related projects. Related projects are projects that have cross-project links with this project or projects that share one or more of the same resources. Since the template will not have cross-project links and will only have generic resources, you will typically find that there are no or very few related projects.

8. Click [Next >]; the **Step 4** dialog appears:

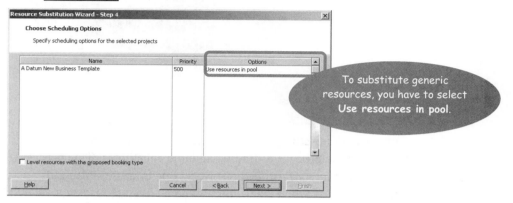

9. Choose the scheduling options. Your options are:

◇ Set the **Priority** level with a number from 0 to 1000. The higher the number, the higher priority the project will have when it competes for resources with other projects. MS Project will load resources into the highest priority projects first.

◇ Under **Options,** you can specify for each project whether MS Project should keep the same resource in a project and only reassign within that project (**use resources in project**) or should consider all resources in the enterprise pool that meet the criteria specified in the **Step 2** dialog (**Use resources in pool**). To replace generic resources, you would typically choose **Use resources in pool** here. If you choose **Use resources in project**, MS Project will not propose any substitutes, because it is only allowed to consider the generic resources that are already in the project.

10. Click [Next >]; the **Step 5** dialog appears:

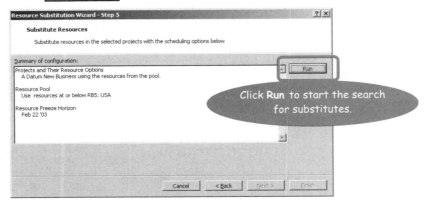

11. This dialog summarizes the settings you chose in the previous steps. Click [Run] to initiate the process of finding suitable substitutes. This process uses a complex algorithm that looks at project priorities, one or more skill fields, availability and other factors when determining which resource to assign. Watch the status line at the bottom of the screen; once it stops flashing, the substitution is done.

12. Click [Next >]; the **Step 6** dialog appears, showing the results of the resource substitution.

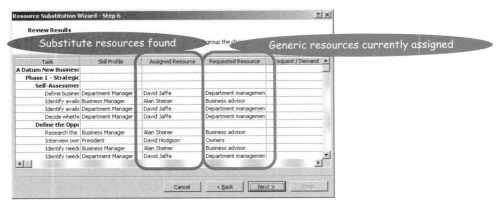

13. You can review the substitutions that Project Server proposes. The fields are as follows:

◇ **Task** contains the detail task name.

◇ **Skill profile** contains the skill profile required for the task. With generic resources assigned, it is the skill set of that generic resource.

◇ **Assigned Resource** is the resource the wizard recommends as a substitute for the generic resource.

◇ **Requested resource** is the resource originally assigned, in this case the generic resource.

◇ **Request/Demand** indicates whether the resource was just requested or was demanded for the task. The generic resources typically should not have this field filled in for their assignments. Only when real people are assigned can the project manager indicate for some of the resources that they are demanded on the job to be successful. Demanded resources are never proposed to be substituted by the wizard.

14. Click [Next >]; the **Step 7** dialog appears:

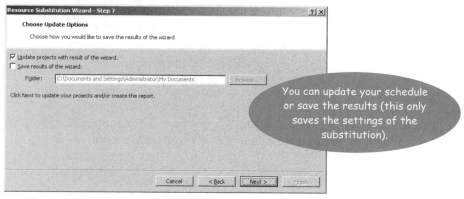

15. Check one or both options:

☑ **Update project with results of wizard**

AND/OR

☑ **Save results of the wizard** in a separate report file. Click [Browse...] to indicate in which subdirectory.

When replacing generic resources, you would normally select the first option. When reallocating resources across projects, you would typically use the second option to store the settings in a report. The report does not contain the detailed substitution suggestions by task as shown in the **Step 6** dialog of the wizard. The report does contain the date on which you created it, the settings you chose (so that you can reproduce the suggested substitutions) and the suggested team members for the project (the highest level result of the wizard). If the report did contain all suggested details, selecting both options would be useful for creating a change log. The report would then register what changes were made at what time, and could also be used as a discussion piece with your team (hope Microsoft picks up on these hints).

16. Click [Next >]; the **Step 8** dialog appears; this is the last dialog.
Click [Finish] and the substitutions of the generic resources will appear in the project schedule.

MS Project may not have replaced all generic resources if you chose the settings too narrow. In particular, the following choices could decrease the number of suggestions:

◆ Choosing a *Resource Breakdown Structure* level that is too low in the organization making the pool of resources that the wizard may consider as substitution candidates too narrow (**Step 2** of the wizard).

◆ If you only allow resources to be considered if they live in the same city or state, but nobody with a certain skill set lives in the area, MS Project can't find substitutes and the generic resource will stay on the task (at least, for now). (**Step 2** of the wizard)

◆ The less related projects you select in **Step 3** of the wizard, the less substitutions will be suggested to you. The wizard will start substituting across all selected projects. This is only relevant when reallocating across projects.

◆ The lower the priority level you give to the project in which to substitute the resources (**Step 4** of the wizard), the fewer substitutes will be suggested.

◆ If in **Step 4** of the wizard you choose **Use resources in project**, MS Project can only swap the resources that are already in the project. It may find some improvements, but that is not guaranteed. If you want to replace generic resources with real people, you have to always select **Use resources in pool**.

Checks on Assignments

Next you will find checks to verify if you have applied best practices to the *assignments* in your schedule:

◆ Are you using the task-related field **Type** for the detail tasks?
The available types in the field *Type* are: **Fixed Duration, Fixed Units** or **Fixed Work**. With this field, you can control what MS Project recalculates: duration, units or work. If you don't monitor the field **Type**, you are not controlling what MS Project does. You are using a software tool, but you have no idea what the tool can do for you. This is similar to having a carpenter's stud finder, but not knowing how to use it. Instead you start drilling many holes in the drywall to find the studs by trial and error as if the wall was hit by a machine gun. If you don't use the field **Type**, you are using MS Project in a trial and error fashion; you change a field here, MS Project recalculates a value there, you don't like what you see and you change it back again … and you start running after your own tail. In IIL's certification curriculum, we expect that people learn to use the field **Type**. If we see the default task type **Fixed Units** still in use for all tasks in the schedule, we know

people are not using this powerful feature in MS Project that makes it a pleasant tool to work with.

◆ Are there no assignments on the summary tasks?
As we discussed on page 396, if you assign resources to summary tasks you can easily end up with over-allocations that cannot be resolved other than by removing the resource from the summary task again. If you assign only to detail tasks, you will never end up with this stubborn type of over-allocation and save yourself time when leveling workloads. Resolving over-allocations is challenging enough.
You can check this easily by applying the filter **09 IIL Summary Tasks with Resources Assigned**.[68]

◆ Does each detail task have at least one human resource assigned?
If there are detail tasks without human resources assigned, you have not captured all the workloads in your project. If workloads are missing, the schedule may be too optimistic, since leveling workloads typically leads to longer schedules and later forecasts. An exception to this rule is that *recurring detail tasks* do not need resources assigned to them. You can check on this in one of two ways:

◇ In the **Resource Usage** view, there should be no detail tasks listed under the first category **Unassigned**.

◇ You can also apply filter **09 IIL Detail tasks without Resources Assigned**.[69] The filter allows you to easily copy the tasks including their ID number into a schedule evaluation report to send back to the project manager.

Note that there may still be detail tasks with only material resources assigned, if you check the **Unassigned** category or apply the filter, so neither check is bullet proof.

---

[68] This filter can be found in the file *IIL Project 2003 tools to check Orange Belt schedules.MPP* available for download at www.jrosspub.com. Please, click the link *WAV Download Resource Center* to enter the download site.

[69] This filter can be found in the file *IIL Project 2003 tools to check Orange Belt schedules.MPP* available for download at www.jrosspub.com. Please, click the link *WAV Download Resource Center* to enter the download site.

Printing the Assignments

Choose **View, Task Usage** to apply the **Task Usage** view, which shows all *assignments* in detail. The assignments appear in this view as resource names, since the task names are indented below their task:

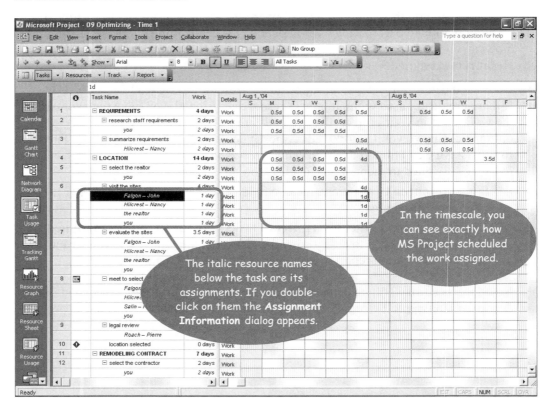

To display the assignments below each resource, choose **View**, **Resource Usage**. Assignments appear in this view as task names, since the resource names are already listed.

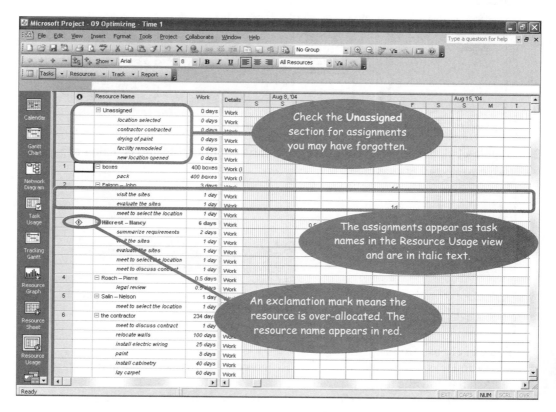

If you don't see the numbers in the timescale, select a resource and click **Go to selected task** (I guess Microsoft forgot to adjust this screen tip!). To change the time unit, use the **Zoom In** 🔍 or the **Zoom Out** 🔍 tool, or choose **Format, Timescale...** to get it exactly right.

 You can now print row totals and column totals in the timescale of the usage views. In the Task Usage or Resource Usage view, you can select these totals by choosing **File, Page Setup**, tab **View** and checking ☑ **Print row totals for values within print date range** and ☑ **Print column totals**.

Alternatively, there are *assignment* reports available.

1. Choose **View, Reports**; the **Reports** dialog appears:

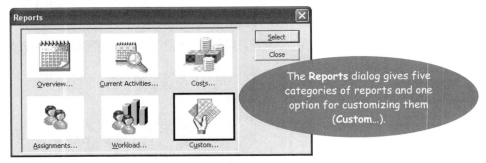

2. Double-click the button **Assignments...**; the **Assignment Reports** dialog appears:

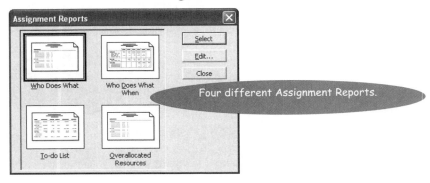

3. You can choose from:
   ◊ **Who Does What** is similar to the Resource Usage view; the assignments are listed below the tasks.
   ◊ **Who Does What When** displays the work on each task spread over time.
   ◊ **To-do List** prompts to select a resource and the report will show all the tasks by week with their start and finish times. You can change this report to show the tasks by month by selecting it and then clicking ▭ Edit... ▭. Note that for each week (or month) the total duration of the task is repeated and the data are not truly time-phased.
   ◊ **Overallocated Resources** shows only the resources that are over-allocated with all their assignments (including the ones that cause the over-allocation).

Here is an example of a **To-do List** report:

To Do List as of Sat Dec 23
Relocation Devom Inc.
Eric Uyttewaal

ID		Task Name	Type	Duration
Week of July 29				
2		research staff requirements	Fixed Work	4 days?
5		select the realtor	Fixed Duration	4 days
Week of August 5				
2		research staff requirements	Fixed Work	4 days?
5		select the realtor	Fixed Duration	4 days
6		visit the sites	Fixed Duration	1 day
7		evaluate the sites	Fixed Duration	1 day
Week of August 12				
7		evaluate the sites	Fixed Duration	1 day
Week of August 19				
8		meet to select the location	Fixed Duration	1 day
12		select the contractor	Fixed Duration	2 days
27		select mover	Fixed Duration	2 days
Week of August 26				
12		select the contractor	Fixed Duration	2 days
27		select mover	Fixed Duration	2 days
Week of September 2				
13		meet to discuss contract	Fixed Duration	1 day
14		revise the schedule	Fixed Duration	1 day
15		negotiate the contract	Fixed Duration	1 day

If you want to produce to-do lists across multiple projects, we recommend you use Project 2003 Professional with *Project Server*. Team members will see their entire task list from multiple projects brought together on one web page with truly time-phased data.

Exercises

Review A

1. What is the definition of an *assignment*?

2. In your own words, describe what the following fields represent:
   a. **Units** field in the Task Form
   b. **Units** field in the **Resource Information** dialog, tab **General**
   c. **Max. Units** field in the Resource Sheet
   d. **Work** field in the Gantt Chart
   e. **Work** field in the Task Form
   f. **Work** field in the Resource Sheet
   g. Task-related **Work** field in the Task Usage view
   h. Assignment-related **Work** field in the Task Usage view

3. In your own words, what is a *Work Contour*?

4. A project manager realizes that she wants to model her project on a high level. She will only enter consolidated resources (pooled resources) in her Resource Sheet. What setting would you recommend to her for **Tools, Options**, tab **Schedule**, field **Show assignment units as**?

5. What are the three task types? How does each task type function? How would you use this feature of MS Project?

6. In your own words, what are the three rules that will help you control what MS Project does when creating and changing assignments?

7. Before you make a change on an assignment, what question should you ask yourself and what field(s) should you check?

8. Describe two different ways of assigning resources to tasks in MS Project. Describe them in detail in terms of mouse clicks or menu items to choose. What are the differences between these two methods in terms of options you have?

9. Would you recommend making multiple, uneven assignments to many tasks in your schedule? Justify your answer in terms of pros and cons.

10. Would you recommend assigning resources to summary tasks? Justify your answer in terms of pros and cons.

11. When you assign a resource to a recurring summary task with the **Assign Resources** dialog, what will MS Project do automatically?

12. A resource is writing two different documents concurrently and you cannot plan or predict when he will be working on one or the other. How would you model this situation in MS Project? In particular, what tasks and assignments would you create and what number of resource units would you assign?

Review B

Read the following situations and determine if you will likely make your first estimate in *person days* work (PD), in *business days* duration (BD) or in *elapsed days* duration (ED) and explain why. Indicate which type of task you recommend: Fixed Duration (FD), Fixed Units (FU) or Fixed Work (FW), and explain why.

	PD, BD or ED? Why?	FD, FU or FW? Why?
1. Writing a 10 page report that normally takes a person 4 hours per page to produce		
2. One load to be transported over a distance of 4,000 miles with one driver		
3. One package that has to be flown a distance of over 4,000 miles and has to arrive in 2 working days		
4. A house painter who is asked for a fixed price quote and the earliest end date for painting a family home		
5. A contractor gives a painter a maximum of 2 weeks to finish painting a building		
6. Backing up a computer system before the conversion to a new operating system, where the backing up requires little supervision once started		
7. A meeting with a presentation to all team members		

Relocation Project — Entering Assignments

Continue to work with your file *Relocation.MPP* or open the file
08 Entering Assignments.MPP available for download at www.jrosspub.com. Please,
click the link *WAV Download Resource Center* to enter the download site. Enter the
assignments as shown in the next table. Some remarks:

◆ First, add the fields **Type, Duration** and **Work** to the Gantt Chart view in such a
   way that the view matches the *task fields* column headings in the next table. Note
   that you cannot add the *assignment fields* shown in the table; you have to enter the
   assignment information in the **Assign Resources** dialog or in the **Task Form**.
◆ Remember that MS Project uses the formula *Duration * Units = Work* and will
   calculate for each detail task the third value that is not provided in the next table.
◆ Think about the easiest way to enter each assignment; decide if you should use the
   Assign Resources dialog or the **Task Form**. The Task Form is best when you want
   to assign multiple resources with specific numbers for units and/or work.
◆ Only the **Fixed Work** tasks are **Effort Driven**.

TASK FIELDS				ASSIGNMENT FIELDS	
Task Name	**Type**	**Dur.**	**Work**	**Resources**	**Units**
REQUIREMENTS	*Fixed Duration*				
research staff requirements	*Fixed Work*		*2d*	*you*	*0.5*
summarize requirements	*Fixed Work*		*2d*	*Hilcrest*	*0.5*
LOCATION	*Fixed Duration*				
select the realtor	*Fixed Duration*	*4 d*		*you*	*0.5*
visit the sites	*Fixed Duration*	*1 d*		*Falgon* *Hilcrest* *the realtor* *you*	*1* *1* *1* *1*
evaluate the sites	*Fixed Duration*	*1 d*		*Falgon* *Hilcrest* *the realtor* *you*	*1* *1* *0.5* *1*
meet to select the location	*Fixed Duration*	*1 d*		*Falgon* *Hilcrest* *Salin* *you*	*1* *1* *1* *1*

TASK FIELDS				ASSIGNMENT FIELDS	
Task Name	Type	Dur.	Work	Resources	Units
legal review	Fixed Duration	0.5 d		Roach	1
REMODELING CONTRACT	Fixed Duration				
select the contractor	Fixed Duration	2 d		you	1
meet to discuss contract	Fixed Duration	1 d		the contractor Hilcrest you	1 1 1
revise the schedule	Fixed Duration	1 d		you	1
negotiate the contract	Fixed Duration	1 d		you	1
REMODELED LOCATION	Fixed Duration				
relocate walls	Fixed Work		100 d	the contractor	10
install electric wiring	Fixed Work		25 d	the contractor	5
paint	Fixed Work		8 d	the contractor	4
drying of paint	Fixed Duration	4 ed			
install cabinetry	Fixed Work		40 d	the contractor	8
install LAN	Fixed Work		60 d	the LAN consultants	5
lay carpet	Fixed Work		60 d	the contractor	6
MOVE	Fixed Duration				
select mover	Fixed Duration	2 d		you	1
pack	Fixed Duration	2 d		the employees boxes	35 400
move	Fixed Work		20 d	the movers	10
unpack	Fixed Duration	2 d		the employees	35

Compare your file with the solution file *09 Optimizing – Time 1.MPP* available for download at www.jrosspub.com. Please, click the link *WAV Download Resource Center* to enter the download site. See page 675 of this book for an automated way of comparing and reporting differences between two versions of one schedule. Notice that the project is missing its November 1 deadline. We will need to optimize the schedule in the next chapter.

Relocation Project — Changing Assignments

Continue to work with your file *Relocation.MPP* or open the file *09 Optimizing – Time 1.MPP* available for download at www.jrosspub.com. Please, click the link *WAV Download Resource Center* to enter the download site.

How should you go about making the following changes to the assignments? You may need to change the **Type** of the task first. The task *install LAN* currently has a duration of 12 days, 5 consultants working on it and 60 days of work.

1. You would like to know how long the task *install LAN* would take if there were 10 *LAN consultants* instead of 5 while keeping the work the same. What task type do you need before you make this change?
   You should get a duration of 6 days. Keep this change.

2. You want to know how many consultants are needed if you want the task *install LAN* done in 3 days while keeping the work the same. What task type do you need before you make this change?
   You should find that 20 *LAN consultants* are needed. Keep this change.

3. You think you over-estimated the work; you will need only 30 days instead of 60 days and you want to keep the duration to 3 days. What is the number of consultants needed now? What task type do you need before you make this change?
   You should find that 10 consultants are needed. Keep this change.

4. You want to keep the number of consultants to 10, but you want to change the duration from 3 to 12 days. How much work is now on the task? What task type do you need before you make this change?
   You should end up with 120 days of work. Keep this change.

5. You want to bring the number of consultants down to 5 while keeping the 12-day duration. How much work is now on the task? What task type do you need before you make this change?
   This brings us back to where we were at the start of this exercise after exploring several scenarios.

Chapter 9 Optimizing the Schedule

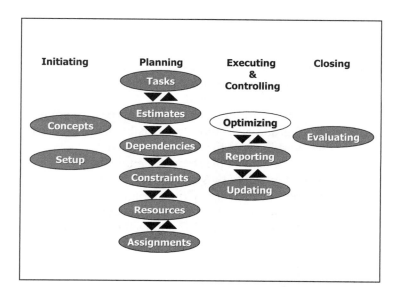

After entering the schedule data, we now have a dynamic model of our project that tells us whether the project is feasible as we envisioned it. In most situations, the draft schedule will show that the duration is too long, the cost is too high, the workloads are unreasonable or any combination of these. With a dynamic model, we can easily develop and explore different scenarios to find the best solution. We can optimize for time, for time and cost or for time, cost and resource availability.

After reading this chapter you will:

◆ be able to choose the appropriate approach for optimizing
◆ be able to optimize the project for time (including scope and quality)
◆ be able to display the Critical Path
◆ be able to solve a fragmented Critical Path
◆ understand the difference between Free Slack and Total Slack
◆ be able to apply several techniques to shorten the project duration (optimize for time)
◆ be aware of the assumptions/shortcomings of the Critical Path Method (CPM)
◆ know what Monte Carlo simulation is and why you would use it
◆ be able to optimize the project for time and cost
◆ be able to optimize the project for time, cost and resource availability
◆ be able to make workloads and over-allocations visible in MS Project
◆ know how to level the workloads of the resources yourself
◆ know how to level the workloads of the resources automatically
◆ know what the Resource-Critical Path is and when it is important
◆ be able to find and shorten the Resource-Critical Path
◆ be able to evaluate the impacts of a change to the schedule (scenario analysis)
◆ be able to check if the schedule is properly optimized using scheduling best practices

Key Resources, the Key to Success

Nob: "Bob, what did you do to meet that deadline? It looked pretty close to impossible to meet it. Everybody was saying that this time you bit off more than you could chew... People made bets against you."

Bob: "You want to know my secrets, don't you?"

Nob: "Oh come on, I share all my secrets with you, don't I?"

Bob: "Well, I am not going to comment on that... but this time, we really got behind. We had to sort out all this new technology stuff ... and it never works the way they advertise it."

Nob: "Yeah, we heard that at one point you were four weeks behind schedule ..."

Bob: "That's right and we almost brought it in on time, mostly, because our team really put in the best they had."

Nob: "Oh come on ... you have some kind of trick up your sleeve ... and you are not willing to share it with me."

Bob: "Well, what we did wasn't rocket science. We just made sure the very best resources were always working on the most critical tasks that drove our project end date. It meant that we sometimes reassigned people when progress shifted among the components. Fortunately, we established a clear understanding with the team up front that we wanted to be able to do that, and they allowed us to."

Nob: "Yeah, we heard some people complain that they had to clean up other people's mess."

Bob: "Our key resources were indeed the key to our success."

The Pulling Forces

Optimizing a schedule is the true art of scheduling. When optimizing, you have to consider the project in all its aspects. The Project Management Institute has identified the dimensions by which projects need to be optimized in its Guide to the Project Management Body of Knowledge (PMBOK® Guide).[70] These knowledge areas are shown with arrows in the illustration. A change in one area often impacts another. Eight forces are at work on each project, and project managers have to consider all of them in an integrated fashion. The PMBOK® Guide calls this *Project Integration Management*, the ninth knowledge area. MS Project provides sufficient features to manage many, but not all, areas:

◆ **Quality**
The quality of deliverables must correspond to the specifications and expectations of the client. You can schedule quality activities in MS Project, but the tool does not provide a full-fledged quality management system. Such a system typically contains the requirements, specifications or acceptance criteria for the deliverables. For software development projects, we recommend you complement MS Project with a requirements tracking system. However, quality impacts can and should always be considered while optimizing, even without a quality tracking system.

◆ **Scope**
The *scope* of a project can be captured using the *Work Breakdown Structure*. It contains the deliverables to be produced and the activities can be derived from them. MS Project is an excellent tool for managing scope. Scope should always be considered when optimizing schedules. The scope of a project is its raison d'être.[71]

◆ **Time**
Deadlines can be scheduled and managed very well in MS Project. Since a project is

---

[70] See the PMBOK® Guide, 2004 edition, published by the PMI.

[71] French for 'reason for its existence'.

a temporary endeavor, every project manager will monitor and manage the duration of their project by definition.

◆ **Cost**

You can manage the expenses for labor, facilities, machines and material with MS Project so they stay within your budget. Not all project managers are given a money budget and therefore, will not monitor the cost of their project as a result. In recent years, more and more organizations are empowering their project managers with a budget, but are also challenging them to stay within it.

◆ **Resources**

The *workloads* have to stay within the availability of the resources. You can do workload leveling with MS Project. One issue we will have to deal with is that when you level resource workloads, the Critical Path can become fragmented. We will therefore introduce a new concept, the *Resource-Critical Path* that is needed to optimize resource-constrained schedules.

In Project Professional with *Project Server*, you can model the resource needs in the longer term using an enterprise resource pool and generic resources. Project Server also allows you to develop skill-based *scenarios* like: *What if we allowed resource substitution between projects; could we then meet the deadlines?* or *What if we added another project to the portfolio and reallocated the resources; how would this impact the finish dates of our current projects?*

◆ **Risk**

Risk is about potential hazards or fortunes that can happen in or to the project. Risk management activities can be scheduled in MS Project and monitored, but it does not have specific features for Risk Management Planning, Risk Identification, Qualitative Risk Analysis, Quantitative Risk Analysis, Risk Response Planning and Risk Monitoring and Control.[72] *Project Server* now has a risk management interface that uses the probability-impact technique to quantify the seriousness of the risk. MS Project does allow you to introduce some probability into the schedule with its *PERT analysis* features, but does not provide *simulation* capabilities. Simulation is the superior technique, and we will discuss it in more detail. There are add-on tools that complement MS Project to perform schedule and cost simulation.

In Project Server, you can collect and manage issues. Team members can easily raise issues as they become aware of them. Managers will see an overview list of raised issues and can respond to them.

---

[72] These are the processes of the Project Risk Management knowledge area in the PMBOK® Guide, 2004 edition.

◆ **Communications**
You can create a variety of paper or online reports with MS Project standalone. *Project Server* enhances the communication features of MS Project tremendously, because it allows you to interact with just about any project stakeholder wherever they may be, as long as they can connect to the Internet or to your Intranet. Project Server also has features that allow you to store several versions of the schedule and designate one version as the official one, which is called the *published version*. Project Server also provides a document management system. Such a system is needed for project communication management in large or complex projects in which often many documents are created.

◆ **Procurement**
You can schedule procurement activities in MS Project, but neither MS Project nor Project Server is a *contract management* system. A separate system may be needed for managing the procurement in projects. Large projects in particular often have many contracts associated with them. Project managers need to have access to the contracts on a moments' notice and may need a contract management system.

Improving one dimension of the project often impacts the others. When the impact is negative, you are *trading off* among the dimensions. For example, if you hire more resources to meet a tight deadline, the impact may be positive on time, but negative on cost. Sometimes, you can find methods that are positive in more than one respect and neutral in others. These are the methods to find and apply first. We will make several suggestions of such methods.

Three Approaches for Optimizing Schedules

We will present to you three different approaches for optimizing schedules. In all three, we include consideration of quality and scope as well. Because these two dimensions do not differentiate the approaches, we have not included the words *scope* or *quality* in the name of each approach. The different approaches are:

◆ *Optimizing for Time*
This approach is also known as *optimizing under the assumption of unlimited resources*. The other approaches will not assume that you have access to unlimited resources. You have access to unlimited resources if you can hire and fire any resources you need when you need them. Instead of firing, being able to release your resources to other projects within the company also meets this criterion. Having *unlimited resources* also implies and assumes that cost is not of primary concern to you and that you only need to consider the forces quality, scope and time. The common technique used in this situation is the Critical Path Method (CPM). Many

industries have been using CPM for decades. Typically, the construction and consulting industries apply CPM. These industries tend to hire and release resources on an as-needed basis, often working with temporary or free-lance resources. Other industries find this optimization too narrow, particularly when cost is a concern or resources are not readily available.

◆ *Optimizing for Time and Cost*
If you have a limited budget and cost is your concern, you should apply this approach. It is also applicable if you can find more money to solve quality, scope or time problems. You could use money to buy better raw materials, rent better equipment or pay penalties for late delivery. However, if you use the extra money to increase resource availability, you should use the next approach instead of just focusing on time and cost, since you are now affecting the resources. You increase availability when you hire more people, subcontract to free-lancers or rent more facilities or equipment.

◆ *Optimizing for Time, Cost and Resources*
If you must also consider the availability and capacity of the resources in order to derive a feasible schedule for your project, you are using this approach. You are making trade-off decisions among quality, scope, time, cost and *resource availability*. An example of optimizing for time, cost and resources is when you consider paying extra to get more overtime from your team. If your resources are scarce, you will have to look at their availability and their workload. You will have to level the resource workloads. Leveling often disjoints the Critical Path, and we cannot expect that CPM will help us any longer. The technique we will suggest is called the *Resource-Critical Path*.

As you can see, we are adding one dimension with each approach to optimization. The optimizations become more complex as we add more dimensions to consider. Including five out of the eight dimensions is the most complex optimization we will discuss in this book. It also is the most complex one MS Project can assist you with as a standalone tool.

Choosing the Options

Choose **Tools, Options** to access the following options that are relevant for all optimizing approaches:

Tab	Option
View	☑ **Show summary tasks** and ☑ **Show project summary task** The project summary task is inserted at the top of the task list and summarizes the entire project, with everything indented beneath it. It has ID number 0 (zero). The project summary task is useful when optimizing, because it displays the total duration, effort and cost of the project. Other schedules are not affected when you (un)check the previous two options, because they are stored in the project schedule; see the label of this section **Outline Options for <schedule name of the project>**.
Calculation	☐ **Calculate multiple critical paths** We recommend you keep this option off, since a single project should only have one ending point in the network logic. If there are multiple ending points, there are multiple critical paths. This option is also stored in the project schedule.
	Tasks are critical if slack is less than or equal to `0` ⬍ **days** This field creates a threshold for marking tasks that are critical. MS Project calculates if a task is critical. Normally, this option is set to zero, which means that MS Project displays tasks as critical with zero or negative slack and shows them in red. This option is also stored in the project schedule.

Optimizing for Time

The three dimensions that we will consider in this type of optimization are *quality*, *scope* and *time*, as indicated by the solid black arrows in the illustration. When you try to decrease the duration of the project and trade-off against quality or scope, you are essentially doing an optimization on the dimension of time. The technique for this type of optimization is the Critical Path Method (CPM). Many project managers have gotten used to keeping their eye on the cost and resources while crashing the Critical Path, but we will not do that. We will discuss the CPM here in its original form, since we discuss including cost on page 466 (Optimizing for Time and Cost) and resources on page 472 (Optimizing for Time, Cost and Resources).

Techniques

◆ **The Critical Path Method (CPM)**

The CPM is a beautiful product of human logic. The beauty lies in the fact that it really helps project managers meet their deadlines by highlighting the tasks that are most likely to affect the project deadline. Finding and highlighting that series of tasks in your schedule is known as the *Critical Path Method*. A critical task does not have buffer time (slack), and any delay experienced on a critical task means your project end date will slip. The CPM uses a single duration estimate for each task.

◆ **The PERT Method**

The *Program Evaluation and Review Technique* (*PERT*) technique is a more sophisticated application of the CPM. Instead of using one duration estimate for each task, PERT uses three estimates for each task: optimistic (O), most likely (ML) and pessimistic (P). These durations are converted to an expected duration with the following formula: Expected Duration = (O + 4 * ML + P) / 6.

After the expected durations have been calculated, CPM can again be applied to the schedule. PERT incorporates probability into the Critical Path. In Project 2003, the PERT feature in MS Project is not installed if you did a typical installation; you have to run setup again to install it as one of the available *COM Add-ins*. MS Project has a toolbar **PERT Analysis** that enables you to apply the PERT-method to your schedule. Right-click on any toolbar and choose **PERT Analysis**. Click the tool

PERT Entry Sheet and enter the estimates. You can even choose the weights for each estimate by clicking **Set PERT Weights**. Then click the **Calculate PERT** to have MS Project calculate the expected durations in the **Duration** field. The PERT calculation often results in durations with decimals. This is one of the reasons why PERT is used less and less. Another reason is that simulation also captures the added risk of paths that converge, which PERT does not.

◆ **Simulation of the Schedule**
Another way to make probability visible is by subjecting the schedule to *Monte Carlo simulation*. This type of simulation creates many versions of the same schedule based on the probability ranges you provide for certain estimates. The simulation software then averages over all the versions of the schedule to arrive at the probability for each possible finish date. Simulation is more powerful than PERT, because it quantifies the compounding effect of parallel paths as well. For more on Monte Carlo simulation, see page 460.

We will further elaborate on CPM and simulation in this book, but leave PERT behind us.

The Critical Path Method (CPM)

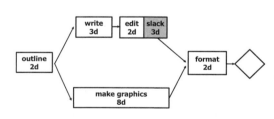

The *Critical Path* in your network of dependencies determines how long your project will take. The concept of the Critical Path is fairly simple. The illustration depicts a simple authoring project: *outline* the document, *write* the text, *edit* the text, while somebody else *makes graphics*. When the text and the graphics are ready, the *format* can be created and the project is finished. All arrows are finish-to-start dependencies and all durations are below the task names. Before we explain the Critical Path theory, you should ask yourself: *What is the minimum duration for this project?*

It does not take a rocket scientist to find that the duration for this project is 12 days. If you came up with the correct answer, you understand the Critical Path concept intuitively. If you came up with a different answer, you can find the Critical Path by comparing the two parallel paths. Add the durations and any lags on each path and compare the totals. The longest one is the Critical Path. In the illustration, you can see that the two parallel alternatives for the Critical Path are the path *write (3d)* and *edit (2d)* which is 5 days long in total versus the path *make graphics (8d)*. It is clear that the *make graphics* path is the longest and determines the project end date. Continue comparing parallel paths until you have checked them all and found the longest path in the whole network; this is the Critical Path. In this case, there are no further parallel paths and we have found the Critical Path: *outline, make graphics,* and *format.*

Parallel chains make up a network, of which all but one chain has *slack.* Sometimes a few chains are equally critical. Slack exists on each chain of tasks when it is performed in parallel with another chain that takes more time. The longest chain in the network is the Critical Path. The Critical Path determines the minimum duration of the project. I call it the *minimum duration* of the project, because the real duration may be longer when some resources are over-allocated. Over-allocations may force tasks to be delayed past the minimum duration. Finding the Critical Path is challenging:

◆ When there are many *parallel paths*
◆ When different types of *dependencies* are used: Finish-to-Start, Start-to-Start, Finish-to-Finish, Start-to-Finish
◆ When there are *lags* or *leads* on the dependencies.

In these cases, it is nice to have the help of a tool like MS Project that will identify the Critical Path for you.

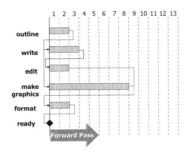

Let's look at how MS Project goes about finding the Critical Path. MS Project starts with all tasks cuddled up to the project start date, as shown in the illustration. Then it schedules them out to the earliest possible dates; *as soon as possible* scheduling. MS Project then performs the forward pass calculation to determine the *earliest possible dates* (*early dates*). Then it schedules all tasks *As Late As Possible* in the backward pass and calculates the *latest allowable dates* (*late dates*) to meet the earliest possible project finish date.

Forward Pass

On the forward pass, MS Project calculates two dates for each task: the early start (ES) and the early finish (EF) date. The result of this forward pass is shown in the illustration. MS Project starts with the first task (*outline*), looks at its duration (*2 days*) and calculates the earliest date it can be ready. This is the **Early Finish** date. The *outline* will be ready at the end of day 2. MS Project will then continue determining the **Early Start** date of the successor(s). *Write* and *make graphics* are the successors; they can start on day 3. The early start date of the successors will be the same as the early finish date of *outline*,

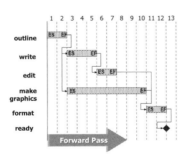

unless other dependencies on the successors cause them to start later. MS Project continues to calculate the early finish for *write* and *make graphics. Format* cannot start until both *edit* and *make graphics* are finished, and the earliest start date for *format* is therefore day 11 even though *format* could start on day 8, if it depended solely on *edit*. MS Project continues through the last task in the chain. The software now knows what the earliest finish date is for the project — day 12 in our example.

Backward Pass

MS Project then goes backward through the network starting at the project end date of day 12 to calculate the late finish dates for the tasks, as shown in the illustration. The **Late Finish** date is the latest date a task should be finished in order to meet the project end date. By subtracting the duration of the task from the finish date, MS Project then calculates the late start date. The **Late Start** date is the latest date you can start working on the task to finish by its late finish date. For *format,* this is day 11, the same as its early finish date. We then continue with the late finish dates of the predecessors. *Edit* can finish on day 10 at the latest and the project will still end on day 12. *Edit* has a late finish date (day 10) that is 3 days later than its early finish date (day 7); therefore, *edit* has a time buffer called *slack* and is not a critical task.

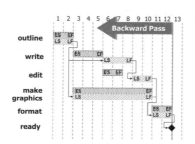

If a task has more than one successor, like *outline,* MS Project has to take all successors into consideration to determine the late date. The start date of the earliest successor determines the late finish date of the task, in this case day 2 (*make graphics*), not day 5 (*write*). So, the latest finish for creating the *outline* is determined by the late start date of *make graphics*, and not the late start date of *write.* As a result, the early and the late dates for *outline* are the same; *outline* does not have slack and is another critical task.

There are two kinds of slack: Total Slack and Free Slack. We will explain both kinds.

Calculating Total Slack

Total slack is the amount of time you can delay a task without affecting the project end date. The total slack (TS) is the *late finish* (LF) date minus the *early finish* (EF) date of a task:[73] TS = LF – EF

It tells you how much a task can slip before delaying the whole project or other *hard constraint* dates in the schedule. For example, the illustration shows that the task *Write* has 3 days of total slack (*TS = 8 – 5 = 3*). If the author calls you and tells you he fell ill, you would ask, "*When do you think you might be better?*" If the answer is more than 3 days, you know you should find somebody else, if you can't permit the project to slip. If the answer is less than 3 days, you may still have a problem, because the editor will now receive the text later, which might cause conflicts in her schedule. You need to communicate!

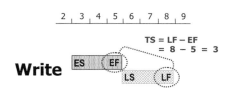

The *total slack* of tasks can be:

♦ Greater than zero: *positive slack*
These tasks have slack and can be delayed for as much total slack as they have. If you delay them more than that, it will slip the project as a whole. You can often level some workloads by using the total slack of a task.

♦ Equal to zero: *zero slack*
Where the *late finish* date is equal to the *early finish* date, there is no slack. Tasks without slack are by definition on the *Critical Path*.

♦ Less than zero: *negative slack*
Tasks with a negative slack are tasks that don't meet the project deadline or hard constraint dates set in the schedule. Slack can only be negative if there are constraints, deadlines or other forces in the schedule that inhibit MS Project from finding and displaying a schedule that meets all those constraints.

---

[73] In fact, MS Project also calculates total slack on the start dates: TS = LS – ES; the lesser of the two total slacks will be the total slack displayed on the task.

Calculating Free Slack

The *free slack* (FS) of a task is the **Early Start** date of the task's successor minus the **Early Finish** date of the task itself. If there is more than one successor, you should take the **Early Start** date of the earliest successor: $FS = ES_{earliest\ successor} - EF$.

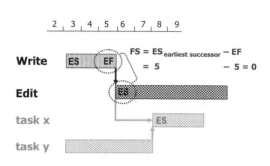

In the illustration, the earliest successor of task *Write* is *Edit* instead of *task x*. The free slack tells you how much you can let the task slip before it affects any of its successors. *Write* does not have free slack, since the successor *Edit* starts immediately after *write* finishes. The free slack of a task is always less than or equal to its total slack.

The difference between total slack and free slack manifests itself in the task *Write*; it has no *free slack* but 3 days of *total slack*. It can use the free slack of its successor *Edit* and slip without delaying the project end date. That is the beauty of the concept of total slack; it tells for each task immediately when the project finish date or other constraint dates are in jeopardy.

MS Project generates all the dates we discussed, and you can find these dates in the task fields **Early Start**, **Early Finish**, **Late Start** and **Late Finish**. The two slack fields are **Total Slack** and **Free Slack**.

The Critical Path

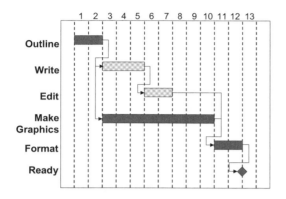

The *Critical Path* can now be found by finding the tasks that do not have total slack. In our example, the tasks *Outline*, *Make Graphics* and *Format* do not have total slack and are the tasks on the Critical Path. They are the dark task bars in the illustration. MS Project can easily highlight the Critical Path for us by displaying it in red. When you apply the **Tracking Gantt** view, you will see the Critical Path highlighted in red. You can also run the **Gantt Chart Wizard** on the Standard toolbar. We need to see the Critical Path to bring our project in on time. If we miss the project deadline, we can find critical tasks and optimize them to shorten our schedule and finish on time.

Constraints and Negative Slack

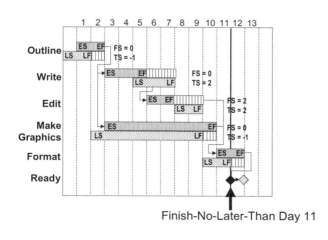

Finish-No-Later-Than Day 11

When you enter constraints into the schedule, all amounts of slack will change. The backward pass is calculated from the Finish No Later Than constraint date instead of the earliest possible project finish date. As a result, the late dates and total slack numbers change when you insert such a constraint. In our sample project, we will introduce a *hard constraint* that is one day before the earliest possible finish date of the project. The illustration shows how this constraint changes the total slack numbers of all tasks.

The forward pass determines the early dates, regardless of constraints. The backward pass takes constraints like Finish No Later Than into account.

You can see that the slack turns negative when the latest allowable dates (LF) are before the earliest possible dates (EF). The critical tasks now have –1 day total slack. When slack is negative, project managers speak of *negative slack*. MS Project identifies this as a *scheduling conflict* and warns you with a dialog:

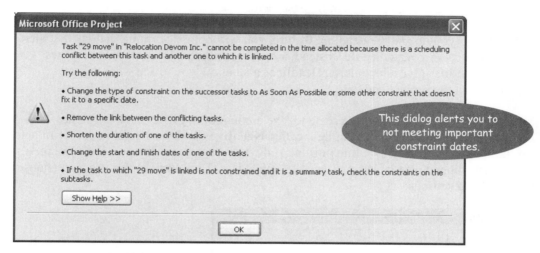

As you can see, MS Project gives concrete advice as to how to solve conflicts.

The constraints that can cause scheduling conflicts, or negative slack, under *forward scheduling* are the constraints that can put pressure on the network of dependencies:
◆ *Must Finish On*
◆ *Must Start On*
◆ *Finish No Later Than*
◆ *Start No Later Than*

In *backward scheduling*, the following constraints can cause negative slack by adding pressure to the network:
◆ *Must Finish On*
◆ *Must Start On*
◆ *Start No Earlier Than*
◆ *Finish No Earlier Than*

Because constraints affect the calculation of slack, you should use them as sparingly as possible without compromising the quality of the model of the project. We recommend entering constraints for very *hard deadlines* only, the do-or-die dates. If the deadline dates are *soft deadlines* or *target dates*, we recommend you use the deadline feature instead, as discussed on page 274. Also, if you have constraints in the middle of your schedule, you will not see by how much the project end date is missed overall, because constraints prevent tasks from floating past them.

Notice that if you do use the deadline feature, you will not get warning dialogs that alert you to conflicts in your schedule. Instead, a red flag will be raised in the **Indicators** column; deadlines give silent alerts. Deadlines also allow you to see what the total slippage is on the project end date.

You can display a line in the timescale for the amount of negative slack a task has. The **Format, Bar Styles** dialog has an item called **Negative Slack** in the list under **From** and **To**. It allows you to display a line in front of the task bars that represents the amount of time a task slipped past its latest allowable finish date (**Late Finish**). To use this, choose the following settings:

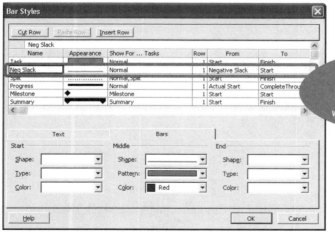

The row **Negative Slack** is inserted to indicate by how much each task is in conflict with deadlines or constraints.

The result would look like this screenshot:

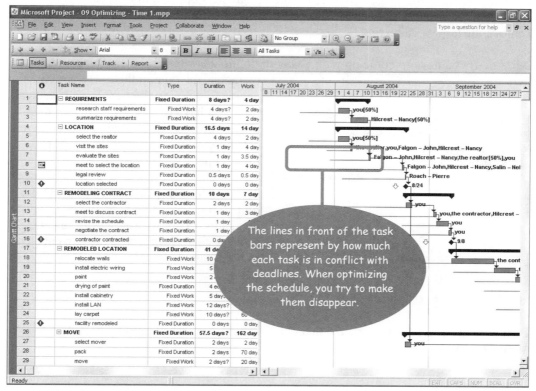

The lines in front of the task bars represent by how much each task is in conflict with deadlines. When optimizing the schedule, you try to make them disappear.

Steps to Optimize for Time

1. Highlight the Critical Path
2. Sort the tasks based on duration
3. Find the longest critical task
4. Make a change on it
5. Consider impacts on quality, scope and time
6. Decide whether you want to keep the change
7. Repeat steps 3 - 7

The rationale behind the steps shown in the process chart is that you first have to find the critical tasks to determine which tasks drive the project duration. If you have MS Project highlight the Critical Path in red you can easily see whether a task is critical or not. If the Critical Path switches to another parallel path while you are optimizing, MS Project will immediately highlight the new Critical Path in red, MS Project continues to show you which tasks are critical.

Then you find out what critical tasks have the longest durations by sorting the tasks. The critical tasks with the longest durations hold the greatest opportunity for saving time. In other words: *Don't sweat the small stuff!* Focus on the long durations that allow you to achieve the largest gains first.

After that, you have to come up with a way to do the work faster. We will suggest

> *1. Highlight the Critical Path*
> 2. Sort the tasks based on duration
> 3. Find the longest critical task
> 4. Make a change on it
> 5. Consider impacts on quality, scope and time
> 6. Decide whether you want to keep the change
> 7. Repeat steps 3 - 7

methods and explain them. Before you decide to go on to the next longest critical task, you have to establish whether the change helped you enough, or if the trade-offs on *quality* or *scope* were too high a price to pay.

The explanation of all the steps will take quite a few pages. To keep the overview and show where we are, we will use the process chart. It indicates the current step in bold italic type.

Highlighting the Critical Path

Switch to the Tracking Gantt view that colors the critical tasks in red by default. Choose **View, Tracking Gantt**.
OR

1. Click **Gantt Chart Wizard** on the **Formatting** toolbar, and a series of dialog boxes follow.

2. Press Next > , and select ⦿ **Critical Path**; the sample box on the left now shows some task bars in red.

3. Click Finish , Format It and Exit Wizard and the task bars of the critical tasks on the Critical Path are now displayed in red.

You can color the text of the critical task names red as well:

1. Choose **Format, Text Styles**.

2. Select from the list **Item to Change** All the item **Critical Tasks**.

3. From the list **Color**, select red.

4. Click [OK]. Notice that all critical task names (except the critical milestones) are colored red.

Displaying the Field Total Slack

1. Insert the column *total slack* in the Tracking Gantt spreadsheet by right-clicking on the column heading before which you would like to insert the total slack column. Choose **Insert Column** from the pop-up menu; the **Column Definition** dialog appears:

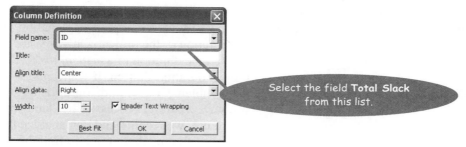

Select the field **Total Slack** from this list.

2. From the list **Field name** [ID ▼] select the item **Total Slack;** you can do this fastest by typing the first few characters of the field name.

3. Click [OK].

4. In Project 2003 Professional, you may get a prompt that **Edits will not be saved** if you try to change an enterprise view supplied and controlled by Project Server. Click [OK] to acknowledge.

5. The field will now be displayed in the Tracking Gantt spreadsheet. You can drag the sliding door bar [▶][◀] (the divider between the spreadsheet and the timescale) to the right to accommodate the new field in the view. To position it exactly between two spreadsheet columns, double-click on the divider.

The total slack explains why some tasks are critical (total slack less than or equal to zero) and other ones are not (total slack greater than zero). If the total slack is negative, you are missing the project *deadline* or one or more *hard constraint dates* in your schedule.

By default, MS Project shows tasks as critical if their *total slack* is less than or equal to zero. This threshold for being critical can be changed in the **Tools, Options**, tab **Calculation**, if necessary.

What you will often see when you display the Critical Path for the first time in a schedule is that it is not a complete chain of tasks that stretches from the project start date to the project end date. Project managers expect to see and need a Critical Path that explains the entire project duration. Instead you will often see a fragmented Critical Path and we will explore the possible causes of fragmentation.

A Fragmented Critical Path: Possible Causes

Normally, the Critical Path provides a complete explanation of what happens between the project start and finish dates. However, the *Critical Path* often looks fragmented as shown in the illustration. The Critical Path may not provide a complete explanation of the duration of the project. Only if you shorten the duration of a *critical task* will the project duration shorten. If you cannot see the complete Critical Path, optimizing becomes a painful process of trial and error. Therefore, we recommend you analyze the causes of fragmentation first to find the complete Critical Path. A complete path runs from the start date to the finish date of the project explaining the entire project duration. We will explore how to reveal the complete chain of critical tasks.

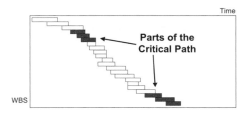

The Critical Path can become fragmented for several reasons:

♦ *Unavailability of resources*
♦ *Schedule constraints and deadlines*
♦ *Elapsed durations*
♦ *Task calendars*
♦ *External predecessors*
♦ *Workload leveling*

We will discuss each of these reasons in more detail and what to do about them.

Unavailability of Resources

In the illustration, the move has to take place on a weekend, and the workweek of the movers is changed so that only Saturday and Sunday are working days. The result is that MS Project will always schedule the *Move* on the weekend, as shown in the illustration. Depending on when the predecessors of the move are done, this could cause slack to be created. When slack is created before the task *Move*, the Critical Path will only start with the task *Move* and therefore, only partially explain the project duration.

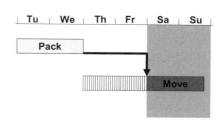

Is this *real slack*? Real slack is time that can be used as a buffer to compensate for slippages. In this case, the slack is real, because if the task *Pack* slips to Friday, this will not impact the project end date.

In this particular situation, slippage would even be desirable, because people may not be productive after they are packed up and ready to go. This could be accomplished by making the schedule constraint *As Late As Possible* for the task *Pack* in the **Task Information** dialog on the **Standard** toolbar. If we were to do this, the slack just moves over to the predecessors of *Pack*, and the Critical Path still needs repair.

Because slack now exists on tasks that are still the most critical tasks, we have to raise the threshold for critical tasks in order to display a complete Critical Path.

Raising the Threshold for Critical Tasks

1. If needed, choose **View, Tracking Gantt**.

2. Insert the column **Total Slack** by right-clicking on a column heading and choosing **Insert Column**. Select **Total Slack** from the list **Field Name** | ID ▾ | and click | OK |. The column should now be displayed in the view.

3. Check to see if you have tasks similar to the task *Move* that are delayed to the date when an assigned resource is available again. Look at what the total slack is on its predecessor. If there is more than one predecessor, take the lowest number. In our

example, there is only one predecessor that has 2 days of slack, and we would raise the threshold for critical tasks to 2 days in that case.

4. Choose **Tools, Options,** tab **Calculation**. Increase the field **Tasks are Critical if Slack is less than or equal to:** `0` to the value you established in step 3.

5. Click `OK`; the Critical Path has now extended to a more complete Critical Path. It still may not explain the entire project duration, and you may have to check on other tasks or other possible causes for a fragmented Critical Path.

Schedule Constraints and Deadlines

We have already seen that constraints can cause negative slack when they are tight, but they can also cause positive slack when they are far out. Positive slack is essentially a *buffer*. Deadlines also affect the slack calculation in a fashion similar to constraints.

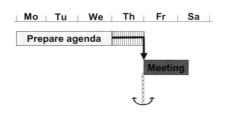

The illustration has two tasks, *Prepare agenda* and *Meeting*. Typically, official meetings, presentations and gatherings occur on a specific date and should be entered with a Must Start On constraint. As soon as you enter these fixed dates, slack can be created on the predecessors of that task, and the Critical Path starts to look disjointed. Only the task *Meeting* will be indicated as critical, because *Prepare agenda* now has slack.

This is another reason why we recommend using as few schedule constraints as possible without compromising the *validity* of the model of your project. In this situation, constraints make it more difficult to find the Critical Path, because they tend to break it. The *constraints* that can cause positive slack in *forward scheduling* are:
◆   *Must Finish On*
◆   *Must Start On*
◆   *Start No Earlier Than*
◆   *Finish No Earlier Than*

In *backward scheduling* these constraints are:
◆   *Must Finish On*
◆   *Must Start On*
◆   *Start No Later Than*
◆   *Finish No Later Than*

The other types of constraints will not fragment a Critical Path. Again, we have to ask ourselves: *Is this real slack?* In this case, the slack is real, because slippage on the predecessor *Prepare agenda* does not impact the end date, unless it slips more than a day. We have to solve this again by raising the threshold for critical tasks, as discussed on page 441.

Under certain circumstances, deadlines can also fragment the Critical Path, for example when there is a tight deadline halfway through the project and a time buffer at the end of the project. In this case, you will only see a partial Critical Path that runs up to the deadline date. This may be a reason to not use many deadline dates in your project schedule. However, if you must set either a constraint or a deadline, we recommend using a deadline. Deadlines allow you to see the compounded effect on the project end date that *hard constraints* obscure.

Elapsed Durations

An elapsed duration is expressed in calendar days as opposed to business days. A task with an elapsed duration can end during nonworking time, whereas its non-elapsed successor cannot start during non-working time; it can only start on the next business

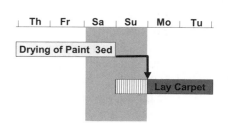

day. This creates slack on the elapsed duration task. In the illustration, the task *Lay Carpet* is scheduled to start on Monday, because it has a regular duration. *Drying of Paint* can slip until 8:00 AM Monday morning without affecting *Lay Carpet*. This creates 1 day of slack on *Drying of Paint*, which has a duration of 3 *elapsed days* (*3ed*).

Once more we have to ask ourselves: *Is this real slack?* The slack is real here, because the *Drying of Paint* could continue for another day without impacting the project. Again, we can resolve this by raising the threshold for critical tasks, as discussed on page 441.

Task Calendars

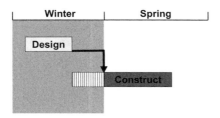

Task calendars can fragment the Critical Path. If the task *Design* can be ready long before the weather is good enough to start construction, it will have slack, and therefore will not be seen as critical. The task *Construct* and its successors will be critical, as shown in the illustration. Just as in the previous examples, the slack is real, and the only way to find a complete path of the most critical tasks is by raising the threshold for criticality (see page 441). If you do this, the Critical Path extends and will explain more of the project duration.

External Predecessors

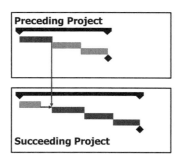

An external predecessor is a task from another project schedule that drives a task in your schedule (see the illustration). If a task has an *external predecessor*, this predecessor could very well drive the task farther out than the other *internal predecessors* that are inside your schedule. If it does, it creates slack on these predecessors. This slack is real slack, because it can be used to compensate for slippages in your schedule. Again, it can be taken care of by raising the threshold for criticality in **Tools, Options**, tab **Calculation**, as discussed before.

Workload Leveling

The illustration shows two tasks, *Print* one document and *Write* another, unrelated

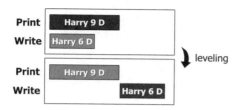

document. The tasks can be done independently of each other and in any order; there is no logical dependency between the two tasks. You have assigned one resource that is over-loaded and you decide to level its workload to make the schedule more realistic. In some instances, you cannot solve the over-allocation in any other way than by delaying a task. As you delay one task, you create slack on the other task that competes for the same resource. As a result, the slack makes critical tasks noncritical, and part of the Critical Path evaporates before your eyes.

One last time, we have to ask ourselves: *Is this slack real?* In this case, the answer is *no*, unlike in all previous situations. The slack is <u>not</u> real slack, because any delay in either task <u>does</u> impact the project end date. If Harry needs more time for *Print*, his other task, *Write*, will slip, because he will have to do that task too. How are we going to solve this?

Harry is assigned full-time to both tasks. Clearly, he cannot do both at the same time. Cloning Harry is not an accepted project management practice yet and hopefully, it never will be, even though it would make our profession of project management much easier. Reassigning one of the tasks to other resources is not an option either when there are no other resources. Therefore, we often have to delay one of the two tasks, but when we delay one, we create slack on the other task. This slack is not real, because if you use it, the project end date will slip. If the task *Print* slips, it will drive the task *Write* farther out, because the same resource does both, and there is a *resource dependency* between the two tasks. Normally, you can use slack to compensate for slippages, but not in this case. Both tasks are resource-critical, even though the current Critical Path algorithm suggests that only the task *Write* is critical. The CPM algorithm only looks at dependencies, not at resource dependencies, when it calculates the early and late dates. CPM does not take resource workloads into account.

We may have conveniently forgotten that CPM assumes that resources are available in unlimited quantities. However, this is only applicable to certain organizations that can quickly hire (and release) extra resources, rendering them unlimited. Construction companies can generally find any number of resources when they need them. Consulting companies consider the entire world as their resource pool.

Should We Add Logical Dependencies?

Some people suggest that you should add dependencies to level out the workloads of the resources. Of course, you could model *resource dependencies* as *logical dependencies* that would be soft dependencies. This works well until you start changing the assignments. In the illustration, if you substitute Harry on one of the two tasks, your schedule could be shorter than it is, because of a soft dependency that has now become obsolete! Adding logic to level workloads in order to keep your Critical Path intact is a static solution for a dynamic problem. As a consequence, the solution will have a short life. That's why we added some question marks to the dependency in the illustration. We recommend keeping your schedule dynamic. We will explain a different method for resolving the over-allocations and for optimizing in this situation on page 472 under Optimizing for Time, Cost and Resources.

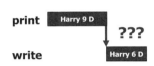

Many schedulers keep the resource workloads reasonable by creating extra logical dependencies. They know the schedule would not be feasible if they didn't use these extra dependencies that really do not reflect a mandatory sequence of tasks. If you are in this category, I invite you to consider a new method instead of setting these extra dependencies: the Resource-Critical Path method. We will discuss it on page 472 and following.

Sorting on Duration

Now that we have highlighted the Critical Path, the next thing to do is find those tasks where we can gain the most time. We can find them by sorting on duration. The sort is just meant to find the long-duration critical tasks. It is smart to focus on long tasks when you optimize your schedule, because long tasks harbor the most opportunity for gaining time in your schedule. We will reset the sort order as soon as we have found them. You may have to sort again after you have made some changes and want to find the next longest critical tasks. You can see in the process graphic on the left that we will do steps 2 and 3 together.

1. Highlight the Critical Path
2. *Sort the tasks based on duration*
3. *Find the longest critical task*
4. Make a change on it
5. Consider impacts on quality, scope and time
6. Decide whether you want to keep the change
7. Repeat steps 3 - 7

1. In the Gantt Chart, choose **Project, Sort, Sort by...**; the **Sort** dialog appears:

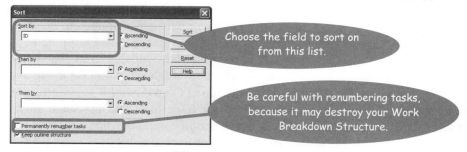

Choose the field to sort on from this list.

Be careful with renumbering tasks, because it may destroy your Work Breakdown Structure.

2. Select from the list **Sort by** `ID` the item **Duration**, and set the sort order to ⦿ **Descending**.

3. Do not renumber the tasks by clearing ☐ **Permanently renumber tasks**. If you were to renumber, you will likely have a catastrophe on your hands, because you have lost the structure of the Work Breakdown Structure. Undo and closing without saving are your last resort!

4. Make sure you sort the detail tasks and not the summary task families by clearing ☐ **Keep outline structure**.

5. Click [Sort]. The longest tasks are now at the top of the screen. The ones that are long and red are the critical long duration tasks which are the prime candidates for optimization. That is where you can realize the biggest gains with the least effort.

After you have identified the first tasks to focus on, you can revert the sort order to its original by choosing **Project, Sort, by ID**.

Shortening the Duration of the Project

Shortening the Critical Path

1. Highlight the Critical Path
2. Sort the tasks based on duration
3. Find the longest critical task
4. *Make a change on it*
5. Consider impacts on quality, scope and time
6. Decide whether you want to keep the change
7. Repeat steps 3 - 7

When the project has to finish earlier than the schedule shows, the Critical Path has to be shortened. At this point in the process we will make a change to the schedule. Any change has to be evaluated in terms of the impact on at least the three driving forces: *quality*, *scope* and *duration* of the project. We could even consider the cost, although we are not obliged to do so, because we assumed that unlimited resources are available to us. The best solutions are those that make the quality (Q) go up (↑), the scope (S) go up (↑) and the time (T) go down (↓). Unfortunately, there are no such ideal solutions and most will cause trade-offs. The next table only provides indications as to what the effect of each action could be in a typical project, but you will have to determine the effects in your own project. If a question mark (?) is shown, you definitely have to look at your specific situation to determine the effect of the measurement. A zero (0) means that there is no expected impact in the typical project.

The table provides ideas on how to improve the schedule. The actions are ranked by overall effectiveness, with the most effective ones first. The first two methods are called *fast-tracking* which will overlap activities. Fast-tracking follows the principle of working smarter instead of harder. If you choose to add resources instead, you will be working harder. Adding resources is called *crashing*.

We recommend you explore whether the first two methods of fast-tracking can be applied to the long critical tasks. Then you move on to the next-longest task, etc. After exhausting the fast-tracking on all tasks, go to the next action in the table. This is the quickest way to find the most time in your project schedule. (Q=Quality, S=Scope and T=Time)

	Action	For	Q	S	T
1.	Change sequential dependencies into partial dependencies (fast-tracking)	critical tasks	0	0	↓
2.	Create parallel paths from a sequential path (fast-tracking)	critical tasks	?	0	↓
3.	Split long tasks into shorter ones	critical tasks	0	0	↓
4.	Change schedule constraints	critical tasks	0	0	↓
5.	Shorten *lags* (waiting periods)	critical tasks	0	0	↓
6.	Split task bars around Must Start On tasks	critical tasks	0	0	↓
7.	Decrease estimates	critical tasks	↓	?	↓
8.	Reduce the scope or delete tasks	critical tasks	↓	↓	↓
9.	Add resources (*crashing*)	critical tasks	?	?	?

It may not be clear why we ranked adding resources at the bottom of the list as the least preferred method, since it is the obvious thing to do for many people. If the resources you add are second-best, they may not do as good a job as the original resources, and quality (Q) may suffer. Also, the new resources need to be trained, and you want to set the right example for them, so typically, you would take your best resources off the task to train the new ones. As a consequence, your progress will slow down (T) in the hope that it will pick up again later. Overall, it is not even clear if you will gain time.

Before making any change, you should check what the current total duration of the project is. You can find this by choosing **Project, Project Information** and clicking

Statistics... OR clicking **Project Statistics** -√r- on the **Tracking** toolbar. In the Statistics dialog, you will find the project duration in the row **Current** and the column **Duration**.

Changing Sequential into Partial Dependencies

There are four types of dependencies that can be combined with a positive *lag* time

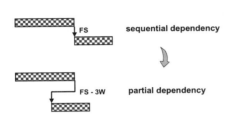

(waiting time/gap) or negative lag time (overlap/*lead*). The illustration on the left shows a Finish-to-Start dependency that is changed into an overlap of 3 weeks (*lead* or *negative lag* of –3w): FS – 3w. The overlap can be entered as an *absolute lag* in a number of days or weeks, like –3w. It can also be entered as a percentage of the duration of the predecessor (*relative lag*), like -40%. Since the start of the successor is dependent upon the partial completion of the predecessor, one could also speak of a *partial dependency*.

1. In the timescale of the Gantt Chart, point with the tip of the mouse pointer to the arrow of the dependency.

2. Wait for one second until the yellow screen tip appears. Check to see if you are pointing to the dependency between the right tasks, because the dependency arrows can overlap one another.

3. Double-click if you have the right one; the **Task Dependency** box appears:

4. You can keep the **Finish-to-Start** and make the lag negative (lead).
   OR
   You can select from the list **Type:** Finish-to-Start (FS) ▼ the
   Start-to-Start or **Finish-to-Finish** to overlap tasks.

5. Type in the **Lag** with absolute time units, like *-2d*, or in a percentage of the duration of the predecessor, like *-30%*. If you type a negative number, the tasks will move to the left in the timescale of the Gantt Chart; a positive lag moves task bars to the

right. In a **Finish-to-Start** dependency, you will overlap the predecessor for the lag you specify. For **Start-to-Start** or **Finish-to-Finish** dependencies, enter zero or a positive lag to create partial dependencies.

6. Click [OK]; you should now see the overlap you wanted between the two task bars in the timescale.

If you can't select the right dependency with the mouse, you can use the Task Form to create the overlap. Click on the successor task in the Gantt spreadsheet. Choose **Window, Split** to display the Task Form, and you can make the lag negative in the **Lag** field of the predecessor.

Creating Parallel Paths

You can cut soft dependencies. Hard, mandatory dependencies should not be cut. If the tasks are critical, the time gain can be large when cutting the soft dependencies. In the top scenario in the illustration, there is no risk of damaging the new carpet, because it is laid after the hanging cabinets have been installed (*sequential dependency*). In the bottom scenario, the carpet layers will have to work neatly and put plastic over the new carpet that has been laid, because the two

tasks are scheduled concurrently (*parallel path*). If they spill glue or paint, it will drop on the plastic sheet.

1. We recommend you set a new dependency into the soft successor first before cutting the dependency, because otherwise the successor task bar might disappear off the screen to the start date of the project.

2. In the Gantt Chart, point with the tip of the mouse pointer to the arrow of the dependency and double-click on it; the **Task Dependency** dialog appears:

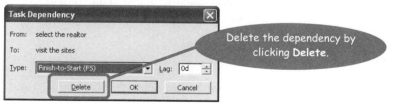

3. Verify whether the right dependency is shown and click [Delete].

4. Click [OK]; the dependency is now removed.

5. You will likely need a new successor for the predecessor, because it is a loose end in the network now unless it still has other successors.

Split Tasks with a Long Duration

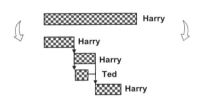

Breaking a long task into smaller tasks gives MS Project more possibilities to optimize, as depicted in the illustration. The benefit is immediate if you can assign portions of the task to other noncritical, and perhaps even cheaper resources. The easiest way to break up a long task is by adding detail tasks below it and changing it into a summary task. You will have to take the assignments and dependencies off the summary task. The advantage of this way is that only the lower level of detail of your schedule has changed, which is not very visible in reports.

Changing Schedule Constraints

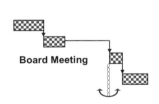

Your project may need authorization for certain matters to proceed. If these decisions are made in board meetings or steering group meetings held on the last Thursday of each month for example, it will slow down the progress on the project immensely.

If you lobby hard, you might get more expedient authorization through executive decisions, which will take some "anchors" out of your schedule. The anchor in the illustration represents a constraint date on the last Thursday of the month.

1. Select the task with the constraint.

2. Click **Task Information** [icon] on the **Standard** toolbar or hold down [Shift] and press [F2]; the **Task Information** dialog appears.

3. Click the **Advanced** tab, and the dialog should now look like:

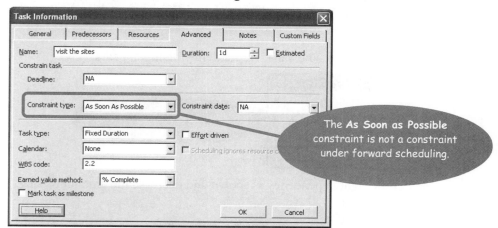

4. Under **Constrain task**, change the **Constraint type** to **As Soon As Possible**.
   OR
   Change the **Constraint date** to an earlier date.

5. Click OK .

Shorten Lag

If you find any *lag* between critical tasks, you might be able to reduce it now that you

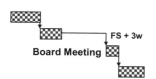

are armed with the argument that the lag is on the Critical Path. In the example in the illustration, you have to wait for the board's decision, and you typically have to wait 3 weeks before the board convenes. You might be able to lobby for an executive decision instead of a full board decision, which would save a few weeks and be a significant gain.

If the wait is for receiving supplies from a vendor, you can often work miracles by offering your supplier extra money for faster delivery.

If the wait is for receiving a building permit from the local government, you can often not influence the process much, unless your company has mighty economical power and political influence. If you start construction without the permit, you add enormous risk to your project.

The steps to decrease lag are:

1. In the Gantt Chart, point with the tip of the mouse pointer to the arrow of the dependency.

2. Double-click on the arrow. The **Task Dependency** dialog appears:

To decrease the **Lag**, lower the number in this field.

3. Verify whether the right dependency is shown and decrease the amount of **Lag**.

4. Click OK .

Split Task Bars around a Short Must Start On Task

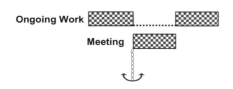

If a team member has a meeting or training to attend, she has to drop her regular work. The meeting or training takes place on an agreed upon, fixed date. You can model this by using schedule constraints, like Must Start On. In the illustration on the left, your ongoing task cannot be completed before the meeting, and could be scheduled entirely after the meeting, but splitting it around the meeting gives the tightest schedule.

To split a task bar:

1. Click **Split Task** 📅 on the **Standard** toolbar. A yellow pop-up window appears, and the mouse pointer now looks like: ⇥

2. Point to a task bar, and click to split it, then drag it to where you want the split to occur. A part of the task bar is split off and in the yellow pop-up, you are shown what the new start and finish dates of the part will be when you release the mouse:

	Task:	
Start:		Wed 4/5/00
Finish:		Sat 4/8/00

3. Drag the split bar to where you want to schedule it, and release the mouse button; the task bar is now split into two parts. Notice that the two parts are connected by dots: ▨▨▨......▨▨

Even though this feature appears to work well at first glance, we do not recommend using it during the planning phase of the project. The predecessors may reschedule the ongoing task, and its split should be moved accordingly to keep it scheduled around the short task with a fixed date. The problem is that the split does not move automatically. You may have to adjust your schedule manually every time a change occurs. That's why we don't recommend using this feature.

There are better approaches:

◆   You can split the task into multiple subtasks. For example, electricians wire a building, but after the inspection, they have to come back to install the switch plates. You could show this as one task with a split task bar, but it would be better to split it into two tasks: *pull cables* and *install switch plates*. Now you can set dependencies between these tasks and keep your model entirely dynamic. If you have a choice between task splitting and bar splitting, we recommend you split the task rather than its bar.

◆   Create a task calendar for those tasks that might be affected. In the task calendar, you indicate nonworking time for the duration of the short Must Start On task. As long as the Must Start On date does not change, the calendar will do a fine job. To find out how to create task calendars, see page 290.

◆   Alternatively, you could allow the over-allocation of the resource to occur and then level the workloads using the **Tools, Level Resources...,** option ☑ **Leveling can create splits in remaining work**. In this case, the leveling will create a split, and when you level again, it will move the split as needed.

◆   Lastly, you could ignore the over-allocation, assuming that the resources will work overtime.

Decrease Estimates

Often when you get closer to the tasks at hand you can provide a more precise estimate. Sometimes, you will find that the team member overestimated and can do a task faster than his original estimate. Sometimes, he finds a better and quicker way to do it. In both cases, you can sharpen the estimate and cut off some of the duration. In many cases, however, decreasing the estimate goes at the expense of the *quality* or the *scope* of the project, and the trade-off will have to be closely examined.

Reduce the Scope or Delete Tasks

Reducing the scope is a matter of deleting deliverables. If you delete deliverables that are on the Critical Path, you will reduce the duration of the project. Perhaps you are thinking at this point that you cannot delete deliverables that are *critical*. However, a critical deliverable does not necessarily mean it is an important deliverable; the word *critical* simply means in project management that it is driving the project end date. If there were critical deliverables qualified as nice-to-have, these would be good candidates. For example, in a course manual the deliverables *index* and *glossary* are often left out. However, not delivering on what you promised may be dangerous from a contractual point of view, not to mention your reputation.

Alternatively, you could focus on the level below deliverables and find critical tasks to delete, as shown in the illustration. Again, *critical tasks* are not necessarily important tasks. Sometimes you can find activities in the realm of nice-if-we-get-around-to-it. These are the candidates to cut. This may happen at the expense of the *quality* of the deliverables. If the quality requirement is a nice-to-have, you could cut the task. Deleting tasks is as easy as clicking on their row heading (ID number) and pressing [Delete].

However, if you have set the *baseline* already, you should keep the task and its baseline data and add "CANCEL" to the task name. You can delete the dependencies, **Work, Cost, Fixed Cost**, and the assignments. Leave the fields **Baseline Work** and **Baseline Cost** alone to maintain the integrity of the baseline.

Once you get a formal approval to change the baseline, you can remove the task in its entirety. For more on this, see chapter 11 on updating schedules (page 611).

Add Resources

Often, managers start asking for more resources when they start to feel the heat of their deadlines. In the illustrated example, the project manager asked for and got Ed to help out. If you add resources, you choose to work harder instead of smarter, and it may cost you more money. I have often observed that when new resources arrive, the best resources are taken off their jobs to train the new ones. This causes the slippage to increase at first instead of decrease.

How many people can you add to tasks? When optimizing for time only, we could in theory add an unlimited number, but in practice, there are limits of course. If you add too many people, eventually nothing will get done. People will be in each other's way and keep each other from being productive. The *law of diminishing returns* is applicable when adding resources. How many carpenters can work in one 10-by-15-foot room? The classic example: adding another mother to carry the child does not shorten the pregnancy. There are simple practical limits. Even though we have assumed we have access to unlimited resources, it definitely does not seem reasonable to add more than the maximum units available as entered in the resource sheet.

Make sure you change the task type to **Fixed Work** before adding resources. This will ensure that the duration decreases when you add them.

Considering Impacts on Quality, Scope and Time

As the next step, you have to evaluate the impact on *quality*, *scope* and *time* of the change you made. You can see the new duration of the project in one of two ways:

1. Highlight the Critical Path
2. Sort the tasks based on duration
3. Find the longest critical task
4. Make a change on it
5. *Consider impacts on quality, scope and time*
6. *Decide whether you want to keep the change*
7. Repeat steps 3 - 7

◆ View the **Duration** of the *project summary task*.
◆ View the **Current Duration** in the project statistics dialog.

We will discuss the steps for both in the next two sections. From the new project duration, you can see how much time you have gained, and whether it is worth the sacrifices you made on the scope of the project or the quality of the deliverables. Realize that if you have used constraint dates or odd resource calendars in the back end of your schedule, the project end date may be held captive. Only if you have an entirely dynamic model will you see that changes immediately pull the project end date back. If you find that the change did not yield the result expected, simply click undo ↩ to get rid of it.

You then continue to repeat steps 3 to 7 in the process of optimizing until you have solved the scheduling conflict.

Inserting a Project Summary Task

The project summary task is task number 0 and summarizes the entire project, because everything is automatically indented beneath it. MS Project will summarize the whole project in its fields **Start, Finish, Duration, Work** and **Cost**. It will show us the duration of the project before we make a change. To see the project summary task, you have to jump to the top of the project every time. In order to make what-if analyses, you need to see the possible impact of any idea you try out. Take note of the duration of the project before making a change, then compare afterward.

1. Choose **Tools**, **Options**; the **Options** dialog appears.

2. Click the **View** tab; the dialog should now look like:

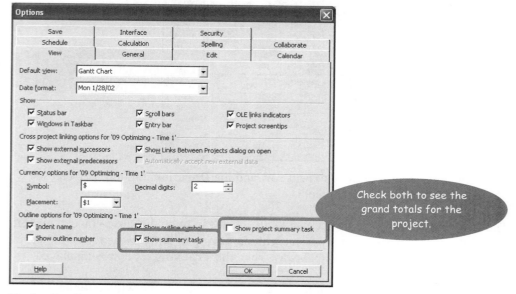

3. Under **Outline Options** check both ☑ **Show Summary Tasks** and ☑ **Show Project Summary Task**.

4. Click [OK]; the project summary task now shows the duration, total cost and work for the project. The task name of the project summary task is the **Title** of the project that can be found in **File, Properties**, tab **Summary**. If no title is filled in, the file name or schedule name from Project Server will stand in for it. We recommend, however, using the project **Title** field; it makes a better name for the project.

5. The Project Summary task forces you to jump to the top of the schedule every time you want to check on the project indicators. We will show you another way that you can use wherever you happen to be in your schedule.

To View the Project Statistics Dialog

1. Right-click on any toolbar and choose **Tracking** from the pop-up menu. The tracking toolbar is displayed:

2. The dialog is now available by clicking on **Project Statistics** 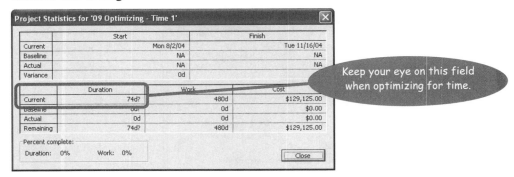 on the **Tracking** toolbar. The dialog looks like:

3. In the intersection of the **Current** row and the **Duration** column, you can see what the new duration of the project is.

The **Project Statistics** dialog seems like the best way to go, because you can view it from wherever you are in your project without having to jump to the top of the project every time. It also is just one click away when the **Tracking** toolbar is displayed.

This concludes our discussion of the Critical Path Method. We will continue with simulation, as promised.

Monte Carlo Simulation

One thing is certain: unforeseen events <u>will</u> happen and you <u>will</u> need a time buffer to compensate for those events. This is generally accepted project management.

Once you have optimized the Critical Path, you should ask yourself: *How much buffer should I reserve in my schedule in order to protect the project deadline?* A *time buffer* is also known as *time contingency*. The harder your project deadline is, the more careful you need to assess how much buffer you need. *Monte Carlo simulation* can help you determine that. Without simulation, you will have to guess what the size of the buffer should be.

What Is Monte Carlo Simulation?

The best-known simulation technique is *Monte Carlo simulation*. For tasks that are hard to predict, you specify the lower and upper limits of an estimate and choose a probability curve between those limits. Some tasks are renowned for their wide range between the lower and upper limit, for example *debug code* in a *software development* project. By the way, we don't recommend you determine ranges for every task (even if you have enough time to do that).

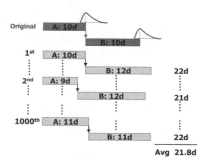

The simulating software generates estimates for all the tasks using these parameters. It uses number generators that produce estimates that comply with the range and the distribution curve you have chosen for the estimate. It creates the first version of the entire schedule and calculates the Critical Path. In the illustration on the left, the *original* schedule is shown as well as the *1st*, the *2nd* and the *1000th* version created by the simulation software.

Simulation will create as many *versions* as you want, but after many versions, every next one has less and less added value. Simulations often create up to a thousand versions of the schedule. In each version, the Critical Path of the schedule is calculated. The simulation software will then calculate average project duration and probabilities for a range of finish dates.

Output of Monte Carlo Simulation

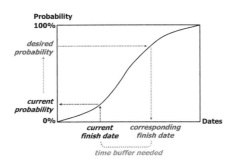

Simulation software creates an s-curve from the many versions of the schedule. An *s-curve* shows projected finish dates charted against the probability of meeting those dates. The illustration shows such an s-curve. The benefit of the s-curve is that you can see the chance of completing your project by the date that MS Project indicates as the project finish date in your schedule (see *current finish date* in the illustration and its *current probability*).

Alternatively, you can choose the level of probability you feel comfortable with, and derive the project finish date, or you can let executives choose it for you (see *desired probability* in the illustration). With the desired probability, you can find the *corresponding finish date*. You can quote this date to the client while knowing the degree of confidence that it can be met. There may still be other risks that you do not know about (*unknown unknowns*), but at least you have quantified *known unknowns* that we will discuss in the next section on why we need simulation.

You can also calculate the size of the time buffer you need in your project. If you read from the s-curve that you need to add 3 weeks as a buffer to your current MS Project schedule to have 90% probability, you should insert this as a *buffer "task"* just before the *project finish milestone* and have it push out the milestone. Alternatively, you could hide the buffer in your schedule if you need to, but this is the least preferred way. For more on that, see page 543.

MS Project does not have simulation capabilities, but there are good *add-ons* on the market with which you can simulate MS Project schedules. One add-on is *Risk+*[74] and another is *@Risk* for MS Project.[75]

---

[74] C/S Solutions (www.cs-solutions.com).

[75] Palisade Corporation (www.palisade.com). Note that @Risk also exists as a standalone tool and that you have to buy the *@Risk for MS Project* edition to simulate schedules.

Why Do We Need Simulation?

Let me try to convince you why using *Monte Carlo simulation* is necessary. It is necessary, because:
- Forecasts from one-point estimates tend to be too optimistic.
- Converging paths compound the time risk.

We will discuss both in more detail.

Optimistic One-Point Estimates

If you ask many different people for an estimate on one task, you can plot the estimated durations on the x-axis against the number of times you hear each estimate on the y-axis. The result will be a distribution curve that depicts the probability of a range of finish dates according to those estimators. It will look like the curve in the illustration. The estimate that you hear most often is the mode, which is why the mode is shown under the top of the curve. The median divides the surface under the curve into two equal parts; there are as many estimates to the left as there are to the right of it. The mean is the mathematical average of all estimates you collect.

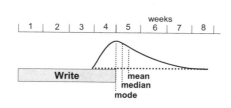

If you do this a few times, you will typically find that the resulting curve is skewed to the right. In other words, durations tend to stretch, rather than shrink. You probably knew that already if you have been a project manager for some time. Even if you don't have project management experience, it probably makes sense. What the skewed curve means is that the duration of the task is more likely to increase 1 week than decrease 1 week. In other words, tasks will more likely take longer than shorter.

However, the Critical Path consists of many tasks. It could be that a task early in the schedule ran late. This overrun can be compensated for by later under runs. The overall effect of the skewing of estimates is therefore not that dramatic. Nevertheless, you can safely state that schedules made with single estimates per task are optimistic in nature. The PERT technique captures the cumulative effect of the skewed estimates along the critical path. However, converging paths have a more dramatic impact which we will discuss next.

Converging Paths Compound the Time Risk

Converging paths decrease the probability of meeting a milestone date. The chance that the milestone will be accomplished on time decreases with every path that is added leading into the milestone. In the illustration, each path has an admirable chance for on time delivery of 90%, but the chance of delivering the milestone on time is exactly 81%. If one path is early, the other may be late and vice versa. When two paths both have to be finished for a milestone, you have to multiply their chances: 90% * 90% = 81%.

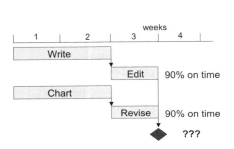

The more parallel paths you have in your schedule, the greater the time risk. The more equal the durations of the paths are, the greater the time risk. This phenomenon is known as *path convergence* or *merge bias*. The aggregated effect of many merging paths of different lengths is very difficult to predict; simulation is the only way to find out. The more parallel paths you see in your schedule, the more you will need to simulate the schedule. This need is even greater if those paths have similar durations.

The paths make it unlikely that your end date, as shown by your MS Project schedule, will be met. That is why project managers developed the habit of padding their schedules. You need to do simulation in order to find the compounded effect of the parallel paths. You can use simulation to quantify how much padding you will need in your schedule. As you can see, we do recommend using simulation in combination with the *Critical Path Method*.

Assumptions of the Critical Path Method

In summary, the Critical Path theory is based on three assumptions:
◆ Assumption 1: Task *estimates* are *normally distributed.*
◆ Assumption 2: There is no *merge bias* or *path convergence*.
◆ Assumption 3: You have *unlimited resources* available.

We saw on page 463 that assumption 1 does not hold true, but we can determine the magnitude of its effect by applying PERT or simulation.

As for assumption 2, we proved before that merge bias (path convergence) does exist. This effect often causes the largest slippages in projects. Simulation is the only technique that can make the compounded effect of converging paths visible. Applying the Critical Path Method (CPM) is good, as long as you simulate it as well. Many overruns can actually be foreseen and quantified when simulation is applied to schedules.

Assumption 3 is more difficult to deal with. Both the CPM and the PERT techniques assume that resources are available in unlimited quantities. This assumption holds true, if workload is not your problem. For example:

◆ If resources are readily available, workload is not an issue.
◆ If you intend to subcontract the work, workload is not your issue. Resource allocation is the contractor's problem.
◆ For a consulting firm that can hire free-lance resources easily in the quantity and with the expertise needed, workload is not a problem.

In these cases, the assumption can stand and the Critical Path Method is the technique to use.

However, many project managers do not have access to unlimited resources in this day and age. In this era of global competition, many organizations cannot afford to supply unlimited resources to projects; neither can they afford not tracking the usage of their resources. Today in the global market, a 1% change in *return on investment (ROI)* can be the difference between a viable and a nonviable company.

If you are managing the workload of your own scarce, internal resources, workload is your concern. In that case, both the CPM and the PERT techniques are of limited value. For example, if you are managing IT resources, you probably are in a *resource-constrained* situation. You need a new technique to optimize such schedules.

Extra resources can be bought with money. We will therefore first introduce cost into the optimization (optimizing for time and cost), and then we will add the limited availability of resources (optimizing for time, cost and resources).

Optimizing for Time and Cost

When you optimize for *time* and *cost*, you should consider the dimensions *scope* and *quality* as well. In the illustration, we are adding cost as the fourth dimension in our quest for the optimal schedule. We will discuss this dimension before the resource dimension, because most resource decisions impact the cost side of our model. So the logical progression in our view is optimizing for time (see page 427), then time and cost (see next), then time, cost and resources (see page 472).

Steps to Optimize for Time and Cost

Any project manager who has a budget in dollars or in person hours should apply this type of optimization. The steps for optimizing for time and cost are very similar to the

1. Highlight the Critical Path
2. Sort the tasks on **Cost**
3. Find the **most expensive** task
4. Make a change on it
5. Consider impacts on quality, scope, time and **cost**
6. Decide whether you want to keep the change
7. Repeat steps 3 - 7

steps for optimizing for time. The differences are highlighted in bold in the illustration. Because you should not lose sight of the time dimension of the project, you still have to find the Critical Path as well. If you want to bring the duration of the project down, you should also apply the optimizing for time methods discussed in the previous section. Keeping the duration of a project as short as possible will also keep the cost of overhead expenses down. To keep the discussion on the process for optimizing for time and cost simple, we will focus mainly on cost in the text that follows.

If you find that the restricted availability of resources is driving your finish date out, you will need to optimize for time, cost and resources, which is the third approach of optimizing (see page 472). In that case, you should read this section as well, because in the next approach we will not discuss any methods to reduce cost.

After you have highlighted the Critical Path, sort on cost to find the most expensive tasks. Develop ideas for how you might bring down the cost with no or minimal compromise on time, scope or quality. Enter the change and check the results to see whether you want to keep the change. We will discuss how to accomplish some of these steps in MS Project.

Sorting on Cost

To find the tasks on which we can make significant savings, we should sort the tasks on cost.

1. Choose **View, Gantt Chart**.

2. Choose **Project, Sort, Sort by...**; the **Sort** dialog appears:

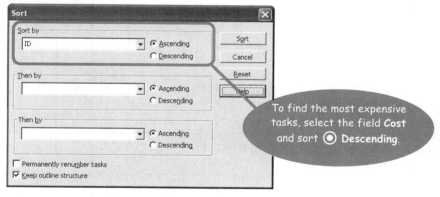

To find the most expensive tasks, select the field **Cost** and sort ⦿ **Descending**.

3. In the **Sort by** list, select **Cost** and set the sort order to ⦿ **Descending**.

4. Do not renumber the tasks; clear:

   ☐ **Permanently renumber tasks** and
   ☐ **Keep outline structure**.

5. Click 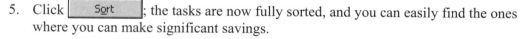 ; the tasks are now fully sorted, and you can easily find the ones where you can make significant savings.

6. You can revert to the original sort order by choosing **Project, Sort, by ID**.

Lowering the Cost of a Project

The best measurements are those that make the *quality* (Q) go up (↑), the *scope* (S) go up (↑), the *time* (T) go down (↓) and the *cost* (C) go down (↓). Unfortunately, there are no such ideal measurements. However, we will give you ideas about what you can do. The following table shows actions to lower the cost (C) and their likely impact on quality (Q), scope (S) and time (T). A question mark (?) indicates that you need to look at your specific situation to determine the effect of the measurement. A zero (0) means that there is no expected impact.

	Action	For	Q	S	T	C
1	Find cheaper contracts	External contractors, consultants	?	?	?	↓
2	Reassign to cheaper resources	Expensive resources	?	?	?	↓
3	Break up a long task and reassign portions to cheaper resources	Long (critical) tasks	0	0	↓	↓
4	Shorten the project duration to decrease overhead cost	Critical tasks	?	?	↓	↓
5	Prevent overtime work	Resources with a higher overtime rate	0	0	↑	↓
6	Smooth the workloads	Resources with erratic workloads	?	?	?	↓
7	Decrease the estimate	Any tasks with labor costs	↓	0	↓	↓
8	Reduce the scope or delete tasks	Any tasks with costs involved	↓	↓	↓	↓

The actions are listed in order of overall perceived effectiveness. You should start at the top of the table and work your way down. If you need to bring down the duration of your project as well, use the optimizing for time methods as discussed on page 448. Make sure you select those methods that do not increase the cost again. If you shorten the project duration, the overhead costs will also decrease (see method 4). You will save on expenses for project management, facilities, support staff and other overhead costs.

If you are to manage the cash flow of your project as well, another measurement might be to renegotiate when the costs accrue and change the resource field **Accrue at** accordingly. Delaying the accrual of expenses will improve your cash flow.

Finding Cheaper Contracts

The question you should ask yourself is: *Do I always solicit more than one bid or proposal?* If the answer is *no*, then this method may create significant savings for you. After all, contractors and consultants are quick to find out whether or not they are in a competitive situation and will quote accordingly. Another option is to research whether there are specialized firms that are quicker or better at their trade than other suppliers. If a specialized firm is using better technology, techniques, equipment or resources, it may be cheaper, even at a higher hourly rate.

1. Create the new resource in the resource sheet. For the how-to, see page 323: Entering Resources.

2. Choose **View, Gantt Chart** where we will change the *assignments* to the new resource.

3. Select the task, and click **Assign Resources** on the **Standard** toolbar; the **Assign Resources** dialog appears:

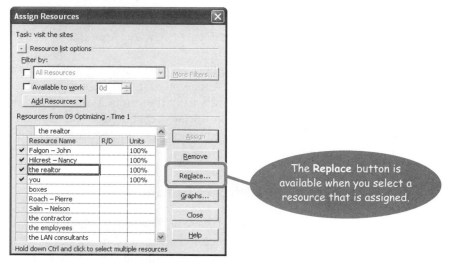

4. Resources that are assigned have a check mark in front of their name in the list. Click on the assigned resource to replace. In MS Project, these resources will always appear at the top of the list.

5. Click Replace... ; the **Replace Resource** dialog appears on top of the **Assign Resources** dialog:

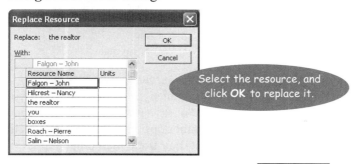

6. Click on the substitute resource, and click OK ; the resource is now replaced on the task.

Reassigning to Cheaper Resources

The best view to find cheaper resources that can substitute expensive resources is the Resource Usage view. Insert the column with the rates (*Standard Rate*) and find which assignments you can move to cheaper resources. You can do this by simply dragging the assignment. Make sure you don't increase the project duration by too much.

Breaking Up a Long Task and Reassigning Portions

If you decide to break up a long task, perhaps the best way is to insert subtasks below it, thereby promoting it to become a summary task. Then you *assign* the cheaper resources to these subtasks and remove the expensive resource from the summary task. The cost should decrease as a result. Don't forget to set appropriate dependencies, so as not to leave any *loose ends* in the network logic. If you can hook up some portions to much earlier tasks, you would be saving time as well.

Shortening the Project Duration

If you decrease the project duration, the overhead costs will decrease. The longer a project takes, the longer the project manager and team leaders need to stick around, and the longer support, facilities and equipment have to stay available. The shorter a project is, the less overhead costs you will incur. To save cost, you therefore have to maintain or bring down the time as well. We discussed the methods to shorten the project duration on page 448.

Preventing Overtime Work

Preventing overtime work will only bring down the cost if you are actually paying a higher rate for overtime. For the how-to steps for decreasing overtime, refer to the section on how to create it in the first place, see page 516. Of course, if you reduce overtime, you may be extending your project duration, which is a simple trade-off against the time dimension. You can only do that if saving cost is more important than finishing as early as possible.

Smoothing the Workloads

In the illustration, the total workload before and after smoothing is the same 100 person days, which would cost the same. However, you should raise the question: *Would the eventual cost for an erratic workload be more or less than the eventual cost for a smooth workload?* If a resource has an erratic workload, there may be days or weeks when the resource is not needed. The resource may have other employment during those valleys for which he is paid from funds other than the project budget. If this is not the case, the project manager will likely keep the resource around, particularly if his skill set is scarce. The project manager then assumes extra cost for the idle time. The answer to the question in this case is that with erratic workloads, the *actual cost* is higher. The project budget does not show this cost, because it only shows the cost of the planned assignments. The extra cost of an erratic workload is hidden cost in the plan. If you smooth the workload, you will decrease this hidden cost of the project. You will therefore not see the cost of the project decrease while you are smoothing the workload. This hidden cost is difficult to quantify during the planning phase, but in general, you can say that the more erratic the workload, the higher the hidden cost in the project plan.

An intriguing paradox is that the scarcer a resource is, the more the resource should be shared between projects from the organization's point of view, but the less likely that project managers actually will share this scarce resource, particularly if they don't have cost responsibility.

Reducing the Scope or Deleting Tasks

We discussed this method on page 456. Remember that the integrity of the original *baseline* may be compromised when you rebaseline after deleting tasks. Instead of removing the task, we recommend you simply add "CANCEL" to the task name. You can delete the dependencies, **Work, Cost, Fixed Cost**, and the *assignments*. Leave the fields **Baseline Work** and **Baseline Cost** alone to maintain the integrity of the baseline.

Once you get a formal approval to change the baseline, you can remove the task in its entirety. For more on this, see chapter 11 on updating schedules (page 611).

This concludes the second approach of optimizing for time and cost. We will now add the next dimension of resources.

Optimizing for Time, Cost and Resources

The next black arrow in the illustration is the dimension *resources*. We add it to the ones we already monitor: *quality*, *scope*, *time* and *cost*. Inclusion of the resources means that we will start monitoring the workload of the resources relative to their availability. If you find that the limited availability (or unavailability) of resources affects the forecast dates, you are in a *resource-constrained* or *resource-limited* situation. In this case, you need to include resources in your optimization. If you don't, your schedule will be too optimistic.

The resource dimension may make trade-offs with:
◆ Cost, when you have to pay for extra resources or pay more for overtime
◆ Time, when you cannot solve over-allocations in any other way than by delaying tasks

In this section, we will only discuss how to trade off between time and resources to keep the discussion simple. If you also need to bring down the cost of your project at the same time, you should consider the methods discussed in optimizing for time and cost (see page 468).

The optimization becomes more complex, but if we manage to handle this complexity, we will have confidence that the project is feasible as far as the resources are concerned. This will increase the *validity* of our forecasts.

Steps to Optimize for Time, Cost and Resources

As the steps in the process chart show, the first thing we have to do is *resource workload leveling* or *workload leveling*. Some people refer to it as *resource leveling*, but personally I find those words too macabre. We have to check:

1. **Check the workloads and level them**
2. Highlight the **Resource Critical Path (RCP)**
3. Find the **most critical resource**
4. Make a change on it
5. Consider impacts on quality, scope, time, cost and **resources**
6. Decide whether you want to keep the change
7. Repeat steps 3 - 7

- whether the workloads are within the availability of the human resources,
- whether the demand for facilities is within the availability of the facilities, and
- whether the work is within the capacity of the equipment.

When resources are scarce, you will often find that the schedule extends when you level the workloads. This renders the *Critical Path* fragmented, and we will need to find the *Resource-Critical Path* (*RCP*). The differences between this method of optimization and the optimizations previously discussed (see page 437) appear in bold type in the process box. There are quite a few pages on this approach to optimizing, so we will show our progress using this process chart regularly. Once you have found the RCP, optimization is very similar to the methods we used with the *Critical Path Method*.

Workload Leveling

The first step in optimizing for time, cost and resources is checking the workloads. If there are over-allocations, the workloads need to be leveled. Ideally, you will have prevented over-allocations in the first place, since they are always painful to solve, particularly when you are sharing resources with other project managers. We explained how you can prevent over-allocations when you use the **Assign Resources** dialog on page 390. If you have *Project Server*, you can even prevent over-allocations across all enterprise projects. Organizations without an infrastructure to prevent over-allocations can end up with towering workloads across projects. We teach how to deal with this in our Black Belt Professional course.[76]

Within a single project, each project manager has the responsibility to make sure that the workloads are reasonable. Of the 1,000 schedules we evaluated, we found that this

---

[76] For more details on this course, see www.iil.com and follow the link *Microsoft Project*.

responsibility is often neglected; about 50% of the schedules we evaluated had over-allocations.

We will discuss how to level workloads in two different ways:
◆ Making manual changes to the schedule (see page 476), or
◆ Letting MS Project automatically solve all over-allocations for you (see page 484).
You will often insert delays for certain tasks when leveling. These delays will influence the calculation of the Critical Path, which we will discuss as well. First we will explore how we can check the workloads.

Checking the Workloads: Resource Graph

1. Choose **View**, **Resource Graph** OR click **Resource Graph** [icon] on the view bar.

2. Hold down [Alt] and press [Home] to make the timescale jump to the start of the project.

3. Use **Zoom Out** [icon] and **Zoom In** [icon] on the **Standard** toolbar to adjust the timescale.

4. Press [Page Dn] to go to the next resource OR press [Page Up] to go to a previous resource.

The *Resource Graph* is also known as the *resource histogram.*[77]

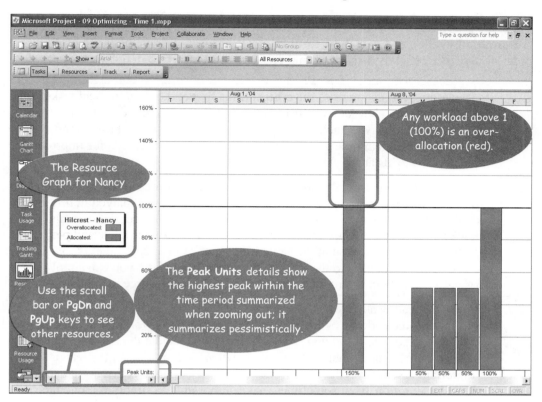

 The Resource Graph shows, by default, the **Peak Units**. **Peak Units** allow you to find over-allocations very easily by zooming out; if you see any red bar appear, you have found an over-allocation. On the other hand, **Peak Units** present an inflated picture of the real work when zoomed out, because it shows the highest bar during the time period summarized. Choose **Format, Details, Work** to get a more realistic view of the workloads suited to forward to your HR-department.

[77] See the PMBOK® Guide, 2004 Edition, published by the PMI.

Level the Workloads Yourself

There are many ways in which you can level the workloads by hand without using the **Automatic Leveling** or **Level Now** features of MS Project. The methods are listed in order of perceived effectiveness. The first ones are most effective in our view.

1.	Reassign the best resources to the critical tasks first and only to critical tasks. You can take non-critical tasks away from the best resources and reduce their workloads in that way. Matching people to the tasks so that the best person does the task also results in time gained, and is one of the rare methods for improving time and workloads at the same time.
2.	Reassign tasks from critical resources to noncritical resources. Critical resources are resources that force critical tasks to be delayed in order to keep their workloads sane. Critical resources extend the project duration and if you take some of their tasks away, you are leveling their workloads and perhaps shorten the project duration at the same time. You can reassign quickly in MS Project by switching to the Resource Usage view, where you can simply drag *assignments* (without ID number, italic text) from one resource to another.
3.	Take the critical resource off a task. Sometimes you can do this when more than one person is working on the task, or you do this as soon as you know who will be able to handle the task other than the critical resource. Remember that the word *critical* does not mean the resource is an important resource on the task; it just means the resource is driving the task and project duration. That sometimes makes it possible to simply remove the critical resource from the task to bring their workload down. Some critical resources simply have a tendency to pull too much work towards them.
4.	Hire extra resources. If you hire extra resources, you can reassign the tasks from your critical resources to the new resources. This works well if the new resources have skills similar to or better than your existing resources.
5.	Contract work out to subcontractors. One definition of a subcontractor is someone who solves your workload problems in exchange for money.
6.	Negotiate more resources from subcontractors. If you can get more resources from subcontractors, the workload of existing resources can be reduced.

7.	Fine-tune the number of units assigned to the tasks involved in the over-allocation. For example, you could keep two tasks scheduled in parallel if you decrease the involvement of the resource to 50%, but make sure you keep the resources working with 100% focus on a critical task.
8.	Split long tasks into many shorter ones and reassign the short tasks to noncritical resources. Splitting tasks increases the number of scheduling possibilities dramatically.
9.	Delay vacations until after the deadline. This is where you start to trade-off against resources and will require a lot of goodwill from your resources. Be careful to not put unreasonable demands on your resources, because they will either burn out or leave.
10.	Work during the weekend. If an over-allocation occurs on a Friday, you can easily solve such a situation by asking the resource to work some hours over the weekend. Again you are trading off against the resource dimension.
11.	Assign overtime. Even though this does not solve the over-allocation, it shows that it has been dealt with. Again you are trading off against the resource dimension.
12.	Change dependencies. Decrease overlaps between tasks that are done by the same resource. Or, in the special case in which you have a team of people going from one city to another to install a system, consider setting extra, soft dependencies to prevent the team from being in two spots at the same time. This solidifies the order in which locations are rolled out and keeps the workloads of the teams reasonable.
13.	Lower quality standards and lower work estimates, which will decrease the workload. You can often cut corners in the category of nice-to-have requirements without jeopardizing the project product too much.
14.	Split task bars when multiple resources are assigned to move the workloads of the individual resources to where the workloads fit into their availability.

15.	Delay tasks
	Slip one of the tasks that compete for the same resource. If you decide to delay one task, choose the task that has the most slack and the least number of resources assigned. If you delay a task with other resources assigned, you may cause many new over-allocations. The less other resources are assigned, the less checking on workloads you need to do. Through the dependencies, successors may cause new over-allocations; you can never really tell what will happen when you start delaying tasks. You have to do it week by week.

MS Project cannot replace you as a manager to make these decisions and will never be able to, because it cannot:

◆ Adjust the units on assignments; how can software determine what a reasonable level of involvement is for all assigned resources?

◆ Find out if more external resources can be found and if they are qualified substitutes.

◆ Talk to resources and find out what non-working time they are willing to sacrifice for the betterment of the project.

◆ Determine which quality standards can be lowered without jeopardizing commitments or contracts.

◆ Determine who the best resource is; this would require an extensive historical database of similar projects. Projects are hardly ever similar enough to provide meaningful data.

◆ Determine who the most critical resource is. Software could possibly figure this out, but currently doesn't; it would be nice if the software suggested who to substitute to improve the schedule.

◆ Reassign tasks to less critical resources. MS Project cannot do this by itself; only with access to the enterprise resource pool from Project Server can it now find substitutes if all of the skills of the resources and skill requirements on the assignments are coded. See page 402. Reassigning is often better than delaying tasks.

What MS Project can only do for you is:

◆ Split task bars where multiple resources are assigned (method number 14), or
◆ Delay task bars (method number 15).

MS Project can only apply the last two methods listed in the table; it cannot handle any of the other methods to level the workloads that are often more effective.

Therefore, we have to conclude that you will have to level the workloads by hand if you want the tightest schedule possible. Let's explore the steps to do this in the easiest way possible.

Use the Resource Allocation View When You Level

Right-click on any toolbar and choose **Resource Management** from the pop-up menu. Click **Resource Allocation View** on the **Resource Management** toolbar to display the **Resource Allocation** view.

OR

1. Choose **View, More Views…**; the **More Views** dialog appears:

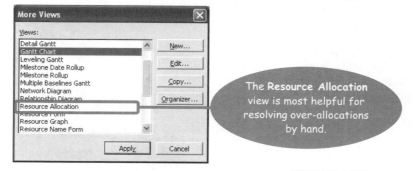

2. Select the **Resource Allocation** view and click Apply; a combination view appears with the **Resource Usage** view in the top pane and the **Leveling Gantt** in the bottom pane. The top view shows the over-allocated resources and the bottom view shows the conflicting tasks, which helps in resolving the over-allocation.

The Steps to Level Workloads Yourself

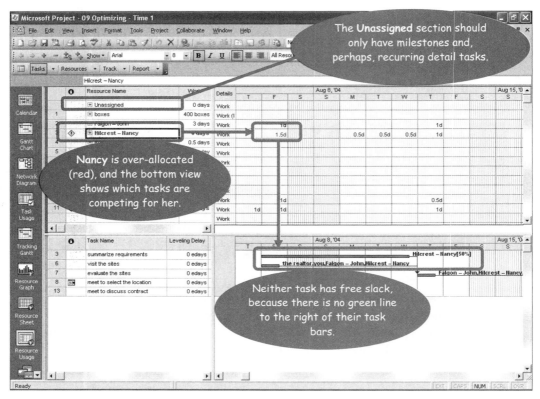

1. Check to see if you forgot any *assignments*; if you did, there is no use in starting the workload leveling. The heading ⊞ **Unassigned** at the top contains the unassigned tasks. Click on the button ⊞ to expand them, and click ⊟ to hide them again. Typically, only the *milestones* and perhaps the *recurring detail tasks* should be listed in the **Unassigned** category. If you have not assigned resources to all detail tasks, you have not captured all the workloads, and you should not start the manual leveling. Manual leveling is a lot of effort which will be wasted effort.

2. Hide all assignments in the top view by clicking on any column heading and then **Hide Assignments** ⬚ on the **Formatting** toolbar.

3. The over-allocated resources are shown in red. Position your mouse pointer over the icon ◈ in the **Indicators ❶** column. The screen tip that pops up gives advice. If you are advised to level on a day-by-day basis, then zoom in the timescale until you see the days, and the over-allocations will become obvious to you.

4. Scroll to the start of the project by dragging the scroll box on the horizontal scrollbar of the timescale to the far left. This step is important, since the tool will only look for over-allocations forward in time. Unfortunately, [Alt] + [Home] does not work in the Resource Usage view.

5. Go to the first over-allocation by clicking **Go To Next Overallocation** on the **Resource Management** toolbar. MS Project starts at the date you have in view and searches forward day by day to find the next over-allocation. It does not stick to the selected resource.

6. Determine if the over-allocation is serious enough that it needs resolution. MS Project highlights tasks even when they overlap only for one hour, which you could ignore. In our certification curriculum, we required project managers to resolve over-allocations when they exceeded 150% of a person's availability on a day-to-day basis and 120% on a week-by-week basis. Thresholds like these should be established within your organization. Please consult with your project office. Resolve the serious over-allocations one by one by applying one of the methods provided on page 476.

Some remarks about the tool **Go To Next Overallocation** :

◆ It often finds over-allocations that are not important. If two 1 hour tasks are scheduled concurrently, it will highlight this as an over-allocation. You can easily skip such over-allocations. Such short overlaps will not affect your project end date in a significant way.

◆ It skips over-allocations that happened in the past, which is okay. You have probably already experienced a slippage in your schedule resulting from over-allocations that were left unresolved.

◆ It sometimes does not find over-allocations that are serious.

Nevertheless, we recommend this tool as the best tool available in MS Project.

In the next illustration, you can see how the over-allocation is solved by delaying one of the tasks that was competing for the same resource:

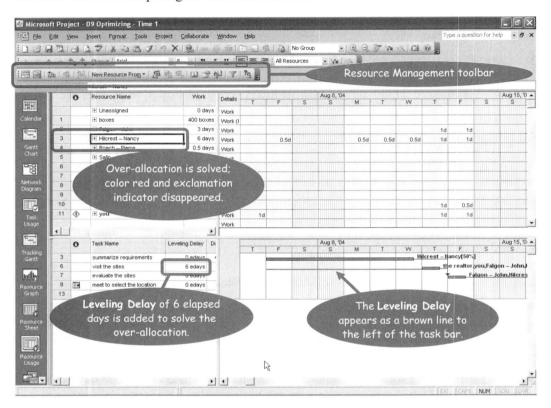

The bottom view can be improved by displaying a line for the total slack as well; see page 432 for an explanation on the two types of slack. If the free slack is not large enough, the total slack may provide possibilities to resolve the over-allocation. We will have to add a colored line for total slack to each task bar. Click in the bottom view and choose **Format, Bar Styles**.

Scroll down until you see the **Slack** line item which depicts free slack. Cut the **Slack** line and paste it back in twice. Change the **Name** of the first one to **Total Slack** and under **To** select **Total Slack** from the list. Change the name of the second one to **Free Slack** and change the **Shape** to the second last item in the list (bar in middle) and change the color to **Lime** (light green) as shown in the following screenshot:

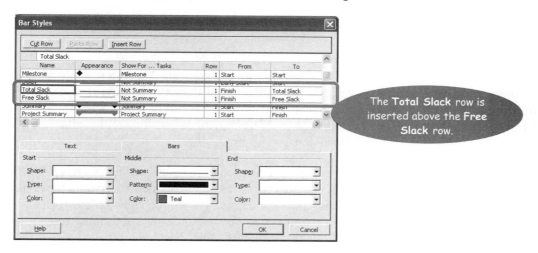

The **Total Slack** row is inserted above the **Free Slack** row.

 If you keep the same **Shape**, the lines will fall on top of one another. If you insert the total slack item above the free slack item, the shorter free slack line will be superimposed on the total slack line. MS Project creates the bars in the order they are listed. Now you can see how far you can delay tasks without affecting the next constraint date or the project end date.

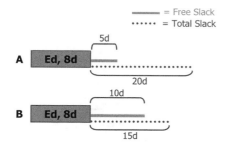

If a task does not have enough *free slack* to solve over-allocations, you can use its *total slack* to solve the work overload. The total slack is always greater than or equal to the free slack. In the illustration, task *A* does not have enough free slack to solve the over-allocation, but it does have enough total slack. If you go beyond the total slack, you are slipping a constraint date or increasing the project duration. In the illustrated example, I would prefer to delay task *B*, since it resolves the over-allocation within the free slack, even though task *B* has less total slack. This assures me that no other successor is affected, which keeps the rest of the schedule the same. That is why I suggested the bright green for free slack and darker green for total slack. If I delay task *A,* successors will be affected. The art of project management is often to minimize the turbulence.

Have MS Project Level the Workloads

Leveling of Facility and Machine Resources

Human resources can do more than one task at a time, which is also known as *multi-tasking.* Whether this affects the productivity is a separate discussion. To level human resources, you fill the workload up to the limit of their availability. If someone is only used 80% of their time, another small part-time task could be added without causing over-allocation. I call this *percentage leveling,* since you try to fill availability up to 100%. This is what MS Project does.

In general, facilities and machines are either occupied or not and need *yes/no leveling.* Unfortunately, MS Project does not consider facilities and machines as separate types of resources. If you only *assign* facilities and machines at 100%, you can emulate yes/no leveling. Many people create a reservation system for boardrooms and training rooms outside of MS Project to keep their "workload" reasonable. You want planned availability to affect the forecasts in your project model.

Materials are consumable and don't need leveling. You can exclude materials by setting the resource field **Can Level** to *No.* MS Project does this for you, in fact, for material resources.

Choosing the Leveling Options

Choose **Tools, Level Resources** to access the *leveling options* when you are resolving *over-allocations.* We will discuss the options section by section:
Leveling calculations
◆ We recommend you select ⊙ **Manual.** If you select manual leveling, you can still have MS Project level the workloads whenever you want by clicking Level Now at the bottom of the same dialog. You can also delete any traces of leveling by clicking Clear Leveling... in this dialog; which will change all values in the task field **Leveling Delay** to zero.

Automatic leveling continuously levels the workloads and makes the task bars jump all over the place with every change you make in the schedule. MS Project levels mostly by delaying tasks. This option is a global option that takes effect in all your project schedules. Also, because you can often find better schedules by hand, we don't recommend using automatic leveling.

◆ In the list, **Look for overallocations on a ... basis,** you can choose the granularity with which MS Project combs through the data to find over-allocations. A double workload on Monday, but a total workload of 16 hours in a week, constitutes an overload on a day-by-day basis, but not on a week-by-week basis. The setting is about the granularity of leveling. We recommend using **Day by Day** or **Week by Week** for most projects.

◆ Check ☑ **Clear Leveling values before leveling** if you want to clear the field **Leveling delay** of values left by previous leveling. Clear it if you want MS Project to add to the leveling delays incrementally; this often leads to unnecessarily long project durations.

Leveling range for <name of project>

◆ Select ◉ **Level entire project**. You normally would level the entire project, but you can also indicate a date range.

Resolving overallocations

◆ Check or clear **Level only within available Slack**.
You can check this option to develop a scenario when you want to know how many of the over-allocations MS Project can resolve within a certain time frame. Clear it if you want MS Project to resolve all your over-allocations; if you have kept the schedule dynamic, it will definitely solve them all.

◆ ☑ **Leveling can adjust individual assignments on a task**
Check this option if you want to find the shortest, leveled schedule. If you have more than one person assigned to a task, this option will reschedule the individual *assignments* rather than all assignments as a group. The result is that task bars are often split into multiple parts, because each assignment on the task will be scheduled separately. This option is not applicable to tasks on which people are supposed to collaborate live in real time. If you use this option, you can still override it for certain tasks by entering **No** in the task field **Level Assignments**. Notice that MS Project sets this field by default to **No** for *fixed duration* and *recurring detail tasks*; for all other tasks it is set to **Yes**. If you clear it, MS Project will schedule the task only when the whole group is available.

◆ ☑ **Leveling can create splits in remaining work**
Check this option if you want to allow MS Project to split task bars. Splitting may generate a tighter schedule, because if you allow splitting, MS Project can schedule around tasks that have fixed dates. The drawback is that task bars become fragmented. If you want to exclude certain tasks from being split, clear their task field **Leveling can split**. Fixed duration tasks have this field set to *No* and will not be split by MS Project, because it would increase their duration.

Three Automatic Leveling Scenarios

Again, we have to check first if we forgot to assign resources to detail tasks; if we did, there is no use in starting automatic leveling. In the Resource usage view, the heading ⊞ **Unassigned** at the top contains the unassigned tasks. Click on the button ⊞ to expand them, and click ⊟ to hide them again. Typically, only the milestones and perhaps the recurring detail tasks should be listed in the **Unassigned** category. If you have not assigned resources to all detail tasks, you have not captured all the workloads, and the forecasts after leveling would be too optimistic.

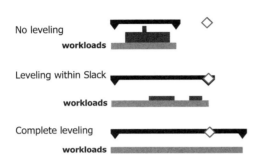

There are three scenarios you can develop with MS Project, and you can switch back and forth among them as many times as you need to. Each scenario provides some useful information. The illustration shows all three. The black workloads are the over-allocations. The more the workloads are leveled, the fewer over-allocations. Without doing anything, you currently have the first scenario of *No leveling*.

◆ **No leveling**

If you look at the timescale of Gantt Charts, you often see several tasks scheduled concurrently. Where two concurrent tasks have the same resource assigned, the workloads can exceed the availability of the resource. If there are no over-allocations, you will not need to level. In that case, only the task durations and dependencies drive the duration of the project. This scenario answers the question: *What is the project duration when the workloads are not leveled?* This scenario tells us the minimum duration for the project.

◆ **Leveling within the slack of the project**

If you create a milestone with a Must Finish On constraint on the proposed target date, you can level within the slack this hard date creates. This scenario answers the question: *What workload will critical resources have while meeting the project target date?* This scenario tells you how many extra resources you should hire in order to meet the target date. As you can see in the illustration, you may need an extra programmer for a few months and an extra tester for one month in a software development project, for example.

◆ **Complete leveling**

This answers: *What is the end date of the project if the workloads of all resources are entirely leveled?* This shows a comfortable deadline for the project and the team.

All three scenarios provide useful information when negotiating deadlines with upper management or clients:

◆ The no-leveling date from the first scenario is your resistance point in negotiations; you should not commit to an earlier date. You will still have to resolve all over-allocations if you commit to this date without delaying the project finish date, which can be challenging depending on how many over-allocations you have.

◆ The remaining over-allocations from the second scenario may provide the common ground in your negotiations with the client. You can ask MS Project to resolve as many over-allocations as it can while staying within a certain time frame. You can then easily find out how many extra resources you need to hire to meet the target date and calculate what that would cost. If the client is willing to pay for these extra resources, you may have a date that meets the mutual needs of your client and yourself.

◆ The finish date of the third scenario of complete leveling is the date we recommend you first quote to your client. It is a date that is nice to have, and that you will likely not get. It could be your starting position in negotiations.

For each of these scenarios, it is nice to see what changes MS Project has made to the schedule, and the **Leveling Gantt** view is best suited for this purpose. To apply this view, choose **View, More Views**, select **Leveling Gantt** from the list and click .

The view looks like this:

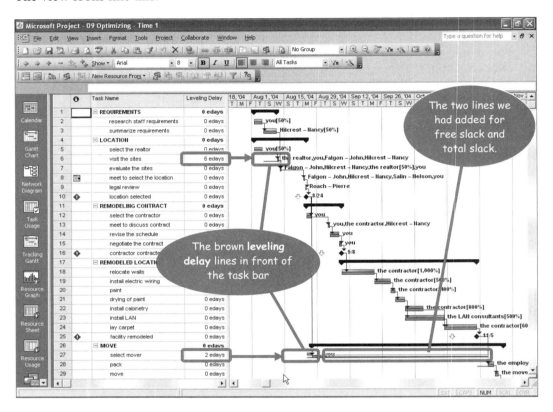

This view includes the field **Leveling Delay** as one of the columns, and it also shows the delay graphically with a brown line to the left of any task bars that were delayed.

You can even make the three scenarios show up side by side in one Gantt Chart, which we will explain in detail on page 492.

No Leveling or Clearing the Leveling

1. You can only clear the leveling if you are in one of the task views. Change to a task view first, if necessary.

2. If you have leveled workloads before, the field **Leveling Delay** will have entries. To check if this is the case, make sure you see this column.

3. To remove the leveling delay, choose **Tools, Level Resources...**; the **Resource Leveling** dialog appears:

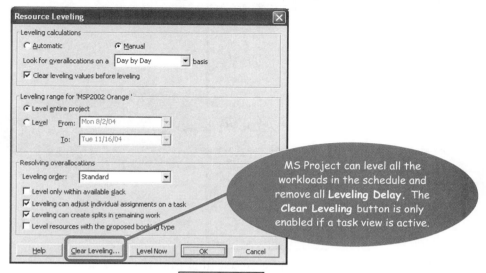

4. Select ⦿ **Manual** and click Clear Leveling... ; the **Clear Leveling** dialog appears:

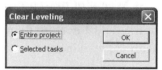

5. Select ⦿ **Entire Project** and click OK ; you are now back in the task view. The numbers in the field **Leveling Delay** should all be zero.

6. If you want to compare all three scenarios in one Gantt Chart, you should at this point save the dates of this version. Choose **Tools, Tracking, Save Baseline** and select ⦿ **Save interim plan** and **Copy Start/Finish into Start1/Finish1**.

You now know the minimum duration for your project; there can be over-allocations in the schedule that need to be taken care of.

Leveling within the Slack of the Project

1. Make sure you have a project finish milestone at which all dependencies come together. The project milestone should have a *Must Finish On* constraint on the proposed target date; a Finish No Later Than constraint does not work here. Make sure you have as few as possible other constraint dates, since they hinder the automatic leveling.

2. Choose **Tools, Level Resources...**; the **Resource Leveling** dialog appears:

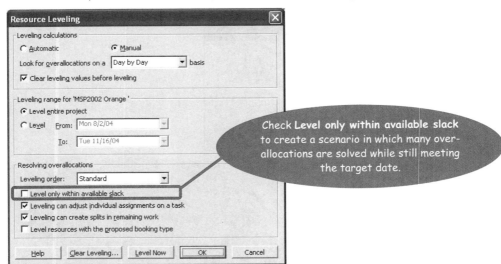

3. Choose the granularity of the leveling by selecting from the list **Look for overallocations on a … basis** the time unit in which MS Project should find over-allocations. We recommend **Day by Day** or **Week by Week** for most projects.

4. Check ☑ **Clear leveling values before leveling** to clear the field **Leveling delay** of old leveling values; MS Project will make a fresh start with the leveling.

5. Check ☑ **Level only within available slack**.

6. Clear ☐ **Level resources with the proposed booking type** unless you want the workloads of resources that are *proposed* but not *committed* on potential projects to be leveled as well.

7. Click **Level Now**. MS Project may alert you that it cannot resolve certain over-allocations, which is what we expected, since we gave it a fixed time frame.

8. Click **OK**.

9. Check the workloads of the resources; there are often some over-allocations left.

10. If you want to compare all three scenarios in one Gantt Chart, you should at this point save the dates of this version. Choose **Tools, Tracking, Save Baseline** and select ◉ **Save interim plan** and **Copy Start/Finish into Start2/Finish2**.

The workloads of the resources are likely still too high to meet the deadline, and you can analyze how much extra expense you would have to solve the over-allocations by hiring temporary workers. Or you can explore other methods to make the workloads reasonable; see page 480.

Complete Leveling

1. Check if you have many hard scheduling constraints, because they will hinder this process of complete leveling.

2. If needed, insert the column **Leveling Delay** by right-clicking on the column heading **Duration**, choosing **Insert Column** and selecting the field **Leveling Delay** from the list. This field allows us to see the result of the leveling.

3. Choose **Tools, Level Resources...**; the **Resource Leveling** dialog appears:

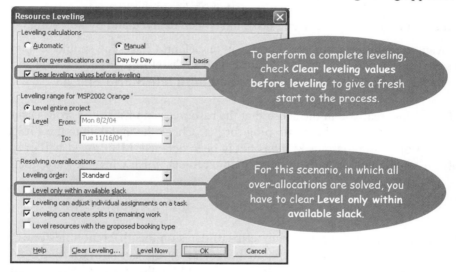

4. Choose the precision of the leveling by selecting from the list **Look for overallocations on a** the granularity with which MS Project should find over-allocations. We recommend **Day by Day** or **Week by Week** for most projects.

5. Check ☑ **Clear leveling values before leveling** if you want to clear the field **Leveling delay** of old leveling values, which we recommend.

6. Select ◉ **Level entire project**.

7. Clear ☐ **Level only within available slack**; otherwise MS Project may not solve all over-allocations.

8. Check ☑ **Leveling can adjust individual assignments on a task** if you want to find the shortest leveled schedule. MS Project schedules the assignments

individually instead of as a group. You may end up with split task bars, but you can redo the leveling and clear the option to prevent bar splits, or you can set the task field **Level assignments** to *No* for task bars you don't want to be split.

9. Check ☑ **Leveling can create splits in remaining work** if you want to allow MS Project to split task bars. The drawback is that the task bars become fragmented. If you want to exclude certain tasks from being split, set their task field **Leveling can split** to *No*. Fixed duration tasks have this field already set to *No*.

10. Clear ☐ **Level resources with the proposed booking type**, unless you want resource workloads that are *proposed* but not *committed* on potential projects to be leveled as well.

11. Click [Level Now]. MS Project delayed certain tasks. In the column **Leveling Delay**, you can see which tasks have been delayed and by how long.

12. If you want to compare all three scenarios in one Gantt Chart, you should at this point save the dates of this version. Choose **Tools, Tracking, Save Baseline** and select ⊙ **Save interim plan** and **Copy Start/Finish into Start3/Finish3**.

The schedule is now realistic in the sense that the resources can finish the work assigned to them without the project end date slipping further. Check the end date in the **Finish** column of the project summary task; it has likely been delayed. MS Project will only be able to solve over-allocations without delaying the project finish when they are small.

Comparing the Three Scenarios in One Gantt Chart

In order to compare the three scenarios in terms of dates on the different milestones, you should create a new view and select separate bar styles for the Start1/Start2/Start3 data sets. These steps assume that you have already captured the three scenarios as shown in previous procedures and executed the last step of all three procedures.

1. Choose **View, More Views...**; the **More Views** dialog appears:

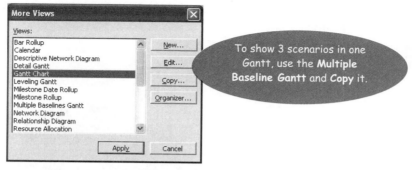

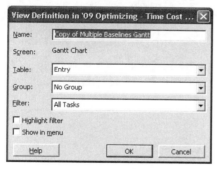

2. Select **Multiple Baselines Gantt** and click Copy....

3. The **View Definition** dialog appears:

4. Change the name of the new view to *Leveling Scenarios* or something that is descriptive. You can keep the rest of the settings and click OK.

5. Check ☑ **Show in menu**; the view will be available with only two mouse-clicks.

6. Click OK; you are now back in the **More Views** dialog.

7. Click Apply.

8. Choose **Format, Bar Styles** and change the settings so that instead of the baseline dates the *Start1/Finish1 - Start3/Finish3* dates are shown. The changes you need to make are shown in the following dialog:

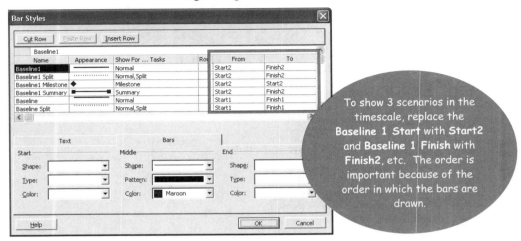

To show 3 scenarios in the timescale, replace the **Baseline 1 Start** with **Start2** and **Baseline 1 Finish** with **Finish2**, etc. The order is important because of the order in which the bars are drawn.

9. Notice the order in which the dates are entered into the dialog. This order is a deliberate choice, since items listed higher are overlaid by lower items. Click OK once done.

10. You should now see the three task bars for each task and have the three scenarios next to each other in the timescale:

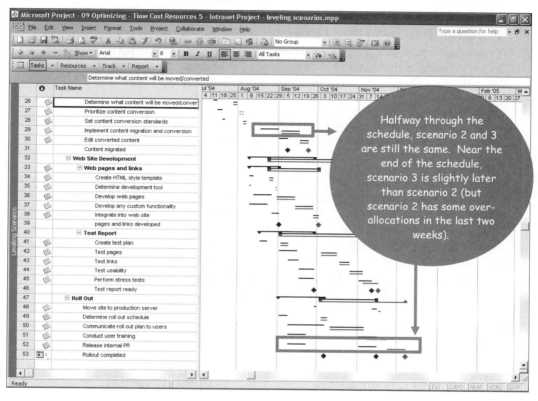

Influencing MS Project's Leveling

How can you predict which tasks will be postponed when resources are over-allocated? When you ask MS Project to level your schedule, it will try to intelligently choose which tasks to delay. It looks at the amount of slack on both tasks that compete for the same resource. It will delay the one task that has most slack. This is smart, because the tasks with most slack are least likely to affect your project end date. However, it does not always delay the task you would prefer. MS Project offers you three choices to influence which tasks are delayed. You will find these in the **Tools, Level resources..., Leveling order** list.

Here are some suggestions on when to use each:

◆ **ID Only**
MS Project will level tasks based upon their ID numbers. It will give priority to the task higher up in the list of tasks. Use this setting to prioritize projects in a consolidated schedule. Put your highest priority projects at the top of the list and then level your consolidated schedule using this option. Dragging projects up and down the list is less effort than maintaining priority numbers.

◆ **Standard**
This is the default setting and is used for regular leveling. Under standard leveling, the task with the most slack will be delayed, which makes sense.

◆ **Priority, Standard**
When you are not entirely happy with MS Project's leveling, you can enter a priority number for certain tasks in the field **Priority**. In this way, you can influence which task is delayed in the leveling. This involves a fair bit of work if you do it on a task-by-task basis; if you fill down a priority number for all tasks of a deliverable, you may be done a lot faster. Priority numbers can range from 0 to 1000. The higher the number, the higher the priority, and the more likely it will be that the task keeps its current dates. MS Project will not delay the higher priority task when you level using the leveling setting **Priority, Standard**.

Another way to influence leveling is to exclude certain tasks or resources as candidates for leveling.

Excluding Tasks from MS Project Leveling

If the priority number is set to *1000*, MS Project will not delay the task, and will effectively exclude it from the leveling process. This is even the case if you use the **ID** or **Standard** setting in the **Tools, Level resources, Leveling order** list.

Excluding Resources from MS Project Leveling

Typically, you would exclude subcontractor resources from leveling, because the workload of people external to your organization is normally not your problem.

You can exclude human resources by entering **No** in the resource field **Can Level**.
OR

1. In the *Resource Sheet* view, select the resources you want to include first, then choose **Tools, Level Resources…**; the **Resource Leveling** dialog appears.

2. Upon clicking , you will see the following dialog:

3. Select the option ⦿ **Selected resources** and click OK . MS Project will now only level the workloads for those resources you selected. This allows you to quickly develop several scenarios.

Should I Level Myself or Have MS Project Do It for Me?

At this point we have discussed both ways of leveling workloads: doing it yourself or having MS Project do it for you. If you struggle with which to choose, here are some guidelines:

◆ If you have few over-allocations in your schedule, you could probably resolve them all yourself without puzzling for hours. We recommend you do it yourself by hand and don't use MS Project's leveling features. MS Project would likely push out your project end date unnecessarily.

◆ If there are many over-allocations in your schedule, resolving them all by hand is a lot of work, and in that case, it may be easier to perform a complete leveling. This will likely push your project end date far out. You can then improve that date by finding the Resource-Critical Path in your schedule and focusing on the resource-critical tasks. We will explain the concept of the Resource-Critical Path in the next section.

How Leveling Affects the Critical Path

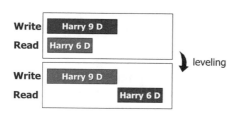

In the illustration, there are two tasks *write* a report and *read* another unrelated document. The tasks are not dependent upon each other; Harry can choose to do them in any order. Before leveling, the Critical Path is the task *write*. After leveling, *read* is the only critical task. Try this out in MS Project! Don't worry, there is nothing wrong with your software; this is how the Critical Path algorithm works, is supposed to work and works in other scheduling software as well.

The Critical Path theory assumes that you have access to unlimited resources.

In MS Project, the leveled mini-schedule looks as follows:

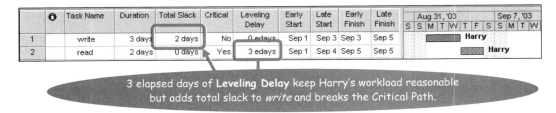

3 elapsed days of **Leveling Delay** keep Harry's workload reasonable but adds total slack to *write* and breaks the Critical Path.

Let me explain the mathematics of the algorithm in this simple example:

◆ On the forward pass, the *early start* for *write* is day 1 and the *early finish* is day 3 given the duration of 3 days. For *read* the early start is day 1; remember that there is no dependency between the tasks, and the early finish is at the end of day 5, given the delayed start date of day 4.

◆ On the backward pass, the *late finish* for *read* is also day 5; the *late start*, therefore, is day 4. *Write* has to be finished on the project finish date; the late finish date is day 5, since there is no dependency between the two. It has to start, at the latest, on day 3 to meet this date.

Total slack can be calculated by subtracting the early finish date from the late finish date. The total slack of the task *read* is 5 − 5 = 0 days; the task is critical and highlighted in red. The total slack for *write* is 5 − 3 = 2 days; the task is not seen as critical by the algorithm. However, common sense dictates that there really is no slack on the task *write*, because it competes for the same resource, *Harry*. And if the task *write* takes longer, the task *read* will be moved out. This example demonstrates the weakness of the Critical Path algorithm. The algorithm does not take resource dependencies into account, because it is built on the assumption that you have access to unlimited resources.

Access to unlimited resources is not the current reality any longer for many organizations that are competing in the global marketplace. Organizations that use their resources well gain a competitive edge. Resources are often stretched to their limits and drive the project end date. An organization that does not optimize the usage of its resources will soon notice this in its bottom line. In other words, many organizations find themselves having to level the workloads of their resources, and upon doing so, the Critical Path often becomes fragmented. The leveling of tasks can make the calculated total slack value of tasks meaningless and therefore the Critical Path as well. In fact, tasks with total slack may be driving the project end date, as is the case with the task *write* in the previous example. If *write* slips, it will move *read,* because of the resource dependency of *Harry* assigned to both tasks. The slack is false slack.

Critical Path or Resource-Critical Path?

We need a smarter Critical Path that takes logical dependencies as well as resource dependencies into account. Such a path is called the *Resource-Critical Path (RCP).*

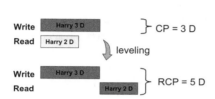

Given the example in the illustration, what should a project manager monitor, the *Critical Path (CP)* or the *RCP*? The answer is obvious. The Critical Path in the unleveled schedule forecasts unrealistic finish dates, because there is a work overload for Harry. In the leveled schedule, the Critical Path is fragmented and useless. Both tasks are resource-critical, because Harry is assigned to both tasks; this is called a *resource dependency*. One should try to find the RCP in *resource-constrained* projects, rather than the Critical Path. Only the RCP provides a complete explanation of the project duration. It shows what drives the project end date at any time during the project duration, just like the Critical Path in *logic-constrained* projects. The RCP is more helpful in a leveled schedule.

In general, any project that uses expert resources tends to be a *resource-constrained* or *resource-limited* project. *Experts* are by definition scarce; otherwise, you would not call them an 'expert'. Examples of projects in which resources are scarce are pharmaceutical, information technology, military, R&D and biotechnology projects. If you are the project manager of such a project, you should find and monitor the Resource-Critical Path in your schedule instead of the Critical Path.

The Resource-Critical Path

Let us first define this new concept of RCP. An *RCP* is the series of tasks that determines the project duration while taking logical dependencies and resource dependencies into account.[78] A task can be *resource-critical* because of a logical dependency or a resource dependency with another task. Notice the definition is not very different from the Critical Path definition. However, other common descriptions of the Critical Path, like *the sequence of tasks without slack*, do not apply to the RCP, because resource-critical tasks can have slack. In the example we just discussed, the task *write* has slack, but still drives the project end date and is therefore as critical as *read*. Both are resource-critical tasks, however, because the same resource works on them. When two tasks compete for the same resource at any point in time, those tasks have a *resource dependency*.

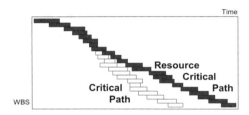

The RCP, in other words, is the chain of tasks that drives the project end date while taking into account that resources have limited availability. When you have relatively few resources, you should focus on the RCP instead of the Critical Path. Any project manager who has experts on the team may need to find the RCP instead of the Critical Path. An easy way to find out if you are in a resource-constrained situation is by leveling the workloads completely; if your project end date slipped and if the over-allocations are gone, you are in a *resource-constrained* project. If the end date did not slip, you are in a *logic-constrained* project. See page 491 for the steps on complete leveling.

You can see in the illustration that the RCP often includes some early critical tasks and then resource-critical tasks that are delayed, because of leveling. All those tasks drive the project end date. *Resource-critical tasks* are tasks that, when delayed, make the project end date slip. I would like to introduce an acronym here to help you remember this fundamental message for resource-constrained projects. The acronym is **ERIC** (**E**ach **R**esource **I**mplies **C**riticality). In a leveled schedule, any resource can be so limited in availability, or needed so much, that it could drive the project finish date. I propose calling this the ERIC-principle. [79]

---

[78] See my article in the magazine *PM Network*, December 1999, PMI: *Take the Path that is Really Critical*.

[79] Hey, that's my first name!

Finding the Resource-Critical Path

1. Check the workloads and level them
2. **Highlight the Resource Critical Path (RCP)**
3. **Find the most critical resource**
4. Make a change on it
5. Consider impacts on quality, scope, time, cost and resources
6. Decide whether you want to keep the change
7. Repeat steps 3 - 7

The next step is to find and highlight the RCP. We will discuss two methods to find the RCP: a manual process and an automatic process. There is no feature in MS Project that highlights the RCP for you, like with the Critical Path. Therefore, it will involve some effort from you to understand the concept of the RCP. In order to optimize the schedule, it is imperative that you do identify the RCP. Now, IIL provides a macro that will automate finding your RCP. [80] This is the first edition of this book in which we provide an automated way to identify the RCP. If you manage *resource-constrained* projects, it will make your life much simpler.

◆ **Manual process**

We recommend this process for small projects. Also, this process will make you truly understand the concept of an RCP. If you can identify the RCP in a schedule by hand, you really understand this concept. When you first learned the Critical Path concept, you were also challenged to find it by hand before you started to rely on automated tools. We recommend you try this process first to enhance your understanding of RCPs.

◆ **Automatic process**

After you understand the concept of the RCP, you can use our macro that identifies the RCP in your schedule very quickly. This macro is included in the download files that come with this book.[81]

---

[80] IIL owns the copyright of this macro that was developed by Ken Jamison. This macro is provided for personal use only. If you would like to use this macro for business purposes, please contact our USA sales staff (212-758-0177) to purchase a corporate license.

[81] See www.jrosspub.com

Manual Process

It is easiest to identify resource-critical tasks by starting at the project end milestone and tracking backward. You look for driving predecessors or resources that are shared between the tasks. Tasks that are resource-critical have either a logical dependency or a resource dependency with earlier tasks. A logical dependency, as you know, is shown as an arrow between the task bars in the Gantt timescale. A resource dependency occurs when two tasks are competing for the same resource. In the Gantt Chart view you can see in the timescale to the right of the task bars which resources are assigned. We recommend you use this view to identify the RCP.

Once you understand the process, you can find the RCP in a small schedule of up to one hundred tasks within minutes with this manual process. In larger schedules, we recommend you use the automatic process.

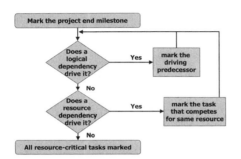

The flowchart gives an overview of the process. You will work backward starting with the project finish milestone. This milestone is by definition resource-critical, so you mark it right away. You then ask yourself for this milestone: *Does a logical dependency drive it?* You check all the predecessors of the project milestone and determine which one is driving it to the date on which it starts. You will find a predecessor that has a finish date that is just before the start date of the finish milestone. Once you have found the driving task, you mark it as a resource-critical task. Then you go back to the top of the flowchart and start all over again with the marked task as the next task to analyze.

You start with the first question again: *Does a logical dependency drive it?* You check all its predecessors and check which predecessor finishes just before the detail task starts; this is most likely the driving predecessor. You may have to check for *lags* on dependencies to determine if the link is driving. If you find a driving predecessor, you mark it and go back to the top of the chart and continue with that task.

If you did not find a driving predecessor, which is often the case for detail tasks in a *resource-constrained*, leveled schedule, you ask yourself the second question in the flowchart: *Does a resource dependency drive it?* Now you look at the resources that are assigned to the task, and you look for another task that finishes just before it that uses the same resource. Once you have found the driving task, you *Mark the task that competes for the same resource* and go back to the top of the flowchart and continue with that task. You continue until you have arrived at the project start date at which point all resource-critical tasks are marked.

We recommend the following view for the RCP-analysis:

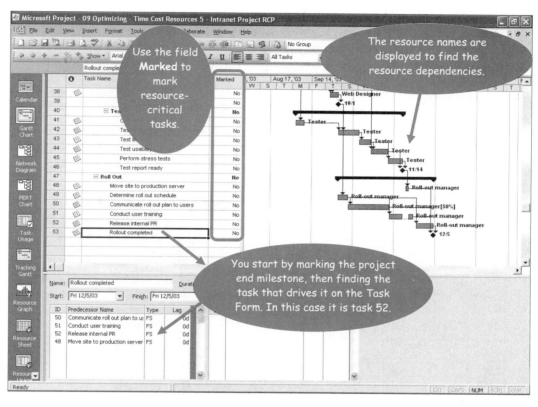

As you can see in the screenshot, we recommend using the **Gantt Chart** with the **Task Form** displayed at the bottom of the view to find the RCP. Make sure you insert the task field **Marked** to tag the tasks that you find to be resource-critical.

The steps to identify the RCP in your schedule are:

1. Choose **View, Gantt Chart** that displays the resource names next to the task bars, which is useful for finding resource dependencies. Also, choose **Window, Split** to display the **Task Form** with the dependencies and their lag. Insert the field **Marked** and enter **Yes** for those tasks that you identified as resource-critical tasks. Mark all resource-critical tasks using the process explained.

2. Switch to the **Tracking Gantt** view, because it already has **Format, Bar Styles** settings that color certain tasks red; the critical tasks. Choose **View, Tracking Gantt**. Notice that the Critical Path is entirely fragmented; it does not explain the entire project duration, but the RCP does.

3. We will now make changes to the bar styles of the view, but we probably want to preserve the original Tracking Gantt view as well. Therefore, we will copy the Tracking Gantt view first. Choose **Views, More Views**. The **More Views** dialog appears and **Tracking Gantt** is selected in the list. Click ⟨ Copy... ⟩ and enter a new name for the view, for example *Resource-Critical Path*. Click ⟨ OK ⟩ and ⟨ Apply ⟩. You are now back in the main screen with the new view displayed.

4. We will make the RCP look the same as our good old Critical Path. Choose **Format, Bar Styles...** We will make changes to the bars so that all normal tasks have a blue task bar, except for tasks that are marked; they will appear in red. These changes are circled in the following screenshot:

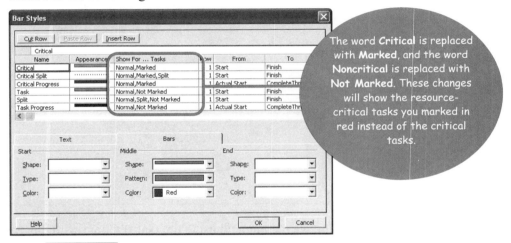

5. Click ⟨ OK ⟩; you can now color task bars red if you change their field **Marked** to **Yes**, or you can change them back to blue by entering **No** in the **Marked** field. This is useful if you need to make corrections to your RCP.

6. Click **AutoFilter** ⟨Y=⟩, and buttons appear in the column headings. Click ⟨▾⟩ in the column heading **Marked** and from the list that appears choose **Yes**. This filters and displays the resource-critical tasks only. Notice that the column heading title is now blue to remind you that an auto filter is on.

7. Replace the % complete to the right of the task bars with the resource names. Choose **Format, Bar Styles** and select the item **Critical**, click tab **Text** and replace

% Complete with **Resource Names**. You may want to get rid of the **% Complete** on the **Summary** tasks as well.

8. Make the dependency arrows disappear by choosing **Format, Layout...** and under **Links**, select the first option.

If you follow these steps with the file *09 Optimizing - Time Cost Resources 5 - Intranet Project.MPP*, the schedule should look at this point like:

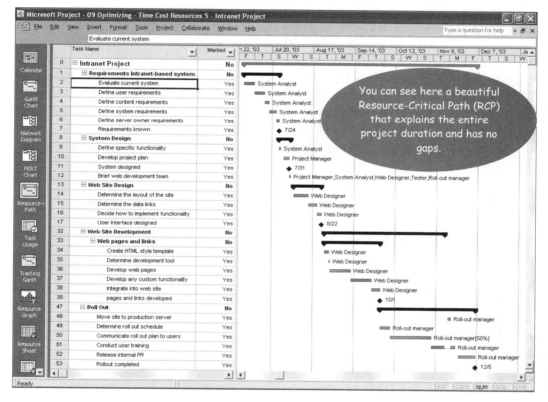

To the uninitiated, the schedule now looks as if the regular red Critical Path is shown, except that it really is the RCP. The RCP drives the project end date, just like the Critical Path. The RCP provides a complete explanation for the project duration, just like the Critical Path would in a *logic-constrained* project. You could present this as your "Critical Path" to people who are not familiar with the concept of the RCP. They will not argue about the correctness of it, because you can easily prove that all red tasks drive the project end date. After all, if any of the tasks on the RCP slips, the project will take longer.

Automatic Process

Identifying the RCP should be done in an automated fashion, because when you are making changes to the schedule during optimization, you need to find the new RCP over and over again, just like the good old Critical Path.

IIL now provides a macro that can identify the RCP in your schedule. You can run this macro by opening the file *IIL Project 2003 tools to check Orange Belt Schedules.MPP* available for download at www.jrosspub.com. Please, click the link *WAV Download Resource Center* to enter the download site.

After you have opened this file, you should open the schedule in which you want to find the RCP. Make sure the workloads in the schedule are completely leveled, see page 491. Then you are ready to run the macro by choosing **Tools, Macro, Macros**. Select the macro **RCP** from the list and click [Run]. The macro now lists the resource-critical tasks at the top of the task list. (Before saving your schedule, make sure it is still intact, since IIL does not provide any warranties and cannot be held liable for damage to your schedule.)

Why Should I Care About the Resource-Critical Path?

Since understanding the RCP-approach requires some effort, I feel compelled to raise your motivation. There are five reasons why applying the RCP-approach is worthwhile in any resource-constrained schedule:
◆ The RCP drives the project end date.
◆ The RCP reveals the critical resource(s).
◆ The RCP allows finding domino effects.
◆ The RCP allows workload smoothing.
◆ The RCP helps to fast-track smarter.
We will discuss each of these reasons.

The RCP Drives the Project End Date

Typically, somewhere along the Critical Path, the resources start to constrain the

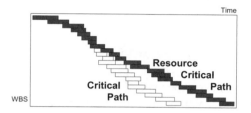

schedule more than the logic, and the RCP overtakes the Critical Path. If that happens, the RCP drives the project end date. As you can see in the illustration, the white tasks constitute the regular Critical Path, but leveling delayed many of them. The result of leveling is shown as black tasks. The RCP is the combination of the critical tasks early in the schedule and all the resource-dependent tasks later on. If any of these tasks slip, the project will finish later; the resource-critical tasks drive the project end date.

Can we give the *CPM* a well-deserved retirement? The answer is no, because there are many situations that are not resource-constrained, and situations in which organizations decide that they will not allow (lack of) resources to drive the schedule out. In those situations, the RCP is not needed and CPM will do.

The RCP Reveals the Critical Resource(s)

The RCP shows who the critical resources are. It also shows when the resources are critical. It is important for the project manager to know at any time which resource

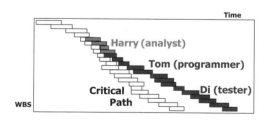

determines the speed of progress in the project. Only if project managers know who is critical can they pay special attention to providing a work environment for those resources that is free of interruptions and disruptions. And they know that if those resources present an issue, they better deal with it right away. Better yet, the project manager can let everybody know who is critical each week and ask the team to leave the critical resource alone. The project manager should even ask the team for full and immediate cooperation when the critical resource calls. Having been a critical resource myself at times, I can speak from experience that my productivity is much higher if my team members immediately help me out in any way they can. It becomes a team effort instead of sole heroism or … a *burn-out*.

Managers get things done through others. The RCP shows project managers which resources they should pay attention to. The RCP allows project managers to focus on people instead of tasks. The RCP puts the focus of managers back where it belongs: on people. Project managers already have a bit the image that they force reams of tasks down people's throats.

The RCP Allows Finding Domino Effects

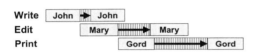

Have you ever experienced an avalanche of changes after you made one small change? If you make one change to a schedule, you may trigger a disastrous *domino effect*. The illustration shows that when *John* became sick, his task slipped. Mary had planned to finish her part just before her holiday. When John finished late, *Mary* had left for her holiday, so her part slipped even more. When she returned, finished her part and handed off to *Gord*, he was temporarily reassigned to another project and would return in 3 weeks. You decide not to wait for *Gord* and assign a new person. The new person will need 1 week of introduction and training, and so forth and so on… One little slip that seems innocuous can cause big delays, because of resource dependencies. As I wrote before, minimizing the turbulence is often the art of project management.

The RCP makes the most important resource dependencies visible. If you make the relationships between the resources visible, you can make changes to the schedule in a more educated fashion. If you monitor only the conventional Critical Path, you will not realize that you are creating an avalanche of changes.

The RCP Allows Workload Smoothing

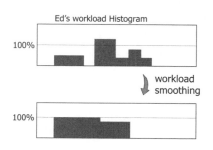

There often is a huge amount of cost involved with erratic workloads, as discussed on page 471 and shown in the illustration. How much does Ed's workload cost before and after smoothing? He has periods when he can twiddle his thumbs and other periods when he is overloaded (and may be wishing he had another job). I often see companies *burn out* their *critical resources*, especially in time-to-market organizations. If a critical resource burns out, the individual and the organization are severely hurt. For organizations, this often has expensive consequences in terms of dissatisfied employees, demoralized work culture, sick leave, attrition, as well as the cost of finding new, highly specialized people. It also costs money when deadlines are missed or contracts are lost.

The RCP keeps an eye on the workloads continuously, because workloads drive the RCP. Therefore, it allows you to monitor and manage workloads better. The eventual cost of a smooth workload is often less than the cost of an erratic one, see page 471.

The RCP Helps to Fast-Track Smarter

When fast-tracking your schedule, you may create workload problems if you only focus

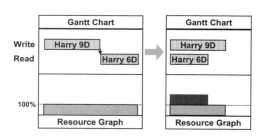

on the Critical Path. You may work a long time to find a shorter schedule, and just when you think you have a better schedule, you may find you have only replaced time problems with workload problems. In the illustration on the left, the dependency was cut, and this created an over-allocation for Harry. The schedule is now infeasible. If you ignore the resource dependencies and just focus on logical dependencies, you may create short schedules. However, because of new over-allocations, these schedules may not be feasible.

What Is the Nature of the Beast?

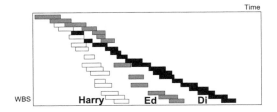

Now that we fully understand why it is important to find the RCP, we should explore the nature of the RCP a bit further. First of all, it is important to realize that each resource has its own RCP.

In the illustration, the schedule is leveled every time for only one of the resources. This creates as many RCPs as there are resources. Harry, Ed and Di are all critical resources, but when leveled, Di pushes the end date out farther than Harry or Ed does. Di is the most critical resource. When shortening Di's RCP, you will arrive at a point after which Ed is more critical than Di. At that point, you have to shift your focus to Ed's workload instead of Di's. A similar thing can happen when crashing the Critical Path; another path can take over from the one we are working on any time. If you use the Critical Path Method in practice, you are probably familiar with that phenomenon.

What we left out of this picture is that there are hand-off points between resources. The RCP may be pushed out farther than you would expect simply based on the RCPs of individuals. These hand-off points always run over a logical dependency. The logical dependencies link the chains of the resource dependencies together. The RCP has tasks that may be resource dependent on each other or logically dependent. The RCP typically reveals that multiple resources are on the RCP.

I will present three different specific situations in which finding the correct RCP can be challenging:
◆ The RCP with multiple critical resources
◆ When multiple resources are assigned
◆ *Logical dependencies* and *resource dependencies*

Scheduling software will have to find the right RCP in all three situations before one can reasonably state that a solid RCP algorithm has been found and this challenge has been met.

The RCP with Multiple Critical Resources

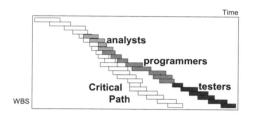

Several different resources typically work on tasks on the RCP. In the typical software development project, the analysts drive the front end of the schedule, the programmers the middle part and the testers the back end, as shown in the illustration. Every time there is a hand-off to the next resource, there is a logical dependency. Again, logical dependencies connect the chains of resource-dependent tasks. The RCP clearly shows who is driving the project duration and when they are driving it.

When Multiple Resources Are Assigned

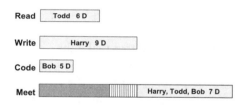

Multiple resources on a task pose a challenge for the algorithm that can find the RCP. The illustrated example on the left has resources assigned full-time to the tasks shown and multiple resources assigned to the last task, *Meet*. The algorithm has to pick the right resource as the critical one. In this case, *Harry* is the critical resource. Comparing this to the traditional Critical Path Method, it is similar to a task that has multiple predecessors and the algorithm has to identify the driving predecessor.

Logical Dependencies and Resource Dependencies

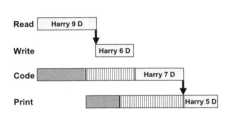

In the illustration, leveling has delayed the tasks *Code* and *Print*. The difficulty in this situation is that there is no hard dependency between *Write* and *Code*, only a resource dependency. An algorithm that identifies the RCP has to be able to handle a combination of logical dependencies and resource dependencies. In the flowchart on page 502, we therefore ask both questions. First, does a logical dependency drive the schedule? If not, does a resource dependency drive the schedule?

Methods to Optimize for Time, Cost and Resources

1. Check the workloads and level them
2. Highlight the Resource Critical Path (RCP)
3. Find the most critical resource
4. *Make a change on it*
5. Consider impacts on quality, scope, time, cost and resources
6. Decide whether you want to keep the change
7. Repeat steps 3 - 7

As you can see in the process chart, we are now finally at the step to make changes on the resource-critical tasks. When the project has to finish earlier than the current schedule, it has to be shortened. The best measurements are those that make the *quality* (Q) go up (↑), the *scope* (S) go up (↑), the *time* (T) go down (↓), the *cost* (C) go down (↓) and the *resource workload* (R) go down (↓). Unfortunately, there are no such ideal measurements. The next table provides indications as to what the effect of each action could be in a typical project. Even though we indicate what the impact might be in a typical project, you have to ask yourself what the possible impacts in your own project might be.

Because we now have limited resources, we should also assess each method and its impact on the resource workload in the project. Where a question mark (?) appears in the resources column (R), you have to check on new over-allocations after applying the measure. Where a zero (0) is shown, no impact is expected. The actions are ranked in order of overall effectiveness to reduce time. We recommend starting at the top of the table with the two fast-tracking methods. After exhausting the fast-tracking, go to the next action in the table. (Q=Quality, S=Scope, T=Time, C=Cost, R=Resource workload)

	Action	For	Q	S	T	C	R
1.	Change sequential dependencies into partial dependencies (fast-tracking)	resource-critical tasks	0	0	↓	0	?
2.	Create parallel paths from a sequential path (fast-tracking)	resource-critical tasks	?	0	↓	0	?
3.	Split long tasks into many shorter ones	resource-critical tasks	0	0	↓	↓	?
4.	Change schedule constraints	resource-critical tasks	0	0	↓	0	?
5.	Shorten *lags* (waiting periods)	resource-critical tasks	0	0	↓	0	?
6.	Split task bars around a Must Start On task	resource-critical tasks	0	0	↓	0	?
7.	Decrease estimates	resource-critical tasks	↓	?	↓	↓	↓
8.	Reduce the scope or delete tasks	resource-critical tasks	↓	↓	↓	↓	↓
9.	Reallocate the best resources to the most critical tasks	resource-critical tasks	0	0	↓	?	↓
10.	Increase assignment units to full-time assignments for critical resources	resource-critical, fixed work tasks	0	0	↓	0	?
11.	Assign overtime hours to critical resources	resource-critical, fixed work tasks	↓	0	↓	?	↑
12.	Add noncritical resources	resource-critical, fixed work tasks	0	0	?	↑	?
13.	Replace critical resources with noncritical resources	resource-critical, fixed work tasks	↓	?	↓	?	↓
14.	Remove a critical resource when multiple resources are assigned	resource-critical tasks	?	0	↓	↓	↓
15.	Postpone vacation of critical resources to after the deadline	resource-critical tasks	0	0	↓	↑	0

Some remarks about optimizing an RCP:

◆ The methods discussed on pages 449 are repeated in this table, because they are also valid in situations with limited resources. The difference is that these methods will now only work on resource-critical tasks instead of critical tasks. The actions are ranked by overall effectiveness.

◆ Fast-tracking on the RCP is not as effective as it was on the Critical Path. However, it still is the preferred method to start with, because it is *quality*, *scope* and *cost* neutral. Fast-tracking is less effective on the RCP, because:

   ◇ There are fewer dependencies on a RCP, because it consists of logical dependencies and resource dependencies.

   ◇ You cannot fast-track two tasks if the same resource is working on both tasks and they are linked. Fast-tracking is changing the dependencies in such a way that more tasks take place concurrently. When you overlap tasks, workloads are moved as well, and you may be creating over-allocations. Fast-tracking has to be applied with greater care. The RCP will show you which tasks have the same resources assigned that will cause new over-allocations when you overlap them. You should focus your fast-tracking efforts on tasks that are done by different resources. For example, when you remodel an office, the tasks of carpenters and electricians can overlap each other, as long as the carpenters start a few days ahead and finish a few days earlier. Fast-tracking is typically effective at hand-off points between critical resources.

◆ Actions 10 through 13 can shorten the durations of resource-critical tasks. These methods will work for all task types except *Fixed Duration* tasks. Before using one of these methods, you have to change its task type to *Fixed Work*, assuming the amount of effort required stays the same.

◆ Overhead tasks or support tasks should not be on the RCP. Overhead tasks support the real work and should not drive the project end date. If you see the project manager, team leaders, or technical support or administrative support people on resource-critical tasks, you may have found an easy way to shorten your project. In most cases, these people can and should be taken off the RCP. After all, they are managing or supporting the real critical resources (or at least that is what they are supposed to do).

We discussed the first eight methods starting on page 448; we will discuss the remainder of them next.

Reallocating the Best Resources to the Most Critical Tasks

This is the best and most basic principle to apply when trying to find the shortest schedule possible while keeping quality up and cost down. Only after you have created the detailed schedule and leveled the workloads, do you have a better idea which tasks are driving your project duration. These are the resource-critical tasks. As soon as you know that, you should ask yourself: *Have I assigned my best resources to my most critical tasks?* If you review your current resource-critical tasks and see resources working on them who are not the fastest to create quality deliverables, you have an opportunity to shorten your project duration by moving your best resources to these tasks. In the illustration the project manager has reassigned his best resources, Jack, Paula and Rino, to the resource-critical tasks.

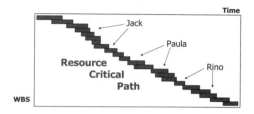

Increasing Assignment Units

When you notice that a resource is working half-time on a critical task, you can finish the task earlier if you can get the resource to temporarily work full-time on it. Again, the right task type has to be applied if you want to see the duration decrease. The task type has to be fixed work. If the work takes 10 person days and Harry could work full-time instead of half-time on it, he would finish the task twice as fast, as depicted in the illustration. You might say that you will not be able to get Harry full-time when you need to ask another project manager, but don't forget that when Harry is done on your task, he is now full-time available instead of half-time for that other project manager.

1. In the Gantt Chart, select a resource-critical task.

2. Choose **Window, Split** to display the **Task Form** at the bottom of the screen:

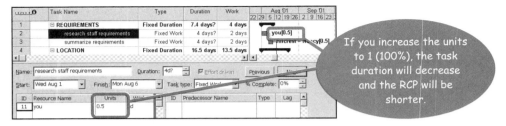

3. Determine which assignment drives the duration of the task if more than one resource is assigned to the task.

4. Select from the list **Task type** Fixed Units the type **Fixed Work** and click OK . This assures that MS Project will shorten the duration when you increase the resource units.

5. Increase the resource units on the task so that the resource works full-time on the critical task. Click OK ; the duration should be decreased.

Assigning Overtime Hours

If you can get resources to put in overtime, critical tasks can often be finished earlier. In the illustration, the second bar shows a shorter duration. Two situations can arise:

◆ If overtime will not be charged to the project, then change the resource calendar of that particular resource. You can increase the working hours or change holidays to working days. You can compensate by giving the resource time off later.

Harry: 40h

Harry: 30h + 10h overtime

◆ If overtime will be charged to the project at a higher overtime rate, then overtime should be entered in the overtime field (**Ovt. Work**) in the Task Form. The cost of the project will increase. The detailed steps are:

1. Select a resource-critical task.

2. Pull up the **Task Form** in the bottom pane and choose **Format, Detail, Resource Work** to display the **Ovt. Work** field. The form should now look like:

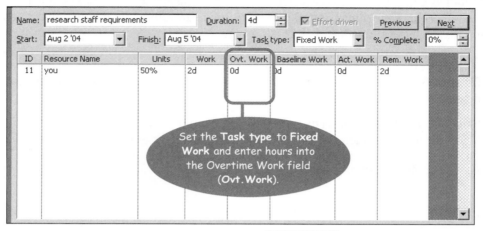

3. Set the **Task type** to **Fixed Work** and click ⬚ OK ⬚.

4. Determine which resource drives the duration of the task, and enter the overtime hours to be worked in the field **Ovt. Work**.

5. Click ⬚ OK ⬚; MS Project schedules the hours worked in overtime outside the regular working time and automatically calculates a shorter duration.

Do not lower the original work estimate; MS Project subtracts overtime from the original estimate before calculating the new duration.

Adding Noncritical Resources

Two resources can normally finish a task faster than one resource. When you add a resource, the duration will decrease, but it will only decrease if you have the right task type applied to the task before adding the resource. When you add a resource to a fixed work task, the same amount of work is now performed by two resources and can be done twice as fast. MS Project will calculate this for you.

Let's think about what happens in practice. When you hire new resources, you have to train them. You would typically take your best resources off their crunching to train the new ones. At first, you will see a short-term decrease in the rate of progress hoping that, in the longer term, the progress accelerates. For this reason we have marked this method with a "?"for the *Time* dimension in the table. Look carefully at your situation to see if adding resources would indeed help.

1. Select a resource-critical task.

2. Choose **Window, Split** to pull up the **Task Form** in the bottom of the screen and determine which resource drives the duration of the task.

3. Select from the list **Task type** Fixed Units ▼ the type **Fixed Work**; this ensures that MS Project will shorten the duration when a resource is added. Click OK .

4. Assign another resource and click OK ; the duration should decrease.

Replacing Critical Resources

If you replace a *critical resource* with a noncritical resource, it may be possible to schedule more tasks in parallel. In the illustration, Ted replaces critical Harry on the second task, which can now be done in parallel with the first one. The gain in time equals the duration of the second task.

Some people argue that you cannot substitute critical resources; otherwise they would not be critical (as in *important*). Remember that the word *critical* has a different meaning in project management. *Critical* does not mean that the resource is important to the task. It merely means that the resource is driving the project duration. In fact, the resource could be a second-choice resource, and it is not a good idea to have your project duration be driven by second-choice resources if you are working against time. Your project will take long enough with first-choice resources. That is why we started by having you check if you applied your best resources to your most critical tasks.

1. In the Gantt Chart select a resource-critical task on which you can replace a critical resource.

2. Choose **Window, Split** to display the Task Form at the bottom of the screen.

3. Click on the name of the critical resource in the Task Form and use the list
   ☐ ▾ to select the substitute resource.

4. Click ▢ OK ▢ .

If you prefer to use the **Assign Resources** dialog instead:

1. Click **Assign Resources** on the **Standard** toolbar, and the floating dialog
   appears:

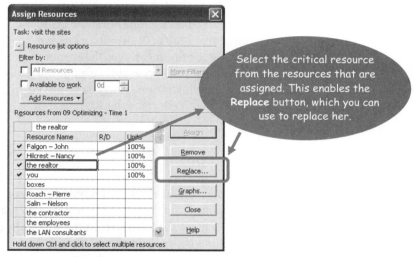

2. Click on the critical resource in the **Assign Resources** dialog.

3. Click ▢ Replace... ▢ ; the **Replace Resource** dialog overlays the Assign Resources
   dialog.

4. Click on the replacement resource, and click ▢ OK ▢ .

Level your schedule again and keep the change if the duration of the project decreased;
otherwise, return to the previous version by closing the schedule without saving.

Removing a Critical Resource When Multiple Are Assigned

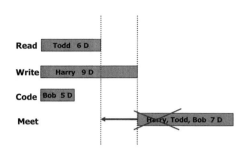

If there are multiple people working on a task, and one of them is a critical resource who has a lot of other work at the same time, you should ask yourself how important the involvement of the critical resource is on this task. If the other people could do without the critical resource, you should consider removing the critical resource from the task. Again, a *critical* resource does not mean that the resource is important for the successful completion of the task. In the illustration, Harry is removed from the task, which shortens the RCP.

Postponing Vacations to After the Deadline

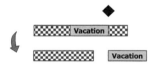

If you can convince your resource to postpone a vacation until after a critical deadline, you may be able to meet the deadline. In the illustration, the deadline is depicted as a diamond. The vacation happens to be scheduled just before the deadline. If it can be moved, the deadline can be met. It is not uncommon for vacations to happen just before deadlines, since projects tend to shift back and forth, whereas vacations don't. Also, some resources seem to have a talent for planning their vacations just before deadlines. The detailed steps for moving vacations are next.

1. Choose **Tools, Change Working Time…**; the **Change Working Time** dialog appears:

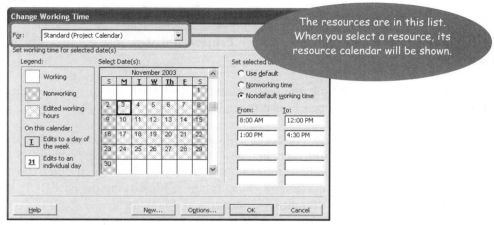

2. Under **For**: `Standard (Project Calendar)` ▾ select the resource.

3. Move the vacation for this resource to later dates after the deadline. Select the current dates for the vacation by dragging over them and then select ⊙ **Use default**. Then select the new vacation dates and select ⊙ **Nonworking time**.

4. Click `OK`. The schedule should now be shorter.

Considering the Impacts

1. Check the workloads and level them
2. Highlight the Resource Critical Path (RCP)
3. Find the most critical resource
4. Make a change on it
5. *Consider impacts on quality, scope, time, cost and resources*
6. *Decide whether you want to keep the change*
7. Repeat steps 3 - 7

After making changes, you have to consider the impacts on *quality*, *scope*, *time*, *cost* and *resource workload* (see the process box on the left). You will have to evaluate the impact on quality and scope yourself. The impact on time and cost can be concluded from the project statistics dialog.

To display the statistics dialog, choose **Project, Project Information,** `Statistics…`. You will save some mouse clicks if you display the **Tracking** toolbar, which has a tool on it to display this dialog.

Right-click on any toolbar and choose **Tracking** from the pop-up menu. The **Tracking** toolbar is displayed:

The dialog is now available with one click on **Project Statistics** -∿- , the first tool on the **Tracking** toolbar.

You can now see how much time you have gained, and whether it is worth any sacrifices you may have made on the scope of the project or the quality of the deliverables.

Whenever you make a change to a resource-critical task, the workloads may move or change. You can check to see if this created new over-allocations by displaying the Resource Usage view. You may have to level the schedule again and determine the new RCP once more. You could make several changes before identifying the new RCP. It may very well be an entirely different series of tasks at this point.

Before identifying the RCP-tasks again, it is recommended to unmark all resource-critical tasks first. To unmark all, click on the column heading **Marked** and choose **Edit, Clear, Contents** or press Control + Delete . Then run the macro again or enter **Yes** for each task that you find to be resource-critical (see the process on page 502). Optimizing for time, cost and resources is challenging and practitioners are greatly helped now that the RCP can be found automatically.

Simulation of the Resource-Critical Path

We discussed *simulation* of the *Critical Path* on page 460. You can also simulate Resource-Critical Paths in *resource-constrained* schedules. The only thing you need to do in this case is change the leveling to automatic leveling so that the simulation software does not forget to keep the workloads reasonable. Choose **Tools, Level Resources…**, select ⦿ **Automatic** and clear ☐ **Level only within available slack**. This ensures that for each scenario of the schedule the workloads are entirely leveled before the project duration is calculated. As you can imagine, simulating RCPs requires major computing power, so make sure you run this on the fastest computer in your office, or simulate a nice long coffee break…

The reasons why you should consider simulating RCPs are the same as for simulating the Critical Path:
◆ Durations are more likely to extend than shrink. Estimates do not follow a normal distribution, but have a distribution that is typically skewed to the pessimistic side.

◆ The more parallel paths you have, the more delays will compound at the merge points (*path convergence* or *merge bias*).

If you simulate the *RCP*, you have taken care of all three assumptions that cripple the utility of the traditional *Critical Path*: the previous two reasons and the fact that the Critical Path assumes access to unlimited resources. This is what we recommend for *resource-constrained* projects.

Apart from that, there are extra factors that are quantified when you simulate resource-constrained schedules. We referred to these factors previously as *domino effects* (see page 508):

◆ The average effect of fixed date personal vacations on the project duration. It is hard to predict how much the project end date will change when some tasks are moved a little bit. The simulation software will run many scenarios and will eventually average the impact of the hard-date vacations.

◆ The average effect on the project duration of asynchronous working hours of resources: *What overall delay will you experience from some resources working a regular workweek and some a compressed workweek?* This effect is also hard to predict other than through simulation.

◆ When you identify activities that have time risk, you should also identify those activities where exact resource availability is not entirely certain. When you decide what distribution curve you need on those tasks, you can incorporate the likelihood of resource availability in the range of estimates and the curve you choose for these tasks.

The s-curve output from the simulation (see page 462 for an example) will indicate the probability by date for a range of project finish dates. Our experience is that most people tend to underestimate the overall effect of all the factors discussed. We prove this over and over again in classes where we ask participants to estimate the outcome of a simulation on a tiny project while showing them the exact inputs of the simulation. We therefore recommend you quantify the factors we discussed that can throw your schedule off its baseline by simulating your schedules. After all, as a project manager, it is prudent to minimize so-called *known unknowns*. We will still have to deal with enough *unknown unknowns*.

Checks on the Optimized Schedule

Here are checks to verify if you have applied best practices when optimizing your schedule.

Optimizing Workloads

◆ Is the total effort within the person hour budget of the project (if a person hour or person day budget is available)?
You can find the total effort of the project by clicking **Project Statistics** ⌁ on the **Tracking** toolbar and looking in row **Current** and column **Work**.

◆ Are the workloads for the resources reasonable?

◇ We had to set arbitrary limits; the limits may differ for your organization. The workload for individuals should not exceed 150% of their regular availability within any week. The workload should not exceed 120% for periods longer than a week. These upper bounds may differ for your organization. We have arbitrarily set them at these levels to prevent burnout, attrition and dramatic loss of productivity.

◇ The workload of consolidated resources (groups) should not exceed their availability.

◇ The workloads should be fairly smooth, since there are hidden costs involved with erratic workloads. See page 471.

Note that it is not enough to just check if there is any red in the Resource Usage view. MS Project often highlights more resources in red than are truly over-allocated. If there is an over-allocation during only one business hour, the resource will already be shown in red. Use the **Go To Next Overallocation** tool on the **Resource Management** toolbar to check the over-allocations. This tool is more selective and more reliable. However, even this tool does not always find all over-allocations, and it also highlights the 1-hour over-allocations. For more information, see the discussion starting on page 480.

Optimizing Costs

◆ Is the cost modeled using the right fields and in the appropriate way?
See page 344 for a discussion of which fields are right and their appropriate use. The following fields are available in MS Project:

◇ Resource Sheet fields: **Type, Material Label, Standard cost, Overtime cost, Cost per use** and **Accrual**. A resource can also have a **cost rate table**.

◇ Gantt Chart fields: **Fixed cost** and **Fixed cost accrual**.

◆ Is the total cost within the budget of the project (if a cost budget is available)?
You can find the total cost of the project by clicking **Project Statistics** ⩘ on the **Tracking** toolbar and looking in row **Current** and in column **Cost**.

Optimizing Time

◆ Are there as many parallel paths as logically possible in the network of dependencies?
Novice schedulers tend to schedule all tasks in one long sequential chain. In that situation, there are many soft dependencies that make the duration of the project unnecessarily long. When optimizing for time, it is important to schedule in parallel what logically can happen simultaneously.

◆ Are there any unresolved conflicts between the task calendars and resource calendars?
If there are conflicts, the forecasts may be too optimistic. You can find the conflicts by looking in the **Indicators** ❶ column for the icon 📆. See page 290.

◆ Are the deadline dates and other constraints met in the schedule?
You can check this by applying filter **10 IIL Deadlines or Constraints not met**.[82]
It displays tasks with deadlines or constraints that have negative slack. When deadline or constraint dates are not met, the schedule may forecast a project end date that is too optimistic.

◆ Does the schedule have a Critical Path or a Resource-Critical Path?
You can check the Critical Path by applying the **Tracking Gantt** view. This view highlights the Critical Path in red by default.

◇ If a schedule is extended when the workloads are leveled, a Resource-Critical Path needs to be identified. Resource-critical tasks need to be marked manually.

◇ The (Resource) Critical Path can only consist of detail tasks and milestones. It should not contain level-of-effort tasks (overhead tasks or recurring tasks) or summary tasks (since the logic and the resources should be kept on the detail tasks).

[82] This filter can be found in the file *IIL Project 2003 tools to check Orange Belt schedules.MPP* available for download at www.jrosspub.com. Please, click the link *WAV Download Resource Center* to enter the download site.

◆ Does the (Resource) Critical Path provide a complete explanation for the project duration?
You can check the completeness by displaying the (Resource) Critical Path and then checking if it has gaps. Normally, there are no gaps, and every business day has at least one critical task (unless there are lags on critical dependencies). If you find gaps, the (Resource) Critical Path is fragmented, and the tasks that are most critical need to be identified in the schedule. See page 440 for possible causes of Critical Path fragmentation and what to do about them.

Exercises

Review

1. We distinguished three optimization approaches in this chapter: optimizing for time, optimizing for time and cost, and optimizing for time, cost and resources.
   a. What are the main differences between these approaches?
   b. Describe the situations in which you should apply each.
   c. What are common techniques used in each approach?

2. Choose one of four answers. Total slack is:
   a. The amount of time a task can move freely without affecting its successors.
   b. The difference between the late finish date and early finish date of the task.
   c. The amount of time in which the resource has to complete the task.
   d. The difference between the early start of the earliest successor and the early finish date of the task.

3. You receive a schedule and notice that the project finish milestone has a negative **Total Slack** of *–10 days*. In your own words, what does this mean?

4. There are six possible causes for fragmentation of the Critical Path; list four of those six causes.

5. When optimizing for time:
   a. What are the seven process steps for shortening the Critical Path?
   b. What are at least six of the nine possible methods to shorten the Critical Path?

6. One of your team leaders suggests that the duration of one of her critical tasks could be decreased if you can provide her with more people to do the work. What factors should you consider?

7. What is Monte Carlo simulation? What benefits can project managers derive from simulating their schedules?

8. What methods are available to decrease the cost of a project? Give at least four of the eight methods discussed.

9. Will the eventual actual cost of smooth workloads be higher or lower compared to erratic workloads? Why?

10. If you have MS Project level the workloads in your schedule, would the project duration be longer or shorter than if you leveled the workloads yourself? Why?

11. There are many ways to level workloads manually. Name at least eight ways.

12. What is the best view in MS Project to level the workloads manually?

13. What three scenarios can MS Project create for you when leveling the workloads? What is the nice-to-know thing from each scenario? Why?

14. In your own words, how does MS Project leveling affect the calculation and the display of the Critical Path?

15. Describe one of the two processes to identify the Resource-Critical Path. What is the major disadvantage of this process?

16. We discussed five reasons why finding the Resource-Critical Path might be a good idea. Name three.

17. There are 15 methods with which you can shorten the Resource-Critical Path. Name as many as you can.

18. Why is the s-curve of a simulated Resource-Critical Path the most reliable information you can present to executives about resource-constrained projects?

19. A project is experiencing a lack of progress during execution.
    a. How would you determine which resources you should ask to work overtime in order to make up the slippage? They will not be paid a higher rate for overtime.
    b. What menu items do you need to choose and what mouse-clicks do you need to make to enter overtime into MS Project?

Relocation Project — Understanding the Gantt Chart

1. Open the file *09 Optimizing — Time 1.MPP* available for download at www.jrosspub.com. Please, click the link *WAV Download Resource Center* to enter the download site. Display the field **Total Slack** in the spreadsheet of the Gantt Chart.

2. Is the total slack expressed in calendar days, business days or person days?

3. Why does the negative slack change from task 13 *meet to discuss contract* to task 14 *revise the schedule*? Hint: Nancy is on holiday in the third full week in August.

4. Why does the negative slack change from task 20 *paint* to task 23 *install LAN*? Hint: there is a task with an elapsed duration between them.

5. Why does the negative slack change from task 25 *facility remodeled* to task 29 *move*? Hint: there is a deadline on task 25.

6. Why does the negative slack change from task 29 *move* to task 30 *unpack*? Hint: the movers only work on the weekend.

Relocation Project — Shorten the Duration

In this exercise, you will use the optimizing for time approach.

1. Open the file *09 Optimizing — Time 1.MPP* available for download at www.jrosspub.com. Please, click the link *WAV Download Resource Center* to enter the download site. Currently, the forecasted finish date is November 16, but your CEO insists that the office should be moved by November 1.

2. Display the Critical Path in your schedule. Make sure you understand all the total slack numbers on each task. If you do not understand the total slack numbers, first do the previous exercise *Relocation Project — Understanding the Gantt Chart*.

3. The objective of this exercise is to bring down the duration (time) of the project as much as is reasonably possible. Use the methods that were discussed in this chapter to get ideas. Come up with your own ways to bring down the duration of the project as much as you can. Try them out and see how much time they save. Try to:

   ◇ make the project end date as early as possible, or

   ◇ if you have a hard constraint on the project end milestone, make the **Total Slack** on the project end milestone *new location opened* positive and as large as possible.

4. Try your ideas out and see if they work. If you keep a change, make a note of it, in order to compare your measures against the solution.

5. Prepare to defend the changes you made in the schedule to the other students.

6. Compare your results against the ideas we will discuss in the next exercise.

Relocation Project — Ideas for Shortening the Duration

In this exercise you will use the optimizing for time approach.

1. To illustrate how a schedule can be optimized, we will explain a complete optimization that will bring the project duration down to less than half the original duration! A similar reduction can be achieved in many projects by applying all of the techniques discussed in this chapter.

2. Open the file *09 Optimizing — Time 2.MPP* available for download at www.jrosspub.com. Please, click the link *WAV Download Resource Center* to enter the download site. The current duration of the project is 74 days.

3. When sorting the tasks on duration, it shows that the tasks *drying of paint, install LAN, relocate walls* and *lay carpet* are the longest tasks. All of these tasks are critical and seem to be a good starting point to find time in the schedule.

Enter the following changes to shorten the relocation project:

4. Create an overlap in the dependency on *relocate walls*, so that *install electric wiring* is done mostly in parallel with relocating the walls. Overlap *relocate walls* and *install electric wiring* with a finish-to-finish plus 1 day dependency. The electricians can start on a wall as soon as the carpenters have it up. What is the duration of the project now?

5. Cut the dependency between *lay carpet* and *install cabinetry* and cut the dependency between *lay carpet* and *install LAN*. Instead, make *lay carpet* dependent on *drying of paint*. Create new dependencies from *install cabinetry* and *install LAN* to *facility remodeled* to get rid of the loose ends in the network. You can lay carpet in parallel with installing cabinets and installing the LAN. What is the duration of the project now?

6. Notice that the Critical Path is fragmented at this point. We have to make sure that we continue making changes to critical tasks only. Make the necessary changes to the schedule in such a way that you see the most critical path in the schedule again. Change the type of dependency between *install electric wiring* and *paint* to finish-to-finish plus 1 day. The painters can start on a wall as soon as the electricians finish it. What is the duration of the project now? Why did the duration not come down?

7. Change the type of dependency between *paint* and *drying of paint* to finish-to-finish plus 1 day. The paint starts drying as soon as the first wall is painted. What is the duration of the project now?

8. Change the type of dependency between *facility remodeled* and *pack* into finish-to-finish. The packing should ideally be ready when the facility is ready. What is the duration of the project now?

9. Cut the dependency between *location selected* and *select the contractor*, and make *select the contractor* dependent on *evaluate the sites*. Create a new dependency between *location selected* and *meet to discuss contract*. You can select the contractor when you have an idea which location will be chosen. What is the duration of the project now?

10. Get rid of the Start No Earlier Than constraint on task 8 *meet to select the location* and arrange for a conference call or internet meeting with the CEO, who is abroad. What is the duration of the project now?

11. Overlap *summarize requirements* and *research staff requirements* finish-to-finish plus 1 day. You can start summarizing as soon as you receive some completed questionnaires. What is the duration of the project now? Notice that the duration did not come down, because task 13 was split even further, because of Nancy's holiday.

12. Get rid of the lag on the dependency between task 12 *select the contractor* and task 13 *meet to discuss contract*. Make sure that you give advance notice of 5 days to the participants you expect at the meeting, so the 5-day time frame for calling the meeting is not needed anymore. What is the duration of the project now?

13. Change the task *install LAN* into a summary task by adding the following subtasks:
   install LAN cables (20 d of Fixed Work, predecessor *relocate walls),*
   install LAN hardware (20 d of Fixed Work, predecessor *install LAN cables),* and
   install LAN operating system (20 d of Fixed Work, predecessor *install LAN hardware,* successor *facility remodeled).*
   Cut the dependencies between *drying of paint* and *install LAN* and between *install LAN* and *facility remodeled*. Keep the resource units at 5 units for all subtasks; remove the *LAN consultants* from the summary task. The result is a more refined and shorter schedule. What is the duration of the project now?

14. Increase the resource units of the *contractor* for the task *lay carpet* from 6 to 12. This decreases the duration of *lay carpet* to 5 days, which is now done entirely in parallel with *install cabinetry*. What is the duration of the project now?

15. You decide to ask the *LAN consultants* to work with 8 consultants instead of 5. Change all assignments of the *LAN consultants* to 8 units on the subtasks of *install LAN*. This will reduce the duration of the subtasks to 2.5 days. What is the duration of the project now?

16. MS Project changed the duration of the task *meet to discuss contract*, because of Nancy's vacation in the third week of August. Set its duration back to 1 day. What is the duration of the project now?

Please answer the following questions:

17. Check the duration of the project. We have reduced it from 74 to 31 days! This is <u>less than half</u> of the original duration and most changes are quite defendable. You have seen here an example of how you can find time in your project schedule if you create a dynamic model of your project in the first place. Could you apply similar methods to your own project schedule?

18. Were trade-offs made against the scope or quality of this project? What are they? Would you undo some proposed changes? Why?

19. If you arrived at a different final duration, find the differences between your file and the solution file *09 Optimizing — Time 3.MPP* available for download at www.jrosspub.com. Please, click the link *WAV Download Resource Center* to enter the download site. See page 675 of this book for an automated way of comparing and reporting differences between two versions of one schedule.

Relocation Project — Lowering the Cost

In this exercise, you will use the optimizing for time and cost approach.

1. Open the file *09 Optimizing — Time Cost 1.MPP* available for download at www.jrosspub.com. Please, click the link *WAV Download Resource Center* to enter the download site.

2. The objective now is to bring down the cost of the project while maintaining or decreasing the duration. Use the methods that were discussed in this chapter to get ideas. Come up with your own ways to bring down the cost of the project as far as you can. Try them out and see how much money they save.

3. Log each change and the total cost of the project after each change you keep.

4. Prepare to defend the changes you made to the other students.

5. Compare your results against the ideas that we will discuss in the next exercise.

Relocation Project — Ideas for Lowering the Cost

In this exercise you will use the optimizing for time and cost approach. Open the file *09 Optimizing — Time Cost 2.MPP* available for download at www.jrosspub.com. Please, click the link *WAV Download Resource Center* to enter the download site.

You found some new resources:

Name	Type	Position	Function	Max. Units	Std. Rate	Accrue at
Carpeteers	*Work*	*contractor*	*external*	*20*	*$140/d*	*End*
cablers	*Work*	*contractor*	*external*	*5*	*$40/h*	*End*
students	*Work*	*contractor*	*external*	*5*	*$80/d*	*End*

You find a specialized carpet company, *Carpeteers* that is willing to do the job. Create this new resource. Carpeteers estimates the work will take 30 person days, and they will do it with 10 employees. Reassign the task *lay carpet* to the new resource *Carpeteers*:

1. What is the current cost of the project?
   What is the current cost for the task *lay carpet*?
   What is the current duration of the project?

2. Reassign the task to Carpeteers.
   What is the new forecasted cost for *lay carpet*?
   How much did we save on this task?

3. What is the new total cost of the project?

4. What is the new total duration of the project? Why is it lower?

5. What consequences does this change have for the scope and quality of the project? Why?

6. Would you keep the reassignment to *Carpeteers*?

Enter the following additional changes to lower the cost of the relocation project:

7. Delete the task *revise the schedule;* it is a nice-to-have task. How much is the total cost now?

8. Delete the task *select the realtor* and hire the one you know. Is there a possible trade-off in doing this? How much is the total cost now?

9. Delete the task *select the contractor* and hire the one you know. Add a new dependency to keep the original logic. Is there a possible trade-off in doing this? How much is the total cost now?

10. Make the task *install LAN* a summary task by adding the following subtasks: *install LAN cables (20 d of Fixed Work,* predecessor *relocate walls)*, *install LAN hardware (20 d of Fixed Work,* predecessor *install LAN cables)*, and *install LAN operating system (20 d of Fixed Work,* predecessor *install LAN hardware,* successor *lay carpet)*.
    Keep the resource units at 5 units for all subtasks; remove the *LAN consultants* from the summary task. Cut the dependencies between *drying of paint* and *install LAN*. You ask the LAN consultants to use cheaper resources to do the cabling. They offer you specialized *cablers*, as shown in the table at the beginning of the question. Reassign the task *install LAN cables* to the cheaper resource *cablers*. How much is the total cost now?

11. You ask the contractor to come up with sharper estimates to save cost. He offers to provide students who can help the carpenters relocate walls. He proposes to replace half of the carpenters with *students* as per the table. Are there possible trade-offs on time, scope or quality? How much is the total cost now?

12. In your search to save cost you decide that the 35 employees should pack all their stuff in 1 day instead of 2 days. Are there possible trade-offs on time, scope or quality? How much is the total cost now?

Please, answer the following questions:

13. The cost should now be $97,950.00, down from $129,125.00. If you found a different answer, compare it with the solution file *09 Optimizing – Time Cost 3.MPP* available for download at www.jrosspub.com. Please, click the link *WAV Download Resource Center* to enter the download site. See page 675 of this book for an automated way of comparing and reporting differences between two versions of one schedule. Make sure you insert column **Cost** before comparing.

14. What is the forecasted duration for the project now?

15. Are there trade-offs in the scope or quality? What are they? Will you keep the proposed changes? Why?

Relocation Project — Leveling Manually

In this exercise, you will use the optimizing for time, cost and resources approach and level the workloads manually.

1. Open the file *09 Optimizing — Time Cost Resources 1.MPP* available for download at www.jrosspub.com. Please, click the link *WAV Download Resource Center* to enter the download site.

2. Set **Tools, Level Resources...** to ⊙ **Manual** leveling.

3. Which view do you recommend to check the over-allocations?

4. You find that a few resources are over-allocated: *Nancy Hilcrest* and you. What changes would you recommend to level the workloads manually for Nancy?

5. What changes would you recommend to level the workloads manually for your own over-allocation?

6. Compare your file with the solution file *09 Optimizing — Time Cost Resources 2.MPP* available for download at www.jrosspub.com. Please, click the link *WAV Download Resource Center* to enter the download site. See page 675 of this book for an automated way of comparing and reporting differences between two versions of one schedule.

Relocation Project — Leveling Automatically

In this exercise you will try the optimizing for time, cost and resources approach and level the workloads automatically.

1. Open the file *09 Optimizing — Time Cost Resources 3.MPP* available for download at www.jrosspub.com. Please, click the link *WAV Download Resource Center* to enter the download site. What is the current duration of the project?

2. Use automatic leveling to resolve all the over-allocations. Which view do you recommend for analyzing the results of automatic workload leveling?

3. Which field does MS Project change when leveling automatically?

4. Which tasks were delayed? By how much?

5. Has MS Project increased the duration of the project? Why?

6. Are there any trade-offs in scope or quality? Would you keep the solution proposed by MS Project? Why?

7. Compare your file with the solution file *09 Optimizing — Time Cost Resources 4.MPP* available for download at www.jrosspub.com. Please, click the link *WAV Download Resource Center* to enter the download site. See page 675 of this book for an automated way of comparing and reporting differences between two versions of one schedule. Make sure you insert the column **Leveling Delay** before comparing.

Intranet Project — Shorten the Duration

In this exercise, you will use the optimizing for time, cost and resources approach using the Resource-Critical Path (RCP).

1. Open the file *09 Optimizing — Time Cost Resources 5 — Intranet Project.MPP* available for download at www.jrosspub.com. Please, click the link *WAV Download Resource Center* to enter the download site.[83]

2. How many resources do you need by month?

3. Would you level this schedule manually? Why?

4. What is the current duration of the project?

5. Level the workloads automatically. What is the duration now?

6. Check the Critical Path in the schedule. Does it make sense?

7. Mark the RCP by entering **Yes** in the field **Marked** for each resource-critical task.

8. While in the Tracking Gantt view, choose **Format, Bar Styles** and change the settings to show a blue bar for all **Normal** tasks (critical and noncritical) and a red task bar for all **Normal, Marked** tasks (instead of for **Critical** tasks). You should now see red task bars for all tasks on the RCP in the schedule.

9. Compare your file against the file *09 Optimizing — Time Cost Resources 6 — Intranet Project.MPP* available for download at www.jrosspub.com. Please, click the link *WAV Download Resource Center* to enter the download site; the files should look the same. See page 675 of this book for an automated way of comparing and reporting differences between two versions of one schedule.

10. The objective now is to bring down the duration of the project as much as possible (time), while maintaining or lowering the cost and keeping the workload reasonable (resources). Bring down the duration by shortening the RCP. Log each change and the resulting total duration of the project for each change you decide to keep. Make a few changes before you find the new RCP. Prepare to defend the changes you made to the other students.

11. Compare your results against the ideas that we will discuss in the next exercise.

---

[83] We will use a different project here, because we saw in the previous exercise that the workload leveling did not affect the project end date. In other words, the Critical Path is identical to the Resource-Critical Path.

Intranet Project — Ideas for Shortening the Duration

In this exercise, you will use the Optimizing for Time, Cost and Resources approach using the Resource-Critical Path (RCP).

1. Open the file *09 Optimizing — Time Cost Resources 6 — Intranet Project.MPP* available for download at www.jrosspub.com. Please, click the link *WAV Download Resource Center* to enter the download site.

2. What is the current duration and cost of this project schedule?

The challenge is to find methods to decrease the duration of the project that do not cost more and that do not cause new work overloads. You have to focus on the resource-critical tasks on the RCP. The following changes are examples of such measures. Enter these changes into the schedule:

3. It is somewhat peculiar that the project manager is on the RCP. We should be able to take him off the RCP. In general, a project manager should never be on the Critical Path, except in very small projects perhaps where he does tasks as a resource as well. Cut the dependency between task *9 Define specific functionality* and task *10 Develop project plan*. Give the task *10 Develop project plan* a new predecessor task *3 Define user requirements*. Give task *9 Define specific functionality* a new successor, task *11 System designed*. Is task 10 still resource-critical? Are there new work overloads? Level the workloads again. Determine the new RCP. What are the duration and cost of the project now?

4. Notice that the *Roll-out manager* is working only 50% on task: 50 *Communicate roll out plan to users*. Increase this to 100% while keeping the work on the task the same. Level the workloads in the schedule again. What is the duration and cost of the project now?

5. You see that the longest resource-critical tasks are tasks *36 Develop web pages* and *37 Develop any custom functionality*. They take 20 days in the current schedule. If you can find an extra web designer for task 37 *Develop any custom functionality*, you can schedule those two tasks in parallel. You ask the resource manager for an extra designer and you get one for that one task. Create a new resource *Web Designer 2*, with the same rate as the first designer and assign her to task 37 *Develop any custom functionality*. Set a new dependency between task 35 *Determine development tool* and 37 *Develop any custom functionality*. Are there new work overloads? Level the workloads again. Determine the new RCP. What are the duration and cost of the project now? Are tasks 36 and 37 still resource-critical?

Please answer the following questions:

6. We started with a schedule of 66 days that was not leveled. We then leveled and ended up with 114 days. We then shortened the schedule again to 90 days without increasing the cost and without (new) work overloads. Does the current RCP make sense? Why?

7. Compare your file with the solution file *09 Optimizing — Time Cost Resources 7 — Intranet Project.MPP* available for download at www.jrosspub.com. Please, click the link *WAV Download Resource Center* to enter the download site. See page 675 of this book for an automated way of comparing and reporting differences between two versions of one schedule.

Case Study — Multinational IT

The client is the IT department of a large multinational company. Recently, the organization made the corporate decision to use MS Project for all its projects. It used Project Workbench before. The project managers still work very much as they did when they used Project Workbench; they like to enter actual hours worked and remaining hours. The organization has a separate time sheet system that reports actual hours worked by project or by category over many projects (e.g., "maintenance").

Managers in the IT department are using the MS Project schedules as checklists. Many of them become frustrated using the scheduling features of MS Project and revert to using Excel instead. When this was acknowledged, the client decided to organize basic training in MS Project using a local training provider. Since the training, one year ago, the situation has not improved a lot, and many people are still using Excel. The ones who use MS Project are not taking advantage of all the features of the application.

In interviews with several users you find that they experience the following problems:

◆ Double data entry of actual hours into the time sheet system and into the project scheduler.

◆ IT executives impose tight deadlines and use cost-payback arguments to successfully defend these challenging project deadlines. Your clients, the IT project managers, told you, "*We have not been able to prove that these deadlines are not feasible.*"

◆ The organization has a matrix structure; many resources are working part-time on the project and are shared across several projects. There are many over-allocations, so many in fact that the project managers were advised by Project Workbench consultants to use AutoSchedule (automatic workload leveling), after which they should try to shorten the schedule.

◆ The organization experiences ripple effects between projects; a change in one project can have impacts on other schedules.
◆ Most projects are independent and do not have cross-project dependencies.
◆ The training did not teach participants how to apply MS Project to their own real life projects.

There is a need for more guidance for the project managers to lower the threshold using the more beneficial features of MS Project.

QUESTIONS

1. Which feature of MS Project should be used to address the ripple effect across projects?

2. What optimization method do you recommend in this situation? Why?

3. Will they then be able to prove that the imposed deadlines are not feasible?

4. What would you recommend in order to:

   ◇ Get more project managers to use MS Project?

   ◇ Get project managers to use more features of MS Project?

Troubleshooting

1. Open the file *09 Sure Critical.MPP* available for download at www.jrosspub.com. Please, click the link *WAV Download Resource Center* to enter the download site. Why are only tasks 3, 4, 5 and 6 shown as critical and not 1 and 2?

2. Open the file *09 Why Overload.MPP* available for download at www.jrosspub.com. Please, click the link *WAV Download Resource Center* to enter the download site. Why is the resource *you* over-allocated in the week of September 2 to 9 with only 1.5 days of work for the entire week?

3. Open the file *09 MSF Application Development.MPP* available for download at www.jrosspub.com. Please, click the link *WAV Download Resource Center* to enter the download site. Level the workloads completely. You may be prompted that MS Project cannot solve an over-allocation; choose **Skip All**. Why is the project duration now extended to the year 2049?

Chapter 10 Reporting

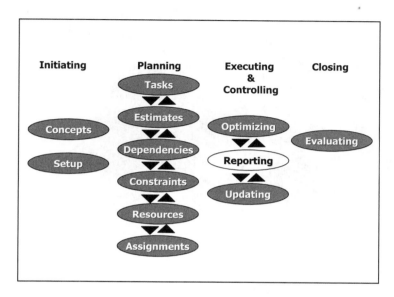

In the previous chapter, we ensured that the schedule meets the project deadline and that the cost stays within the budget. We are now ready to publish the schedule to the world.

After reading this chapter you will:
- ◆ be able to determine if you need to hide the buffer in your schedule
- ◆ be able to print your schedule
- ◆ know the standard reports of MS Project
- ◆ be able to customize a standard report
- ◆ be able to customize views for reporting with a custom table, filter and grouping
- ◆ know how to create one-page reports always
- ◆ be able to check if you used scheduling best practices for project reporting
- ◆ know how to create some useful and hard-to-get-at reports
- ◆ know how to use the organizer to copy custom objects between projects

Micro-Management

Nob was in a good mood. Nob was grinning from ear to ear. He had just gotten the best project he had ever been assigned. Nob told Bob: "The project charter specifies very little oversight by executives. In fact, the charter does not specify any reporting or reporting period. It looks like I can just do what I want, and that is exactly what I am going to do."

Bob just smiled and thought to himself, "And you see that as your best project, okay…"

A few months later when Bob met Nob, Bob asked: "What happened to the project from heaven?" Nob lowered his head and voice: "Well, I'm still working on it, but the project sponsor is in my office and on my back all the time! He walks in every day and wants to know what is going on. He talks to my team members as well. He is the micro-manager from hell!"

Bob asked: "How often do you submit reports to him?" Nob scoffed and said the sponsor never asked for one, so he does not get any. Bob smiled: "How can the sponsor keep track of your project, if you don't provide him a written status regularly? A verbal update every day, will keep the micro-manager away!"

Project Communications Management

Is This a Peak Performance?

Performance measurement by itself is impossible; of course you can measure the quality of the performance, but you are always measuring the quality of the planning as well. Both the baseline and the performance relative to the baseline are the products of the project manager. For example, if a project manager deliberately pads his schedule by 50% and then boasts that he delivered his project in 30% less time; is this good performance or poor planning? Does this project manager deserve a raise? In my view, he should be scolded, because he could have saved his organization a lot of money and time. Executives can't measure performance by itself; they need to measure the quality of the planning as well. When they measure the quality of planning, they will move their position as observer and come to a different conclusion, which is known as *parallax* in astronomy. Executives need to be involved in the planning phase of the project as well and make sure they get a solid baseline. With a good baseline, the executive can delegate the *execution phase* entirely and measure the real performance.

Therefore, the project manager has to deal with an important dilemma: *Will I hide my time buffer or not?*

Hiding Your Time Buffer?

When we optimized the schedule in the previous chapter, you may have found a healthy amount of time as a buffer to accomplish the deadline. The dilemma of whether or not to hide the buffer can be one of the most difficult choices. As a project manager, you are in a double bind here. If you show the buffer, you may lose it. If you hide the buffer, you enter into a game of secrecy, and you may have to do double bookkeeping with your schedule. We recommend you consider the following about upper management:

◆ What is the dominant pulling force in the project?
   Is the project driven by time, cost, quality or availability of resources? What is the interest of upper management? If time is the dominant force, everybody will be scrutinizing your schedule to find time. The more people who look for it, the less the chance you will succeed in keeping it hidden. In many software and hardware projects, the sole focus is to be the first one to market. If that is the case, you will not likely succeed in keeping the time buffer for yourself.

◆ How mature is upper management in terms of project management?
Does management accept that, as the project manager, you should own a buffer to meet the hard deadlines? It is generally accepted project management practice that project managers who are responsible for meeting hard deadlines own a buffer in their projects. However, greedy executives may try to confiscate it.

◆ How centralized is your organization?
Your organization may be very centralized. If that is the case, you will likely lose visible buffers. Project management thrives well in a decentralized organization. In these organizations, executives establish a contract with the project manager through a project charter, scope statement and project plan. These formal documents should clearly spell out the rules of the game. If your organization doesn't use these formal project documents, you risk losing buffers that you make visible. The performance contract is not clear.

Similar questions can be asked when it comes to the client if you are a manager of *external projects* where the client of the project is external to your organization, which is typical for consulting companies:

◆ What is the dominant pulling force in the project?
What is the interest of the client? Does the client want the project product as soon as possible, or is high quality or low cost more important?

◆ How mature is the client in terms of project management?

◆ What is the type of contract with the client?
In dealing with the client it is important to be aware of the type of contract that is established. If it is a time and materials contract, the client will be looking over your shoulder, and you won't need a buffer at all. If the contract is a firm fixed price contract, you will need a buffer that you don't need to show to the client. You can hide it from the client, as well as your profit margin.

Methods to Hide the Time Buffer

If you are in an *external project* on a firm fixed price contract, you should hide your time and cost buffer from the client, but not from your own executives. If you are in an *internal project* and you deem it impossible to show and defend your time buffer to your executives, you could hide it in your schedule. The following are methods to hide a buffer. Most of them are the opposite of the optimizing methods we discussed in the previous chapter. They are ranked in order of ascending sophistication. The likelihood that a buffer will stay hidden from examining eyes increases as you move down the list:

1. **Overestimate lags**

   Lags are gaps between task bars of dependent tasks. Lags are used to model waiting time that is out of your control, as when you are waiting to receive a construction permit. It is smart to estimate these lags on the (very) safe side. For the how-to, see page 223. However, they can easily be noticed in the Gantt Chart. It is cost neutral.

2. **Insert extra holidays in the project calendar**

   You can insert extra common holidays in the project calendar. The task bars that span these days will simply stretch. This can be noticed in the Gantt Chart by sharp analysts. For the how-to, see page 120. It is cost neutral.

3. **Decrease the working hours in the project calendar**

   This is frequently applied. Managers know that resources are not focused and productive 8 hours a day, even though their workday is 8 hours. In the project calendar, start the business day later or finish it earlier. For the how-to, see page 118. This may make the calendar inconsistent with the **Hours per day** setting in **Tools, Options, Calendar**. Durations may start to show decimals and will be obvious. Therefore, use caution with this method. It is cost neutral.

4. **Ignore the benefits of learning curves**

   If you have repetitive activities in your schedule, you will likely benefit from the decreasing learning time with every repeat. Your estimate should be lower with every repeat. If you ignore this effect of the learning curve, you are in fact keeping a buffer in your schedule. See page 200. The cost of the project will also be overstated with this method.

5. **Introduce ramp-up and wind-down factors**

   If your resources are involved in more than one project at a time, your resources will be less productive, because of setting up and closing down work when moving from project to project. You can include this time in your estimates, which will also affect the cost. See page 195.

6. **Introduce distraction factors for high-focus tasks**

   Certain tasks require your full focus, but the world around will not stop spinning. Writing a report or a book is a situation in which most people need to concentrate fully and need consecutive, uninterrupted time. Dear colleagues, this is why you always get my voicemail when I am writing. Increase the estimate on these tasks with a distraction factor, which will affect the cost as well.

7. **Introduce extra revision cycles**
Every revision cycle has two tasks: *revise* and *modify*. For writing, you could add tasks like *edit* and *rewrite*. You might even get away with another cycle of *re-edit* and *re-re-write*, but you may want to call it something else. For the how-to of inserting tasks, see page 161. Inserting extra revision cycles increases the cost as well, but could have a positive impact on quality.

8. **Keep maximum units of resources low**
In a resource-constrained schedule you can influence the forecasted project end date by changing the availability of resources (**Max. Units**). If you are not entirely sure how many you will receive, you can create a time buffer in your schedule if you keep the maximum units on the low and safe side. For the how-to, see page 334. This will only affect the duration of the project, not the cost.

9. **Assign one scarce expert to more tasks than needed**
If one expert is in great demand, she will likely drive the project finish date. If you *assign* her to more tasks than strictly needed, she will drive out the forecasted finish date even further, thus creating a time buffer for you. It is hard to argue with using the best resource on many tasks and is therefore often effective. For the how-to, see page 386. If the expert is paid at a higher rate than other resources, you are also increasing the cost.

10. **Create extra inconspicuous tasks**
One of my students once confided that he always creates the task *Find alternative resources* in the task list, wherever it is slightly appropriate. I won't mention his name so as not to spoil his fun. Other good ones that are hard to argue with are *Apply quality check* or *Update the project plan*. Who can argue about those? These extra tasks increase the cost as well.

11. **Pad the duration and work estimates**
As one project manager once put it, *To pad or not to pad* is similar to the Shakespearian *To be or not to be*. However, you are entering into a culture of secrecy and padding also increases cost.

12. **Don't use overtime yet**
If you know you can count on your resources working some overtime, don't enter it into the schedule during the planning phase. Whenever your team members work a weekend, the 2 days will be pure gain. For the how-to, see page 516. Be careful with this method if you pay a higher rate for overtime, since the planned cost of the project may be understated, because it is calculated based on regular rates. You may gain time but run over budget.

13. **Set extra soft dependencies**

    Soft dependencies are dependencies that are not absolutely needed, but that can be defended with an argument such as: *"We prefer to do it like this, because it has the following advantage ..."* and you rationalize away. For the how-to, see page 231. This method is cost neutral.

14. **Be pessimistic about material delivery dates**

    When you are dependent upon receiving a shipment before you can do your work, create a delivery milestone on a date that is later than the date you were promised by the supplier. In this way you create some buffer on other people's performance you depend on. Now you face a new dilemma: *Will you tell your supplier?* For the how-to, see page 229. This method is cost neutral.

15. **Insert extra holidays for your critical resources**

    Determine who the most critical resources are in your schedule and insert extra holidays in their resource calendar. For the how-to, see page 330. This cannot be easily seen in the Gantt Chart and is a very sophisticated way of hiding buffer time. This method is cost neutral.

As you may have noticed, all these methods boil down to not fully optimizing your schedule. If you don't use all the methods of optimization or if you don't apply them to their fullest, you may keep a hidden time buffer in your schedule. We recommend you try to optimize your schedule to the maximum first, to be sure about the real amount of buffer you have. Then you can hide it again in other hard to find places if you really need to.

Why You Should Make Buffers Visible in Internal Projects

As we stated before, it is <u>highly preferable</u> to keep the buffer you own visible in your schedule in internal projects. There are several reasons for this:

◆ It is the professional thing to do, because it is generally accepted project management practice that when upper management asks project managers to commit to hard deadlines, project managers are allowed to own time buffers.

◆ The big drawback of hiding time buffers from executives is that it creates a culture of secrecy in *internal projects*. If the different levels of management stop communicating openly with each other, the situation may worsen over time. Ideally, the time and money buffers should be on the table instead of under it. If a project manager habitually hides time buffers and an executive happens to find out, the executive may start cutting time off future schedules for this project manager. In turn, the project manager will then hide bigger buffers in harder to find places. The executive may start slashing the schedules more, making arbitrary cuts. The situation deteriorates in a downward spiral. As a consultant, I have been witness to organizations that continuously play this game, instead of conducting projects in an open and professional manner. If you think you can defend the buffer in your project successfully, we recommend you do that. Openness is greatly preferred over a culture of secrecy that can create a vicious downward spiral.

◆ More importantly, your team members will follow your example as the project manager and start hiding their buffers to you. They will start padding their estimates and their time sheets as their report to you, since you also pad your schedule as you report to executives. Whether you like it or not, you are leading by example. This will make it impossible to come out ahead of schedule, and at best, you will finish on time. More likely, you will finish a little late every time. Finishing a little late every time is typical for a culture of secrecy that may have developed slowly over a long period within your organization. From a statistical point of view, it is abnormal if your internal projects always run a bit late. Statistically, it is normal if several projects run over and several under, some much over and some much under. This is typical for a healthy organization where a culture of openness and integrity reigns.

◆ Last and most important, if project managers start to hide time buffers and money buffers, executives will never get clarity on the true return on investment (ROI), true profit margins and true time-to-market gains. Isn't it neat to know how much you contributed as a project manager to the bottom line? That would be a nice point to talk about during your performance appraisal.

How to Defend Visible Buffers

There are several ways for project managers to defend buffers that are explicitly visible in the schedule and who want to be *professionally responsible*:

◆ Monetary budgets have financial reserves as a generally accepted budgeting practice. Why can't schedules have time reserves?

◆ Create a separate line item for the time buffer in the task list, instead of leaving it as an undefined, gaping hole in your schedule. You can *assign* yourself as the resource, so it becomes clear to everybody that you own it (and this also adds a buffer of effort and cost). Make sure this line item is dependent on the last tasks. Set the project end milestone as its sole successor.

◆ Name the time buffer line item *Time Contingency Reserve* which is a technical term that may impress some to such a degree that they let you keep it, or if they don't understand it, they might be too afraid to ask you what it means, and you will keep it. Or simply call it *TCR* and wait if they ask what that means.

◆ You can split the big buffer into smaller ones that you spread across your schedule. Visually, this will look more acceptable.

◆ Another, entirely scientific, method that will prove that you need a reasonable amount of time buffer in your schedule is *Monte Carlo simulation*. We discussed it on page 460. You can use simulation to create a probability curve of project end dates. When you have the curve, you can decide which probability you feel comfortable with and find out what buffered end date results. This dictates how much time you need as a buffer. Or you can ask upper management with what level of confidence they feel comfortable and quote the corresponding date from the *S-curve*. You then add the buffer as a line item that makes the schedule extend to this date.

◆ If executives still try to steal your time buffer, you may start to feel that you cannot be held responsible any longer for meeting the non-buffered deadline. If that is the case, make it clear that you do not accept this responsibility any longer and that you will just do your best. If deadline accomplishment is an item in your performance appraisal, state clearly that you don't want to see missing this particular deadline brought up in your performance appraisal, and ask for agreement on this. If a verbal understanding did not work last time, ask for this in writing. This will make it perfectly clear that you don't appreciate being made accountable for doing the impossible. Your family and friends don't appreciate it, either.

◆ If all else fails, you can try to provide only reports on such a high level that buffers are not visible at all. One-page milestone reports, for example, don't reveal buffers.

Choosing the Options

There are some options to be well aware of when reporting. For example, you may have noticed questions marks in the duration column. These question marks signify that you did not enter the duration yourself, but had MS Project enter the default duration (*1 day?*) or a calculated duration based on the formula $D * U = W$. MS Project calls this *estimated durations*. I am pretty sure that executives don't appreciate seeing question marks next to all your estimates in the schedule; it decreases their level of confidence and they may start asking questions. You can make the question marks disappear by choosing **Tools, Options, Schedule**:

Tab	Option
Schedule	☑ **Show that tasks have estimated durations** Clear it if you want to hide the question marks in the duration field. Executives may start asking questions if you leave question marks in your reports.
	☑ **New tasks have estimated durations** Clear if you don't want to see question marks for any new tasks you create.
Edit	You can change the time units for **Minutes, Hours, Days, Weeks, Months, and Years** to one character to save space on the screen.

Communication Features in Project 2003

The word *report* refers to a specific feature in MS Project (menu **View, Reports**). I will therefore also use the words *printout*, *output* and *performance report*[84] to refer to what people normally call a *report*.

You can either print a report or print a view to publish your schedule. Since Project 2002, you have a third option to publish your schedule through Project Server on a website with restricted access.

◆ **Reports**
   Several different standard reports are available in MS Project in the
   View, Reports... menu. All reports are table-like with precise, numeric information. Only the reports allow you to print the project calendar and resource calendars. For a detailed discussion, see page 552.

◆ **Views**
   A view is what you see on the screen; MS Project always has a view applied. A printout of a view shows on paper whatever you created on the screen: WYSIWYG (What You See Is What You Get). MS Project is very user-friendly in this respect; rarely will you see differences between screen and paper. You can print any view from the menu except for any of the form views (Task Form, Resource Form and Relationships Diagram). Graphical charts, like the Gantt Chart, Network Diagram and Resource Graph can only be printed through views. And only in views

---

[84] See the PMBOK® Guide, 2004 Edition, published by the PMI.

can you apply the feature of grouping (**Project, Group by**). For a detailed discussion, see page 557.

◆ **Project Server**
Project Server is the companion application for Project 2003 Professional, even though when you realize the magnitude of Project Server you would state it the other way round. It is a separate application that works with MS Project. It allows you to communicate with stakeholders via a website and is therefore the way of the future. Project Server is not only a communication tool; it facilitates *collaboration* and *delegation* as well. For an overview of the reporting features in Project Server, see page 582.

The following table provides a comparison of your reporting options. This may help you determine which option is best suited for you:

Reports	Views	Project Server
Paper based	Paper based	Online
One-way communication	One-way communication	Two-way collaboration
No edits (Print Preview)	Edits possible	Some edits possible
Somewhat customizable	Highly customizable	Highly customizable
Quick and easy	More effort	Most effort
Tables only	Tables & timescale charts	(Pivot) tables & all charts

In this chapter, we will discuss printing reports and views on paper in detail and give an overview of the vast online reporting possibilities with *Project Server*.

Using Reports

Choose **View, Reports**; the **Reports** dialog appears:

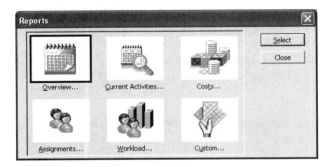

To print a report, first select the report category you want and then select a specific report to view in the print preview window. You can choose one of the standard reports from the following categories:

◆ **Overview**
Overview reports show information for the entire project duration, including summary tasks, critical tasks, project milestones, cost and schedule information.

◆ **Current Activities**
Current activity reports show a variety of task information, such as tasks that are not started, in progress, completed or behind schedule (slipping).

◆ **Costs**
Cost reports show budgets by task for the entire project duration; time-phased budget (*cash-flow*), tasks and resources that are over budget; and *earned value* information for all tasks.

◆ **Assignments**
Assignment reports show assignments by resource for the entire project duration, assignments for only the resources you specify, assignments displayed by week or resources that are over-allocated.

◆ **Workload**
Workload reports show task usage or resource usage information.

There is also a **Custom** category, which allows you to create a new report, customize an existing report or copy any of the reports just discussed.

Certain outputs can only be created if you use the report feature in MS Project:

◆ **Project Summary**: Gives statistics on the entire project. You can find it in the section **Overview**. It provides project health indicators like current **Finish** date versus **Baseline Finish** date and current **Cost** versus **Baseline Cost**. It is similar to the **Project Statistics** dialog (**Project, Project Information**, Statistics...).

◆ **Project Calendar**: Prints the holidays and working hours. You can find it in the section **Overview** listed as *Working Days*.

◆ **Resource Calendars**: Print the resource-specific calendars that can be included in any resource report. To include the resource calendar information, double-click on **Custom...** and select any of the resource-related reports (e.g. **Resource**) and click Edit... , on the tab **Details** check ☑ **Calendar**. This is a good way to check if the vacations of the team members were captured in the schedule. Vacations require little effort to enter, but can throw projects off track in a major way, particularly with deadlines in September.

Previewing Reports

1. Choose **View, Reports...**; the **Reports** dialog appears:

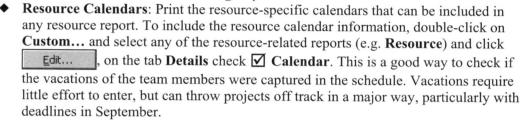

2. If you double-click on **Overview** reports, the **Overview Reports** dialog appears:

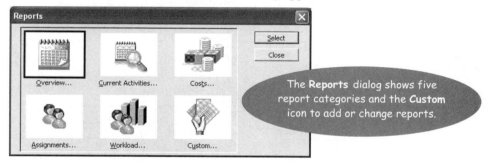

3. Some performance reports, like the **Project Summary** report, cannot be produced in other ways. If you double-click on it, you will see the report in print preview:

Relocation Devom Inc.		
Devom Inc.		
Eric Uyttewaal		
as of Jan 28 '03		

The Project Summary report shows total Duration, Work and Cost, as well as dates relative to the baseline.

Dates

Start:	Aug 2 '04	Finish:	Nov 16 '04
Baseline Start:	NA	Baseline Finish:	NA
Actual Start:	NA	Actual Finish:	NA
Start Variance:	0 days	Finish Variance:	0 days

Duration

Scheduled:	74 days?	Remaining:	74 days?
Baseline:	0 days?	Actual:	0 days
Variance:	74 days?	Percent Complete:	0%

Work

Scheduled:	480 days	Remaining:	480 days
Baseline:	0 days	Actual:	0 days
Variance:	480 days	Percent Complete:	0%

Costs

Scheduled:	$129,125.00	Remaining:	$129,125.00
Baseline:	$0.00	Actual:	$0.00
Variance:	$129,125.00		

Task Status

		Resource Status	
Tasks not yet started:	31	Work Resources:	8
Tasks in progress:	0	Overallocated Work Resources:	2
Tasks completed:	0	Material Resources:	1
Total Tasks:	31	Total Resources:	11

4. You will get an error message when proceeding to print preview if you don't have a printer set up on your computer. You can set one up through Windows, even if it is only for print preview purposes:

◇ In Windows XP click **start**, **Printers and Faxes, Add a Printer**.

◇ In Windows 2000 click **Start**, **Settings, Printers, Add Printer**.

5. When hovering over the page, the mouse pointer looks like 🔍. If you click on an area of the page, you can zoom in on the details, and with another click you will zoom out again.

6. To change the margins, header or footer, click **Page Setup...** at the top of the screen.

7. To print the report, click .
    To return without printing, click ⬛Close⬛.

To Customize a Report

1. Choose **View, Reports…**; the **Reports** dialog appears:

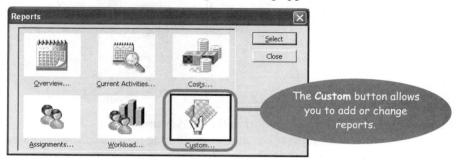

The **Custom** button allows you to add or change reports.

2. Double-click on **Custom…** ⬛; the **Custom Reports** dialog appears:

The **Custom Reports** dialog allows you to **Copy** or create a **New** report or to select and **Edit** one.

3. Select from the list a report that is closest to what you want and click ⬛Copy…⬛ to copy the report while leaving the original intact.
    OR
    Click ⬛Edit…⬛ to edit the report itself.

4. Some reports cannot be copied, for example the **Base Calendar** and the **Project Summary** report. You can only edit the font and style in these reports.

5. If you select a task-related report, the **Task Report** dialog appears:

There are separate dialogs for task (shown in screenshot), resource, assignment and crosstab reports. Each gives different options.

6. Enter a descriptive name for your report in the field **Name:**.
   Depending on what type of report you choose, the dialog provides the appropriate choices. For an explanation of your choices, see the next section on *Report Customization Options* or click | Help | (if available).

7. Click | OK | when done.

8. Click | Select | to display the report in print preview.

9. If it looks good, click | Print... | and the **Print** dialog appears.

10. Click | OK | to print the report.

Report Customization Options

We will discuss the most common options for customizing reports:

◆ **Definition** tab
   Choose the table and the filter.
   Check ☑ **Gray bands** to print gray bands separating individual tasks or resources. This improves readability.

◆ **Details** tab
   Choose the data to include in the report. If you are editing a task-related report, you can include certain task fields. In resource reports, you can include resource fields. In both resource and task reports you can include assignments.
   Check ☑ **Border around details** to print borders around the details you include in the report.

Check ☑ **Show totals** for any fields that should be added up; the totals are shown at the bottom of the report.

◆ **Sort** tab
Specify a sort order for the records in the report.

On all tabs you can click [Text...]. This button opens the **Text Styles** dialog, where you can choose the font and type styles for the report.

Over the years, I have found that **Views** provide more options to create the output my clients expect than **Reports**. We will discuss using **Views** in the rest of the chapter.

Using MS Project Views

The view can be changed in many ways depending on the need for information. The steps to tailor views to your reporting needs are given next. It may seem like an elaborate process, but there are advantages:
◆ You will use them regularly and the custom views are only two mouse-clicks away
◆ You may also be able to re-use them in other projects.

The process is:

1. Customize **Fields**
   In the extra fields in MS Project (like **Text1**, **Number1**, **Flag1** among others) you can enter Excel-like formulas. You can even add graphical indicators, like red/yellow/green, to indicate status.

2. Design a new **Table**, which fields do you want?

3. Design a new **Filter**, which tasks or resources do you want to show?

4. Create a new **Group** to categorize the tasks or resources.

5. Create a new **View** that also applies the newly created **Table, Filter** and **Group**.

6. Sort the records.

7. Apply any formats such as text styles or bar styles.

8. Choose the **Page Setup** settings.

9. Draw using the **Drawing** toolbar.

A view applies a table (that may contain custom fields), a filter and a group. Because the definition of the view calls for what table, filter and group to use, it is best to create those first. A view contains many other settings:

◆ The sorting order through the menu items **Project, Sort**.
◆ Any formats applied through the **Format** menu.
◆ All page setup settings from the **File, Page Setup** dialog.
◆ Any objects created with the **Drawing** toolbar.

Since these are stored in the **View** object, we recommend creating the new view before doing the sort, format, page setup and drawing; otherwise they end up in another view object that you have now messed up. The **Table, Filter** and **Group** also exist as separate objects in the **Tools, Organizer**. If you want to create a new view, for example a one-page *Executive Overview*, you can create a table and call it *Executive Overview*, a filter called *Executive Overview* and a group called *Executive Overview*, as well. When you apply the view, it will apply all its *Executive Overview* components. If you name them all the same, it is clear that they belong together. This helps when you want to give the view to somebody else with the organizer; you can easily see which objects belong together.

You can start the name of certain objects with an * (asterisk) or a number to shuffle them to the top of the list. Or you can use an acronym to indicate they are customized for your organization (for example, at the International Institute for Learning, we use IIL).

New views can be created using a *single view* or a *combination view*. A combination view applies two other views, one in the top and one in the bottom pane. Combination views are useful for analyzing projects, because what you select in the top view is always shown in more detail in the bottom view.

Since the 2002 release you can print the row and column totals in the timescale of the **Usage** views by choosing **File, Page Setup**, tab **View**, ☑ **Print row totals for values within print date range** and ☑ **Print column totals**. The **Print Range** is set in the **File Print** dialog.

Fields

MS Project has many extra fields in the project database that are called Text1-Text30, Flag1-Flag20, or Number1-Number20. You can claim and rename these extra fields. You can even enter Excel-like formulas in them so that they calculate values that are of your interest. You can design performance measurement metrics specific to your organization. You can go one step further and choose graphical indicators for the metrics (red/yellow/green) to reveal the health of the project quickly. In the illustration, the **Number1** field was changed to traffic light indicators. Executives tend to like traffic lights; they can quickly find the problem areas. There are many fields that can be customized, but this does not mean you should go wild with it.

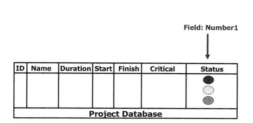

The steps to customize fields are:

1. Choose **Tools, Customize, Fields...**; the **Customize Fields** dialog appears:

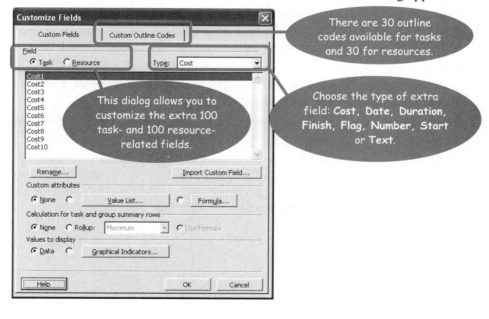

2. Click the tab **Custom Fields** or the tab **Custom Outline Codes**. With **Custom Outline Codes** you can create breakdown structures other than the deliverable-oriented Work Breakdown Structure (WBS). If you have Project Server, you have another 150 *enterprise fields* and also 30 *enterprise outline codes* available for projects, tasks and resources.[85] We will focus in this book on the **Custom Fields** instead of outline codes and only discuss the non-enterprise ones.

3. First decide if you want to customize a ⊙ **Task** or a ⊙ **Resource** field.

4. Then select the **Type** of field from the list | Cost   ▼ |. There are a total of 100 task-related fields and 100 resource-related fields, in addition to the extra enterprise fields and outline code fields that can also be customized by the project office staff:

    ◇ **Cost1 - Cost10** fields can capture extra dollar information like *committed cost*, which is useful if you have a budget to commit dollars from. Project managers do need to keep track of the dollars they committed in order to find the dollars they can still spend. You could use another cost field to calculate the amount of *available budget*, which is the total budget minus the committed amount. The accounting system typically does not help here, because it only becomes aware of expenditures when invoices are received.

    ◇ **Date1 - Date10** fields can store dates that we used to find the Resource Critical Path (see page 501).

    ◇ **Duration1 - Duration10** fields can be used to store durations of interim plans. You have to copy them yourself, since saving an interim plan (**Tools, Tracking, Save Baseline, ⊙ Save interim plan**) only saves the start and finish dates.

    ◇ **Finish1 - Finish10** fields are used to store finish dates in interim plans. We used **Start1-Start10** and **Finish1-Finish10** to display the three workload leveling scenarios in one Gantt Chart; see page 492.

    ◇ **Flag1 - Flag20** fields are used to save *yes/no* type of information, for example to indicate if a resource is willing to travel.

    ◇ **Number1 - Number20** fields are often used to enter formulas that calculate with other numeric fields. For example, you create a formula that calculates the time performance with an under/over percentage; this formula could look like: **Duration Variance / Baseline Duration * 100%**.

---

[85] We discuss the *enterprise fields* and *enterprise outline codes* in the Black Belt Professional course. For more information visit www.iil.com and follow the link *Microsoft Project*.

◇ **Start1 - Start10** fields are used to store finish dates in interim plans. See Finish1-Finish10.

◇ **Text1 - Text30** fields are used to store extra textual information, like the *performing organization* for tasks or the *position* or *department* for resources. Text fields can be enriched with a pick list, known as a **Value List** in MS Project.

5. Select the field in the list. The list is refreshed when you choose the **Type**.

6. Click | Rename... | to give the field a more descriptive name that reveals its purpose. Click | OK |. Eventually you will see that the field is now listed under both names in the database. For example, if you changed the name *Cost1* to *Committed Budget*, you will see that the field is listed as *Cost1 (Committed Budget)* and *Committed Budget (Cost1)*.

7. Set **Custom attributes**:

◇ You can create a pick list for the field. Click | Value List... |.

◇ You can enter an Excel-like formula in the field. Click | Formula... |.

8. Decide if you want MS Project to calculate values on summary tasks or on group headings by selecting your preferences under **Calculation for task and group summary rows**.

9. Under **Values to display** you can create | Graphical Indicators... | by specifying a **Test** and choosing a cute **Image** for the range of **Value(s)**. You can add tests and images for each different range of values. By default, summary and detail tasks will use the same tests, but you can create separate tests, values and images for:

◇ **Nonsummary rows**

◇ **Summary rows**, if you clear the option:

☑ **summary rows inherit criteria from Nonsummary rows**

◇ **Project summary**, if you clear the option:

☑ **project summary inherits criteria from summary rows**

MS Project has some unique functions that can be very useful when creating formulas. For example, the **ProjDateDiff** function can give you the number of business days between two dates and even base it on a *base calendar* of your choice. These functions are often better than using your own arithmetic, like *[Baseline Finish] – [Finish]*, since the function will give you the number of calendar days instead of business days. Most data in MS Project is expressed in business days.

When you develop formulas, you can neither put any letters in number fields, nor put numbers in flag fields, etc. You have to stay within the type of data that corresponds to the **Type** of field you choose to customize.

You can also rename columns in the **Insert, Column, Column Definition** dialog, field **Title**. If you do this, the field will only be renamed in the active table, since the column titles are stored in the table object. If you use this process, the field will be renamed in the entire database and will be listed under its old and new name in every column pick list, which is a better practice.

There are also **Enterprise fields** available for customization by the administrator of *Project Server*. Enterprise fields are fields reserved for standardization across the entire enterprise. The use of enterprise fields is typically determined centrally by the project office, since they are a means to standardize data capture for enterprise reporting purposes. Organizations typically standardize on performance reports, project rollup reports and project archiving. When we discuss reporting using Project Server, we will elaborate further (see page 582).

Because the number of possibilities for customizing fields is almost without limit, a more detailed description is beyond the scope of this book.[86]

Tables

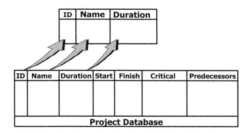

A table is a selection of fields from the project database, including their order of display. You can use the fields you may have customized in the table. A table does not contain project data; it is only a layout. MS Project is different from other applications, because tables in Word or Excel do contain data. In the illustration, the table at the top displays only the fields *ID, Name* and *Duration* out of all the fields present in the MS Project database.

Using an Existing Table

1. Make sure you are in one of the table views; a table view has a spreadsheet with columns and rows. The *Network Diagram* and the *Resource Graph* do not use tables. There are also views that are fill-in forms; they do not use tables either.

---

[86] We discuss them in great detail in the Black Belt Professional course. See www.iil.com and follow the link *Microsoft Project*.

2. Choose **View, Table <name of current table>** and choose the table you want to apply. The currently displayed table (if listed) has a check mark in front of it.
    OR

    Right-click on the **Select All** area where the column headings intersect with the row headings in the spreadsheet. A pop-up menu appears from which you can choose the table to apply.

3. The layout of columns is now replaced by a new layout which follows the definition of the table object you applied.

 Since the 2002 release, you can now rearrange the columns very quickly by clicking on a column heading, releasing the mouse and dragging the column when you see the mouse pointer.

Some worthwhile tables to draw attention to are:

◆ **Cost** table contains the **Fixed Cost** fields that are handy for when you have subcontracts.

◆ **Schedule** table contains all the fields related to the *Critical Path Method*.

◆ **Summary** table which brings date, duration, cost and effort data together in one table. Most other tables have either cost or schedule data.

◆ **Tracking** table will be used when we update the schedule in the next chapter.

◆ **Work** table is useful when you track the work (effort) completed rather than the task completion.

There are more tables available if you choose **View, Table, More Tables...**. Some extra ones in this list are:

◆ **Baseline** table that shows all baseline fields.

◆ **Constraints** table shows the fields **Constraint Type** and **Constraint Date** that allows you to view any constraints you might have in your schedule.

◆ **Earned Value** table if you do this type of progress reporting.

Designing a New Table

Instead of constantly changing the **Entry** table for reports you want to create, there are advantages to creating a new table object for each report need. That way you will not have to reinvent the wheel every time.

1. Choose **View, Table <name of current table>, More Tables...**; the **More Tables** dialog appears:

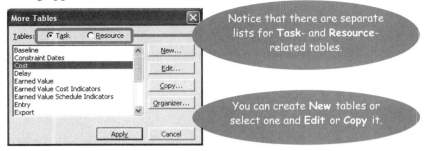

Notice that there are separate lists for **Task**- and **Resource**- related tables.

You can create **New** tables or select one and **Edit** or **Copy** it.

2. To list the task tables, select ⊙ **Task**; for resource tables select ⊙ **Resource**.

3. Select the table in the **Tables** box that is closest to what you want, and click

   Copy... to create a duplicate with which to work. The **Table Definition** dialog appears:

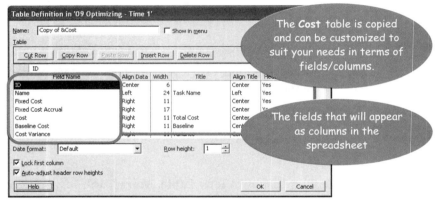

The **Cost** table is copied and can be customized to suit your needs in terms of fields/columns.

The fields that will appear as columns in the spreadsheet

4. In the **Name** box, type a new name for the table.

5. To delete a field in the table, click the row to delete and click Delete Row .
   To insert a new field in the table, click the row before which you want the new field to appear and click Insert Row .
   To replace a field, click on its field name and select the new field from the list that appears.

 6. In MS Project, you can choose to wrap the text in each column heading by setting **Header Wrapping** to **Yes**.

7. If you want to list the new table in the menu, check ☑ **Show in menu**.

8. If you want to lock the first field, check ☑ **Lock first column**. There are advantages to having a locked first column; it allows you to select an entire task or resource record in the database and the locked title will not scroll off the screen. The data cannot be edited in the locked column, which is just fine for ID numbers, which are maintained by MS Project anyway.

9. In MS Project, you can choose to ☑ **Auto-adjust header row heights**.

10. Click ⸢ OK ⸥; you are now back in the **More Tables** dialog.

11. To apply the table and return to your project, click ⸢ Apply ⸥.

You can now adjust the column width of a column by pointing anywhere on the right-hand side of the column, not any longer in the column heading only.

Filters

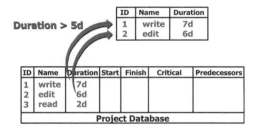

Duration > 5d

ID	Name	Duration
1	write	7d
2	edit	6d

ID	Name	Duration	Start	Finish	Critical	Predecessors
1	write	7d				
2	edit	6d				
3	read	2d				

Project Database

A *filter* selects and displays records from the project database that meet the criteria that you set. You can filter tasks or resources. MS Project allows you to create criteria that look in any field in the database. The filter does not contain the project data; it is just the screen applied to the project database. In the illustration, the tasks with a duration greater than 5 days have been filtered from the database, which renders only 2 records from the database.

A filter does not display any detail tasks that are collapsed under their summary task, even if they meet the criteria. If a filter does not display the right tasks, they are probably collapsed. Expand all summary tasks first, using the ⸢ **Show ▾** ⸥ tool, before applying a filter. As you can see, collapsing and filtering interfere with each other.

10

The filter **All Tasks** is the default filter in task views to show all tasks; the filter **All resources** is comparable in resource views. As their names suggest, these are not real filters, because they display every record present in the project database. To get rid of a filter in a view, reapply the **All tasks** or **All resources** "filter" or press ⸤F3⸥.

Applying an Existing Filter

1. Choose **Project, Filtered for <name of current filter>**.
    OR
    Click the ▾ of the tool `All Tasks ▾` in task views, or `All Resources ▾` in resource views, on the standard toolbar and the list of filters appears.

2. Select a filter from the list. Only the records that meet the criteria in the filter definition are now displayed. If you want to see its definition, choose **Project, Filtered for <name of current filter>, More Filters…** and click `Edit…`.

There are some very useful filters included in MS Project such as these task filters:

◆ **Critical** displays all tasks that drive your project end date. Note that the word *"critical"* does not necessarily imply that the task is important. It looks for *Yes* in the calculated field **Critical**.

◆ **Cost Overbudget** displays the tasks that cost more than their baseline cost.

◆ **Date Range…** displays tasks that fall in whole or in part within the period you indicate. This allows you to focus on the tasks in the coming weeks.

◆ **Milestones** displays all important events in your schedule, the delivery dates for the deliverables in your project. It looks for *Yes* in the calculated field **Milestone**.

◆ **Slipping Tasks** displays all tasks that are forecasted to finish later than their baseline.

◆ **Summary Tasks** displays all summary tasks and gives you a high-level view of the project. It looks for *Yes* in the calculated field **Summary**.

◆ **Using Resource…** displays tasks assigned to a resource of your choice. This allows you to create simple to-do lists. It looks for tasks that contain the name of the resource in the **Resource Names** field.

Some useful resource filters to be aware of are:

◆ **Overallocated Resources** displays resources with too much work at certain times. Realize though that it will display resources that may only have an over-allocation during 1 hour in the project. It normally displays more resources than you need to worry about. It looks for resources with *Yes* in the calculated field **Overallocated**.

◆ **Slipping Assignments**, when applied in the Resource Usage view, displays those resources with assignments that are late.

Just as with tables, there are advantages to creating a new filter object for each reporting need, so you will not have to change or recreate your filter every time.

Designing a New Filter

1. Choose **Project, Filtered for <name of current filter>, More Filters...**; the **More Filters** dialog appears:

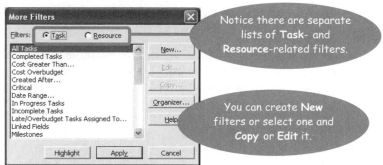

Notice there are separate lists of **Task**- and **Resource**-related filters.

You can create **New** filters or select one and **Copy** or **Edit** it.

2. Select ⊙ **Task** to see a list of task-related filters or ⊙ **Resource** for resource-related filters.

3. Click on a filter that is close to what you want and click [Copy...]; this will keep the original intact. The **Filter Definition** dialog appears:

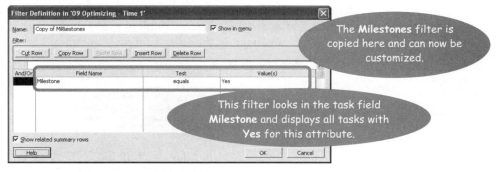

The **Milestones** filter is copied here and can now be customized.

This filter looks in the task field **Milestone** and displays all tasks with **Yes** for this attribute.

4. Enter a name for the filter; keep it the same as the table you created.

5. To list the new filter in the menu, check ☑ **Show in menu**.

6. Change the filter definition:
   Select the field to filter on from the list under **Field Name**.
   Select the comparison from the list under **Test**.
   Enter the **Value(s)**; for an explanation of your many options in this field, see after these steps.

7. You can add more conditions by adding **And** or **Or** in the **And/Or** field and entering the second condition on the second line. **And** results in fewer records displayed, whereas **Or** results in more records displayed.

8. Click  OK .

9. Click Apply .

The **Value** field in the **Filter Definition** dialog can contain:

◆ Other field names that you select from the list
   This allows you to make comparisons between fields and, for example, display all tasks that slipped. The definition of such a filter would be: *Finish is greater than [Baseline Finish]*. Notice that in the field **Value** field names are enclosed in square brackets.

◆ Literal values that you type in, for example:
   ◇ *Yes* to filter on a flag field
   ◇ *$10,000* to filter on a cost field
   ◇ *5 days* to filter on duration or work
   ◇ *Jan 15, 2003* to filter on dates

◆ Prompts for the user to enter a value
   This creates a totally customized, interactive filter. You have to enter the prompt in a format similar to: "<text of the prompt>"? where <text of the prompt> is the question to display. An example is *"Enter the minimum duration"?*. Notice that you need to include the quotation marks and the question mark at the end. As a result, the following dialog appears when you apply the filter, and after clicking
   OK the desired records are displayed:

Example of a totally customized, interactive filter

   An item from an *enterprise outline code lookup table*. New in the 2003 release is that the entire tree list will appear in the **Value(s)** field of the **Filter Definition** dialog box. This makes life much simpler when filtering on the custom enterprise fields.

Groups

Groups allow you to categorize the tasks (or resources) on certain attributes. When you apply a grouping to the task list, the original structure of the WBS will be temporarily hidden and the new grouping will be displayed. In the illustration, you can see that the tasks are categorized on the attribute *Critical* in two groups of *Yes* and *No*. The task-related field *Critical* is a calculated yes/no field that indicates whether or not a task is critical. When you apply **No Group** again, the grouping will disappear, and the *Work Breakdown Structure* will reappear.

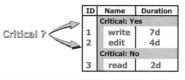

ID	Name	Duration
	Critical: Yes	
1	write	7d
2	edit	4d
	Critical: No	
3	read	2d

ID	Name	Duration	Start	Finish	Critical	Predecessors
1	write	7d			Yes	
2	edit	4d			Yes	
3	read	2d			No	

Project Database

Grouping can be done on multiple levels. You can create alternative breakdown structures by grouping on a field. You can even create multi-level breakdown structures that are an alternative to the WBS. You can do so using an outline field (e.g., **Outline Code1**) in which you code the levels of the new breakdown.

For example, your finance department may request a breakdown of tasks by *accounting codes* for *Team member*, *Manager* and *Subcontractors*:[87]

Accounting Code	Task Name	Accounting Code	Baseline Cost	Cost	Cost Variance	Actual Cost
1	⊟ **Labour cost**	**1**	**$129,125.00**	**$135,875.00**	**$6,750.00**	**$11,025.00**
1.1	⊟ **Team member (employee)**	**1.1**	**$32,918.75**	**$32,918.75**	**$0.00**	**$4,743.75**
1.1	research staff requirements	1.1	$1,125.00	$1,125.00	$0.00	$1,125.00
1.1	summarize requirements	1.1	$525.00	$525.00	$0.00	$525.00
1.1	select the realtor	1.1	$1,125.00	$1,125.00	$0.00	$1,125.00
1.1	legal review	1.1	$281.25	$281.25	$0.00	$281.25
1.1	select the contractor	1.1	$1,125.00	$1,125.00	$0.00	$1,125.00
1.1	negotiate the contract	1.1	$562.50	$562.50	$0.00	$562.50
1.1	select mover	1.1	$1,125.00	$1,125.00	$0.00	$0.00
1.1	pack	1.1	$13,925.00	$13,925.00	$0.00	$0.00
1.1	unpack	1.1	$13,125.00	$13,125.00	$0.00	$0.00
1.2	⊟ **Manager (overhead)**	**1.2**	**$6,281.25**	**$6,281.25**	**$0.00**	**$6,281.25**
1.2	visit the sites	1.2	$1,312.50	$1,312.50	$0.00	$1,312.50
1.2	evaluate the sites	1.2	$1,181.25	$1,181.25	$0.00	$1,181.25
1.2	meet to select the location	1.2	$2,175.00	$2,175.00	$0.00	$2,175.00
1.2	meet to discuss contract	1.2	$1,050.00	$1,050.00	$0.00	$1,050.00
1.2	revise the schedule	1.2	$562.50	$562.50	$0.00	$562.50
1.3	⊟ **Subcontractor (external)**	**1.3**	**$89,925.00**	**$96,675.00**	**$6,750.00**	**$0.00**
1.3	relocate walls	1.3	$22,500.00	$29,250.00	$6,750.00	.00
1.3	electric wiring	1.3	$5,625.00	$5,625.00		
1.3	paint		$1,800.00	$1,800.00		
1.3	drying of paint		$0.00	$0.00		
1.3	install cabinetry		9,000.00	$9,000.00		
1.3	install LAN		3,750.00	$33,750.00	$0.	
1.3	lay carpet		$13,500.00	$13,500.00	$0.00	$0.00
1.3	move		$3,750.00	$3,750.00	$0.00	$0.00

Field used for the new grouping of task records.

The grouping even displays sub totals on each group level.

As you can see in the screenshot, the original *WBS* is entirely hidden and all task records follow a new breakdown structure. The grouping feature even calculates totals on the group headings.

---

[87] This screenshot was created using the *Relocation Project* exercise files. We discuss custom outline codes in detail in the Black Belt Professional course. See www.iil.com and follow the link *Microsoft Project*.

This grouping feature almost gives MS Project the power of a relational database. An example of a grouping of resources is shown in the following screenshot. You can try to reproduce this screenshot by doing the exercise on page 610:

	Resource Name	Position	Function	Cost
	⊟ **employee**			**$28,500.00**
2	Palgon – John	employee representative	employee	$675.00
3	Hilcrest – Nancy	planner	employee	$1,575.00
7	the employees	employees	employee	$26,250.00
	⊟ **external**			**$90,825.00**
4	Roach – Pierre	lawyer	external	$281.25
6	the contractor	contractor	external	$52,650.00
8	the LAN consultants	LAN consultants	external	$33,750.00
9	the movers	movers	external	$3,750.00
10	the realtor	realtor	external	$393.75
	⊟ **manager**			**$9,000.00**
5	Salin – Nelson	CEO	manager	$1,125.00
11	you	project mngr.	manager	$7,875.00
	⊟ **material**			**$800.00**
1	boxes		material	$800.00

The resources are grouped by **Function** (resource-related field).

Notice that if an item falls in more than one group, the item is repeated. For example, if you assigned two resources to a task and then grouped the tasks by resource, the task name will show up under both resources. In this case, the subtotals would be meaningless.

Applying an Existing Grouping

1. Choose **Project, Group by: <name of current group>**; a submenu appears.
   OR
   Click ▾ on the list No Group ▾ on the standard toolbar; the list with different groupings appears.

2. Select a group from the list; the task or resource records are sorted and displayed within their groups.

Just as with tables and filters, there are advantages to creating a new group object for each reporting need, so you will not have to recreate your group every time.

Some worthwhile standard *Groups* that are available are:

◆ **Complete and Incomplete Tasks** which separates the past tasks from the future tasks.

◆ **Milestones;** many people want the milestones at the top of the list and this grouping does that for you in two clicks. If you need more sophistication, for example only hand-picked milestones, you will have to mark them in one of the extra **Flag** fields and develop a custom filter.

Designing a New Grouping

1. Choose **Project, Group by: <name of current group>, More Groups…**; the **More Groups** dialog appears:

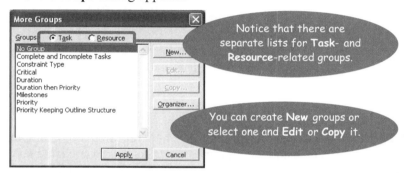

2. Select ⦿ **Task** to see a list of task-related groupings or ⦿ **Resource** for resource-related groupings.

3. Click on a group that is close to what you want and click 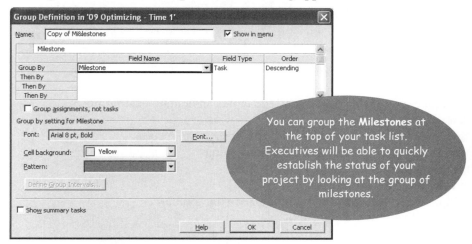 Copy... ; this will keep the original intact. The **Group Definition** dialog appears:

Group Definition in '09 Optimizing - Time 1'

Name: Copy of Milestones   ☑ Show in menu

	Field Name	Field Type	Order
Group By	Milestone	Task	Descending
Then By			
Then By			
Then By			

☐ Group assignments, not tasks

Group by setting for Milestone

Font: Arial 8 pt, Bold   Font...

Cell background: ☐ Yellow

Pattern:

Define Group Intervals...

You can group the **Milestones** at the top of your task list. Executives will be able to quickly establish the status of your project by looking at the group of milestones.

☐ Show summary tasks

Help   OK   Cancel

4. Enter a name for the group; keep it the same as the name of the table you created.

5. To list the new group in the menu, check ☑ **Show in menu**.

6. Change the group definition:
Select the field to group by from the list under **Field Name**.
Select **Descending** or **Ascending** from the list under **Order**.
If you choose a numeric field, it is important to select the intervals as well by clicking Define Group Intervals... . If you skip this, MS Project will group on each value, which is useless most of the times.

7. Click OK ; you are now back in the **More Groups** dialog.

8. Click Apply .

 Notice that, since Project 2002, you can group on assignment fields in the Task Usage view instead of tasks; the tasks will disappear temporarily. Instead of grouping on the task-related **Cost** field, for example, you can group the *assignments* instead. In the **Group Definition** dialog, check ☑ **Group assignments, not tasks**; this enables the list under **Field Type**. From this list, select **Assignment**. The grouping will now use the assignment-related rows instead of the task-related rows and hide the task-related rows. In the Resource Usage view, you can group the assignments instead of resources.

You can now also print the row and column totals in the timescale of the **Usage** views by choosing **File, Page Setup**, tab **View**, ☑ **Print row totals for values within print date range** and ☑ **Print column totals.**

Views

A view contains:
- A reference to the table it uses, and the table can contain custom fields
- A reference to the filter it applies
- A reference to the group by which it categorizes the records
- Any formats applied through the **Format** menu
- The sorting order applied via **Project, Sort**
- The **File, Page Setup** settings
- Any drawing objects created with the **Drawing** toolbar

The following illustration depicts this:

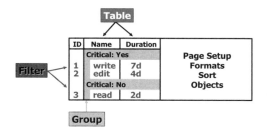

Perhaps you noticed that the **Format** menu looks different in each view. For example, the Calendar view provides different format menu items than the Gantt Chart view. Also, the **File, Page Setup** dialog contains different options for each view. The fact that the menus change when you switch views can be confusing to the occasional user of MS Project. The reason for the changes is that the settings are specific to each view and are stored in the view object. Thanks to it, the view provides a steady display and printout of the project information.

It is a good idea to create a new view for each of your reporting needs. The view can also be added to the **View** menu. If you do so, the view ean be accessed from then on with two simple mouse-clicks. The appearance of views can be fine-tuned using the sorting and format menus.

Creating a New View

1. Choose **View, More Views...**; the **More Views** dialog appears:

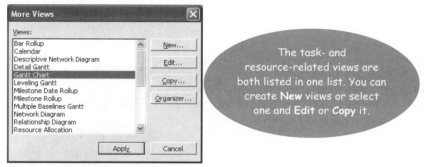

The task- and resource-related views are both listed in one list. You can create **New** views or select one and **Edit** or **Copy** it.

2. Choose the view that is closest to what you want and click [Copy...].
   OR
   Click [New...]; the **Define New View** dialog appears, which allows you to choose between creating a ⦿ **single view** or a ⦿ **combination view**. We will focus on a single view in the rest of the steps. Click [OK].

3. The **View Definition** dialog appears:

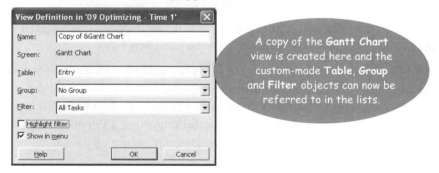

A copy of the **Gantt Chart** view is created here and the custom-made **Table**, **Group** and **Filter** objects can now be referred to in the lists.

4. Fill in the name of the new view and select the **Table**, the **Group** and the **Filter** from the lists. It helps if all the components of the view have the same name, as we recommended before. With identical names, it is obvious they belong together. You can still return to the definition dialogs for table, group and filter to rename them.

5. If you want this view to show in the menu, check ☑ **Show in menu**; the view will be available with only two mouse-clicks.

6. Click [OK]; you are now back in the **More Views** dialog.

7. Click [Apply].

Sort the Records

Choose **Project, Sort** and pick one of the listed sort orders; the sort will be applied immediately. What you will find though is that it does not sort all individual line items, but the summary task families. Please follow the next steps to change this.
OR

1. If you want to customize the sort order, make sure you are in a *task view* to sort tasks and in a *resource view* to sort resources. In the steps that follow we will explain sorting tasks. Choose **Project, Sort, Sort by...**; the **Sort** dialog appears:

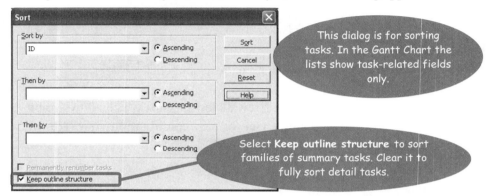

2. Select the first sort order key from the **Sort by** list; if you think you will need a second sort key to break any ties, select it from the list **Then by**.

3. An important choice is whether you want to ☐ **Keep outline structure**. If you do, MS Project will only sort the families of summary tasks. If you don't keep the outline structure, MS Project will do a complete and continuous sort of all line items, ignoring the breakdown structure. Be careful to never ☐ **Permanently renumber tasks**; this is the quickest way to wreck the structure of your *WBS* completely.

4. Click [Sort] and the sort will be applied.

5. To reset the sort order (if you did not renumber), simply resort by ID number by choosing **Project, Sort, By ID**.
OR
If you did accidentally renumber, click **Undo** ↶ to set it straight, close your schedule without saving or resort and renumber on the field **WBS**.

The sort order is stored in the view object in which you applied the sort. Each view can have a different sort order.

Apply Any Formats

The **Format** menu offers many options to improve the appearance of the output. Any change you make through the format menu will be stored in the view object that you have on the screen when you make the change.

The format menu changes when you apply another view. For example, when you are in a view without a timescale, the menu item **Format, Timescale** is grayed out and inaccessible. When you realize that each view has its own format menu, you understand that MS Project is a much bigger application than it first appears to be.

We reviewed the different format options when we discussed printing each view:
◆ Gantt Chart was discussed starting on page 294.
◆ Network Diagram was discussed starting on page 254.
◆ Resource Spreadsheet was discussed starting on page 355.
◆ Resource Graph will be discussed on page 591.
◆ Calendar view will be discussed on page 593.
◆ Tracking Gantt view will be discussed on page 663.

I will summarize only the important choices here:
◆ What text and bar formats do you want?
You can customize the text for individual tasks you select using the menu items **Format, Font** or format the individual bar with **Format, Bar**. You can do it faster by applying a style to each type of task by choosing **Format, Text Styles** or **Format, Bar Styles**. We recommend you use the styles first before overriding the styles for single tasks using **Format, Font** or **Format, Bar**.

◆ Which date formats do you want in the spreadsheet and in the timescale?
First of all, choose the default date format for all date fields in MS Project by choosing **Tools, Options**, tab **View, Date Format**. If you want to change the date order (e.g., from mmddyy to ddmmyy), you have to go to the **Control Panel, Regional Options** (Windows 2000) or **Regional and Language Options** (Windows XP).
To override the default date format in the spreadsheet, choose **View, Table <name of current table>, More Tables**, click Edit... and select the format you want from the **Date Format** list at the bottom.
To override the default date format in the timescale when you display dates next to the task bars, choose **Format, Layout** and select the date format from the list **Date Format**.

◆ Do you want to show dependencies in the Gantt Chart or Tracking Gantt? Make your choice using the menu **Format, Layout, Links**. You can also choose between straight and hooked arrows.

◆ Do you want to roll up detail task bars into their summary task bars in the Gantt Chart?
A regular summary task bar looks like ▼━━━━▼ . Rolled-up summary task bars look like ▼■━■▼ with detail task bars rolled up onto it or like ▼━◇━▼ with milestones rolled up.
You have to choose between:
◇ No rolling up (default)
◇ Rolling up certain hand-picked detail task bars
Hand-pick the task bars by selecting them, clicking the **Task Information** tool 📋 and checking ☑ **Roll up Gantt bar to Summary**. Take similar steps for the summary task, but check ☑ **Show rolled up Gantt bars**
◇ Rolling up all detail task bars onto their summary task bars
Choose **Format, Layout,** ☑ **Always roll up Gantt bars**. To make the rollup appear only when summary tasks are collapsed, you can then also check ☑ **Hide roll up bars when summary expanded**.

◆ What fields do you want to show in the timescale of the **Task Usage** and **Resource Usage** views? You can select fields other than the default **Work** field. Choose **Format, Details** for a quick pick list or **Detail Styles...** for a complete list; better yet, right-click in the yellow area of the timescale and a menu will pop up that allows you to quickly pick a field listed or other ones through the menu item **Detail Styles...** .

◆ In the Resource Graph view, you can also choose to graph details other than the default **Peak Units** by choosing **Format, Details**. Notice that the peak units allow you to find over-allocations quickly, but give an inflated impression of the workloads when you zoom out from days to weeks to months in the timescale. Workloads seem to inflate, because MS Project takes the highest bar (the peak unit) of the 4 weeks in a month to summarize the entire month. You should consider changing to the details **Work** for a more realistic depiction of the expected workload over time.

Choose the Page Setup Settings

The page setup settings are stored in the view object that you have on the screen when you choose **File, Page Setup**.

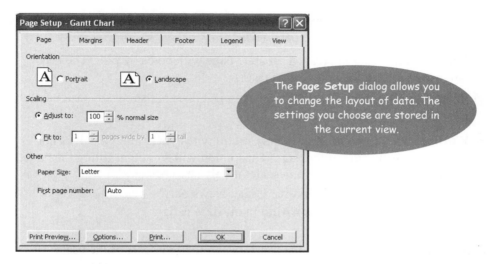

We will only summarize the important options in the **File, Page Setup** dialog, since we discussed many of them in previous chapters:

◆ **Page** tab
  ◇ **Orientation**: When you print the timescale, it is often best to change from ⦿ **Portrait** to ⦿ **Landscape**. This will allow you to keep the entire timescale on one page and prevent you from having to tape pages together.
  ◇ The **Scaling** option will shrink or enlarge the print image, but is only available if your printer can handle scaling; the range is from 10% to 500%.

◆ **Header, Footer, Legend** tab
  Choose the position first: **Left, Center** or **Right**. You can type in any header text, or better, use the lists **General** or **Project Fields** at the bottom of the dialog to select standard phrases. Select the item from the list and then click [Add]; this will add a cryptic code for it in the header, footer or legend. These codes refer to entries you made in the **File, Properties** dialog. If you make changes in that dialog, all headers of all views will be updated automatically.
  The font size is small by default for a header. To increase it, select the text by dragging over it and clicking [A]; the **Font** dialog appears, where you can choose the font, style and size.

◆ **View** tab

The important options for *task views* (except the Calendar view) are:

◇ ☐ **Print all sheet columns** will print all columns, even if they are hidden behind the timescale.

◇ ☐ **Print first** 3 ⬍ **columns on all pages**: You should not have to use this option if your report is only one page wide.

◇ ☑ **Print Notes**: This will create a separate page with notes by task. The task IDs are used to relate the notes to the tasks.

◇ ☑ **Print blank pages** will print a page even if it does not show any task bars (timescale) or nodes (Network Diagram).

◇ ☑ **Fit timescale to end of page** is only useful when your timescale does not reach the right-hand side of the page. This option will stretch it, filling the page. Note that it does not shrink the timescale; it only stretches.

◇ Available in Task Usage or Resource Usage views only:

☑ **Print row totals for values within print date range**

☑ **Print column totals**

These options allow you to add the row totals to the timescale of the usage views on the right-hand side and column totals at the bottom by day, by week or by month, depending on the current time unit.

Copying Views Between Projects

Once you have created a view object, you can use it in other projects or share it with other people. You can even put it in your *Global.MPT* file and use it in all your other project schedules.

1. Open the schedule that contains the object, and open the schedule to copy the object to.

2. Choose **Tools, Organizer…**; the **Organizer** dialog appears:

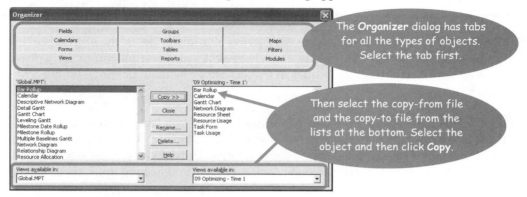

3. Activate the tab **Views** as the type of object to copy.

4. In the list on the left at the bottom of the dialog, select the schedule from which to copy the object and in the list on the right, select the schedule to copy to.

5. Then select the view object to copy and click | Copy >> |.

6. Click the tab **Fields** and copy the fields the view uses in its table.

7. Click the tab **Tables** and copy the table that the view uses.

8. Click the tab **Filters** and copy the filter object that the view uses.

9. Click the tab **Groups** and copy the group object that the view uses.

10. Click | Close | when done.

 It is a lot easier to see which objects are the components of one view if they all have the same name. That's why we recommended naming them the same.

 The organizer allows you to copy objects into the *Global.MPT* file. Any objects you put into this global template are visible in all your projects, unless there is already an object in the project schedule that has the same name. Give objects unique names if you want to see them in any schedule you copy them to.

 If you use Project Server, the Project Server administrator can easily make a successful view available to every project manager by creating *enterprise views*. Ask your administrator to change the *Enterprise Global*.

Using Project Server Views

The *Project Server* views aggregate data across multiple projects, the *project portfolio*. In this book, we focus on managing a single project and we will therefore only provide an overview of reporting capabilities of Project Server without delving into the how-to steps.[88]

In order to create informative views in Project Server, you have to set up enterprise fields in what is called the *Enterprise Global*. The enterprise global is a container of fields and views standardized across the enterprise. Only if you capture organization-specific attributes will you be able to report on them. You need to think about and then customize enterprise fields. Project Server has the following enterprise fields:

◆ Project
◆ Task
◆ Resource

Each of these fields can be single level or multi level (*Outline Code*) fields. The multi level fields allow you to drill into the data on multiple levels, for example by country, by state (province) or by city. There are also ten enterprise resource fields that allow you to enter multiple values. These are suitable to capture the skills of each resource and do *skill-based scheduling*.

Enterprise views are outputs you standardize on across the enterprise. The *project office* within your organization would think about what views would benefit project managers, resource managers and executives. The project office will publish these views as *Enterprise* Views. Only people with *Project Server* administrative privileges can create and change the enterprise views; these people are typically not project managers. Of course, you can always request extra views to be added.

Centrally designed enterprise views provide several benefits for your organization:

◆ They prevent project managers and resource managers from having to spend time and energy developing appropriate report formats, reinventing the same wheel over and over again.

---

[88] In the Blue Belt Professional and Black Belt Professional courses, we focus on managing multiple projects with Project Server. See www.iil.com and follow the link *Microsoft Project*.

◆ They provide the capability to have all project managers and resource managers create reports in the same format. With a standard format, executives will be able to analyze portfolios faster and compare projects better.

We will now discuss a selection of Project Server views.

Resource Manager Workload View

In this view, a resource manager can assess the workloads and find any over-allocations, both on the level of a team and the individuals in the team. In the next screenshot, the team workload looks reasonable apart from some peaks exceeding the availability. However, if you look closer at individual workloads, you will see that Brad Sutton is heavily over-allocated. In certain weeks, he has over 200 hours of scheduled work. It is likely that all projects in which Brad is involved will slip.

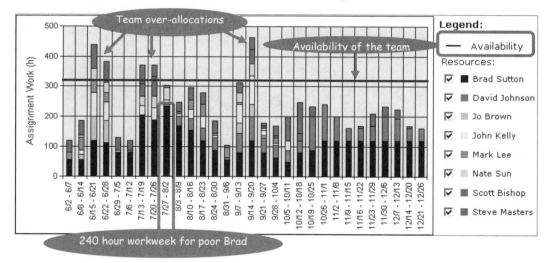

Notice that the resource manager can use the check boxes on the right hand side to zoom in on one resource; the view is interactive.

Resource Manager Resource Utilization View

The following view shows the resource utilization for the different regions of the company:

Very high utilization in Malaysia, and low numbers elsewhere

Level 02 ▾	Level 03	Level 04		Years ▾ Quarters 2003				Total
				⊞ Q1	⊞ Q2	⊞ Q3	⊞ Q4	
⊟ Asia	⊟ Southeast	⊞ Korea	Availability	9,728.0h	9,880.0h	10,032.0h	10,032.0h	39,672.0h
			% Res. Util.	1.48%	5.95%	0.72%	1.18%	2.32%
		⊞ Malaysia	Availability	9,728.0h	9,880.0h	10,032.0h	10,032.0h	39,672.0h
			% Res. Util.	28.45%	56.52%	97.91%	79.21%	65.84%
	Total		Availability	29,184.0h	29,640.0h	30,096.0h	30,096.0h	119,016.0h
			% Res. Util.	9.98%	20.82%	32.88%	26.79%	22.72%
⊟ USA	⊞ Central		Availability	8,704.0h	8,840.0h	8,976.0h	8,976.0h	35,496.0h
			% Res. Util.			2.14%	6.77%	2.25%
	⊞ East		Availability	18,944.0h	19,240.0h	19,536.0h	19,536.0h	77,256.0h
			% Res. Util.				1.31%	0.33%
	⊞ West		Availability	40,448.0h	41,080.0h	41,712.0h	41,712.0h	164,952.0h
			% Res. Util.	0.61%	7.29%	19.26%	10.38%	9.46%
	Total		Availability	68,096.0h	69,160.0h	70,224.0h	70,224.0h	277,704.0h
			% Res. Util.	0.36%	4.33%	11.71%	7.40%	6.00%
Grand Total			Availability	99,328.0h	100,880.0h	102,432.0h	102,432.0h	405,072.0h
			% Res. Util.	3.18%	9.09%	17.69%	12.94%	10.79%

As you can see, the utilization is unbalanced within the company and this company should look into relocating resources, selective hiring in the Malaysia region and perhaps releasing resources elsewhere.

Executive Traffic Light Portfolio View

The following screenshot shows a portfolio view for executives with budget and schedule traffic lights for the projects that are grouped by project manager:

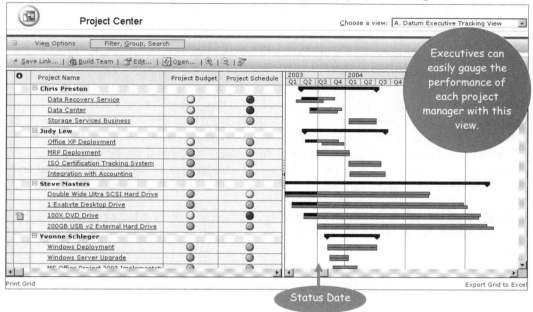

This view would be ideal for executives as input for status meetings and performance appraisals of their project managers. Notice that the baseline is also visible, which helps assessing the status. *Project Web Access* even allows executives to drill down into each project to have a look at the cause of slippages.

If you want to do traffic light reporting with red, yellow and green indicators to give a quick impression of the health of a project or portfolio, you have to think about the business rules that determine which of the three colors is shown for each project, deliverable and task.

You can use traffic lights for:

◆ *Budget performance*: What are the threshold values for well within budget (green), close to the original budget (yellow) and running dangerously over budget (red)?

◆ *Schedule performance*: What are the threshold values for well within schedule (green), close to on schedule (yellow) and slipping dangerously (red)?

◆ *Quality performance*: Project Server does not have features for quality management. You will need a separate quality management system to determine or calculate the quality values. In software development projects, you could develop a quality indicator that, for example, reveals if one or more must-have requirements are not met (red), one or more nice-to-have requirements are not met (yellow) and all requirements are met (green). In *Project Server*, you can definitely present these quality indicators next to schedule and budget indicators in a project portfolio view. Executives would probably be very grateful.

The *Earned Value* performance indicators are worth exploring as a basis for budget and schedule performance reporting.[89]

The business rules typically differ from organization to organization; even within an organization they can, perhaps even should, differ from business unit to business unit. It is not uncommon for them to even differ from one department to the next; the IT department can have different standards for healthy projects than the engineering department. This is particularly true if the average budget for IT projects is $50,000 and for engineering projects $1 million.

No matter what criteria you use, it should be clear to everybody what a red light means, just like driving a car. If red traffic lights weren't clearly understood by everybody, the streets wouldn't be very safe …

---

[89] See for more information on Earned Value:
- Guide to the PMBOK®, 2004 Edition, published by the PMI.
- Earned Value Project Management, Fleming, Quentin W. and Joel Koppelman, second edition, Project Management Institute Inc., Newton Square, PA, USA, 2000.

Executive Portfolio Bubble Chart

The following chart is a very nice view for analyzing the health of a project portfolio. The diameter of the bubble represents the total amount of money to be invested in the project (*project budget*). The Y-axis shows the level of *alignment with strategic* objectives. The X-axis shows the expected percentage of *Return on Investment* (*ROI*). Executives can assess which projects are their *stars* and which ones just eat the money without ever producing revenues (I tend to call them *black holes*). In the next chart, the stars are in the top right quadrant:

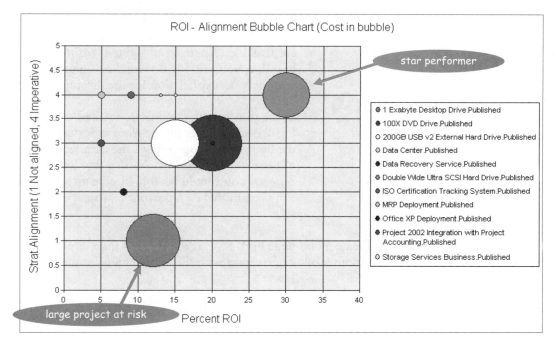

 This view requires several customizations of enterprise fields, views and *OLAP-cube*. *OLAP* stands for *Online Analytical Processing* and refers to the capability to drill down and slice and dice in *Project Web Access* views.

Creating One-Page Reports ... Always!

This heading may seem pretentious if you are juggling a schedule with thousands of tasks. Regardless of the size of the project, you can always surprise your executives and clients with one-page performance reports. There is a simple technique to do this, and it will make your stakeholders happy, if not euphoric. Executives typically don't have the time to dig through pages and pages of schedules, and they will never start taping them together. They expect you to provide concise information, i.e., one-page reports. The first one-page report should only show the major milestones. That is all you need if all the milestones are on schedule and the budgets are feasible. Where a milestone is off its baseline, you provide a second one-page report that gives an explanation for the discrepancy.

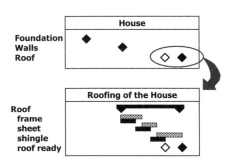

In the illustration, the milestone chart at the top shows slippage on the *Roof* milestone. In the bottom one-page report, the detailed cause of the slippage is shown. With a few *one-page reports*, you should be able to give an adequate status and forecast report for a project of any size.

In a similar fashion, you can create a one-page high-level cost report. If there are discrepancies, you can create another one-page report with the explanation for the differences.

You will have to master the filters feature of MS Project to accomplish this (see page 565).

Checks on Reporting

We would like to suggest the following checks to verify if you used best practices for project reporting. The checks pertain to what custom view objects you developed in your schedule. We discussed creating custom views on page 557.

◆ Is there a one-page status report available as a separate **View** object in your project schedule that displays the *major milestones* relative to the baseline?

◇ Are the milestones filtered in this view instead of listed together in the WBS? Many project managers put the major milestones at the top of their schedule to create a one-page overview of the project. This makes the network of dependencies very complex in the Gantt Chart, because the dependencies run up and down with long arrows. This makes it very difficult to check if the network of dependencies is complete. Instead, we advocate using a separate view that displays all milestones using the **Milestones** filter.

◇ Are the appropriate milestones chosen to represent the status and to forecast a large project?
If you have many milestones, you may end up with multiple pages. Instead of reporting on all milestones, you can mark certain milestones as major milestones using a flag field (Flag1 - Flag20). The filter of the view should display these major milestones. If you use the **Flag1** field, the filter definition would be: *Flag1 equals Yes.* You then make this filter part of the view in **Views, More views**, select the view in the list and click | Edit... |. Select your newly created filter to replace the default filter in this view and click | OK |. When you switch to the view, the filter will automatically be applied. Identifying the right milestones is the challenge here, and you could print all milestones the first time and ask the executive to highlight the 30 most important milestones once. About 30 lines fit within one page.

◇ Does the one-page view report give an appropriate impression of the health of the project?

◆ If your schedule has a *Resource-Critical Path*, is there a separate view object that displays it?
The view should have the resource-critical tasks flagged in the field **Marked** or a **Flag** field. See page 501 for a detailed discussion of the Resource-Critical Path and how to create this view.

Examples of Useful or Hard-to-Get-At Reports

We will discuss the following special reports in more detail. Some are very useful, others are just hard to get at:
◆ Responsibilities by department (see next section)
◆ Workload histogram for individuals and groups (see page 591)
◆ To-do lists in the Calendar view (see page 593)
◆ Reports that include the notes (see page 596)
◆ The time-phased budget (see page 599)

Responsibilities by Department

With the new *Group* feature, it is easy to communicate lists of responsibilities by department or resources by type. The next screenshot shows a resource by type grouping:

	Resource Name	Work	Details	Aug	Sep	Oct	Nov
	⊟ **Group: No Value**	**0 days**	Work				
	⊞ Unassigned	0 days	Work				
	⊟ **Group: employee**	**148 days**	Work				
2	⊟ Falgon – John	3 days	Work	3d			
	visit the sites	1 day	Work	1d			
	evaluate the sites	1 day	Work	1d			
	meet to select the location	1 day	Work	1d			
3	⊞ Hilcrest – Nancy	5 days	Work	5d			
7	⊞ the employees	140 days	Work				140d
	⊟ **Group: external**	**316 days**	Work				
4	⊞ Roach – Pierre	0.5 days	Work	0.5d			
6	⊞ the contractor	234 days	Work	1d	133d	94d	6d
8	⊞ the LAN consultants	60 days	Work			60d	
9	⊞ the movers	20 days	Work				20d
10	⊞ the realt...	...	Work	1.5d			
	⊟ **Group: man...**	...days	Work				
5	⊞ Salin – Nelson	1 day	Work	1d			
11	...3 days	Work	14.43d	0.87d			
	⊟ **Group: material**		Work				
1		0 boxes	Work (				

Effort needed by department, by resource and by assignment

Third level: assignments

Second level: resources

First level: departments

1. Choose **View, Resource Sheet**.

2. Enter the department in which each person works in the field **Group**.

3. Choose **View, Resource Usage**.

4. Select from the list `No Group` ▾ on the **Standard** toolbar the item **Resource Group**; the result will show three outline levels:

   ◇ The first level shows the resource groups, i.e., departments.

   ◇ The second level shows all resources working in each department.

   ◇ The third level shows all the *assignments* for each resource.

Workload Histogram for Individuals and Groups

Workload histogram is synonymous with *Resource Graph* in MS Project. When you enter the group or department the resource works in, you can create interesting workload histograms. You can create a graph that compares the workload of an individual with the total work for that group (department). The next screenshot shows the total work of the *LAN consultants* relative to the total workload of all *external* resources (as characterized in the field **Group**) displayed using the **Group...** filter. Other resources, like *contractor, movers, Pierre Roach*, and *realtor* also belong to the **Group** external resources, as you can see in the exercise solution files for the relocation project at the end of this chapter.

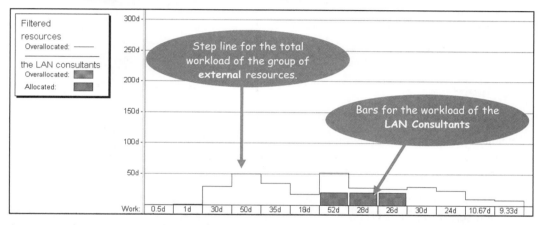

1. Enter the department in the **Group** field for each resource, as we did for the previous sample output.

2. Choose **View, Resource Graph**.

3. Press [Page Dn] until you see the graph of the individual for whom you want to compare the workload to the total workload of the department or group.

4. Notice that the Resource graph displays **Peak Units** by default. The **Peak Units** format always displays the highest over-allocation in red, even if it is just one 200% over-allocation during one hour in an entire year. Choose **Format, Details, Work**, which exchanges the **Peak Units** for **Work** numbers. **Work** provides a more accurate picture than **Peak Units**. The format **Work** displays the total number of person days of effort per time unit.

5. Choose **Format, Bar Styles**; the **Bar Styles** dialog appears:

Select under **Filtered Resources** to show a **Step Line** for **Overallocated Work** and for **Allocated work**. You will see the resource versus the total of the group if you filter on the group it belongs to.

6. Select the settings as shown in the previous screenshot, and click [OK]; the view now shows stepped bars for the workload of the resource and a red line for the total work in the project (filter is still **All Resources**).

7. Make sure you have filled in the resource-related field *Group* in the resource sheet. Then select the filter **Group...** from the list | All Resources ▼ | on the **Formatting** toolbar; the **Group** dialog appears:

Enter the name of the group for which you want to see the total charted.

8. Enter the name of the group the resource belongs to in the field **Group name** and click [OK]. Now you see the workload of the resource relative to the total workload of the department the person belongs to.

9. Create the header and footer in the **File, Page Setup** dialog.

10. Print the report by choosing **File, Print**.

You can display different data in the Resource Graph more quickly by making it the bottom view, with the Resource Usage view in the top. Select in the Resource Usage the data to chart and it will immediately appear in the Resource Graph at the bottom.

Note that, unfortunately, you cannot change the y-axis; MS Project often creates a y-axis that is too long.

To-Do Lists in the Calendar View

The calendar view does not show many tasks within one day. When we first discussed this view on page 81, we stated that the calendar view is particularly suited for creating to-do lists by resource. There are several reasons for this:

◆ Typically, a resource has only one or two tasks on any given day. Two tasks can easily be displayed in the calendar view, but not more.

◆ Not all people understand Gantt Charts, but most people can read calendars. To-do lists in the calendar view are generally easier to understand than in the Gantt Chart.

◆ You can show the resource-specific holidays and vacation days in this view.

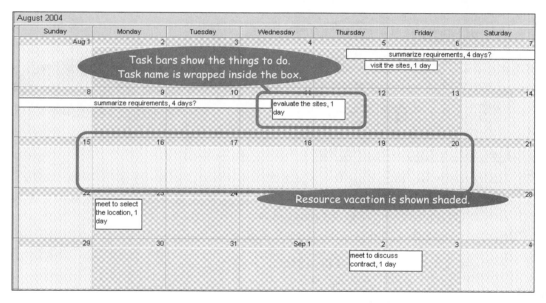

Creating a To-Do List for a Resource

1. Choose **View, Calendar**.

2. Select from the filter list 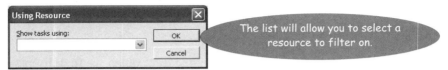 on the **Formatting** toolbar the **Using Resource...** filter; the **Using Resource** dialog appears:

3. Select from the list **Show tasks using** the resource for which to create the to-do list. Click OK .

4. To create the shading for vacation time, choose **Format, Timescale...**; the **Timescale** dialog appears. Click the tab **Date Shading**:

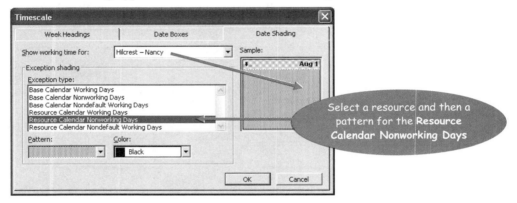

5. Under **Show working time for,** select the resource of this to-do list and choose the appropriate pattern and color settings. Click OK . The view now colors or shades the nonworking days for the resource.

6. Create the header and footer in the **File, Page Setup** dialog.

7. Print the report by choosing **File, Print**.

To Adjust the Row Heights and Column Widths

While in the **Calendar** view, choose **View, Zoom** and select the number of weeks to display within one screen to adjust the row heights of the days.
OR
Point to the horizontal divider that separates the weeks; the mouse pointer changes to ✢. Click and drag the divider up to decrease the height of all rows. Drag it down to increase the height.

Double-click the right-hand side of the column dividers between the days to adjust the column widths so they best fit in the entire screen. You can also drag them, but this usually takes several trial and error attempts.

To Change the Timescale

While in the **Calendar** view, choose **Format, Timescale** OR simply double-click on the timescale; the **Timescale** dialog appears. Click tab **Week Headings**:

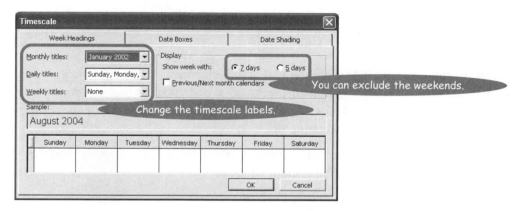

On the page tab **Week Headings** you can:
- ◆ Change the titles shown for the months, weeks and days.
- ◆ Select **Show week with** ◉ **5 days** as opposed to the default 7 days if your team never works weekend days.

To Format the Calendar View

While in the **Calendar** view, choose **Format, Bar Styles** and you can:
- ◆ Choose the appearance of the different types of tasks.
- ◆ Add text labels inside the task bars by selecting the labels in the **Field(s)** dropdown list. You can even add multiple labels, like "**Name, Resource Name**", but you will find that in short task bars, the text is often cut off to fit inside the bar, which brings me to my next point.
- ◆ When task names are too long for the task bars, which they likely are for one-day tasks, use ☑ **Wrap text in bars**.

To Improve the Layout of the Task Bars

1. While in the **Calendar** view, choose **Format, Layout...**; the **Layout** dialog appears:

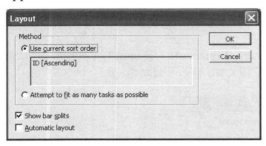

2. Under **Method** you can select different layout arrangements for the task bars:

    ⦿ **Use current sort order** will list the task bars based upon the active sorting.

    ⦿ **Attempt to fit as many tasks as possible** tries to optimize the use of space by displaying more than one bar horizontally.

3. If you check ☑ **Automatic layout,** the task bars will be rearranged every time the sort order changes or tasks are inserted or deleted.

Reports That Include the Notes

The **Notes** field can hold a lot of text; there is virtually no limit to it. You may need to capture a lot of text when:

◆ Creating a *WBS dictionary*, which is a narrative description of the major deliverables in the WBS

◆ Capturing *checklist items* or *reminders* to yourself

To include the notes in a report, you have two options:

◆ Print all the notes together on a separate notes page using a View

◆ Print the notes in between the tasks they relate to using a Report.

Print a View with a Separate Notes Page

The following is an example of a separate notes page using views:

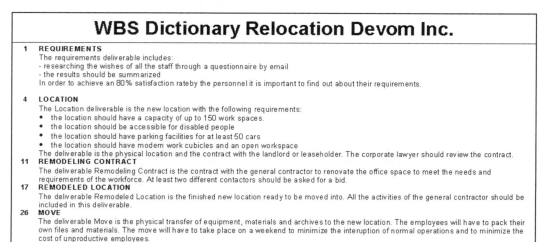

To create it, follow these steps:

1. In the Gantt Chart, choose **File, Page Setup**; the **Page Setup** dialog appears:

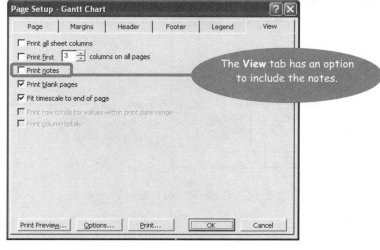

The **View** tab has an option to include the notes.

2. Click the tab **View**.

3. Check ☑ **Print notes**.

4. Click Print Preview... , Print... or OK .

Print a Report with Notes in Between the Tasks

The following report shows the notes inserted in between tasks:

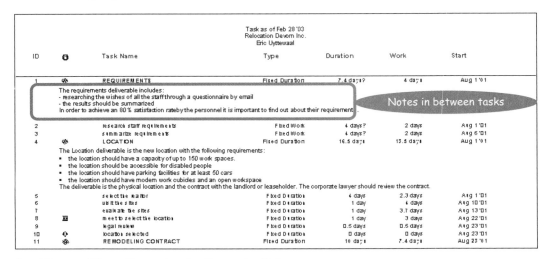

1. Choose **View, Reports**; the **Reports** dialog appears:

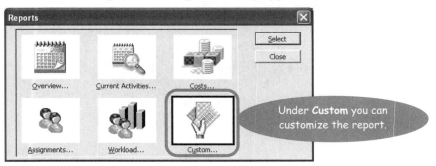

2. Double-click on **Custom** ; the **Custom Report** dialog appears.

3. Scroll down the list and select **Task**; the dialog should now look like:

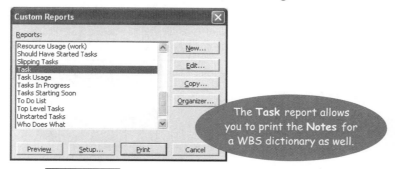

The **Task** report allows you to print the **Notes** for a WBS dictionary as well.

4. Click [Edit...]; the **Task Report** dialog appears.

5. Click the tab **Definition**, if needed, and check ☑ **Show summary tasks** to include the deliverables.

6. Click the tab **Details** and check ☑ **Notes**, as in the following screenshot:

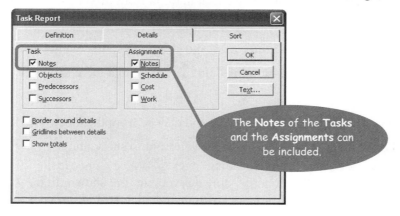

The **Notes** of the **Tasks** and the **Assignments** can be included.

7. The notes will now appear in between the tasks in the printout. Click [OK] and click [Preview] to see the report, or click [Print...].

The Time-Phased Budget

If your financial department asks you as the project manager to predict how much money your project needs each month, you can print a time-phased budget. You have two options:

◆ Time-phased budget by resource: Use the **Resource Usage** view
◆ Time-phased budget by task or deliverable: Use the **Task Usage** view

The following sample report shows expenses by deliverable by month:

| | ❶ | Task Name | Cost | Details | Qtr 3, 2004 | | | Qtr 4, 2004 | | |
					Jul	Aug	Sep	Oct	Nov	Dec
1		⊞ REQUIREMENTS	$1,650.00	Cost		$1,650.00				
4		⊞ LOCATION	$6,075.00	Cost		$6,075.00				
11		⊞ REMODELING CONTRAC	$3,300.00	Cost		$1,125.00	$2,175.00			
17		⊞ REMODELED LOCATION	$86,175.00	Cost			$28,125.00	$44,550.00	$13,500.00	
26		⊞ MOVE	$31,925.00	Cost		$1,125.00			$30,800.00	
				Cost						

The deliverable *remodeled location* costs *$86,175* in total that will have to be paid in *Sep, Oct* and *Nov.*

The steps to create this view are:

1. Choose **View, Task Usage** (or **Resource Usage** if you want the report by resource.)

2. Click **Go to selected Task** to scroll the numbers into view; you will see the details **Work** displayed by default, which is the required effort spread over time.

3. Choose **Format, Details, Cost**. Notice the check mark in front of **Work**; the work details are currently shown in the chart.
   OR
   Right-click in the yellow area of the timescale, and choose from the menu **Cost**.

4. Choose **Format, Details, Work** to turn this field off; notice that there is now a check mark in front of **Cost**.
   OR
   Right-click in the yellow area of the timescale, and choose from the menu **Work**.

5. Adjust the level of detail of the outline structure you want to show. In the Task Usage view, click on any column heading, click **Show ▾** and choose the appropriate level of detail. In the example, only deliverables are shown. In the Resource Usage view, click on any column heading and click **Hide Subtasks** ▬ on the **Format** toolbar.

6. Adjust the timescale to show the time unit your financial department would like to see by using **Zoom in** 🔍 and **Zoom out** 🔍.

7. Make sure can read all the numbers in the timescale; if the columns are too narrow, you will see ####. You can now adjust the column width of the bottom tier timescale units by dragging their right-hand border OR you can choose **Format, Timescale** and adjust the **Size** %.

8. Create the header and footer in the **File, Page Setup** dialog.

9. Print the report by choosing **File, Print**.

Printing

We will discuss some final things to do and settings to choose before sending the schedule to the printer.

Inserting the Project Logo into the Header or Footer

1. Choose **File, Page Setup**.

2. Click the tab **Header** or **Footer**.

3. Click **Insert picture** ; the **Insert Picture** dialog appears:

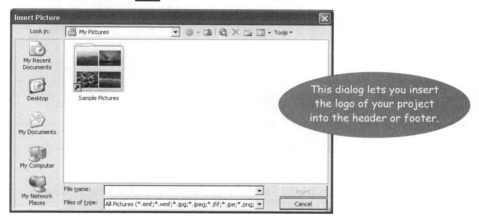

This dialog lets you insert the logo of your project into the header or footer.

4. Navigate through your directory system and select the image file with the logo of your project.

5. Click ![Insert]; the logo is now displayed in the header.

6. If the logo image is too big, you can click on it and selection handles will appear around the image. Point to a corner selection handle and drag it to resize the picture.

Specify Columns to Spell-Check

1. Before you start the spellchecker, you should prevent MS Project from highlighting abbreviations or codes you used. Choose **Tools, Options...** and click tab **Spelling**.

2. Keep **Yes** for those columns you want the spell-checker to check; set the rest to **No**.

3. Check ☑ **Ignore words in UPPERCASE** and
   ☑ **Ignore words with numbers** to eliminate stopping on abbreviations or codes.

4. Click | OK |.

To Check the Spelling in the Schedule

1. Choose **Tools, Spelling**.

2. When the spell-checker displays a misspelled word in the **Not In Dictionary** field, you can:

   ◇ Click | Ignore | to ignore the misspelled word, or click | Ignore All |.

   ◇ Type the correction in the **Change To** field and click | Change | or click | Change All |.

   ◇ Click | Add | to add the word to the user dictionary.

Inserting Page Breaks Manually

1. Select the task or resource to push onto the next page.

2. Choose **Insert, Page Break**; a dashed line will appear that represents the page break.

3. Choose **File, Print** and check ☑ **Manual page breaks** to make the breaks appear in the printout.

The page breaks, set in the table also insert breaks in other reports that are based on the same table. Therefore, use them only when really needed.

To remove page breaks position your cursor in any cell below the dashed line (e.g. same cell when you inserted it) and choose **Insert, Remove page break**.

Adjusting the Column Width

When you see railroad tracks like ##### in cells, it just means that the column is not wide enough for the value to display. You can easily best fit the column width by double-clicking on the right-hand divider in the column heading. Point to it first, and when you see the mouse pointer ↔ , double click. This best fits the column for all rows in the schedule, not just the visible rows. Please note that the **Predecessor** and **Successor** columns can become very wide when best fitted.

The Timescale Is Too Short or Too Long

The timescale often has to be adjusted, because it spills over onto the second page, and you want to shorten it, or it occupies only a small part of the page, and you want to stretch it.

To Shorten the Timescale

1. Choose **Format, Timescale** or double-click on the timescale; the **Timescale** dialog appears.

2. On any of the tier tabs, decrease the **Size** percentage, which will shorten the timescale. Check the sample box at the bottom to see how far you can go.

 In the task and resource usage views, you can drag the width of the time unit columns to the size you want.

To Stretch the Timescale to One Page

1. Choose **File, Page Setup**.

2. Click the tab **View** and check ☑ **Fit timescale to end of page**.
    This will stretch the timescale to fill the page.

Print Preview

Use print preview to check the header, footer, legend, margins and the timescale before printing or to check the position of the boxes on a Network Diagram.

1. Apply the view you want to print.

2. Click 🔍 or choose **File, Print Preview**:

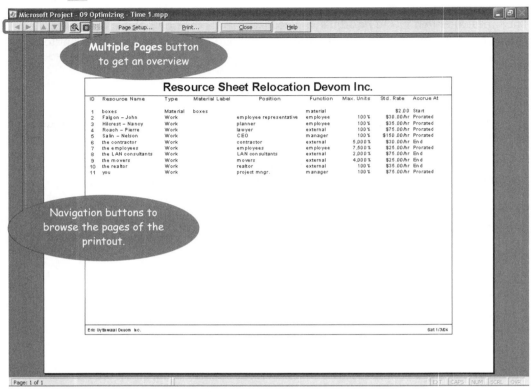

3. Use the multi-page button 🔡 to zoom out and get an overview of all the printed pages, and then click on one of the pages to zoom into that page.
   OR

   Hold down [Alt], and use the arrow keys to browse through the pages of the printout.

4. On the print preview, click where you would like to zoom in to see part of a page in more detail. Click again to zoom out.

5. To change the margins, header, footer or legend text, click [Page Setup...].

6. To print the view, click [Print...].
   To exit print preview without printing, click [Close].

Printing the Current View

 Use the new tool **Print current view as a report** on the Project Guide toolbar called **Report**. The guide will present a series of prompts and take you through the process.
OR

Apply the view to print and click to send the schedule directly to the default printer.
OR

Choose the print options using these steps:

1. Choose **File, Print**; the **Print** dialog appears:

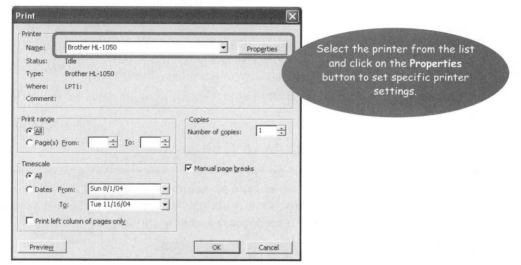

2. Select a printer in the **Name** list.

3. Click **Properties** to select the options available for the printer, such as paper source and orientation. Note that the choices you make here apply to all applications. Click **OK** when finished to go back to the **Print** dialog.

4. Select from the options available for your printer; see the next page for an explanation.

5. Click **OK** to start printing, or click **Close** to return to your project without printing.

 Colors you may have used are automatically replaced by hatch patterns on a black-and-white printer.

Print Options

◆ **Print range**
Select ⦿ **All** to print the entire project.
OR
Type the page numbers of the first and last page to print in the **Page(s) From** and **To** fields.

◆ ☑ **Manual page breaks**
Check to use the manually set page breaks. Clear to use automatic page breaks set by MS Project.

◆ **Timescale**
If you are printing a view with a timescale (Gantt Chart, Task Usage, Resource Graph and Resource Usage view), the **Timescale** section is active.
To print the project from project start date to finish date use ⦿ **All**;
for a particular period select ⦿ **Dates From To** and fill in the dates for the period you want.

Sending a Project Schedule to Colleagues

1. Choose **File, Send To, Mail Recipient (as Attachment).** The schedule will be attached to the e-mail. The **Choose Profile** dialog may appear: select a user profile, and click [OK]. The new e-mail message dialog appears:

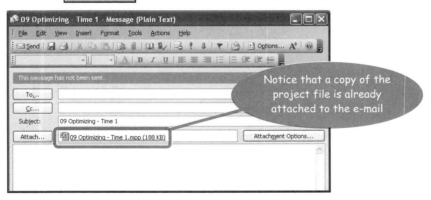

2. Fill in the **To** and the **CC** fields, and send the message.

 Notice that you don't even need to save your schedule before sending it; the feature always sends the schedule as it appears on your screen.

Instead, you can use the **File, Send To, Routing Recipient** feature to send the schedule to a chain of people, each of whom will receive the schedule for review.

If you don't want your colleagues to be able to change your project schedule, you should create a Portable Document File (PDF) using *Adobe Acrobat*.[90] Adobe Acrobat sets itself up as if it were a printer, so you can create PDF files simply by choosing **File, Print** and then selecting as the printer either **Acrobat PDFWriter** or **Acrobat Distiller**.

---

[90] Adobe Acrobat (www.adobe.com) is not free software, although the PDF reader is.

Exercises

Review Questions

1. Is it possible to create a one-page report for a 1,000-task schedule that reflects the performance of the project? Would you recommend doing this?

2. We discussed 15 ways to hide a buffer in your schedule. Mention six ways.

3. What are the three communication features in MS Project?
   What are their main differences?

4. What other objects does a view object refer to and apply?
   What other settings are stored inside the view object?

5. How can you transfer an object to another project schedule?

6. Can you print the following items?
   Would you do this through a report or through a view?
   Please indicate the exact name of the report or view.

Can you print?	Yes/No	Through Report or View? Which?
a. Gantt Chart		
b. Project calendar		
c. Resource calendar		
d. Project statistics (as shown in the **Project, Project Information,** Statistics... dialog)		
e. Cash outflow report		
f. Notes		

Relocation Project — Reporting an Executive Overview

1. Open the file *10 Reporting 1.MPP* available for download at www.jrosspub.com. Please, click the link *WAV Download Resource Center* to enter the download site. We will create a custom view that provides executives with a high-level overview of the project.

2. Create a new task table named *Executive Overview*. Use the columns **ID, Name, Duration** and **Cost**.

3. Create a new filter, *Executive Overview*, to display milestones and their summary tasks.

4. Create a new view, *Executive Overview*, and show it in the menu. Make sure that when you apply the view *Executive Overview*, the corresponding table and filter are both applied.

5. Hide the question marks in the duration column by choosing **Tools, Options,** tab **Schedule** and clearing the option ☐ **Show that tasks have estimated duration**.

6. Apply the following **Format, Timescale** settings:

	Middle Tier	**Bottom Tier**
Units	*Months*	*Days*
Label	*Jan '00*	*1,2,...*
Count	*1*	*7*
Align	*Center*	*Center*
Size	*100 %*	*100 %*

7. Format the **Header, Footer** and **Legend** of the Gantt Chart as follows:

Page Tab	Section	Set to	Font
Header	*Center*	*&[View] &[Project Title]*	*Arial, Bold, 20*
Footer	*Left*	*&[Manager] &[Company]*	*Arial, Regular, 8*
	Right	*&[Date]*	*Arial, Regular, 8*
Legend	*Legend on*	⊙ *None*	

8. Compare your file with the view *Executive Overview* in the solution file *10 Reporting 2.MPP* available for download at www.jrosspub.com. Please, click the link *WAV Download Resource Center* to enter the download site. See page 675 of this book for an automated way of comparing and reporting differences between two versions of one schedule.

Relocation Project — Reporting Cost by Function

1. Open the file *10 Reporting 2.MPP* available for download at www.jrosspub.com. Please, click the link *WAV Download Resource Center* to enter the download site.

2. Switch to the **Resource Sheet** view.

3. Create a new resource table *Cost by Function* that shows the fields **ID, Resource Name**, **Position**, **Function** and **Cost**.

4. Create a grouping *Cost by Function* so that you can easily read the total cost by function category of the project.

5. Create a new resource sheet view named *Cost by Function* that is shown in the menu. The view should apply the corresponding table and grouping.

6. Set the **Page Setup** settings to the following:

Tab	Section	Set to
Page	*Orientation*	*Portrait*
	Scaling	*Fit to: 1 page wide by 1 tall*
Margins	*top,bottom,left,right*	*1 inch or 2.5 cm*
	Borders Around	*every page*
Header	*Center* *Arial, Bold, 20*	*&[View] &[Project Title]*
Footer	*Left*	*&[Manager] &[Company]*
	Center	*none; delete the default entry*
	Right	*&[Date]*

7. Compare your file with the solution file *11 Updating the Schedule 1.MPP* available for download at www.jrosspub.com. Please, click the link *WAV Download Resource Center* to enter the download site.

Chapter 11 Updating the Schedule

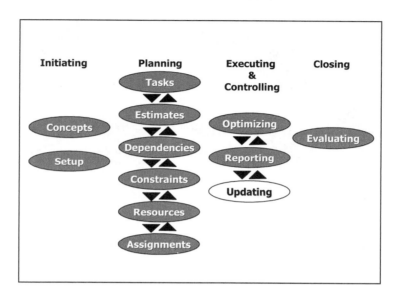

In the previous chapter on Reporting, we printed or published our optimized schedule to gain approval for it. In this chapter, we will explore what you need to do after you have the go-ahead and can start the work in the project.

After this chapter you will:
- ◆ be able to prepare your schedule for updating
- ◆ be able to set the baseline and know how to maintain it
- ◆ be able to choose the appropriate way of updating your schedule:
  - ◇ updating the tasks, or
  - ◇ updating the assignments (time sheets)
- ◆ be able to update on the task level using actual start and finish, actual and remaining duration
- ◆ be able to update on the assignment level using Project Web Access or Microsoft Office Outlook time sheets
- ◆ be able to handle the wide variety of update situations that occur in practice
- ◆ know how to communicate the status and the forecasts of the project
- ◆ be able to check if the schedule is updated properly using scheduling best practices
- ◆ be able to optimize the schedule after updating to compensate for slippages

"I am already 90% complete!"

Nob is bent over his paper schedule. "What are you doing Nob?" is Bob's question while he walks into the office.

Nob: "I am trying to figure out if I will meet the project deadline or not."

Bob: "And ... what are you finding?"

Nob: "I am not sure yet ... if Joe delivers on time I will be fine, but his percentages are going up very slowly."

Bob: "Where is he at right now?"

Nob: "Well, he tells me that he is now at 90% complete. Last week he was at 80%."

Bob: "What does 90% complete mean?"

Nob: "It means that ... he is almost done, of course!"

Bob: "Have you asked him for an estimate of how many days he still needs?"

Nob: "No, I always just ask for a % complete."

Bob: "That's why you have difficulties trying to figure out if you will meet the deadline or not. If you would ask him for the remaining duration as well, you would know! I never ask for a % complete, because that number does not help me update my forecasts. Also, I find that people mean totally different things when they say it is 90% complete. Programmers often mean that they have figured out the logical puzzle at 90% complete and that they will now start programming it. When busy team members tell me it is 90% complete, they are basically telling me to get off their backs so they can do their work. Other people actually mean that they have spent 90% of the time they were supposed to spend. They may still need as much time to finish it, though. 90% complete is no information as far as I am concerned!"

Overview of Updating

The updating of a project schedule is entering what happened in the past (the *actuals*) and what you forecast for the future of the project.

Executing a project is often a more chaotic experience than anticipated in the project plan:
- The progress can run behind on some tasks and ahead on other tasks relative to the baseline.
- When a critical task slips, corrections to the schedule have to be made in order to meet the deadline.
- Unexpected expenses or sudden budget cuts may have to be compensated for.
- Tasks are completed out of sequence. Team members manage to start working on tasks they logically should not have started, at least according to your plan.
- People fall sick. And worse, sick people who pass deliverables on to healthy people may pass on their bugs as well…

Optimizing methods are important when you plan a project, but even more so when you execute a project.

The process steps for updating schedules can be summarized as follows:
- Baseline the schedule: set it once for the entire schedule and maintain its integrity.
- Choose the client reporting period, see page 618.
- Choose the update strategy, see page 621.
  - ◇ Tasks update:
    Updating tasks is collecting progress information on the task level. It is less effort than updating assignments, see page 623.
  - ◇ Assignments update:
    Updating assignments is collecting actual hours worked by day by resource. When you update assignments, you work with time sheets, see page 639.
- Update the schedule: enter the actual values and remaining estimates. This is discussed separately for each strategy.
- Check if the schedule is updated correctly, see page 660.
- Prepare the status and forecast report, see page 663.
  You may need to re-optimize your schedule before reporting on it.

The Baseline

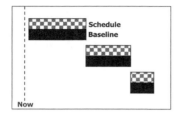

The baseline is a frozen copy of the final approved schedule. The *baseline schedule* is the target to aim for. The baseline should remain the same throughout the project as much as possible. In the illustration on the left, you can see that each task bar is split into two parts. The top part is the current schedule – the dynamic model of the project. The bottom part is the static *baseline* to compare the current schedule against. If you display the status date also as a line in the timescale, you have all you need to visually assess the status of a project.

Viewing the Baseline

1. Choose **View, Tracking Gantt Chart** which displays two task bars for each task the current schedule at the top and the baseline schedule at the bottom, if present.

2. Click on the menu items **View, Table <name of current table>, More Tables**.

3. Choose the table **Baseline** in the list.

4. Click [Apply].

Notice that the fields in the baseline date columns show **NA** when the baseline is not yet set for the tasks.

Setting the First Baseline

1. Choose **Tools, Tracking, Save Baseline**.

2. Select ⦿ **Save Baseline**.

3. To set the baseline for all tasks, select ⦿ **Entire Project**

4. Click [OK]; the original schedule is copied to the **Baseline** fields for comparison. If you get a notification that you do not have the rights to save a baseline to *Project Server*, the administrator has not granted you permission to save baselines.

Remarks:

- Note that the baseline version of the schedule contains only five task-related fields: *baseline start* and *baseline finish* dates, *baseline duration*, *baseline work* and *baseline cost*. It also saves the time-phased work and cost data. Certain resource- and assignment-related fields are also baselined. You can see that a baseline is not a complete version of the schedule; many task-related fields are not captured in baseline fields. Don't use baselines if what you really need is a complete version of the schedule.

  Project Server has *version control* features, like checking in and out. It keeps track of the most current version: the *published* version, as well as other versions of the same schedule.

- Apart from eleven baselines, there are also ten interim plans (*Start1*/*Finish1* through *Start10*/*Finish10*), which are extra sets of only start and finish date fields. In each of these you can store a set of start and finish dates you would like to keep. You can copy a set into any other set at any time, even back into the current schedule (*Start*/*Finish*). However, we don't recommend this, because it affects the **Duration** and **Work** numbers. Be aware that the interim plans only contain the start and finish dates, and hold no duration, work or cost data, unlike the baselines. The interim plans are useful for a quick comparison before and after a series of changes. We used it on page 492 to compare the three different leveling scenarios.

- Since Project 2002, MS Project captures the date in the name of the baseline. You can see the date on which you set the baseline in **Tools, Tracking, Save baseline**.

- Make sure you set the baseline <u>after</u> you have substituted generic resources with real people, because:

  ◇ You have not performed a feasibility check on your schedule from a workload point of view if you still have generic resources in your schedule. The schedule with real people assigned may turn out to be not feasible.

  ◇ The resource-related baseline fields are set back to "*0*" (zero) or "*NA*" when you use the *Resource Substitution Wizard*.

Maintaining the Baseline

The baseline is considered to be a contract between the project manager and the sponsor or client of the project. You would normally set the *baseline* only once, unless:

- There are formal changes approved <u>after</u> the baseline has been set. These changes could be:
  ◇ *Scope* changes that entail addition or removal of deliverables
  ◇ Substantial additions or deletions of *tasks*

◇ Substantial additions or losses of *resources*

◇ Substantial changes in resource *rates* or *fixed cost*

◆ When other *changes* are approved or imposed that force you to re-think and re-baseline your schedule, like budget increases, changes of deadline, or availability of crucial resources.

◆ When *errors* in the schedule turn up unexpectedly, you would need to get formal approval to re-baseline the affected tasks.

◆ There might be exceptional *circumstances*, such as a fire, strike or a sudden economic recession. If they affect your original plan, you should submit a change request to re-baseline.

◆ '*Acts of God*' may affect your project: flood, tornado, hurricane or earth-quake. Even if these happen elsewhere, shipments with supplies for your project may be affected.

In all of these cases, a change request should be submitted to the decision-makers to request approval to change the baseline. If you acquire approval, you should only re-baseline those tasks that are affected. These are, of course, the tasks that are new and inserted, but also their dependent tasks downstream (*successors*). Don't forget these last ones!

It is <u>not</u> a good idea to reset the baseline often, because comparing to a baseline that moves constantly is not meaningful. Your project becomes a target-seeking missile trying to catch up with a constantly moving target. Treat the baseline as a contractual agreement, even if it wasn't formalized with signatures. Insist that changes are brought forward through formal change requests. Incorporate the changes only after they were formally approved. Pay attention to creating a clear and smooth change request process and communicate it to the stakeholders.

If you baseline the entire schedule for a second time in the same way, you overwrite all the values in the baseline fields: start and finish dates, duration, cost, work and the date on which the baseline was set. You may loose valuable (contractual) information if you do this inadvertently.

There is a way to preserve baselines. Since Project 2002, MS Project has fields for ten extra baselines (Baseline1 through Baseline10), and you can copy any of these baselines back into the active **Baseline** fields and between each other. This allows you to compare against any of your ten 'steady states'. Before you copy another baseline back into the baseline fields, make sure you save your most current baseline in the next available set of baseline fields and you document what each baseline set is about.

If you plan on using *Earned Value* this may be of particular importance. The Earned Value calculations can be based on any of these 11 baselines by choosing **Tools, Options**, tab **Calculations** and click Earned Value... to select the baseline from the list **Baseline for Earned Value calculations**.

Here are the steps to change the baseline:

1. To save the current baseline first, choose **Tools, Tracking, Save Baseline**; the **Save Baseline** dialog appears.

2. Select ⊙ **Save interim plan** and select under **Copy** the current **Baseline** and under **Into** the next available set of baseline fields. The first time you revise your baseline this would be **Baseline1**. In that case, the dialog should now look like:

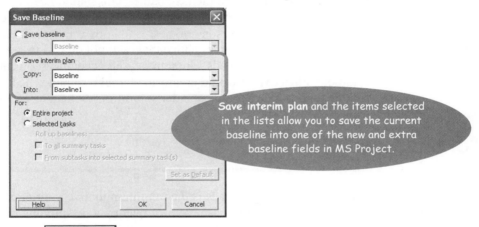

3. Click OK ; the date on which you copied the baseline is captured in the name of the baseline in the list. This will help you manage multiple baselines.

4. Now we can proceed to revise the current baseline. Select the tasks affected by the change request in the Gantt spreadsheet. These can be:

   ◇ Newly inserted deliverables or tasks and any other tasks that are dependent on the new ones that may have shifted

   ◇ Successor tasks affected by canceled deliverables or tasks

5. Choose **Tools, Tracking, Save Baseline**; the **Save Baseline** dialog appears again.

6. Select the option **For: ⊙ Selected tasks**.

7. Under **Roll up baselines**, check:
   ☑ **To all summary tasks** to update baseline information on all the higher-level summary tasks of the detail tasks selected.

☑ **From subtasks into selected summary tasks** to update only the summary tasks that you selected. If you had not selected the specific summary tasks in step 1, and want to use this option, cancel the dialog, include those summary tasks in your selection as well and start at step 5 again.

8. Click [OK].

If there is no formal change request, you have to be careful with deleting tasks that you don't need any longer, particularly when you do *Earned Value* performance reporting. If you simply delete these tasks, you compromise the integrity of the baseline, because it decreases the total *baseline work* and *baseline cost* on the summary tasks the next time you change the baseline and roll up to the summary tasks. Instead of deleting the task, add 'CANCEL' or 'DELETE' in capital letters to the task name. You should keep the work because when you rebaseline you need these numbers for now; set the task **Type** to **Fixed Work**. You need the cost for the same reason and best is to copy it into the field **Fixed Cost**. You can remove the assigned resources, since they will not do this task any longer, and you don't want to keep false workloads for them in your schedule. You can mark the task as 100% complete; otherwise it would create an eternal cost and schedule variance in your Earned Value report. You should consider submitting a change request to rebaseline and delete canceled tasks entirely.

The Client Reporting Period

As we discussed on page 149, ten reporting periods is the minimum to give your client enough possibilities for corrective action. Otherwise, your project may be spinning out of control … without your client knowing it. Clients will often prescribe the reporting period to you.

You don't want too many reporting periods, because each progress report takes time and effort to prepare. Each report therefore adds to the overhead cost of managing the project. With too many reporting periods, it becomes too heavy a burden for the project budget. The overhead cost can run up to 25% of the total cost, which can be a lot of money. Ideally, you should not have to report more than 30 times.

What does this mean for our projects? The next table shows what it means for projects of different durations.

Project Duration	Minimum Client Reporting Frequency	Maximum Client Reporting Frequency
1 month	every other business day	every business day
3 months	weekly	twice a week
1 year	monthly	every two weeks
2 years	every two months	every month
5 years	every half year	every two months

As the project manager you should ask your team to report status back to you at least as frequently as the client needs reports. In practice, team members often report more frequently to you as the project manager than that you report to the client.

Showing Progress

Graphically

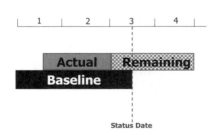

Status Date

The progress can best be seen in the **Tracking Gantt** view. This view shows the task bars as shown in the illustration. The scheduled task will slowly but surely fill in with solid dark blue (*Actual*) to indicate how much progress has been made (*Actual Duration*). Notice that the actual duration represents the number of days a team member has worked on the task so far, even though many people only think of it as the number of days the task took once it has been completed.

Ideally, the actual duration runs up to the *status date*, indicating that the task is progressing as scheduled. In the illustration, you can see that the progress has fallen behind (sickness, under-estimation, other tasks took priority). The rest of the bar in light blue (*Remaining*) represents the *Remaining Duration*. The remaining duration is how many days the task will still take from the status date on. The following formula works

behind the screens, as you can easily see from the illustration:
Actual Duration + Remaining Duration = Duration
You can see that the duration is often recalculated through this formula when you update the schedule, which causes deviations from the baseline duration.

The black *Baseline* allows us to analyze slippages. In the illustration, you can see that:
◆ The task started 0.5 week later (Actual Start) than scheduled (Baseline Start).
◆ The task duration was already revised from 2.5 (Baseline Duration) to 3.5 weeks (current Duration); this is a 1-week difference.
◆ The progress is still behind; the task is also progressing 0.5 week slower, because the Actual Duration (progress) is 0.5 week behind the status date. This 0.5 week of work to be done should be rescheduled to the future. It is likely the slippage will further increase, since progress was slower than expected in the last update period, and the remaining duration may need to be increased again.

Mathematically

You can express progress in terms of the duration progress at the task level. As long as you keep revising the **Remaining Duration** with your latest estimates, the total **Duration** will be recalculated, and MS Project will calculate the **% Complete**. The formula is shown to the left. The *% Complete* is a calculated indicator of progress on tasks. If you want, you can even have MS Project calculate and enter time sheet information based on *Actual Durations* entered. Of course, MS Project will not be as precise at this compared to collecting time sheets with the exact information.

$$\% \text{ Complete} = \frac{\text{Actual Duration}}{\text{Duration}}$$

$$\% \text{ Work Complete} = \frac{\text{Actual Work}}{\text{Work}}$$

Alternatively, you can collect time sheets and enter the *actual hours* worked on the level of assignments from the time sheets. If you revise the **Remaining Work**, the total work will be recalculated. The formula is similar to the one for durations: *Actual Work + Remaining Work = Work*. MS Project will then calculate the **% Work Complete**, which will also be a useful progress indicator. With this information, MS Project can also calculate the Actual Duration and Remaining Duration on the task level, and update the tasks accordingly.

This shows that there are two different updating strategies you can take.

Updating Strategies

There are two different strategies to update your schedule: *updating tasks* or *updating assignments*. An *assignment* is always a combination of a task and a resource, as discussed on page 369. Assignments are on a more detailed level than tasks, since one task can have multiple assignments; there are multiple resources assigned.

◆ Updating tasks means updating a maximum of four fields for each task in the following order:
  ◇ **Actual Start**,
  ◇ **Actual Duration**,
  ◇ **Remaining Duration**, and
  ◇ **Actual Finish**.

◆ When you update assignments with time sheet information, you typically update for every assignment of a resource:
  ◇ *Actual hours by day or by week* in the timescale field *Actual Work* (Note that there is also an assignment-related field **Actual Work** in the spreadsheet that is the total of all the timescale entries; we are not referring to that field here.)
  ◇ *Remaining hours* by assignment in the field *Remaining Work* in the spreadsheet

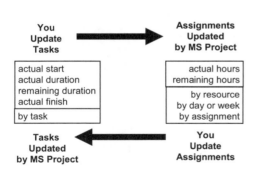

The illustration summarizes the two ways of updating the schedule. If you *update tasks*, MS Project can update the assignments for you. If you update the assignments from the time sheets, MS Project can update the tasks. MS Project will do this for you if you keep the option **Tools, Options**, tab **Calculation, ☑ Updating task status updates resource status** checked.

The strategy of updating the tasks is quick and easy. You only have to enter actual dates and durations, and in most cases, you can do that with the mouse. Since you only specify the **Actual Start** date and not all the dates on which the work took place, MS Project arbitrarily spreads the *actual hours* in the timescale. This makes this method less precise than entering actual hours worked from time sheets when you update assignments, but in many situations it is precise enough. There are new options in **Tools, Options**, tab **Calculation** that can improve the precision of the automatic spreading.

Updating assignments requires more numbers to process and therefore more work during the busy project execution. To illustrate this, consider the following situation. You have a schedule with 300 tasks and 10 weekly reporting periods, which means that every week you have to update an average of 30 tasks, 20 of which are typically completed in that week. If you do a task update, you would have to collect:

◆ For the 20 completed tasks, you collect actual start and actual duration, but if you are not interested in exact dates, you would only have 20 actual durations.

◆ For the 10 tasks in progress, you collect actual start, actual duration, remaining duration and actual finish. If you are not interested in exact dates, you could do with 20 pieces of information (10 actual durations, 10 remaining durations).

The grand total for updating tasks therefore is 20 + 20 = 40 pieces of data (recommended).

For an assignment update, we will have to make more assumptions. We will assume that the average task duration is 4 days and the average number of resources per task is 1.5:

◆ For the 20 completed tasks: 20 tasks * 4 days * 1.5 resources = 120 pieces of data
◆ For the 10 tasks in progress: 10 tasks * 4 days * 1.5 resources = 60 pieces of data

The grand total for updating assignments is: 120 + 60 = 180 pieces of data.

As you can see, if you update assignments instead of tasks, you are processing more than four times as much data during the project *execution phase* when you are very busy. If you don't have an electronic time sheet system in place, we recommend you do task updates instead of assignment updates. The paper time sheets will drown you in data. Data entry takes (too) much effort, and often project managers can't keep up, even if they only need to review the data on a weekly basis. And we haven't even mentioned the double data entry and the probability of errors.

We have observed that too many project managers stop updating their schedules sometime during the project *execution phase*, because they either fail to get that much information from their team members or they drown in the flood of data or errors. If you abandon updating your schedule, you lose the model that provides you with up-to-date forecasts and allows you to do what-if scenarios to determine the best course of action. You lose your grip on the project. It is better to have less precise grip than no grip. We recommend you consider carefully which update strategy fits your situation best.

Project Professional with *Project Server* provides an electronic time sheet system that supports updating assignments as just explained:

◆ It will make collecting status from your team members much easier.

◆ It allows you to transfer the numbers automatically back into your schedule and prevents double data entry. Many time sheet systems currently on the market do not put the update information back into the schedules and are not useful for project managers.

◆ It makes submitting performance reports to executives and client much easier.

If you have Project Server, or an equivalent, updating assignments is the recommended course of action.

We will now discuss updating tasks in detail, and we will discuss updating assignments later on page 639 and following.

Updating Tasks

Here are the things you need to do when *updating tasks*:
◆ Collect the update information by task
◆ Choose the **Tools, Options** (see page 627)
◆ Prepare the view (see page 628):
  ◇ Change the view to **Tracking Gantt**
  ◇ Apply the **Tracking** table
  ◇ Display the **Tracking** toolbar
◆ Set the **Status Date** and the **Current Date** for updating (see page 629)
◆ Set the task **Type** of the tasks you will update to **Fixed Units** (see page 630)
◆ Enter the update information (see page 631)
◆ Check whether the schedule is updated correctly (see page 660)
◆ Prepare the status and forecast report (see page 663)
  You may need to re-optimize your schedule before reporting on it.

What Data to Collect?

Actual Duration + Remaining Duration = Duration

Actual Duration / Duration = % Complete

When we update the tasks in our project, we should keep the formulas shown in the illustration in the back of our minds. They explain the values that MS Project calculates and displays when we enter actuals. Notice that *Actual Duration* is not only the number of days that you worked on a task after it is done. While the task is still in progress, Actual Duration is the number of days that you have worked on the task up until the status date. The *Remaining Duration* is the forecast of how many days a task will still take from the status date forward.

In a tasks update, you enter the **Actual Duration** and allow MS Project to calculate the **Remaining Duration** and the **% Complete** using the formulas shown in the illustration. Once resources have started working on a task they often have a much better idea how long it will take. You may find that the remaining duration calculated by MS Project may be too little or too much time. If so, you should update the **Remaining Duration** field with a more precise estimate. MS Project will then recalculate the total **Duration** (**Actual** plus **Remaining**) and decrease or increase the **% Complete** accordingly.

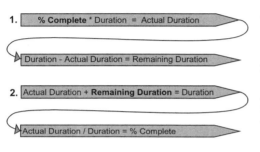

If you want to enter **% Complete** instead of the **Actual Duration**, it will be a longer, two-step process that follows the formulas in the illustration on the left. You can see that it is more complicated. First you enter the **% Complete** (step 1 in illustration), but when you revise the **Remaining Duration** (step 2), MS Project recalculates the **% Complete** you first entered. You may not like that. Why enter a number that will change in most cases?

More importantly, you have to ask yourself what it means if a team member tells you "I am at *90% complete*". Does it mean:

- ◆ *I am almost finished!* (this is what we would like it to mean, of course), or
- ◆ *I have spent 90% of the time I was supposed to spend on this task,* or
- ◆ *I have just figured out how to do this, and now I will do it,* or
- ◆ *I did all the easy stuff, now I will start the difficult stuff!* or
- ◆ *Last week it was 80% complete, so this week it must be 90%,* or
- ◆ *I want the project manager to think that I am at 90% complete!* or
- ◆ *Leave me alone, so I can do my work; I am busy enough!* or
- ◆ *I have started to work on the task!*

I often ask groups of project managers what they have found *90% complete* means, and inevitably they indicate that *90% complete* can mean any of the above! We therefore recommend you ask for **Actual Durations** instead of **% Complete** when collecting update information; ask for facts rather than fiction. Using **% Complete** is less objective than entering the actual number of business days that people worked on a task (**Actual Duration**). The number of days somebody really worked on a task can easily be counted and is factual information. For example, if the resource worked on the task on Wednesday, Thursday and Friday the **Actual Duration** is 3 days so far.

If you choose to enter **% Complete** instead of having it calculated by MS Project as we suggest, we recommend:

◆ You still ask for **Remaining Duration** updates, since they will keep your forecasts accurate. If you only enter **% Complete** your forecasts will be inaccurate.

◆ You allow fairly rough increments in **% Complete** only. We suggest increments such as 0%, 25%, 50%, 75%, 100% as shown on the **Tracking** toolbar, or perhaps only 0% and 100%. In the latter case, you can simply ask: *are you finished with it, or not?* This question does not leave much room for wishful thinking (or outright manipulation). However, you need to have a fairly detailed schedule in order to get good results with rough percentages. The durations of the detail tasks should be near 1% rather than the 10% in the *1%-10% rule*; see our discussion on page 144. If you create tasks that are small enough, you can get to the facts more easily.

◆ You consider the options that will influence how MS Project will spread the *actual hours* worked when entering **% Complete**. Choose **Tools, Options,** tab **Calculation**; the main options are (see for more detail page 627):

☑ **Move end of completed parts after status date back to status date** which moves the actual hours worked to before the status date.

☑ **Move start of remaining parts before status date forward to status date** which moves the remaining durations to after the status date.

Edits to total task % complete will be spread to the status date. If you change a % complete, MS Project can calculate the actual hours and spread them out to the status date when this option is on. When it is off, the actual hours will be entered where they were scheduled or from the **Actual Start** date onward and splits will often appear in the task bars.

We will not discuss updating with **% Complete** any further and will instead explain how to update with **Actual Duration** and **Remaining Duration** in more detail.

Collecting the Data

In order to update your schedule with actual data, you need to gather the data. You need to collect the following information for task updates from your team members. We recommend that you use the following questions:

◆ *On what date did you start on the task?* (**Actual Start**)
This question is only needed if accuracy of actual dates is important.

◆ *How many business days have you worked on the task as per the status date?* (**Actual Duration**)

◆ *How many business days do you still need to finish the task after the status date?* (**Remaining Duration**) You need to ask this question only for tasks that are currently in progress.

◆ *On what date was the task finished?* (**Actual Finish**)
This question is often not needed if you kept the remaining durations up to date in previous updates.

If you don't want to collect and enter this much information, we recommend you choose **Remaining Duration** as the absolute minimum. If you only keep the remaining duration estimates up-to-date and schedule them after the status date, the forecasts will be *valid*. The next thing to add to the mix would be the **Actual Duration**.

Instead of collecting Actual Duration and Remaining Duration, you can also collect *Actual Work* and *Remaining Work* on the task level. If most of your tasks are based on effort (Work), this may make even more sense. This will work in a similar way as with durations, except for that you enter them into the fields **Actual Work** and **Remaining Work** of course.

There are two ways that are commonly used to collect the data for task updates:

◆ Regular status meeting:
In a short meeting of one hour at most, you quickly ask each team member for this information. You then enter it, or have it entered. Some project managers have it entered immediately during the status meeting and display the schedule on a large screen to reveal new schedule conflicts that can be discussed and resolved right away.

◆ To-do list turn-around reports:
You can distribute to each team member paper to-do lists that also contain empty fill-in fields for the status information. Ask the team members to enter the status information and return it to you by the end of the week, at which time they get the next to-do list. If you report weekly, print a to-do list that covers two weeks ahead to show what is coming up, and to allow the resource to make progress ahead of schedule. Note that such a list is not as detailed as a time sheet is.

Choosing the Options for Updating Tasks

Choose **Tools, Options**. Here are the options we recommend for updating tasks using **Actual** and **Remaining Duration**:

Tab	Option
Calculation	☑ **Updating task status updates resource status** Updating the tasks will update the actual work of the assignments. We recommend you keep this option checked for task updates. Only clear it if you want to update the tasks <u>and</u> the assignments.
	☑ **Move end of completed parts after status date back to status date** This moves the actual duration bar to before the status date. Actual work done is moved into the past. We recommend you turn this on. ☑ **And move start of remaining parts back to status date** The remaining duration bar will cuddle up to the status date (unless there are dependencies that keep it where it is). You can turn it off.
	☑ **Move start of remaining parts before status date forward to status date** This moves the remaining duration bar to after the status date. Work still to be completed is moved to the future. We recommend you turn this on. ☑ **And move end of completed parts forward to status date** This moves the actual duration bar to cuddle up to the status date. You can turn it off.
	☐ **Edits to total task % complete will be spread to the status date** If a task is falling behind, the progress entered will be evenly spread to the status date. This option is only relevant if you enter % Complete.
	☑ **Actual costs are always calculated by Microsoft Office Project** Updating the tasks will update the *actual cost*. It is up to you whether you want MS Project to do that.

Tab	Option
	Set as Default Sets the options as the default settings for any new schedules you create. The existing schedules are not affected, because these options are stored in the project schedule as you can see in the label of the section divider **Calculation Options for <schedule name of the project>**.
General	☐ **Automatically add new resources and tasks** Prevents a typo in a resource name from accidentally adding a new resource. Works similarly for tasks.
Edit	☐ **Allow cell drag and drop** Prevents accidentally dragging data on top of other data in your baselined schedule.
Schedule	☑ **Split in-progress tasks** Allows moving the uncompleted portion of a task to after the **Status Date** by splitting the task bar. With this option cleared, the options on the **Calculation** tab cannot split any task bars and will behave quite differently as a result.
	Set as Default Sets the option as the default setting for any new schedules you create. The existing schedules are not affected, because this option is stored in the project schedule as you can see in the label of the section divider **Scheduling Options for <schedule name of the project>**.

Notice that the options in **Tools, Options**, tab **Calculation**, that were new in the 2002 release, help to reschedule in-progress tasks, but they have no effect on tasks that have not started yet, but should have started as per the status date. These tasks may have to be rescheduled to after the status date to put them into the future where they belong, since work can only be done in the future. As you can see, these options help when updating the schedule, but do not guarantee that your schedule will be entirely up to date.

Prepare the View for Updating

1. Choose **View, Tracking Gantt**.
   The current schedule is shown in the top half of the task bars (colored blue or red). The baseline is shown as the gray bottom half of the task bars.

2. The tracking table has all the fields in which to enter data for task updates. To apply it, choose **View, Table <name of current table>, Tracking**. The table looks like the following screenshot in which it is very easy to enter actual information:

	Task Name	Act. Start	Act. Finish	% Comp.	Act. Dur.	Rem. Dur.	Act. Cost	Act. Work
1	⊟ REQUIREMENTS	NA	NA	0%	0 days	7.4 days	$0.00	0 days
2	research staff requirements	NA	NA	0%	0 days	4 days	$0.00	0 days
3	summarize requirements	NA	NA	0%	0 days	4 days	$0.00	0 days
4	⊟ LOCATION	NA	NA	0%	0 days	16.5 days	$0.00	0 days
5	select the realtor	NA	NA	0%	0 days	4 days	$0.00	0 days
6	visit the sites	NA	NA	0%	0 days	1 day	$0.00	0 days
7	evaluate the sites	NA	NA	0%	0 days	1 day	$0.00	0 days
8	meet to select the location	NA	NA	0%	0 days	1 day	$0.00	0 days
9	legal review	NA	NA	0%	0			

Enter actual progress into the **Tracking** table.

3. To display the **Tracking** toolbar: point to any toolbar and click the secondary mouse button. From the pop-up menu, choose **Tracking**. The tracking toolbar is displayed:

The **Tracking** toolbar has all the handy tools for updating.

 Notice that all objects you need for updating the schedule have the word '*tracking*' in their name: *Tracking Gantt* view, *Tracking table* and *Tracking toolbar*. This makes it easy to remember!

Setting the Status Date for Updating

1. Choose **Project, Project Information**.

2. Change the **status date** to the date through which you want to update tasks and compare the schedule against the baseline.

3. The status date does not yet appear as a vertical line in the timescale. Choose **Format, Gridlines** and select **Status Date** in the list as the line to change. Choose a dashed line in a bright color. Click [OK]; the status line is now visible in the timescale similar to:

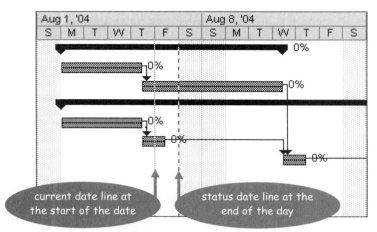

current date line at the start of the date

status date line at the end of the day

 MS Project uses the system date of your computer to continuously update the *current date*. When you open your schedule again tomorrow, you will find tomorrow's date as the current date. The *status date* stays the same, since you last entered it and will refresh your memory about when your last update took place. The line for the status date is displayed at the end of the day, whereas the line for the current date is displayed at the start of the day.

Set the Task Type for Tasks to Update

When you enter update information into MS Project, you will trigger recalculations in the formula D * U = W (Duration * Units of resources assigned = Work). The task **Type** has to be set in such a way that it triggers the right recalculations that are performed by MS Project in an unsolicited way.

When we update tasks, we change the durations. *Fixed duration* is therefore not the right **Type** of task, because we are not controlling what MS Project recalculates. When you extend task durations, you typically want to keep the resources that work on the task the same (units), and see the total work (effort) increase. The type *Fixed Units* is appropriate for that purpose. You could choose *Fixed Work*, if you want the number of *resource units* to be recalculated when the duration changes.

1. Click on any column heading in the Tracking Gantt spreadsheet to select all tasks.
    OR
    Be more selective, and select just those tasks that need to be updated.

2. Click **Task Information** on the **Standard** toolbar; the **Multiple Task Information** dialog appears. Click the **Advanced** tab; the dialog should now look like:

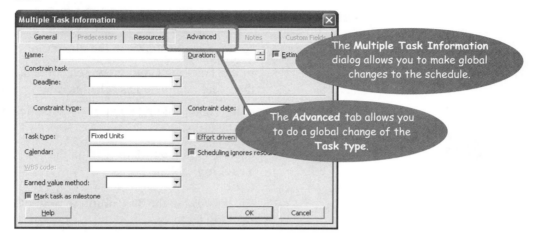

3. Select from the list **Task type** the item **Fixed Units**. Changing the task type does not trigger a recalculation, only a change in one variable in the formula: *Duration * Units = Work* will do that.

4. Clear ☐ **Effort driven** and click | OK |. Please note that summary tasks continue to be **Fixed Duration**.

Task Updating Situations in Practice

The following six situations are all you will ever come across when updating tasks:
- Tasks that Ran as Scheduled
- Tasks that Run as Scheduled
- Tasks that Run Behind
- Tasks that Will Take Longer (or Shorter)
- Tasks that Started Late (or Early)
- Tasks that Finished Late (or Early)

You will encounter all of these situations. They each have their own best way for entering update information. We will detail how-to steps for each situation.

 If you know that your project is almost on schedule, a quick way of updating most of your schedule is by clicking on a column heading to select all the tasks and then clicking **Update as Scheduled** on the **Tracking** toolbar. This updates your entire project as if it is running exactly according to schedule. Now you can tweak the status of some tasks that are off schedule with the next steps.

Tasks that Ran as Scheduled

You simply need to mark these tasks as 100% complete as shown in the illustration.

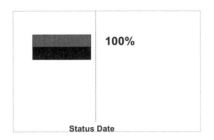

1. In the Tracking Gantt view, select the tasks that were completed as scheduled by dragging or holding down [Control] and clicking on the tasks.

2. Click **100% Complete** [100%] on the **Tracking** toolbar
OR
Enter 100% in the **% Complete** field of the tracking table.
OR
Click **Update Tasks** [icon] on the **Tracking** toolbar and enter 100% under **% Complete**.

Tasks that Run as Scheduled

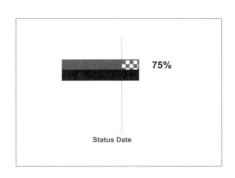

In this case, you want to show actual progress up to the status date as in the illustration.

1. Select the tasks that are on schedule by dragging or by holding down [Control] and clicking on them.

2. Click **Update as Scheduled** [icon] on the **Tracking** toolbar; this updates all selected tasks as if they are exactly on schedule as per the status date.

Tasks That Run Behind

This situation will require more updating effort. You will need to capture the actual

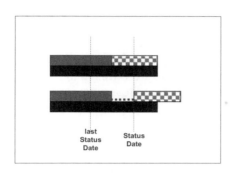

progress, but, because the task is behind, you will also have to bring the incomplete portion of the task bar forward to after the *status date*. Lastly, you will have to review the forecast of the remaining duration. If the task is progressing slower than planned, it was underestimated and you may have to increase the remaining duration.

In the illustration, you can see that the progress is falling behind, because the solid color of the actual progress does not run up to the status date in the task bar at the top. The bottom task bar has a split showing the incomplete portion of work rescheduled to after the status date.

1. Enter the **Actual Duration** of the task (the number of days you have worked on the task); MS Project will calculate the new remaining duration. Revise this calculated **Remaining Duration** (the number of business days still to go) and MS Project will calculate the **% Complete**.

2. If there is remaining duration scheduled in the past, reschedule it to after the status date, to the future. You can do this by dragging that part of the task bar.
OR
Select the task and click **Reschedule Work** on the **Tracking** toolbar. This will split the task bar if the option ☑ **Split in-progress tasks** is in effect in **Tools, Options, Schedule**.
OR
You don't need to do a thing if in **Tools, Options**, tab **Calculations**, you checked ☑ **Move start of remaining parts before status date forward to status date.**

You have to move the remaining duration out to the future, because unfortunately, you can't schedule work-to-be-done in the past. (If only we could…) Only if you move it out and revise it, will the dependent successors be rescheduled. If you forget this, you end up with a *status report* instead of a *forecast report*. A status report is like a report on yesterday's weather instead of a forecast report on tomorrow's weather.

You still have to ask yourself if the forecasted finish date is accurate. If you look at the rate of progress in the illustration, you will notice that it is more or less half of what it should be. Half of the work that should have been completed since the last status is accomplished. If the interruptions or slow progress will continue, the eventual duration will be double the baseline duration. You can see that currently, the forecasted duration is less than double the baseline duration; and the remaining duration should be increased even more if you expect the progress to continue in the same way. Running behind goes hand in hand with taking longer.

Tasks That Will Take Longer or Shorter

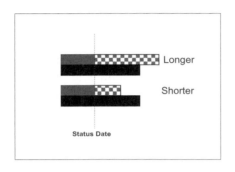

In this situation, good progress was made, but the realization sinks in that the remaining duration will not suffice. We need to increase the remaining estimate, or we may need to shorten it. (Hey, it has been known to happen!)

Since we are going to change the duration, you will trigger a recalculation through the formula $D * U = W$. You should not leave the task type set to **Fixed Duration**, since MS Project might recalculate the units or the work. We recommended changing the task type to **Fixed Units** before you start updating. If you choose **Fixed Units**, the work will change. If you choose **Fixed Work**, the number of resources (units) working on the task will change.

1. If needed, set the **Type** of task to *Fixed Units* tasks (or *Fixed Work*).

2. Enter the **Actual Duration** of the task.

3. Revise the **Remaining Duration**.
   OR
   Change the remaining duration with the mouse by pointing to the right side of its task bar. When you see the single-headed arrow mouse pointer ⏵, drag to change the remaining duration to compensate for the slippage. If you cannot get it on the right date, click **Zoom In** 🔍 on the **Standard** toolbar first.

4. You may have to use the methods to shorten your schedule as discussed in chapter 9 to compensate for the slipped finish date (see page 448).

Tasks That Started Late or Early

In this situation, the task did not start on the day that was planned. The illustration on the left reveals that the top task started late, whereas the bottom task started early. In the *Late* situation, the actual start date (left side of top bar) is later than the baseline start date (the left side of the black bottom bar). If you updated your schedule regularly and if you had a dynamic schedule (with all dependencies and few constraints), the start date may have moved already to the right date. If that is not the case, you have to enter it.

1. Point to the middle of the blue task bar, and when you see a four-headed arrow mouse pointer ✥ , drag the task bar to its new start date. If you cannot get it on the date you want, click **Zoom In** 🔍 on the **Standard** toolbar first.
    OR
    Enter the date in the field **Act. Start** of the tracking table.
    OR
    Select the task with a delayed start, click **Update Tasks** 📅 on the **Tracking** toolbar, then fill in the **Actual Start** date and click [OK] .

2. You may have to use the methods to shorten your schedule as discussed in chapter 9 to compensate for the slipped finish date (see page 448).

Tasks That Finished Late or Early

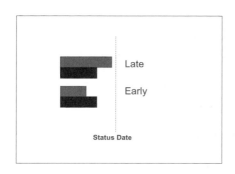

In this situation, you need to enter the finish dates. In the illustration on the left, you can see that the top task finished late relative to the black baseline bar. The bottom task finished early. If you updated your schedule regularly, however, you often don't need to enter finish dates. When you revise the remaining duration, MS Project already changes the finish date to the right date, or close to it. If it still isn't the right date, you can enter that date into the project schedule.

The steps are:

1. Point to the right side of its blue task bar, and when you see a single-headed arrow mouse pointer ⊪ , drag the finish to its new date. Set the task to 100% complete.
    OR
    Enter the date in **Act. Finish** of the tracking table.
    OR
    Select the task with a slipped finish date, and click **Update Tasks** ⊞ on the **Tracking** toolbar and fill in the **Actual Finish** date and click [OK] .

2. You may have to use the methods to shorten your schedule as discussed in chapter 9 to compensate for the slipped finish date (see page 448).

"My Reality Is More Complex..."

There are certain situations that seem more difficult to update in your schedule than discussed before:

◆   Combination of situations
    For example, what to do with a task that started late, runs behind and will take longer?
◆   Updating out of sequence
    What if tasks have been done out of sequence? For example, a task is already in progress that is scheduled to start in the future.
◆   New activities on the fly
    What if you realize while working on a task that it actually consists of more tasks, or what if you decide to reassign resources?

We will discuss each situation in more detail.

Combination of Situations

Your situation can be more complex. No matter what, it is always a combination of the six situations we discussed before. For example, the start date is different from the baseline start and the progress is behind. Let's say, the situation on a two-day task on May 2nd 2000 at 5PM is:

◆   The Actual Start date is May 2nd with a Baseline Start of May 1st
◆   The Remaining Duration is revised from 1 day to 2 days

In a situation like this, we recommend you start with updating the **Actual Start**, then the **Actual Duration** and the **Remaining Duration** last. Graphically speaking, you enter data going from left to right over the task bar. If you keep this in mind, you will never see unexpected results in MS Project. It will help you if you put the columns in the right order.

The resource worked only May 2nd on the task; the Actual Duration is one day. The *% Complete* will be calculated at *50%*. Before entering the Remaining Duration, the schedule will look like:

Task Name	% Complete	Duration	Remaining Duration	Start	Apr 30, 00					
					Apr 30	May 1	May 2	May 3	May 4	May 5
write report	50%	2 days	1 day	May 2			▬▬ 50%			

When you enter the Remaining Duration, you trigger a recalculation of the *% Complete* and it will be *33%*; you have completed one day of a three-day task that was a two-day task. See the next schedule:

Task Name	% Complete	Duration	Remaining Duration	Start	Apr 30, 00					
					Apr 30	May 1	May 2	May 3	May 4	May 5
write report	33%	3 days	2 days	May 2			▬▬ 33%			

Updating Out of Sequence

Occasionally, you may need to show progress on a task that is scheduled in the future. The predecessors of the task may hold it there. If work has started on a future task, you need to show progress on it, regardless of the logic of the dependencies. This is known as *out-of-sequence updating*. Normally, a task can only start when its predecessors are finished.

Out-of-sequence progress often occurs in practice. For example, authors have to wait until they receive the research results before they can start writing the research report. The research takes longer and the authors decide to start developing the outline of the report and creating the format styles for the layout of the document. They don't need to have the results of the research for this.

Updating out of sequence is simple, because actuals are stronger than any other scheduling feature in MS Project. Entering actuals overrides the logic of the dependencies and even schedule constraints, so you can go ahead and update in the same way. The option **Split in-progress tasks** (in **Tools, Options, Schedule**) will affect the result in out-of-sequence situations (assuming **Tools, Options, Calculation**, ☑ **Move end of completed parts after status date back to status date**):

◆ If selected, the remaining duration stays where its dependencies kept the task. This is called *retained logic*

◆ If cleared, the remaining duration is scheduled to start on the status date which pulls the successors back to the status date. This is called a *logic override*, which is also known as *progress override*.

You still need to check the final result, because in some cases, you want to retain the logic and in other cases, you want to override the logic.

New Activities on the Fly

When you are executing the project, you often realize you omitted some tasks. You may have forgotten certain activities that involve discrete effort. Or, you may find better approaches to create the deliverables. Generally it is better to add new activities to show changes rather than attempting to modify existing activities. This is particularly true if you have already reported any progress on the activities. For example, if progress is lagging, you could decide to reassign a portion of a task to somebody else. In that case, you can make this clearer if you leave the baselined activities as they are and create a new activity for this extra resource. The new activities end up without a baseline and are clearly marked as new activities that are inserted on the fly to capture how the project really unfolded. In the case of contract disputes, you need to communicate clearly what the plan was and what happened in reality. Some experts go as far as capturing all impacts by creating new line items.[91] This technique is particularly useful for litigation when a contract dispute erupts, but it also allows you to learn better from the projects you ran. These new line items should only be in the present or past, and not far out in the future.

---

[91] As suggested by Frank Walker, TWG Project Management, LLC.

Updating Assignments

An MS Project schedule is not accessible by multiple users at the same time. Some project managers would like multi-user access in order to have their resources update the project schedule. Giving team members access to my schedules never seemed like a good idea to me; they often don't know MS Project well and can easily wreck my schedule. The time sheet features in MS Project facilitate updating by all team members without giving them access to your project schedule.

Here are the things you need to do when *updating assignments* using *time sheets*. Time sheets are sometimes called *project turn-around reports*. The steps are:

◆ Choose the options in **Tools, Options** (see page 641).
◆ Prepare the view (see page 643):
  ◇ Change the view to **Resource Usage,** and customize it.
  ◇ Apply the table **Work**, and customize it.
◆ Set the **Status Date** for this update.
◆ Set the task **Type** for all tasks to be updated to **Fixed Units** (see page 645).
◆ Collect the data using time sheets.
  For electronic time sheets, you can use the *Project Web Access* or *Microsoft Office Outlook* time sheets that come with *Project Server* (see page 647) or third party time sheets that integrate well with MS Project. You could also work with paper time sheets, but in many cases, such a system is too laborious and therefore abandoned during project execution. I will focus in this book on electronic time sheets only. If you don't have an electronic time sheet system, we recommend updating tasks instead; see page 623.
◆ Transfer the time sheet information into the schedule.
  The effort that you have to expend is reviewing the time sheet numbers and clicking one button to transfer the accepted numbers from Project Web Access back into the MS Project schedule. This is where the Project Web Access time sheet system sets itself apart from many other time sheet systems. Other time sheet systems may not transfer the time sheet information back into the MS Project schedule. If your current time sheet system only serves the purpose of client billing or salary administration (HR), you are not well served as a project manager and we would recommend updating tasks instead, see page 623. Third-party time sheet applications that are highly integrated with MS Project are PSA Solution (Tenrox)[92] or

---

[92] See www.tenrox.com.

TimeControl (HMS Software).[93] These third-party systems can meet other business objectives as well, such as time and attendance tracking for the human resources department or time and billing systems for professional services departments. Another third-party time sheet system is EPK-Suite.[94] This system is unique in that it allows you to collect time sheet information on any level in the project: task, deliverable or project.

◆ Check whether the schedule is updated correctly (see page 660).
◆ Prepare the status and forecast report (see page 663).
You may need to re-optimize your schedule before reporting on it.

What Data to Collect?

Now that we have discussed the process, we will discuss your choices on what data you can collect. You can collect the following data from your team members using Microsoft *Project Web Access*:

◆ **Percentage of work complete**
Resources report the percentage of work complete between 0 and 100%. The *% Work Complete* is a weak metric to collect from team members as we argued on page 623. We therefore don't recommend using this type of time sheet.

◆ **Total actual work done and remaining work by task**
Resources report the running total of actual work done and the work remaining to be done on each assignment. This option has the advantage that it requires the least amount of data entry, just two numbers for each assignment at every status cycle. The disadvantage is that these numbers are running totals that the team members have to calculate themselves. For example, the field may display 17 hours up to last week, and if the person worked 15 hours this week, he has to enter $17 + 15 = 32$ hours. People could easily make mistakes doing this. Also, when the data is transferred into the schedule, MS Project has to spread these hours over the days, since you did not ask the team members on which days the 15 hours were worked. This spread will not be precise, even though there are some options in MS Project that control the spreading better (**Tools, Options**, tab **Calculation**).

◆ **Hours of work done per day or per week** and **remaining work**
Resources report the hours worked on each assignment for each day in a weekly time sheet. This is the most common type of time sheet where resources enter their *actual hours* worked by day. When they enter their hours, the **Remaining Work** for

---

[93] See www.hmssoftware.ca

[94] See www.EPKgroup.com

the assignment is automatically decreased. Just before sending the time sheet back to the project manager, the resource reviews the calculated **Remaining Work** number and adjusts it, if necessary. We recommend you use this type of time sheet; it is the most precise and least prone to errors. This time sheet is known as the traditional or 'real' time sheet.

Project Server has to be configured for the type of time sheet you want to use with your team. The default time sheet is the first option **Percentage of Work Complete** (*% Work Complete*), and if you want to use the traditional time sheet, the Project Server administrator needs to change this (**Admin, Customize Project Web Access**). Otherwise, the actual work fields are grayed out and not editable in the timescale.

Even though we recommend you use the third type of time sheet, we would like to stress that updating the tasks or using one of other types of time sheets is still preferred over not updating your schedules at all. The remainder of this chapter focuses on the third option we recommended, the traditional time sheet.

Choosing the Options for an Assignments Update

Choose **Tools, Options** to set the following options:

Page tab	Set to:
Calculation	☑ **Updating task Status updates Resource Status** We recommend you check this option so that MS Project calculates the **% Complete** on the task level. We also recommend you protect the time sheet numbers by locking them in. Otherwise, the time sheet numbers can be changed from within MS Project when entering a **% Complete**. The Project Server Administrator can lock in actuals by selecting the appropriate settings (**Admin, Customize Project Web Access, ⦿ Managed Periods**) and closing periods that should be final. OR ☐ **Updating task Status updates Resource Status** If you turn it off, you will not see **% Complete** on tasks which allows you to enter them. This is useful if you want to update both tasks and assignments simultaneously. Doing both types of updates is a lot of work.

Page tab	Set to:
	☐ **Move end of completed parts after status date back to status date** This option has no effect when you work with traditional time sheets. See also after this table. ☐ **And move start of remaining parts back to status date** This option has no effect when you work with traditional time sheets. See also after this table.
	☐ **Move start of remaining parts before status date forward to status date** This option has no effect when you work with traditional time sheets. See also after this table. ☐ **And move end of completed parts forward to status date** This option has no effect when you work with traditional time sheets. See also after this table.
	☑ **Actual costs are always calculated by Microsoft Office Project** MS Project will calculate the *actual costs* based upon *actual hours* worked if you keep it on. If you want to enter actual cost numbers yourself, you should turn it off.
Edit	☐ **Allow cell drag and drop** Prevents accidentally dragging data on top of other data in your baselined schedule. We recommend turning it off at this point.
General	☐ **Automatically add new resources and tasks** This prevents accidentally adding resources during updating and re-optimising.
Schedule	☑ **Split in-progress tasks** Allows you to split the task bar and move the remaining duration to after the status date. We recommend keeping this option on.
	☐ **Autolink inserted or moved tasks** Disabling **Autolink** will prevent accidental changes to the network logic in the baselined schedule.

Notice that the options in **Tools, Options**, tab **Calculation** that were new in the 2002 release have no effect when you work with traditional time sheets on which team members fill in their *actual hours* worked by day. These options only make a difference:

◆   when you update tasks and enter **Actual Durations**, see page 623, or
◆   when you use the first or second type of time sheet discussed on page 640. Since you don't indicate on which dates the work actually took place, these options control on

which dates MS Project will put the actual hours worked. The result is that the time-phased spread is fairly rough.

Prepare the View

We will first explain in which view you can see the time sheet information. This is useful for checking the electronic time sheet information once it is transferred back into MS Project. If the time sheet numbers are not locked in, you can make corrections to the time sheet information that is automatically transferred into your project schedule.

In case you receive updates from each resource individually, you should probably use the **Resource Usage** view. Unfortunately, the view cannot display the status date line. Instead, click on the timescale on that date; it stays selected and can act as a status date.

1. Choose **View, Resource Usage**.

2. Create a new table by choosing **View, Table: <name of current table>, More Tables**; the **More Tables** dialog appears:

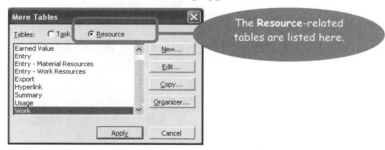

3. Select the table **Work,** and click [Copy...]; the **Table Definition** dialog appears:

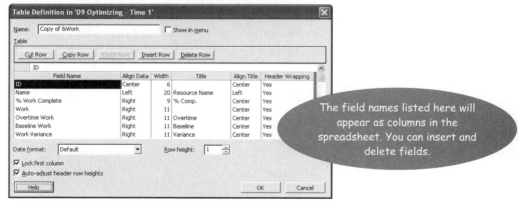

4. Give the table a name, for example *Update Assignments*. After the field **Name**, insert the fields **Baseline Work, Work, Actual Work, Remaining Work** and **% Work Complete**. Abbreviate their column titles in the field **Title** to, for example, *Bas.Work, Work, Act.Work, Rem.Work* and *%Work Comp.* respectively to save space. Click [OK] and [Apply].

5. Change the time to a one-character time unit label in **Tools, Options,** tab **Edit,** under **View options for time units** to save space. Click [OK].

6. In the timescale, only the field **Work** is shown. Right-click anywhere in the yellow area below the timescale and select **Detail Styles...** from the pop-up menu; the **Detail Styles** dialog appears:

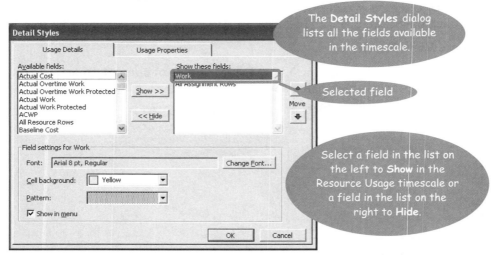

The **Detail Styles** dialog lists all the fields available in the timescale.

Selected field

Select a field in the list on the left to **Show** in the Resource Usage timescale or a field in the list on the right to **Hide**.

7. In the list **Available Fields,** select **Baseline Work** and click on [Show >>]. Do the same for the field **Actual Work,** which will be the input field. Perhaps you should even give this field a different background color. Rearrange the fields so that the **Baseline Work** field is at the top. Click [OK].

The view should now look like:

	Resource Name	Bas.Work	Work	Act.Work	Rem...				M	T	W	T	F	S
1	⊟ Harry	32 h	32 h	0 h	32 h	0%	Base. Work		8h	8h	8h	8h		
							Work		8h	8h	8h	8h		
							Act. Work							
	Write	*32 h*	*32 h*	*0 h*	*32 h*	*0%*	Base. Work		8h	8h	8h	8h		
							Work		8h	8h	8h	8h		
							Act. Work							
2	⊟ Ed	32 h	32 h	0 h	32 h	0%	Base. Work		8h	8h	8h	8h		
							Work		8h	8h	8h	8h		
							Act. Work							
	Read	*32 h*	*32 h*	*0 h*	*32 h*	*0%*	Base. Work		8h	8h	8h	8h		
							Work		8h	8h	8h	8h		
							Act. Work							

View ready for checking assignment updates.

Time sheet information can be entered or changed in the **Act. Work** *fields of the assignments (italic) in the timescale.*

The Formulas Behind the Screens

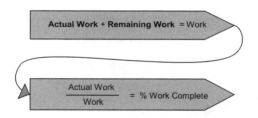

Actual Work + Remaining Work = Work

$$\frac{\text{Actual Work}}{\text{Work}} = \text{\% Work Complete}$$

The illustration shows the formulas that MS Project will use when updating the assignments in your project. You should keep these formulas in the back of your mind, because they explain the values that MS Project calculates and displays.

The formulas define the relationships between the four variables: *Actual Work*, *Remaining Work*, *Work* and *% Work Complete*. If you enter only two out of the four, MS Project will calculate the rest using the formulas.

Set the Task Type for All Tasks

Work changes often during updates!
D * U = W

The task field **Type** has to be set in such a way that it triggers the right recalculations. When working with time sheets, we will be entering **Actual Work** and **Remaining Work** values that cause the **Work** value to be recalculated as shown in the illustration: *Actual Work + Remaining Work = Work*. Fixed work is therefore not the right type of task, because we will not control what MS Project recalculates; will it recalculate the units or the duration? Remember you change one, fix another and have MS project calculate the third one. When updating assignments, you typically want to see the effect on the **Duration** of the task (forecast), while keeping the same resources on the task (**Fixed Units**). Again, **Fixed Units** seems the most appropriate type of task for updating assignments as it was for updating tasks. If the task duration cannot extend, you can consider adding resources.

1. Switch to the Tracking Gantt view by choosing **View, Tracking Gantt**.

2. Click on a column heading in the Gantt spreadsheet to select all the tasks.

3. Click the **Task Information** 🖹 tool; the **Multiple Task Information** dialog appears:

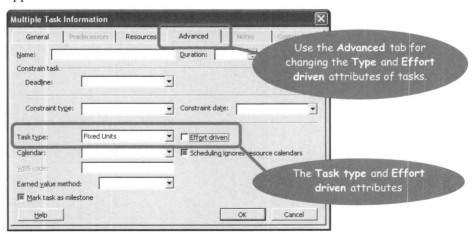

4. Click the **Advanced** tab and select **Fixed Units** from the list
   Task type [⯆].

5. Clear ☐ **Effort driven** and click [OK]. We recommended earlier to keep effort driven turned off, see page 374. Please note that summary tasks continue to be **Fixed Duration**.

Collecting the Data with Project Web Access Time Sheets

In this configuration, there is one focal point for all stakeholders, the Project Server website. The time sheet data are kept in the database that powers the site, *SQL Server 2000*. The project manager publishes the *assignments* from within Project 2003 Professional to the website which displays the assignments in the time sheets of the respective resources. The resources can access their time sheets by browsing to the website with *Internet Explorer* and logging in. They will need a *Client Access License (CAL)* for *Microsoft Project Web Access*. When resources fill in their time sheet, they can send it back to the project manager for approval. The project manager then logs into the Project Server intranet site using *Internet Explorer* to review the time sheet information. He can reject or accept the numbers and transfer the accepted numbers into the MS Project schedule. As you can see, the project managers control entirely what ends up in their schedules.

Publishing the Assignments

When you *assign* resources to the tasks, these assignments need to be communicated to the people involved. In MS Project, this is called publishing assignments. In the **Collaborate, Publish** menu you will find different options. These menu items can also be accessed with a single click with the **Collaborate** toolbar (right-click on any toolbar and choose **Collaborate**). In the **Collaborate** menu, you will find the following items:

◆ **Publish, All Information**
This creates or updates the project and all its assignments in the Project Server database.

◆ **Publish, Project Plan**
This creates or updates only the project-level data in the Project Server database. The project will be visible in the portfolio views. It does not publish assignments.

◆ **Publish, New and Changed Assignments** 🗓
This creates or updates the assignments in the time sheets of the team members. By populating their task lists, you are implicitly asking them to commit to the tasks. A commitment is assumed unless the team member rejects the assignment.
When changes happen to the assignment, such as a cancellation, a change in start date, or the amount of work, MS Project will immediately notice this and keep track of these changes. It displays the icon 🖂 in the **Indicators** column. You can easily keep track of whether you communicated the change to the resources by looking for this icon. To communicate these changes, you would choose **Publish, New and Changed Assignments** once again.

◆ **Request Progress Information** 🗓
This is to remind the team member of submitting progress information. The **Indicators** column ❶ in MS Project will show the icon 🖂. In *Microsoft Project Web Access*, the tasks in the time sheet will be marked with a ❓ in the indicators column ❶. The team member can be sent a reminder by e-mail in parallel.

How MS Project Keeps Track

You may be interested to dig in behind the screens and see how MS Project keeps track of commitments, changes and update requests. If not, you can skip this section.

How MS Project Keeps Track of Commitments

Once you publish an assignment, the assignment will have *Yes* in the assignment-related field *Confirmed*. *Project Server* works on the assumption that a resource accepts a task unless the person undertakes action and rejects it by selecting the task in his time sheet and clicking 🗓 Reject . If a resource does nothing, the task is accepted, and this commitment is visible on the level of assignments.

When a task has more than one resource assigned, MS Project will summarize all commitments on the task level. Only when all resources assigned to the task have committed themselves will MS Project toggle the task-related cell **Confirmed** to **Yes**. For example, when two resources Harry and Ed are both assigned to the same task, the possibilities are:

Harry	Ed	Task field **Confirmed** will show:
Accepted	Accepted	Yes
Accepted	Rejected	No
Rejected	Accepted	No
Rejected	Rejected	No

The task-related cell summarizes all its assignment cells. As you can see, MS Project summarizes the *assignments* in a pessimistic fashion. Only if all resources are *committed*, will **Confirmed** show **Yes** on the task level.

In the Task Usage view, you can see by assigned resource who rejected and who accepted in the **Confirmed** cells. View the commitments in the Task Usage view with the assignments expanded and the field **Confirmed** displayed. The following screen shows this:

ℹ	Task Name	Duration	Confirmed	Update Needed	TeamStatus Pending
	⊟ **REQUIREMENTS**	**7.53 days**	**Yes**	**No**	**No**
	⊟ research staff requirements	4 days	Yes	No	
	you		Yes	*No*	
	⊟ summarize requirements	4 days	Yes	No	
	Hilcrest – Nancy		Yes	*No*	*No*
	⊟ **LOCATION**	**17.5 days**	**Yes**	**No**	**No**
	⊟ select the realtor	4 days	No	No	No
	you		*No*	*No*	*No*
	⊟ visit the sites	1 day	No	No	No
	Falgon – John		*No*	*No*	
	Hilcrest – Nancy		*No*	*No*	
	the realtor		*No*	*No*	
	you		*No*	*No*	

Assignment is published and accepted (not rejected).

Assignments still have to be published or were rejected.

The **Confirmed** field can also be edited manually, but you can only edit the field in the assignment-related cells, not in the task-related cells. You can do this to make corrections.

The other fields **Update Needed** for changes and **TeamStatus Pending** for progress requests, work in a similar fashion.

How MS Project Keeps Track of Changes

Whenever the project manager makes a change, the field *Update Needed* toggles to **Yes.**

You can see the icon ✉ in the **Indicators** column when you need to send out updates to your team members. Point to the icon ✉ for a second and read the screen tip that appears. When the start, duration, work or finish of a task is changed, MS Project will immediately toggle the field **Update Needed** from **No** to **Yes** and display the icon ✉ in the **Indicators** column. This will tell you if you need to publish the changed assignments again.

You can choose **Collaborate, Publish, New and Changed Assignments** to inform team members of the changes. You can do this for selected tasks or for all tasks at once. As a result, team members will find the icon ❶ in front of tasks that have changed in their time sheet.

 MS Project will notice automatically when a resource was removed from a task or if a task was removed entirely and will prompt you if you would like to publish this.

Customizing the Time Sheets

You can customize the time sheet by choosing **Tools, Customize, Published fields …**. The **Customize Published Fields** dialog appears:

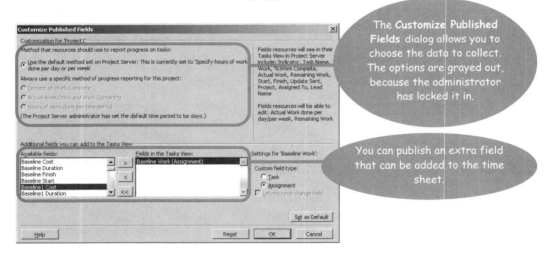

The **Customize Published Fields** dialog allows you to choose the data to collect. The options are grayed out, because the administrator has locked it in.

You can publish an extra field that can be added to the time sheet.

 The default time sheet view has all the fields shown in the list on the top right. These fields cannot be removed; they are the standard time sheet fields. You can add fields to be published from the list in the bottom left. The *Baseline Work* field would be a candidate to add which allows the project manager to see if work has increased when reviewing the time sheets. This field also needs to be added to the time sheet view by the Project Server administrator.

The Resource Fills in the Time Sheet in Project Web Access

A resource logs into the Project Server website and clicks **Tasks** to display the time sheet where *actual hours* can be entered. The time sheet will look similar to:

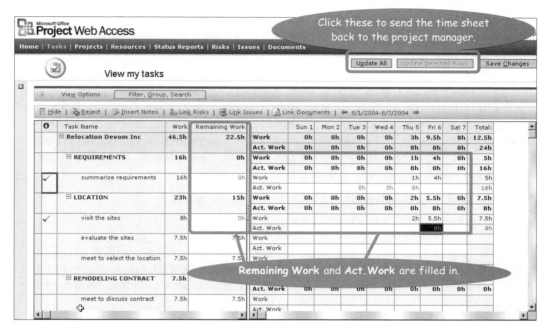

 Resources can enter the hours they worked on each day of the week in the field **Act. Work** assuming that *Project Server* is configured to work with the traditional time sheet, see page 640. Ideally, the resource enters the actual hours worked every day and saves them. The **Remaining Work** hours are automatically decreased every time actual hours are entered. At the end of the week, the resource reviews the **Remaining Work** hours and revises them if necessary. The resource can even add remarks in the **Notes** field if this field is added to the time sheet. To send the time sheet back to the project manager, the resource has two options:

◆ The resource clicks **Update All** to send all numbers entered to the appropriate project manager(s).

◆ The resource selects the rows with numbers to send back to a project manager and clicks **Update Selected Rows**. Note that this button is only available if the highlight is in the spreadsheet on the left as opposed to the timescale on the right.

As an immediate result, the resource will see the icon ▦ in front of the tasks sent to the project manager. The numbers that need to be approved are in red, and as soon as the project manager accepts the numbers, their color will turn back to black and the icon ▦ disappears.

The Resource Fills in the Time Sheet in Microsoft Office Outlook

Instead of using Project Web Access, team members can also fill in their time sheet in Microsoft Office Outlook. You need an add-on to Microsoft Office Outlook. The add-on first needs to be downloaded and setup which can be done in Project Web Access by choosing **Tasks**, and from the side pane click **View and report on your tasks from your Outlook calendar** and then ▢ Download Now ▢. You will need administrative privileges to install the add-on. You will have:

◆ a new toolbar called **Project Web Access** in Outlook, and

◆ an extra tab in the **Tools, Options** dialog.

The resource will first have to download the *assignments* from Project Web Access into Microsoft Office Outlook. Notice that they will appear in the **Calendar** view in Outlook and not in the **Tasks** view, since most people use the calendar view rather than the tasks view. Importing assignments can be done manually by clicking ▢ Import New Assignments ▢ on the new toolbar **Project Web Access** or scheduled to occur automatically using **Tools, Options**, tab **Project Web Access**.

The assignments will appear in the top of the **Calendar** in Outlook:

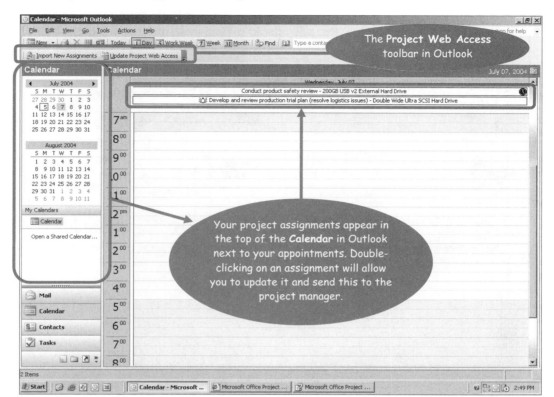

 Notice that you can move assignments to another date in your calendar, but when the next import happens, the dates will reflect the dates in Project Web Access once again. Project Web Access and Outlook have a master-slave relationship, and Project Web Access is the master. Generally, you should not make changes to the assignments except for updating the progress on them.

You can enter the progress information:

1. Double-click on an assignment and click the tab **Project Web Access** which will display the following window that you should maximize in order to see the entire time sheet:

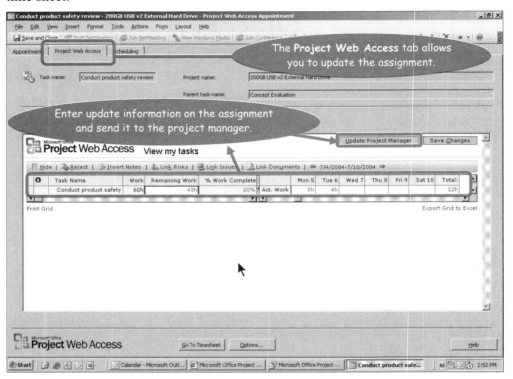

2. Enter the actual hours worked and revise the estimate in the **Remaining Work** column.

3. To send the actual hours worked and revised estimate to the project manager for review, you have three options:

    ◊   You click Update Project Manager to immediately send the entered numbers to the project manager, or

    ◊   You click Save Changes and every week you click Update Project Web Access on the **Project Web Access** toolbar to send all updates to the project manager(s), or

    ◊   You schedule the updates to be sent back automatically to the project manager by selecting the appropriate options in the **Tools, Options**, tab **Project Web**

Access dialog in the section **Update from your Outlook calendar to Project Web Access**.

4. Save and close by clicking on the toolbar.

 Weak points in the Outlook interface are:

◆   You can only enter progress on one task at a time. In Project Web Access, you can see the entire list and can more easily enter progress on multiple tasks. Outlook does have a feature that allows you to view all downloaded tasks. Choose **View, Arrange By, Current View, Active Project-Related Appointments**.

◆   Outlook simply displays the Project Web Access interface, and if you want to rearrange the order of the columns permanently, you will have to do this in Project Web Access. For example, we recommend moving the **Remaining Work** column to the left so that you can easily fill it in. We hope your administrator is on the ball and has done this already.

The Project Manager Checks the Time Sheets

Regardless whether the resource enters the time sheets in Outlook or in Project Web Access, the project manager will receive the time sheets in Project Web Access and can check them there.

Time sheets are received by the project manager as **Updates**, and the page with updates looks like this:

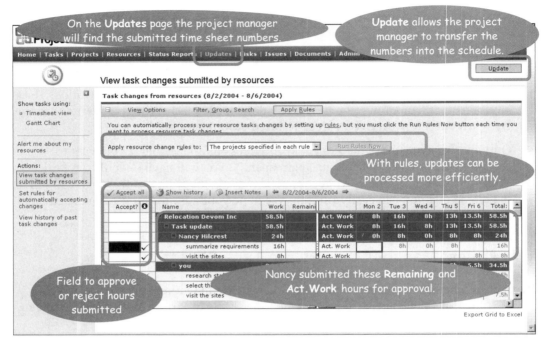

When you review the time sheets as the project manager, you have three options in the column **Accept?**:

◆ Enter **Accept** to approve the line item. After your review, you can transfer the accepted data into your MS Project schedule by clicking [Update]. Any inserted notes will also be transferred into the project schedule and appear in the **Notes** field, complete with the date and name of the resource.

◆ Enter **Reject** to refuse the line item. You should get in touch with the team member to sort the issue out. The team member will receive a notification by e-mail.

◆ Leave it blank to decide later.

You can speed up entering your decisions by accepting:

◆ All at once: if you want to quickly approve all updates, click [✓ Accept all].
◆ By project: where it shows the name of the project, select **Accept** from the list in the column **Accept?.** This marks all updates in this project as accepted.

◆ By type of update message: where it shows the type of update message, e.g. **Task Update** in the screen shot, select **Accept** from the list. This marks all updates in this category as accepted.

◆ Person-by-person: where you see the person's name, select **Accept** from the list. This marks all updates from that resource as accepted.

After you have accepted many items, you can still toggle some items to **Reject**.

You can also apply rules for automatic acceptance of time sheets: click the tab **Apply Rules** and create a rule that will eliminate some mindless clicking. Certain team members may always submit very reliable time sheets. When you want to run your automatic rules, you need to click | Run Rules Now |; the system does not run the rules by itself. The rules only fill in **Accepted**, and you also have to click | Update | to transfer the accepted entries to MS Project.

Viewing the Time Sheet Data in MS Project

After transferring the time sheet hours, you can view the *actual hours* entered in the *Resource Usage* view with the assignments expanded. Choose **Format, Details, Actual Work** to see the exact numbers typed in by the resources as illustrated in the next screen:

	O	Resource Name	Work	Remaining Work	Details	Aug 1, '04 S	M	T	W	T	F	S
3	✉	⊟ Hilcrest — Nancy	46.5 hrs	22.5 hrs	Work			8h	0h	8h	8h	
					Act.W			8h	0h	8h	8h	
	📊	summarize requirements	16 hrs	0 hrs	Work			8h	0h	8h		
					Act.W			8h	0h	8h		
	📊	visit the sites	8 hrs	0 hrs	Work				0h	8h		
					Act.W				0h	8h		
	✉	evaluate the sites	7.5 hrs	7.5 hrs	Work							
					Act.W							
				hrs	Work							
					Act.W							
					Work							
					Act.W							

The **Remaining Work** estimates as submitted by Nancy.

The **Act. Work** hours that Nancy submitted and that were approved.

You can see the exact same numbers here as you saw previously on the **Updates** page in Project Web Access.

When you use material resources, you will notice that the **% Complete** gets stuck on 99% when all labor resources are done with their work. You have to manually mark tasks with material resources assigned as 100% complete. You may get a warning about actuals being out of sync, but you can ignore that.

Updating the Costs

Cost Updating Strategies

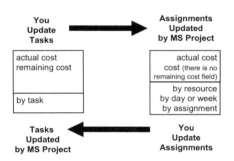

Similar to updating the schedule:

♦ You can update the tasks and have the assignment details automatically updated by MS Project.

♦ You can update the *assignments* and have the tasks automatically updated by MS Project. If you enter the data into the time-phased assignment fields, you can model the actual cash flow very precisely. In order to do so, you have to change a default option.

Setting the Options for Assignment Cost Updates

It is possible to manually enter actual costs in the time-phased *Actual Cost* fields on the task level or on the assignment level in MS Project. This can be a useful way of keeping the cost of your project up to date on a daily or weekly basis, because you can enter expenses for a particular day or week in your schedule and thus create an accurate cash flow report.

 In its default options, MS Project calculates actual costs automatically. It calculates them based on the accrual method you set and the actual time progress you enter. If you want to enter actual costs yourself, you must first turn off the automatic updating of actual costs, which allows you to enter the actual costs.

1. Choose **Tools, Options**, and then click the **Calculation** tab.

2. Clear ☐ **Actual costs are always calculated by Microsoft Office Project**.

3. Click OK .

Preparing the View for Updating Costs

1. Choose **View, Task Usage**.

2. Choose **View, Table: <name of current table>, Tracking**; the fields for updating tasks are displayed.

3. Choose **Format, Detail Styles…**, in the list **Available fields** select **Cost** and click the Show >> . Do the same for **Actual Cost**. Click OK . The **Act. Cost** field is now also displayed in the timescale:

Task Name	Baseline Cost	Cost	Actual Cost	Remaining Cost	Details	25	Aug '04 1	8	15	22
1 ⊟ REQUIREMENTS	$1,650.00	$1,650.00	$0.00	$1,650.00	Cost		$1,343.75	$306.25		
					Act. Cost					
2 ⊟ research staff requirements	$1,125.00	$1,125.00	$0.00	$1,125.00	Cost		$1,125.00			
					Act. Cost					
you	$1,125.00	$1,125.00	$0.00	$1,125.00	Cost		$1,125.00			
					Act. Cost					
3 ⊟ summarize requirements	$525.00	$525.00	$0.00	$525.00	Cost		$218.75	$306.25		
					Act. Cost					
Hilcrest – Nancy	$525.00	$525.00	$0.00	$525.00	Cost		$218.75	$306.25		
					Act. Cost					

Update the running totals in the spreadsheet.

Or enter the cost week-by-week in the timescale.

4. Update running totals on task or assignment level: add the new cost to the running total displayed in the spreadsheet column **Act. Cost,** and enter the new running total of actual cost.
OR
Update in the timescale on a week-by-week basis on task or assignment level: enter expenditures in the **Act. Cost** row in the week you incurred those costs.

Checks on an Updated Schedule

The following checks reflect best practices on updating schedules. A schedule has to be updated if today's date is later than the project start date. If the project should have started, the schedule needs to show actuals and revised forecasts. The following questions help determine if the best practices of updating schedules were applied:

◆ What is the quality of the baseline in the schedule? The schedule needs a good baseline, because it will be the standard for comparing the progress.

◇ Is a baseline present?
Keep in mind that projects planned far into the future that aren't approved yet, do not necessarily need a baseline.

◇ Is the baseline complete?
You can verify the presence and completeness by applying the filter **11 IIL Tasks with missing baseline info.**[95] The filter displays any tasks without entries in **Baseline Start, Baseline Finish, Baseline Duration** or **Baseline Work**. When *assignments* are created after the baseline is set, the Baseline Work field is still empty. Note that the filter does not check on the field **Baseline Cost**.

◇ Is the baseline original?
The baseline cannot be reset without formal approval of the appropriate project stakeholders.

◇ Is the baseline relevant?
If the project deviated too far from the baseline, a new baseline needs to be negotiated. The baseline should provide a meaningful *standard of comparison* for the current schedule. You can check this by looking at how far the current schedule is removed from the baseline. Does the project have a fighting chance to catch up with the baseline again, or is it a lost cause? If it is a lost cause, you should submit a change request.

---

[95] This filter can be found in the file *IIL Project 2003 tools to check Orange Belt schedules.MPP* available for download at www.jrosspub.com. Please, click the link *WAV Download Resource Center* to enter the download site.

◆ Are the appropriate options selected in **Tools, Options** for the chosen updating strategy?

⬦ For task updating (revising the task-related **Actual Duration** and **Remaining Duration** fields), the options should be set as follows:

Tab **Schedule**: ☑ **Split in-progress tasks**

Tab **Calculation**: ☑ **Updating task status updates resource status**

⬦ For assignment updating (entering numbers from the time sheets into the assignment-related **Actual Work** and **Remaining Work** fields), the options should be set as follows:

Tab **Schedule**: ☑ **Split in-progress tasks**

Tab **Calculation**: ☑ **Updating task status updates resource status**

(2003) If you keep this option selected, you should not enter **% Complete** on tasks, because this may override time sheet data. In Project 2003, overriding can be prevented by the Project Server administrator by locking in time sheet periods.

⬦ For updating both the tasks and the assignments, the options should be set as follows:

Tab **Schedule**: ☑ **Split in-progress tasks**

Tab **Calculation**: ☐ **Updating task status updates resource status**

You cannot enter both types of information unless you clear this option.

◆ Is the **Status Date** set to an appropriate date?
The **Status date** in the **Project, Project Information** dialog should be set to a date that is close to today's date. If it is too far in the past, the schedule may be out-of-date. If it is too far in the future, the project manager is guessing the progress instead of entering factual progress.

◆ Is the task type of soon to be updated tasks set to **Fixed Units** and non **Effort-driven**?
When you update the schedule, you change the durations (task updates) or the work (assignment updates). We recommended Fixed Units and non Effort-Driven, because you typically first would like to see what the schedule looks like when the same resources continue to work on the task. You can always re-optimize the schedule, we discussed this in Chapter 9 Optimizing the Schedule, see page 419.

◆ Is the schedule up to date as per the **Status date**?

⬦ Are all actual durations (actual work / actual hours worked) scheduled in the past?
The actuals are scheduled in the past if they are earlier than the status date. Otherwise, the schedule does not have up-to-date forecasts. When you bring actual durations to the past, all their dependent tasks may be rescheduled earlier

as well, which improves the forecasts. This is why rescheduling is important. You can verify this by applying the filter
12 IIL Reschedule Actual Durations...[96]

◇ Are all remaining durations (remaining work) scheduled in the future?
The remaining estimates are scheduled in the future if they are later than the status date. You cannot leave unfinished work scheduled in the past. If you leave unfinished work before the status date, you are scheduling more work to be done in the past even though the past is gone. The work should be moved to the future to update the forecast dates of all dependent tasks. Otherwise, the schedule does not reflect up-to-date forecasts and you have created a *status report*, instead of a *forecast report*. You can verify this by applying the filter
13 IIL Reschedule Remaining Durations...[97]

◇ Are the remaining durations (remaining work) revised?
Otherwise, the schedule may not reflect up-to-date forecasts. If the project manager has been revising the durations of detail tasks, these will be displayed. This filter is different from the other filters in the sense that if it displays tasks, it is good. If the filter does not display any tasks, it is an indication that the project manager is not revising his (remaining) durations while updating. If remaining durations are not revised, the forecasts are not very accurate, and may not even be reliable. You can display the tasks with a revised duration by applying the filter **14 IIL Remaining Durations revised**.[98]

---

[96] This filter can be found in the file *IIL Project 2003 tools to check Orange Belt schedules.MPP* available for download at www.jrosspub.com. Please, click the link *WAV Download Resource Center* to enter the download site.

[97] same

[98] same

Prepare the Status and Forecast Report

Regardless of whether you chose to update *tasks* or *assignments*, the *Tracking Gantt* chart is good for reporting progress and new forecasts. Choose **View, Tracking Gantt** to apply this view.

Choose **View, Table <name of current table>, Variance** to see the current schedule and baseline dates. The screen should now look similar to:

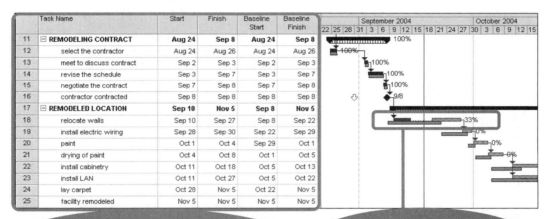

This is the **Variance** table with **Start** and **Finish** (current schedule) and **Baseline Start** and **Finish** (baseline).

The current schedule (top half) is later than the baseline (bottom half): slippage

The Tracking Gantt view depicts progress using the calculated date field **Complete Through**. You can see this field listed by choosing **Format, Bar styles** and looking under **To**. The **Complete Through** field:

◆ Follows closely the **Actual Duration** that is entered by you, when you update tasks
◆ Is the number of days for which actual hours are entered, when you update assignments.

Notice that the Tracking Gantt does not show progress on the tasks (**% Complete** and **Actual Durations**) if you work with time sheets and you cleared the option ☐ **Updating Task Status updates Resource Status** in **Tools, Options,** tab **Calculation**. With the option off, the **% Complete** and **Actual Duration** are not calculated for tasks.

In Project 2003 Professional with *Project Server*, reporting progress is as simple as can be. As the project manager, you just need to keep your schedule up-to-date and save it. The status and forecast can be viewed at any time online by executives; even if it is on a Saturday night at 10PM. Executives will see their entire portfolio of projects in *Microsoft Project Web Access*:

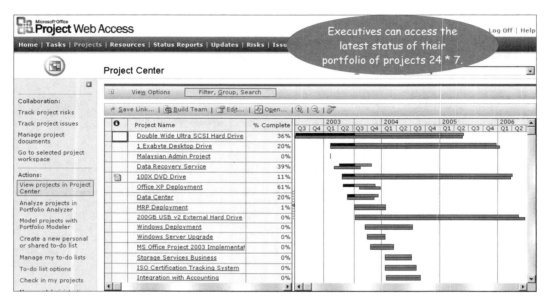

Exercises

Review

1. What are the process steps for updating schedules?

2. a. What benefit can you gain from a baseline in your schedule?
   b. How do you set it in MS Project?
   c. How often do you set it?

3. What are legitimate reasons for changing your baseline?

4. Describe in your own words what the following indicators mean:
   ◇ Actual Duration
   ◇ Remaining Duration

5. How do the following indicators relate to each other? Please describe their relationship using formulas.
   ◇ Actual Duration
   ◇ Remaining Duration
   ◇ Duration
   ◇ % Complete

6. There are two main strategies for updating schedules. What are they and what are the main differences between them?

7. When collecting update data, you could ask for % complete. What are the weaknesses of this metric?

8. a. What menu items do you need to choose to set the status date?
   b. Why do you need a status date?

9. a. What task type do you recommend when updating tasks?
   b. How can you change multiple tasks to this task type?

10. There are six different update situations in practice. Please mention four.

11. A team leader submits the following report to you as shown in the next illustration. Would you accept this report:
    ◇ As a status report? Why?
    ◇ As a forecast report? Why?
    If you would not accept it, indicate what needs to be changed.

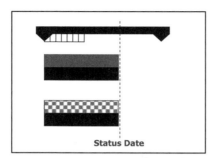

Status Date

12. What are the pieces of data that you will need to collect when you want to update assignments?

13. Which vehicles are available to collect time sheets?

14. When checking whether your schedule is properly updated, what do you look at?

Relocation Project – Updating Tasks

1. Open the file *11 Updating the Schedule 1.MPP* available for download at www.jrosspub.com. Please, click the link *WAV Download Resource Center* to enter the download site.

2. Change to the **Tracking Gantt** view and **Tracking** table. Hide the **% Complete** field. Display the **Tracking** toolbar.

3. Set the baseline for the entire project.

4. Set the **Status Date** and the **Current Date** to *September 17, 2006* and create a gridline for the status date in the Gantt timescale.

5. Set the following options in **Tools, Options, Calculation**:
   ☑ **Updating Task status updates resource status**
   ☑ **Actual costs are always calculated by Microsoft Office Project**

6. Switch the task type to **Fixed Units** and non **Effort-Driven** for all tasks.

7. Enter the status of the project by updating the tasks. As of *September 17, 2006* the situation is:
   All the tasks until *Remodeled Location* are done and ran as scheduled.
   The contractor started late, because he finished his previous contract late. He supplied the following update:

Task	Started	Actual Duration	Remaining Duration
relocate walls	*10 Sept.*	*3d*	*15 d*

   The rest of the tasks are not started yet.

8. Don't forget to check whether there are any remaining durations scheduled before the status date. Reschedule these after the status date. Also check if there are actual durations after the status date and reschedule these before the status date.

9. Describe the status of the project in your own words.

10. Compare your file with the solution file *11 Updating the Schedule 2.MPP* available for download at www.jrosspub.com. Please, click the link *WAV Download Resource Center* to enter the download site. See page 675 of this book for an automated way of comparing and reporting differences between two versions of one schedule.

Relocation Project – Optimizing for Time and Cost Again

1. Open the file *11 Updating the Schedule 2.MPP* available for download at www.jrosspub.com. Please, click the link *WAV Download Resource Center* to enter the download site.

2. You find this schedule too risky; you need to meet the new deadline date of November 16, 2006 and, on top of that, you need a time buffer to meet the project deadline. You decide to explore whether working overtime offers solutions. The overtime rates are:

Name	Std. Rate	Overtime Rate
employees	*$ 25/h*	*$ 50/h*
contractor	*$ 30/h*	*$ 50/h*
LAN consultants	*$ 75/h*	*$ 100/h*
Realtor	*$ 35/h*	*$ 45/h*

3. What is the cost of the project now?

4. Which people would you ask to work overtime first to meet the November 16 deadline? Why?

5. You want to explore whether overtime by the contractor can solve the schedule conflict.
   How many overtime person days do you propose on which tasks to meet the deadline?

6. How much does your project cost if you pay the overtime rates?

7. Could you negotiate to pay regular rates instead?

8. How would you enter the overtime work if you pay the regular standard rate?

9. Compare your file with the solution file *11 Updating the Schedule 3.MPP* available for download at www.jrosspub.com. Please, click the link *WAV Download Resource Center* to enter the download site. See page 675 of this book for an automated way of comparing and reporting differences between two versions of one schedule.

Chapter 12 Evaluating the Project

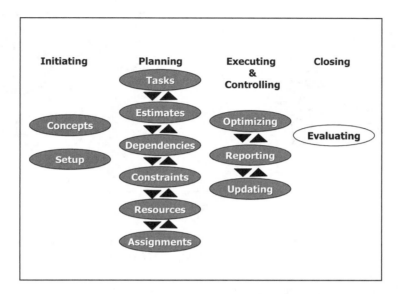

In this chapter, we review how you can become a better project manager for your next projects.

After this chapter you will:
◆ Know why project evaluation is important.
◆ Have a list of questions that will help you learn from a finished project.
◆ Know what to capture in lessons learned.

"Can We Go Now ...?"

Nob and his team members sit down with a pizza to look back at the project they just finished. The pizza is almost finished when Nob kicks off the meeting asking: "What did we learn from this project?"

Harry says: "Well, I learned that I am not going to work with Chris again!"

Chris fires back immediately with: "Likewise ... man!"

Nob straightens his body and asks again: "Folks, we are here to learn from our mistakes and our successes ... what did we learn?"

Mary: "I found out that I am always too optimistic in my estimates! Next time I will not give estimates unless I am forced to ..."

Nob: "Did you ask yourself how you could get more accurate estimates?"

Mary: "I don't like estimating; it's too hard..."

Vern: "Yeah, I agree..."

Nob makes a big gesture to interrupt this exchange and summarizes: "So, what you have learned from this project is that you don't want to provide estimates anymore to the project manager?"

Vern: "That sums it up pretty well!"

Nob: "What else did we learn?"

Veronica: "I learned that filling in time sheets takes a lot of time. Particularly when we were crunching, the time sheets were a nuisance!"

Nob has grown slightly irritated by the negativity that befalls him in this meeting and remarks sarcastically: "I guess you learned you don't want to fill in time sheets anymore?"

Then Harry asks the deadly question: "Can we go now ...?"

Project Evaluation

Evaluating a project when it is completed is often seen as a waste of time. The reason for this seems to be that the atmosphere during an evaluation can be loaded with animosity. When things did not run the way they should have, pointed fingers appear. These evaluations are indeed a waste of time. The little story of Nob on the previous page shows a perfect example of time wasted on an evaluation meeting.

Evaluation is useful when the focus is on, and stays on, the future. Only by learning from the past can you become better prepared for the future. Lessons learned can lead to improvements to the WBS, the accuracy of estimates, the use of dependencies, the use of resources and the appropriateness of assignments in the schedule. The meeting must be directed in such a fashion that people focus on gain for the future instead of on pain from the past. If managed well, the meeting can be a source of valuable information. Evaluating prevents running into the same troubles again.

If you, as the project manager, want to prevent finger pointing, you should start each question with: "*What could I have done to ...?*"

Of course, many projects run well. Even in this case, evaluating is important, because it is the only way to become yet a better project manager. There is always room to deliver projects better. When you stop asking yourself the question: *What could we have done better?*, you will stop learning from your experiences. In this age in which the only constant seems to be that things change rapidly, nobody can afford to stop learning. Life-long learning is the motto for success.

Evaluation Points

After the project is over, you can ask some questions with your team. These are a few suggestions with respect to the schedule as a tool to manage and control the project:

1. Was the schedule clear to all stakeholders? How can we make it clearer in future projects?

2. Was the WBS complete? Was it easy to understand? Did it function as a tool for delegation? Were the deliverables clearly formulated in it, or did some deliverables cause confusion? How can we improve the WBS for similar projects in the future?

3. Were the estimates optimistic or pessimistic? What factors caused the estimates to be optimistic or pessimistic? How can we be better forecast these factors in future projects?
   You can determine the personality factors in the estimates by comparing the resource-related fields **Actual Work** with **Baseline Work**. These numbers are aggregates and will give a good impression if someone tends to be optimistic or pessimistic in estimating. We discussed this in more detail on page 180.

4. Was there enough of a time buffer in the schedule to compensate for unforeseen events? Which tasks consumed most of the buffer? Why? On page 492, we discussed how up to three versions of the schedule can be shown next to each other in the timescale; a view like this would be very helpful for this analysis. What can we do in the future to prevent similar tasks slipping again?

5. Was the schedule easy enough to maintain during project execution? Was the network of dependencies complete, and did it update the forecasts automatically? Could accurate status and forecast reports be generated at each reporting period? How can we produce the reports more easily in future projects?

6. Were the right resources available at the right times? How can we predict or ensure the availability better in future projects?

We recommend you capture these findings in lessons learned on the project.

To prevent painful lessons learned in the school of hard knocks, we recommend you use a checklist to ensure the quality of your schedule. In the next chapter, we will provide a checklist with which you can evaluate your schedule. This list can be used to check the quality of the schedule as soon as it is created. This checklist allows you to be more proactive in your next project.

Chapter 13 Summary

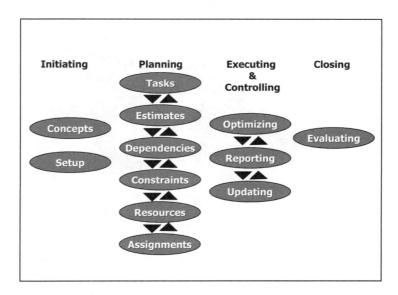

As you can see in the illustration, we have discussed a project throughout its entire life cycle including updating a schedule and closing it out with lessons learned. Throughout the book, we have made many recommendations that reflect best scheduling practices and we will bring these recommendations together by providing two checklists in this summary chapter:

◆ Checklist for Troubleshooting MS Project Schedules, see page 675
◆ Checklist for Dynamic Project Models, see page 678

Certificates Weather the Storm

The economy turned sour and both our friends, Bob and Nob, got laid off. When they accidentally met, they exchanged their experiences. Nob told Bob that he did not get an interview yet, but had some interest from one employer. Bob said that he had one interview coming up. He commented that prospective employers had a special interest in the certificates he had attained over the years.

"What certificates did you get?" asked Nob. "Well, I got my PMP certification from the PMI and then I also became a Black Belt in MS Project through the International Institute for Learning," Bob said with some pride in his voice. "I guess the certificates set me apart!"

Nob asked: "How did you get around to getting these certificates while you were managing your projects? I did not have time for that!"
Bob: "I don't know how I did it, but I did. I am now reaping the benefits from making it a priority at the time."

Nob looked down and said, "I guess I have enough time now to get certified, but nobody is going to pay for the training and certification. Why didn't I spare some time when I could?"

Comparing Two Versions of One Project Schedule

At times you may need to be able to compare two schedules quickly. This can be useful in the following situations:

◆ Learning from the exercises in this book
  To check your results in the Relocation Project exercises, you can compare your MPP file with the solution file available for download at www.jrosspub.com. Please, click the link *WAV Download Resource Center* to enter the download site.

◆ Checking what changes subcontractors made to their schedules.

◆ Troubleshooting a schedule by comparing it to a previous version.

◆ Learning from past projects by comparing successive versions of a schedule.

You can ask Project 2003 to create a report with the differences between two versions of one schedule:

1. Switch to the most recent version of the schedule, and display it on the screen.

2. Right-click on any toolbar and choose **Compare Project Versions**.

3. Click the first button **Compare Project Versions** [image] on the toolbar, and the dialog **Compare Project Versions** appears with your schedule filled in as **Project version 2 (later version)**.

4. Under **Task Table** select the table **Entry** from the list. If you suspect that the table in the most recent version does not have all the fields that you want to compare, cancel and insert the columns first. To find differences in:
   ◇ estimates insert columns **Duration** and **Work**,
   ◇ dependencies insert column **Predecessors** or **Successors**,
   ◇ constraints insert columns **Constraint type** and **Constraint Date**,
   ◇ deadlines insert column **Deadline**, and/or
   ◇ assignments insert column **Resource names**.

5. If you want to compare resource information as well, select a **Resource Table**. The table **Entry** will often meet your needs.

6. Click [OK], and the comparison starts and the screen will flash. Project 2003 displays the dialog **Compare Project Versions – Done** and click [Yes] to view the legend.

7. Click [Close] to close the legend dialog and view the differences. Project 2003 has created a new project file that displays data and difference columns.

8. To zoom in on the differences, select the **Show all differences** and **Show differences columns only** from the respective lists on the **Compare Project Versions** toolbar. This will display only the records that are different and only the **Diff** columns. After you have found the differences, you may like to see the data columns from the schedules again by selecting **Show data and differences columns**.

9. Once you are done with your analysis, you can close the report schedule or save it for future reference.

Now you have found the differences, you may need a checklist for finding the cause of these differences. We will present such a checklist next.

Checklist for Troubleshooting MS Project Schedules

If you don't understand why a task is scheduled on the dates it is, here are some questions to ask yourself. The questions are ranked in terms of precedence: the higher on the list, the stronger the effect. As soon as you find the reason, you don't need to go down the list further. We therefore recommend you start at the top of the list and go down when you are troubleshooting schedules:

1. First of all, press [F9] to force a recalculation. Even if you have automatic recalculation on, I have found that it is not always freshly calculated. Check to see if this solved the problem.

2. Does the task have an actual start date?
   Does one of its predecessors or successors have an actual start date?
   Insert the column **Actual Start** to check this.

3. Is there a *hard constraint* on the task or on its predecessors or successors?
   Insert the column **Constraint Type**.

4. Is there a task calendar on the task or on its predecessors or successors?
Insert the column **Task calendar**. To see what the task calendar has in terms of non-working days, choose **Tools, Change working time**, then select the task calendar from the list at the top under **For:**.

5. Is there a leveling delay on the task (or on its predecessors)?
Insert the column **Leveling Delay**. If the task is delayed for the purpose of leveling the workload of resources, there will be an entry in this field.

6. What predecessors does the task have?
Insert the field **Predecessors**. Is there a *lag* on the dependency?
If there is more than one predecessor, typically only one of them drives the start date of the task you are wondering about.

7. For Fixed Work/Fixed Units tasks: Are there vacation days set on the calendar of the resource who works on the task or on its predecessors or successors?

8. Are there splits in the task bars?
Fixed Duration tasks can have weird splits in their task bars if one of the resources is not available when the task is scheduled. Fixed Duration task bars can also have leading dots before the task bar or trailing dots following the task bar that are a left over of task bar splits. You can often get rid of these dots by changing the task type to Fixed Units or Fixed Work.

9. Task-specific constraint tendencies (ASAP or ALAP):
If you have an ALAP task constraint in an ASAP schedule, it tends to move dependent ASAP tasks out to later dates.

10. Default constraint tendencies (ASAP or ALAP):
You can check the default constraint in **Project, Project Information**. If you **Schedule from Project Start Date**, the default is ASAP. **From the Project Finish Date**, the default is ALAP. Under ASAP scheduling, tasks will tend to stay close to the project start date, unless one of the previous factors overrides this. Under ALAP scheduling, tasks will tend to stay close to the project finish date.

Checklist for Dynamic Project Models

As a summary of this book, we will provide a list of criteria for good schedules. What is a good schedule? A good schedule is a model of the project that provides *valid* forecasts and that is easy to maintain. Only dynamic models are easy to maintain. Let's break the term *valid dynamic model* into its components:

A schedule has to be a model of the project:
◆ A model is a simplification of the reality.
    A model should be a deliberate simplification of the complex reality. We often use the criterion that if you cannot explain the model to your stakeholders, the model is too complex.
◆ A model of the project provides forecasts.

A schedule has to produce forecasts that are *valid*. A schedule will only produce valid forecasts if:
◆ It contains all deliverables.
◆ The basis for estimates (pure work time versus gross work time) is consistent with the working times on the project calendar.
◆ The time estimates seem reasonable for the work to be done.
◆ The schedule produces accurate forecasts.
    Unfortunately, this can only be determined after the project is over.

A schedule has to be *dynamic*. The ideal of a totally dynamic model is that if one thing changes in reality, you should have to change only one field in your MS Project model. Even though this ideal is hard to reach, you can get very close to it if you set your schedule up in the right way. A schedule is dynamic if:
◆ It has as few constraints as possible.
◆ It has a complete network of dependencies.
◆ It is easy to maintain so that it can be kept alive during project execution.
◆ It is up to date in real time.
◆ It continuously provides forecasts.
◆ It is in an electronic format and is accessible online.

Throughout the chapters, we have made many recommendations for making your schedule a valid and dynamic model of your project. These recommendations are compiled in the checklist that follows. The list can be used to evaluate the quality of your project schedule and to check on the use of best practices.

If your schedule meets these guidelines, you have created a valid, dynamic model of your project. You have positioned yourself to bring the project to a successful completion. From experience, we can say that managing a large schedule is a nearly impossible task if it does not meet the requirements of the checklist. Schedules that meet the requirements not only need the least maintenance during the execution of the project, but they are also the easiest schedules to have when you are managing multiple projects. The next level of the IIL certification curriculum, *Managing Multiple Projects* or the Blue Belt level, is targeted at people who manage more than one project. You need the single schedules to meet all requirements on the checklist if:

◆ You need to create an *integrated program schedule* for a large endeavor from subschedules. You need to apply the checklist on the subschedules.

◆ You want to start developing scenarios with a *portfolio* of projects using the *Portfolio Modeler* in *Microsoft Project Web Access*.

◆ You want to monitor and level the workloads across multiple projects.

◆ You want to apply *Monte Carlo simulation* to your schedules.

In Appendix 2, you will find a list of about one hundred examples of schedules that reflect these best practices of scheduling with MS Project. These schedules are from real life projects and are valid and dynamic models. We recommend you have a look at the schedules that are relevant for your business.

We also provide tools with the checklist to check your schedules in an efficient manner, and we will discuss these next.

Copyright of the Tools and Checklist

The tools and checklist are copyrighted material: © 2005 by International Institute for Learning, Inc. This checklist is provided to you for personal purposes only. If you would like to use this checklist for commercial purposes within your organization, please contact IIL and talk to one of our sales representatives about licensing these tools and the checklist, see www.iil.com or call 1-800-325-1533 (USA).

Tools to Check Schedules

We provide several tools to make checking the schedules easier. You will find them in the file *IIL Project 2003 tools to check Orange Belt schedules.MPP* available for download at www.jrosspub.com. Please, click the link *WAV Download Resource Center* to enter the download site.

◆ Small macros to avoid repetitive mouse clicks.
Use the **Tools, Organizer** to transfer the module *IIL_OrangeBeltMacros* into your project schedule. You may have to restore the shortcut keys suggested below by choosing **Tools, Macro, Macros**, select the macro, then click `Options...`:

◇ **CONTROL + A** to run the macro **ExpandAllSummaryTasks_A** that expands all summary tasks (A for All). Every time before you apply a filter, you have to expand all summary tasks.

◇ **CONTROL + L** to run the macro **ListProjectSummary_L** that displays or hides the project summary task (L for List).

◇ **CONTROL + E** to run the macro **ZoomTimescaleToEntireProject_E** that zooms the timescale so that you can see the entire project (**View, Zoom, Entire Project**; E for Entire).

◆ Use the **Tools, Organizer** to copy the following filters into your project schedule:

◇ **01 IIL Level of Detail < 1% of Proj Dur...** : an interactive filter that prompts for the minimum duration for detail tasks to check the level of detail in the WBS using the *1%-10% rule*. The filter displays neither summary tasks nor recurring tasks.

◇ **02 IIL Level of Detail > 10% of Proj Dur...** : an interactive filter that prompts for the maximum duration for detail tasks to check the level of detail in the WBS using the *1%-10% rule*. The filter displays neither summary tasks nor recurring tasks.

◇ **03 IIL Milestones**: allows you to display the milestones without the summary tasks, which makes this filter different from the standard Milestones filter. Without the summary tasks, you can more easily copy them into a feedback email.

◇ **04 IIL Summary Tasks with Dependencies**: this filter displays all summary tasks with dependencies on them. If there are many summary tasks with dependencies, it makes checking the completeness of the network logic and tracing the Critical Path too difficult. We recommend keeping the logic on detail tasks as much as possible.

◇ **05 IIL Detail Tasks without Predecessors**: a filter that displays detail tasks without any predecessors to find the starting points of the network of dependencies. Detail tasks without predecessors may start on the project start date or will have a Start No Earlier Than constraint (SNET). The network of dependencies can have multiple starting points, but only one ending point. This filter displays all starting points of the network. You can then see if there are starting points in the network that should perhaps have a predecessor. Recurring tasks are not shown by the filter. Use this filter to copy all the IDs and task names into the feedback e-mail to the project manager.

◇ **06 IIL Detail Tasks without Successors**: A filter that displays detail tasks without any successor to find tasks that are not incorporated in the network of dependencies (*loose ends*). There should be only one ending point in the network of dependencies, otherwise Critical Path and slack calculations are not likely to be correct. Recurring tasks are not shown. Use this filter to copy all the IDs and task names into the feedback e-mail to the project manager.

◇ **07 IIL Detail Tasks with SS or FF**: this filter displays all tasks involved in a Start-to-Start (SS) or Finish-to-Finish (FF) dependency. SS and FF dependencies can easily have loose ends in the network of dependencies and have to be checked separately and carefully.

◇ **08 IIL Constraints other than ASAP**: A filter that displays any tasks with a constraint other than As Soon As Possible (ASAP). A dynamic model should have as few constraints as possible. Recurring tasks are not shown, because they should have constraints.

◇ **09 IIL Detail Tasks without Resources Assigned**: This filter displays all detail tasks without any resources assigned. You can also check this by looking under **Unassigned** in the **Resource Usage** view, but this filter allows you to copy the task IDs and names into the feedback e-mail. With that information, the person can find the tasks without *assignments* easily. If assignments are forgotten, workloads were omitted and the forecasted dates may be too optimistic.

◇ **10 IIL Deadlines or Constraints not met**: This filter displays items with deadlines or constraints that have negative slack. These deadlines or constraint dates are not met, and the schedule may forecast dates that are wrong. You can copy the task IDs and names into the feedback e-mail.

◇ **11 IIL Tasks with missing baseline info**: A filter that displays any tasks that do not have baseline information in Baseline Start, Baseline Finish, Baseline Duration or Baseline Work. When assignments are created after the baseline is set, the Baseline Work field is often empty on these tasks. Notice that the filter does not check the field Baseline Cost.

◇ **12 IIL Reschedule Actual Durations...**: An interactive filter that prompts you for the status date twice and displays tasks with an Actual Start or Actual Finish date after the status date. All actual dates should be in the past, i.e. earlier than the status date. As the status date, we would enter the date on which the schedule was submitted. With this filter, you can determine if there are actuals in the future, which does not make sense. There should be no Actual Start or Actual Finish dates later than the status date. The filter shows if the schedule is updated properly and thus if the forecasted dates are accurate and reliable.

◇ **13 IIL Reschedule Remaining Durations...**: An interactive filter that prompts you for the status date twice and displays tasks with remaining durations scheduled in the past (earlier than the status date). With this filter you can determine if the schedule is updated properly and if the forecasted dates are accurate and reliable.

◇ **14 IIL Remaining Durations revised**: this filter displays all detail tasks for which the current duration is not equal to the baseline duration. If the filter displays any tasks, it would indicate that the project manager is revising the *Remaining Durations*. Regular revision of remaining durations is important to ensure that the forecasted dates are accurate and reliable. Provide feedback to the project manager only if the filter does not display any detail tasks.

Make sure that all summary tasks are expanded before applying any of these filters, since filters never display detail tasks that are collapsed under their summary tasks. Press [Control] + [A] to expand all detail tasks with the macro. Press [F3] to stop a filter and display all tasks again.

Best Practices Checklist for Schedules

In the checklist, we have used the words "*summary task*" and "*detail task*" very carefully. It is important that the words are interpreted correctly for the guidelines to make sense. A summary task is any task with indented subtasks listed beneath it on a lower level in the WBS. A detail task is any task without indented subtasks in the WBS.

The checklist is a succinct summary of this book. The checklist has a background section and the following categories that correspond to chapters in this book.

◆ Work Breakdown Structure (WBS)

◆ Estimates
◆ Dependencies
◆ Scheduling Constraints
◆ Resources
◆ Assignments
◆ Optimizing
◆ Reporting
◆ Updating

Background Information You Need to Know About the Project

You need to know the answers to the following questions in order to make a thorough evaluation of the schedule:

◆ What is the objective or final product of the project
(if not described in **File, Properties, Comments**)?

◆ What is the deadline date of the project
(if not shown as a deadline date in the schedule)?

◆ Does the project have a cost budget? If yes, how much?

◆ Does the project have a person hour budget (effort)? If yes, how many person hours, person days, person weeks, person months or person years?

◆ Did the project manager gather pure work time estimates or gross work time estimates? For an explanation of these terms, see page 195.

◆ Did the project manager apply the Rolling Wave approach in the schedule? If so, what is the duration of the detail planning window? For an explanation of Rolling Wave, see page 198.

◆ Will the project manager do task updates (durations) or assignment updates (time sheets) or both?

Setup

◆ Does the **File, Properties**, tab **Summary, Comments** field contain a description of the objective or final product of the project?
The description is visible as a **Note** on the project summary task. You need to have some background information on the project to better evaluate the schedule.

◆ Do the working hours on the **Tools, Change Working Time, Standard (Project Calendar)** correspond to the **Tools, Options, Schedule, Hours per day** setting? For example, working times of 8AM-12PM and 1PM-5PM are consistent with 8 hours per day and 40 hours per week. If the settings are inconsistent, your forecasts are either too optimistic or too pessimistic. Also, you will often see decimals in the task durations in that case. See page 117 for a more detailed discussion.

The quickest way to check consistency is by choosing **Tools, Change Working Time**. The button <u>Options...</u> will take you directly to the **Tools, Options, Calendar** dialog. See page 112 for a way to set this straight.

WBS

◆ Are there deliverables in the WBS? Is the WBS a deliverable-oriented breakdown structure?

Deliverable-oriented breakdown structures provide the best control on the project. Deliverables should be captured using nouns (perhaps with adjectives, but without verbs). Verbs change a deliverable into an activity. If there are no nouns in the WBS, we have to conclude that there are no deliverables.

Alternatives for a deliverable-oriented breakdown are a phase-oriented breakdown or an organizational breakdown. From a project control perspective, these are less effective. See page 131 for a detailed discussion.

◆ Is the list of deliverables *complete* but lean?

◇ Are all expected deliverables explicitly included in the WBS? This should also include significant reporting items, like monthly status reports, test plans and test reports.

◇ Are the project management deliverables and activities included in the WBS? See page 156 for different ways of doing that.

◇ Are *out-of-scope* deliverables that may be expected by the client explicitly excluded from the WBS? We recommend you capture exclusions in the **File, Properties,** tab **General, Comments** field.

◇ There are no unnecessary deliverables in the WBS that were not agreed upon with the *client* or *project sponsor*.

◆ Does the WBS have a *logical hierarchy*?

If you don't have a logical hierarchy, you may report the wrong cost and duration by phase or deliverable. You can check if the WBS is a logical hierarchy by expanding the outline structure level by level using the Show ▾ tool on the **Formatting** toolbar. See page 134.

◇ Is the WBS an indented list with multiple hierarchical levels instead of a long list without structure?

◇ Are the most important items on the highest levels in the WBS?
  - Are the phases, if present, on a higher level than the deliverables?
  - Are the tasks, if present, on a lower level than the deliverables?

◇ Does each summary task have at least two subtasks?

◇ Is there any duplication or logical overlap between deliverables?

◇ Does each group of subtasks capture all the work of their summary task (top-down check)?

◇ Does each item logically relate to its summary tasks on all higher levels (bottom-up check)?

◇ Is the feature **Tools, Options, View, Project Summary Task** used instead of a physical project summary task? MS Project's project summary task has ID number 0 (zero) in the first column.

◆ Are there enough *milestones*?
There are enough milestones when there is roughly one milestone for each deliverable. Milestones allow you to create high level, one page reports on the project. Milestone events typically capture when the deliverable is completed, approved, sent, signed-off, published or shipped, for example. You can check this by applying the standard filter **Milestones** and checking if most deliverables have a milestone.

◆ Are the WBS elements properly formulated?
If you apply the following guidelines, you ensure that everybody will be able to understand your WBS (see page 141):

◇ Phases are formulated using the *imperfect tense* (-ing).

◇ Deliverables are formulated using a *noun* (perhaps with an adjective, but without a verb).

◇ Detail tasks are formulated using a *present tense* verb.

◇ Milestones are formulated using the noun of the deliverable and a verb in *perfect tense (*or *past tense* in English). Instead of a verb, the words *ready*, *complete* or

13

sign-off can be used. You can apply the filter **03 IIL Milestones** to display only the milestones without the summary tasks.[99]

◇ Are the names of the deliverables, tasks and milestones used consistently in the WBS?

◆ Does the WBS have the *right level of detail*?
Too little detail does not provide enough control on the project. There may be too few detail levels in the WBS (see page 145):

◇ If you cannot estimate the duration or work on the detail tasks.

◇ If you have difficulties finding the dependencies between the detail tasks.

◇ If you often assign more than one resource per task.

◇ If there are detail tasks that are longer than a reporting period.

◇ If there are detail tasks with durations longer than 10% of the project duration (1%-10% rule). You can check this by applying the filter
02 IIL Level of Detail > 10% of Proj Dur....[100] You will be prompted to enter what 10% of the project duration is. You can find the project duration by looking at the **Duration** field of the project summary task. The filter will display all detail tasks that are longer than 10% of the project duration. We recommend you split all these tasks into smaller ones.
An exception to the 10% maximum is if you created long tasks to capture overhead effort, like *project management* or *technical support.*

Too much detail causes too much work in maintaining the schedule. There may be too many detail levels in the WBS (see page 145):

◇ If you think there are too many levels or if you think the task list is too long.

◇ If you added reminders, to-do items or acceptance criteria into the task list. Transfer these to the **Notes** field.

---

[99] This filter can be found in the file *IIL Project 2003 tools to check Orange Belt schedules.MPP* available for download at www.jrosspub.com. Please, click the link *WAV Download Resource Center* to enter the download site.

[100] This filter can be found in the file *IIL Project 2003 tools to check Orange Belt schedules.MPP* available for download at www.jrosspub.com. Please, click the link *WAV Download Resource Center* to enter the download site.

◇ If you can't guarantee you will be able to update all detail tasks in the schedule during project execution.

◇ If there are tasks with durations shorter than 1% of the project duration (1%-10% rule). You can check this by applying the filter **01 IIL Level of Detail < 1% of Proj Dur...**[101] You will be prompted to enter what 1% of the project duration is. You can find the project duration by looking at the **Duration** field of the project summary task. The filter will display all detail tasks that are shorter than 1% of the project duration. *Recurring detail tasks* will not be displayed, since they typically are short and are allowed to be shorter than 1%. You can keep a few of these, but if you keep many, you will have to spend too much effort on updating your schedule during project execution. You then risk that you will let your schedule become obsolete at some point.

◆ Is the WBS clear to all project stakeholders?
All stakeholders like your customers, suppliers, upper management, team members and support staff need to fully understand the WBS. If you don't understand it as a project manager, nobody will. If an outside reviewer doesn't understand it, chances are some other stakeholders won't either.

◆ Project management overhead tasks, if present, should extend over the entire duration of the project. It does not make sense to stop managing the project halfway.

◇ Do the overhead tasks (like *project management*) extend over the entire duration of the project? See page 156.

◇ Do the *status meetings*, as recurring tasks, continue over the entire duration of the project? See page 154.

◆ Are there as few as possible task bar splits in the schedule at the end of the *planning phase* of the project?
Task bar splits often require a fair bit of maintenance and should be applied with restraint, see page 153. During the *execution phase* you will see enough splits appear when updating your schedule with actuals.

---

[101] This filter can be found in the file *IIL Project 2003 tools to check Orange Belt schedules.MPP* available for download at www.jrosspub.com. Please, click the link *WAV Download Resource Center* to enter the download site.

Estimates

◆ Are the estimates reasonable given the work that needs to be performed?
You will need some technical expertise to verify if the estimates are reasonable. If you don't have this technical expertise, you could review the schedules of previous but similar projects. You can ask your team members who have the technical knowledge to peer review each others' estimates or you can ask a *subject matter expert* (*SME*) to review the estimates.

◆ Are the estimates that you collected consistent with the working hours entered in the **Standard (Project Calendar)**?
If they are not consistent, the resulting schedule may be too short or too long, see page 195.
◇ Gross working time estimates should be entered in a schedule with gross working hours (typically 8:00 AM-5:00 PM).
◇ Pure working time is 100% productive time. Pure working time estimates should be entered in a schedule with pure working hours. Note that 100% productive working hours corresponds to a shorter working day, for example, 8:00 AM-3:00 PM. For most organizations, the percentage of totally productive working time lies between 60% and 80% of the working hours.[102]
Let's say your normal workday has 8 hours. If you estimate that the productive hours are 70% of the hours worked, the working hours should be 70% * 8h = 5.6 hours, let's say 5.5 hours (68.75%). Working hours that correspond to this are, for example, 9:00 AM-12:00 PM and 1:00 PM-3:30 PM. We prefer that you set working hours like these on the project calendar. You can set other working times as long as the total number of hours adds up to 5.5. To review the steps to set working hours, see page 116.

Dependencies

◆ Is the network of dependencies complete?
A complete network allows the schedule to update itself and displays the correct Critical Path. The network is complete if the task bars of all detail tasks are tied up at both ends. However, the network can have multiple starting points, but only one ending point. Only then will the Critical Path calculation be correct. For more

---

[102] This range is based on answers we received in our classes in which we taught thousands of project managers.

discussion, see page 246. The following questions will help determine if the network is complete:

◇ Is the logic only set on detail tasks and milestones?
If dependencies run over summary tasks as well, it takes too much time to check if the network is complete. It is also too hard to trace the Critical Path and understand it. Only with a complete network will the schedule be a fully dynamic model of the project. You can check if there are dependencies on summary tasks by applying filter **04 IIL Summary Tasks with Dependencies**.

◇ Are all the starts of the detail tasks and milestones linked to at least one other detail task or milestone?
You can verify if all starts are linked by applying filter
05 Detail Tasks without Predecessors. Note that if the project manager used SS- or FF-dependencies, the filter is not conclusive; see our discussion on page 246. You can check if there are tasks with SS- or FF-dependencies by applying filter **07 IIL Detail Tasks with SS or FF.**
Exceptions to this rule are:
- All tasks that can start when the project starts and that are driven by external forces or deliveries rather than by hand-offs within the project.
- External delivery milestones with a **Start No Earlier Than** constraint date. (see page 229)
- Recurring tasks (see page 154)
- Overhead tasks (see page 156)

◇ Are all ends of the detail tasks and milestones linked to at least one other detail task or milestone?
A *loose end*, *hanger* or *dangling task* is a detail task that does not have its finish tied to any other task. In any project, there should only be one loose end, the project finish milestone (ignoring the summary, recurring and overhead tasks). You can verify if all ends are linked up by applying the filter
06 IIL Detail Tasks without Successors.[103] Note that if the project manager used SS or FF dependencies, the filter is not conclusive. There will be another check on those.
Exceptions to this rule are:
- The project end milestone

---

[103] This filter can be found in the file *IIL Project 2003 tools to check Orange Belt schedules.MPP* available for download at www.jrosspub.com. Please, click the link *WAV Download Resource Center* to enter the download site.

- Recurring tasks, see page 154.
- Overhead tasks, see page 156.

◇ Do you have SS and FF dependencies properly linked up?
If you used SS or FF dependencies in your schedule, you should filter and display all those tasks with SS and FF dependencies and check on loose ends manually. See page 247 for a more detailed discussion. You can do this check by applying the filter **07 IIL Detail Tasks with SS or FF**.[104] Since the filter will display both the predecessor and successor involved in the SS or FF dependency, you can check if they are hooked up properly to other tasks by revealing the **Predecessors** and **Successors** fields. What you should look for is:
- Does a task with SS in the **Successor** field also have an FS or FF successor that ties up its end?
- Does a task with FF in the **Predecessor** field also have an SS or FS predecessor that ties up its start?

◇ Are there tasks with an unreasonably large amount of *Total Slack*?
You can check this by doing a descending sort on **Total Slack** by choosing **Project**, **Sort**, **Sort by...** and selecting **Total Slack** from the **Sort by** list. Check if the tasks with most slack were expected to have a lot of slack. If not, you have found missing logic.[105] Even after you have given all detail tasks a successor, you should still apply this check, because even if each task has a successor, it does not guarantee that you haven't forgotten important links. Checking the **Total Slack** will actually lead you to where you forgot to set important dependencies in your model of the project. This check is very effective in catching missing logic in schedules. Remember that if you miss just one essential dependency, your critical path is wrong, your forecasts are not *valid* and your model is not dynamic.

◇ When a change is entered into the schedule, does it update the rest of the schedule automatically and appropriately through dependencies?
Is the entire schedule still *valid*? Where the schedule is not valid, an essential dependency might be missing. If you have to check the entire schedule after each change, you don't have a dynamic model. Remember, the logic should be

---

[104] This filter can be found in the file *IIL Project 2003 tools to check Orange Belt schedules.MPP* available for download at www.jrosspub.com. Please, click the link *WAV Download Resource Center* to enter the download site.

[105] This check was contributed by Frank Walker, TWG Project Management, LLC.

helpful, especially during project execution when you update your schedule regularly.

◆ Is the Network Logic simple enough?
If the network is simple you can use it to explain impacts to your team. Project managers should be able to explain the network to their project team, otherwise the network is too complex, see also page 251. Are there redundant dependencies that make the network too difficult to explain and maintain:

◇ Are there dependencies that leapfrog each other?

◇ Are there dependencies that run in parallel on detail tasks and their summary tasks? If that is the case, keep the detail task dependencies and remove the summary task dependencies.

◇ Can you, as the project manager, explain the network to your project team?

◆ Does the network have circular logic?
Circular logic does not make sense, because it is not clear which task should be scheduled first. MS Project warns you not to set circular logic within a single schedule.

◆ Does the logic of the network make sense?
The schedule is now entirely driven by dependencies. After the previous checks on dependencies are done, you should perform one more high level check to see if the resulting schedule actually makes sense. You can check this best by showing only the first outline levels of the Work Breakdown Structure and checking if the timing of the deliverables (or phases) makes sense on this high level. You can use the Show ▾ button on the **Formatting** toolbar to display **Outline level 2** or **Outline level 3** depending on the size of your project. Even though you may not be an expert in the field of this project, you can always pick up on common sense things like *design* scheduled before *construction*, *write* before *print*, etc. Realize that if you followed our recommendations and minimized the number of constraints and entered all dependencies, the start and finish dates of the tasks are entirely driven by the network of dependencies. If the resulting schedule does not make sense, you probably overlooked an essential dependency. See page 245 for more.

Deadlines, Constraints and Task Calendars

◆ Is the project deadline date captured in the schedule?
It can be set using the **Deadline** feature date or using the **Constraint** feature in MS Project. The deadline or constraint date needs to be set on the project finish

milestone. Using a deadline date or a constraint date depends on how hard the project target finish date is, see our discussion on page 282.

◆ Are there as few *Task Calendars* as possible in the schedule?
Task Calendars have a very specific purpose as we discussed on page 290 and should only be used in those situations.

◆ Does the schedule have as few as possible schedule constraints?
Constraints make the schedule rigid and jeopardize a dynamic schedule, see also page 277. However, constraints are legitimate on:

◇ *Recurring detail tasks*, like *status meetings 1, status meetings 2,* etc.

◇ *External dependencies*, such as *delivery of supplies* or *arrival of materials*.

◇ Activities that have to take place on a certain agreed-upon date, like *deliver presentation* and *conduct training*. In general, these are activities in which a group of people is involved.

◇ Do-or-die-by dates, like the *December 31, 1999* deadline for Y2K projects as we all perceived it before that date.

◇ Activities affected by (winter) weather conditions, i.e., in Canada asphalting the streets *Starts No Earlier Than April 1ˢᵗ*, because of the cold. You can also use the feature of **Task Calendars** for these situations in MS Project (see page 290). Task Calendars would be a better way in the case of the multi-year planning of infrastructural works; unlike constraints, task calendars will push a job automatically out to the next year if it does not fit within this year any more.

You can display all tasks that have constraints by applying the filter **10 IIL Constraints other than ASAP**.[106] The filter will not display recurring detail tasks, because recurring detail tasks should have constraints.

Resources

Resources and assignments are important in projects in which it can be expected that limited resource availability or huge workloads will influence the project end date. They are also important if there is a budget and the cost needs to be managed.

---

[106] This filter can be found in the file *IIL Project 2003 tools to check Orange Belt schedules.MPP* available for download at www.jrosspub.com. Please, click the link *WAV Download Resource Center* to enter the download site.

◆ Are all resources identified in the Resource Sheet?
This is the case if all resources that could have a potential impact on the project are entered into the Resource Sheet. There can be impacts on *scope*, *quality*, *duration* or *cost* of the project, see page 314. Resources and assignments should be entered for projects:

◇ Where it can be expected that limited resource availability or huge workloads will affect the end date of the project.

◇ If you have a cost *budget* for the project and you are responsible for staying within that budget.

◇ If you have a budget expressed in *person months* and you have to stay within this *effort budget*. This is quite common in government IT projects.

◇ If you foresee a quality or scope impact on the project depending on which resources you will get.

◆ Are all resources named completely and consistently using a naming convention like *<first name> <last name>* or *<last name>-<first name>*?

◆ Are there no overlaps between the resources or duplication of resources?
If there are overlaps or duplications, MS Project will still aggregate the workloads of the resources, but these total numbers will be useless when you check on over-allocations. If Bill Tan is listed twice as a resource (as Bill Tan and William Tan), you would have to sum all time-phased workloads in order to determine if he is over-allocated. The workloads in the Resource Graph and in the Resource Usage can appear to be smaller than they really are when duplicate or overlapping resources exist. See also page 474.

◆ Is the availability of the resources appropriately modeled?
This can be assessed by asking you the following questions. For a detailed discussion on each question, see page 334.

◇ Does the availability of individuals not exceed 120% as captured in the resource field **Max. Units** or the availability profile in the **Resource Information** dialog, tab **General**?
At the International Institute for Learning, we set an arbitrary limit and choose the maximum to be 120%. We think it is unreasonable to ask resources for more than 120% availability for periods longer than one week. When you ask resources to work overtime for extended periods of time, their productivity goes

down dramatically.[107] So, apart from the fact that it is unreasonable to ask resources for much overtime over extended periods, it does not make sense either. In your organization, the actual threshold may be different from 120%.

◇ If the **Max. Units** are less than 100%, is there a valid reason for this? Valid reasons are that the project manager works with pure work time estimates (see page 195) or that the resources have other ongoing work or other concurrent projects. Or the resource may be a part-time resource.

◇ Are the vacations of individual resources captured in their resource calendar? Vacations need to be entered, particularly when there are important deadlines close to the vacations. To check if they are entered, choose **View, Reports, Assignments…, Who does what**, click ⬛ Edit… , click tab **Details**, check ☑ **Calendar**, and click ⬛ OK . In print preview, you will now see individual vacations listed under **Exceptions**, as well as the exceptions from the *project calendar*. Look carefully to verify if the individuals' vacations are listed. You can copy this changed report back into your *Global.MPT* using **Tools, Organizer** to have it ready for future schedule analysis.

◆ Are the costs of the resources appropriately modeled? See page 344 for more. The following guidelines will help determine this:

◇ Are human resources entered as **Work** resources in the resource field **Type**? Are facilities, machines and materials entered as **Material** resources (see our discussion on page 349)?

◇ Do **Material** resources have an appropriate **Material Label** to indicate their unit of measure? For *bulk resources* or *consumable resources* the *material label* should reflect the unit of measure, for example, the material label for cabling could be *yards* or *meters*.

◇ Are the rates entered in the appropriate fields?
- Time-related costs for **Work** resources in the **Std. Rate** field
- Unit-related cost for **Material** resources in the **Std. Rate** field
- Time-related cost for facilities and machines as **Material** resources using two fields: the **Std. Rate** field, where you enter the per-unit cost, and the assignment-related *Units* field, where you indicate the number of units used

---

[107] The OSHA (Occupational Safety & Health Administration) of the U.S. Department of Labor, see www.osha.gov

per time unit, for example, 2 rooms each day should be entered as *2/day* (for *consumption rate* see page 349)

- Use-related costs in the **Cost/Use** field
- Overtime costs in the **Ovt. Rate** field, but only if the overtime is paid and paid at a higher rate than the standard rate. See page 341 for more detail.
- Rates that vary over time in the **Cost Rate Tables**, see page 351
- Multiple rates per resource in the five **Cost Rate Tables** and the appropriate cost rate table (A, B, C, D or E) selected for each assignment
- Task- or deliverable-related fixed costs in the **Fixed Cost** field in the Gantt Chart. See page 352 for more.

◇ Is the cost scheduled appropriately?
This is important for managing the cash-flow of the project: *Can bills be paid when they are supposed to be paid?*
- Does the resource-related **Accrue At** field reflect when the cost occurs: at the **Start** or at the **End**, or **Prorated** with the time-phased amount of work?
- Does the task-related **Fixed Cost Accrual** field reflect when the fixed cost will be incurred?

Assignments

◆ Are you using the task-related field **Type** for the detail tasks?
The available types in the field *Type* are: **Fixed Duration, Fixed Units** or **Fixed Work**. With this field, you can control what MS Project recalculates: duration, units or work. If you don't monitor the field **Type**, you are not controlling what MS Project does. See page 379 for three rules that make your MS Project life easier.

◆ Are there no *assignments* on the summary tasks?
As we discussed on page 396, if you assign resources to summary tasks, you can easily end up with over-allocations that cannot be resolved other than by removing the resource from the summary task again. If you assign only to detail tasks, you will never end up with this stubborn type of over-allocation and save yourself time when leveling workloads. Resolving over-allocations is challenging enough. You can

check this easily by applying the filter **09 IIL Summary Tasks with Resources Assigned.**[108]

◆ Does each detail task have at least one human resource assigned?
If there are detail tasks without human resources assigned, you have not captured all the workloads in your project. If workloads are missing, the schedule may be too optimistic, since leveling workloads typically leads to longer schedules and later forecasts. An exception to this rule is that *recurring detail tasks* do not need resources assigned to them. See page 398 for more. You can check on this in one of two ways:

◇ In the **Resource Usage** view, there should be no detail tasks listed under the first category **Unassigned**.

◇ You can also apply filter **09 IIL Detail tasks without Resources Assigned.**[109]
The filter allows you to easily copy the tasks including their ID number into a schedule evaluation report to send back to the project manager.

Note that there may still be detail tasks with only material resources assigned if you check the **Unassigned** category or apply the filter, so neither check is error proof.

Optimizing Workloads

◆ Is the total effort within the person hour budget of the project (if a person hour or person day budget is available)?
You can find the total effort of the project by clicking **Project Statistics** -∿- on the **Tracking** toolbar and looking in row **Current** and column **Work**.

◆ Are the workloads for the resources reasonable?
If the workloads are too high, the forecasts are too optimistic. See page 473 for detailed steps on leveling workloads.

---

[108] This filter can be found in the file *IIL Project 2003 tools to check Orange Belt schedules.MPP* available for download at www.jrosspub.com. Please, click the link *WAV Download Resource Center* to enter the download site.

[109] This filter can be found in the file *IIL Project 2003 tools to check Orange Belt schedules.MPP* available for download at www.jrosspub.com. Please, click the link *WAV Download Resource Center* to enter the download site.

Chapter 13 Summary

◇ We had to set arbitrary limits; the limits may differ for your organization. The workload for individuals should not exceed 150% of their regular availability within any week. The workload should not exceed 120% for periods longer than a week. These upper bounds may differ for your organization. We have arbitrarily set them at these levels to prevent burnout, attrition and dramatic loss of productivity.

◇ The workload of consolidated resources (groups) should not exceed their availability.

◇ The workloads should be fairly smooth, since there are hidden costs involved with erratic workloads. See page 471.

Note that it is not enough to just check if there is any red in the Resource Usage view. MS Project often highlights more resources in red than are truly over-allocated. If there is an over-allocation during only one business hour, the resource will already be shown in red. Use the **Go To Next Overallocation** tool on the **Resource Management** toolbar to check the over-allocations. This tool is more selective and more reliable. However, even this tool does not always find all over-allocations, and it also highlights the 1-hour over-allocations. For more information, see the discussion on page 480.

Optimizing Costs

◆ Is the cost modeled using the right fields and in the appropriate way?
See the checks on resources on page 692 for more detail on this.

◆ Is the total cost within the budget of the project (if a cost budget is available)?
You can find the total cost of the project by clicking **Project Statistics** -ᐱⱱ- on the **Tracking** toolbar and looking in row **Current** and in column **Cost**.

Optimizing Time

◆ Are there as many parallel paths as logically possible in the network of dependencies?
Novice schedulers tend to schedule all tasks in one long sequential chain. In that situation there are many soft dependencies that make the duration of the project unnecessarily long. When optimizing for time, it is important to schedule in parallel what logically can happen simultaneously.

◆ Are there any unresolved conflicts between the task calendars and resource calendars?

13

PAGE 697

If there are conflicts, the forecasts may be too optimistic. You can find the conflicts by looking in the **Indicators** ❶ column for the icon 🖳. See page 293.

◆ Are the deadline dates and other constraints met in the schedule?
You can check this by applying filter **10 IIL Deadlines or Constraints not met**.[110]
It displays tasks with a deadline or constraint that have negative slack. See page 434 on why this is. When deadline or constraint dates are not met, the schedule may forecast a project end date that is too optimistic.

◆ Does the schedule have a Critical Path or a Resource-Critical Path?
The (Resource) Critical Path tells you which tasks drive your project end date. You can check the Critical Path by applying the **Tracking Gantt** view. This view highlights the Critical Path in red by default, see page 438.

◇ If a schedule is extended when the workloads are leveled, a Resource-Critical Path needs to be identified. Resource-critical tasks need to be marked manually.

◇ The (Resource) Critical Path can only consist of detail tasks and milestones. It should not contain level-of-effort tasks (overhead tasks or recurring tasks) or summary tasks (since the logic and the resources should be kept on the detail tasks).

◆ Does the (Resource) Critical Path provide a complete explanation for the project duration?
You can check the completeness by displaying the (Resource) Critical Path and then checking if it has gaps. Normally, there are no gaps, and every business day has at least one critical task (unless there are *lags* on critical dependencies). If you find gaps, the (Resource) Critical Path is fragmented, and the tasks that are most critical need to be identified in the schedule. See page 440 for possible causes of Critical Path fragmentation and what to do about them.

Reporting

◆ Is there a one-page status report available as a separate **View** object in your project schedule that displays the *major milestones* relative to the baseline?

---

[110] This filter can be found in the file *IIL Project 2003 tools to check Orange Belt schedules.MPP* available for download at www.jrosspub.com. Please, click the link *WAV Download Resource Center* to enter the download site.

◇ Are the milestones filtered in this view instead of listed together in the WBS? Many project managers put the major milestones at the top of their schedule to create a one-page overview of the project. This makes the network of dependencies very complex in the Gantt Chart, because the dependencies run up and down with long arrows. This makes it very difficult to check if the network of dependencies is complete. Instead, we advocate using a separate view that displays all milestones using the **Milestones** filter. See page 588.

◇ Are the appropriate milestones chosen to represent the status and to forecast a large project?

◇ Does the one-page view report give an appropriate impression of the health of the project? Executives like to see one page reports.

◆ If your schedule has a *Resource-Critical Path*, is there a separate view object that displays it?
The view should have the resource-critical tasks flagged in the field **Marked** or a **Flag** field. See page 501 for a detailed discussion of the Resource-Critical Path and how to create this view.

Updating

The following guidelines are important if the project should have started, which is the case if today's date is later than the project start date. The schedule needs to show updated information with actuals and revised forecasts.

◆ What is the quality of the baseline in the schedule? The schedule needs a good baseline, because it will be the standard for comparing the progress. See page 614 for the how-to set a baseline.

◇ Is a baseline present?
Keep in mind that projects planned far into the future and that aren't approved yet, do not necessarily need a baseline.

◇ Is the baseline complete?
You can verify the presence and completeness by applying the filter **11 IIL Tasks with missing baseline info.**[111] The filter displays any tasks

---

[111] This filter can be found in the file *IIL Project 2003 tools to check Orange Belt schedules.MPP* available for download at www.jrosspub.com. Please, click the link *WAV Download Resource Center* to enter the download site.

without entries in **Baseline Start, Baseline Finish, Baseline Duration** or **Baseline Work**. When assignments are created after the baseline is set, often the Baseline Work field is still empty. Note that the filter does not check on the field **Baseline Cost**.

◇ Is the baseline original?
The baseline cannot be reset without formal approval of the appropriate project stakeholders.

◇ Is the baseline relevant?
If the project deviated too far from the baseline, a new baseline needs to be negotiated. The baseline should provide a meaningful *standard of comparison* for the current schedule. You can check this by looking at how far the current schedule is removed from the baseline. Does the project have a fighting chance to catch up with the baseline again, or is it a lost cause? If it is a lost cause, you should submit a change request.

◆ Are the appropriate options selected in **Tools, Options** for the chosen updating strategy? See page 627 and 641.

◇ For task updating (revising the task-related **Actual Duration** and **Remaining Duration** fields), the options should be set as follows:

Tab **Schedule**: ☑ **Split in-progress tasks**

Tab **Calculation:** ☑ **Updating task status updates resource status**

◇ For assignment updating (entering numbers from the time sheets into the assignment-related **Actual Work** and **Remaining Work** fields), the options should be set as follows:

Tab **Schedule**: ☑ **Split in-progress tasks**

Tab **Calculation:** ☑ **Updating task status updates resource status**

If you keep this option selected, you should not enter **% Complete** on tasks, because this may override time sheet data. In Project 2003, overriding can be prevented by the Project Server administrator by locking in time sheet periods.

◇ For updating both the tasks and the assignments, the options should be set as follows:

Tab **Schedule**: ☑ **Split in-progress tasks**

Tab **Calculation:** ☐ **Updating task status updates resource status**
You cannot enter both types of information unless you clear this option.

◆ Is the **Status Date** set to an appropriate date?
The **Status date** in the **Project, Project Information** dialog should be set to a date

that is close to today's date. If it is too far in the past, the schedule may be out-of-date. If it is too far in the future, the project manager is guessing the progress instead of entering factual progress.

◆ Is the task type of soon to be updated tasks set to **Fixed Units** and non **Effort-driven**?
When you update the schedule, you change the durations (task updates) or the work (assignment updates). We recommended Fixed Units and non Effort-Driven, because you would typically like to see what the schedule looks like when the same resources continue to work on the task. You can always re-optimize the schedule; we discussed this in Chapter 9 Optimizing the Schedule, see page 419.

◆ Is the schedule up to date as per the **Status date**? See page 629 and page 660.

◇ Are all *actual durations* (*actual work / actual hours* worked) scheduled in the past?
The actuals are scheduled in the past if they are earlier than the status date. Otherwise, the schedule does not have up-to-date forecasts. When you bring actual durations to the past, all their dependent tasks may be rescheduled earlier as well, thus improving the forecasts. This is why rescheduling is important. You can verify this by applying the filter
12 IIL Reschedule Actual Durations...[112]

◇ Are all remaining durations (remaining work) scheduled in the future?
The remaining estimates are scheduled in the future if they are later than the status date. You cannot leave unfinished work scheduled in the past. If you leave unfinished work before the status date, you are scheduling more work to be done in the past even though the past is gone. The work should be moved to the future to update the forecast dates of all dependent tasks. Otherwise, the schedule does not reflect up-to-date forecasts and you have created a *status report*, instead of a *forecast report*. You can verify this by applying the filter
13 IIL Reschedule Remaining Durations...[113]

---

[112] This filter can be found in the file *IIL Project 2003 tools to check Orange Belt schedules.MPP* available for download at www.jrosspub.com. Please, click the link *WAV Download Resource Center* to enter the download site.

[113] This filter can be found in the file *IIL Project 2003 tools to check Orange Belt schedules.MPP* available for download at www.jrosspub.com. Please, click the link *WAV Download Resource Center* to enter the download site.

◇ Are the remaining durations (remaining work) revised?
Otherwise, the schedule may not reflect up-to-date forecasts. If the project manager has been revising the durations of detail tasks, these will be displayed. This filter is different from the other filters in the sense that if it displays tasks, it is good. If the filter does not display any tasks, it is an indication that the project manager is not revising his (remaining) durations while updating. If remaining durations are not revised, the forecasts are not very accurate and may not even be reliable. You can display the tasks with a revised duration by applying the filter **14 IIL Remaining Durations revised**.[114]

---

[114] This filter can be found in the file *IIL Project 2003 tools to check Orange Belt schedules.MPP* available for download at www.jrosspub.com. Please, click the link *WAV Download Resource Center* to enter the download site.

In Closing

If you have any further questions, don't hesitate to contact us. If you have any feedback on this book, please e-mail me at: EricU@iil.com.

This book contains the entire content for the first and second level of the certification curriculum (White Belt and Orange Belt). We would like to invite you to take on the challenge of becoming certified in MS Project. You can do this through self-study, live Web-based training or through traditional classes, public or onsite. Please visit our Web site, www.iil.com, to read up on the entire certification curriculum. I hope to personally welcome you into one of these courses.

Please find the files available for download at www.jrosspub.com. Please, click the link *WAV Download Resource Center* to enter the download site. The files that are available to all readers of this book are: the solution files of the Relocation Project exercises, the answers to the sample exam questions in Appendix 1, the filters and macros with which you can check the quality of your own schedule and the about one hundred certified schedules as real life examples.

Professors that use this book in their courses can even get a solution manual from the publisher J. Ross Publishing that provides the solutions for all remaining questions: review questions, some relocation project exercise questions, the case study discussion questions and the troubleshooting situations.

I thank you for the time you spent reading this book. I hope you found it worth your valuable time.

Eric Uyttewaal, PMP
Executive Director, Microsoft EPM Division
International Institute for Learning
www.iil.com

Appendix 1: Certification Curriculum Sample Exam Questions

The Testing Process for Certification

In this appendix you will find exam questions that are representative of the Orange Belt online exam in the certification curriculum of the International Institute for Learning (IIL). Candidates need to know this entire book in preparation for the Orange Belt exam.

The certification curriculum is designed so that it complies with the standards of the American Council on Education (ACE). The ACE protects the interests of American universities when auditing certification curricula offered by a private industry, see www.acenet.edu. The ACE has audited our curriculum and has accredited it. This means that participants should be able to get (elective) university credits with their certificate from IIL.

The Orange Belt exam:
- The exam is an open-book and open-computer exam; candidates can keep this book at hand when taking the exam and can use the MS Project application interface and help system.
- The online exam consists of 30 multiple-choice questions and takes one hour. The participants know their score immediately at the end of the exam. The passing mark is 70%.
- In the first twelve months of the online exams, 67% of the people who took the Orange Belt exam passed it. Over all our online exams, including the White Belt, Orange Belt and Blue Belt, 69% of the people passed the exams. ACE promotes the guideline that at a 70% passing mark, ideally 70% of the people should pass the exam. As you can see, the statistics of our exams look very healthy.
- The exam is carefully crafted in terms of coverage of all chapters and difficulty of the exam questions, just like all other exams in the curriculum.
- Each exam question directly relates to one of the learning objectives stated at the start of each chapter.
- Most answers are objectively right or wrong, and the use of good-better-best answers is minimized.

The exam has the following three main test objectives:

◆ Test your <u>readiness</u> to use the basic features of MS Project in practice.
In other words, it tests your active knowledge of the complete how-to steps for the basic features of MS Project. Basic features are those features most project managers need when modeling their projects, regardless of their industry.

◆ Test your <u>understanding</u> of MS Project.
It tests your understanding of the behind-the-screens working of the tool. You have to understand some of the formulas that MS Project uses in the background in order to be able to predict what will happen on the screen. In order for a tool to be a real tool, you have to be able to predict what it does; only then will it be a tool for you. If you could not predict what a hammer does, the hammer would not only be useless, but also dangerous. MS Project can be dangerous too, if you don't understand it. A fool with a tool is still a fool.

◆ Test your <u>practical</u> knowledge and skills.
It tests you on how to model real life situations rather than theoretic examples. We provide real life situations that lead into the question and ask you to make a recommendation about what the project manager should do in that situation.

The test questions are subject to continuous improvement. All answers given by participants are captured in the database, and periodically, the performance of the questions is analyzed. If a question is answered wrong all the time or never answered wrong, the question is either dropped from the database or modified. When a question is modified, it receives a new ID-number, so it can be tracked as if it were a new question.

Next, you will find 40 sample exam questions; the real exam only has 30 questions. If you want to see whether you are ready to go for the exam, you should be able to answer 30 questions in 60 minutes and attain a score of 70% or higher. You should pace your work at 2 minutes per question. The correct answers can be found in the files available for download at www.jrosspub.com. Please, click the link *WAV Download Resource Center* to enter the download site.

We recommend you read all answers before picking the best one. If you don't know the answer, you have a 25% scoring chance if you just fill in any answer.

40 Orange Belt Sample Exam Questions

1   Project templates are used …
    A. As sample projects from which project managers can learn
    B. As a jumpstart for creating schedules for repetitive projects
    C. For ensuring everybody uses the same resource names
    D. For ensuring everybody uses the same milestones

2   The summary tasks summarize their detail tasks. Which of the following fields of detail tasks do NOT necessarily add up to a total shown on the summary task?
    A. Duration
    B. Cost
    C. Work
    D. None of the fields mentioned

3   If you want to transfer a single view from one project to another, how many objects may you have to copy at most in the Organizer?
    A. 1 view object
    B. 2 objects: 1 view object and 1 table object
    C. 4 objects: 1 view object, 1 table object, 1 group object and 1 filter object
    D. 5 objects: 1 view object, 1 table object, 1 group object, 1 filter object and 1 report object

4   What is a true statement about slack?
    A. The amount of Total Slack is always greater than or equal to the amount of Free Slack.
    B. Delaying a task within its Total Slack will never affect its successors.
    C. Free Slack is synonymous to Float.
    D. The slack of a task is the amount of buffer you give a task.

5   The type of resources that is normally excluded from leveling is:
    A. Group Resources
    B. Individual Resources
    C. Facilities
    D. Materials

6   You want to create a schedule that needs the least maintenance while the project is executed, because you will be busy enough managing the project. You decide to follow these guidelines:
   A. Enter as many dependencies and schedule constraints as possible.
   B. Enter as few dependencies and schedule constraints as possible.
   C. Enter as many dependencies as needed and as few schedule constraints as possible.
   D. Enter as few dependencies as possible and as many schedule constraints as possible.

7   Which statement is true?
   A. Optimizing of the schedule should preferably be done only once.
   B. Refining the Gantt Chart should be done only once to win the bidding process.
   C. Setting the baseline for the entire project should be done only once in a project.
   D. Entering milestone constraint dates should preferably be done only once in a project.

8   Project schedules can contain:
   A. Only tasks, estimates, dependencies, constraints, resources and assignments.
   B. Schedule data (such as tasks, estimates) and objects (such as views, filters, tables, maps).
   C. Schedule data, but no objects. Objects are contained in project templates only.
   D. Schedule data (such as tasks, estimates) and global options.

9   You want to shorten your project by creating an overlap between two tasks that are Finish-to-Start (FS) dependent on each other. How can you best accomplish this?
   A. You set a lead time on the dependency, or you change the type of dependency.
   B. You set a negative lag time on the dependency, or you change the type of the dependency to SS or FF.
   C. You cut the FS dependency; this will schedule both tasks in parallel
   D. You change the dependency to an SS-dependency with a 100% lag.

10 You are using forward scheduling, and you have to install new computers, install software on the computers and train people in the use of the software. You want the users to be trained just before May at the latest. How would you schedule this situation?

 A. The task "train people" needs an ALAP constraint and a milestone is needed with a Must Finish On constraint on May 1st.

 B. All tasks need ALAP constraints and a milestone is needed with a Must Finish On constraint on May 1st.

 C. The task "train people" needs an ALAP constraint and a milestone is needed with a Finish No Later Than constraint on May 1st.

 D. The task "train people" needs an ALAP constraint and a milestone is needed with a Finish No Later Than constraint on April 30th.

11 You have a task with a Fixed Duration of 5 days. Two resources are working full-time on the task. The Work field shows 10 days. You want to change the duration while keeping the work on the task the same. How can you accomplish this?

 A. You change the task type to Fixed Work, then you enter the new duration. MS Project will adjust the number of resource units working on the task.

 B. You change the task type to Fixed Units, then you enter the new duration. MS Project will adjust the number of resource units working on the task.

 C. You keep the task type Fixed Duration and you enter the new duration. MS Project will adjust the number of resource units working on the task and keep the Work the same.

 D. The task type does not matter. You enter the new duration. MS Project will adjust the number of resource units working on the task and keep the Work the same.

12 When you have to level workloads, you can do this manually, or you can have MS Project do it automatically. Which of the following statements is true?

 A. Automatic leveling results in tighter schedules than leveling manually.

 B. With automatic leveling, you can create three different scenarios: no leveling, leveled by a target date, and full leveling. You cannot go back and forth between the scenarios, but they make automatic leveling better than manual leveling.

 C. Leveling manually involves more work than automatic leveling, but can lead to shorter schedules.

 D. Manual leveling methods are reassigning resources, moving vacations, assigning in overtime and delaying tasks. Automatic leveling is assigning in overtime and changing non-working time into working time.

13 The differences between Views and Reports in MS Project are:
   A. The data in Views is editable, but the data in Reports is not. Views are customizable. Reports are not customizable.
   B. Reports always show numeric information. Views do not. The Reports are highly customizable. Views are less customizable.
   C. The Views are highly customizable. Reports are less so. The data in Views is editable. The data in Reports is not.
   D. Reports are quicker and easier for printing Gantt Charts and Time-Phased Budgets than Views.

14 A person complains that it always takes too much effort to create print-outs of the schedule regularly, such as Gantt Charts and to-do lists for each resource. What would you recommend?
   A. Use Reports instead of Views.
   B. Create separate views for each print-out you need. Separate the views in which you do the scheduling from the views you use for reporting. Use the Calendar view as a basis for the to-do lists in combination with the "Using Resource..." filter.
   C. Use Project Server to communicate to-do lists to resources. Use the Reports feature to create the Gantt Charts.
   D. Use the fit-to-one page feature to make the data quickly fit on one page.

15 A scheduler left some uncompleted work scheduled before the status date. The updated schedule shows that all the deadlines are met. What statement is appropriate about this status report?
   A. The report is wrong; the work should be brought forward to after the status date using the "Update as Scheduled" button on the Tracking toolbar.
   B. Who cares, as long as the deadlines are met?
   C. The portion of work should be moved to after the status date using the "Reschedule Work" button, because this may affect meeting future deadlines.
   D. As long as the scheduler has entered all the Actual hours worked for each resource, the report is OK.

16 It is important to keep a time buffer in your project schedule. Why is this?
   A. Unforeseens
   B. Murphy's Law
   C. Path convergence
   D. Unforeseens, path convergence and the fact that task durations tend to extend, rather than shrink

17 Which of the following statements about project calendars is TRUE?
   A. Changing the Standard Project Calendar changes all the base calendars in the project.
   B. Changing the Base Calendar changes all the resource calendars in a project.
   C. You cannot create a workweek with seven work days.
   D. On the Standard Project Calendar you enter the statutory holidays and the work hours.

18 You are monitoring two milestones:
   "Report sent" shows a Total Slack of 2 days.
   "Test done" shows a Total Slack of -5 days.
   These figures indicate:
   A. Both milestones will slip
   B. The milestone "Report sent" can be met easily, but "Test done" cannot be met without taking corrective action
   C. The milestone "Test done" can be met easily, but "Report sent" cannot be met without taking corrective action
   D. Both milestones can easily be met

19 You want to update your project during project execution. Which steps should you follow and in which order?
   A. You set the baseline, the options and the status date in every status period. Then you enter actuals.
   B. You set the baseline and the options once, you enter the status date, display the Tracking Gantt, then you enter % Complete.
   C. You set the baseline and the options once, and you maintain the baseline, if needed. You enter the status date, you display the Tracking toolbar and the Tracking Gantt view, and then you enter actuals.
   D. You set the baseline once, and you never touch it again. You enter the status date and the options in every status period, you display the Tracking toolbar and the Tracking Gantt view, and then you enter actuals.

20 In which ways can you set schedule constraints?
   A. By driving a nail through a task bar on the Gantt Chart that hangs on the wall in your office.
   B. By entering start or finish dates, or by setting dependencies on the task.
   C. By entering actual start or finish dates, or by using the Task Information dialog box.
   D. By using the Advanced tab on the Task Information dialog box or using the task fields "Constraint Type" and "Constraint Date".

21 Two resources are working full-time on the task with 10 days of Work. You want to add an extra resource to the task, but keep the Work the same. How can you accomplish this?
    A. First you change the task type to Fixed Work, then you add the extra resource and the duration will decrease as a result.
    B. First you set the task to Fixed Duration, then you add the extra resource.
    C. First you change the task type to Fixed Units, then you set the task to non-Effort-Driven and add the extra resource.
    D. First you set the task to Fixed Duration and non-Effort-Driven, then you add the extra resource.

22 What do the "maximum units" of a resource represent?
    A. The number of part-time resources in a group resource.
    B. The percentage workload of a part-time resource.
    C. The maximum availability of the resource.
    D. The overall workload of the resource.

23 Which of the following statements is most accurate?
    A. For Summary Tasks, only the task name needs to be entered. For Detail tasks, the Task Name, Duration and/or Work need to be entered. For Milestones, the duration needs to be set to 0.
    B. For Summary Tasks, the name and the duration need to be entered. For Detail tasks, the Task Name and Duration need to be entered. For Milestones, the duration has to be set to 0.
    C. For Summary Tasks, the task name needs to be entered. For Detail tasks, the Task Name and Duration need to be entered. For Milestones, the 'Mark Task as Milestone' needs to be set.
    D. For Summary Tasks, the task name and the cost need to be entered. For Detail tasks, the Task Name, Duration and/or Work need to be entered. For Milestones, the schedule constraint needs to be set.

24 In general, what factor(s) should you consider when deciding whether or not to add a resource to the resource list?
    A. Whether the resource will add to the total cost of the project
    B. The impact the resource will have on the duration of the project
    C. The impact the resource will have on the workload histograms
    D. Whether the resource is available and whether the resource will have an impact on the duration or the cost of the project

25 Suppose you have several tasks to which you want to add John to the resources assigned. You can save time entering the assignments by:
   A. Selecting multiple tasks and using the Multiple Task Information dialog box.
   B. Using the Edit, Fill feature and fill John down in the field Resource Names.
   C. Copying a cell and pasting it into many other cells.
   D. Choosing the default Options appropriately.

26 Which of the following statements is true about dependencies and dates?
   A. Entering dependencies makes your schedule rigid and is worse than entering dates.
   B. If your situation allows you to enter dependencies rather than exact dates, it is better to do so, because the schedule can be maintained more easily with dependencies.
   C. Dependencies are better, because it is easier to enter and to explain dependencies.
   D. Entering Start and Finish dates is better, because most tasks (like milestones, meetings and training) have a fixed start or finish date.

27 Which of the following statements is FALSE?
   A. A Start No Earlier Than constraint will make sure that the Start and Finish date of the task will always be on or later than the date specified.
   B. A Finish No Later Than constraint will make sure that the Start and Finish date of the task will always be before or on the date specified.
   C. A Finish No Earlier Than constraint will make sure that the Start and Finish date of the task will always be on or after the date specified.
   D. A Start No Later Than constraint will make sure that the Start date of the task will always be before or on the date specified.

28 Which of the following statements about Views is TRUE?
   A. The Network Diagram shows the work breakdown structure clearly.
   B. The Usage views show the workloads of the resources in a histogram.
   C. The Resource Graph shows the workloads in numbers over time.
   D. A Gantt Chart shows tasks over time in a graphical format.

29 You contracted a painter on a fixed-price contract of $1300. In which view and in which field would you enter this cost?
   A. In the Resource Sheet in the field Fixed Cost
   B. In the Resource Sheet in the field Fixed Cost Accrual
   C. In the Gantt Chart in the field Fixed Cost
   D. In the Gantt Chart in the field Fixed Cost Accrual

30 You pay an electrician $70 per hour, and for overtime, $90 per hour. In which views and in which fields would you enter these rates?
A. In the Resource Sheet, enter $70/h in the Standard Rate field. MS Project does not have features for capturing overtime.
B. In the Resource Sheet, enter $70/h in the Standard Rate field. The rate of $90/h does not need to be entered, because MS Project will charge over-allocated hours automatically at the overtime rate.
C. In the Resource Sheet, enter $70/h in the Standard Rate field and enter $90/h in the Overtime Rate field.
D. In the Resource Sheet, enter $70/h in the Standard Rate field.

31 Which of the following statements is true about filtering Milestones?
A. The Milestone filter will show all the milestones in your plan except for the milestones of summary tasks that were collapsed.
B. The Milestone filter will show only those milestones that are marked as a milestone in your plan.
C. Milestones cannot be filtered out.
D. You need to create a new custom filter. You can create it through the menu items Project, Filtered For ..., More Filters. It should display tasks that have 'Yes' in the Milestone field.

32 Which of the following statements about Work and Duration is TRUE?
A. Work and Duration are essentially the same.
B. Work relates to human effort applied, whereas Duration relates to working time.
C. The amount of Work always determines the Duration of a task.
D. The Duration is always greater than or equal to the amount of Work.

33 Which of the following statements best characterizes the difference between pure work estimates and gross work estimates?
A. Pure work estimates are based only on the effort necessary to perform the task. Gross work estimates include typical distractions that occur during the normal course of the day.
B. Pure work is preferable to gross work in that gross work includes tasks like cleaning restrooms.
C. Pure work estimates are more pessimistic in nature and create typically longer projects than gross work estimates.
D. Pure work estimates are based on the effort to complete the task; whereas gross work takes the time constraints into consideration.

34 Being able to distinguish which task is the predecessor is crucial in determining the appropriate dependency between two tasks. Which of the following guidelines will help you identify which task is the predecessor?
   A. Ask yourself: which task occurs first in time? The task that comes first chronologically is always the predecessor.
   B. Ask yourself: which task is driving the other one? The driving task is always the successor.
   C. Ask yourself: which task follows the other one? The follower task is always the predecessor.
   D. Ask yourself: which task is driving the other one? The driving task is always the predecessor.

35 You have negotiated with a computer consulting firm to provide on-line technical support to your company for one month (20 working days) for a fixed fee of $5,000. What is the easiest way to capture this cost?
   A. Plan on about one call per day and assign one unit of the consultant resource to each. Set the Cost Per Use field to $250. (20 days times $250 = $5,000).
   B. Assign one full-time consultant resource to your "technical support" task and set the Standard Rate for the consultant to $250/day (20 days times $250 = $5,000).
   C. For the "technical support" task with a 20-day duration, set the task field called Fixed Cost to $5,000.
   D. Set the task type to Fixed Cost and enter $5000 in the Cost field.

36 When making resource assignments, which view or dialog box listed below gives you most control over the variables that influence the resource assignment calculations?
   A. Task Form view
   B. Task Sheet view
   C. Assign Resources dialog box
   D. Gantt Chart view

37 Which of the following techniques, when applied appropriately to your project model, will typically yield the most accurate prediction of the end date of your project (assuming forward scheduling with unlimited resources)?
   A. Critical Path Method (CPM) combined with Monte Carlo simulation
   B. Critical Path Method (CPM)
   C. Resource Critical Path (RCP)
   D. Program Evaluation and Review Technique (PERT)

38 In which of the following situations would the concept of the Resource Critical Path (RCP) be most beneficial to you?
   A. A project in which you have unlimited resources.
   B. A project in which you require several hard-to-get resources.
   C. A project in which your resources are easily replaceable.
   D. A project in which most of your resources are subcontracted out.

39 Assuming you are optimizing for time and you've highlighted the Critical Path, which of the following methods or techniques for shortening the duration of your project is recommended as a first course of action?
   A. Breaking up long tasks into shorter tasks.
   B. Removing or softening constraints and reducing lags.
   C. Reducing scope or deleting non-value-added tasks.
   D. Changing sequential dependencies into partial dependencies or parallel paths.

40 You are using forward scheduling and you want to:
   1 Install new computers
   2 Install software on the computers
   3 Train people in the software while the software is installed on their computers
   4 Everything finishing before May at the latest.
   The dependencies you need are:
   A. 1 Finish-To-Start to 2, 2 Finish-To-Start to 3, 3 Finish-To-Start to 4
   B. 1 Finish-To-Finish to 2, 2 Finish-To-Start to 4, 3 Finish-To-Start to 4
   C. 1 Finish-To-Start to 2, 2 Finish-To-Finish to 3, 3 Finish-To-Start to 4
   D. 1 Finish-To-Start to 2, 2 Finish-To-Start to 4, 3 Start-To-Start to 4

Appendix 2: Files Available to Readers

The download files are available for every owner of this book; see the next list of files. Apart from the download files, there is a solution manual for college professors (PDF-file). The solution manual contains all answers to review questions and the questions in the Relocation Project exercises. It also contains the answers to the troubleshooting challenges. Finally, the solution manual contains discussions of the case studies in this book. This solution manual can only be downloaded by professors who have their students use this book in their courses as mandatory reading.

J. Ross Publishing has created a resource download center on the Web site www.jrosspub.com. Click the link *WAV Download Resource Center* and you will find the following files:

◆ **Filters and macros to check the quality of your own schedule**
(MPP file: *IIL Project 2003 tools to check Orange Belt schedules.MPP*)
These filters and macros can be used to evaluate the quality of schedules. You can use these same filters and macros for your personal benefit. Please contact IIL about licensing these tools if you want to use them for business purposes within your organization.

◆ **Relocation Project Solution Files** (MPP files)
This download contains the start- and finished-exercise files for the Relocation Project that is featured throughout the exercises in all the chapters in the book. The Relocation Project is taken through a complete project life cycle from inception to updating.

◆ **Troubleshooting Exercise Files** (MPP files)
This contains files that are used for the troubleshooting exercises. Each file has a problem. The problems are representative of the kind for which technical support might be called. See the troubleshooting exercises at the end of the chapters.

◆ **Answers to the sample exam questions of appendix 1** (PDF-file)
The multiple-choice questions in appendix one are exam questions that were really used in the certification curriculum. This download contains the right answers and brief explanations.

◆ **Best Practice Schedules** (about one hundred MPP files in total)
In the past, we used to certify schedules as the Orange Belt certification criterion. You will find certified schedules here of the people who allowed us to publish their schedule. You will find several different ZIP-files for downloading. Each file contains the certified schedules for a particular industry. Feel free to download as

many as you want to explore. The files are a selection of excellent schedules that have proven valuable to the individuals that created them and to their organizations. The criteria I used to select the schedules are:

◇ The schedules meet the requirements of the checklist discussed in the summary chapter. This chapter contains an overview of all the best practices discussed throughout the book. All of them have been passed for certification and are excellent schedules.

◇ The schedules display a wide variety of projects and industries in which MS Project and our scheduling guidelines are implemented.

◇ The schedules may have value for you personally for your own projects.

I wish to extend a special thank you to all individuals and organizations that were so kind in allowing me to share their schedules with you. They provide insight into how the corporate world uses MS Project to deliver their projects successfully. See the next table with all the names of the individuals, the names of their organizations (if allowed) and the name of the MPP file. They are all Project 2003 files.

CREATOR	FILE NAME
Automotive Projects	
Aytekin Bozkan	Aytekin Bozkan – TEHCM DV testing Automotive parts
Patty Amsden EPW, Inc., USA	Patty Amsden – Dew Model
Carl Koerschner Simpson Industries, Inc., USA	Carl Koerschner – Steering Knuckle Design
Steve Magee Dura Automotive, USA	Steve Magee – Recliner
Construction Projects	
Sandra J. Perko GS XXI, Inc.	Sandy Perko – Expansion of Suite101a
Dale Dawson Central Lincoln PUD, USA	Dale Dawson – Transformer House
Alberto Alcala General Services Administration, Auburn, WA, USA	Alberto Alcala – Phased Construction
Eric Marois Algonquin College, Canada	Eric Marois – Voice and IP Installation

CREATOR	FILE NAME
Hardware Projects	
Jim McCluskey	Jim McCluskey – EDI links for Pharmacies
Dick Lane WeBeGeeks, Inc.	Dick Lane – Network Installation
Wayne Broich	Wayne Broich – Install PCs
Bill Reinhart SBC/Ameritech, USA	Bill Reinhart – Router Installation
Tim Schell	Tim Schell – Install Web Hardware
Eddie Perez	Eddie Perez – Office Move
Charlie Milstead	Charlie Milstead – IT Infrastructure
Robertson Young	Rob Young – PC Deployment
Home Projects	
Nancy Tighe	Nancy Tighe – Master Bathroom
Larry Smith	Larry Smith – Landscape yard
Kenny Liss, PMP La-Z-Boy Incorporated	Kenny Liss – Building a Deck
Karel Swinnen EDS	Karel Swinnen – Garden works
Ken Taylor, PMP	Ken Taylor – Build Log Home
	Windows Restoration
Dohn Kissinger, PMP	Dohn Kissinger – Backyard Landscape Project
Ann Hardie	Ann Hardie - Summer 2001 Cleanup
Joy Barnitz	Joy Barnitz – House sale
John Rouster	John Rouster – Vacation
Tom Cappel	Tom Cappel – First Floor Remodel
John Koepke	John Koepke – Build Fence
Kevin Gore	Kevin Gore – Build Deck
New Product Development Projects	
Chris Benson	Chris Benson – Autonomous Lawn Mower
Lisa James Pharmacia	Lisa James – Design and build air compressor
Plant Development & Maintenance Projects	
Todd A. Daily PCT Engineered Systems, LLC	Todd Daily – PCT Shop Test for Mill
	Refurbishing a Plant

CREATOR	FILE NAME
	Installation Remstar equipment for comp tooling
David Peeters, PMP Alliant Energy	David Peeters – Facility Center Database
Steven Stricklin	Steven Stricklin – Heat Rolls Rebuild
Daniel Zook	Daniel Zook – Process Plant
Donald Martin Walker & Associates, Inc., USA	Donald Martin – Plant Development
Project Management	
Roy L. Ragsdale	Roy Ragsdale – Time-Keeping Project
Stephanie Ghingher AEGON USA	Stephanie Ghingher – PMO Software Selection
Kristin Horhay	Kristin Horhay – Establishing a PMO
Derek Scoble, PMP SGR Inc.	Derek Scoble – Montana State PMO
Greg Callahan	Greg Callahan – Planning Process Development
	Project Portfolio Mgmt
Stephanie Iverson Marriott Vacation Club International, USA	Stephanie Iverson – Project Mngt System Implementation
Daniel Vitek	Daniel Vitek – HW&SW Purchase Process
Linda Lawlor Linda Lawlor Consulting, Canada	Linda Lawlor – Automated Project Office
Ann Russell	Ann Russell – Project Charters
Software Development Projects	
Alan Bearder	Alan Bearder – W2K Active Directory SMS Schedule
Allie Darr	Allie Darr – Insurance SW development
Allie Fairfax	Allie Fairfax – AEF Data Application
Amy Schoenherr ProjectSavvy	Amy Schoenherr – Proposed Citrix Schedule
Beth Devroy Access Business Group	Beth Devroy – Skin Care System-COGS
Chas Eddingfield	Chas Eddingfield – Software Modification

CREATOR	FILE NAME
Darrell Little North American Mortgage Company	Darrell Little – MERS TOSR software development
Doug Winters, PMP	Doug Winters – Data Retrieval
Frank A. Stillo, PMP OneWorld Inc.	Frank Stillo – SW Development Concert
Isabella M. Stengele Marsh	Isabella M Stengele – RMX Enhancements
James P. Crowell Marsh	James P Crowell – Detailed Analysis of Placement Repository
Joanne M. Greene-Blose Eastman Kodak Company	Joanne M Greene-Blose – ReMan release 4 Reprinted with permission from Eastman Kodak Company
	Full Flight Simulator Upgrade for Company XYZ
	Sales Forecasting Database
Carla Carter Levi, Ray & Shoup, USA	Carla Carter – Monthly checkwriting
Kathy Convery Levi, Ray & Shoup, USA	Kathy Convery – Database
	Requirements and Specifications
	SW Development
David Kempster Centrefile, Ltd. UK	David Kempster – Customer Database
Charlotte Mensah Centrefile, Ltd. UK	Charlotte Mensah – Develop Cube
Ron Ainsworth Centrefile, Ltd. UK	Ron Ainsworth – Software Development
Michael Jordan Great American Insurance, USA	Michael Jordan – Claims Software
Software Implementation Projects	
Brad Jones Mount Carmel Health	Brad Jones – Software Installation
Bonnie Heinecke Fortis, Inc.	Bonnie Heinecke – Cognos suite deployment
Bob Herman	Bob Herman – Software Transition
	Beta Testing
Carol A. Ergen, PMP	Carol A Ergen – SuperMontage Implementation

CREATOR	FILE NAME
Dino Nosella SAP Canada Inc.	Dino Nosella – SAP Performance and Balancing
Jim Schuster, PMP Fortis, Inc.	Jim Schuster – Implementation of DB2
Larry Wentzel	Larry Wentzel – Automate Benefit Enrollment
Len Maland, PMP HP Consulting & Integration Services	Len Maland – Computer-Aided Dispatch System
Mark Cimon Cognos	Mark Cimon – Logistics Software
Nicholas Scott	Nicholas Scott – PROMPT Implementation Project Seven
Ronald Sonnabend	Ronald Sonnabend – SAP Upgrade Workplan
	SW Selection and Procurement
Beth Pollard	Beth Pollard – Emulation Evaluation
Training and Organization Projects	
Tommie G. Cayton, Ph.D.	Tom Cayton – Incentive Standardization
Tara T. Miller	Tara Miller – training
Peter Avery Capital Defender Office, NY	Peter Avery – Newsclips for Capital Defender Office
	Translation Japanese
Gail Angel Cognos	Gail Angel – Document Writing
Chris Baeten EDS	Chris Baeten – MS Project training
Caroline Robison EDS	Caroline Robison – Communications Project
Annie Nuyts EDS	Annie Nuyts – Security Organization and Governance delivery
Michael Starkey	Michael Starkey – Training Process Development
Regulation Implementation Projects	
Chetna Mathur	Chetna Mathur – Health regulation implementation

References

1. Guide to the Project Management Body of Knowledge, 2004 Edition, Project Management Institute, Inc., Newtown Square, Pennsylvania, USA.

2. Practice Standard for Work Breakdown Structures, 2001, Project Management Institute, Inc., Newtown Square, Pennsylvania, USA.

3. Work Breakdown Structure Practice Standard Project – WBS vs. Activities, Project Network, April 2000, Berg, Cindy and Kim Colenso, Project Management Institute, Inc., Newtown Square, Pennsylvania, USA.

4. Earned Value Project Management, Second Edition, 2000, Fleming, Quentin W. and Joel M. Koppelman, Project Management Institute, Inc., Newtown Square, Pennsylvania, USA.

Glossary

Activity See *task*. In this book, the terms *task* and *activity* are used interchangeably since the interface of MS Project uses the word *task* often.

Actuals The actuals is the set of data that represents how the project ran. It shows the final duration (*Actual Duration*), the hours that were spent (*Actual Work*), the real start date (*Actual Start*), the real finish date (*Actual Finish*) and the final cost (*Actual Cost*) of each task.

Assignment An assignment is a combination of a task and a resource. It can be a resource scheduled to work on a particular task or a task assigned to a specific resource. Assignments have their own specific fields, such as start and finish, work, units, work contour and cost rate table.

Bar Chart See *Gantt Chart*.

Baseline The baseline is the originally approved schedule, plus the approved changes. The baseline schedule is meant to be compared against. The baseline contains the start and finish dates, durations, work and cost numbers and their time-phased spread. The baseline values are static unless you baseline again. See also *interim plan*.

Base Calendar is any calendar that can be used as the project calendar, task calendar or resource calendar. See also *project calendar* and *resource calendar*.

Business Day A business day is a working day, normally a weekday. See also *person day* and *calendar day*.

Calendar day A calendar day is a 24 hour day. Unlike a business day, a calendar day disregards non-working time. See also *business day* and *person day*.

Critical Path The Critical Path is the sequence of tasks that determines the duration of the project. The tasks on the Critical Path are often scheduled tightly; upon finishing one, the next one immediately starts. In other words, there is often no slack between critical tasks. See also *resource-critical path*.

Critical Path Method (CPM) The Critical Path Method is an approach for optimizing schedules that is based on identifying the Critical Path in a schedule. The method is based on the assumption that there is access to unlimited resources. See also *Critical Path* and *resource-critical path*.

Critical Resource A critical resource is a resource that drives the duration of the project, because of its limited availability. A critical resource is assigned to a (resource) critical task and drives the duration of the task. See also *Critical Path* and *resource-critical task*.

Critical Task A critical task is a task on the Critical Path. See also *Critical Path* and *resource-critical task*.

Delaying Delaying is rescheduling one of two tasks that compete for the same resource to a later date in order to resolve a resource over-allocation. The over-allocation is caused by the concurrent scheduling of both tasks and the use of the same resource. See also *leveling*.

Dependency A dependency is a logical cause-and-effect relationship between two tasks. If a task cannot start until another task is finished, it is 'dependent' on the completion of the other task. For example, the start of printing a report is dependent on finishing the writing of it. See also *resource dependency*.

Detail Task A detail task is a task on the lowest outline level or any task without subtasks. Detail tasks are done by a person, and it should be possible to estimate the duration and the cost of each detail task. See also *summary tasks*.

Duration The duration is the number of business hours or business days estimated to complete a task or deliverable. See also *work*.

Earned Value The earned value is the value of the completed work, the sum of the approved budget numbers of the completed work. Earned value analyses are often made during the execution of the project to evaluate the progress and to forecast the trend of the project duration and cost.

Effort See *work*.

Elapsed Duration Elapsed duration is the time it takes to perform a task expressed in calendar hours or calendar days (which includes evenings, weekends and holidays). Elapsed time is used for tasks like *dry paint* or *back up computers*, typically tasks without human resources assigned. See also *duration*.

Enterprise An enterprise can be your entire organization, or any subset thereof. The boundaries of the enterprise are determined with the purpose of modeling its project portfolio and pool of resources. The term is used by Microsoft to position the professional edition of MS Project in the marketplace. See also *workgroup*.

Filter A filter is a condition that determines whether a task or resource is displayed. A filter is an object that can be transferred between project schedules using the organizer. See also *organizer*.

Fixed Duration Task A fixed duration task has a duration that will stay the same regardless of how many additional resources are assigned to the task. For example: *drying of paint, teaching a course*.

Fixed Units Task A fixed units task is a task that keeps the number of resources assigned the same when a change is made to the *duration* or the *work*. The duration will change if the work is changed, and vice versa.

Fixed Work Task A fixed work task is a task that is effort-driven; the amount of *effort* (*work*) will be the same, regardless of the number of resources doing the task. For example, *coding a computer program, writing reports* and *painting walls* entail a relatively fixed amount of effort. The work can be estimated up-front.

Float See *slack* and see also *free slack* and *total slack*.

Free Float See *free slack*.

Free Slack Free Slack is the time that a task can be delayed without influencing the start of any dependent tasks. On the *Critical Path* there is no free slack. Free slack is synonymous to *free float*.

Gantt Chart A Gantt Chart is a graphical presentation of tasks over time. Bars in a timescale represent the durations of the tasks. The chart is named after Henry L. Gantt, who invented it in the early 20th century. The Gantt Chart is also called a *bar chart*.

Global.MPT The Global.MPT file is the default template file that is always open when MS Project is running. It contains the default objects that are accessible in new and existing project schedules. Each object in the Global.MPT is accessible in all project schedules, unless there is an object with the same name in the existing project schedule.

Group A group is an object that categorizes task or resource records in the MS Project database. A group can be transferred between project schedules using the organizer. There is also a resource-related field *group* in which the department of a resource could be captured. See also *organizer*.

Interim Plan An interim plan is a set of start and finish dates that is used to compare. Interim plans only contain start and finish dates and are therefore only a partial schedule and different from the baseline. See also *baseline*.

Lag A lag is the duration of a dependency. In a finish-to-start dependency, it is the time you have to wait after the independent task is finished before the dependent task can start. Lag shows as a gap between task bars in the timescale of a Gantt Chart. Lag time pushes the dependent task to later in time.

Lead A lead is a negative duration of the dependency. In a finish-to-start dependency, it is the amount of time by which the dependent task starts earlier than the finish of the independent task. The two task bars will overlap in the timescale and create a partial dependency. Lead time pulls the dependent task to earlier in time. See also *partial dependency*.

Leveling Leveling the workload of resources is bringing workload peaks of resources down within their availability or increasing workload valleys to their availability. Resources can have too much work when they happen to be assigned to two tasks at the same time. Reassigning one of the tasks to another resource is one of the possible solutions. A last-resort solution is to reschedule one of the two tasks to later in time. This is called delaying a task. See also *delaying*.

Logical dependency See *dependency*.

Milestone A milestone is an event with a zero-duration. A milestone is an important point in time, often an evaluation point. It can be a date on which a deliverable has to be ready or a meeting in which Go/No Go decisions are made. Events like the opening of a new facility can be milestones. Milestones appear as diamonds in the timescale of the Gantt Chart and are visual reminders of these important dates.

Network Diagram The network diagram shows the logical dependencies between the tasks. Dependencies are shown in the network diagram as arrows between task boxes. Each arrow depicts a dependency and points from the driving task to the follower task. See also *dependency*.

Object Objects are things that change the appearance of the schedule data (tables, filters, groups, views, fields, reports, maps, calendars) or components of the MS Project interface (modules, toolbars, menu bars). All objects can be seen in **Tools, Organizer**. See also *organizer*.

Open DataBase Connectivity (ODBC) ODBC is a standard set to foster the exchange of data between database applications. Databases that adhere to ODBC allow other database software to read and write the data.

Organizer The organizer is a feature in MS Project through which objects can be transferred between project schedules and even the *Global.MPT* file. Examples of objects are: tables, filters, groups, views, calendars and toolbars. You can access the organizer by choosing **Tools, Organizer**.

Outline Structure The outline structure refers to the profile of the indented task list. Detail tasks are indented under their summary task, to form an indented list of tasks, also called the outline structure. See also *work breakdown structure*.

Partial Dependency A partial dependency occurs when a task is dependent upon the partial completion of its predecessor. As a result, the tasks will overlap each other in the Gantt Chart. A finish-to-start dependency with lead time (negative lag) is an example of a partial dependency. See also *dependency*, *lead* and *lag*.

Person Day A person day is one person working for one full business day. See also *business day* and *calendar day*.

PERT PERT stands for Program Evaluation and Review Technique, a technique used to analyze and optimize network logic.

PERT Chart The PERT chart used to be a view in MS Project, but was renamed to *network diagram* in the Project 2000 version. The PERT Chart showed the network of dependencies between the tasks. See *network diagram*.

Predecessor The predecessor is the independent task or driver in a dependency relationship. In the example of *writing* and *printing*, the task *writing* is the predecessor of *printing* and *printing* is the successor of *writing*. See also *successor*.

Project Calendar It is the same as the *standard project calendar*. The project calendar is the calendar on which you specify which days are working days and non-working days for everybody involved in the project. It restricts the scheduling by MS Project. You can base the *resource calendars* on the standard project calendar, which will copy all the holidays into the resource calendars. It is a time-saving device for creating resource calendars See also *base calendar* and *resource calendar*.

Project Database All the data that are entered in the project are stored in the project database. Data can be extracted from this database as needed for a view or a report using filters.

Project Summary Task The project summary task is the project title at the top of the task list that displays summarized totals for the entire project. Its task ID number is zero, and all other tasks are indented below it, so that it summarizes the duration, work and cost for the entire project. It can be toggled on and off by choosing **Tools, Options**, tab **View**.

Project Template A project template is a standardized schedule that is typical of a kind of project run by an organization. It contains a standard WBS with dependencies; often, generic resources are assigned to the tasks. A contractor who builds houses uses the same schedule over and over again for every house. He could use a project template as a boilerplate schedule. Template schedules can decrease the necessary data entry for creating similar schedules over and over again, and are protected from accidentally being changed. Project template schedules copy themselves when you open them.

Recalculation A recalculation is a refresh of the entire schedule based upon changes made. Whenever a task is inserted or changed, the project cost and work change, as well as the dates of other dependent tasks. All these figures have to be recalculated by MS Project.

Report A report in MS Project is a tabular and numeric presentation of the project. Many reports are shipped with MS Project and are ready-to-go. Reports are customizable only to a certain degree. See also *view*.

Resource Calendar A resource calendar is an individualized calendar with the working days and times defined for the resource, as well as the non-working days and times. See also *project calendar* and *base calendar*.

Resource-Critical Path The resource-critical path is the sequence of tasks that determines the duration of the project given a limited availability of resources. The resource-critical path takes logical dependencies and resource dependencies into account. Unlike the Critical Path, the Resource-Critical Path is not based on having access to unlimited resources. See also *Critical Path, logical dependency* and *resource dependency*.

Resource-Critical Task A resource-critical task is a task on the resource-critical path. See also *resource-critical path* and *critical task*.

Resource Dependency A resource dependency is a relationship between two tasks through a resource that is assigned to both tasks. If the resource needs more time to finish the task that is scheduled first, it will cause the other (resource-dependent) task to start later. See also *logical dependency*.

Resource A resource is a person, team, facility, machine or material used in a project to accomplish tasks. Anything that can influence the timing, cost or quality of tasks should be defined as a resource in the project.

Resource Leveling, see *leveling*.

Responsible A responsible person is the person who is accountable for deliverables of the project. Responsible people only become resources to the project if they work on any tasks in the project. See also *resource*.

Schedule A schedule is a set of start and finish dates of all deliverables, tasks and milestones of the project. An MS Project schedule typically contains the WBS, the dependencies between the tasks, some date constraints, the estimates, the resources and assignments, based upon which it calculates the start and finish dates.

Sequential Dependency When two tasks are sequentially dependent upon each other, it means that the driver task has to be finished entirely before the follower task can start. See also *partial dependency*.

Slack see *float* and see also *total slack* and *free slack*.

Sort A sort is a ranking of tasks or resources based on one or more fields in the project database.

Standard (Project Calendar) It is the calendar that acts as the project calendar. See *project calendar*.

Successor The successor is the dependent task or follower in a dependency relationship. In the example of *writing* and *printing,* the task *writing* is the predecessor of *printing* and *printing* is the successor of *writing*. See also *predecessor*.

Summary Task A summary task is an item in the WBS with subtasks and shows the duration, total cost and total amount of work of its subtasks. To make a schedule easier to understand for stakeholders, you can group tasks and give each group a descriptive summary task name. Summary tasks are often deliverables and give the plan a logical structure. If tasks are scheduled in parallel, the summary duration is not necessarily the sum of the durations of the subtasks. See also *detail tasks*.

Table A table is a selection of task- or resource-related fields that appear as columns in the spreadsheet of a view. A table is an object that can be transferred between project schedules using the organizer. See also *organizer*.

Task A task is a concrete piece of work that has to be done and that can be assigned to a resource. It should be possible to estimate the duration of a task. In this book, the word *task* is used interchangeably with *activity*. See *activity*.

Task bar Each task has a task bar in the timescale of the Gantt Chart that represents the duration of the task.

Total Float See *total slack.*

Total Slack Total slack is the total amount of time a task can be delayed without influencing the end date of the project (or any earlier constraint date). Total slack is synonymous to *total float*.

Tracking progress Tracking progress is comparing the current schedule to the baseline. Comparisons can be made on the start and finish dates, duration, work and cost.

Updating The updating of a project schedule is entering what happened in the past (the *actuals*) and what you forecast for the future of the project. Actuals are the actual start date, the actual days or hours spent on a task and the actual finish date.

View A view is an arrangement of project data in MS Project. A view applies a table, filter and group object, and also contains the sort order, format settings, page layout choices and drawing objects. A view is an object that can be transferred between project schedules with the organizer. See also *report, organizer, table, filter* and *group*.

WBS The WBS is a deliverable-oriented hierarchical decomposition of the work to be executed by the project team to accomplish the project objectives and create the required deliverables.[115] See also *outline structure, summary tasks* and *detail tasks*.

What If Analysis This is a way of finding out by trial and error what a better schedule may be.

Work The work is the estimated number of person hours or person days a resource spends on a task or deliverable. In MS Project, *work* is synonymous to *effort*. See also *duration*.

Work Breakdown Structure See *WBS*.

Workgroup A workgroup is a limited number of people that work closely together performing projects. See also *enterprise*.

Workload leveling See *leveling*.

---

[115] See the PMBOK® Guide, 2004 Edition, published by the PMI.

Index

Some remarks on the index. The name of fields and the enumerated values (attributes) that you can find in the fields are listed in the index. We have also grouped them together under certain headings:

◆ Assignment-related fields are also listed under *fields (assignment-related)*
◆ Resource-related fields are also listed under *fields (resource-related)*
◆ Task-related fields are also listed under *fields (task-related)*
◆ Values in assignment fields are also listed under *attributes (assignment-related)*
◆ Values in resource fields are also listed under *attributes (resource-related)*
◆ Values in task fields are also listed under *attributes (task-related)*

as late as possible, 106, 276, 278, 280, 281, 430, 441

as soon as possible, 106, 205, 246, 276, 278, 280, 281, 430

ASAP. See 'as soon as possible'

assign, 145, 156, 166, 184, 187, 189, 311, 313, 314, 346, 348, 379, 386, 396, 398, 470, 484, 546, 548, 647

Assign Resources, 320, 346, 350, 371, 383, 386, 387, 391, 393, 397, 402, 469, 473, 519

assignment units, 137, 176, 183

assignments, 66, 89, 94, 369, 372, 373, 378, 380, 382, 386, 396, 398, 399, 401, 408, 410, 412, 446, 469, 472, 476, 480, 485, 552, 566, 573, 590, 621, 647, 649, 652, 658, 660, 663, 681, 695, 725

  multiple, uneven assignments, 378, 399

  part-time, 371

  updating assignments, 621, 639

assumptions, 202

attributes (assignment-related)

  Demand, 389

  Request, 389

attributes (resource-related)

  End, 322

  Material, 317, 318, 345, 350

  Prorated, 322

  Start, 322

  Work, 317, 318, 345

attributes (task-related)

  As Late As Possible, 441

  As Soon As Possible, 205

  Finish No Earlier Than, 435, 442

  Finish No Later Than, 435, 442

  Fixed Duration, 184, 186, 188, 189, 374, 377, 379, 384, 395, 634

  Fixed Units, 184, 374, 377, 386, 395, 634

  Fixed Work, 184, 187, 188, 190, 374, 377, 379, 385, 395, 634

  Must Finish On, 435, 442

  Must Start On, 435, 442

  Prorated, 352

  Start No Earlier Than, 435, 442

  Start No Later Than, 435, 442

  Type, 378

authentication

  Project Server authentication, 70

  Windows authentication, 70

AutoFilter, 248

Autolink, 163, 221

automatic leveling, 114, 484

availability, 317, 335

availability profile, 336, 341

available budget, 560

B

backward scheduling, 106, 226, 276, 280, 286, 435, 442

bar chart, 725

bar styles, 140

base calendar, 725

base calendars, 322, 329, 330, 339, 561

baseline, 90, 202, 457, 471, 614, 620, 725

  baseline schedule, 614

  changing the baseline, 615

  standard of comparison, 660, 700

Baseline Work, 650

Black Belt Professional, 16

Black Belt Standard, 16

black holes, 587

Blue Belt Professional, 16

Blue Belt Standard, 16

budget, 61, 202, 353, 693

principle of, 217, 218

E
earliest possible dates, 430
early dates, 430
early finish, 430, 432, 433, 498
early start, 430, 433, 498
Earned Value, 51, 552, 586, 617, 618, 726
editions
    Microsoft Office Project 2003
    Professional, 57
    Microsoft Office Project 2003
    Standard, 57
effort. See 'work'
effort budget, 353, 693
effort driven, 374, 383, 394, 631
elapsed days, 227, 394, 415, 443
elapsed duration, 193, 726
elapsed lag, 224
elapsed time, 191, 224, 394
employees, 322
entering dependencies, 220
enterprise, 57, 71, 81, 727
enterprise calendars, 118, 119, 120
enterprise fields, 324, 560
Enterprise Gantt Chart, 81
Enterprise Global, 71, 121, 581, 582
enterprise outline codes, 560, 568
enterprise project management, 3, 17, 18, 57
enterprise resource planning, 44
enterprise resource pool, 108, 319, 323, 324, 327
enterprise templates, 106, 110
enterprise views, 162, 581, 582
entry bar, 88
enumerated, 319

EPM, 3, 57, See 'Enterprise Project Management'
ERP. See 'Enterprise Resource Planning
errors, 616
estimated durations, 178, 549
estimates, 145, 202, 464
    business days, 175, 183, 193
    business hours, 183
    calendar days, 193
    dates, 183
    elapsed duration, 193
    estimated durations, 178
    function points, 186
    gross work time, 195, 196
    law of averages, 181
    living document approach, 202
    metrics, 186
    most difficult estimate, 183
    owning them, 179
    parameters, 186, 190
    parametric estimating, 186
    person days, 175, 183, 192
    person hours, 183
    personality factor, 181
    pure work time, 195, 196
    quantity surveyors, 186
    range estimate, 179
    Rolling Wave, 198
    single point estimate, 179
    worst-case, 180
exceptions, 335
execution phase, 26, 31, 146, 167, 219, 221, 247, 252, 335, 340, 345, 543, 622, 687
executives, 325
experts, 315, 499
eXtended Markup Language, 1, 4
external dependency, 229
external projects, 544

law of diminishing returns, 457
lead, 223, 224, 226, 235, 237, 241, 260, 429, 450, 728
legend, 305
level of effort tasks, 148
leveling, 114, 473, 728
    automatic leveling, 114, 484
    Can Level, 484
    cross-project leveling, 5
    granularity, 485
    level assignments, 485
    level the workloads yourself, 476
    Leveling Can Split, 485
    Leveling Delay, 485
    leveling options, 484
    manual leveling, 484
    MS Project levels the workloads, 484
    over-allocations, 484
    percentage leveling, 484
    Priority, 204
    workload leveling, 114
    yes/no leveling, 484
Leveling Gantt, 96, 487
Link Tasks, 233
Link tool, 231
living document approach, 202
local resources, 323, 335, 347
logic, 220, 245
    logic override, 637
    progress override, 637
    retained logic, 637
logic override, 637
logical and, 301
logical dependency, 230, 510, 728
logical hierarchy, 134, 164, 684
logic-constrained schedule, 29, 30, 499, 500, 505
logo

project logo, 306
lookup table, 568
loose ends, 248, 470, 681, 689

M
machine resources, 318
machines, 313, 315, 317, 318, 344
manage-points, 149
manual leveling, 484
margins, 304
material, 93, 317, 318
material label, 320, 355, 694
material resources, 318
materials, 313, 315
    consumption rate, 346
    time-related cost, 347
matrix organizations, 6
Max. Units, 93, 198, 317, 321, 329, 334, 337, 341, 354, 369, 370, 388, 546, 693
maximum units. See 'Max. Units'
meetings, 154, 186, 189
mentoring, 24
menu bar, 58, 76
merge bias, 464, 523
methodology, 24
Microsoft, 19
Microsoft Learning, 19
Microsoft Office, 65, 77
Microsoft Official Curriculum, 19
Microsoft Partners, 105
Microsoft Project. See 'Project 2003'
Microsoft Project Server. See 'Project Server'
Microsoft Project Web Access. See 'Project Web Access'
middleware, 3
migrate, 58
milestone diamond, 140

published version, 73, 424
pure work time, 195, 196
PWA. See 'Project Web Access'

Q
quality, 29, 47, 52, 202, 353, 424, 427,
438, 448, 456, 458, 466, 468, 472, 512,
514, 521, 693
quality control, 156
quality management, 47
quality performance, 585
quantity surveyors, 186

R
R&D. See 'Research and Development'
R/D. See 'Request/Demand'
RAM. See 'Responsibility Assignment
Matrix'
rate escalation, 351
rate profile, 346
rate tables, 346
rates, 616
RBS. See 'Resource Breakdown
Structure'
RCP. See 'Resource-Critical Path'
readiness, 22
real slack, 441
real time status, 219
recalculation, 730
recurring task bars, 141
recurring tasks, 142, 148, 154, 156, 251
    important questions, 155
    recurring detail task, 148, 155, 167,
    251, 294, 398, 409, 480, 485, 687,
    692, 696
    recurring summary task, 155, 397,
    398
    remarks, 154
relationship. See 'dependencies'

relative lag, 450
relocation project, 32
remaining duration, 619, 623, 682
remaining hours, 621
remaining work, 626, 645
reminders, 596
reports, 355, 550, 730
    Earned Value, 618
    enterprise views, 582
    forecast report, 662, 701
    GIF, 3
    one-page reports, 588
    PDF, 3
    portfolio analyzer, 4
    portfolio modeler, 4
    portfolio views, 4
    project calendar, 553
    project summary, 553
    reports that include the notes, 596
    resource calendars, 553
    responsibilities by department, 590
    status report, 662, 701
    time-phased budget, 599
    to-do lists, 593
    working days, 553
    workload histogram, 591
reports that include the notes, 596
Request, 389
request progress information, 648
Request/Demand, 389, 407
required, 319
Research & Development, 44, 177
resource
    resource loading, 369
    resource management, 325
    resource managers, 325
    resource modeling, 325
    resource name, 320
    resource pool, 323

zoom in, 233